New York and Los Angeles

New York and Los Angeles

The Uncertain Future

Edited by

David Halle

Andrew A. Beveridge

OXFORD

UNIVERSITY PRESS

OXFORD
UNIVERSITY PRESS

Oxford University Press is a department of the University of Oxford.
It furthers the University's objective of excellence in research, scholarship,
and education by publishing worldwide.

Oxford   New York
Auckland   Cape Town   Dar es Salaam   Hong Kong   Karachi
Kuala Lumpur   Madrid   Melbourne   Mexico City   Nairobi
New Delhi   Shanghai   Taipei   Toronto

With offices in
Argentina   Austria   Brazil   Chile   Czech Republic   France   Greece
Guatemala   Hungary   Italy   Japan   Poland   Portugal   Singapore
South Korea   Switzerland   Thailand   Turkey   Ukraine   Vietnam

Oxford is a registered trade mark of Oxford University Press
in the UK and certain other countries.

Published in the United States of America by
Oxford University Press
198 Madison Avenue, New York, NY 10016

© Oxford University Press 2013

Library of Congress Cataloging-in-Publication Data
New York and Los Angeles : the uncertain future / edited by David Halle, Andrew A. Beveridge.
   p. cm.
Includes bibliographical references and index.
ISBN 978-0-19-977838-6 (hardcover : alk. paper)—ISBN 978-0-19-977837-9 (pbk. : alk.
paper)—ISBN 978-0-19-977842-3 (ebook)   1. New York (N.Y.)—Social policy.   2. New York
(N.Y.)—Social conditions—21st century.   3. New York (N.Y.)—Economic policy.   4. Los Angeles
(Calif.)—Social policy.   5. Los Angeles (Calif.)—Economic policy.   6. Los Angeles (Calif.)—Social
conditions—21st century.   I. Halle, David.   II. Beveridge, Andrew A., 1945–
HN80.N5N524 2013
303.309747′1—dc23
2012030386

9 8 7 6 5 4 3 2
Printed in the United States of America
on acid-free paper

To Louise, Fredrica, and the rest of our families

ACKNOWLEDGMENTS

Bringing new, thoughtful, and comprehensive analysis to the nation's two largest urban centers requires drawing out the best of a large team of diverse researchers. We would like to thank the talented chapter authors, who worked so hard and cooperatively, including attending several conferences to discuss the project. We also appreciate Rick Bell's help in hosting two of these gatherings at the American Institute of Architects facility in New York City.

Financial support for the volume came from UCLA's Faculty Senate to Halle and from the following National Science Foundation grants to Andrew Beveridge (DUE 0919993, BCS 0647902, and SES 0940804). Social Explorer, Inc. helped defray some costs as well. Many of the volume's contributors also acknowledge support for their work in their specific chapters. Any opinions, findings, and conclusions expressed here are those of the authors and do not necessarily reflect the views of these financial supporters or the organizations with which they are affiliated.

Sydney Beveridge contributed excellent editing and organizational support, working with many of the authors on the final revisions of their chapters, as well as making numerous useful suggestions and conducting supplemental research. Brittney Wagner and Samantha Hammer helped in final editing.

James Cook, our editor at Oxford University Press, was supportive throughout this project.

Others who contributed suggestions and comments during the authoring of this volume include James Jasper, Phil Kasinitz, Robert Kapsis, Ahmed Lacevic, Wilfredo Lugo, Peter Mullan, John Torpey, Susan Weber-Stoger, and Kathyrn Wylde.

David Halle
Andrew A. Beveridge

CONTENTS

LIST OF FIGURES

LIST OF TABLES

LIST OF CONTRIBUTORS

Helmut K. Anheier, Professor of Sociology and Dean at the Hertie School of Governance, Berlin, and Professor of Sociology, Heidelberg University

Rick Bell, Executive Director, New York Chapter of the American Institute of Architects

Andrew A. Beveridge, Professor of Sociology, Queens College and Graduate Center, City University of New York and President, Social Explorer, Inc.

Sydney J. Beveridge, Media and Content Editor, Social Explorer, Inc.

Margaret M. Chin, Associate Professor of Sociology, Hunter College and the Graduate Center, City University of New York

Andrew Deener, Assistant Professor of Sociology, University of Connecticut

Andrea Dinneen, Doctoral Candidate in Sociology, University of California Los Angeles

Jameson W. Doig, Professor of Politics and Public Affairs, Emeritus, Woodrow Wilson School of Public and International Affairs, Princeton University; Research Professor in Government, Dartmouth College

Beth Leavenworth DuFault, Doctoral Candidate, University of Arizona, Eller College of Management

Ingrid Gould Ellen, Professor of Urban Planning and Public Policy, New York University's Wagner Graduate School of Public Service

Steven P. Erie, Professor of Political Science, University of California, San Diego

Jeffrey Fagan, Isidor and Seville Sulzbacher Professor of Law, Columbia University School of Law

Susan Fainstein, Senior Research Fellow in Urban Planning, Harvard University

Nancy Foner, Distinguished Professor of Sociology, Hunter College and the Graduate Center, City University of New York

David Gladstone, Associate Professor of Planning and Urban Studies, University of New Orleans

Robert Gottlieb, Professor of Urban & Environmental Policy, Occidental College

David Halle, Professor of Sociology, University of California, Los Angeles

David Howard, Director of Research and Innovation, The Doe Fund, Inc.

Rebecca Y. Kim, Associate Professor of Sociology, and Frank R. Seaver Professor in Social Science, Pepperdine University

Vladimir Kogan, Assistant Professor of Political Science, Ohio State University

William Kornblum, Professor of Sociology, City University of New York, Graduate Center

Marcus Lam, Assistant Professor, Social Enterprise Administration, Columbia University School of Social Work

Steve Lang, Professor of Sociology, Laguardia Community College

John MacDonald, Associate Professor of Criminology, University of Pennsylvania

Scott A. MacKenzie, Assistant Professor of Political Science, University of California, Davis

Martha M. Matsuoka, Assistant Professor of Urban & Environmental Policy, Occidental College

John Mollenkopf, Distinguished Professor of Political Science, City University of New York, Graduate Center

Theodore Glen Nitschke, Office Manager, Kaplan Stahler Agency

Brendan O'Flaherty, Professor of Economics, Columbia University

Jan Reiff, Associate Professor of History, University of California, Los Angeles

Raphael Sonenshein, Executive Director, Pat Brown Institute for Public Affairs, California State University, Los Angeles

Forrest Stuart, Assistant Professor of Sociology, University of Chicago

George Sweeting, Deputy Director, New York City, Independent Budget Office

Edward Telles, Professor of Sociology, Princeton University

Kristen Van Hooreweghe, Assistant Professor in Environmental Studies and Sociology at State University of New York, Potsdam

Eric Vanstrom, Doctoral Candidate of Cinema and Media Studies, University of California, Los Angeles

Roger Waldinger, Distinguished Professor of Sociology, University of California, Los Angeles

Julia Wrigley, Associate University Provost and Professor of Sociology, City University of New York, Graduate Center

Min Zhou, Professor of Sociology, University of California, Los Angeles

New York and Los Angeles

CHAPTER 1

New York and Los Angeles

The Uncertain Future

DAVID HALLE AND
ANDREW A. BEVERIDGE

THE UNCERTAIN FUTURE

The direction of New York and Los Angeles, the nation's two largest cities and urban regions, is hugely uncertain, more so than it has been for decades. This suggests the need for new thinking and interpretation over a range of key topics, and that is the purpose of this book. The volume includes contributions from foremost experts across a variety of relevant fields—politics, economics, education, environmental studies, criminology, demography, architecture, culture, and history. It is also the first book to use the 2010 Census and the initial releases of the five-year file from the American Community Survey (ACS) for an in-depth discussion of New York and Los Angeles.

WHY NEW YORK AND LOS ANGELES

Our book focuses on New York and Los Angeles because of their size—together the regions contain about one-eighth of the population of the United States—and because they are often seen as quite different from each other. Whatever trends appear in both cities and regions need to be taken seriously. The discussions illuminate broad issues and themes as they relate to these two centers of power and influence.

Still, the chapters throughout ask how representative our findings are of urban America and draw from other cities where appropriate. For example, the most popular film about any United States city is *The Sting* (1973), set in Chicago, as David Halle, Erik Vanstrom, Jan Reiff, and Ted Nitschke point out in chapter 18. To help place our findings in a broader context of other US cities and regions as well as major historical changes, the book is coordinated with *Social Explorer*, developed by Andrew Beveridge, which offers online tools to display demographic change in the United States from 1790 through the present. *Social Explorer* also enables users to create interactive maps and reports.

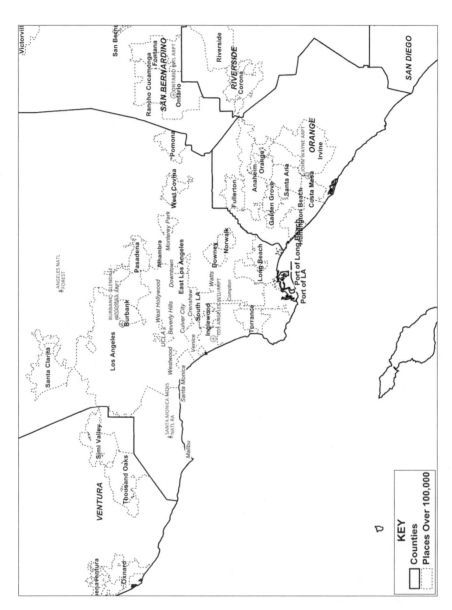

Figure 1.1
Los Angeles and Vicinity, Places with 100,000 or More in Population, and Selected Neighborhoods
Source: Andrew A. Beveridge based on 2010 Census boundary files.

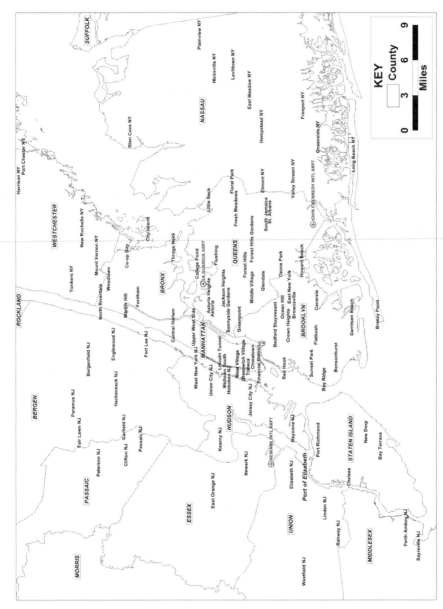

Figure 1.2
New York City and Vicinity, Counties, Selected Places and Neighborhoods
Source: Andrew A. Beveridge based on 2010 Census boundary files.

OVERVIEW: THE NEW DEMOGRAPHY

The latest demographic data underline the need to keep modifying older urban ste-reotypes, as Andrew Beveridge and Sydney Beveridge detail in chapter 2. Latinos and Asians continue to grow as a percentage of each city and region. By 2010 Latinos made up 48.5 percent of the City of Los Angeles (up from 46.5 percent in 2000), and 28.6 percent of New York City (up from 27 percent in 2000), and now surpass blacks there with whom they were roughly coequal in 2000. (See table 1.1.) The Asian popu-lation too has increased steadily to 11.4 percent of the City of Los Angeles and 12.7 percent of New York City.

The peripheral zones (mostly suburban) of both regions are also becoming more diverse in their Latino, Asian, and black composition. For example, Latinos increased by an astounding 43 percent in New York's outer suburbs from 2000 to 2010. Likewise in the Los Angeles region, the most rapid growth of Latinos occurred in the outer suburbs, roughly 28 percent. The Asian population too has shown its largest increase in the outer suburbs of each region during that time, roughly 18 percent in New York and 9 percent in Los Angeles. The often affluent, heavily Chinese global "ethnoburbs," such as Monterey Park and Alhambra in the San Gabriel Valley east of the City of Los Angeles offer fascinating case studies, as Min Zhou and colleagues show in chapter 13. First attracting affluent Taiwanese in the 1970s, by the 1980s they were increasingly drawing often well-to do mainland Chinese including families of Chinese officials and businessmen, some of whom come in on finance visas and go into business in the United States.

Meanwhile, the African American population continues to decline in both cities, though it retains a more substantial base in New York than in Los Angeles. African Americans now represent just 9.7 percent of the City of Los Angeles, down from 11.3 percent in 2000. In New York City, African Americans now constitute 25.6 percent of the city, down from 26.6 percent in 2000. The change in once iconic black neighbor-hoods is striking and reveals major shifts in the urban ghetto. In retrospect, 1950–80 was the "classic" period of the now waning African-American urban ghetto. Watts, for example, the epicenter of Los Angeles's 1965 mega riot, went from 91 percent black and just 9 percent Latino in 1970, to just 29 percent black and 70 percent Latino in 2010. Compton, also once considered a quintessentially black ghetto, now looks like a neighborhood blacks were just passing through. So Watts and Compton resemble one classic inner-urban pattern, whereby an initially poor group achieves the means to move out and is replaced by a different, newly arrived poor group. Indeed, "black flight" in Los Angeles has long been a common term referring to the movement to the suburbs from once predominantly black neighborhoods that are now mainly Latino—immigrant and poor.[1]

New York City's Harlem, once America's most iconic black "ghetto," is in transi-tion too, though somewhat differently than Compton and Watts. "Black flight" is not a Harlem issue, while "gentrification" is. In 1901 "Central Harlem" (basically from Central Park at 96th Street up to 155th Street) was just 10 percent black. By 1930, during the Harlem Renaissance, it was a definably black area—70 percent black while the rest of the city was less than 2 percent black. By 1950, Central Harlem was

Table 1.1 POPULATION SIZE AND CHANGE IN LOS ANGELES AND NEW YORK CITY REGIONS, 1990 TO 2010

	1990	2000	2010	Change 1990–2000 (%)	Change 2000–2010 (%)
New York City	7,322,564	8,008,278	8,175,133	11.6	2.1
% Hispanic/Latino	24.4	27	28.6	4.2	1.6
% Black	28.7	26.6	25.6	–3.1	–1
% Asian (including Pacific Islands and Hawaii)	7	9.8	12.7	5.7	2.9
% White	52.3	44.7	44	–8.3	–0.7
% Non-Hispanic white	43.2	35	33.3	–9.9	–1.7
New York CSA (including New York City)	19,686,925	21,361,797	22,085,649	12.2	3.4
% Hispanic/Latino	14.5	18.1	21.7	7.2	3.6
% Black	17.6	17.1	16.9	–0.7	–0.2
% Asian (including Pacific Islands and Hawaii)	4.6	6.8	9.1	4.5	2.3
% White	71.4	64.3	61.6	–9.8	–2.7
% Non-Hispanic white	64.8	56.6	51.7	–13.1	–4.9
City of Los Angeles	3,485,398	3,694,820	3,792,621	8.8	2.6
% Hispanic/Latino	39.9	46.5	48.5	8.6	2
% Black	14	11.3	9.7	–4.3	–1.6
% Asian (including Pacific Islands and Hawaii)	9.8	10.1	11.4	1.6	1.3
% White	52.8	47	49.8	–3	2.8
% Non-Hispanic white	37.3	29.8	28.7	–8.6	–1.1
Los Angeles County (including City of Los Angeles)	8,863,164	9,519,338	9,818,605	10.8	3.1
% Hispanic/Latino	37.8	44.6	47.7	9.9	3.1
% Black	11.2	9.8	8.7	–2.5	–1.1
% Asian (including Pacific Islands and Hawaii)	10.8	12.1	13.9	3.1	1.8
% White	56.8	48.7	50.3	–6.5	1.6
% Non-Hispanic white	40.8	31.1	27.8	–13	–3.3
Los Angeles CSA (including LA County)	14,531,529	16,373,645	17,877,006	23	9.2
% Hispanic/Latino	32.9	40.3	44.9	12	4.6
% Black	8.5	7.6	7	–1.5	-0.6

(Continued)

Table 1.1 (CONTINUED)

	1990	2000	2010	Change 1990–2000 (%)	Change 2000–2010 (%)
% Asian (including Pacific Islands and Hawaii)	9.2	10.7	12.6	3.4	1.9
% White	64.6	55.1	55	-9.6	-0.1
% Non-Hispanic white	49.8	39	33.6	-16.2	-5.4

Source: 1990, 2000, and 2010 Census Data from *Social Explorer*. For the NY and LA CSAs, see figures 2.1 and 2.2 and page 35 discussion.

about 98 percent black and through 1980 the black population was never below 94 percent. Yet by 2010 the black population had dropped to 58.6 percent, well below its 1930 level, and the current rate of decline is stunningly rapid. Meanwhile, the Hispanic population of Central Harlem rose from 4.3 percent in 1980 to 23.6 percent by 2010. Non-Hispanic whites rose in number too, from about 0.6 percent of the Central Harlem population in 1980 to 11.8 percent by 2010. The deconcentration of the black population is happening in many different areas of Harlem and is unlikely to reverse. The transition of New York and Los Angeles from cities with large inner-city African American neighborhoods to new kinds of racial and ethnic compositions is ongoing.

Changes in women's earnings and labor market position are also consequential. In every area of the two metro regions, a higher proportion of women now hold Bachelor's degrees than men, and median earnings of women in their twenties working full-time are higher than for their male counterparts. The ideal typical lifestyle of a nuclear family where the husband works and the wife is a "homemaker" continues to erode. Partly as a result, a significant fraction of affluent, non-Hispanic white parents are staying in the more desirable parts of the city near their jobs, instead of moving to the suburbs. Manhattan has experienced a baby boom, and in the most sought after areas for wealthy families, such as the Upper West Side and Downtown, kindergarten classrooms are packed and parents struggle to find space in both public and private schools.

This book considers a host of other key topics; in some of which one city has lessons for the other. The book's interdisciplinary approach also produces many insights. For example, holding other factors constant, neighborhoods with large concentrations of immigrants turn out to have markedly lower crime rates than neighborhoods with fewer immigrants, and immigrants often outperform natives within the schools. Crime has plummeted in both cities after the epidemic that ran from the late 1960s to the early 1990s, so that community–police relations are now center stage. Commissioner William Bratton played a critical role in police reform in both cities, in New York from 1994 to 1996 and in Los Angeles from 2002 to 2009. Bratton's more recent stint in Los Angeles may be one reason that today Los Angeles's community-police relations seem to be doing better than New York's. In Los Angeles Bratton instituted COMPSTAT Plus, an interestingly different, and possibly superior, version of the famous COMPSTAT program he introduced in the 1990s in New York, as discussed by Jeffrey Fagan and John Macdonald in chapter 8. Now a resident of Manhattan, Bratton is an intriguing possibility as Commissioner to serve whoever is elected New York's mayor in 2013.

Economic issues include financial reform (e.g., post-Dodd-Frank challenges to bank power and Wall Street); the housing crisis (e.g., efforts to address the "death spiral" of falling prices and rising foreclosures); inequality (e.g., issues raised by the Occupy Wall Street movement); and infrastructure (e.g., challenges posed by a new class of mega-ships that will stream through the refurbished Panama Canal in 2015). There are also issues of neighborhood integration and segregation (e.g., Brooklyn and Queens are the two most segregated counties in the country by race); environmentalism; urban planning (e.g., how to balance growth and preservation); the latest architectural developments; and changing depictions of the two cities in popular culture.

Comparing the two city's political regimes is also fascinating. For example, although each city's population is among the most racially and ethnically heterogeneous in the country, since 1965 Los Angeles has had a five-term African American mayor (Bradley) and now a two-term Latino mayor (Villaraigosa), but never a Jewish mayor, while New York has had just a one-term African American mayor (Dinkins) and three Jewish mayors, contrasts that John Mollenkopf and Raphael J. Sonenshein address in chapter 5. They also highlight a difference in what each city considers iconic leadership, with New York City selecting moderate Republicans (both former Democrats) as mayors (Giuliani and Bloomberg) in recent elections, while Los Angeles prefers liberal, Democratic leaders, although the nuances of this argument are complex and the future is open.

Social issues include education and especially the quest among reformers for the "silver bullet" to fix the schools. Such highly promoted reforms as mayoral control and charter schools are no longer, at least alone, the clear solution.

LIMITS OF "THE CLASSIC PERSPECTIVES"—URBAN "DECLINE," URBAN "RESURGENCE"

The book's overall goal is to assess the various directions of these two cities and regions over a range of key topics. We do not see a single direction that can serve to summarize trends, a simplification that was sometimes appropriate in the past. For example, for several decades after World War II the overall direction of major US urban areas was clear—the decline of central cities and the expansion of the suburbs. This motif of urban decline was associated with large African American, urban "ghettos," now on the wane as mentioned, and with notions of "white flight" and suburbanization based on massive tract housing developments, notably in the Los Angeles region's "Inland Empire" of San Bernardino and Riverside counties, and in Long Island's Nassau and Suffolk counties.

A reversal of this trend can be increasingly identified for urban regions in the early years of the twenty-first century, namely the growing attraction of urban life.

Also the environmental movement's critique of auto-dependent "sprawl" combined with high gas prices increasingly called the suburban lifestyle into question. In New York City these trends were reflected in a revitalization of the city's "outer boroughs," especially Brooklyn and Queens, and more modestly the Bronx (Staten Island never really flagged in the twentieth century). In the City of Los Angeles these trends produced a resurgence of the downtown, spearheaded by mega entertainment projects such as Disney Concert Hall, the Staples Center, and L.A. Live, but also new urban apartment buildings that were heavily driven by the unwillingness of suburbanites, operating through Los Angeles's new neighborhood councils, to permit apartments and associated development in their locales, as Andrew Deener, Steven Erie, Valdimir Kogan, and Forrest Stuart show in chapter 14 on development. Part of downtown's change is the city's attempt to "clean up" Skid Row, the largest such area in the United States, an effort into which officials poured huge resources—by 2009 Los Angeles's Skid Row had more police per square mile than any other US location. This urban revival triggered a new concern, especially in New York City, that more sections of the city were becoming places where only the wealthy could reside, not unlike Paris and some other European cities. Illustrating this perceived danger, more and more parts of the city were said to be "gentrifying," a term often used too vaguely to be valuable analytically but whose typically negative connotations reflected widespread unease about the city's future as a place where all social classes could live. The economic and financial crisis that began in 2007 has cast doubt on parts of this urban resurgence, at least for now, though some elements are on track, including the tendency for well-to-do whites to stay in the city to raise families.

The course of cities such as New York and Los Angeles is now fluid and subject to multiple forces, providing the context for this volume's assessments. Each chapter's authors discuss the latest developments and suggest the likely future direction in a particular, key area, and they reach beyond the more standard narratives of decline and resurgence. The rest of this introduction discusses findings from some of the major topics of the book in more detail.

THE FINANCIAL/ECONOMIC CRISIS

A volume such as this must foreground the ongoing 2007–08 economic and financial crisis and its associated uncertainties, which, in one way or another, affect almost every topic discussed here, and which chapters 6 and 7 consider in detail.

Banks and other institutions based in New York and Los Angeles each helped to create the crisis, but in very different ways. Los Angeles was an epicenter of the real estate lending spree. For example, seven of the top 10 lenders of subprime loans nationwide were based in either Orange County or Los Angeles County, including Countrywide, the largest. New York's Wall Street firms, in turn, pushed deregulation and also created key financial instruments that fueled the lending spree. Crucial here were Credit Default Swaps, invented by J. P. Morgan Chase in 1995, which allow lenders to buy insurance policies that reimburse them if loans they make go sour, thus passing the entire risk of borrower default to a third party that receives regular payments from the lender (similar to insurance premiums). As applied to mortgage loans, the result was that many lenders, rather than focusing on loans to people who could likely afford to repay them, instead just maximized the number and size of loans they made, and therefore their commission and other fees. Warren Buffett famously called Credit Default Swaps "weapons of financial mass destruction."

Such products were also a key reason why a collapsing housing bubble in 2007–08 threatened the entire international financial system, since trillions of dollars in risky mortgages had become embedded throughout that system as mortgage-related securities were given triple A grades by the rating agencies, repackaged, and sold to investors around the world.

Managing the Crisis

Both mayors Bloomberg and Villaraigosa have shown creative and skillful leadership during the 2007–08 financial crisis. That contrasts with Washington's congressional deadlocks that have hampered Obama's administration, and with Europe's arguably counterproductive response to the crisis, led by Germany's Chancellor Merkel who insisted on fiscal austerity, at the cost of economic growth, to remedy excessive government deficits and debt in countries such as Greece, Spain, and Italy. This fiscal austerity had, by May 2012, worsened the already depressed economies of these countries and thus exacerbated their fiscal problems as government tax revenues fell, an outcome many economists had predicted (Summers 2012). Still, New York City has fared somewhat better than the City of Los Angeles. For example, by March 2012 unemployment in Los Angeles, at 13.6 percent, was substantially above the nation's rate of 8.6 percent, while New York City's at 9.8 percent was just somewhat above it, though moving higher.

New York City's better condition has several causes, as George Sweeting and Andrea Dinneen explain in chapter 7. Crucial is luck—the federal government bailed out the city's financial sector using the Troubled Asset Relief Program and other funds. (This could be viewed as a deserved payback for the city's history of contributing far more in taxes to the federal government than it receives in benefits, and for the federal government's history of funneling military expenditures to Southern California.)

Another key reason New York has fared better than Los Angeles is the different impact, positive for New York and negative for Los Angeles, of two seminal historical events—New York's near bankruptcy and California's Proposition 13. In 1975 New York City came so close to bankruptcy that the President of France and Chancellor of West Germany both expressed concern to US President Ford at the time about the effect of default on the international banking system. Underlining leadership's importance, New York City's Mayor Beame was out of his depth, and the city was basically saved when New York State Governor Hugh Carey (advised by financier Felix Rohatyn) assembled a broad coalition of groups willing to make concessions while also putting tight restrictions on the city's fiscal policies. Mindful of that history, a generation of policymakers imposed fiscal caution on the city including a legal requirement to balance its budget over a four- to five-year period, a countercyclical financial prudence that has served the city well in the current crisis.

History, by contrast, hampered Los Angeles in the form of Proposition 13, the radical 1978 ballot initiative that not only capped local property tax rates but also required a two-thirds majority vote for legislative passage of any tax increase. Then-Governor Jerry Brown called the proposition "the biggest can of worms the State has ever faced," though after it passed he did what was needed to make it work, with the state "bailing out" localities by taking responsibility for a share of their local expenditure especially on education (Skelton). Ironically, Brown was reelected governor during the current crisis in time to see his gloomy prediction for the long run vindicated. Hamstrung by Proposition 13 and other issues, the California state government not only struggled to resolve its own fiscal problems but in 2009 it also redirected an estimated $113 million in Los Angeles City property tax revenues to cover its own operating costs.

California leads in many trends—positive and negative—and Proposition 13 was a damaging manifestation of the latter, namely the "something for nothing" syndrome (Sears 1982, 216–18, 243). Surveys at the time showed that the voters (illogically) wanted lower taxes and less government but also constant or increased spending on specific services, and somehow believed they could have both. The message was "Taxes, No! Big government, No! Services, Yes!" Similar sentiments, exploited by poor leadership, clearly contribute to Washington's current deadlocks.

Still, in a much-heralded change, in November 2012 California voters passed Proposition 30, Governor Brown's ballot initiative that raised the State sales tax by a quarter-cent and increased taxes on wealthier residents/households (those earning over $250,000 a year.) Several observors argued that this returned California to the cutting-edge of positive trends by challenging the view that government deficits shoud be mainly addressed by major cuts in services and programs rather than also by some tax increases. An elated Governor Brown urged just re-elected President Obama to likewise "stand his ground" in demanding a national tax increase on the wealthy to help fund the US budget deficits. The November election also gave the Democrats a two-thirds majority in both State leglislatures, enough to now pass tax increases, though Brown cautioned that this should not be the occasion for a "State spending spree."

Two Ongoing Uncertainties: Homeowners and Wall Street

The real estate sector and the financial sector remain central areas of focus and contention. On the real estate front, the federal government has done far less to help homeowners than economists such as Nouriel Roubini, Robert Shiller, and Kenneth Rogoff recommended. So the future of the housing market remains highly uncertain.

On the Wall Street/financial sector side, outrage over bank bonuses fuelled passage of the Dodd Frank Act in June 2010, the most far-reaching legislation to control banks since the 1930s Securities and Exchange Act. Dodd-Frank introduced an array of potentially powerful arsenals that have scarcely had time to be tested. Above all, a major challenge to the most profitable sector of the banking world is the Volcker Rule that prohibits banks with retail customers that use government-insured accounts from "proprietary trading" (i.e., engaging in investment banking using the bank's own money). Naturally banks are trying to find ways around this (technically they have until 2014 to comply), but it will not necessarily be easy. For example, J. P. Morgan's chief executive, Jamie Dimon, suffered a huge embarrassment in May 2012 as the bank's London office, apparently using "hedging" as a backdoor way to conduct "proprietary trading," revealed over $2 billion of losses amidst huge blunders. Overall, the power of the financial sector will likely remain somewhat diminished, especially compared to its pre-crisis peak in 2006–07, though struggles over bank power will be a major, unsettled issue for years.

A corollary is that Wall Street will probably be less dominant in New York City's economy than in the recent past. By early 2012 reports predicted that education, health services, and professional and business services would drive employment growth in the city, as Wall Street continued to shed jobs. On the upside, the city's tech and creative sectors (professionals in fashion, media, law, and entertainment) have been the big surprises, including young entrepreneurs/techies from Silicon Valley, Boston, and elsewhere relocating to New York. In 2011, of those renting in Manhattan below 96th street, people in tech accounted for 12.8 percent and in the creative sector 13.5 percent, up from 7.2 percent and 8.6 percent in 2005, respectively (Fung 2012).

HURRICANE SANDY

Hurricane Sandy[2] hit the New York-New Jersey region on October 30, 2012, as one of the worst natural disasters since the original Dutch settlers arrived. In New York City alone there were 43 deaths. Almost 1 in 10, about 775,000, city residents saw some flooding in the building they lived in, and about 1 in 20 lived where flooding was over six feet. (See table 15.4). Lower Manhattan including Wall Street's financial district and subway and automobile tunnels, like many areas of the city and region, was almost completely unprotected from Sandy's twelve to fourteen foot surge. Many offices and apartment buildings lost power for at least two weeks and were uninhabitable much longer because of flood damage (figure 15.7 documents the flood areas in the region, while figure 15.8 shows the flood depth in New York City). The city's subways and commuter rail lines were halted, in some cases for a week or more. Schools were closed, and about 40,000 households became homeless. Among massive damage to the region, Sandy crippled Newark's sewage plant, the fifth largest in the country, and over 4 billion gallons of raw or partially treated sewage spilled into waterways including New York's Upper Bay. New York Governor Cuomo and New Jersey Governor Christie, preparing preliminary requests for federal disaster aid a month later, estimated damage at roughly $60 billion (about $30 billion to each state), not counting loss to economic activity.

The city and region were woefully unprepared for the disaster, even when it was believed precautions were in effect. For example the owners of a new building downtown at 2 Gold Street designed it to protect against flood by installing 3.5 foot flood gates, which Sandy simply went over, crushing an oil tank and destroying more than 40 cars in the basement.

The extent to which Sandy was related to global warming was a matter of debate. On the one hand according to the New York City Panel on Climate Change, while the New York Harbor rose just 1 foot in the last 100 years it was projected to rise 1 to 2 feet by 2050, and 3 to 4 feet by 2080. Also, of the top 10 high-water marks at the Battery on the southern end of Manhattan since 1900, three have occurred in the past two years – Hurricane Irene, Hurricane Sandy and the 2010 spring flood. On the other hand the hurricane that gave birth to Sandy was technically only category 1. But it merged with another weather sytem, so the storm was an unlucky result of two weather systems.

New York's waterfront location, like most global cities, has been the foundation of its commercial success. Still, with four of its five boroughs located on islands (only the Bronx is part of the continental mainland), it currently ranks number five among 140 port cities around the world in terms of susceptibility to storm surges, and its future as a major global city is in doubt without new protective measures (Gapper 2012). Cities such as London, Rotterdam, Hamburg and Tokyo have all built storm barriers, levees and sea walls.

After Sandy many people, including Governor Cuomo and Christine Quinn, a leading contender to replace Mayor Bloomberg in the November 2013 elections, concluded that the city should implement a far more aggressive set of preventive measures. Its heavy reliance on just evacuating people in flood risk areas when dangerous storms were expected, plus "soft" ecological solutions such as reconstructed wetlands for coastal protection, were insufficient.

There had certainly been earlier warnings that far more protection was needed. Participants at a 2009 seminar in New York City organized by the American Society of Civil Engineers (and attended by the city's Office of Emergency Management and the United States Army Corps of Engineers) had asked officials to consider surge barriers and tide gates to protect the city. Malcolm Bowman, a professor of oceanography at Stony Brook University, after Sandy argued, as he had before, for building a roughly five-mile barrier from Sandy Hook, New Jersey to the Rockaway Peninsula, with locks and sluiceways to allow ships and water to pass during ordinary times, and costing over $10 billion. Another, smaller barrier could stretch across the top of the East River to protect against surges from Long Island Sound, and could rise from the ocean floor using hydraulics as a threat approached. (See chapter 15 by Van Hooreweghe, Lang, and Kornblum, including figure 15.7).

Still, such proposals face the daunting set of obstacles that typically doom "mega projects" in New York and elsewhere (Halle and Tiso 2013). These obstacles include cost; political issues (will New Jersey's governor agree to a storm barrier that might protect the New York harbor but deflect water towards New Jersey); government agencies with over-lapping jurisdictions; cronyism and incompetence; NIMBYism; and the weakening of the Port Authority of New York and New Jersey which should have a leading role in issues affecting the bistate port.

Another group of those now warning against just returning to "business as usual" opposed simply rebuilding all homes close to the beach and restoring the shorelines to where they were. The federal government encourages this "let's come back stronger and better" attitude by making billions available to replace roads, pipelines and other infrastructure. Instead, it was argued, government should discourage the reconstruction of destroyed or badly damaged beachfront homes in New Jersey and New York. While taxpayers might then be forced to compensate homeowners, it should save taxpayers money in the long run by ending the cycle of repairing and rebuilding properties in the path of future storms (Pilkey 2012).

Alongside many examples of efficiency and heroism among key organizations, Sandy also revealed plenty of incompetence, sometimes gross. Among the worst was the Long Island Power Authority (LIPA), a crony-filled government entity answerable to New York State which utterly failed to prepare for Sandy (e.g. failing to cut down trees liable to fall on power lines during a storm, e.g relying on a paper map system of the location of lines), and left over 1m customers without power for over two weeks. Poor decisions made by other organizations included Con Edison waiting too long, as Sandy approached, to shut off power at its 14th st station in Lower Manhattan, leading to an explosion that blacked out hundreds of thousands of customers downtown for a week and for some much longer; the Port Authority's excessively complex, and insufficiently protected, signalling system for its PATH trains which meant that, when the key tunnels flooded, the system could not be restored for over three weeks; and New Jersey Transit allowing almost a quarter of its trains to be damaged by failing to move them from low-lying yards in Kearny and Hoboken which were flooded, even though forecasts from the National Weather Service had warned that Sandy could damage these areas. (By contrast, the MTA moved much of its stock of subway and railroad cars to higher ground as the storm approached.)

Meanwhile Sandy, and especially these defects in the organizational response, should be a reminder that while the Los Angeles region remains prone to its own threats especially earthquakes, the City of Los Angeles's ability to address catastrophic events is uncertain, as Scott MacKenzie and Steve Erie warn. Since 1912, approximately 20 earthquakes of magnitude 6.0 or more have occurred in Southern California, most recently the 1994 Northridge Earthquake, which claimed 57 lives, injured thousands more and resulted in $20 billion in economic damages. With several fault lines running below the region's most densely populated areas, even small quakes can cause damage. In response to the Federal Disaster Mitigation Act of 2000, the city and county of Los Angeles have prepared local hazard mitigation plans to reduce the risk of various threats and provide direction to local agencies and residents. In 2000, the City of Los Angeles created the Emergency Management Department (EMD) to coordinate the local response to and recovery from earthquakes, wildfires, floods, landslides, acts of terrorism and other significant events. Yet in 2008 a city controller audit found significant gaps in the city's level of preparedness for a catastrophic event. Mayor Villaraigosa responded with an Emergency Management Initiative to enhance local planning efforts, train city employees in disaster response and modernize the city's antiquated emergency management structure. However, the EMD remains understaffed and underfunded relative to similar agencies in other large cities. A follow up review of the City's Emergency Management Plan in May 2012 found that many of the city controller's 2008 recommendations have not been implemented. Recent budget cuts have reduced the city's workforce and threatened its ability to effectively coordinate emergency preparedness activities, with fire and police particularly hard hit and the former facing criticism over reduced response times. In November 2012, the City Council voted to place a half-cent sales tax hike on the March 2013 ballot, which would raise $215 million to avert further service cuts, as discussed in chapter seven. Still, the plan is opposed by the major candidates running to replace Mayor Villaraigosa.

EDUCATION: NO SILVER BULLET

Education is a central issue for each city. The school systems of New York City and the City of Los Angeles are the first and second largest districts in the nation—New York with 1.1 million students and Los Angeles with 710,000—and they offer fascinating case studies, as Julia Wrigley discusses in her wide-ranging chapter. Each system has experienced large immigrant influxes and has had problems of severe underachievement, racial segregation, overcrowding, crumbling infrastructures, and declining political support.

Each system has experimented with reforms as it tries desperately to improve. Examples in recent decades have included the "small schools" movement, charter schools, and mayoral control of the education system. Under Bloomberg, New York City has been an epicenter of reform attempts. At the start of his mayoralty, Bloomberg was handed "mayoral control" of the schools, becoming the first ever New York mayor with the ability to appoint and dismiss the chancellor of the city's public schools on his own.

The results have been mixed. The "small schools movement" experiment was the initial major project of Bloomberg's first schools Chancellor, Joel Klein. It was heavily supported by the (Bill) Gates Foundation, but after a 2009 study showed that the students had weak math scores (small schools did not have many math teachers) Gates switched to supporting charter schools. For example, the Harlem Children's Zone has now received over $200 million from private philanthropists. A characteristic of the current period in US education is the large role played by wealthy foundations in developing ideas for public education, reflecting a view that the schools are adrift and that foundations and other nonprofits need to fill the government lacuna (the classic case for nonprofits, as Helmut Anheier, David Howard, and Marcus Lam discuss in chapter 19). By 2011 perhaps the dominant conclusion of New York school reform was sobering—no single approach offers a "silver bullet." Progress likely requires a combination of measures, and even then it is not assured.

Another sobering conclusion is that even adequately measuring success is difficult. Bloomberg, in line with the stress he generally placed on measurable accountability, had said his school reforms should be judged by two metrics—student test scores and graduation rates. The schools under his mayoralty seemed to have shown some improvement in both of these marks, but a heralded narrowing gap between black and white students turned out not to be true. Also, New York City students' gains on state tests (in some grade levels) seemed questionable when compared with the National Assessment of Educational Progress (NAEP) exams, the gold standard of tests. Now New York State is redoing its tests to try to have better measures of outcome based upon so-called value added. In Los Angeles the system is far more adrift. The LA mayor could never achieve mayoral control, and sadly the Los Angeles district did not even claim major test score advances. Its students' NAEP scores showed little or no improvement.

CRIME

Fagan and MacDonald's crime discussion shows that this issue too is a fascinating story, of changing policing and changing crime. Los Angeles and New York each suffered a crime epidemic from the late 1960s to the early 1990s, visible in homicide and robbery trends. Drugs were crucial to the crime wave, but so were guns—nearly all the increase and decline in homicides across the fifty-year window represented changes in the number of gun-related homicides. Demographically, the violence was rooted among adolescents and young adults, ages 13–24.

Crime has now plummeted in both cities to levels not seen since the early 1960s. The reasons are a complex mix, from changing police tactics to long-term demographics. The former included the famous COMPSTAT program, introduced by Commissioner Bratton in interestingly different forms in both cities. The essence of COMPSTAT is using geographical mapping of crime to make strategic decisions about officer deployment, and setting police division benchmarks for crime reductions. Under the NYPD COMPSTAT, each division captain was basically responsible for crime trends and formulating a response in his or her police area, and performance was noted in monthly, central command staff meetings. When Bratton was appointed LAPD police chief in 2002, he instituted COMPSTAT Plus (i.e., the LA version). This created a centralized audit team of LAPD commanders, who then worked with each local police division to develop its own strategic plan to meet crime reduction goals. This was a sea change for the LAPD and also for COMPSTAT. Previous LAPD approaches to reducing crime, dating back to the Parker administration, relied on sending specialized units and tactical responses to local divisions. Never before had reducing crime focused on a locally based, community-wide approach that relied primarily on line-officers and command staff, in consultation with a central audit division. Los Angeles witnessed a significant reduction in crime rates after the implementation of COMPSTAT plus, as New York had under the original COMPSTAT (i.e., the version without a central audit).[3]

Fagan and MacDonald also foreground demographic, non-police related, causes of the crime drop. These include immigration, as mentioned earlier. In both cities, neighborhoods with high immigrant concentrations show larger crime declines than similar neighborhoods without heavy influxes of immigrants. (There are also interesting differences between immigrants groups—for example, in New York, neighborhoods settled by Mexican immigrants have lower crime rates than areas settled by Dominican newcomers.) Among the ways that immigrants affect crime is bringing commercial development in the form of local services to the newly arrived groups; immigrants also tend to occupy dwellings that are undesirable and/ or abandoned, giving the space new meaning. Perhaps recognizing this relationship in both cities, police patrol neighborhoods with high concentrations of immigrants less aggressively than other economically comparable neighborhoods.

The quality of police–community relations is clearly a key issue. Accusations of unconstitutional policing have resulted in major civil litigation in Los Angeles and New York during the past decade, and both cities have operated under consent decrees. Still, Fagan and MacDonald argue that a central reason the NYPD seems to have reduced abuses less under the consent decree than its LA counterpart is that the NYPD, unlike the LAPD, was not subject to court-ordered monitoring of its behavior during this period. In 2009, Los Angeles emerged from nine years under a consent decree. In lifting the decree the US District Court Judge noted, "The LAPD has become the national and international policing standard for activities that range from audits to handling of the mentally ill to many aspects of training to risk assessment of police officers and more." The LAPD has entered into new partnerships with various community organizations, and in recent polls nearly 80 percent of LA residents expressed strong approval for the performance of the department. Remarkably, this included 76 percent and 68 percent of the black and Latino respondents respectively, and doubtless partly reflected the fact that Bratton's COMPSTAT Plus approach, unlike that of the NYPD, did not result in the rapid reallocation of line officers to impact zones.

New York City, by contrast, emerged from the Daniels civil litigation in 2007, which did not involve court-ordered monitoring of the NYPD's behavior, only to become immediately mired in three new separate lawsuits alleging both racial discrimination and a pattern of unconstitutional street stops. The NYPD has intensified its spectrum of Order Maintenance Policing tactics, including trespass enforcement in public housing, street stops, and misdemeanor marijuana enforcement. All three approaches have led to litigation against the NYPD. The divided response of the City's diverse communities to the Stop and Frisk program, the centerpiece of the NYPD strategy, shows the depth of the racial breach between citizens and police: white voters approve 59 to 36 percent, while disapproval is 68 to 27 percent among black voters and 52 to 43 percent among Hispanic voters.

Finally, both cities are confronting the threat of terrorism, and both have responded with strategies that have transformed policing. This policy involves intensive surveillance and intelligence gathering targeted at terror suspects, and relies on an implicit form of racial profiling. The emphasis on terror complicates things immensely. There is no legal mandate for local police to undertake terror investigations other than to address crimes committed within their jurisdictions. Aggressive policing of terror creates tensions with citizens in targeted populations that undermines police legitimacy and may ruin community relationships and incentives for citizens to cooperate with police in investigations.

INNOVATION, COMPETITION, AND ENVIRONMENTALISM AMONG PORTS—SEA, AIR, AND LAND

Measured by the value of international trade, fully half the nation's leading global gateways (ports, airports, and land ports-of-entry) are in the Los Angeles and New York regions—the two Ports of Long Beach and Los Angeles and Los Angeles International Airport, and the Port of NY/NJ and John F. Kennedy International Airport. With $417 billion in global trade in 2010, Los Angeles ranked first in the value of vessel cargo and third in air cargo shipments. With $354 billion in global trade, New York ranked first in air cargo and third in vessel cargo.

The United States is widely recognized as facing major infrastructure challenges. In 2010 the American Society of Civil Engineers estimated that the United States needed to spend $2.2 trillion just to maintain the quality of its mostly second-rate infrastructure. The port-related facilities (docks, airports, rail lines, and associated facilities) in each region present important challenges, as analyzed by Jameson W. Doig, Steven P. Erie, and Scott A. MacKenzie in chapter 4. Based on current infrastructure and policy, as well as future trends, the two cities are in very different positions in maintaining their status as prime port cities.

Since early in the twentieth century, the crucial trade infrastructure assets in both regions have been handled by powerful public agencies designed to be insulated from local and state elected officials. These specialized institutions have aided New York and Los Angeles in building economies strongly shaped by trade opportunities. In the New York region, a large portion of these transportation networks has been constructed and managed by the bi-state Port Authority of New York and New Jersey, created in 1921 after years of conflict between the two states. The Port Authority's empire includes the major airports (Kennedy, LaGuardia, and Newark), the region's largest marine terminals (Newark and Elizabeth), major bridges and tunnels (Lincoln and Holland tunnels and George Washington Bridge), and the PATH railroad. In contrast, the Los Angeles system is decentralized with separate municipal agencies created to govern its major airports and seaports.

Nowadays, though in somewhat different ways, both the Port Authority and the LA region's port and airport agencies face new pressures threatening their current positions. Other regions have started to take traffic from the largest ports, while the New York and Los Angeles agencies must devote increased attention to environmental standards and security threats.

The Port Authority faces at least three huge challenges—preparing for the new class of mega-ships, completing the World Trade Center, and resisting political pressures that lead to staff appointments based on patronage and to funding projects that add to agency deficits while also (in some cases) diverting staff energies and funds from its core transportation mission.

The New Mega-Ships

Around 2015 the Panama Canal is scheduled to open a new channel that will accommodate ships carrying double the cargo of those that currently fit the canal. So the main Atlantic ports—New York (Newark-Elizabeth), Savannah, Charleston, Baltimore, Norfolk, and Miami—are competing to prepare themselves to capture as large a share of that traffic as possible since all but one (Norfolk) cannot accommodate the new ships without substantial physical changes.

In the New York area, it is the height of the new mega ships, more than their depth, that poses a major problem. Right now, the eighty-year-old Bayonne Bridge between Staten Island and New Jersey has such a low clearance that container ships sometimes have to wait for low tide before they can pass. The situation will get worse when ships with containers stacked nine high, rather than the current six, start coming through the Panama Canal. The Port Authority is solving that problem by raising the roadway on the Bayonne Bridge by some six stories, a challenging task that the agency hopes to complete by 2015, when the bigger ships will cross through the Panama Canal.

By contrast, Los Angeles and Long Beach, the two ports in California's San Pedro Bay, are already positioned to handle the new generation of cargo ships. Nonetheless, competition, whether from developing West Coast ports like Port Prince Rupert in Vancouver or from East Coast ports, which can receive direct shipments from Asia via the Suez Canal and, by 2014–15, through the Panama Canal, will continue to threaten Los Angeles's position as the premier gateway to Pacific Rim trade. Los Angeles has responded to this challenge by upgrading its freight-rail infrastructure to cut transit times for goods headed toward the nation's interior. But these new challenges come at a difficult time. Budget problems in California and Los Angeles have reduced the amount of money available to finance infrastructure upgrades. And increasing pressure from environmental groups and local communities means that all future investments will have to address quality of life concerns while navigating ever tighter financial constraints.

Rebuilding the World Trade Center

The Port Authority's executives, engineers, and other staff are heavily absorbed in the effort to rebuild the World Trade Center. In 2006 the Port Authority assumed overall management of the complex effort, which involves constructing up to five new skyscrapers, the third-largest transit hub in New York City, a performing arts center, restoration of two city streets, a memorial and museum, and a retail complex. In 2011 alone, the Port Authority's capital budget related to the World Trade Center was $1.9 billion— more than three times the amount allocated for airport modernization and ten times the funds made available for port improvements. The World Trade Center costs were an important factor in the Port Authority's decision in August 2011 to seek gubernatorial approval (soon granted) for a substantial increase in bridge and tunnel tolls and local PATH train fares. The World Trade Center is certainly moving ahead, but at substantial cost in diverting Port Authority resources from other essential transportation projects.

Revenue Diversions and Political Patronage
at the Port Authority

As the authors of chapter 4 note, the Port Authority has faced insistent political demands that it allocate funds to activities outside its main mission (e.g., construction of the Newark Legal Center) and to programs that it does not control (as in money to fill gaps in New Jersey's transportation budget). Staff energies and money have also been diverted in increasing amounts to complete the World Trade Center, which is largely a real-estate venture.

The agency has also, especially in the past two years, been forced to appoint a large number of staff members based on patronage, not competence. In January 2012, Shawn Boburg and John Reitmeyer of the Bergen County *Record* described at length Republican Governor Chris Christie's extensive use of patronage appointments at the Port Authority (Boburg and Reitmeyer 2012). Their research revealed that fifty people had been hired by the Port Authority after referrals by the Christie administration since he became governor in 2010. The jobs ranged from federal affairs director to toll collector. Eleven of the fifty employees hired had donated to Christie's gubernatorial campaign or had an immediate relative who did. Five came directly from his administration or worked on his campaign.

This is probably the greatest example of patronage abuse in the Port Authority's history. As described in chapter 4, the structure of the Port Authority's Board of Commissioners is supposed to shield it from narrow political interests. For example, although governors from New York and New Jersey each select the agency's top two executives, as well as the twelve-member board of commissioners, the latter have overlapping six-year terms so that no single governor can exercise disproportionate control over the agency through appointees. The governors have veto power over the unpaid commissioners' decisions but no official authority to hire employees.

While patronage is not new at the Port Authority, Christie's patronage is extreme. "I don't know of any instance in which a governor has [recommended] 50 people for the Port Authority staff," said Martin E. Robins, director emeritus of Voorhees Transportation Policy Institute at Rutgers University, and planning director at the Port Authority in the 1980s. Despite press stories detailing his patronage appointments, Christie continued to recommend the hiring of political loyalists to the Port Authority and the firing of those unwilling to compromise professional standards for political considerations. By the fall of 2012, the total number of Christie patronage appointees exceeded eighty.

Los Angeles Ports and Environmentalism
Problems: The Clean Trucks Program

The chapters on environmentalism in each region highlight a challenge especially acute for the Ports of Los Angeles and Long Beach. For years Los Angeles had the reputation as the most environmentally problematic city in the country, with the worst air quality (occasionally challenged by Houston in recent years). The ports of Los Angeles and Long Beach turned out to be key toxic hot spots, together generating over 20 percent of Southern California's diesel particulate pollution, much of it from idling trucks loading and unloading cargo.

Martha Matsuoka and Robert Gottlieb in chapter 16 discuss two tested approaches for dealing with diesel fumes at the ports. The first attempted to reduce diesel emissions from trucks and remains embroiled in controversy. It consisted of The Clean Trucks Program, adopted in late 2006 as part of the joint San Pedro Bay Ports Clean Air Action Plan (discussed in chapter 4 also). Its goals were straightforward: replace and retrofit approximately 16,000 trucks to meet the 2007 federal EPA emissions standards by 2012. A central problem was how to pay for replacing these trucks, since the costs of doing so for independent truck drivers, who on average netted just $30,000 in income annually, were steep. So the Clean Trucks Program instead required trucking companies who service the Port to hire truck drivers as employees in return for securing transport contracts with the Port. The trucking companies would now pay the costs of the clean air program including purchasing new, cleaner trucks.

The policy was immediately opposed by the American Trucking Associations, which filed an injunction blocking the implementation of the program. In August 2010, a federal court judge cleared the way for full implementation of the Clean Trucks Program but ruled that during the appeals process the employee concessionaire component could not proceed. So right now individual truck drivers are required to retrofit their trucks but without any financial help in doing so.

The Port Authority of New York and New Jersey, mindful of the problems of the Clean Trucks Program at the Los Angeles and Long Beach ports, introduced a more moderate program to deal with diesel truck pollution. In January 2011, it banned 1994 and older trucks (Los Angeles's plan bans 2004 and older trucks) without the requirement that trucking firms hire drivers as employees. With funds including a grant from the US EPA, plus $23 million of its own funds, the Port Authority set up a loan program for drivers to make the required retrofits to get the estimated 640 old trucks off the road. Still, many drivers are ineligible and are expected to be out of work as a result.

A second, different approach to the problem of pollution at Los Angeles's ports was more successful, allowing infrastructure growth while using a community mitigation fund to address environmental concerns. This approach evolved as an eventual compromise over a dispute regarding a new proposed terminal project at the Port of Los Angeles. The new terminal would add 76 acres by 2038 and expand the terminal's throughput to a level that equals the current operations of the Port of Oakland, one of the ten busiest container ports in the United States. The Los Angeles Harbor Commission (with the Mayor's blessing) approved the expansion in early December 2007, despite strong community criticism. A week later, fifteen organizations and two Harbor residents wrote to the City Council appealing the decision.

In April 2008, the City of Los Angeles and the Port of Los Angeles agreed to a settlement and in October of the same year established the nonprofit Port Community Mitigation Trust Fund to address long-term approaches to the health and community impacts of port growth and expansion. The off-port mitigation fund, financed by future expansion projects, provided over $50 million in off-port, property community mitigation projects. These include air purification and sound proofing systems

NEW YORK AND LOS ANGELES (21)

in public elementary schools and residents' homes; public respiratory healthcare services at local community clinics and health services providers; and potential wetlands restoration projects in Wilmington and San Pedro.

This was a textbook model of successfully dealing with NIMBYism, a huge problem for each city and region (Dear 1992; Garvin 2002). NIMBYism can be very complex, but its core consists of conflicts over projects that produce widely dispersed benefits but also geographically concentrated costs (usually on a particular neighborhood), such as those that result from transportation projects, homeless shelters, prisons, airports, sports stadiums, and waste disposal sites. This inequality of cost distribution almost guarantees local opposition. The benefits associated with these facilities are both broadly distributed and, compared to the local costs, more meager. Consequently, few individuals aside from a project's developer have an incentive to advocate on behalf of a particular project.

A central solution, in theory, is for government to propose transfer payments that compensate an adversely affected neighborhood. The idea is that the localized project creates a public surplus (hopefully economic), hence it is both fair and politically sensible (in terms of getting the project accepted) to redirect part of that surplus to those disproportionately bearing the project's costs, as with the Port of Los Angeles's successful mitigation fund.

HOUSING AND NEW YORK'S "PRODUCTION EXTERNALITY" GOAL

Ingrid Gould Ellen and Brendan O'Flaherty's comprehensive account of housing policies in the two cities underscores the usefulness of the comparative approach. Considering America's ten largest cities by population, New York and Los Angeles have the largest proportions of renters by far, 70 percent in New York and 61 percent in Los Angeles, followed by Chicago with 56 percent and Houston with 54 percent (2000 data). In none of the other ten largest cities do renters constitute a majority of households. Also New York and Los Angeles are the only two US cities with over a million people that still regulate rents on most apartments. Nor is New York rent regulation necessarily stricter than in Los Angeles, as is often thought. For example, the reach of Los Angeles rent regulation is wider than that of New York, since in Los Angeles rent regulation applies to all units with two or more apartments, while, with minor exceptions New York covers only buildings with six or more apartments. (The vast majority of regulated units in New York City fall under the less strict rent stabilization regime, rather than under traditional rent control.)

Still, a huge difference comes when considering subsidized housing, not just rent regulation. New York far exceeds Los Angeles and any other major city in spending on subsidized housing, for example, in 1995 spending $107 per capita on housing, compared to an average of $13 per capita in the next largest thirty-two cities (Schwartz 2009, 230). For one, the public housing version of subsidized housing is successful in New York City, with, historically, a reputation for being better managed and maintained than in most other large cities. The New York City Housing Authority is by far the largest city housing authority in the country, currently maintaining roughly 180,000 units of public housing, almost twice as many as the next nine largest cities combined. Also, almost no units have been torn down, since public housing is viewed more positively in New York than in other cities. By contrast, the second largest housing authority, Chicago, which managed 21,442 units of public housing in 2008, is planning a huge net reduction of 13,000 public units. In general US public housing is highly subsidized and affordable, with tenants paying 30 percent of their income for rent (known as the "30 percent standard").

Another feature of New York City's housing policy is that subsidized housing is not confined to the poor or working class, but often includes the lower-middle and middle class too. For example, the City oversees 60,000 Mitchell Lama rental units that are aimed at moderate- and middle-income households. The city also offers tax breaks for developers who build rental housing for moderate and middle-income households, and compared to other cities has traditionally reserved a greater share of its public housing units for working families, not just the unemployed poor. Also, rent-regulated apartments are not means-tested (the only exception is the rule freeing an apartment from rent-regulation if the rents rises above $2,400 or the tenant's income rises above $200,000 for two years). So in New York some households living in housing units with below-market rents have relatively high incomes.

Ellen and O'Flaherty argue that the goals of housing policy in New York City account for its distinctiveness. New York City's attention to subsidized housing is above all due to a perception by leaders of the importance of particular, "externality-related" goals, in addition to, or even over, redistributive goals, which are probably the most frequent justification usually offered for rent regulation and subsidized housing. Many New York business and other city leaders have long known that major productivity advantages accrue from the city's huge population and job density. These advantages come both from having lots of jobs and economic sectors close together where people can easily interact, and from having many of those who work in these jobs living reasonably close by, minimizing commutes. For example, in 2010, the geographically small chunk of Manhattan south of 61st Street generated 35 percent of the payroll by value, and contained 25 percent of the jobs, in the entire New York Metropolitan Statistical Area, a huge, twenty-three-county, geographic area.[4]

New York's leaders have repeatedly stressed the value of and need to support these production externalities. Back in 1980 the New York Chamber of Commerce (later renamed the New York Partnership) surveyed businesses asking what their major problems were. The largest turned out to be the difficulty their employees and job recruits faced in finding housing within their means. That was a key finding that led Governor Rockefeller to start state-run affordable housing initiatives, followed soon after by the city.

Mayor Bloomberg's 2002 housing plan likewise emphasizes production externalities: "In order for New York City to remain competitive and to ensure that its record growth can continue; significant housing issues must be addressed." Still, by the time Bloomberg took office, the main earlier options for creating substantial amounts of affordable housing were mostly no longer available, leaving "inclusionary housing," which incentivizes the private sector to build affordable housing, as the main option. Classic public housing was hardly possible anymore, since the federal government had long ago drastically reduced funding for new public housing. Also, the stock of housing units and land owned by the city for possible sites to create more affordable housing had dwindled.

"Inclusionary housing" works by giving financial incentives to developers of residential projects if they include a certain percentage of "affordable" housing units (usually rental units, not ownership) for low- and moderate-income households. The financial incentives basically allow the developer to construct a larger building, or give the developer tax-exempt financing, or both in return for including some affordable units. So another advantage of "inclusionary housing" is that it avoids segregating the poor into their own buildings, as happens with public housing. By contrast, there are few if any records of Los Angeles mayors or city officials similarly arguing that providing new, affordable, housing for the middle and lower-middle class, not just for the poor, is important to the city's well-being.

ARCHITECTURE

In a tour de force, Rick Bell, Executive Director of the New York section of the American Institute of Architects, argues in chapter 17 that six trends capture the main directions of architecture in Los Angeles and New York. These trends are reuse, sustainability, transparency/openness, fun, connectivity, and spirit. New York's High Line, a disused, above ground rail line now converted to a park and the city's most talked-about new project for decades, exemplifies three of these themes—reuse, connectivity, and fun. This doubtless helps explain its popularity. Further, a slew of innovative new buildings around the High Line have led the re-emergence of New York's architecture after a long period of doldrums. The *Los Angeles Times* architecture critic greeted the opening in 2011 of LA architect Neil Denari's innovative condo (HL23) cantilevered over the High Line, as having reversed assumptions about New York and LA architecture:

> It used to be that for young, experimental or otherwise untested architects, L.A. was the place to get an unorthodox design built. In New York, on the other hand, opportunities for those architects tended to be limited to residential or commercial interiors that had no impact on the skyline.... HL23 ... is a sign of how dramatically that equation has changed in recent years.... To complete the first ground-up building of his career, the 53-year-old Denari [one of the city's most prominent architects] had to go to Manhattan the island that was for decades known among architects as the place visionary dreams went to die (Hawthorne 2011).

THE POLITICS OF TOLERANCE IN CITY
AND SUBURBS: CHANGING PATTERNS

The growing racial and ethnic diversity of the suburbs beyond the city limits, mentioned earlier, does not, of course, necessarily translate into greater tolerance there or mean that these suburbs are increasingly integrated. These days, the New York region's outer-suburban environment can be openly hostile to immigrants in those towns and cities with a more recent immigration history, reflecting tensions between the fast-rising Latino population and the still numerically dominant non-Hispanic whites. These tensions are reminiscent of outer Los Angeles in the early days of the post-1960s immigrant inflow there.

For example, bitter conflicts have arisen over day-labor sites and overcrowded immigrant housing in towns in Westchester County and Long Island, as Nancy Foner and Roger Waldinger document in chapter 12. An example is Steve Levy, the County Executive of Suffolk County, the fast-growing eastern half of Long Island, which has witnessed a dramatic growth in its foreign-born, mostly Latino population in recent years. Levy's crusade against undocumented immigrants helped make him virtually unbeatable. Elected as a Democrat in 2003 in a county dominated for years by Republicans, four years later Levy had an 80 percent approval rating and endorsements from both the Republican and Democratic parties. In 2007, he supported a bill, dubbed "Standing While Latino," which had it passed the county legislature would have banned day laborers from seeking employment along county roadways. On Long Island in Farmingville, a largely white community in Suffolk County about 50 miles from New York City, two Mexican day laborers were beaten nearly to death in 2000 by two men from nearby towns. Both cities, New York and Los Angeles, pride themselves on their tolerance these days. Still, at the level of neighborhoods and residential settlement too, New York's liberalism has limits. One of the clearest findings from the 2010 data is the continuing high residential separation of blacks from non-Hispanic whites in New York City and Nassau County, among the starkest divides in the country. In order to measure how separated/segregated one population is residentially from another, demographers use a D score, which can range from 0 to 1, with D scores of 0.7 or above indicating very high separation levels. Of the eight counties with the highest black/non-Hispanic white D scores in both regions, six are New York City's five counties plus adjoining Nassau County, with Brooklyn and Queens topping the list, as Andrew Beveridge and colleagues show in chapter 11. None are in the Los Angeles region. Of the thirty-five counties in the New York and Los Angeles region, only two score above 0.8 on separation between blacks and non-Hispanic whites. They are Brooklyn (0.83) and Queens (0.80). Incredibly, both these scores are down slightly from their 2000 level, but Brooklyn is still the most segregated county in the nation.

Segregation also exists, and is growing moderately, with respect to the very affluent from the rest of the population. Finally, at least in both regions, it is plain that the segregation is not fueled by income but is mostly related to racial differences, especially with respect to the black population. Simply put, affluent blacks are segregated from affluent whites at very high levels.

Los Angeles's earlier reputation as a focus of anti-immigrant sentiment was solidified in the early 1990s when 56 percent of the voters in Los Angeles County supported the statewide Proposition 187, which would have made undocumented immigrants ineligible for government-funded social and health services. (Most of the provisions were invalidated by California court decisions.) In stark contrast, around the same time as Proposition 187 was passed in California, New York City Mayor Rudolph Giuliani issued an executive order protecting undocumented immigrants from being reported when they used city services.

However, nowadays the City of Los Angeles is at least as likely to lead in demonstrating tolerance. Right after Arizona enacted a harsh law against undocumented immigrants in 2010 that allowed police to detain people on the suspicion that they were in the country illegally and made the failure to carry immigration documents a crime (mostly invalidated at the end of the Supreme Court term in 2012), New York City's Mayor Bloomberg sharply attacked it, saying that with this law "we are committing national suicide.... This is not good for the country. We love immigrants here." In Los Angeles, Mayor Villaraigosa went even further, backing a boycott of Arizona in response to the immigration crackdown.

Indeed, on the level of political liberalism, measured by the Americans for Democratic Action score of a city's congressional delegation, the City of Los Angeles is now more liberal than New York City (so are Philadelphia, San Diego, and Detroit), as Ingrid Gould Ellen and Brendan O'Flaherty point out in chapter 10.

These differences played out in regard to the Occupy Wall Street movement. When it began, New York Mayor Bloomberg cautiously accepted a judicial ruling confirming that Occupy's presence, camping in Zuccotti Park one block from Wall Street, was legal (the park was by law required to be open 24/7). Los Angeles Mayor Villaraigosa, by contrast, openly welcomed the Occupy Los Angeles contingent, as did the City Council, despite the fact that its presence was technically illegal since the park outside City Hall where the occupiers slept was legally supposed to be closed during the night. Villaraigosa even donated 100 ponchos for the occupiers when it rained and sometimes served them breakfast. It is true that a week after Bloomberg eventually forcibly evicted the New York protestors in a pre-dawn police operation, LA city officials also told its protestors they could not stay indefinitely. Yet, reflecting the LA mayor's generally more liberal proclivities compared to New York's, the city offered the protestors a generous package of incentives to leave, including a $1-a-year lease on a 10,000 square-foot office space near City Hall, and land elsewhere for those wishing to farm.

INEQUALITY

The topic of inequality is both simple, as Occupy Wall Street's hugely successful slogan, "we are the 99 percent," demonstrated, and complex, as David L. Gladstone and Susan S. Fainstein show in chapter 3. On the simple side, the main measures of income inequality show New York and Los Angeles as among the most unequal US cities in one of the most unequal countries in the world. For example, considering all thirty-three OECD countries in the mid-2000s, inequality in the United States, as measured by the Gini index from lowest, 0, to highest, 1, was exceeded only by Mexico, Chile, and Turkey. Inequality in the United Kingdom was almost as high as the United States, suggesting the importance in inequality of a dominant financial sector. (See table 1.2.) In 2010, levels of income inequality—again as measured by the Gini index—of the twenty-five largest US cities, including Washington, DC, were highest in Boston, New York, Washington, DC, and Los Angeles in that order. (See table 1.3.)

Table 1.2 GINI COEFFICIENTS FOR INCOME FOR OECD
COUNTRIES

	Gini coefficient	
	Level	Rank
OECD average	**0.313**	—
Australia	0.336	9
Austria	0.261	26
Belgium	0.259	29
Canada	0.324	12
Chile	0.494	1
Czech Republic	0.256	31
Denmark	0.248	33
Estonia	0.315	14
Finland	0.259	27
France	0.293	23
Germany	0.295	20
Greece	0.307	17
Hungary	0.272	25
Iceland	0.301	19
Ireland	0.293	22
Israel	0.371	5
Italy	0.337	8
Japan	0.329	11
Korea	0.315	15
Luxembourg	0.288	24
Mexico	0.476	2
Netherlands	0.294	21
New Zealand	0.330	10
Norway	0.250	32
Poland	0.314	16
Portugal	0.353	6
Slovak Republic	0.257	30
Slovenia	0.236	34
Spain	0.317	13
Sweden	0.259	28
Switzerland	0.303	18
Turkey	0.409	3
United Kingdom	0.345	7
United States	0.378	4

Source: OECD Factbook 2011: Economic, Environmental and Social Statistics.

Table 1.3 INCOME INEQUALITY IN 25 LARGEST CITIES, 5 LARGEST METROS, AND UNITED STATES IN 2010

	Total Population	Mean Income Bottom Quintile	Mean Income Top Quintile	Mean Income Top 5%	Ratio Mean of Top Quintile to Bottom Quintile	Gini Coefficient	Rank of Gini among Top 25 Cities
25 Largest Cities							
New York, New York	8,184,899	$9,022	$214,592	$419,734	23.8	0.535	2
Los Angeles, California	3,797,144	$9,661	$203,469	$395,275	21.1	0.525	4
Chicago, Illinois	2,698,831	$8,269	$176,762	$323,358	21.4	0.510	8
Houston, Texas	2,107,208	$9,405	$178,069	$333,823	18.9	0.511	7
Philadelphia, Pennsylvania	1,528,306	$5,692	$130,101	$223,845	22.9	0.505	10
Phoenix, Arizona	1,449,481	$8,824	$158,626	$274,407	18.0	0.485	17
San Antonio, Texas	1,334,359	$9,487	$144,117	$243,232	15.2	0.460	21
San Diego, California	1,311,886	$12,392	$208,873	$371,374	16.9	0.478	18
Dallas, Texas	1,202,797	$9,392	$178,542	$344,955	19.0	0.519	5
San Jose, California	949,197	$15,980	$221,017	$331,906	13.8	0.434	25
Indianapolis, Indiana	824,199	$9,288	$136,405	$236,293	14.7	0.468	20
Jacksonville, Florida	823,316	$10,370	$147,605	$267,451	14.2	0.459	22
San Francisco, California	805,463	$11,527	$266,447	$472,606	23.1	0.507	9
Austin, Texas	795,518	$9,923	$178,828	$315,314	18.0	0.488	14
Columbus, Ohio	789,939	$8,325	$130,292	$217,939	15.7	0.456	23
Fort Worth, Texas	744,114	$11,113	$153,778	$262,252	13.8	0.453	24
Charlotte, North Carolina	734,418	$11,170	$194,778	$380,009	17.4	0.501	11
Detroit, Michigan	711,910	$4,721	$92,933	$151,247	19.7	0.488	15
El Paso, Texas	652,113	$9,011	$136,285	$232,452	15.1	0.474	19
Memphis, Tennessee	647,870	$7,462	$136,112	$248,400	18.2	0.489	13
Boston, Massachusetts	621,383	$6,219	$211,148	$385,857	34.0	0.543	1

(Continued)

Table 1.3 (CONTINUED)

	Total Population	Mean Income Bottom Quintile	Mean Income Top Quintile	Mean Income Top 5%	Ratio Mean of Top Quintile to Bottom Quintile	Gini Coefficient	Rank of Gini among Top 25 Cities
Baltimore, Maryland	620,583	$6,977	$142,166	$246,008	20.4	0.497	12
Seattle, Washington	610,710	$11,840	$220,090	$388,153	18.6	0.488	16
Washington, District of Columbia	604,453	$9,062	$259,204	$473,343	28.6	0.532	3
Denver, Colorado	604,414	$9,027	$186,279	$341,037	20.6	0.515	6
5 Largest Metros							
New York-Newark-Bridgeport, NY-NJ-CT-PA	22,111,682	$12,450	$238,929	$441,041	19.2	0.500	5
Los Angeles-Long Beach-Riverside, CA	17,920,862	$12,709	$197,775	$346,881	15.6	0.472	27
Chicago-Naperville-Michigan City, IL-IN-WI	9,699,178	$12,715	$192,288	$338,089	15.1	0.466	34
Washington-Baltimore-Northern Virginia, DC-MD-VA-WV	8,605,658	$17,511	$237,849	$391,560	13.6	0.442	88
Boston-Worcester-Manchester, MA-RI-NH	7,569,282	$12,750	$209,255	$361,602	16.4	0.467	31
United States	309,349,689	$11,307	$171,741	$299,770	15.2	0.469	NA

Source: American Community Survey Data, 2010 from *Social Explorer.*

In New York and Los Angeles, relative inequality appears to grow as the geographic unit of reference becomes smaller and more central. Thus, New York City is more unequal than the larger New York metropolitan area, while Manhattan is substantially more unequal than the larger city or metropolitan area. Los Angeles demonstrates a similar pattern: the City of Los Angeles is more unequal than Los Angeles County, which in turn is more unequal than the Los Angeles metropolitan area.

On the more complex side of the inequality discussion, highly skewed income distributions in New York and Los Angeles in part reflect their laudable openness, as Gladstone and Fainstein point out in their chapter. Both cities and regions host huge numbers of low-skilled immigrants willing to accept work at very low levels of wages and benefits. Meanwhile, at the top, New York especially, but also Los Angeles, offers extraordinarily high earnings possibilities due to the disproportionate presence of industries (investment banking, corporate law, broadcasting, and motion pictures) that pay their top executives and performers exceptionally well. Finance is key here. By 2008 the average wage and salary for those employed in Finance and Insurance in New York City was $197,441, almost twice as high as the next best paid NY sector (Management of Companies, $114,790). By contrast, the highest paid sector in Los Angeles, measured by average wage and salary, was Management of Companies ($73,020). Further, the 2008 wages and salaries of Finance and Insurance in New York were 54 percent higher than ten years ago, the largest increase by far in either New York or Los Angeles (Art, Entertainment, and Recreation in New York was the second largest increase at 28 percent). Still, the future of finance is unclear and not likely to return to those peaks soon.

Overall, inequality increased substantially in global cities during the last three decades, not so much because the poor have become poorer and more numerous—although this has occurred—but because the rich became so much richer, as Gladstone and Fainstein point out.

THE UNCERTAIN FUTURE OF GLOBAL CITIES

A final uncertainty relates to the core reasons underpinning the dynamism of these two cities. That dynamism rests on New York and Los Angeles being magnets for certain industries key to the global economy, as well as for extraordinarily diverse populations. The future of their economies depends on the continuing need of these industries to be close to each other and able to draw on a local labor force (the "production externalities" that Ellen and O'Flaherty stress). Saskia Sassen contends that this drive for cohesiveness and closeness has increased in the last decade and predicts that it will continue to do so.

Still, this is not assured. As recently as the early 2000s several astute urban observers were arguing the opposite, namely that the then-new Internet would make such closeness unnecessary, and that major urban centers were obsolete. Likewise, for two decades before the Internet the "Los Angeles School" of urban studies had been predicting the demise of mega urban centers, to be replaced by "edge cities" dispersed from the core and each containing substantial office and commercial sectors, as well as residential development, as part of suburbanization's ongoing dynamic. These gloomy predictions for the future of global cities did not happen. Still, Gladstone and Fainstein strike a sensibly cautious note of uncertainty, while also stressing the difference that positive political leadership and innovation can make to a city's future. As they argue, "It is our view that firms involved in servicing the international economy do not necessarily require close contact with each other, and the faster growth rates outside these two central cities, even in producer services, weakens [Sassen's] argument. We do not, however, see the outcome as predetermined by either technology or cost structures but rather a contingent consequence of political leadership and economic innovation."

NOTES

1. Already back in 1992 the *Los Angeles Times* ran an article stressing "L.A.'s Loss: 'Black Flight'" complaining that "an exodus to distant suburbs is depriving the inner city of active, involved families."
2. Hurricane Sandy made landfall in Atlantic City on the evening of October 29th. It was then called a Post Tropical Cyclonic Event by the National Weather Sevice. It then merged with a Nor'easter and was dubbed by many in the media as Superstorm Sandy.
3. Crime had also fallen in Los Angeles after the appointment in June 1992, following the Rodney King riots, of former Philadelphia Police Commissioner Willie Williams, the first African American police chief of Los Angeles, who took some steps toward a community policing model. Still, intense resistance to community policing within the LAPD middle and upper management ranks eventually cost Williams his job, and his 1997 replacement Bernard Parks focused on tactical units to combat crime, which rose again.
4. The data are based on estimates by the New York City Economic Development Corporation, provided by Merrill Pond of the New York Partnership. The Metropolitan Statistical Area is composed of the following counties: Essex County, NJ, Hunterdon County, NJ, Morris County, NJ, Sussex County, NJ, Union County, NJ, Middlesex County, NJ, Monmouth County, NJ, Ocean County, NJ, Somerset County, NJ, Nassau County, NY, Suffolk County, NY, Bergen County, NJ, Hudson County, NJ, Passaic County, NJ, Bronx County, NY, Kings County, NY, New York County, NY, Putnam County, NY, Queens County, NY, Richmond County, NY, Rockland County, NY, Westchester County, NY, Pike County, PA.

PART ONE

Overview

CHAPTER 2

The Big Picture

Demographic and Other Changes

ANDREW A. BEVERIDGE AND
SYDNEY J. BEVERIDGE

N ew York City and Los Angeles are two iconic US cities of the twenty-first century.[1] Both are coastal cities, and both dominate their surrounding regions. They
serve as cultural and media centers for the nation and the world. They have diverse
populations and are home to some of the richest and poorest people in the United
States. They have been destinations for young people who want to strike it rich, be
discovered, and "make it." New York and its region became, in the words emblazoned
on signs around Wall Street near Zuccotti Park, where the Occupy Wall Street movement was once encamped, the "Capitol of Capital." Not too far from Zuccotti Park is
Ground Zero, now the site of the 9/11 memorial. Since the end of World War II, Los
Angeles has been synonymous with the rapid expansion of suburban development as
new arrivals quickly settled many areas inside and outside of Los Angeles City proper
and developed office complexes and downtown amenities. Freeways and traffic jams
were a natural by-product of this growth.

The images of New York City and Los Angeles have been reflected and reinforced
by well-known lyrics to popular songs, as well as portrayals in movies and television.
Both cities inspired songs that reinforce the notions of unparalleled success next
to those who have not made it and either leave or slip into poverty or worse. These
include two now used at sporting events, Randy Newman's "I Love LA" and Jay Z and
Alicia Keys "Empire State of Mind." Both make reference to the wealthy and successful, as well as "the bum over there."

The complex images of New York and Los Angeles portrayed in such songs and
throughout the popular media play out in many realms in both cities. Politics and
planning, the educational system, housing policy, arts and culture, the place of
various immigrant groups, and most especially the economy and the impact of the
financial crisis are complex and give rise to ambiguous outcomes. Although out-
wardly positive, the notion that "if you can make it here you can make it anywhere"

from the old Frank Sinatra lyric betrays a dark alternative: you might not actually make it. The feeling of optimism, that the Dow would go to 44,000, that history was at an end and there was a triumph of liberal democracy (Fukuyama 1992) including the market system, and that the Internet bubble would usher in a new economy all were dampened in the spring of 2000 after the stock market crash. Then came 9/11 and notions of security and the inevitability of triumph were shaken.

This was followed by a housing boom and the emergence of "structured finance," which allegedly minimized or eliminated risk while creating huge profits, and funded the massive housing bubble. While "exotic" (read risky and misleading) loan products based upon housing mortgages were developed by Countrywide Financial and many other lenders based in Southern California, many of their enablers were at the large banks in New York City which used a variety of methods to package and sell the loan products throughout the world to investors, mutual funds, government pension funds, and even other banks at a handsome short-term profit. (See discussion in chapter 6.)

The financial crisis has cast a pall over the fate of New York, Los Angeles, and much of the rest of the world. But Los Angeles, with its strong dependence on real estate and construction, and New York, still the world banking center, have been especially affected but in different ways. Particularly, the ongoing fallout has been the rash of foreclosed properties and the collapse of much of the real estate industry, which has had a huge effect locally, especially in Los Angeles, but also in certain areas in New York. This chapter will look at long-term trends in both cities and regions, and tease out what effects the recent economic reversals are having on the population, housing, and incomes of their residents.

LOS ANGELES AND NEW YORK CITY: THE FIRST AND SECOND CITIES AND REGIONS ARE STILL GROWING

New York City and Los Angeles are big. This is true both of the cities and the regions of which they are the center. In 2010 New York City was the largest city in the United States with a population of 8,175,133, while Los Angeles was second with 3,792,621. As for the region, New York City's Combined Statistical Area (CSA) (the Census Bureau's current term for big region) was number one at 22,085,649, while Los Angeles's CSA was number two at 17,877,006. Together these regions make up one-eighth of the nation's population. Chicago, the traditional "second city" had a population of 2,695,598, while its region had 9,686,021. Chicago was the iconic city of urban development for most of the twentieth century, studied in depth by the sociology department at the University of Chicago, and often used as a proxy for urban development in the United States. Yet viewing Chicago (the city or region) in this way was no longer reasonable by the late twentieth century.

New York City was consolidated into its present form in 1897 and includes five counties, while Los Angeles County, with a population of 9,818,605, includes many municipalities besides Los Angeles, and even some areas that are still unincorporated. New York City, of course, always was big. According to the first Census in 1790, the 33,000 people in New York City made New York the largest of the thirteen colonies, while Los Angeles entered the top 100 cities a century later at 57 with 50,395, when number one New York City already was over 1.5 million, and number two Chicago was just under 1.1 million. In 1940, the last Census before the postwar boom and the massive move to the suburbs, New York City was still number one with 7,454,995 while Los Angeles grew to number five with 1,504,277. The regional populations were 13,484,919 for New York and 3,252,720 for Los Angeles.

REGIONS OF LOS ANGELES AND NEW YORK CITY

Exactly where urban agglomerations begin and end and what areas they encompass are always difficult and sometimes controversial questions. Since 1940 the Census Bureau has tried to make sense of the urban regions in the United States. In 2010 it promulgated a new concept called the Combined Statistical Area or CSA, which replaced the consolidated areas that they used in the past. To understand and compare the demographic and other trends that are occurring in Los Angeles and New York it is important to be able to subdivide these two CSAs, which we will also often refer to as "regions." [2]

The Los Angeles CSA includes the counties shown in figure 2.1 (Ventura, Riverside, Los Angeles, Orange, and San Bernardino). We then divided the CSA into four parts, which we call "Defined Areas." These include the following:

1. *West of Downtown*, which goes from Downtown Los Angeles through Malibu, and also includes some other territory. It is used as a proxy for the most affluent and fashionable parts of Los Angeles.
2. An area called *LA Urban*, which includes most of the rest of LA City and some unincorporated areas (e.g., East Los Angeles).
3. The *Rest of LA County*.
4. The *Rest of the LA Region*, which includes Ventura, Orange, Riverside, and San Bernardino counties.

Figure 2.2 presents our defined areas for the NYC region, which, with one small exception, is the New York City CSA.[3]

1. *Manhattan* is used as the area to compare to Los Angeles's *West of Downtown*.
2. The four counties that make up the outer boroughs of New York—Queens, Brooklyn, the Bronx, and Staten Island—are combined as *Outer Boroughs* for comparison with *LA Urban*.
3. The suburbs that are near to New York City, as well as some that include areas of urban density—Stamford, Bridgeport, Newark, and New Haven—are included in the *Inner Suburbs*. This area can be compared to the *Rest of LA County*.

4. The balance of the thirty-county region is considered *Outer Suburbs*. These areas are further away from the city and include some low density suburbs and can be compared to the *Rest of the LA Region*.

Figure 2.3 presents population change from 1970 through 2010 based upon the decennial censuses. Several striking results are visible and are shown in table 2.1. Growth in the LA Region overall was steady and continued during each of the four decades. The growth peaked at 26.4 percent between 1980 and 1990. By contrast, the New York City region barely grew from 1970 to 1980, the period of the city's fiscal crisis and near bankruptcy. Indeed, Manhattan, the Outer Boroughs, and the Inner Suburbs all suffered declines during that period. Overall the region only grew 0.9 percent in that decade, and that came primarily from the 32.4 percent growth in the Outer Suburbs. Indeed, in both the LA and NYC regions, the most substantial growth occurred in the Rest of the LA region or the NY Outer Suburbs in every decade, demonstrating more and more settlement away from the regions' cores.

From 2000, with the end of the Internet boom, until 2010, after the financial crisis, both regions grew, but the bulk of that growth was outside Los Angeles City and New York City. The Los Angeles region grew 9.2 percent to almost 17.9 million while the New York City region grew 3.3 percent to about 22.1 million. The cities fared less well. Los Angeles City grew 2.6 percent to about 3.8 million and New York City grew 2.1 percent to 8.2 million.

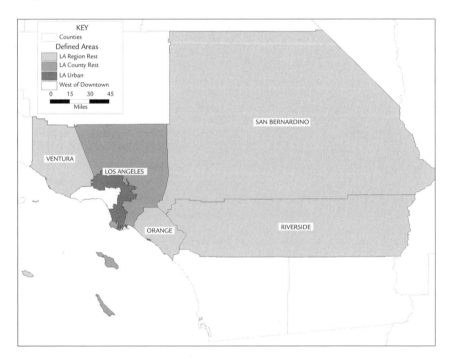

Figure 2.1
Defined Areas for Los Angeles Region and Counties
Source: Andrew A. Beveridge based upon 2010 Census boundary files.

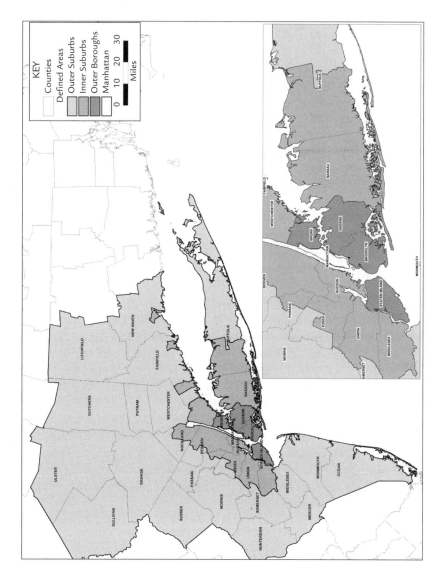

Figure 2.2
Defined Areas for New York City Region and Counties
Source: Andrew A. Beveridge based upon 2010 Census boundary files.

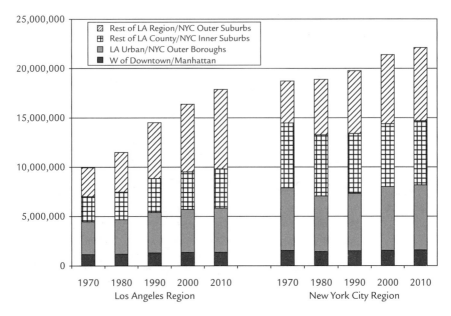

Figure 2.3
Los Angeles and New York City Regions Population Change 1970 to 2010
Source: Andrew A. Beveridge based upon Census data 1970 to 2010 from *Social Explorer*.

Considering the period just since the 2010 Census, the Los Angeles region gained 1.1 percent in the fourteen months from April 2010 to July 2011, while the New York City region gained 0.6 percent. Digging deeper, New York City's gain of 0.85 percent means the city is now growing faster than its surrounding region and the fourteen-month gain represents about one-third of the gain in the last decade, while LA City's gain of 0.71 percent and larger gains in all of the counties except Los Angeles means that unlike the New York City region, growth is occurring in the LA Region away from the core. (Census Bureau 2012b, c).

The population density of both regions is shown in figures 2.4 and 2.5. Manhattan has some of the highest population densities in the United States. In the Los Angeles region, of course, the mountainous areas are difficult to build in. Still, in terms of urbanized areas (a Census classification) Los Angeles's urban areas are the densest in the United States in terms of average persons per square mile, even more so than those in the New York City region.[4]

RACIAL AND HISPANIC CHANGE AND
THE FOREIGN BORN

There have been massive changes in terms of the racial and ethnic composition of both regions, as well as an increase in the foreign-born population. These trends have affected the various defined areas in each of the regions somewhat differently, but the emergence of a very desirable near center city place to live is true in both regions.

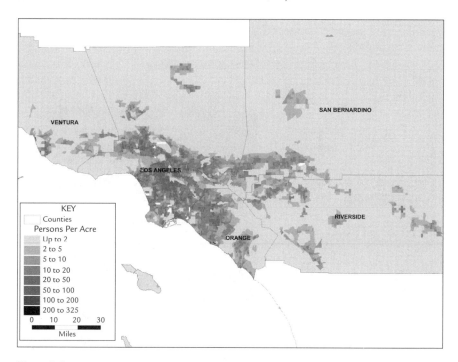

Figure 2.4
Population Density by Census Tracts, Los Angeles Region, 2010
Source: Andrew A. Beveridge based upon 2010 Census data from *Social Explorer* and 2010 Census boundary files.

This and the slowing of population migration and "white flight" to the suburbs, which are becoming increasingly diverse, represents a real reversal of a nearly half-century trend that became well established after World War II.

A major trend in both regions has been the general decline of the non-Hispanic white population, as shown in figure 2.6 and table 2.2. This decline is in the face of an overall population increase and points up the massive changes in the population composition of both regions. However, in what is an obvious reversal of trend and perhaps a harbinger of a large change, from 2000 to 2010 there was growth in the non-Hispanic white population in West of Downtown in the LA region (1.7 percent), and in Manhattan in the NYC region (8.2 percent).

Figure 2.7 shows the distribution of the non-Hispanic white population in the LA region. In general, areas away from West of Downtown and the LA Urban area have the highest concentrations of non-Hispanic white population. At the same time, there are sections throughout the region where the concentration of the non-Hispanic white population is relatively low.

The non-Hispanic white population in the NYC region is concentrated in a few areas in the city and in many of the suburban areas, both inner and outer, as is shown in figure 2.8. There is a set of older urban areas—Yonkers, Newark, Patterson, Bridgeport, and New Haven—where parts of the area have very low concentrations of non-Hispanic whites. We will look explicitly at levels of segregation in the two regions and how they have changed in chapter 11.

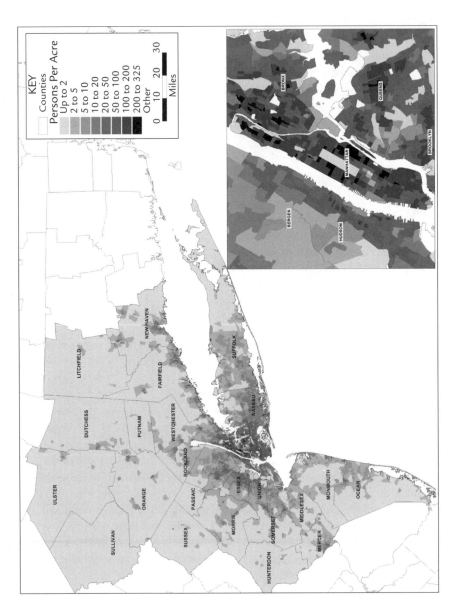

Figure 2.5
Population Density by Census Tracts, New York City Region, 2010
Source: Andrew A. Beveridge based upon 2010 Census data from *Social Explorer* and 2010 Census boundary files.

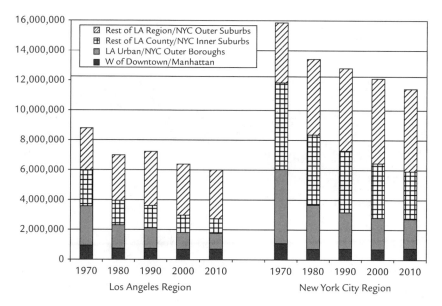

Figure 2.6
Los Angeles and New York City Regions Non-Hispanic White Population Change 1970 to 2010
Source: Andrew A. Beveridge based upon Census data 1970 to 2010 from *Social Explorer.*

The growth of the black or non-Hispanic African American population follows a roughly similar pattern in both regions through 2010. For each of the decades up to 2000 there was consistent growth in each region, but from 2000 to 2010 the African American population actually declined by 1.1 percent in the NYC region, while it grew in the LA region, but only by a tiny 0.4 percent. In both regions the most desirable near center city areas, West of Downtown and Manhattan, experienced sharp declines in the non-Hispanic African American population of over 11 percent in each between 2000 and 2010. There were declines too in the LA Urban area (almost 11 percent) and in the Outer Boroughs of New York City (about 5 percent). Somewhat offsetting this was the rapid growth of the non-Hispanic African American population in the Rest of the LA region (23.9 percent) and the NYC Outer Suburbs (15.4 percent). These changes are shown in figure 2.9, and table 2.3. In short, in the dense urban areas the non-Hispanic African American population is declining, and this is especially so in the most desirable areas—Manhattan in the NYC region and West of Downtown in the LA region.

As shown in figure 2.10, the non-Hispanic African American population in the LA region is still quite concentrated, but there are also concentrations of African American population outside of LA Urban and West of Downtown. Comparing the patterns in the NYC region (shown in figure 2.11), high concentrations of non-Hispanic African American population are much more evident in the NYC region than in the LA region, including areas outside of New York City. These patterns are consistent with the recent increases of the African American population in the Rest of the LA Region and in the Outer Suburbs of the NYC region. (African American segregation in the two regions is examined in chapter 11.)

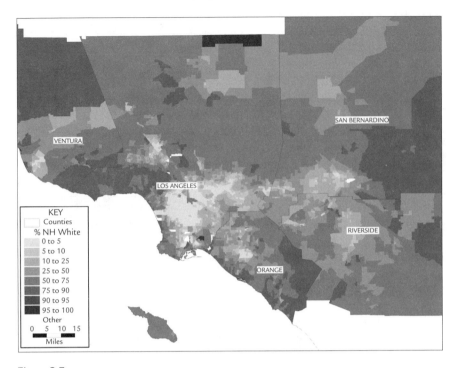

Figure 2.7
Percent Non-Hispanic White by Census Tract, Los Angeles Region, 2010
Source: Andrew A. Beveridge based upon 2010 Census data from *Social Explorer* and 2010 Census boundary files.

One of the major changes in both regions has been the massive increase in the Hispanic population. Hispanics have been consistently coded by the Census since 1980. The changes in all eight defined areas were mostly positive through all four decades and quite large in the early decades analyzed, especially in the outer areas, either the Rest of the LA Region or the NYC Outer Suburbs. (See figure 2.12 and table 2.4.) However, during the last decade the growth of the Hispanic population in the desirable urban areas of West of Downtown and Manhattan slowed to a crawl (2.1 percent) or declined (–3.4 percent), respectively. Despite this, the overall increase in Hispanics from 2000 to 2010 in both regions was more than 20 percent. The bulk of this growth occurred away from the center of both regions and out in the suburbs.

The spread of Hispanics in both regions is evident in figures 2.13 and 2.14. In the LA region there are a number of locations where the area is predominantly or almost entirely Hispanic. By contrast, the NYC region does not appear to have many such areas.

One should bear in mind differences in the diversity of the various Hispanic groups in the two regions. Mexicans account for 81.3 percent of the Hispanics in the LA region, but only 12.8 percent in the NYC region. Puerto Ricans are number one in the NYC region at 31.0 percent, but they represent only 1.0 percent of the Hispanics in the LA region. Dominicans are number two in the NYC region at 18.2 percent with less than 1 percent in the LA region. Mexicans are number three in the NYC region (12.8 percent), followed by Ecuadorians (7.7 percent), and Colombians

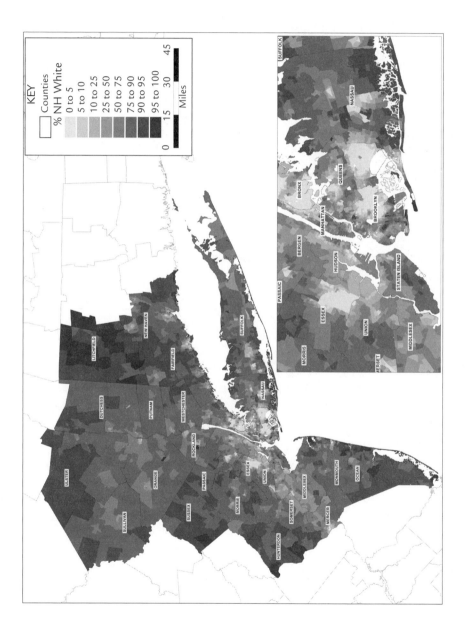

Figure 2.8
Percent Non-Hispanic White by Census Tract, New York City Region, 2010
Source: Andrew A. Beveridge based upon 2010 Census data from *Social Explorer* and 2010 Census boundary files.

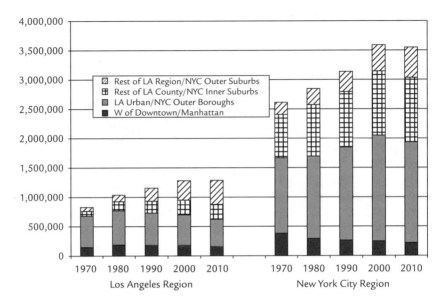

Figure 2.9
Los Angeles and New York City Regions Non-Hispanic Black Population Change 1970 to 2010
Source: Andrew A. Beveridge based upon Census data 1970 to 2010 from *Social Explorer*.

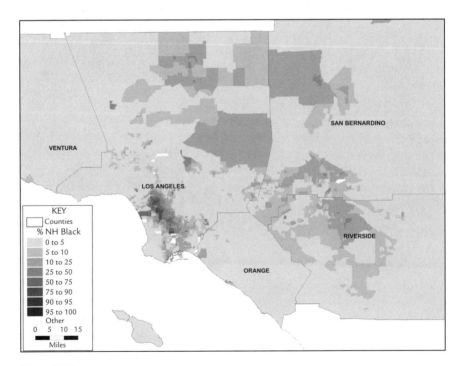

Figure 2.10
Percent Non-Hispanic Black by Census Tract, Los Angeles Region, 2010
Source: Andrew A. Beveridge based upon 2010 Census data from *Social Explorer* and 2010 Census boundary files.

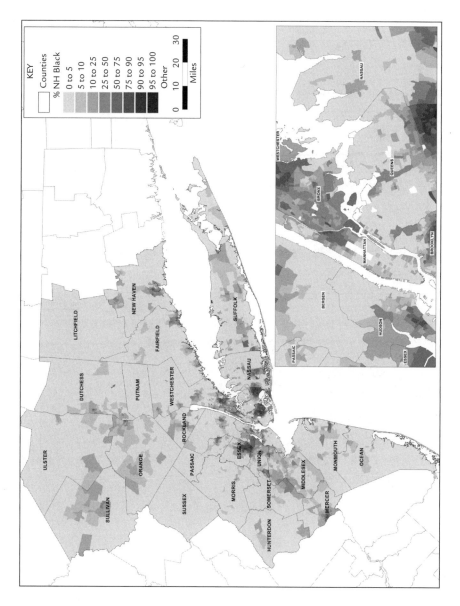

Figure 2.11
Percent Non-Hispanic Black by Census Tract, New York City Region, 2010
Source: Andrew A. Beveridge based upon 2010 Census data from *Social Explorer* and 2010 Census boundary files.

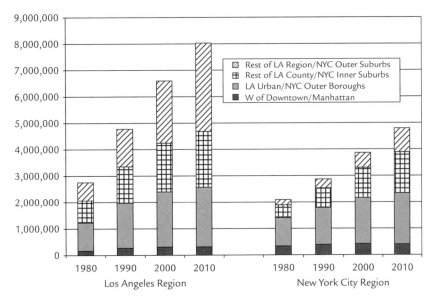

Figure 2.12
Los Angeles and New York City Regions Hispanic Population Change 1980 to 2010
Source: Andrew A. Beveridge based upon Census data 1970 to 2010 from *Social Explorer*.

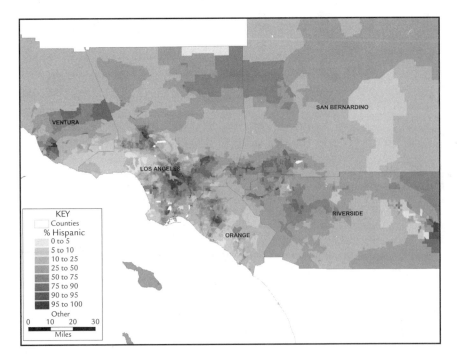

Figure 2.13
Percent Hispanic by Census Tract, Los Angeles Region, 2010
Source: Andrew A. Beveridge based upon 2010 Census data from *Social Explorer* and 2010 Census boundary files.

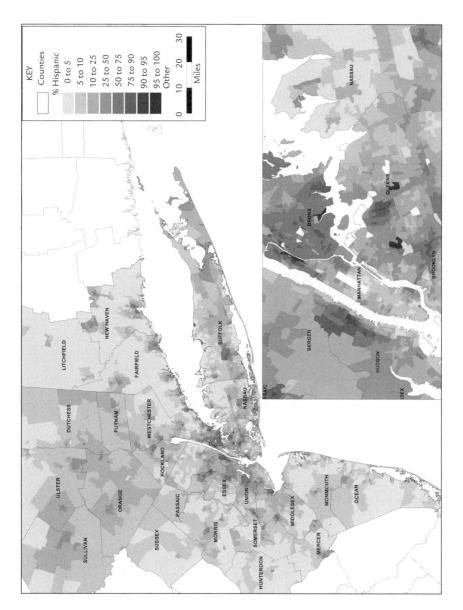

Figure 2.14
Percent Hispanic by Census Tract, New York Region, 2010
Source: Andrew A. Beveridge based upon 2010 Census data from *Social Explorer* and 2010 Census boundary files.

(5.4 percent). Salvadorans are number two in the LA Region at 5.7 percent while they are number six in the NYC region at 4.2 percent. (All of the other Hispanic groups have lower percentages.) So, in the LA region to be Hispanic is usually to be Mexican, while in the NYC region, Hispanic can mean many different origins.

Asians have grown rapidly in all areas of both regions in every decade from 1970 through 2010. Growth was especially rapid when there were only a few Asians in both regions. As the base increased, the rate of growth overall went from 117.9 percent in the decade of the 1970s to 29.3 percent in the last decade in the LA region, and from 151.8 percent to 38.5 percent in the NYC region. Although their percent growth has slowed somewhat, Asians are still increasing rapidly in both regions. This is displayed in figure 2.15, and it also is reflected in table 2.5.

As figures 2.16 and 2.17 show, there are areas of very high Asian population concentration in both regions. However, in general, the Asian population is more spread out than either Hispanics or non-Hispanic African Americans. The rapid growth of the Asian population and the fact that they, as with the Hispanics, have diverse origins means that Asians live both dispersed among other groups and in concentrated conditions. (Further discussion of the Chinese communities in both regions is in chapter 13 and patterns of Asian segregation are discussed in chapter 11.)

The foreign born population is driving the changes in the Hispanic and Asian populations, as well as in some other groups more common in the NYC region, including the Russians and Irish. Figure 2.18 and table 2.6 show the growth and composition of the foreign born in the two regions. To understand the scale of the change, in 1970 the LA region had fewer than one million foreign born, and now has about 5.5 million.

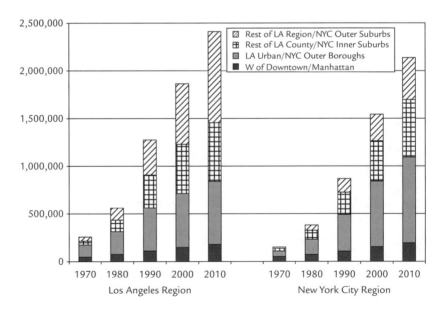

Figure 2.15
Los Angeles and New York City Regions Non-Hispanic Asian Population Change 1970 to 2010
Source: Andrew A. Beveridge based upon Census data 1970 to 2010 from *Social Explorer*.

In the NYC region the numbers more than doubled from about 2.4 million to 5.7 million. Although slightly smaller in total number, the proportion of foreign born in the LA region is somewhat higher than in the NYC region overall: a little under one-third compared to one-quarter. Still, in both West of Downtown LA and Manhattan there has been a decline in the foreign born population in the last decade. Once again, the area in each region that is both relatively near the center of the city and the most desirable is diverging from the rest of the region in terms of group population trends.

Overall, the demography of the two largest regions in the United States has been transformed from 1970 to 2010. The Hispanic and Asian populations of both regions grew rapidly throughout the period and in almost every area. By contrast, the African American population is declining overall in the NYC region and is barely growing in the LA region. It is declining in the core areas of both regions. Again, a major development is the differentiation of population in the areas in both regions that are near the center but very desirable: Manhattan in the NYC region and West of Downtown in the LA region. In both these areas, there is an increase in the non-Hispanic white population, a decline or very slow growth in the Hispanic population, and a decline or minimal growth in the foreign-born population. In short, just like the suburbs right after World War II through much of the twentieth century, these neighborhoods have become areas of growth for non-Hispanic whites. At the same time, the conventional suburban areas are becoming increasingly diverse. This dual trend is

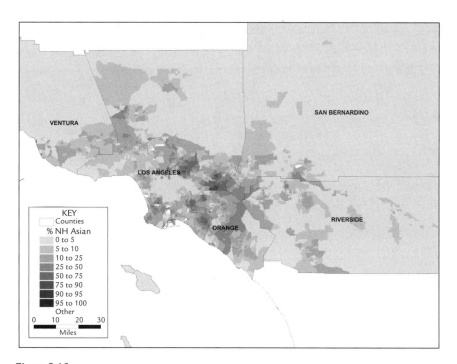

Figure 2.16
Percent Non-Hispanic Asian by Census Tract, Los Angeles Region, 2010
Source: Andrew A. Beveridge based upon 2010 Census data from *Social Explorer* and 2010 Census boundary files.

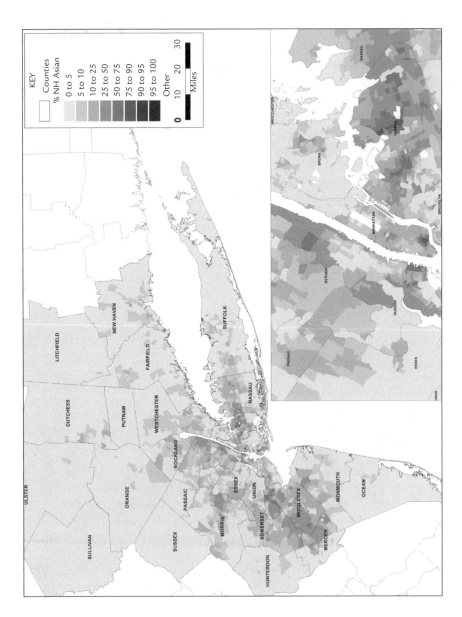

Figure 2.17

Percent Non-Hispanic Asian by Census Tract, New York City Region, 2010

Source: Andrew A. Beveridge based upon 2010 Census data from *Social Explorer* and 2010 Census boundary files.

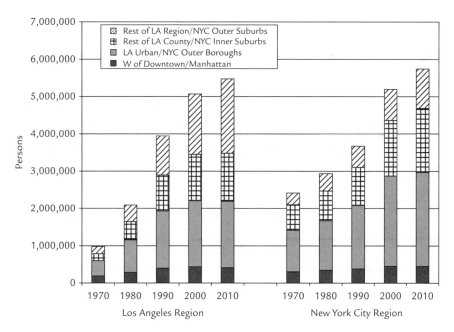

Figure 2.18
Los Angeles and New York City Regions Foreign Born Population Change 1970 to 2010
Source: Andrew A. Beveridge based upon Census data 1970 to 2000 and American Community Survey data from 2010 from *Social Explorer.*

very significant and may be a real harbinger of a changing pattern of settlement in the two largest regions of the United States and in other regions too.

HOUSING, INCOME, AND THE FINANCIAL CRISIS

As with population groups, there is great diversity in both regions in terms of housing and income. It is also possible to begin to track the extent to which the recent financial crisis has had effects. Both regions have large numbers of rich and poor, and both regions have generally seen stagnation or decline of median household income since 1990, but have also experienced gyrations in house values. Of course, the housing bubble and ensuing collapse have been highly consequential in both regions, with foreclosures having had a massive effect in the LA region because of the dependence of a large sector of the economy on residential construction, real estate, and mortgage finance. These trends will be a major focus of this section of the chapter, the financial impacts of these trends on government finance are discussed in chapter 7, and the genesis and expected trajectory of these trends are the subject of chapter 6.

As with the rest of the United States, median household income in the LA and NYC regions followed uneven and often divergent trajectories since the 1980s. From 1980 to 1990, both regions gained substantially, 14.2 percent in the LA region and 23.2 percent in the NY region. From 1990 to 2000, there was a decline in the LA region of about 6.9 percent overall, and a small decline in the NYC region of 1.8 percent overall. From 2000 to 2008–10 these declines continued. (See table 2.7.) This is even more marked with respect to wages, since the number of dual earner households in both areas has increased, which should, other things being equal, lead to a rise in household income. Bucking this trend dramatically is the continued growth of median income in Manhattan and (to a lesser extent) West of Downtown. For instance, while the NYC region was experiencing a small decline in median income overall from 2000 to 2008–10, Manhattan experienced growth of 5.9 percent. (Patterns of income change are shown in figure 2.19 and table 2.7.)[5]

The geographic distribution of median household income is shown in figure 2.20 for the LA region and in figure 2.21 for the NYC region. Notwithstanding the wealth in Manhattan and West of Downtown, in both regions it is plain that as one goes away from the city to the suburban or less urban areas, incomes tend to be higher. Areas of concentrated poverty are in the portions of the regions that are associated with the inner city. In the NYC region, these areas include part of the Bronx, northern Manhattan, Brooklyn, and areas in Newark in New Jersey, as well as Bridgeport and New Haven in Connecticut. In the LA region, poverty is concentrated in East Los Angeles, Downtown Skid Row, and parts of South Central and Compton, as well as poverty pockets outside of the LA County. (Whether the rich and poor are becoming more or less concentrated will be addressed in chapter 11.)

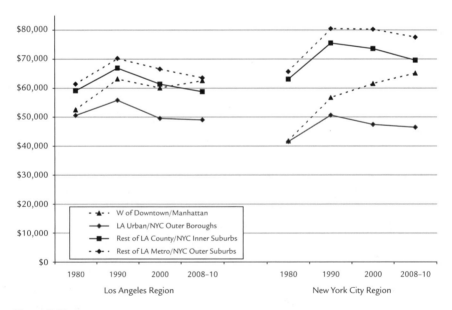

Figure 2.19
Median Household Income (in 2010 dollars) Los Angeles and New York City Regions by Region, 1980 to 2000 and 2008–2010
Source: Andrew A. Beveridge based upon Census Data and American Community Survey Data for the dates indicated from *Social Explorer.*

Both the NYC and LA regions participated in the most recent housing boom, which began around 2000. Using data from the Census Bureau on self-reported housing value (the only publicly available data that can be disaggregated to small geographical areas), the LA region had an overall 66 percent gain in median house value from 2000 to 2008–10, while the NYC region had an overall gain of 61 percent. It also seems to be the case that self-reports become unreliable when prices are falling and houses are not selling. In that situation it is difficult to gauge exactly what houses are worth. The Census data are shown in figure 2.22 and summarized in table 2.8.[6] The geographical distribution of reported median house value by location in the two regions is shown in figures 2.23 and 2.24.

In the Los Angeles region those areas with very high median house values include the West of Downtown area, those near the coast in Orange and Ventura counties, as well as a few in the Valley. In the NYC region house values are very high in Manhattan. Indeed, the median reported value in 2008–10 is $841,800, which is higher than any other defined area in either region. This also represents an increase of 94.6 percent in real terms from the values in 2000, a larger increase than any other area. Other areas in the NYC region with high median house values are the North Shore of Long Island, the Sound Shore area of Westchester County, the wealthy Connecticut towns of Greenwich, New Canaan, and Darien, and some parts of Central Jersey. Areas further out from the city center generally have lower reported median house values. This is consistent

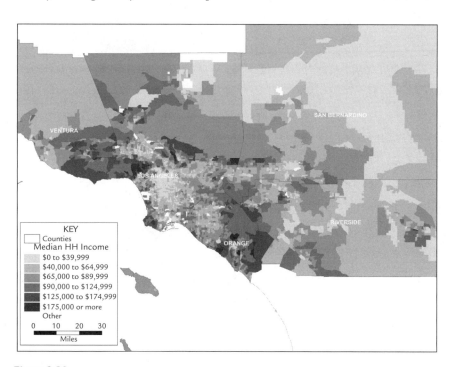

Figure 2.20
Median Household Income by Census Tract, Los Angeles Region, 2010
Source: Andrew A. Beveridge based upon 2006-2010 American Community Survey data from Social Explorer and 2010 Census boundary files.

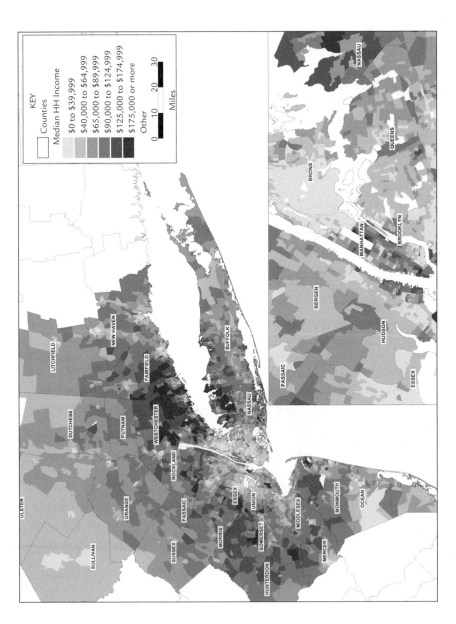

Figure 2.21
Median Household Income by Census Tract, New York City Region, 2010

Source: Andrew A. Beveridge based upon 2006–2010 American Community Survey data from *Social Explorer* and 2010 Census boundary files.

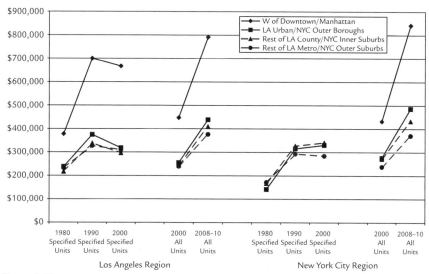

Figure 2.22
Median House Value (in 2010 dollars) Los Angeles and New York City Regions by Defined Areas, for Specified Owner Occupied Units 1980 to 2000 and All Owner Occupied Units 2000 to 2008–2010
Source: Andrew A. Beveridge based upon Census data 1980, 1990, and 2000, and 2008-2010 American Community Survey data from Social Explorer.

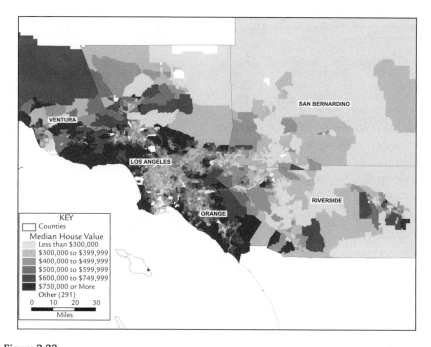

Figure 2.23
Median House Value by Census Tract, Los Angeles Region, 2006–2010 (ACS Data)
Source: Andrew A. Beveridge based upon 2006–2010 American Community Survey data from Social Explorer and 2010 Census boundary files.

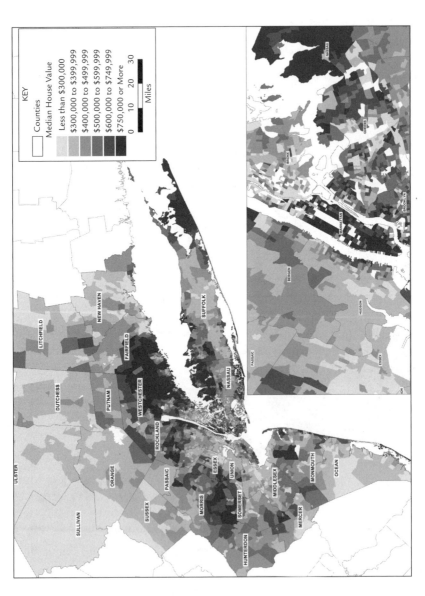

Figure 2.24
Median House Value by Census Tract, New York City Region, 2006–2010 (American Community Survey data)
Source: Andrew A. Beveridge based upon 2006-2010 American Community Survey data from *Social Explorer* and 2010 Census boundary files.

with the other changes that are being seen in the NYC region and with the trend that wealthier residents are no longer moving in just one direction out to the suburbs.

The Census reported house values are those that household members voluntarily report to a census enumerator. Another index is by Case-Shiller, which is now part of Standard and Poor's. Reported monthly, it is a more accurate measure of house values since it is based upon sales of the same houses over time. The Case-Shiller index was set at 100 in January 2000, thus it allows one to track house value change (but not actual house value) comparatively across a large variety of regions. Figure 2.25 presents the Case-Shiller index for the New York and Los Angeles regions, as well as a composite of ten regions from January 1987 to July 2012, adjusted for inflation and for seasonal price changes in both housing and other items. During that period, the LA region peaked at 230.1 in February 2006, the NYC region peaked at 182.4, and the composite index reached a height of 191.4. In July 2012 the indexes stood at 124.3 for the LA region, 119.9 for the NYC region, and at 113.9 for the composite. Thus, after peaking well above the NYC region, the LA region has since fallen almost to the NYC region average. In short, the Los Angeles boom and subsequent bust was much larger than that in the NYC region. Note that housing prices showed a small peak in the late 1980s, but nowhere near the prices at the height of the most recent bubble. The genesis of this run-up and its consequences for the two regions are discussed further in chapter 6. Here it should be noted that the increases and decreases

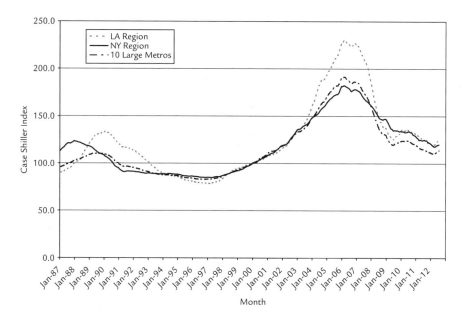

Figure 2.25
Case-Shiller Housing Price Index for LA and NYC Region and Composite 10 Large Regions, January 1987 through July 2012 (Seasonally and Inflation Adjusted)
Source: Andrew A. Beveridge based upon Case-Shiller Housing Price Index for Los Angeles and New York City Regions and Composite 10 Large Regions, seasonally adjusted. Inflation adjustment used Bureau of Labor Statistics Consumer Price Index.

of price associated with the inflation and deflation of the bubble are unprecedented in US history and the history of the two regions.

It is also important to examine one consequence of the collapse of the bubble—the foreclosure crisis. Other studies have looked at different aspects of foreclosures in various regions; here we will simply compare the rate and pattern of foreclosures in the LA and NYC regions. Because of the rapid pace of new construction in Los Angeles compared to New York City, many more of the mortgages that led to foreclosures or foreclosure starts, which means filing a notice of delinquency to start the process, were issued in Los Angeles. Figure 2.26 and table 2.9 make this plain. Figure 2.26 computes a rate of foreclosures over the number of owner occupied houses in a given tract. The data are based upon one year of foreclosure records from RealtyTrac, including foreclosure starts and completed foreclosures (where the bank takes ownership of the property). The foreclosure start process is somewhat different in California than New York, but the process whereby the bank takes the house is identical.

Using these data, which do have some inaccuracies and duplications, it is plain that the rate of foreclosure starts and foreclosures completed in the NYC region is far below that for the LA region. Overall, the rate of foreclosure starts in the NYC region is 1.6 percent of owner occupied houses, while it is 5.6 percent in the LA region or more than three times as great. For completed foreclosures, the rate is 0.3 percent in the NYC region, but 4.1 percent in the LA region, or about fourteen times the rate in the NYC region. When one examines the geographic pattern of foreclosures in the two regions, as is shown in figures 2.27 and 2.28, the differences are glaring. In Los

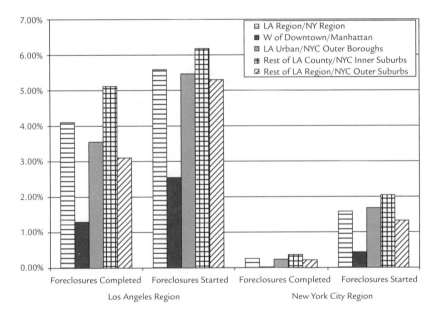

Figure 2.26
Foreclosure Rates April 1, 2008, to March 31, 2009, Los Angeles and New York City Regions by Defined Areas
Source: Andrew A. Beveridge based upon RealtyTrac individual level foreclosure data aggregated to census tracts, and American Community Survey Data 2006–2010 from *Social Explorer*.

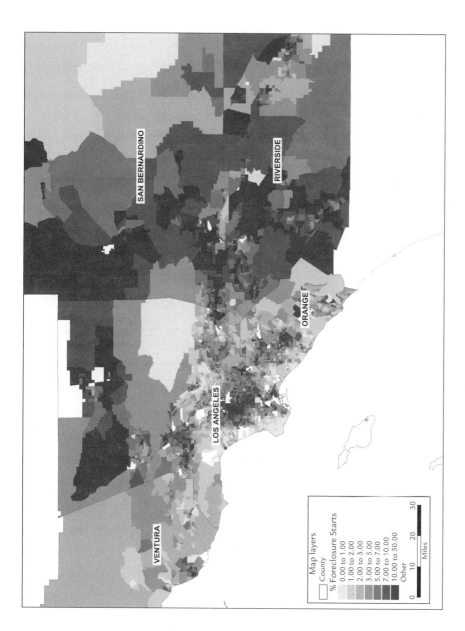

Figure 2.27

Percent Foreclosure Starts by Census Tract, Los Angeles Region, May 1, 2008, to April 30, 2009

Source: Andrew A. Beveridge based upon RealtyTrac individual level foreclosure data aggregated to census tracts, and American Community Survey data 2006-2010 from *Social Explorer.*

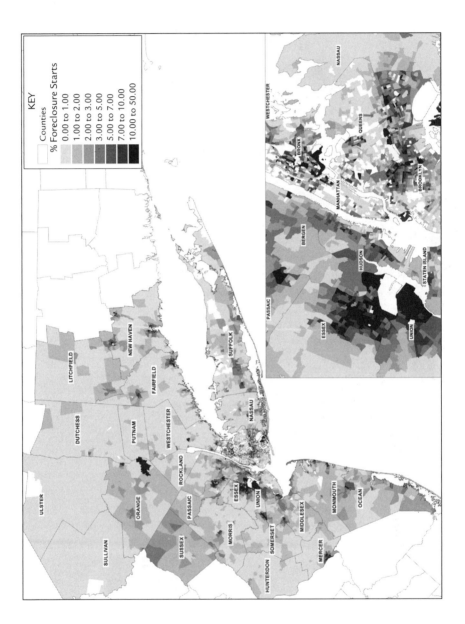

Figure 2.28
Percent Foreclosure Starts by Census Tract, New York City Region, May 1, 2008, to April 30, 2009

Source: Andrew A. Beveridge based upon RealtyTrac individual level foreclosure data aggregated to census tracts, and American Community Survey Data 2006–2010 from *Social Explorer*.

KEY

Counties
% Foreclosure Starts

0.00 to 1.00
1.00 to 2.00
2.00 to 3.00
3.00 to 5.00
5.00 to 7.00
7.00 to 10.00
10.00 to 50.00

Angeles, there are some concentrations of foreclosures in the denser parts of the LA region, a much lower rate in West of Downtown, and high rates of foreclosures in areas away from the center of the LA region. These areas had much new construction in the first decade of the twentieth century. By contrast, the NYC region has had far fewer foreclosures in general, and they are much more clustered in minority areas (e.g., Jamaica, Queens) and in relatively low-income level areas. These include the Bronx, parts of Brooklyn, Northern Manhattan, and Newark, as well as the centers of New Haven and Bridgeport. Such a pattern suggests that in the NYC region, lower-income minorities, who may have been first-time homeowners, were targeted with subprime or high-cost mortgages. In the LA region it seems the foreclosure crisis, though including minority areas, also included many areas beyond where conventional subprime lending patterns victimized minorities, demonstrating that the crisis was much more widespread.[7]

The patterns of change in rent in the various areas are shown in figure 2.29 and table 2.10. As that figure and table make plain, while rent did increase substantially from 1980 to 2008–2010, the increase overall is dwarfed by the change in house value. Median rent increased slightly more than two-thirds over three decades in both regions. (Housing policy and housing patterns are the subject of chapter 10.)

The patterns of housing and income in the LA and NYC regions are emblematic of the patterns of change in much of urban America but with nuances of their own. First, household median income has increased only modestly since 1970, and actually

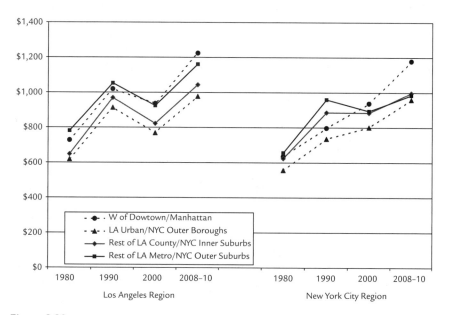

Figure 2.29
Median Contract Rent (in 2010 dollars) Los Angeles and New York City Regions by Defined Areas, 1970 to 2000 and 2000 to 2008–2010
Source: Andrew A. Beveridge based upon Census Data 1970 to 2000 and American Community Survey Data 2008–2010 from Social Explorer.

declined overall in both regions since 1990. At the same time, the housing bubble and its aftermath seriously affected a number of neighborhoods and communities, first by involving the building and selling of housing that was actually not affordable to the residents, and then by either foreclosing on that housing or causing a massive falloff in value. It is plain that the housing bubble and its aftermath affected many more neighborhoods and communities in the LA region, and affected them more seriously, than in the NYC region.

THE RISE OF WOMEN AND CHANGES FOR CHILDREN

Since 1970 the role of women in the United States and within the two major regions has changed radically. These changes are having massive effects on the two regions in every aspect, including the organization of workplaces and neighborhoods, as well as the rearing of children. With the change in the status of women signaled by the Civil Rights Acts in the 1960s, which mandated equality of educational opportunity and job opportunities for women, the changing roles of men and women, particularly younger men and women, have been marked. By tracking these changes for those in their twenties we can begin to see what the future may hold as the 20-somethings go through the rest of their life courses.

The incredible increase in women with college degrees compared to men has been a very striking reversal. A larger proportion of younger women than younger men hold bachelor's degrees in the two regions in every area for which data existed. This is shown in table 2.11. For instance, while the percent of men age 20 to 29 with a college degree increased from 20.0 to 31.0 percent in New York City between 1970 and 2010, for women the figure grew from 14.4 to 40.9 percent. Indeed, in every single area of the region shown in table 2.11, a higher proportion of women hold a bachelor's degree. This fact has been true since the 1990 Census in every area, and the educational gap between male and female 20-somethings has only grown since then.

This has led directly to a large increase in 20-something women working full time, as shown in table 2.12. Traditionally, women were much less likely to work full time outside the home than men, but that gap is closing for 20-somethings. Even more striking is the fact that for 20-somethings in New York City, Los Angeles, and the rest of LA County, the median earnings of women working full time are higher than the median earnings of men working full time. This does not mean that women in the same occupational category will necessarily make more than a male worker. Instead, it reflects the fact that working women are better educated than working men and therefore more likely to be in occupations that pay somewhat better than those held by men. In many ways, this represents a sea change for these cities and urban settings, and is directly related to the increased desirability of certain urban areas as places to live.

As is well known, the marriage age is much higher than it used to be and has increased from the very early twenties to the mid-late twenties for both men and women nationwide.[8] The number of children born to each woman has declined from 3.65 in 1960 to 2.05 in 2009 (World Bank 2012), and the number of women in the labor force has increased, as shown in table 2.12. Together these trends mean that the ideal typical lifestyle of a nuclear family with a husband and wife with two children, where the husband works and the wife is a "homemaker" that had been envisioned in earlier decades is breaking down. Indeed, recent work by Eric Klinenberg (2011), as well as other discussions, makes this abundantly clear.

As has been seen, though there was modest growth in household income over the four decades discussed here, when one looks at wages, especially male wages, that picture reveals much worse realities about earnings. These results are shown in table 2.13. Indeed, in every area male wages for 20-somethings are lower in 2006–10 than they were in 1970 and even in 2000. The wage gains for the 20-somethings, where they exist at all, are incredibly modest and are all among females. Furthermore, even here there is an overall decline in each geographic area between 2000 and 2006–10. In other words, a better educated workforce is earning less now than a less educated workforce was earning one, two or four decades ago. No doubt this reflects the impact of the financial crisis, as well as other trends over the last several decades.

Not only are families now composed differently, they have also changed their settlement patterns. In earlier decades after World War II, most of those families who were having children went to the suburbs to rear them. Now, however, it is plain that more children are living in desirable parts of the city. Among the affluent non-Hispanic white parents, who account for a large fraction of this population gain, it appears that at least a fraction of them are choosing to stay in the city instead of moving out to the suburbs. Indeed, Manhattan has experienced a baby boom, and in the most desirable areas for wealthy families, such as the Upper West Side and Downtown, kindergarten classrooms are packed and parents struggle to find space at both private and public schools. This is reflected in table 2.14, as the median household income of non-Hispanic white children zero to four years old is over $220,000 in Manhattan, compared to about $90,000 for all children in Manhattan and over $141,000 in the West of Downtown area of LA compared to $81,500 for all groups. Not only is there a greater gap in Manhattan between the non-Hispanic white children and other children in terms of income, but there are also more of such children. Instead of a move to the suburbs to find grass and schools, more and more of the better off (especially non-Hispanic white) families are staying in the more desirable parts of the two cities. The suburban dream of lawns and schools has apparently faded for such households, many with two career couples, so the bright lights of the big city, even with the hassle of finding schools, play dates, and the like, now are much more attractive than they were in years past. But remember, these are the families that can afford the "luxury product" of Manhattan and West of Downtown.

CONCLUSION

At the end of the HBO television show *Sex and the City*, Miranda moves with her husband, child, dog, and cat to Brooklyn (no doubt either to Brooklyn Heights or Park Slope), from an upscale but small Manhattan apartment to a house with a backyard. Miranda, of course, is a very successful lawyer and her husband is a bartender with an income far below hers, making them emblematic of the shifting education and income levels of men and women. Moving out of Manhattan was seen as a huge step for her and her husband, but once they did it they were satisfied. However, they never considered moving to the suburbs. Not that one should base a demographic analysis on a media stereotype, but the fact is that *Sex and the City*, as well as other media images, do strike a responsive chord if they reflect either some of the aspects of reality or of people's aspirations.

Here is a recap of some important demographic trends in New York and Los Angeles explored in this chapter:

1. A slowing of growth in the outer areas of both regions, and some growth in the more urbanized segments of both, particularly higher income and higher home value areas.
2. The increasing diversity in the defined areas outside of Los Angeles and New York cities, coupled with a decline in the African American population and a slowing of the growth of Hispanics in the cities, along with continued growth of the Asian population.
3. The emergence of very desirable areas in or near the city center that for some eclipse the traditional attraction of the suburbs. In New York City, these include most of Manhattan and some Manhattanesque neighborhoods near to Manhattan (Park Slope, Williamsburg, Long Island City, and Brooklyn Heights). In Los Angeles, many are in the West of Downtown area, including Westwood and Century City.
4. An unprecedented housing bubble that inflated and then deflated in less than seven years, prompting massive foreclosures and declines in Wall Street bonuses and employment, as well as a huge construction and real estate crash in the LA region and layoffs (followed by bailouts) in the financial sector in the NYC region.
5. Stagnant wage growth and modest household income growth for the last four decades.
6. The emergence of women as a major economic force as they outperform men with higher levels of education, higher status occupations, and higher incomes with a larger proportion in the labor force. An increase in the marriage age, a decline in the marriage rate, as well as an associated increase in the age of the mother when the children are born made this possible.
7. An increase of affluent families with children living in the desirable areas of the city instead of moving to the suburbs.

Taken together, these trends upend most of the conventional stereotypes about the NYC and LA regions. The two iconic regions are in flux, and the futures of both are quite uncertain. Not only are the economic prospects of both regions clouded, but so are who the major groups will be, where they will live, and what they will do.

NOTES

1. This chapter relies upon tabulated data from the US Census Bureau, including data derived from *Social Explorer*, a website created under the direction of Andrew A. Beveridge and Ahmed Lacevic. Other material is cited as appropriate. The analyses presented were performed by Andrew Beveridge.

2. We used data from the 1970, 1980, 1900, 2000, and 2010 Census, as well as data from the 2006–2010 and 2008–2010 ACS for the rest of the analyses in this chapter. In this way, it is possible to look at comparable trends in comparable areas. All tables and figures in this chapter were produced by the authors.

3. Sullivan County was substituted for Pike County, Pennsylvania to keep the New York City region within three states and make it possible to divide it more easily by PUMA. Pike County has a population of 57,369, while Sullivan County has population of 77,547, so this change would have an insignificant effect on any results, but makes it possible to have comparable areas for the forty-year period.

4. This is based upon a simple analysis of the 2010 Census Urban Lists Records provided by the Census Bureau.

5. Since the American Community Survey (ACS) was readjusted to conform to the 2010 Census starting in 2010, it is especially difficult to track income, house value, or rent changes using the ACS data released before and after the Census 2010 release. To create the tables and figures in the chapter, the PUMAs, in the case of the ACS, and the tracts, in the case of the Census, were allocated to the defined areas. At that point, the values for income, house value, and rent were totaled for each defined area and region, and then a median was computed by doing a linear interpolation based upon the tabulated data. The result was then adjusted based upon the cost of living index from the BLS. For this reason, the calculated median numbers should be seen as a reasonable approximation to the actual median.

6. It is also the case that the Census Bureau changed how they collected house value. Through 2000 it was mainly based upon so-called specified owner occupied units, which were defined as single-family detached units. Condos, coops, and units with rental space were excluded. Manhattan has so few specified units, slightly more than 1,000, that reporting would be misleading. The change in median value of such units from 1980 through 2000 is shown in table 2.8.

7. Other work has demonstrated this, such as Vesselinov and Beveridge 2011.

8. The median age at first marriage in the United States rose for men from 23.2 in 1970 to 28.7 for men in 2011 and for women from 20.8 to 26.5 (US Census Bureau 2011d).

Table 2.1 POPULATION IN LOS ANGELES AND NEW YORK CITY REGIONS AND DEFINED AREAS, 1970 TO 2010

LA Region	1970	1980	1970–80	1990	1980–90	2000	1990–2000	2010	2000–2010
West of Downtown	1,139,206	1,179,850	3.6%	1,306,359	10.7%	1,349,581	3.3%	1,364,600	1.1%
LA Urban	3,317,725	3,491,618	5.2%	4,089,211	17.1%	4,350,069	6.4%	4,468,224	2.7%
Rest of LA County	2,555,345	2,802,109	9.7%	3,459,907	23.5%	3,819,394	10.4%	3,985,781	4.4%
Rest of LA Region	2,933,989	4,019,857	37.0%	5,668,718	41.0%	6,854,588	20.9%	8,058,401	17.6%
LA Region	9,946,265	11,493,434	15.6%	14,524,194	26.4%	16,373,632	12.7%	17,877,006	9.2%

NYC Region	1970	1980	1970–80	1990	1980–90	2000	1990–2000	2010	2000–2010
Manhattan	1,537,940	1,427,640	–7.2%	1,487,267	4.2%	1,537,195	3.4%	1,585,871	3.2%
Outer Boroughs	6,349,611	5,641,557	–11.2%	5,832,943	3.4%	6,471,083	10.9%	6,589,260	1.8%
Inner Suburbs	6,584,211	6,188,146	–6.0%	6,072,529	–1.9%	6,373,345	5.0%	6,505,911	2.1%
Outer Suburbs	4,244,076	5,620,260	32.4%	6,351,509	13.0%	7,007,838	10.3%	7,424,783	5.9%
NYC Region	18,715,838	18,877,603	0.9%	19,744,248	4.6%	21,389,461	8.3%	22,105,825	3.3%

Source: 1970 to 2010 Decennial Census Tabulations from Social Explorer. Defined area allocations of census tracts by Andrew A. Beveridge.

Table 2.2 NON-HISPANIC WHITE POPULATION IN LOS ANGELES AND NEW YORK CITY REGIONS AND DEFINED AREAS, 1970 TO 2010

LA Region	1970	1980	1970–80	1990	1980–90	2000	1990–2000	2010	2000–2010
West of Downtown	938,843	745,040	−20.6%	736,742	−1.1%	689,621	−6.4%	701,127	1.7%
LA Urban	2,634,720	1,556,688	−40.9%	1,369,313	−12.0%	1,108,435	−19.1%	1,060,660	−4.3%
Rest of LA County	2,415,521	1,648,750	−31.7%	1,507,706	−8.6%	1,161,327	−23.0%	966,534	−16.8%
Rest of LA Region	2,806,336	3,037,078	8.2%	3,611,597	18.9%	3,427,700	−5.1%	3,276,033	−4.4%
LA Region	8,795,419	6,987,557	−20.6%	7,225,359	3.4%	6,387,083	−11.6%	6,004,354	−6.0%

NYC Region	1970	1980	1970–80	1990	1980–90	2000	1990–2000	2010	2000–2010
Manhattan	1,088,227	713,360	−34.4%	726,553	1.8%	703,873	−3.1%	761,493	8.2%
Outer Boroughs	4,954,636	2,954,082	−40.4%	2,435,759	−17.5%	2,097,394	−13.9%	1,961,411	−6.5%
Inner Suburbs	5,799,220	4,698,869	−19.0%	4,124,134	−12.2%	3,645,276	−11.6%	3,196,500	−12.3%
Outer Suburbs	4,016,208	5,063,963	26.1%	5,515,158	8.9%	5,664,356	2.7%	5,512,221	−2.7%
NYC Region	15,858,291	13,430,274	−15.3%	12,801,604	−4.7%	12,110,899	−5.4%	11,431,625	−5.6%

Source: 1970 to 2010 Decennial Census Tabulations from *Social Explorer*. Defined area allocations of census tracts by Andrew A. Beveridge.

Table 2.3 NON-HISPANIC BLACK POPULATION IN LOS ANGELES AND NEW YORK CITY REGIONS AND DEFINED AREAS, 1970 TO 2010

LA Region	1970	1980	1970–80	1990	1980–90	2000	1990–2000	2010	2000–2010
West of Downtown	145,596	181,440	24.6%	181,025	−0.2%	179,647	−0.8%	159,121	−11.4%
LA Urban	531,015	586,175	10.4%	547,169	−6.7%	518,335	−5.3%	462,348	−10.8%
Rest of LA County	84,970	158,320	86.3%	205,174	29.6%	252,778	23.2%	255,043	0.9%
Rest of LA Region	66,891	111,900	67.3%	222,855	99.2%	330,731	48.4%	409,812	23.9%
LA Region	828,472	1,037,835	25.3%	1,156,223	11.4%	1,281,491	10.8%	1,286,324	0.4%

NYC Region	1970	1980	1970–80	1990	1980–90	2000	1990–2000	2010	2000–2010
Manhattan	380,306	290,126	−23.7%	261,091	−10.0%	245,939	−5.8%	217,102	−11.7%
Outer Boroughs	1,286,668	1,403,432	9.1%	1,584,997	12.9%	1,804,825	13.9%	1,714,787	−5.0%
Inner Suburbs	739,849	878,442	18.7%	945,295	7.6%	1,091,031	15.4%	1,099,455	0.8%
Outer Suburbs	206,470	274,300	32.9%	343,657	25.3%	448,983	30.6%	518,250	15.4%
NYC Region	2,613,293	2,846,300	8.9%	3,135,040	10.1%	3,590,778	14.5%	3,549,594	−1.1%

Source: 1970 to 2010 Decennial Census Tabulations from *Social Explorer*. Defined area allocations of census tracts by Andrew A. Beveridge.

Table 2.4 HISPANIC POPULATION IN LOS ANGELES AND NEW YORK CITY REGIONS AND DEFINED AREAS, 1970 TO 2010

LA Region	1980	1990	1980–90	2000	1990–2000	2010	2000–2010
West of Downtown	159,869	270,242	69.0%	307,552	13.8%	314,131	2.1%
LA Urban	1,068,005	1,698,850	59.1%	2,089,679	23.0%	2,253,940	7.9%
Rest of LA County	838,000	1,381,486	64.9%	1,844,927	33.5%	2,119,818	14.9%
Rest of LA Region	689,812	1,427,920	107.0%	2,356,328	65.0%	3,340,942	41.8%
LA Region	2,755,687	4,778,497	73.4%	6,598,487	38.1%	8,028,831	21.7%

NYC Region	1980	1990	1980–90	2000	1990–2000	2010	2000–2010
Manhattan	336,215	386,602	15.0%	417,816	8.1%	403,577	-3.4%
Outer Boroughs	1,069,566	1,396,459	30.6%	1,742,738	24.8%	1,932,499	10.9%
Inner Suburbs	482,418	749,930	55.5%	1,140,808	52.1%	1,553,170	36.1%
Outer Suburbs	205,296	334,333	62.9%	564,236	68.8%	906,677	60.7%
NYC Region	2,093,495	2,867,324	37.0%	3,865,598	34.8%	4,795,923	24.1%

Source: 1980 to 2010 Decennial Census Tabulations from *Social Explorer*. Defined area allocations of census tracts by Andrew A. Beveridge.

Table 2.5 NON-HISPANIC ASIAN POPULATION IN LOS ANGELES AND NEW YORK CITY REGIONS AND DEFINED AREAS, 1970 TO 2010

LA Region	1970	1980	1970–80	1990	1980–90	2000	1990–2000	2010	2000–2010
West of Downtown	48,018	74,705	55.6%	111,764	49.6%	147,706	32.2%	178,318	20.7%
LA Urban	126,714	239,302	88.9%	451,224	88.6%	566,032	25.4%	661,477	16.9%
Rest of LA County	40,406	120,707	198.7%	344,400	185.3%	514,534	49.4%	616,248	19.8%
Rest of LA Region	42,633	126,997	197.9%	367,168	189.1%	635,583	73.1%	954,599	50.2%
LA Region	257,771	561,711	117.9%	1,274,557	126.9%	1,863,856	46.2%	2,410,642	29.3%

NYC Region	1970	1980	1970–80	1990	1980–90	2000	1990–2000	2010	2000–2010
Manhattan	51,799	72,863	40.7%	106,297	45.9%	152,498	43.5%	193,332	26.8%
Outer Boroughs	57,407	158,538	176.2%	383,431	141.9%	689,102	79.7%	898,885	30.4%
Inner Suburbs	27,625	94,552	242.3%	235,358	148.9%	422,846	79.7%	603,866	42.8%
Outer Suburbs	14,631	55,480	279.2%	143,508	158.7%	278,667	94.2%	440,975	58.2%
NYC Region	151,462	381,433	151.8%	868,594	127.7%	1,543,113	77.7%	2,137,058	38.5%

Source: 1970 to 2010 Decennial Census Tabulations from Social Explorer. Defined area allocations of census tracts by Andrew A. Beveridge.

Table 2.6 FOREIGN-BORN POPULATION IN LOS ANGELES AND NEW YORK CITY REGIONS AND DEFINED AREAS, 1970 TO 2010

LA Region	1970	1980	1970–80	1990	1980–90	2000	1990–2000	2010	2000–2010
West of Downtown	186,928	286,563	53.3%	400,231	39.7%	437,920	9.4%	413,683	-5.5%
LA Urban	412,344	877,451	112.8%	1,527,179	74.0%	1,771,965	16.0%	1,781,621	0.5%
Rest of LA County	187,520	481,893	157.0%	967,031	100.7%	1,239,511	28.2%	1,282,519	3.5%
Rest of LA Region	191,011	446,523	133.8%	1,049,811	135.1%	1,618,219	54.1%	1,992,606	23.1%
LA Region	977,803	2,092,431	114.0%	3,944,251	88.5%	5,067,614	28.5%	5,470,429	7.9%

NYC Region	1970	1980	1970–80	1990	1980–90	2000	1990–2000	2010	2000–2010
Manhattan	306,588	348,530	13.7%	383,857	10.1%	452,440	17.9%	452,102	-0.1%
Outer Boroughs	1,107,970	1,321,277	19.3%	1,698,659	28.6%	2,418,592	42.4%	2,519,041	4.2%
Inner Suburbs	683,390	800,887	17.2%	1,020,359	27.4%	1,490,923	46.1%	1,711,855	14.8%
Outer Suburbs	320,423	466,246	45.5%	567,472	21.7%	832,750	46.7%	1,056,748	26.9%
NYC Region	2,418,371	2,936,940	21.4%	3,670,347	25.0%	5,194,705	41.5%	5,739,746	10.5%

Source: 1970 to 2000 Decennial Census Tabulations from *Social Explorer*, 2006–2010 American Community Survey Tabulations from *Social Explorer*. Defined area allocations of census tracts by Andrew A. Beveridge.

Table 2.7 MEDIAN HOUSEHOLD INCOME (IN 2010 DOLLARS) LOS ANGELES AND NEW YORK CITY REGIONS AND DEFINED AREAS, 1980 TO 2008–2010

LA Region	1980	1990	1980–90	2000	1990–2000	2008–10	2000 to 2008–10
West of Downtown	$52,505	$63,182	20.3%	$60,062	-4.9%	$62,594	4.2%
LA Urban	$50,585	$55,789	10.3%	$49,540	-11.2%	$49,030	-1.0%
Rest of LA County	$59,124	$66,940	13.2%	$61,399	-8.3%	$58,799	-4.2%
Rest of LA Region	$61,437	$70,234	14.3%	$66,588	-5.2%	$63,548	-4.6%
LA Region	$56,517	$64,555	14.2%	$60,081	-6.9%	$58,766	-2.2%

NYC Region	1980	1990	1980–90	2000	1990–2000	2008–10	2000 to 2008–10
Manhattan	$41,761	$56,733	35.9%	$61,556	8.5%	$65,184	5.9%
Outer Boroughs	$41,563	$50,649	21.9%	$47,427	-6.4%	$46,452	-2.1%
Inner Suburbs	$63,089	$75,518	19.7%	$73,591	-2.6%	$69,597	-5.4%
Outer Suburbs	$65,678	$80,489	22.6%	$80,291	-0.3%	$77,510	-3.5%
NYC Region	$54,896	$67,656	23.2%	$66,417	-1.8%	$63,970	-3.7%

Source: 1980 to 2000 Decennial Census Tabulations from *Social Explorer*, 2008–2010 American Community Survey Tabulations from *Social Explorer*. Defined area allocations of census tracts by Andrew A. Beveridge.

Table 2.8 MEDIAN HOUSE VALUE (IN 2010 DOLLARS) IN LOS ANGELES AND NEW YORK CITY REGIONS AND DEFINED AREAS 1980 TO 2000, AND 2000 TO 2008–2010 FOR SPECIFIED OWNER OCCUPIED UNITS AND ALL OWNER OCCUPIED UNITS

LA Region	Specified Owner Occupied Units					All Owner Occupied Units		
	1980	1990	1980–90	2000	1990–2000	2000	2008–10	2000 to 2008–10
West of Downtown	$377,364	$699,968	85.5%	$666,794	-4.7%	$447,474	$791,203	76.8%
LA Urban	$237,872	$374,145	57.3%	$317,920	-15.0%	$255,157	$438,897	72.0%
Rest of LA County	$216,667	$337,753	55.9%	$296,537	-12.2%	$243,970	$409,902	68.0%
Rest of LA Region	$232,312	$326,894	40.7%	$310,071	-5.2%	$239,797	$375,888	56.8%
LA Region	$235,029	$353,156	50.3%	$320,454	-9.3%	$253,078	$421,700	66.6%

NYC Region	Specified Owner Occupied Units					All Owner Occupied Units		
	1980	1990	1980–90	2000	1990–2000	2000	2008–10	2000 to 2008–10
Manhattan	NA	NA		NA		$432,651	$841,800	94.6%
Outer Boroughs	$142,226	$315,822	122.1%	$330,612	4.7%	$276,319	$486,505	76.1%
Inner Suburbs	$167,898	$327,166	94.9%	$341,272	4.3%	$272,531	$433,374	59.0%
Outer Suburbs	$172,084	$293,400	70.5%	$284,489	-3.0%	$238,178	$370,524	55.6%
NYC Region	$166,440	$310,962	86.8%	$318,258	2.4%	$259,899	$419,429	61.4%

Source: 1980 to 2000 Decennial Census Tabulations from *Social Explorer*, 2008–2010 American Community Survey Tabulations from *Social Explorer*. Defined area allocations and imputations of median from census tracts and PUMA tabulations by Andrew A. Beveridge.

Note: From 1980 to 2000 the Census Bureau computed house value just for single-family detached houses, which it called "specified owner occupied units." There were not enough such units in Manhattan for a reliable estimate of house value. Starting in 2000, the Census Bureau broadened this to all owner occupied units, which include condos and co-ops, producing reliable Manhattan data.

Table 2.9 FORECLOSURE RATES IN LOS ANGELES AND NEW YORK CITY REGIONS
AND DEFINED AREAS, MAY 1, 2008, THROUGH APRIL 30, 2009

LA Region	Foreclosures Completed	Foreclosure Started
West of Downtown	1.30%	2.54%
LA Urban	3.55%	5.47%
Rest of LA County	5.12%	6.18%
Rest of LA Region	3.10%	5.30%
LA Region	4.11%	5.59%
NYC Region	Foreclosures Completed	Foreclosure Started
Manhattan	0.02%	0.44%
Outer Boroughs	0.24%	1.68%
Inner Suburbs	0.37%	2.04%
Outer Suburbs	0.22%	1.33%
NYC Region	0.26%	1.59%

Source: RealtyTrac Foreclosure Data Allocated to Defined Areas, Number of Owner Occupied Homes
2006–2010 American Community Survey Tabulations from *Social Explorer*. Defined area allocations
and rate computations of census tracts by Andrew A. Beveridge.

Table 2.10 MEDIAN CONTRACT RENT (IN 2010 DOLLARS) LOS ANGELES AND NEW YORK
CITY REGIONS AND DEFINED AREAS, 1980 TO 2008–2010

LA Region	1980	1990	1980–90	2000	1990–2000	2008–10	2000 to 2008–10
West of Downtown	$728	$1,019	40.07%	$936	–8.18%	$1,224	30.77%
LA Urban	$619	$913	47.37%	$769	–15.74%	$978	27.18%
Rest of LA County	$648	$969	49.51%	$822	–15.20%	$1,044	27.01%
Rest of LA Region	$781	$1,053	34.85%	$924	–12.23%	$1,161	25.65%
LA Region	$685	$981	43.13%	$845	–13.86%	$1,089	28.88%
NYC Region	1980	1990	1980–90	2000	1990–2000	1089	2000 to 2008–10
Manhattan	$635	$797	25.56%	$937	17.50%	$1,179	25.82%
Outer Boroughs	$556	$736	32.39%	$802	8.95%	$959	19.64%
Inner Suburbs	$625	$886	41.85%	$884	–0.23%	$997	12.80%
Outer Suburbs	$656	$959	46.17%	$894	–6.81%	$984	10.07%
NYC Region	$595	$821	37.86%	$850	3.55%	$994	16.94%

Source: 1980 to 2000 Decennial Census Tabulations from *Social Explorer*, 2008–2010 American Community
Survey Tabulations from *Social Explorer*. Defined area allocations of census tracts by Andrew A. Beveridge.

Table 2.11 PERCENT BA DEGREE AMONG THOSE 20 TO 29 IN VARIOUS AREAS OF LOS ANGELES AND NEW YORK CITY REGIONS, 1970 TO 2006–2010

	LA Rest of Region Males	LA Rest of Region Females	Ratio Females to Males (%)	LA County Males	LA County Females	Ratio Females to Males (%)	LA City Males	LA City Females	Ratio Females to Males (%)
1970	13.2%	9.6%	72.8%	15.3%	10.8%	70.6%			
1980	15.1%	12.6%	83.4%	14.3%	12.0%	83.5%	17.4%	15.7%	90.1%
1990	13.2%	13.9%	105.2%	15.0%	15.8%	105.2%	15.9%	17.3%	109.3%
2000	12.9%	15.8%	122.7%	14.9%	18.0%	120.6%	18.1%	21.2%	116.9%
2006–10	14.5%	19.8%	136.8%	17.4%	23.3%	134.0%	23.0%	28.0%	121.5%

	NYC Rest of Region Males	NYC Rest of Region Females	Ratio Females to Males (%)	NY City Males	NY City Females	Ratio Females to Males (%)
1970	19.2%	13.9%	72.7%	20.0%	14.4%	72.0%
1980	22.0%	19.7%	89.7%	23.1%	21.1%	91.3%
1990	23.7%	25.5%	107.6%	23.1%	25.5%	110.6%
2000	25.0%	31.2%	124.7%	26.9%	31.8%	118.5%
2006–10	26.2%	34.7%	132.1%	31.0%	40.9%	131.9%

Source: 1970 to 2000 Decennial Census Tabulations from *Social Explorer*, 2006–2010 American Community Survey Tabulations from *Social Explorer.*

Table 2.12 PERCENT OF 20-SOMETHINGS WORKING FULLTIME BY SEX IN VARIOUS AREAS OF LOS ANGELES AND NEW YORK CITY REGIONS, 1970 TO 2006–2010

	LA Rest of Region Male	LA Rest of Region Female	Ratio Females to Males (%)	LA County Male	LA County Female	Ratio Females to Males (%)	LA City Male	LA City Female	Ratio Females to Males (%)
1970	58.6%	23.1%	39.5%	55.0%	27.6%	50.1%			
1980	57.5%	35.2%	61.2%	57.9%	37.5%	64.7%	50.9%	35.9%	70.5%
1990	58.0%	39.3%	67.7%	55.7%	39.4%	70.7%	50.1%	36.5%	72.8%
2000	50.5%	33.5%	66.4%	46.3%	31.6%	68.2%	43.6%	31.5%	72.2%
2006–10	50.1%	35.4%	70.7%	49.4%	37.7%	76.4%	50.5%	38.6%	76.5%

	NYC Rest of Region Male	NYC Rest of Region Female	Ratio Females to Males (%)	NY City Male	NY City Female	Ratio Females to Males (%)
1970	62.1%	26.8%	43.1%	55.9%	30.7%	54.8%
1980	59.2%	40.9%	69.0%	47.3%	34.0%	71.9%
1990	61.1%	47.2%	77.3%	47.9%	38.2%	79.7%
2000	54.4%	42.6%	78.4%	44.1%	33.7%	76.3%
2006–10	51.5%	42.2%	81.9%	48.9%	40.7%	83.3%

Source: 1970 to 2000 Decennial Census Tabulations from Social Explorer, 2006–2010 American Community Survey Tabulations from Social Explorer.

Table 2.13 MEDIAN EARNINGS (IN 2010 DOLLARS) OF 20-SOMETHINGS IN VARIOUS AREAS OF LOS ANGELES AND NEW YORK CITY REGIONS, 1970 TO 2006–2010

	LA Rest of Region Male	LA Rest of Region Female	Ratio of Female to Male Earnings (%)	LA County Male	LA County Female	Ratio of Female to Male Earnings (%)	LA City Male	LA City Female	LA City Ratio of Female to Male Earnings (%)
1970	$47,858	$30,023	62.7%	$44,885	$31,228	69.6%			
1980	$39,676	$29,761	75.0%	$38,775	$31,370	80.9%	$38,231	$31,437	82.2%
1990	$36,951	$31,672	85.7%	$35,192	$36,010	102.3%	$36,932	$34,832	94.3%
2000	$31,813	$30,111	94.7%	$30,111	$34,601	114.9%	$35,670	$35,288	98.9%
2006–10	$30,006	$30,000	100.0%	$28,459	$33,185	116.6%	$33,973	$34,691	102.1%

	NYC Rest of Region Male	NYC Rest of Region Female	Ratio of Female to Male Earnings (%)	NY City Male	NY City Female	Ratio of Female to Male Earnings (%)
1970	$39,981	$21,699	54.3%	$41,913	$34,779	83.0%
1980	$30,061	$22,550	75.0%	$36,070	$31,834	88.3%
1990	$35,192	$27,449	78.0%	$38,711	$37,611	97.2%
2000	$30,111	$24,874	82.6%	$39,275	$39,275	100.0%
2006–10	$23,412	$20,328	86.8%	$34,435	$37,767	109.7%

Source: 1970 to 2000 Decennial Census Tabulations from *Social Explorer*, 2006–2010 American Community Survey Tabulations from *Social Explorer*.

Table 2.14 MEDIAN HOUSEHOLD INCOME (IN 2010 DOLLARS) FOR CHILDREN 0–4 IN VARIOUS AREAS OF LOS ANGELES AND NEW YORK CITY REGIONS (ACS 2006–2010)

	LA Rest of Region All Groups	LA Rest of Region Non-Hispanic White	% Non-Hispanic White or All Groups	LA County All Groups	LA County Non-Hispanic White	% Non-Hispanic White or All Groups	LA City All Groups	LA City Non-Hispanic White	% Non-Hispanic White or All Groups	West of Downtown All Groups	West of Downtown Non-Hispanic White	% Non-Hispanic White or All Groups
1980	$57,568	$64,719	112.4%	$54,368	$66,116	121.6%	$45,084	$72,126	160.0%			
1990	$70,383	$81,600	115.9%	$65,104	$88,155	135.4%	$49,708	$92,906	186.9%			
2000	$64,149	$85,096	132.7%	$57,472	$91,641	159.5%	$43,202	$95,569	221.2%	$63,363	$132,225	208.7%
2006–10	$63,525	$91,054	143.3%	$60,013	$101,279	168.8%	$45,744	$110,887	242.4%	$81,500	$141,280	173.3%

	NYC Rest of Region All Groups	NYC Rest of Region Non-Hispanic White	% Non-Hispanic White or All Groups	NY City All Groups	NY City Non-Hispanic White	% Non-Hispanic White or All Groups	Manhatta All Groups	Manhatta Non-Hispanic White	% Non-Hispanic White or All Groups
1980	$63,157	$69,136	109.5%	$36,724	$57,103	155.5%	$33,066	$83,213	251.7%
1990	$80,940	$87,979	108.7%	$49,441	$79,181	160.2%	$47,509	$160,121	337.0%
2000	$87,976	$101,722	115.6%	$48,439	$78,550	162.2%	$58,912	$202,920	344.4%
2006–10	$87,300	$106,417	121.9%	$50,000	$89,390	178.8%	$90,000	$220,498	245.0%

Source: 1980 to 2000 Decennial Census Tabulations from *Social Explorer*, 2006–2010 American Community Survey Tabulations from *Social Explorer*.

CHAPTER 3

The New York and Los Angeles Economies from Boom to Crisis

DAVID L. GLADSTONE AND SUSAN S. FAINSTEIN

New York and Los Angeles are two of the three American cities with the strongest claims to global city status.[1] Their position in the world rests on the structure and size of their economies, substantial proportions of which involve activities with global reach. These include the provision of financial and other services to businesses around the world, the production of cultural transmissions with worldwide audiences, and the accommodation of visitors from other countries. Their global influence expresses itself in terms of their disproportionately large shares of certain industries relative to other American cities and, especially, in the sheer magnitude of employment in these sectors. The large number of employees and amount of value added within financial and producer services and the hospitality industries, as well as motion pictures and other entertainment media, give New York and Los Angeles their special character as global centers.[2]

Despite their similarities, New York and Los Angeles do not occupy identical places in the world system of cities nor do they possess the same economic geographies. Their birth at different stages in American economic development led to different industrial structures (Abu-Lughod 1999). Even though both grew up around major ports, the effect of involvement in international trade differed. In New York it gave rise to dense development around the docks and an enormous financial industry supporting shipping activities, soon extending into a whole range of industries nationwide. By the time Los Angeles's port began to challenge New York's in size, eastern banking institutions had acquired a dominant position that limited serious competition and, to the extent a West Coast financial rival developed to New York, it was San Francisco not Los Angeles. In the meantime, Los Angeles benefited from a mild climate, nonexistent topographical boundaries to expansion, and, eventually, federal spending during World War II. These factors stimulated the growth of its vast aerospace industry and the development and wide dispersal of both commercial and manufacturing sites. Jewish producers seeking a more open society than existed in the East moved to the West Coast; their decision to locate the motion picture studios in Hollywood also contributed to differences between the two cities (Gabler 1988). In the postwar years, as we will discuss below, the critical path set in the earlier period led to the emergence of further dissimilarities.

If the two cities thus do differ in terms of industrial composition and spatial arrangements, they strongly resemble each other in labor force characteristics. Both display highly skewed income distributions, in part because both are hosts to huge numbers of low-skilled immigrants willing to accept work at very low levels of wages and benefits. At the same time, each offers extraordinarily high earnings possibilities due to the disproportionate presence of industries (investment banking, corporate law, broadcasting, and motion pictures) that pay their top executives and performers exceptionally well. In fact, inequality has increased substantially in global cities since the 1970s, not so much because the poor have become poorer and more numerous—although this has occurred—as because the rich have become so much richer (Fainstein 2001).

In previous work, we compared the chief industrial and economic characteristics of New York and Los Angeles (Gladstone and Fainstein 2003). We argued that because global cities have much higher concentrations of financial institutions and property development firms than nonglobal cities, they are more sensitive to the effects of financial cycles. This shared sensitivity led to similar responses to business cycles in the two cities. New York has been especially affected by volatility in financial markets, while Los Angeles, which has long depended for growth on the activities of land developers, is especially susceptible to falling real estate prices. In this chapter we consider whether the two were similarly affected by the crash of 2007–09, examine the effects of ballooning real estate prices during the early part of the last decade, and discuss the impact of the subsequent foreclosure crisis. We also assess the consequences of the global economic crisis on the urban fabrics, income distributions, public revenue situations, and economic futures of both cities at the end of the 2000s. Although the freezing of credit markets, the steep drop in real estate values, and the decline, subsequent rebound, and continued volatility of Wall Street stock indices are related phenomena, we will consider how each component of the crisis and its aftermath has affected the two cities. We focus especially on the employment effects associated with ongoing financialization of economic activity that occurred

Table 3.1 POPULATION AND LABOR FORCE, LOS ANGELES COUNTY AND
NEW YORK CITY, 2010

	Los Angeles			New York	
	City	County	Metropolitan Area (MSA)	City	Metropolitan Area (MSA)
Population	3,797,144	9,830,420	12,849,383	8,184,899	18,919,983
Labor Force	2,010,951	5,019,215	6,610,058	4,170,694	9,806,374

Source: US Census Bureau, 2011a, from American Community Survey 2010.
Note: The Los Angeles Metropolitan Statistical Area (MSA) consists of Los Angeles and Orange counties, and the New York City MSA consists of 22 counties in New York and New Jersey. The MSA in both regions is smaller than the Consolidated Statistical Area (CSA), which is used in Chapters 1, 2, and 11 to define the regions. All figures estimated; margins of error not shown.

throughout the 2000s and the differential impact on the two cities of the federal government's response to the financial crisis. Although we describe some attributes of the metropolitan economies to which these two cities belong, we mainly restrict our discussion to the five boroughs of New York City and Los Angeles County. Of the two, Los Angeles County has a population about 20 percent larger than New York's (9.83 million versus 8.18 million), but is at the center of a smaller metropolitan area (12.85 million versus 18.92 million) (table 3.1).

GLOBAL CITY FUNCTIONS IN THE TWO ECONOMIES

Global-city theorists generally point to three sets of characteristics that distinguish truly global cities from national or subglobal urban centers (Sassen 2001; Castells 1989; Friedmann 1986). The first is the global city's role as a command-and-control center in the international political economy. Global cities are places where key decisions get made; as such, they are home to large numbers of corporate head-quarters, banks, financial exchanges, and associated producer services, such as management consulting and major accounting firms, as well as national and inter-national economic and political institutions. As a consequence of the space needs of these organizations and their employees, they are also loci of relatively larger capital inflows into the real estate sector and built environment more generally. Money flowing into property markets in New York and Los Angeles represents a significant share of all international mortgage investment; to the degree that finan-cial institutions in these cities redirect investment into other property markets, they influence the form of nonglobal urban centers around the world (Fainstein 2001). Second, global cities are centers of global culture (Sassen and Roost 1999), accounting for a disproportionate share of the world's motion picture, music, news, entertainment, and artistic production. Third, global cities possess a distinctive industrial base; a decline in "traditional" manufacturing employment has been off-set by rapid growth in the producer services, telematics, media, tourism, retail, and other service industries.

The three major characteristics of a global city—command-and-control functions and associated investments in property development, along with cultural production and a distinctive industrial base—are present in varying degrees in the two metropo-lises. New York clearly exceeds Los Angeles in the first category. Few Fortune-500 firms are headquartered in Los Angeles—in fact, New York City is home to nearly three times as many Fortune-500 headquarters as Los Angeles County (CNN/Money. com 2011). There are virtually no large banks or investment houses headquartered in Los Angeles and, although neither city is a state or national capital, New York pos-sesses the United Nations and a large complex of nongovernmental organizations relating to it. Los Angeles is highly specialized in global cultural production, and in terms of employment, substantially more so than New York; in 2008 its motion pic-ture and sound recording industries accounted for about 3.4 percent of total employ-ment and 4.7 percent of the total annual payroll of all firms operating in Los Angeles County. Nevertheless, New York houses the headquarters of the major television

Table 3.2 OVERNIGHT VISITORS TO NEW YORK CITY AND
GREATER LOS ANGELES AREA, 2010

	Visitors	Domestic	International	International (%)
Los Angeles	25,800,000	20,600,000	5,200,000	20.2
New York	29,250,000	19,550,000	9,700,000	33.2

Source: The Los Angeles Convention and Visitors Bureau 2010; NYC & Company n.d.

networks. Both cities have very large tourism industries with a strong global component (Gladstone and Fainstein 2001). New York and Los Angeles are among the
leading destinations for foreign visitors to the United States. Of the 29.25 million
overnight tourists who visited New York in 2010, an estimated 9.7 million (about
one-third) were international travelers. In Los Angeles, 5.2 million international visitors made up more than 20 percent of all overnight visitors (table 3.2).

INDUSTRIAL STRUCTURE

Global-city theorists point to a particular type of service industry, producer services, as a key characteristic of global cities. According to Sassen (2001), global cities are production sites for highly specialized financial, business, and legal services.
Consequently, global cities like London, Tokyo, and New York will have much higher
concentrations of businesses and employment in these sectors than nonglobal cities like Manchester, Osaka, and Houston. An analysis of New York's financial and
producer services industries underscores Sassen's contention that, by her definition,
New York is a truly global city. It has a disproportionately large share of employment, as measured by location quotients,[3] in nearly every producer services industry,
including "finance and insurance" (2.0), "real estate rental and leasing" (1.7), and
"securities, commodity contracts, and other financial investments and related activities" (7.4) (table 3.3). Moreover, New York's producer services are highly concentrated
in space: location quotients for each producer service are higher in Manhattan than
they are for the city as a whole. In some categories, such as security and commodity
brokers, they are much higher. This centrality implies that these firms are primarily
serving other businesses rather than retail customers.[4]

In 1998 the US Census Bureau changed the way it classified industries for statistical
and measurement purposes; it replaced the former Standard Industrial Classification
(SIC) system with a new North American Industry Classification System developed
in conjunction with the governments of Canada and Mexico. Therefore, direct comparisons with pre-1998 years are not exact in most cases, particularly at higher levels
of aggregation. With this caveat in mind, one notable difference between employment figures for 2008 and 1997 is the relatively higher location quotient of "motion
picture and sound recording industries" for New York in 2008. In that year, New York

Table 3.3 LOS ANGELES COUNTY AND NEW YORK CITY, LOCATION QUOTIENTS FOR
MOTION PICTURES AND PRODUCER SERVICES, 2008

Industry/ Employment	Los Angeles	New York	United States	Los Angeles, LQ	New York, LQ
	3,910,429	3,406,402	120,903,551		
Information	227,414	178,438	3,434,234	2.05	1.84
Finance and Insurance	185,587	376,379	6,511,616	0.88	2.05
Real Estate and Rental and Leasing	88,787	106,118	2,196,314	1.25	1.71
Professional, Scientific, and Technical Services	365,627	318,278	8,032,847	1.41	1.41
Management of Companies and Enterprises	76,200	89,804	2,887,407	0.82	1.10
Administrative and Support and Waste Management Services	288,361	216,431	10,224,557	0.87	0.75
Arts, Entertainment, and Recreation	85,996	83,607	2,069,346	1.28	1.43
Accommodation and Food Services	354,147	268,114	11,926,329	0.92	0.80
Motion Picture and Sound Recording Industries	133,340	26,984	351,533	11.73	2.93
Securities, Commodity Contracts, and Other Financial Investments and Related Activities	27,204	203,758	973,920	0.86	7.43

Source: US Census Bureau 2011b.
Note: For industries with employment expressed as a range, median values used.

registered a relatively high location quotient for information industries, of which "motion pictures and sound recording industries" is a part. (Although "motion pictures and sound recording industries" in New York employ a significant number of people, the publishing firms in New York employ nearly three times as many.) New York did not appear as specialized in financial services and real estate in 2008 as it did in 1997 under the SIC code classification, but it was the clear leader in people employed in securities-related industries with about eight times more people employed in them as in Los Angeles and with nearly 30 percent of the city's total annual payroll due to the single subindustry of "securities, commodity contracts, and other financial investments and related activities."[5] As government rescues of financial firms "too big to fail" (and based in New York) have demonstrated, that high dependence led to New York being the principal beneficiary of the federal government's Troubled Assets Relief Program (TARP), as well as a host of other US Treasury Department and Federal Reserve programs targeted at stabilizing financial-sector firms.[6] The result is that New York has fared better than many other cities in the wake of the Great Recession.

If we restrict our definition of a global city to one with a very high concentration of producer services, financial establishments, and law firms, then New York is far more "global" than Los Angeles, which conforms to the national pattern much more than does New York. Moreover, in all but two categories, miscellaneous business services and legal services, the location quotients for Los Angeles's producer services industries declined from the late 1970s to the late 1990s (US Census Bureau 1977–97).[7] In other words, by the late 1990s Los Angeles had become less specialized in the industries that Sassen defines as global. However, a less restrictive view of global city functions than Sassen's that instead places more emphasis on cultural influence would consider Los Angeles's entertainment industries as heightening its global importance. As shown in table 3.3, Los Angeles has an astonishing location quotient of 11.73 in the category "Motion Picture and Sound Recording Industries." Not only does this greatly surpass New York's value for this industry, but it reflects the continued, and probably growing, importance of Los Angeles's entertainment production in the world. Regardless of where one travels, Hollywood films constitute a major portion of movie and television fare.

SERVICE AND MANUFACTURING SECTORS

In both New York and Los Angeles, as in the United States as a whole, the service sector, including consumer, producer, and public services, has been the driving force of employment growth. During the 1977–97 period, service-sector employment increased by 137 percent in Los Angeles, 77 percent in New York, and 165 percent nationally (US Census Bureau 1977–97). Service-sector employment retained its importance in both cities during the 2000s, as employment in education, health care, arts and entertainment, real estate, information, and accommodation all registered double-digit increases over the 1998–2008 period (table 3.4). Although the service-sector did not grow as fast in New York or Los Angeles as it did in the country as a whole during either the 1977–97 or 1998–2008 periods, services have historically represented a higher share of employment in Los Angeles and New York than in the nation as a whole (since at least the late 1970s), and in New York they represented a much larger share in 2008—76.3 percent versus 62.1 percent for Los Angeles and 60.5 percent for the United States (US Census Bureau 1977–97; US Census Bureau 2011b).

A still significant difference between New York and Los Angeles is the size of each city's manufacturing sector. In 1997, Los Angeles's manufacturing industries

Table 3.4 LOS ANGELES COUNTY AND NEW YORK CITY, EMPLOYMENT GROWTH IN SELECTED INDUSTRIES, 1998–2008

	1998		2008		Growth (%), 1998–2008	
	Los Angeles	New York City	Los Angeles	New York City	Los Angeles	New York City
Industry / Total employees	3,693,537	3,079,430	3,910,429	3,406,402	5.9	10.6
Mining	2,942	227	2,114	148	−28.1	−34.8
Utilities	7,500	17,359	17,500	17,106	133.3	−1.5
Construction	119,985	99,968	153,858	131,166	28.2	31.2
Manufacturing	638,389	185,787	453,162	91,607	−29.0	−50.7
Wholesale trade	263,110	183,583	280,991	168,037	6.8	−8.5
Retail trade	349,666	231,879	413,506	284,861	18.3	22.8
Transportation and warehousing	139,224	114,179	164,246	113,199	18.0	−0.9
(Total Services)	2,145,074	2,236,285	2,427,558	2,600,733	13.2	16.3
Information	164,267	149,730	227,414	178,438	38.4	19.2
Finance and insurance	177,067	372,354	185,587	376,379	4.8	1.1
Real estate and rental and leasing	80,535	92,651	88,787	106,118	10.2	14.5
Professional, scientific, and technical services	383,371	285,405	365,627	318,278	−4.6	11.5
Management of companies and enterprises	80,298	94,266	76,200	89,804	−5.1	−4.7
Administrative and support and waste management	311,818	216,448	288,361	216,431	−7.5	0.0
Educational services	95,074	128,871	124,486	178,186	30.9	38.3
Health care and social assistance	360,703	507,450	460,082	618,236	27.6	21.8
Arts, entertainment, and recreation	69,033	57,003	85,996	83,607	24.6	46.7
Accommodation and food services	264,368	186,320	354,147	268,114	34.0	43.9
Other services (except public administration)	158,540	145,787	170,871	167,142	7.8	14.6

Source: US Census Bureau 2011b.
Notes: Employment in "Auxiliary" industries not included; Forestry, mining set to zero for Richmond County, New York (no data reported); for industries with employment expressed as a range, median values used.

employed nearly one in six workers. At the same time, New York's manufacturing firms employed only one in twelve workers, or just over 8 percent of the city's total workforce (US Census Bureau 1977–97). In the late 1990s, Los Angeles had become the largest manufacturing center in the United States in terms of employment, surpassing both Chicago and Detroit (Swertlow 1999). It differed from the country's other major manufacturing centers in terms of its output: whereas Chicago and Detroit had specialized in heavy machinery, farm equipment, and automobiles, Los Angeles was producing a wide range of products, "from ball bearings and flywheels, to medical devices and silicon chips, to elegant glassware and apparel" (Swertlow 1999, 16). Among manufacturing subindustries in Los Angeles, apparel firms still employed the largest number of workers, but metal fabricating and heavy industry together represented a much larger source of employment. Indeed, as we will point out later, one reason for the lessening of income inequality in Los Angeles during the 2000s may be the decline in relatively low-paying apparel and textile industry jobs in Los Angeles and a corresponding increase in unionized service-sector employment.

Even though the sector remained significant, manufacturing employment plummeted in Los Angeles in the first decade of the new century—by nearly 30 percent— while in New York the slide was greater (table 3.4). The degree of change in the two cities differs from that of the nation: whereas manufacturing employment declined by 5 percent nationally from 1977 to 1997 and by 22 percent from 1998 to 2008, it declined even more in New York and Los Angeles (US Census Bureau 1977–97; US Census Bureau 2011b). There were fewer manufacturing jobs in New York in 2008 than there were construction jobs, which increased by more than 30 percent over the same period. Although manufacturing industries in Los Angeles declined in the 2000s, they did so from a much larger base than in New York; manufacturing in Los Angeles still accounts for nearly five times the number of jobs as in New York, close to 450,000, and Los Angeles remains one of the largest manufacturing centers in the United States.

More revealing are the relative shares of manufacturing and service-sector employment in the two metropolitan economies, with Los Angeles again mirroring national developments and New York sharply diverging from the national pattern (table 3.5). In Los Angeles, the share of manufacturing employment declined from just over 30 percent of all employment in 1977, to under 19 percent in 1997, to less than 12 percent in 2008 (US Census Bureau 1977–97; US Census Bureau 2011b). In New York, the plunge in manufacturing employment has been precipitous; its share of total employment fell from 22 percent to less than 3 percent during the same period. New York's divergence from the national pattern has only emerged during the last thirty years;[8] well into the twentieth century, New York had the largest number of manufacturing jobs of any city in the nation.

The continuing, albeit shrinking, importance of manufacturing in the Los Angeles economy, and its relative lack of significance in New York, is underscored by a comparison of the two cities' largest companies (table 3.6). In 2010 the ten largest firms by revenue in New York included only one manufacturer: the pharmaceutical company, Pfizer, although headquartered in New York, had no production facilities there and thus had little employment impact. In contrast in 2010 three of the ten largest employers in Greater Los Angeles were manufacturing firms: Northrup-Grumman,

Table 3.5 LOS ANGELES COUNTY AND NEW YORK CITY, EMPLOYMENT SHARE IN SELECT
INDUSTRIES, 1998–2008 (ALL FIGURES ARE %)

	Los Angeles		New York	
Employment Share by Industry	1998	2008	1998	2008
Total	100	100	100	100
Forestry, fishing, hunting, and agriculture support	0.0	0.0	0.0	0.0
Mining	0.1	0.1	0.0	0.0
Utilities	0.2	0.4	0.5	0.5
Construction	3.2	3.9	3.2	3.9
Manufacturing	17.3	11.6	6.0	2.7
Wholesale trade	7.1	7.2	6.0	4.9
Retail trade	9.5	10.6	7.5	8.4
Transportation and warehousing	3.8	4.2	3.7	3.3
(Total Services)	58.1	62.1	72.6	76.3
Information	4.4	5.8	4.9	5.2
Finance and insurance	4.8	4.7	12.1	11.0
Real estate and rental and leasing	2.2	2.3	3.0	3.1
Professional, scientific, and technical services	10.4	9.4	9.3	9.3
Management of companies and enterprises	2.2	1.9	3.1	2.6
Administrative and support and waste management and remediation services	8.4	7.4	7.0	6.4
Educational services	2.6	3.2	4.2	5.2
Health care and social assistance	9.8	11.8	16.5	18.1
Arts, entertainment, and recreation	1.9	2.2	1.9	2.5
Accommodation and food services	7.2	9.1	6.1	7.9
Other services (except public administration)	4.3	4.4	4.7	4.9
Unclassified	0.1	0.0	0.2	0.0

Source: US Census Bureau 2011b.
Notes: Employment in "Auxiliary" industries not included; Forestry, mining set to zero for Richmond County, New York (no data reported); for industries with employment expressed as a range, median values used.

Amgen, and Western Digital. That the largest of the three is a military contractor is no accident. Throughout the postwar period, and particularly during the 1960–90 period, Los Angeles received above-average levels of Pentagon dollars, a factor that also has contributed to growth in the city's producer services industries (Markusen and Gwiasda 1994; Markusen et al. 1991).

As we have pointed out, the decline in share of manufacturing jobs has meant an increase in the proportion of service-sector jobs in both cities, but the share of service-sector employment in New York has been larger than in Los Angeles: from the late 1970s to the late 1990s service-sector employment increased its share in Los

Table 3.6 LARGEST COMPANIES IN GREATER LOS ANGELES AND NEW YORK CITY, 2010

Los Angeles County

Company	Revenues ($1,000,000)	Fortune 500 rank	Industry
Walt Disney	36,149.0	57	Entertainment
Northrop Grumman	35,291.0	61	Aerospace/defense
Ingram Micro	29,515.4	80	Wholesalers
DirecTV Group	21,565.0	116	Telecommunications
Health Net	15,713.2	146	Health care
Occidental Petroleum	15,531.0	150	Mining/crude oil production
Amgen	14,642.0	159	Pharmaceuticals
Edison International	12,361.0	187	Utilities
Jacobs Engineering Group	11,467.4	203	Engineering/ construction
Western Digital	7,453.0	304	Computer peripherals

New York City

Company	Revenues ($1,000,000)	Fortune 500 rank	Industry
J. P. Morgan Chase & Co.	115,632.0	9	Commercial banking
Citigroup	108,785.0	12	Commercial banking
Verizon Communications	107,808.0	13	Telecommunications
American International Group	103,189.0	16	Insurance
Goldman Sachs Group	51,673.0	39	Commercial banking
Pfizer	50,009.0	40	Pharmaceuticals
MetLife	41,098.0	51	Insurance
New York Life Insurance	34,014.3	64	Insurance
Morgan Stanley	31,515.0	70	Commercial banking
News Corp.	30,423.0	76	Entertainment

Source: CNN/Money.com 2011.

Angeles from 25 to 40 percent of all employment, while New York's share increased from 28 percent to nearly 45 percent of total employment. Nationally, service-sector employment increased during the same period from 21 percent to 35 percent (US Census Bureau 1977–97). The trend has continued over the 1998–2008 period, with service-sector employment in Los Angeles representing nearly 60 percent of all employment in 2008, and in New York representing more than 75 percent of total employment (US Census Bureau 2011b).[9] Even over the 2007–09 recessionary period service-sector industries continued to grow in New York, increasing by 0.7 percent, or by about 17,000 jobs (US Census Bureau 2011b) (table 3.7).

Table 3.7 LOS ANGELES COUNTY AND NEW YORK CITY, EMPLOYMENT GROWTH IN
SELECT INDUSTRIES, 2007–2009

| Industry | New York City | | | Los Angeles County | | |
| | Employees | | | Employees | | |
	2007	2009	2007–2009 Change (%)	2007	2009	2007–2009 Change (%)
Total for all sectors	3,332,440	3,281,929	−1.5	3,866,150	3,703,233	−4.2
Construction	119,119	120,440	1.1	161,885	128,698	−20.5
Manufacturing	98,033	77,300	−21.1	456,722	420,013	−8.0
Wholesale trade	166,864	153,847	−7.8	267,958	264,342	−1.3
Retail trade	289,746	278,312	−3.9	428,286	389,604	−9.0
Transportation and warehousing	112,870	106,390	−5.7	161,843	148,059	−8.5
(All Services)	2,503,123	2,519,781	0.7	2,372,461	2,333,937	−1.6
Information	175,383	168,573	−3.9	212,458	213,757	0.6
Finance and insurance	340,702	337,046	−1.1	187,241	171,200	−8.6
Real estate and rental and leasing	105,892	102,520	−3.2	91,233	82,142	−10.0
Professional, scientific, and technical services	320,849	314,122	−2.1	368,125	347,225	−5.7
Management of companies and enterprises	94,835	85,613	−9.7	79,103	81,799	3.4
Administrative and support and waste management services	204,792	195,373	−4.6	281,310	256,970	-8.7
Educational services	171,644	180,923	5.4	117,347	124,427	6.0
Health care and social assistance	602,359	632,873	5.1	447,922	472,035	5.4
Arts, entertainment, and recreation	72,923	78,217	7.3	76,785	84,742	10.4
Accommodation and food services	246,522	259,289	5.2	341,645	338,653	−0.9
Other services (except public administration)	167,222	165,232	−1.2	169,292	160,987	−4.9

Source: US Census Bureau 2011b.

Throughout the 2000s, New York/New Jersey and Los Angeles maintained their positions as two of the nation's and the world's largest ports. The Port of Los Angeles is significantly larger than the Port of New York and New Jersey, particularly with respect to containerized cargo. Nearly twice as many containers pass through the Port of Los Angeles as through New York, although the amount of cargo moving through their respective airports is about the same. Los Angeles's manufacturing industries benefit from their strategic position along the Pacific Rim, with large shipments of manufactured goods heading to both Latin America and East Asia. In fact, the enormous growth in trade with China over the last two decades gives West Coast ports a significant advantage over their eastern counterparts. However, passenger volume in the New York airports exceeded that of Los Angeles airports by approximately 80 percent, reflecting that city's greater importance as a business and tourist destination, as will be discussed below.[10]

DISTRIBUTIONAL EFFECTS

Wage and Salary Income

Economic change in the two cities has resulted in the growth of a top, extremely high-income sector, a shrinking middle, a vast working class, and a smaller, very poor lower class—an income distribution that has largely remained in place during the 2000s, even though the two cities have diverged somewhat with respect to trends in inequality. Expansion in both numbers of people and income at the top stems from the types of industries present in the two cities; likewise, the low-wage working class is a product of the new occupational structure, characterized by the decline of unionized jobs and the broadening of the poorly paid service sector. Service-sector jobs, including many in the advanced producer-services industries, pay lower-than-average wages and in some service industries, such as tourism, they pay about one-third the average wage. In both New York and Los Angeles, tourism industry jobs have grown faster than jobs in other industries, and tourism employment has increased its relative share, growing in both cities over the last three decades. At the same time, average wage and salary increases in tourism-related industries have lagged behind wage increases in other industries (Gladstone and Fainstein 2001).[11] What is true of tourism jobs is also true of jobs in the retail services industry and manufacturing.

A comparison of aggregate wage and salary income over the 1998–2008 period reveals relatively strong growth for both cities, but with the rise in New York (17.4 percent) more than double that of Los Angeles (7.5 percent). It also shows that wages in New York are much higher on average—by more than 50 percent overall—than they are in Los Angeles. In fact, manufacturing, arts and entertainment, and health services are the only industries in which average wage and salary income was higher in Los Angeles than New York in 2009. Finance and management were among the highest paying industries in both cities and also registered the highest income gains between 1998 and 2008—not an unexpected outcome given the strong run up in the stock market during the 2000s and the income polarization that has come to characterize both cities and the country as a whole. The financial and arts-related industries were among those with high wage and salary growth in New York (with finance and insurance registering the highest increase of 55.0 percent), whereas in Los Angeles the largest increases occurred in the professional services (50.1 percent), finance (22.6 percent), and real estate (11.1 percent) sectors. A comparison of average wage and salary income for different industries over the 2008–09 period shows the clear effects of the national recession. Overall wage and salary income dropped in New York (a 9.7 percent decline), while in Los Angeles it grew slightly (by 1.5 percent). As we have noted, however, average wage and salary income in Los Angeles is relatively lower than in New York and for most industries substantially lower. Finance and management are among the industries most affected by the recession in both cities, but in New York the financial industries were, on average, much more negatively affected or at least appeared to be, possibly due to deferred payouts to traders and financial firm executives in 2009. Although comparable census data for 2010 was unavailable as of this writing, we would expect that the decline in average wage and salary income for financial services firms has more than reversed itself (table 3.8).

Poverty

Although poverty rates for the country as a whole remained fairly steady throughout the 1980s and 1990s, they increased sharply in Los Angeles and New York in that period. But during the 2000s, and despite a near doubling of the unemployment rate between 1999 and 2009, the share of the population with incomes below the poverty level appeared to have declined in both cities, as did the share of the population in extreme poverty (income less than half the poverty level). The share of people living in families with incomes between one half the poverty level and the poverty level increased in New York, and the share of people with incomes between one and two times the poverty level increased in both cities (table 3.9). So while poverty may be less extreme, it is still substantial. Not surprisingly, there are significant variations within each city. In the case of New York, for instance, there was a large increase in people earning between 50 and 99 percent of poverty incomes in Manhattan.[12] In Los Angeles the efforts of union and community organizers to increase the wages of those at the bottom of the wage scale—hotel workers, for instance—may be part of the reason for the decline in people with incomes falling significantly below the poverty line (table 3.9).[13] So far, efforts to introduce living wage requirements in New York have failed to gain passage.

Unemployment

During the 2000s the unemployment rates in the two cities diverged dramatically, with Los Angeles more closely approximating the national average and New York significantly deviating from both Los Angeles and the nation as a whole (table 3.10;

Table 3.8 AVERAGE WAGE AND SALARY INCOME FOR SELECT INDUSTRIES,
NEW YORK CITY AND LOS ANGELES COUNTY, 1998–2009

	Average Salary 1998		Average Salary 2008		Growth (%) 1998–2008		Growth (%) 2008–2009	
	New York	Los Angeles	New York	Los Angeles	New York	Los Angeles	New York	Los Angeles
Total for all sectors	$50,634	$33,513	$59,449	$36,011	17.4	7.5	−9.7	1.5
Construction	$46,565	$35,765	$48,344	$36,081	3.8	0.9	0.4	1.8
Manufacturing	$30,102	$34,534	$30,890	$35,440	2.6	2.6	−4.0	8.8
Wholesale trade	$49,458	$37,987	$50,255	$38,417	1.6	1.1	−2.2	1.2
Retail trade	$21,920	$21,317	$22,628	$19,897	3.2	−6.7	−1.8	1.8
Transportation and warehousing	$33,661	$35,718	$32,719	$33,331	−2.8	−6.7	3.0	0.3
Services								
Information	$66,437	$57,084	$72,095	$54,012	8.5	−5.4	4.8	4.9
Finance and insurance	$127,913	$58,569	$198,218	$71,801	55.0	22.6	−21.5	−10.8
Real estate and rental and leasing	$38,251	$32,413	$45,195	$36,016	18.2	11.1	−6.2	−0.4
Professional, scientific, and technical services	$64,465	$36,527	$71,913	$54,830	11.6	50.1	−1.6	0.1
Management of companies and enterprises	$95,403	$70,458	$113,153	$73,302	18.6	4.0	−3.1	−7.0
Administrative and support and waste management services	$28,383	$20,170	$32,848	$21,895	15.7	8.5	−3.1	6.7
Educational services	$29,630	$26,292	$32,540	$25,679	9.8	−2.3	3.0	2.7
Health care and social assistance	$34,654	$32,083	$34,906	$35,174	0.7	9.6	1.5	3.1
Arts, entertainment, and recreation	$39,982	$61,471	$38,455	$61,173	−3.8	−0.5	8.1	−0.7
Accommodation and food services	$19,242	$12,880	$19,316	$13,265	0.4	3.0	−0.3	0.1
Other services (except public administration)	$27,588	$20,529	$29,250	$20,761	6.0	1.1	0.4	1.0

Source: US Census Bureau 2011b.
Note: All salaries in 1998 dollars; figures may not sum due to rounding.

Table 3.9 RATIO OF INCOME TO POVERTY LEVEL, LOS ANGELES COUNTY AND
NEW YORK CITY, 1999–2009 (ALL FIGURES % OF POPULATION)

	Los Angeles			New York		
	1999	2009	+/−	1999	2009	+/−
Under.50	8.02	6.68	−1.33	11.35	8.38	−2.97
.50 to.74	4.53	4.27	−0.26	4.57	4.58	0.01
.75 to.99	5.36	5.11	−0.25	5.33	5.77	0.44
Under.99	**17.91**	**16.07**	**−1.84**	**21.25**	**18.73**	**−2.52**
1.00 to 1.24	5.99	5.64	−0.35	5.02	4.97	−0.05
1.25 to 1.49	5.96	5.86	−0.10	4.83	4.97	0.15
1.50 to 1.74	5.31	5.31	0.00	4.44	4.40	−0.04
1.75 to 1.84	2.09	2.27	0.18	1.85	1.92	0.07
1.85 to 1.99	2.68	2.96	0.28	2.40	2.56	0.15
2.00 and over	60.05	61.89	1.84	60.22	62.45	2.23

Source: US Census Bureau 2011a. Census 2000 and 2009 American Community Survey.
Note: 2000 and 2009 figures estimated; margins of error not shown. Figures may not sum due to rounding.

Table 3.10 LOS ANGELES AND NEW YORK, UNEMPLOYMENT RATES, 2000–2012

Year	Los Angeles (City)	Los Angeles (Metropolitan Area)	New York (City)	New York (Metropolitan Area)	United States
2000	6.0	4.9	5.8	4.4	4.0
2001	6.3	5.3	6.1	4.9	4.7
2002	7.5	6.3	8	6.5	5.8
2003	7.7	6.4	8.3	6.6	6.0
2004	7.2	6.0	7.1	5.7	5.5
2005	5.9	5.0	5.8	4.9	5.1
2006	5.3	4.4	5	4.6	4.6
2007	5.6	4.8	4.9	4.4	4.6
2008	8.3	6.9	5.5	5.3	5.8
2009	12.8	10.9	9.2	8.6	9.3
2010	13.9	11.8	9.5	9.0	9.6
2011	13.6	11.4	9	8.5	8.9
2012 (March)	13.1	10.9	9.8	8.9	8.4

Source: United States Bureau of Labor Statistics 2000–2012. *Note*: All rates not seasonally adjusted; March 2012 figures for New York (city and metropolitan area) and Los Angeles (city and metropolitan area) are preliminary estimates.

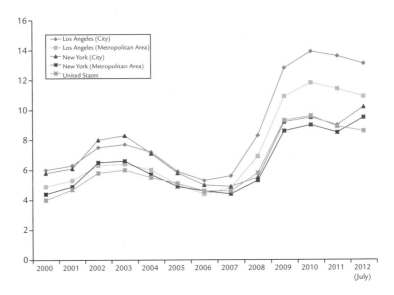

Figure 3.1
New York and Los Angeles Metropolitan Region Unemployment Rates, 2000 to 2012.
Source: Bureau of Labor Statistics 2000–2012.

figure 3.1). New York's unemployment rate exceeded that of both Los Angeles and the nation during the early part of the decade, but it fell below both after the financial crisis, seemingly a direct consequence of the federal government's rescue of the financial sector under TARP, as well as other US Treasury Department, Federal Reserve, and Federal Deposit Insurance Corporation programs. Interestingly, although the highest earning households reside in Manhattan, job increases in the outer boroughs outpaced those in Manhattan, perhaps reflecting a diversification of the New York economy. In fact, the total net job loss incurred between 2000 and 2009 took place in Manhattan where, despite the public money flowing into the financial industry, heavy layoffs occurred within it. At the same time, gentrification in the outer boroughs led to an increased demand for services, and firms seeking cheaper space also moved outside the Manhattan core (Giles 2011, 9).

Inequality

Although measures of inequality vary according to the data used, all measures of income inequality with which we are familiar indicate that both New York and Los Angeles are among the most unequal US cities and have also shown a clear trend of growing inequality over the past three decades, but with some notable differences. In New York, the richest and poorest groups gained in number at the expense of the middle throughout the 1980s and 1990s, a trend that appears to have continued during the past decade. Whereas 43.6 percent of all New York City households were middle class in 1977 (households with income between 80 percent and 200 percent of the city median), by 1997 they numbered less than 40 percent of the city's population by this measure (McMahon et al. 1998). During the 1980s, the city's upper income groups grew rapidly, from 8 percent to nearly 16 percent of all families; during that decade the number of low-income households declined. Throughout most of the 1990s, however, the number of lower-income households increased, leading McMahon et al. (1998, 16) to conclude, "after seven years of a national economic expansion New York City's middle class is still waiting for the economic recovery to begin."

Other measures tell a similar story. Over the 1990–2010 period, for example, inflation-adjusted median household income in New York, as reported by the Census Bureau, declined by 2.0 percent while average income increased by 9.6 percent, one sign of a polarizing social structure. Another way of looking at relative income inequality is by comparing the growth of households in specific income categories from census to census. In New York, the number of households in the middle class— households reporting incomes between $25,000 and $100,000—fell from 50.6 percent of all New York households in 1990 to 48.7 percent of all households in 2010. Trends in New York State tax data are also indicative of increasing income polarization: from 1993 to 1997 the highest income tax filers increased their share of total income from 35.1 percent to 44.8 percent; and from 36.6 percent in 1998 to 49.9 percent in 2006 (New York State Department of Taxation and Finance 2012; US Census Bureau 2011a). The richest 1 percent of New Yorkers accounted (in 2007) for 44 percent of all income in the city, up from about 12 percent in 1980 (Fiscal Policy Institute 2010). The authors of a Fiscal Policy Institute report on income inequality in the city note: "The lopsided growth during the 2002–2007 expansion meant that while the inflation-adjusted income of the average New York City household in the bottom 95 percent declined slightly, the average income among the city's top five percent increased by 85 percent. And among the richest one percent of New York City, average real income more than doubled, increasing by 119 percent" (Fiscal Policy Institute 2010, 9). The authors of the report go on to note that were New York City a nation, it would rank "15th worst among 134 nations with respect to income concentration" (Fiscal Policy Institute 2010, 15).

Although Los Angeles is also characterized by high levels of inequality, its manifestation differed there. Growing inequality in Los Angeles was not a straight line trend from 1990 to 2010, and Los Angeles diverges in this regard from New York and the United States as a whole, where the growth in inequality continued unabated from the late 1980s to the late 2000s. Rather, inequality grew much more rapidly in Los Angeles during the 1990s, peaked in the mid-1990s, and then leveled off in the 2000s (still growing, just not as fast). Thus, a report issued by the Assembly Select Committee on the California Middle Class in the late 1990s documents that between 1994 and 1996 the fastest growing groups of households in Los Angeles were those with income below $40,000 and those with income exceeding $100,000 per year. While the number of households with incomes between $40,000 and $100,000 declined in absolute terms, the greatest expansion (120 percent) occurred among households earning in excess of $25 million dollars per year. As the authors of the report bluntly state, "whether the measure is relative inequality or actual income, the seven years from 1989 to 1996—from recovery to recession to recovery again—saw the decline of the middle and working classes" (Assembly Select Committee on the California Middle Class 1998, 5). Not surprisingly then, the Gini coefficient (a common measure of inequality) for Los Angeles rose much more rapidly during the 1990s than it did for the nation as a whole, and by the late 1990s was about 40 percent higher, a level approaching highly unequal Third World societies (Nickelsburg 2007).

During the 2000s, however, Los Angeles deviated from the trend of increasing inequality characteristic of New York and the United States as a whole. Even so, Los Angeles is similar to New York in that the middle class declined both relatively and absolutely over the 1990–2010 period, with the number of households in the middle strata (those with incomes between $25,000 and $100,000) declining by more than 20,000 and falling from 56.6 to 52.3 percent of all households in Los Angeles County. At the same time and in a similar manner to New York, median income in Los Angeles fell more sharply (by 9.7 percent) than average income (3.6 percent), yet another indication of an increasingly unequal society (US Census Bureau 2011a).

One explanation for the crescendo of inequality in Los Angeles in the 1990s is the city's changing labor market in the aftermath of the early 1990s recession—a recession that hit southern California particularly hard due to cutbacks in national defense spending—as the number of higher-paying jobs in the aerospace and high-technology manufacturing sectors declined while employment in low-er-wage apparel and sweated industries increased (Nickelsburg 2007). Similarly, the recent relative decline in inequality may also be traced back to the labor market, as relatively low-paying apparel jobs diminished, while higher-paying jobs in the hospitality, health care, and other service-sector industries grew (Nickelsburg 2007).

In more general terms, three factors explain the contraction of the middle class in both cities: some middle class families leave the city as household costs increase or as jobs disappear; some fall into lower income categories; and some see their incomes increase. Income polarization in New York and Los Angeles is also fueled, at least in part, by the arrival of large numbers of immigrants from poor countries who accept work in low-wage jobs and replace the departing middle classes. In 2008, 36.4 percent of New York City's population was foreign born, while the proportion for Los Angeles was 39.4 percent (US Census Bureau 2011c).

In 2010 the cities of New York and Los Angeles were, according to the US Census Bureau, the two most unequal of the fifteen largest cities in the United States (See table 3.11). In New York, 1 percent of income tax filers accounted for nearly half the income and one part of the city—the Bronx—had more people living in poverty than any other county in the United States (New York State Department of Taxation and Finance 2012; US Census Bureau 2011a).

The metropolitan areas to which the two cities belong are also among the most unequal in the country, with New York once again heading the list and with Los Angeles in third place, trailing only the New York and Miami metropolitan areas. In both New York and Los Angeles, relative inequality appears to grow as the geographic unit of reference becomes smaller and more central. Thus, New York City is more unequal

Table 3.11 GINI COEFFICIENTS FOR THE FIFTEEN LARGEST US CITIES AND METROPOLITAN AREAS, 2010

City	Population	Gini Coefficient	Metropolitan Area	Population	Gini Coefficient	Metropolitan Area/City/County or Borough	Gini Coefficient
New York	8,184,899	0.535	New York	18,919,983	0.501	New York County (Manhattan)	0.594
Los Angeles	3,797,144	0.525	Miami	5,582,351	0.500	New York City	0.535
Dallas	1,202,797	0.519	Los Angeles	12,849,383	0.483	Los Angeles city	0.525
Houston	2,107,208	0.511	Boston	4,560,689	0.473	New York Metropolitan Area	0.501
Chicago	2,698,831	0.510	Houston	5,977,092	0.472	Los Angeles County	0.490
San Francisco	805,463	0.507	San Francisco	4,345,320	0.472	Los Angeles Metropolitan Area	0.483
Philadelphia	1,528,306	0.505	Philadelphia	5,971,483	0.471	Bronx Borough	0.480
Austin	795,518	0.488	United States		0.469	United States	0.469
Phoenix	1,449,481	0.485	Chicago	9,474,211	0.467	Queens Borough	0.440
San Diego	1,311,886	0.478	Detroit	4,291,843	0.461	Staten Island Borough	0.438
United States		0.469	Dallas	6,402,922	0.459		
Indianapolis	824,199	0.468	Atlanta	5,288,302	0.459		
San Antonio	1,334,359	0.460	Phoenix	4,211,213	0.454		
Jacksonville	823,316	0.459	Seattle	3,449,059	0.439		
Columbus	789,939	0.457	Washington, DC	5,610,082	0.434		
San Jose	949,197	0.434	Riverside	4,245,773	0.434		

Source: US Census Bureau 2011a. 2010 American Community Survey.
Note: The Gini coefficient, expressed as a number from 0 (perfect equality) to 1 (perfect inequality), is a common measure of inequality. All Gini coefficients shown are estimates; margins of error not shown.

than the larger New York metropolitan area, while New York County (the borough of Manhattan) is substantially more unequal than the city or metropolitan area of which it is a part. In fact, were Manhattan a separate country, it would rank number seven in the world in terms of inequality according to the Central Intelligence Agency, behind only the Central African Republic, Sierra Leone, Botswana, Lesotho, South Africa, Seychelles, and Namibia, and just ahead of Haiti (Central Intelligence Agency 2011). Los Angeles demonstrates a similar pattern: the City of Los Angeles is more unequal than Los Angeles County, which in turn is more unequal than the Los Angeles metropolitan area.

Stability and Instability

New York and Los Angeles both suffered sharp recessions at the beginning of the 1990s, doing worse than the nation. Then, once recovery began, they shared in the country's growing prosperity, albeit with the rewards distributed extremely unequally. In the immediate aftermath of the World Trade Center disaster, the future of the two economies, and particularly of New York's, was difficult to predict. Even without the events of September 11, 2001, the extent to which the two cities could hold onto the gains of the 1990s was an open question.[14] The broader base of the Los Angeles economy made its prospects appear stronger in the early 2000s, as New York's reliance on the securities industries had increased substantially. In 1998, finance and insurance firms accounted for just over 12 percent of the city's workforce (372,354 employees) but represented more than 30 percent of total earnings ($47.6 billion). A decade later, in 2008, the same sector accounted for relatively fewer workers—just over 11 percent of the city's workforce, or 376,379 employees—but nearly 37 percent of the total payroll ($98.1 billion). By this one measure at least, the city became even more dependent on financial services than previously (table 3.4; US Census Bureau 2011b).

In contrast to New York, the fortunes of Los Angeles are not as dependent upon a single industry or related group of industries. Even the "motion pictures and sound recording industries," with a location quotient of over 11.5 in 2008, represented only about 5 percent of total payroll in 2008 (133,340 employees and a payroll of $8.8 billion), and information industries, of which motion pictures is a part, comprised less than 9 percent in 2008 (227,414 employees and a payroll of $16.2 billion). Significantly, manufacturing remains one of the city's leading sectors in both payroll and employment terms (453,162 employees and a payroll of $21.1 billion) (table 3.3; US Census Bureau 2011b).

In New York the rather surprising efflorescence of the "new economy" based in information services during the 1990s indicated a widening of the city's economic base. Although the dot.com firms that gave part of New York the nickname Silicon Alley flourished only briefly, there are signs now of a revival of information technology related industries, which have located in the southern part of Manhattan (below Times Square and above the financial district). Other industries also came along to pick up the slack, including a fledgling biotech industry. Synergies between New York's fashion, entertainment, and arts sectors have further strengthened the dynamism of the city's economy (Currid 2007). A sharp decline in the crime rate over the preceding two decades accompanied economic and population rises, and some of the city's increased attractiveness to people and businesses can be attributed to the changed perception of its safety. One of the qualities of a global city not captured by quantitative measures is its attractiveness to creative people—it is this strength that perennially seems to make New York rebound from sharp economic downturns (Fainstein, Gordon, and Harloe 2011).[15]

New York experienced substantial job losses in the early 1990s and again at the beginning of the new century. By 2004, however, the city and the wider metro area had replaced all the jobs lost in the preceding decades (New York State Department of Labor 2009), although the city, unlike the metro area, never regained its 1969 peak. Rapid recovery from the 2001 downturn stemmed from the special attributes of the city's economic base: "Despite the magnitude of the losses, the sheer size of New York's economy kept the effects relatively small as a fraction of total economic activity, and the flexibility of markets in New York...enabled the city to recover much of its economic vibrancy" (Chernick 2005, 3). The strength of the area's economy rested on the financial and business services sector, but it continued to add jobs in fashion, cultural industries, and a variety of service occupations (US Dept. of Commerce 2009). The recession of 2008–09 led to a doubling of the unemployment rate, but in the aftermath of the financial crisis New York's unemployment rate declined more rapidly than that of the country, fell below the national level, and for 2010 was 4.4 points below Los Angeles's (table 3.10; figure 3.1). Accordingly, over the 2007–09 period the number of jobs in New York declined by 1.5 percent, as compared with a decline of 4.2 percent in Los Angeles (table 3.7).

Another reason New York has arguably weathered the post-2007 recession better than Los Angeles or the nation as a whole is the structure of the city's real estate industry. Although both New York and Los Angeles have extensive employment in real estate and large inflows of mortgage capital, the foreclosure crisis has affected New York much less than it has Los Angeles, as the previous chapter showed. From January 2007 to July 2008, the US Department of Housing and Urban Development estimated that more than 2.5 times as many mortgages were in foreclosure in Los Angeles as in New York. Notably, the borough with the highest real estate values—Manhattan—also had the lowest number of foreclosures in the city (only 533). The difference between New York and Los Angeles with respect to foreclosures is most likely due to a much larger number of single family detached residences in Los Angeles compared to the large number of cooperative housing units in New York—co-op boards routinely vet the financial resources of prospective owners and have limited the ability of borrowers to obtain adjustable rate mortgages. That Los Angeles has been hit much harder by the slump in real estate is clear from an analysis of employment in the construction sectors of both cities: whereas construction jobs declined in Los Angeles by more than 20 percent from 2007 to 2009, they increased in New York by more than 1 percent (table 3.7).

Public Revenue Impacts of the Financial Crisis

As in almost all American cities, Los Angeles and New York's governments have been experiencing fiscal stress. New York, however, had a less serious shortfall than had been expected initially. The city's Independent Budget Office (IBO) found that the city would receive $525 million more in tax revenues in 2011 and $790 million more in 2012 than projected by the Mayor and that in the fiscal year 2011 it would end up with a surplus of nearly $1.7 billion (IBO 2010). The IBO projected gaps in the subsequent years, but not of a size sufficient to be a crisis. Los Angeles's fiscal situation was more serious, with a projected shortfall for 2011–12 of $350 million, amounting to approximately 8 percent of anticipated revenues. Nevertheless, the city's situation appeared manageable (Los Angeles, City of 2011). At the same time, the states of New York and California were both experiencing severe budgetary deficits, which were likely to affect municipal budgets negatively. New York State reduced its grants in aid to New York City by $870 million (about 7 percent) between 2009 and 2011, while the 2011–12 California budget included deep spending cuts to health and human services, higher education, and environmental protection (California Department of Finance 2012).

Super Storm Sandy

At the time of this writing, a new threat to New York's economic stability arose from Hurricane Sandy, which swept over the city at the end of October, 2012. Although it is premature to arrive at any firm prediction of the hurricane's effect, its estimated cost in damage to property and infrastructure is in the tens of billions. The immediate impact on public and private revenues results from a week in which few businesses were operating, the transit system was shut down, and millions of people in the metro area were without electricity. Non-salaried employees mostly went without pay, although other workers engaged in storm-related work drew in overtime wages. In the medium term many businesses will remain closed for months while their facilities are returned to normal, and some number will lose their patronage altogether as a consequence of business interruption. In the longer term, federal aid and insurance money will provide work for those in the construction trades for repairs and upgrades to infrastructure. Much will depend on the as-yet unknown extent of federal largesse, which could have a major multiplier effect. Although Manhattan's midtown business district was largely unaffected by the storm, both the downtown financial district and the area to its north, which houses many of the new technology-based firms, lost power, and a number of downtown office buildings were flooded. The result may be to discourage further interest in occupying property in these areas.

CONCLUSION

Cities throughout the world have been promoting themselves as global cities. The implication is that strong linkages to the world economy will increase a city's well-being. The cases of New York and Los Angeles, however, make this faith questionable. They are enormous powerhouses of wealth, attributable to their dominance in certain industries. But whether much of this wealth trickles down to the majority of the population is questionable. Meanwhile, their large, poor populations constitute a continual strain on public sector budgets, while their function as a haven for immigrants is double-edged in its contribution to economic strength.

The sheer size of the populations and economies of the two cities, the glamour associated with their leading industries, and their history of generativity mean that they will probably retain their places within the American system of cities. At the same time, if the past is any guide, they are likely to suffer high levels of volatility. They will continue to be destinations for international travelers and aspiring migrants from the heartland. But they will also continue to be the locations of the country's largest aggregations of impoverished people and to display extreme differences of wealth. The diversity of occupations and groups in New York and Los Angeles and the extent of both geographic and social mobility make the commonly used imagery of a dual city inappropriate. Other tropes that have been applied include fragmentation, quartering, division, and layering (Marcuse 1989; Marcuse and van Kempen 2000; Mollenkopf and Castells 1991). We see in these two cities an ongoing dynamism, causing these more active descriptors to fit better the relationship between economy and society within their boundaries.

In conclusion, then, our analysis points to certain commonalities of the two cities that distinguish them from other American metropolises: the absolute size of their leading industries; their sensitivity to perturbations in the world economy; and the extraordinary diversity of their populations. Despite the expansion of their suburban hinterlands and the flight of firms to other, less expensive locations around the world, they continue to be magnets for certain industries key to the global economy. The future of their economies depends on the continuing need of these industries for proximity to each other. Sassen (2000) contends that this cohesiveness has increased in the last decade and predicts that it will continue to do so. It is our view that firms involved in servicing the international economy do not necessarily require close contact with each other, and the faster growth rates outside these two central cities, even in producer services, weakens her argument. We do not, however, see the outcome as predetermined by either technology or cost structures but rather a contingent consequence of political leadership and economic innovation.

NOTES

1. Chicago is a more significant financial center than Los Angeles, but it is nowhere near as culturally dominant.
2. This chapter uses some material that was originally published in Gladstone and Fainstein (2003), © 2003 by The University of Chicago. All rights reserved.
3. A location quotient is a ratio of ratios. In our analysis the numerator is the ratio of employment in a specific industry divided by total employment in Los Angeles County or New York City and the denominator is the ratio of nationwide employment in the industry divided by total national employment. A location quotient with a value greater than one indicates a higher-than-average representation of employment in the particular industry in the local economy.
4. Information on firms drawn from the Census does not differentiate between those primarily serving other businesses and those serving consumers. In fact, most serve

both, although different branches may specialize in one or the other customer group. Only a few types of firms (e.g., advertising agencies) have only business customers.

5. At just under 5 percent of total annual payroll, Los Angeles was much less dependent on its most specialized global industry in 2008 ("motion pictures and sound recording industries") than New York was on its most specialized global industry (the subindustry "securities, commodity contracts, and other financial investments and related activities") (US Census Bureau 2011b).

6. Nomi Prins and Krisztina Ugrin have compiled a series of "bailout tallies," which are available at http://www.nomiprins.com/reports/.

7. Based on the authors' analysis of US Census Bureau data.

8. Markusen and Gwiasda (1994, 171) point out that "in 1960, New York [sic] region led the nation in total numbers of jobs yet mirrored the nation's economic structure: New York's manufacturing shares of all jobs exactly matched the national average of 31%." By the New York region, Markusen and Gwiasda are referring to the New York Metropolitan Region.

9. Due to changes in the way the Census Bureau defines industry groups, our pre-1998 figures with respect to the share of the workforce employed in service-sector industries are not directly comparable to 1998 and post-1998 data.

10. Information obtained from web pages of the Port Authority of New York and New Jersey, the Port of Los Angeles, and Los Angeles World Airports, March 13, 2011. Containerized cargo is measured in 20-foot equivalent units (TEUs). In 1995 the number of TEUs passing through the two ports was roughly equal (2.3 million in New York/New Jersey; 2.5 million in Los Angeles). By 2009, while the number of TEUs going through New York/New Jersey had doubled to 4.6, the number passing through Los Angeles in 2010 had tripled to 7.8 million. In addition to LAX, Los Angeles World Airports operates Ontario Airport; the amount of cargo and number of flights passing through it is not substantial. In contrast, New York's three airports—JFK, LaGuardia, and Newark—are all among the nation's busiest.

11. Nevertheless, not all tourism jobs in New York and Los Angeles are low paying. Income and occupational polarization is evident even within the tourism industry itself, with some industries and occupational groupings characterized by low wages and others by much higher wages. "Arts, entertainment, and recreation" and "accommodation and food services" are among the fastest growing components of the tourism industry in New York and Los Angeles, yet they stand at opposite ends of the spectrum with respect to average wage and salary income of their employees.

12. While the situation of the upper 80 percent of the income distribution curve can be explained in terms of labor market characteristics, the very poor owe their plight primarily to the failure of welfare measures. Their status is a consequence of processes of social exclusion—they are unemployed or detached from the labor force and suffer from serious deficiencies of language, education, and access to social networks.

13. See, for example, Los Angeles Alliance for a New Economy 2009.

14. The 2001 national economic downturn was affecting both cities before September 11. Some of Los Angeles's key industries, including apparel/textile manufacturing, international trade, and motion pictures were already suffering (LAEDC 2001 Press Release. July 30. http://www.laedc.org/pressreleases/PR42.html [inactive link]). In New York heavy dependence on the securities and commodities industry meant that the sharp decline in stock market capitalization that preceded the attacks had a strongly negative effect on the city's economy for a few years.

15. The title of John Mollenkopf's (1992) book on New York City politics in the 1980s is *A Phoenix in the Ashes*; along with the city's penchant for generating new political coalitions is its capacity for spawning new industries and transformed neighborhoods.

CHAPTER 4

America's Leading International Trade Centers and their Entrepreneurial Agencies

Challenges and Strategies in the New York and Los Angeles Regions

JAMESON W. DOIG, STEVEN P. ERIE,
AND SCOTT A. MACKENZIE

Los Angeles and New York are linked by their preeminent role in international trade.* They are the nation's top two centers of foreign commerce, far exceeding other international gateways. Table 4.1 shows 2011 US merchandise trade by shipping mode for the top 10 customs districts. With $467 billion in global trade, Los Angeles topped the list, ranking first in the value of vessel cargo and third in air cargo shipments. With $418 billion in global trade, New York was right behind Los Angeles, ranking first in air cargo and third in vessel cargo. As domestic manufacturing and other traditional sources of economic growth either slow or decline, international trade will become an increasingly important component of economic performance in the United States. Thus, trade activities in the NY-NJ and LA metropolitan areas have both local and national importance.

The vital international commerce that pours through these two regions is supported by extensive networks of airports, seaports, and freight-rail lines. Table 4.2

*The authors wish to thank the following individuals for assistance and helpful comments: Robert Beard, Tom Clyne, Robert James, Donald Lotz, Maureen McManus, Connie Nardella, William Nurthan, Beth Rooney, Ralph Tragale, Christopher Ward, Peter Zantal, and their colleagues at the Port Authority of NY-NJ; also, Lillian Borrone, David Halle, Anthony Shorris, Kristina Stillman, Steve Strunsky, Vladimir Kogan, Rumman Chowdhury, Norm Emerson, Michael Armstrong, Geraldine Knatz, and Michael DiBernardo. A special note of thanks to Stephen Marshall for a close reading, which helped us to correct several errors. For research support, we thank the John Randolph Haynes and Dora Haynes Foundation and the Woodrow Wilson School, Princeton University.

Table 4.1 US MERCHANDISE TRADE BY SHIPPING MODE, 2011 (IN BILLIONS OF DOLLARS BY CUSTOMS DISTRICT)

Rank	District	Vessel	Air	Land	Total
1	**Los Angeles**	**381.7**	**83.7**	**2.0**	**467.4**
2	**New York**	**208.0**	**206.8**	**3.3**	**418.2**
3	Houston	242.5	20.2	0.3	263.1
4	Detroit	4.6	6.1	227.4	238.2
5	New Orleans	153.3	64.9	4.3	222.6
6	Laredo	1.2	0.4	212.5	214.2
7	Seattle	87.7	14.2	52.6	154.7
8	Chicago	1.6	115.6	30.6	147.9
9	Savannah	85.7	36.1	1.8	123.7
10	San Francisco	69.2	50.9	0.1	120.3

Source: US Department of Commerce, Bureau of the Census, FT 920 US Merchandise Trade: Selected Highlights (Washington, DC, December 2011).

Table 4.2 TOP US GLOBAL GATEWAYS, 2010 (MERCHANDISE TRADE IN BILLIONS OF DOLLARS)

Rank	Gateway	Type	Exports	Imports	Total
1	**Port of Los Angeles**	**Water**	**33.7**	**202.6**	**236.3**
2	**Port of NY-NJ**	**Water**	**46.3**	**125.1**	**171.3**
3	**JFK Int'l. Airport**	**Air**	**81.9**	**77.7**	**159.6**
4	Port of Houston	Water	70.7	60.2	130.9
5	Laredo bridges	Land	57.3	63.7	121.0
6	Detroit bridges	Land	62.8	48.2	111.0
7	Chicago airports	Air	35.3	75.3	110.7
8	**Port of Long Beach**	**Water**	**31.8**	**56.6**	**88.4**
9	**L.A. Int'l. Airport**	**Air**	**36.9**	**40.5**	**77.4**
10	Port Huron bridges	Land	34.7	38.7	73.5

Source: US Department of Transportation, Research and Innovative Technology Administration, Bureau of Transportation Statistics, *Pocket Guide to Transportation 2012*, table 4–10.

displays the nation's top 10 global gateways for 2010. In terms of the value of international trade, one-half of the nation's leading global gateways (ports, airports, and land ports-of-entry) are located in the Los Angeles and New York regions: the Port of Los Angeles; the Port of NY-NJ; JFK International Airport; the Port of Long Beach; and Los Angeles International Airport.[1] The Ports of Los Angeles and Long Beach are collectively known as the ports of San Pedro Bay.

The expansion of these transportation networks in the past century was essential to the central national role now occupied by these two regions; and expanding trade with domestic and international trading partners has been a driving force in the past

100 years in stimulating (and justifying) the building of docks, freight-rail lines, airports, and associated facilities.

Since early in the twentieth century, the crucial trade infrastructure assets in both regions have been planned, constructed, and maintained by powerful public agencies that were designed to be insulated from both local and state elected officials. Geography and global market conditions have been important, but these insulated agencies—operated by creative regional public entrepreneurs—have enabled New York and Los Angeles, more than most regions, to build local economies strongly shaped by trade opportunities. In 2008, New York and Los Angeles were the nation's leading export regions as measured by the value of locally produced exports (services and goods) and the number of export-related jobs (Istrate, Rothwell, and Katz 2010).

The two regions also lead the nation in the number of import-related jobs. In the NY-NJ region, port-related activities (primarily imports) generate more than 400,000 jobs each year. In the Los Angeles area, the estimated total is more than 550,000 jobs. Many of these are well-paid, blue-collar jobs in regions with declining opportunities in manufacturing. And through their efforts to build, maintain, and improve airports, seaports, and freight-rail systems, these agencies have had a positive impact in shaping economic development in their metropolitan areas.

Because New York Harbor is shared by New Jersey and New York, the efforts to improve shipping efficiency required cooperative action across state lines. These efforts culminated in the creation in 1921 of the bi-state Port Authority of New York and New Jersey (Port Authority). Its creators endowed the agency with broad powers, permitting its leaders to construct and control not only seaport operations but airports throughout the region, as well as bridges, tunnels, and other functions. In contrast, the Los Angeles system is decentralized; separate municipal agencies were created to govern its major airports and seaports. More recently, other LA-area communities have acquired greater voice through the creation of new authorities to govern inland airports and freight-rail facilities.

The appointed boards of these agencies reflect (albeit imperfectly) the political orientations of the local and state elected officials who appoint them. In Los Angeles, the decisions of governing boards are subject to public veto via the initiative process; and recently, elected officials have been able to exercise greater influence over the commissions governing airports and marine terminals. In the New York region, the Port Authority is spared public referenda, but the governors of New York and New Jersey appoint the agency's commissioners—who generally bring a mix of private- and public-sector experience to their review of the agency's agenda—and governors have at times used their appointing and veto powers to bend the agency to their will.

Transportation politics and policy outcomes have been powerfully shaped by the functional missions of these agencies. In Los Angeles, the separation of seaport and airport facilities encourages a narrow policymaking focus; resources gathered in one area cannot be used to develop and modernize in other fields. The multifaceted Port Authority, in contrast, must balance priorities and resources across many transportation and other development arenas. In doing so, it faces demands to alter its plans from numerous competing constituencies.

Despite the severe economic downturn that began in late 2008, the volume of international trade is expected to grow substantially over the next ten to twenty years. Traffic in and out of LA seaports and airports is likely to double between now and 2020, and the New York region may see similar growth. Existing facilities will need to be modernized and expanded, and new facilities will have to be developed. In Los Angeles, this means improving underutilized suburban airports to take the load off Los Angeles International Airport (LAX) and upgrading existing rail facilities to mitigate the burden on local roads. In the New York region, the Port Authority has taken control of 115 acres in Jersey City for new rail and port terminal space, and it has purchased a rail-float barge, which will be used to convey rail cars across New York Bay, reducing truck movements along congested highways in the region. The recent addition of Stewart Airport, 60 miles north of Manhattan, should help to meet expanding air-travel demand. With future passenger traffic being attracted to outlying airports, solving ground access issues will become vitally important in both regions.

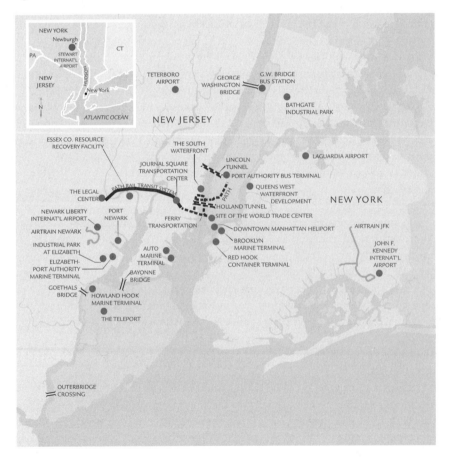

Figure 4.1
Facilities of the Port Authority of New York and New Jersey
Source: Port Authority of New York and New Jersey. Used by permission.

Figure 4.1 displays the airport, seaport, and other facilities operated by the Port Authority. Of particular importance are JFK International Airport, Newark Liberty International Airport, and Port Newark/Elizabeth. Figure 4.2 shows the Los Angeles area's airport system, which is the most decentralized in the world. Of particular significance are the two international airports currently operated by Los Angeles World Airports, a semi-autonomous municipal department: Los Angeles and LA/Ontario International Airports. Figure 4.3 shows the ports of San Pedro Bay (Ports of Los Angeles and Long Beach), the region's major rail lines and yards, the Alameda Corridor rail line from the ports to the downtown LA railyards, and the Alameda Corridor East project of planned separated-grade rail lines from the downtown railyards to the region's eastern boundary.

Can these metropolitan areas manage the expected trade growth while dealing with more expansive environmental regulations, the greater costs imposed by post-9/11 security concerns, and escalating demands by increasingly restive local communities? The entrepreneurial agencies discussed in this essay will occupy a central role in meeting these challenges. In doing so, the public officials leading these agencies will need to foster greater cooperation among public- and private-sector stakeholders.

In their varying structures and range of responsibilities, these entrepreneurial agencies illustrate distinctive ways in which large regions can design and operate transportation networks. Their successes (and failures)—and the opportunities and obstacles they face—offer useful lessons to cities and regions grappling with economic development challenges in an increasingly competitive global environment.

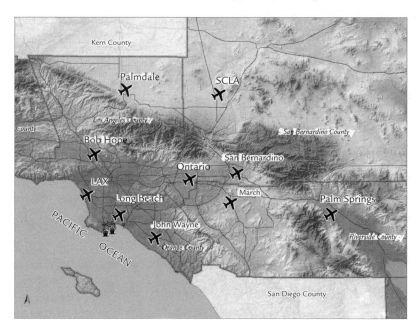

Figure 4.2
Airports and Sea Ports in the Los Angeles Region
Source: Southern California Association of Governments. Used by permission.
Note: SCLA is Southern California Logistics Airport.

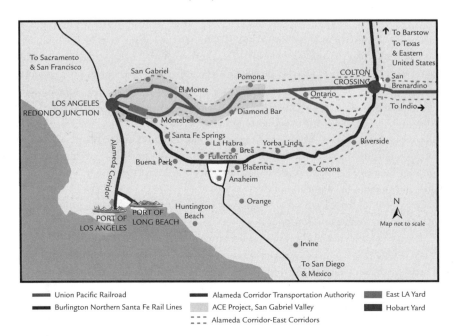

Figure 4.3
The Ports of Los Angeles and Long Beach (San Pedro Bay Ports), the Alameda Corridor, and Alameda Corridor East Project
Source: Alameda Corridor-East Construction Authority. Used by permission.

Our analysis is divided into three parts. The first examines the creation of the major trade infrastructure agencies in both regions and their development up to 1990. We then explore the mounting challenges these agencies have faced in the past twenty years. Finally, we consider strategies needed to grapple with current and future demands, including expanding air and sea traffic, security needs, and environmental concerns.

CREATING NEW AGENCIES AND FACILITIES

In summarizing the historical evolution of the port and airport agencies in the New York and Los Angeles regions, we devote special attention to how institutional autonomy was initially achieved and how it has (to varying degrees) been maintained. We also examine the contribution of bureaucratic entrepreneurs in planning, constructing, and maintaining the key components of each region's trade infrastructure portfolio. And we explore the concerns that such autonomy raises for democratic norms of accountability.

The Port Authority Story: The Search for Autonomy, Power, and a Wide Portfolio

The Port Authority of New York and New Jersey was created in 1921 after years of conflict between the two states (Doig 2001).[2] Resisting demands that local officials in New Jersey and New York City have important roles in controlling transportation developments in the region, state officials created a bi-state agency via interstate compact. Initially titled the Port of New York Authority, the agency was governed by commissioners appointed by the states' chief executives. Under the compact, the Port Authority would operate in a "Port District" of 1,500 square miles, including the largest city in both states and more than 300 cities and towns in seventeen counties.[3] As stated in the compact, the agency's overall goal was to aid in the development and coordination of "terminal, transportation and other facilities of commerce" in the Port region.

The Port Authority soon devised a plan centered on railroad tunnels to carry freight from the West and South under the Hudson River and Upper Bay to New York's piers.[4] The railroad executives resisted, and in the late 1920s, negotiations collapsed. However, under the creative hand of Julius Henry Cohen, counsel for the New York State Chamber of Commerce and later general counsel for the Port Authority, the interstate compact had been written in broad terms. The agency was given "authority to purchase, construct, lease and/or operate any terminal or trans-portation facility" within the port district, and though it had no taxing power, it could charge for the use of any facilities it constructed and operated. With the states' approval, the Port Authority embarked on a program of vehicular crossings in the mid-1920s. It soon constructed three spans between New Jersey and Staten Island, completed the George Washington Bridge in 1931, and built the first tube of the Lincoln Tunnel (finished in 1937); two more tubes were added later. The Holland Tunnel, built by another bi-state agency, opened in 1927 and was transferred to the Port Authority in 1930–31.[5]

All these crossings generated toll revenue from trucks and passenger vehicles, and once the Great Depression and wartime gas rationing ended, the agency began to look beyond bridges and tunnels. Led by a new executive director, Austin Tobin, and aided by the surge of postwar traffic (generating millions of dollars of "excess" toll revenue), the Port Authority employed an array of strategies to wrest control in 1947 over Newark's seaport and airport, Hoboken's piers, and New York City's LaGuardia and Idlewild (now Kennedy) airports from their reluctant municipal own-ers. In 1948–49, the agency also sought control of New York City's extensive piers, but city officials successfully resisted these overtures.

Using funds from bridge and tunnel tolls, Tobin and his aides modernized the Newark and Hoboken marine terminals. During the 1950s, freight tonnage increased sharply. More pier space was needed, and New Jersey state officials approved a plan to extend the Newark port facilities south into Elizabeth, with new terminals to be built on 640 acres of tidal marshlands. Most of the new terminal berths were designed for transporting containers, and by 1962, the Port Authority's container operations car-ried goods to terminals in LA-Long Beach and Oakland; in 1966, European ports were added. By 1970—when 300,000 loaded 20-foot containers were handled at Newark/ Elizabeth—the Port Authority operated the world's largest container operation, fol-lowed in order by Oakland, Rotterdam, Sydney, and Los Angeles. The vast open areas needed for efficient container storage and handling were available at Newark and Elizabeth but nonexistent on New York's side of the Harbor.

Once the Port Authority had captured all three of the region's major airfields—Newark, LaGuardia, and Idlewild—competition among airport operators within the nation's largest metropolitan area ended. But in air transport as in seaport activity, modernization and expansion required partners across the nation and overseas. The Port Authority played the lead role in forming the Airport Operators Council, which soon included airports in Los Angeles, Boston, London, and other large American and European cities. The Airport Operators Council successfully pressed Pan American, United, and other major carriers to accept higher landing fees, generating funds to modernize and expand airport facilities. Airport operators would no longer be dependent on the willingness of elected officials to allot moneys to airfield operation and modernization.[6]

In New York as in Los Angeles, expanding air travel generated conflict with local residents. In the 1950s, community protests were important in the imposition of noise limits for planes departing from the three NY-NJ airports, but in the 1970s the Port Authority joined forces with local groups in opposing plans to land the supersonic Concorde at Kennedy Airport. By the mid-1990s, Port Authority officials were engaged in frequent discussions with local officials and residents as they developed rail links to JFK and Newark airports. Close cooperation on noise and congestion issues has continued during the past fifteen years, as the Port Authority has expanded a small airport and modernized terminals at the three major airports. In 2011, however, residential complaints regarding overnight arrivals at JFK escalated, leading to active negotiations with town noise-abatement committees (Herbert 2012).

By the 1990s, the Port Authority had expanded its domain to include a wide array of facilities and functions—the Newark and Elizabeth terminals plus smaller port facilities at Hoboken, Brooklyn, and Staten Island; the three major airports plus a small airfield in Teterboro, NJ, and the Manhattan Heliport; six interstate bridges and tunnels; two bus terminals in Manhattan; industrial parks in the Bronx and at two New Jersey sites; and real estate developments in Newark and at the World Trade Center. The agency had also agreed in 1962 to take control of a bankrupt commuter rail system—renamed the Port Authority Trans-Hudson system (PATH)—and modernize it at great expense.

Until the early 1960s, the primary criterion in acquiring or building a facility had been that it would—in the long run—be self-supporting. That standard was set aside when political pressure led the Port Authority to take control of PATH, a project certain to generate large, continuing deficits. The agency reluctantly accepted that burden on its revenues in return for the two states agreeing to allow it to devote some of its surpluses to building the Trade Center—a project of great interest to Tobin and his colleagues, though it had only a thin justification as a "transportation-related" project. Tobin and his aides justified the Trade Center as an important step in competing for international trade and as crucial in revitalizing lower Manhattan. Also, committing large sums to building the Trade Center would, the Port Authority hoped, protect it from demands that it devote more funds to the region's rail system. Moreover, the 110-story twin towers would symbolize the importance of New York as a world commercial power and of the Port Authority as crucial to the region's success.[7]

Revenue streams from the George Washington Bridge, the Lincoln and Holland tunnels, and the airport parking lots have far exceeded the funds required at those

facilities, providing essential moneys needed at deficit-producing operations, notably the marine terminals and PATH. In 2009, for example, PATH produced a deficit of more than $60 million and the marine terminals lost about $45 million. The
Newark-Elizabeth terminals generate more than $200 million in annual revenue, but
operating expenses and dredging costs absorb most of that total; the Staten Island
piers operate in the red, but they are justified by the Port Authority as helping to
meet the agency's overall need for containership capacity.

Most of the decisions on how to allocate funds at these many facilities have been
made objectively, based on careful staff studies; however, political reality has required
continual efforts to spread capital spending fairly evenly between the two states.
Moreover, by the 1970s, pressure from the governors and local officials led the Port
Authority to provide substantial sums to aid these officials' own favored projects,
such as the Newark Legal Center, planning studies in several cities, and the Hudson-
Raritan Estuary program, under which the Port Authority provides funds to nonprofit
organizations that acquire property for environmental mitigation in both states.

Los Angeles: Strategies for Building Powerful,
Semi-Autonomous Municipal Departments

Construction of the Ports of Los Angeles and Long Beach and Los Angeles
International Airport were improbable and remarkable achievements. Their creation
and development required strong public–private partnerships and innovative institutional arrangements. In the beginning, private interests predominated. Local business groups such as the LA Chamber of Commerce played major roles in the creation
and early development of the region's global gateways. Later, durable public–private
partnerships formed, as bureaucrats fashioned close working relationships with
their clientele groups—shippers, carriers, and airlines—and with the federal government. In the late twentieth century, this system of bureaucratic clientelism—in
which these agencies focused primarily on serving their customers with low fees and
terminal leases—was altered significantly as a result of challenges by community,
labor, minority, and environmental groups seeking greater influence over transportation planning, policymaking, and facility development.

The story of Los Angeles's early harbor development is a riveting tale of urban
rivalries, railroad hegemony, and political revolt (Deverell 1994). In the 1870s, after
the transcontinental rail line was completed, Los Angeles and San Diego (120 miles
to the south) fiercely battled to secure the rail connection to San Francisco that would
ensure regional growth and supremacy. As a price for placing a trunk line through
Los Angeles, the Southern Pacific Railroad demanded a king's ransom in subsidies. In
1876 local voters approved the expensive deal and Los Angeles secured the vital rail
connection to San Francisco and the East. This proved to be a Faustian bargain, as the
Southern Pacific soon saddled the region with high shipping rates and poor service.

In the 1890s an epic battle over the siting of the harbor, which pitted the railroad against the local business community, set the trajectory of Los Angeles's transportation future. The Southern Pacific wanted a railroad-controlled harbor at Santa

Monica. The LA business community countered with a proposal for a municipally owned harbor at San Pedro. Southern Californians embraced municipal ownership—and the financing, land-use, and other powers of local government—as a counter to Southern Pacific dominance. After a lengthy battle, the San Pedro site received needed federal assistance for a breakwater and harbor dredging. Thereafter, Los Angeles annexed the cities of San Pedro and Wilmington, secured local control of the tidelands, created a municipal Harbor Department to operate what would become the Port of Los Angeles, and voters subsequently approved the bonds needed to fund port development (Queenan 1983).

In the 1920s LA port officials secured passage of voter-approved city charter amendments enhancing their authority and autonomy. One hallmark of Los Angeles (and later Long Beach) city government was the citizen commission system. Major municipal departments, such as Harbor, Water and Power, and eventually Airports were governed by five-member citizen boards appointed by the mayor with the approval of the city council. Commissioners were appointed for fixed terms, giving them some policy independence from elected officials. Another hallmark featured proprietary revenue funds earmarked for agency projects and operation. This made it difficult for elected officials to divert funds for other city purposes. In 1926 the LA Harbor Department achieved further autonomy with financial self-sufficiency.

In Long Beach, the business community played a similar supportive role in that city's lengthy transition from private to public port development (Queenan 1986). By the early 1930s Long Beach had developed a municipal port system (albeit on a smaller scale than in Los Angeles) and adopted a governance structure comparable to Los Angeles's. Oil revenues generated by drilling in the harbor ultimately made Long Beach a true competitor for San Pedro Bay trade. It could offer lower prices and thereby lure port business from its larger neighbor.

In the sixty-year period from the New Deal through the administration of LA Mayor Tom Bradley (1973–93), the region's ports were fundamentally transformed from small-scale, local-market-oriented facilities to major wartime arsenals of democracy and, finally, to world-class trade portals serving diverse regional, national, and global markets. The hallmark of the two San Pedro Bay ports was their public entrepreneurship, which featured long-term strategic planning and development, agile responses to market forces stemming from trade globalization and containerization, and public–private partnerships. The region's visionary harbor entrepreneurs included LA port manager Clarence Matson, who devised a Pacific Rim trade strategy in the early 1920s, and Long Beach mayor and city manager Charles Windham, who facilitated early Port of Long Beach development.

Significantly, Los Angeles and Long Beach port competition and entrepreneurship in the postwar era affected planning and development at the Port Authority of New York and New Jersey. With the launching of the containerization revolution in the 1960s—initially prompting bicoastal cooperation between West Coast ports and the Port Authority—a fierce battle for container traffic erupted among West Coast ports, particularly Los Angeles and Long Beach. In the early 1960s, the Port of Los Angeles allotted $51 million in revenue bonds to constructing container facilities. Long Beach responded by creating a 310-acre landfill to accommodate its expanding container operations. This competitive battle would in time relegate the NY-NJ ports to third place, behind Los Angeles and Long Beach.

By the 1970s, the two San Pedro Bay ports' terminals were diverting a substantial amount of Far East shipping that had formerly traveled via the Panama Canal to Port Authority piers. Western ports had important advantages—proximity to Asia's expanding trade; deep harbors to handle the increasingly large container ships; and the best transcontinental rail access (the Southern Pacific, Union Pacific, and Santa Fe lines) of all West Coast ports (Erie 2004; Levinson 2006). The Port Authority responded by asking that the main ship channel between New York Bay and the Newark/Elizabeth terminals be deepened; but that urgent request was held up for more than a year by New York's governor, George Pataki, who demanded that more attention be given to increasing freight traffic through smaller marine terminals which the Port Authority had acquired—to demonstrate that it was involved on both sides of the Hudson—in Brooklyn and on Staten Island.

The result of these several efforts can be seen in the figures for number of containers handled—expressed in 20-foot equivalent units, or TEUs (see table 4.3).[8]

During the past several decades, the Port Authority and its LA–Long Beach counterparts have paid close attention to developments at each other's ports—and at other ports on both coasts—much as they would if they were private competitors in a loosely regulated market. At times, their efforts have been constrained by political pressures, and all three agencies have found portions of their revenues diverted to other purposes. But as partially independent "profit centers," all three have attempted to maximize income, which has entailed a sustained focus on modernization and skillful marketing strategies.

In the Los Angeles metropolitan area, the late twentieth century witnessed active collaboration between the two San Pedro Bay ports on landside ground-access projects—while they remained fierce seaside competitors. Of particular note was the Alameda Corridor, a $2.4 billion separated-grade rail project linking the ports and the downtown railyards (see figure 4.3). In 1989 the cities of Los Angeles and Long Beach agreed to use their joint-powers authority to create a consolidated rail-corridor agency—the Alameda Corridor Transportation Agency (ACTA). In the mid-1990s, the project passed environmental review despite conflicts between the ports and cities along the corridor's 19-mile route. The project was completed in 2002, with the help of $400 million in funding from the two ports and a federal loan guarantee (to be repaid from container fees). Soon thereafter planning began on the ambitious Alameda Corridor East project, an effort to separate grade crossings along 70 miles of

Table 4.3 HISTORICAL PORT TRAFFIC (MILLIONS OF TEUS)

	1990	2000	2006	2011
Los Angeles	2.1	4.9	8.5	7.9
Long Beach	1.6	4.6	7.2	6.0
New York/New Jersey	1.9	3.0	5.1	5.5

Sources: Compiled by Authors from Data from the Port Authority of New York and New Jersey, Port of Los Angeles, Port of Long Beach.

mainline railroad in the San Gabriel Valley between downtown Los Angeles and the eastern fringes of the metropolitan area (see figure 4.3).

The Alameda Corridor did not happen quickly or smoothly. Project financing was a major problem, as were ACTA governance conflicts between the two ports and the corridor cities. With the global economic downturn beginning in late 2008 and the accompanying sharp drop in container traffic and Alameda Corridor revenues, critics have questioned whether the project should be considered a success. Notwithstanding its recent financial troubles, the Alameda Corridor is generally considered a model public–private partnership because of the involvement of the railroads and the use of a novel container charge paid by private shippers to repay its federal loans.

Los Angeles International Airport (LAX) followed a similar public–private partnership trajectory. In 1926 the LA Chamber of Commerce, recognizing the emergence of a burgeoning aviation market, began lobbying the city council for the siting and development of a municipal airport. One location actively promoted by local boosters was a relatively small 3,000-acre swath of bean field known as Mines Field, near the coast and 16 miles from downtown. This site, which was soon approved by the city council, would become the home of LAX. Like the ports, early airport development required substantial federal assistance. During the 1930s the city purchased the then-leased airport site to meet federal requirements for New Deal Works Progress Administration grants. During World War II, the federal government assumed control of the airport and improved the landing field.

In the postwar era, the city's business, civic, and labor groups actively supported LAX modernization and expansion, which was overseen by skilled airport managers such as Francis Fox and Clifton Moore. Airport officials, much like their counterparts at the port, encouraged bureaucratic clientelism, in which the airlines received low landing fees and other concessions as growth inducements. However, beginning in the 1960s, stakeholders less friendly to airport modernization emerged, making airport expansion more difficult. As LAX grew to meet the needs of the jet age, nearby communities organized to oppose airport expansion because of its adverse local environmental impacts—air pollution, noise, traffic, and residential relocation (Friedman 1978). In the 1990s, efforts to develop a new LAX Master Plan, which had the support of both business and labor groups, were stymied by strong community, environmental, and minority group opposition (Erie 2004). For Los Angeles's local elected officials, who in earlier times had been staunch advocates of airport development, the political lesson was clear. Today, local officials are scrupulously mindful of vocal anti-growth sentiment.

MOUNTING CHALLENGES, 1990–2010

The Port Authority under Duress: Recent Projects and Political Demands

During the past two decades, the Port Authority has faced major political and financial challenges, confronted two disasters at the World Trade Center, and added several projects to its portfolio. On the financial side, PATH has continued to generate large deficits—more than $200 million a year in the 1990s and more than $300 million annually in the past several years. And the pressure to help local officials with planning and other projects, described earlier, has continued; the Port Authority's budget for 2012 lists $120 million for these purposes in the two states, plus $340 million to be spent on roads in New Jersey.

Meanwhile, the agency's staff has continued to develop its own plans to meet the region's transportation needs. A monorail was constructed joining the terminals and parking lots at Newark Airport; later it was extended to meet the main rail line between New York and Trenton/Philadelphia. A new rail line was built from Kennedy Airport through Queens to connect with the Long Island Railroad and the City's subway system. In 1991, the Port Authority began constructing tracks that permit railroad cars to travel onto its docks, allowing containers to be loaded directly from ships to railroad cars that then enter the national railroad system. Labeled ExpressRail, the system is now in operation at the Port Authority's three major container terminals (Newark, Elizabeth, and Staten Island).

However, when the agency's staff recommended extending the runways at Newark Airport in the 1990s and dredging the channel leading to the marine terminals at Newark and Elizabeth, New York officials balked. Arguing that the Port Authority should devote more of its energies and funds to airports and port operations on the New York side of the Hudson River, New York's governor Pataki blocked action on these projects for several years. In 1994, New York City's Mayor Rudolph Giuliani attacked the Port Authority's alleged bias toward New Jersey and urged that the agency be broken up so New York City could take control of "its own" airports and marine terminals. These were two of many recurring skirmishes between the two states for economic and political advantage. In the 1980s and 1990s, for example, New Jersey officials offered tax concessions to businesses willing to move to New Jersey, a strategy that gained them several firms and a measure of hostility from New York's governors and mayors. The successful efforts to persuade the New York Giants and the Jets to abandon New York to play in the Meadowlands rubbed salt in the interstate wound.

By the year 2000, conflicts such as these had become ingrained. In recent years, the relationship between the two states has been much less cooperative than it was in earlier decades. Public officials in both states have come to view the Port Authority less as an institution with a mission to aid *regional* economic development, and more as a source of projects that will be helpful to their particular state or city.

One object of interstate contention has been the World Trade Center. This project generated problems from the start. When first proposed in the 1960s, it was destined for the Lower East Side and estimated to cost $350 million. Criticized by New Jersey officials as an office building with no benefit for their state, it was then shifted to the west side and connected to a passenger rail line from New Jersey (now PATH). As the twin towers rose to their final 110 stories, costs rose sharply, reaching more than $1 billion in 1980. The project was attacked on esthetic grounds, and the Port Authority was criticized for pouring vast sums into a real estate venture, money that might have been used instead to improve transportation systems in the bi-state region.[9]

In February 1993, a bomb exploded at the twin towers, creating a crater five stories in depth and killing five people. On September 11, 2001, two planes crashed into the towers, bringing them down and killing nearly 3,000 people. During the past ten years, much of the Port Authority's energy has been devoted to grappling with politics, planning, and construction at the 16-acre World Trade Center site. These efforts, discussed further below, have diverted billions of dollars—and the time of senior Port Authority officials—that could have been devoted to modernizing marine terminals and airports, and in meeting other transportation challenges that form the agency's central mission.

The Los Angeles Area Agencies under Siege: Fiscal, Environmental, and Community Challenges

In the past two decades, the Los Angeles port, airport, and freight-rail agencies have also faced major challenges. The first crisis was fiscal, stemming from a severe recession in the early 1990s. The State of California diverted $3.6 billion in city and county property-tax revenue in order to honor the state's commitment to education. A companion state law gave charter cities authority to shift revenue from their ports into their general-fund budgets for two years. In this permissive environment, fiscally strapped cities also sought to divert revenue from other municipal revenue-producing departments (e.g., airports, water, and power) in order to make up for the recession- and state-induced budgetary shortfalls. Los Angeles took the lead. Under Mayor Richard Riordan, substantial revenues were siphoned off from the city's three proprietary departments: Harbor, Airports, and Water and Power.[10] Long Beach followed suit with smaller revenue diversions from its Harbor Department (Erie 2004). Significantly, the LA and Long Beach ports and LAX had just launched massive and costly expansion programs, making their built-up cash reserves tempting targets.

Municipal revenue diversions from the region's global gateways ultimately were thwarted. Los Angeles overreached in terms of its excessive port diversions and was successfully sued by the State Lands Commission, which oversees public trust lands (tidelands, submerged land, and navigable waters) in California. Under state law, these lands, which are managed by local agencies like the ports of San Pedro Bay, must be used for statewide as opposed to purely local purposes. Similarly, Los Angeles was forced to return diverted LAX airport funds after Congress (at the behest of the airlines) blocked that ploy. The bleak fiscal situation and changing national political dynamics also affected funding for the Alameda Corridor project. When Republicans captured control of Congress in 1994, a planned project grant became instead a federal loan. Project planners scrambled to find a repayment arrangement, which culminated in a rail container fee.

The second set of challenges involved mounting environmental and community opposition. The ports and airports were the LA region's leading toxic hotspots, generating severe air pollution from vessels, trucks, and airplanes, as well as substantial noise and traffic congestion. As the two ports and LAX announced major expansion plans to handle the anticipated growth in international trade and air passenger traffic, neighboring communities and environmental groups fought back. The LAX

Master Plan was halted by NIMBY ("Not in my Backyard") community and environ-mental activists, who successfully contested the Plan's environmental impact report and advocated the use of new criteria for evaluation, such as "environmental justice." Since the neighborhoods underneath the LAX flight path were heavily minority, the environmental costs (air pollution, traffic, and noise) of LAX expansion would be dis-proportionately borne by minority residents. Under a Settlement Agreement, LAX expansion was capped at 78 MAP (million annual passengers) and future air traffic growth would occur, it was hoped, at outlying airports.

Port expansion, particularly at the Port of Los Angeles, was also buffeted by growing community and environmental opposition. In the late 1990s the restive harbor com-munities of San Pedro and Wilmington launched a campaign, taking their lead from activists in the San Fernando Valley, to legally separate from the City of Los Angeles and create new municipalities with greater control over their own destinies. (For a discus-sion of the secession movement that was launched and centered in the San Fernando Valley, see Deener et al., this volume.) While the secession movements failed, they had salutary community effects. For example, the Port of Los Angeles launched an ambi-tious harbor-side revitalization project to aid the economically distressed community of San Pedro. Under the terms of a new voter-approved LA city charter designed to head off the secession movement, the commissions governing the port and airport were expanded, with new seats reserved for members residing near these facilities. As a result, the two commissions have become more sensitive to community sentiment.

CURRENT AND FUTURE CHALLENGES AND STRATEGIES

The Port Authority and the LA region's port and airport agencies face significant new competitive pressures that—combined with increasing environmental and security costs—threaten to erode their current positions as the premier centers for marine and air cargo in the United States. Other regions have improved their operations and have begun to bite into traffic at the largest ports. To respond to these threats, the Port Authority and the LA-area agencies are working on expansion programs for their facilities in order to meet increasing demand for rapid and efficient transfer and distribution of exports and imports.[11] At the same time, they will have to devote sus-tained effort to achieving environmental standards, which are becoming ever-more stringent, and to responding to possible security threats.

After a decade of prodigious growth, container traffic through the Ports of Los Angeles and Long Beach slowed during the recession but picked up again as the recovery gained strength. Container traffic through Port Authority facilities—which grew at a brisk 7 percent annual rate for nearly a decade—has also slowed during the recession. In contrast, the ports at Oakland, Tacoma, and Vancouver have seen measurable growth, and on the East Coast, Savannah now challenges NY-NJ as the premier East Coast port. In 2007, Savannah ranked fourth in the nation in annual container volume, just behind NY-NJ. The expansion of the Panama Canal, to be com-pleted by 2014, will permit ships that are too wide to go through the Canal in its cur-rent dimensions (post-Panamax ships) to use the Canal to bypass San Pedro Bay and

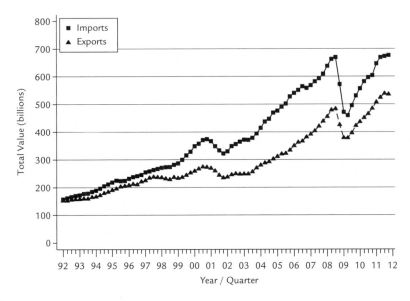

Figure 4.4
US Trade with the World
Source: Created from U.S. Census Bureau, FT920 - U.S. Merchandise Trade: Selected Highlights (Washington, DC, December 2011).

deliver goods to the East Coast—with the Port Authority's piers competing for the new traffic with Savannah, deep-water terminals at Norfolk and Halifax, and other ports.[12]

The recession has affected trade at all ports, and in the year ending in March 2009, American imports dropped 27 percent (Healy 2009; Healy and Wassener 2009). Figure 4.4, which tracks America's trade with the rest of the world, captures the dramatic effects of the crisis and the ongoing recovery from it. In January 2009, American imports stood more than 35 percent below their 2008 peaks, a level not seen since early 2004. Exports dropped by 27 percent. Combined, US trade with the rest of the world was down more than 30 percent in less than a year. Starting in early 2009 and continuing through 2011, there has been a rise in trade as the American and global economies began slowly recovering. By the end of 2011, trade activity had finally reached and exceeded pre-2008 levels (Landler 2008; Miller 2009).

How NY-NJ, LA-Long Beach, and their competitors respond to trading opportunities as the downturn abates could alter the relative rankings of the West Coast and East Coast ports and, by implication, influence the economic performance of their respective regions.

Tensions between Growth and Other Goals in the New York Region

The Port Authority expects marine traffic will expand steadily in the years ahead. Figure 4.5 shows the volume of container traffic flowing through its terminals in recent

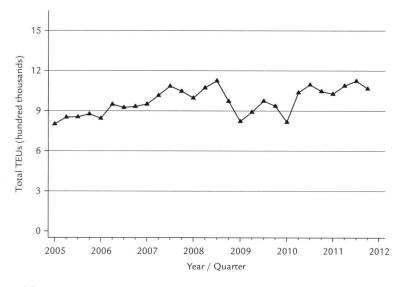

Figure 4.5
Port of New York-New Jersey Container Traffic
Source: Compiled by authors from data from the Port Authority of New York and New Jersey.

years. The drop in container traffic was not as steep in 2008 as at the West Coast ports. Moreover, the increase in container traffic since 2009, sustained through 2011, suggests that the region is well on the way to recovery. In Los Angeles, the economic downturn, coupled with California's fiscal crisis, continues to pose major obstacles to financing future projects. In New York, smaller traffic losses and the ability to draw upon revenue from bridge tolls and other sources have helped to insulate the Port Authority from the difficulties faced by West Coast rivals; however, its financial capacity is constrained by declines in travel through its facilities—and by the financial demands at the World Trade Center, as well as investments to aid vehicular and rail movement in the region.

In 2007, the Port Authority's terminals handled more than 5 million TEUs, a 250 percent increase since 1993. By 2015 the total may well approach 6 million. To meet this demand, the agency must improve the ability of post-Panamax ships, carrying 8,000–12,000 containers each, to reach its Newark and Elizabeth terminals by dredging the main shipping channels to 50 feet or more—and by raising the deck of the Bayonne Bridge from 151 to 215 feet above the water. Dredging, a joint effort of the Port Authority and the Army Corps of Engineers, was begun in 2005 and is expected to cost $1.5 billion, with half to be paid by the Port Authority. The dredging effort, which generates environmental concerns associated with the loss of shallow-water habitat, should be largely completed prior to expanded Panama Canal operations in 2014–15. The Bridge project will begin in 2013 but will not be completed until 2015.

In meeting challenges from West and East Coast ports, the Port Authority must take steps to reduce the total transit time to the final destination. For goods from the Far East, the Panama Canal expansion will be helpful. But the agency must increase the efficiency with which goods are moved between ship and shore, and through distribution centers. Typically, containers arriving in Newark via ship have been offloaded to trucks, which navigate congested roads to reach rail cars on the mainline (New York-to-Philadelphia) tracks. To speed the transfer process—and reduce highway congestion—the Port Authority has constructed on-dock "double stack" rail facilities at Newark and Elizabeth. Containers are offloaded from ships onto railroad cars, which are standing on tracks in the terminal; marshaled fifty cars or more deep, they are then hooked to an engine and the assemblage enters the mainline rail system without significant delay. (The Port Authority's Staten Island terminal has a similar rail connection.) The project—labeled ExpressRail—is now complete; costing $600 million, it should remove 500,000 truck trips annually from the roadways. Here reduced air pollution and improved efficiency of the cargo-handling process go hand in hand, rather than being in conflict.

The Port Authority has also provided funds to each state to improve truck and rail-freight routes across the region; and it has acquired 115 acres along a Jersey-City peninsula to aid rail access to port and carfloat facilities. In addition, the agency is once again studying the proposal (first made in 1921) to build a rail tunnel to carry goods between Brooklyn and Jersey City, where railroads would emerge to connect with the national system. That project seems unlikely to go beyond the drawing board because of its cost (two billion dollars or more), limited space for terminals and truck access in Brooklyn, and the reluctance of the railroads to help pay for the project. As an alternative, to reduce truck congestion and pollution in the region, the Port Authority has expanded the use of rail-float barges to convey goods between Brooklyn and the New Jersey shore, across Upper New York Bay.

The New York region's marine facilities have lost their once-commanding position in US maritime transport (table 4.3),[13] but the Port Authority's three airports still dominate in the total value of air cargo. In 2011, the New York airports shipped $206 billion in merchandise trade compared to the Los Angeles airports' $83 billion. However, as table 4.4 shows, the major LA airports have caught up with New York, but both regions' airports have experienced declines since 2000.

Although this analysis is mainly focused on issues of freight transportation, ease of passenger travel and the numbers of passenger movements are highly relevant to economic development in the region. The 9/11 disaster and the current recession

Table 4.4 HISTORICAL AIR CARGO TRAFFIC (THOUSANDS OF TONS)

	1994	2000	2003	2011
LAX	1,516	2,002	1,924	1,773
ONT	379	511	571	417
Los Angeles Total	1,895	2,513	2,495	2,190
JFK	1,499	1,864	1,709	1,387
EWR	872	1,070	890	811
LGA	40	20	12	7
New York Total	2,412	2,955	2,612	2,222

Sources: Compiled by Authors from data from the Port Authority of New York and New Jersey, Los Angeles World Airports.

have been accompanied by downturns in passenger travel, yet the general trend at the three Port Authority airfields is positive. In 2000, 33 million passengers used Kennedy Airport; the number was 47 million in 2011; and the agency expects to handle 54 million in 2020. The comparable totals at Newark are 34 million, 33 million, and 38 million; at LaGuardia the numbers are essentially flat (25, 24, and 25 million). To handle the increases at Kennedy, the agency has constructed Terminal 5, with 26 gates; it can handle 20 million passengers per year and is linked to a new parking garage, with a capacity of 1,500 vehicles. The Port Authority is also studying how best to redevelop Terminals 2 and 3 at Kennedy; Newark's Terminal B is currently being modernized at a cost of $280 million. These changes have faced less community resistance than have developments at LAX, in part because of active Port Authority efforts to engage the community, described earlier. Also, the Port Authority is not as subject to direct influence by local officials and voters as are the LA-area agencies; in addition, the sensitivity to air pollution is greater in Los Angeles, with its long tradition as smog capital of the nation.

In 2007, the Port Authority added Stewart Airport, 60 miles north of New York City, to its air-transport complex. Stewart's cargo and passenger operations currently connect with only a few cities, and in 2011 it handled only 400,000 passengers. The Port Authority expects to expand the airport slowly, to take pressure off Newark and LaGuardia. Sensitive negotiations are underway locally, as the agency develops plans to improve runways and to meet the inevitable challenge of highway congestion as the airport becomes more heavily used. The PA plans to invest $500 million in Stewart during the next ten years. By 2035, annual passenger volume may reach 7 million.

Early in 2011, the Regional Plan Association (RPA) released an extensive report analyzing the likely future demand at the three major NY-NJ airports and concluded that substantial improvements are needed. The RPA report noted that the region's airports are now limited to 110 million passengers per year, but that by 2030 the likely demand will be 150 million annually. It proposed that the Port Authority increase capacity by constructing new runways at Kennedy Airport and by relocating the three terminals at Newark. The RPA also supports changes in the air-traffic control system (called NextGen) that will allow more planes per hour to take off and land safely (Regional Plan Association 2011). However, NextGen is likely to increase air and noise pollution significantly, prompting community criticism. The other changes recommended by RPA will also generate local concern regarding noise and require active Port Authority measures to involve local officials and community groups.

Since 9/11, security against terrorists and other threats has been an important focus at the airports. The Port Authority has spent more than $4 billion in capital and operating funds on security measures. In 2006, the agency began a pilot program at Newark Airport using biometric fingerprint technology to better identify workers authorized to work in secure areas. In 2007, bollards were introduced at Newark and LaGuardia, to stop vehicles with explosives from gaining access to the terminals, and this protective strategy has now been introduced at other sites. With a $400 million grant from the federal government, improved in-line baggage screening is being implemented at the three large airports.

However, efforts to make the marine-container supply chain secure from terrorist threats are lagging, in part due to the sheer complexity of the task. The Port Authority has added extensive physical- and employee-screening improvements at the Port—including radiation-detection monitors at the exit gates. Some of its security efforts have been subsequently applied throughout the industry. Like other ports, however, it is in the midst of a controversial federally mandated effort to install screening for each container by 2012—even though no system yet exists that would fully screen these containers without seriously disrupting marine commerce.

As suggested earlier, the Port Authority has taken a number of initiatives to reduce negative environmental impacts from its operations. These include ExpressRail, use of rail-car floats to cut down truck congestion, and modernization efforts at PATH. In 2008, the agency began giving toll reductions for drivers of low-emission vehicles. Looking ahead, the Port Authority has set an ambitious agenda—including the goals of becoming "carbon neutral" in the near future, developing Stewart Airport as a carbon-negative airfield, and reducing greenhouse-gas emissions by 80 percent by 2050 (compared with 2006 levels). However, these goals will be met in part by purchasing carbon offsets.

At the port, the agency is engaged in cooperative programs with environmental agencies and tenants. The Port Authority report "Clean Air Strategy for the Port of New York and New Jersey" lays out a series of steps needed to reduce diesel and greenhouse gas (GHG) emissions. These include replacing the oldest, most polluting trucks serving the port, retrofitting switcher locomotives that handle on-dock rail operations, and modernizing cargo-handling equipment.

Two challenges with no counterparts at West Coast agencies deserve brief mention. One is the continuing effort to grapple with passenger-rail needs, at its own facilities and in nearby portions of the region. In recent years, the Port Authority has been actively involved in efforts to construct a new commuter rail tunnel connecting mid-Manhattan and New Jersey. These efforts have been blocked, at least temporarily, by New Jersey's Governor Chris Christie. Meanwhile, the agency is replacing its entire fleet of 340 PATH cars, at a cost of $3.3 billion.

In addition, the Port Authority's executives, engineers, and other staff are absorbed in the effort to rebuild the World Trade Center. In 2006 the Port Authority assumed overall management of the complex effort, which involves constructing up to five new skyscrapers, the third-largest transit hub in New York City, a performing arts center, a memorial and museum, and a retail complex. A crucial challenge facing the Port Authority is the great number of organizations and individuals involved—nineteen public agencies, two private developers, thirty-three architects and consulting firms, and 101 contractors and subcontractors. It is no wonder the Port Authority concluded in 2008 that rebuilding the Trade Center has become "a major focus of the Port Authority's efforts." In 2011 alone, the Port Authority's capital budget related to the World Trade Center was $1.8 billion—more than three times the amount allocated for airport modernization and ten times the funds made available for port improvements; in 2012 the budgeted total is $2 billion, more than the total for all other Port Authority activities taken together. The Trade Center costs were an important factor in the Port Authority's decision in August 2011 to seek gubernatorial approval (soon granted) for a substantial increase in bridge and tunnel tolls and PATH fares.

Skeptics have asked whether the Port Authority's funds and energies should be so heavily absorbed in this massive project, which—except for the underground transit links to PATH and New York City subways—is not clearly connected with the agency's transportation program.[14] And observers in New Jersey have begun to wonder whether the agency's commitment to devote equal funding and attention to their state is being undermined by the extraordinary effort to rebuild a portion of downtown Manhattan. This is an interstate tension that will continue to confront the Port Authority in the years ahead.

In October 2012, Hurricane Sandy underscored the human and economic challenges likely to be part of a "climate-change future." Sandy hit the New York-New Jersey region with great force on October 29–30, demolishing houses and beaches, knocking down power lines, and sending surges of water that covered LaGuardia Airport's runways and poured into subway and PATH stations as well as the Holland Tunnel, while fierce winds toppled containers stacked at Ports Newark and Elizabeth. The region slowly recovered during the next month; a week after Sandy, the port facilities began operating at near capacity, and PATH was functioning at most stations, while the Holland was cleared for regular traffic a few days later. Port Authority and municipal officials began to consider what preventive steps – such as large barriers at surface and below-ground entrances – might be taken to reduce disruption when the next major storm hits.

All these efforts may be compromised by the willingness of the states' governors to give substantial priority to patronage. Since Chris Christie became New Jersey's chief executive, in 2010, he has demanded that the Port Authority hire dozens of his friends, party workers, and political associates; and the agency's commissioners have passively acquiesced. By late 2012, more than eighty of his preferred candidates had been hired—though several of them have been forced to leave due to ethical and other transgressions. Among the Christie appointees are the manager of one of the marine terminals, whose main qualification appears to be donations to Christie's campaign; a senior financial analyst who was a leader in a county Republican Committee (and a former gourmet food broker); and the director of "interstate capital projects," who went to school with Christie and was the Republican mayor of a small town in New Jersey. Governor Cuomo, who has the power to block unqualified appointments, has sat passively, occupied by other priorities, although he has not—except for two or three recommendations—played the patronage game.[15]

The key role in protecting the Port Authority from patronage and other forms of favoritism lies with the twelve-person Board of Commissioners. Appointed for fixed six-year terms, they can ensure staff integrity; any significant Port Authority action requires a majority of the six commissioners from each state, and the Board can take the obligation to maintain staff quality into its hands at any time. The commissioners showed some tendency to exert leadership when they authorized a study of the Port Authority's management by two outside consultants. The first set of reports from these consultants sharply criticized past management practices; the second set, released in September 2012, included much useful information on the financial pressures facing the agency, and praised the accomplishments of the new staff executives and the leadership of the Board, which paid for the studies. Although outside observers had urged that the consultants and the Board come to grips with the problems of patronage that had been sharply criticized in the press, and the impact of patronage and other factors on staff morale, the consultants avoided exploring these issues, and the Board received the reports with gratitude and remained silent on the patronage issue.[16]

Economic, Environmental, and Security Challenges in the Los Angeles Region

The ability of Los Angeles's infrastructure agencies to maintain the region's status as the premier international gateway on the West Coast will depend on how public officials respond to the challenges posed by international markets and local political forces. The challenges are threefold. First, the global economic downturn that began in late 2008 resulted in unprecedented drops in traffic while Los Angeles's trade infrastructure agencies have faced increasing competition from rival West Coast ports. Second, in recent years, local communities surrounding Southern California's port and airport facilities, supported by elected officials and environmental groups, have formed a formidable obstacle to efforts to expand existing facilities. Third, the terrorist attacks of September 11, 2001, exposed the vulnerability of the global economy to security threats that are difficult to detect and prevent.

Economic Challenges

Because a large majority of foreign-made consumer goods arrive into the country via waterborne vessels, the sharp economic decline in international trade depicted in figure 4.4 resulted in large drops in maritime business for West Coast ports. Figure 4.6 shows the sharp decline in containerized cargo shipments at the Ports of Los Angeles and Long Beach in 2007–08, with recovery beginning in 2009. During the final two quarters of 2008, volume at the Port of Los Angeles dropped nearly 30 percent. At the Port of Long Beach, the decline was only slightly less severe. By the end of the second quarter, combined traffic at the two ports had fallen 25 percent from the highs set in 2006.

To retain current customers and attract new ones, both ports quickly cut their cargo rates. Anecdotal evidence suggests that their aggressive response was effective. Although both ports posted significant declines in shipping volume, their losses fell short of those at other West Coast ports, from Oakland to Seattle, and the most recent quarters show a significant uptick in traffic at both Los Angeles and Long Beach. In addition, the San Pedro Bay ports appeared well positioned to capitalize from optimistic signs of stabilization and potential economic recovery that emerged in late 2009. A survey by Moody's Investors Service showed that the two ports remained the highest-ranked by shippers, suggesting that they would be the first to experience at least partial recovery. By late 2010, container traffic at the two ports had returned

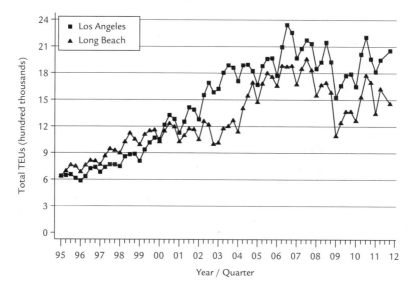

Figure 4.6
San Pedro Bay Port Traffic
Source: Compiled by Authors from data from the Port of Long Beach and Port of Los Angeles.

to pre-2008 levels. Traffic levels mostly held steady in Los Angeles in 2011, while the Port Authority saw its cargo volume reach its highest level ever (White 2009a, c).

The costs of the downturn have, nonetheless, cut deep across the LA region. During the boom times of 2006, the two ports had enough work for more than 1,000 laborers for every day shift. By February 2009, the ports were employing only 660 laborers. The Inland Empire, a major hub for goods imported through the ports of Los Angeles and Long Beach, saw its workforce reduced by more than 80,000 jobs. Citing the decline at the ports, credit rating agencies threatened to cut their ratings on $2 billion in bonds from the Alameda Corridor Transportation Authority (ACTA). In the first quarter of 2009, ACTA saw its revenues fall 21 percent, and it warned that without a significant rebound in trade, both ports would need to help pay for its operations. (The ports are contractually obligated to help ACTA meets its debt obligation if the agency's revenues fall short.) Fortunately for port officials, traffic rebounded in 2010 and 2011, and a loan from the Federal Rail Administration has, so far, allowed ACTA to maintain its operations without shortfall payments from the ports (Semuels 2009; White 2009b).

For the region's airports, dark clouds were forming before the financial crisis hit. Still recovering from the attacks of September 11, 2001, airport operators were under growing strain in mid-2008, as domestic airlines cut capacity by as much as 20 percent in the face of historically high fuel costs. Usually resilient, international carriers soon followed suit. In addition, billions of dollars of investment by other cities were coming online and Los Angeles faced serious new competition from upgraded airports in San Francisco, Las Vegas, Houston, and Miami. Finally, German-owned shipping company DHL announced in November 2008 that it would slash US operations in the face of stiff competition and mounting financial losses and would shut its West Coast hub in Riverside. Just two months earlier, the company had given the region's economy a vote of confidence by announcing plans to launch a new international route out of LAX (Maynard 2008).

In the last quarter of 2008 and the first quarter of 2009, the number of passengers passing through LAX dropped 20 percent, but passenger traffic has seen a partial rebound since then. Similarly, air freight dropped more than 25 percent. The situation has been even worse for Ontario International Airport (ONT). Between July 2008 and July 2009, passenger traffic at the airport dropped more than 25 percent, one of the largest declines among midsize airports in the United States (Weikel and Pae 2008). With the sharp drop in traffic at Ontario Airport, Ontario city officials in 2010 launched a campaign to take over the facility from Los Angeles World Airports (LAWA), which has managed it since 1967. Ontario officials claimed that LAWA had a conflict of interest and was focusing on restoring traffic at LAX at the expense of Ontario Airport (Weikel 2010). Similarly, the Port Authority has in recent years faced pressure to return Newark Airport to city control (Milo 2012).

The impact of the economic downturn has been exacerbated by the fiscal crisis in California, which has endangered funding for upgrades at the San Pedro Bay ports and highway improvements across the region. Prior to the recent downturn, Los Angeles's infrastructure agencies were moving forward on an ambitious portfolio of projects, including repairs to the aging Gerald Desmond Bridge (over which 10 percent of the nation's containerized trade travels), elimination of choke points along the Alameda Corridor East, and an expressway to speed trucks and trains traveling between the ports and downtown rail yards. These projects will enhance the LA region's ability to cope with the anticipated growth of international trade traffic over the next twenty years. Container traffic at the ports of San Pedro Bay is expected to grow to 42.5 million TEUs by 2030 (Los Angeles County Economic Development Corporation 2008).

Finally, Los Angeles's port complex faces fiercer competition from other ports. Of particular concern is Port of Prince Rupert, north of Vancouver, which is closer to Asian markets and has the deepest port on the West Coast. The Prince Rupert Port Authority has joined forces with the Canadian National Railway and the Canadian government to expand its marine terminals and rail links into the United States, with the goal of handling four million TEUs by 2015. In 2009, the Canadian government launched a $7 million marketing campaign designed to divert Asian imports from other West Coast ports to Prince Rupert (Marroquin 2009). Increased competition will further undermine the ability of San Pedro Bay ports to raise money to pay for facility upgrades. Increased container fees at the San Pedro Bay ports, which would pay the bulk of the costs for new facilities, could further increase diversion to competing ports.

Greening Los Angeles

By the early 2000s, the Ports of Los Angeles and Long Beach were playing defense with respect to environmental groups and local elected officials representing communities impacted by port operations. In 2001, for example, a challenge by the Natural Resources Defense Council held up the opening of the China Shipping Container Line terminal at the Port of Los Angeles by more than a year and a half. In 2004, the city council of Long Beach refused to sign off on an environmental impact statement for a project at Pier J. The project would have added 115 acres to a 270-acre terminal, improving efficiency at the port and perhaps reducing emissions from idling trucks. Nonetheless, environmental groups were uninterested in expansion projects that paid lip service to the environment while failing to address the problem of increasing emissions from the ports (Hall 2008).

In October 2001, the Board of Harbor Commissioners that oversees the Port of Los Angeles gave port officials a new directive: hold emissions from future port operations at or below 2001 levels. The Commissioners, which included three members living near the harbor, also directed port officials to address concerns from surrounding communities. In 2001, the Commission created an advisory committee to assess the impacts of port development. In 2003, the Port of Los Angeles implemented an environmental mitigation program using $50 million in port revenues. As part of this program, $23.5 million was earmarked for "community aesthetic" projects, $20 million for reducing air quality impacts, and $10 million was given to the Gateway Cities Council of Governments—an association representing cities in southeast Los Angeles County, including Long Beach and other communities located along the Alameda Corridor and major highways near the San Pedro Bay ports—for incentives to replace or retrofit existing diesel-powered trucks.

Similar developments were being considered and implemented in Long Beach. After the council rejected the Pier J project in 2004, the Board of Harbor Commissioners that oversees the Port of Long Beach directed port officials to develop a comprehensive environmental policy. The port submitted a draft Green Port Policy in December 2004, which was formally adopted in January 2005. The policy establishes environmental stewardship and compliance, sustainability, community engagement, and education as guiding principles for the port (Port of Long Beach 2005). In 2005, the port formed a Sustainability Task Force to develop recommendations for operational improvement, which would integrate the Green Port Policy into all aspects of its day-to-day operations.

The election of LA Mayor Antonio Villaraigosa in 2005 was a boon to environmental groups in Southern California. Villaraigosa pledged to make Los Angeles "the cleanest, greenest big city in America." Once in office, he immediately set about delivering on his campaign promise. He selected an environmental lawyer and labor official to serve on the Harbor Commission and, in December 2005, appointed Geraldine Knatz as Executive Director at the Port of Los Angeles. Knatz had served as Director of Development at the Port of Long Beach and was in charge of developing its Green Port Policy.

In November 2006, officials from both port agencies approved the San Pedro Bay Ports Clean Air Action Plan (CAAP). The $2 billion CAAP directs the ports, in collaboration with public agencies and private industry, to adopt programs and technologies to reduce port-related pollution by 45 percent over five years. It outlines a comprehensive environmental program that is unmatched among port authorities worldwide.

As part of the plan, the two agencies have agreed to implement a package of tariffs, lease requirements, grants, and incentive programs to curb harmful air emissions. Shippers, for example, were offered incentives to reduce the speed of vessels in and out of San Pedro Bay. CAAP called for hundreds of millions of dollars in new spending by the ports and local governments for air quality improvement programs, including extensive monitoring around the port. Under CAAP, all major cargo and cruise ship terminals are being equipped with shore-side electricity, so that vessels can shut down diesel-powered auxiliary engines and plug into clean electricity while docked in San Pedro Bay (Port of Los Angeles and Port of Long Beach 2006).

The most controversial element of the Plan has been the Clean Trucks Program, which targets 16,800 old diesel trucks for retrofit or replacement. The program levies a ban, phased in over CAAP's five-year life, on trucks that fail to meet the Federal Clean Truck Emission Standards adopted in 2007. To finance the replacement and retrofitting of trucks, the ports have imposed a fee on loaded containers ($35 per loaded TEU and smaller; $70 for larger containers).

The Trucks Program has attracted opposition from transportation and shipping groups. The Pacific Merchant Shipping Association called the program "ill-advised and unlawful" in a letter to the Federal Maritime Commission urging federal intervention. Particularly egregious to shippers and truckers is a provision adopted by the Port of Los Angeles that requires drivers to obtain licenses, which the port will only grant to trucking companies. The provision, which the US Court of Appeals for the Ninth Circuit threw out in September 2011, would have shut out individual owner-operators (those not employed by a drayage company), currently 88 percent of harbor truck drivers. Critics regarded the provision as a nod to organized labor. The Port of Long Beach's refusal to adopt a similar provision opened up a crack in the San Pedro Bay ports' up-to-now united front on environmental improvement.

On the airport side, the concerns of local environmental and community groups have focused as much on noise pollution as on air quality and sustainability. In 2000, LAWA created a Community Noise Roundtable to ensure the airport's cooperation in addressing the concerns of nearby communities. In 2001, LAWA signed an agreement with the City of Inglewood, pledging to cooperate to reduce noise, improve air quality, and help local residents find jobs at the airport. In 2004, the Board of Airport Commissioners unanimously passed a proposal to spend $500 million in nearby communities to soundproof homes and schools, create job-training programs, reduce airport noise, control traffic and study the health effects of airport operations. In exchange, a coalition of twenty-two community groups agreed to drop their opposition to LAWA's $11 billion expansion plan.

Through initiatives like CAAP, the culture of Los Angeles's infrastructure agencies is changing. No longer can public officials ignore the environmental impact of proposed projects. Indeed, environmental groups have become adept at using state environmental regulations to hold up port and airport projects. To get projects through the environmental review process, public officials typically have to negotiate side payments to prevent time-consuming and costly lawsuits. In 2008, for example, the Port of Los Angeles finally obtained approval for expanding the China Shipping Container Line terminal. The project will double the size of the terminal and generate more than 8,400 new jobs. Attached, however, is a host of environmental and "community beautification" initiatives that will increase project costs. The main terminal building will be constructed according to "gold" certification-level Leadership in Energy and Environmental Design standards. Yard tractors will use alternative fuel sources, and all ships entering the facility will comply with the Port of Los Angeles's speed reduction program (a package of incentives for operators of incoming vessels designed to lower emissions at the port). Finally, the project will pay for a new community park in San Pedro and landscaping improvements along nearby Front Street.

Security Challenges

In the wake of September 11, 2001, LA port and airport officials have undertaken extensive review and modification of security procedures. In 2007, the Port of Los Angeles adopted a strategic plan to enhance public safety at the port and in nearby communities, improve the ability to prevent or detect actions intended to disrupt port operations or the flow of cargo, and bolster emergency preparedness procedures for responding to security events. Nineteen initiatives were adopted, including the establishment of a new police substation in nearby Wilmington, addition of two 24-hour vessels to patrol the harbor, and creation of a vehicle and cargo inspection team. Cameras have been installed at critical locations and port officials have established controlled access areas where unauthorized personnel are not permitted to enter (Port of Los Angeles 2007).

Port of Long Beach officials have similarly beefed up security procedures in recent years. In 2004, for example, Harbor Commissioners agreed to spend $3 million for radiation detectors at every port gate. The eighteen radiation portals scan all containers leaving the port by truck or train. In February 2009, the Port of Long Beach opened a $21 million command-and-control center to house its security division, as well as units from the Long Beach Police Department, US Coast Guard, US Customs and Border Protection, and Marine Exchange (Port of Long Beach 2009).

Since then, enrollment has increased, though delays in deploying biometric card readers has slowed full implementation of the program. In addition to developing its own new plans and protocols, the San Pedro Bay ports have implemented a host of federal security procedures adopted after 2001. The Ports of Los Angeles and Long Beach are currently cooperating with the US Coast Guard and the Transportation Security Administration (TSA) to implement the federal Transportation Worker Identification Credential (TWIC) program. Under the TWIC program, workers with unescorted access to secure US port areas must have biometric identification cards that include a photo and fingerprints. In order to obtain an ID card, workers must be legal residents and pass a background check. Enrollment for the program began in late 2007; by April 2008, more than 15,000 workers had signed up to receive an ID card. Port officials estimated, however, that more than 100,000 local truck drivers, longshore workers, port employees, and others would need cards to gain access to port facilities. Slow progress at the ports led federal authorities to extend the deadline for workers to April 2009 (Marroquin 2008).

One side effect of implementing both the TWIC and Clean Trucks Program has been a reduction in the number of owner-operator truck drivers serving the ports.

While exact numbers are difficult to gather, a 2007 port-commissioned study estimated that 15 to 22 percent of drivers would not quality for a TWIC card. The program disqualifies undocumented workers and those with previous criminal convictions. Similarly, the strict emissions requirements of the Trucks Program, which forced many drivers to purchase newer and more expensive vehicles, has raised the costs of hauling containers. The declining number of drivers was not a problem in 2008 and 2009, when traffic levels at the ports were low. As traffic levels recover, however, both ports could experience a shortage of qualified port truck drivers (Koren 2012).

Security concerns at LAWA became paramount after September 11, 2001. Less than two weeks after the attacks, LA Mayor James Hahn directed airport officials to refocus the LAX Master Plan from expansion to better security. The revised plan advocated a massive redesign to reduce the airport's exposure to terrorist attacks. More recently, LAWA officials have stepped up efforts to improve security at LAX and Ontario Airport. In February 2009, LAWA officials announced the opening of the nation's first independent air cargo screening facility, Mercury Air Cargo, which participated in TSA's Certified Air Cargo Screening Program. Under federal guidelines adopted in the Implementing the 9/11 Commission Recommendations Act of 2007, the air cargo industry was required to screen 50 percent of cargo on wide-body passenger aircraft at levels commensurate with passenger-checked baggage by February 2009. By August 2010, the industry was supposed to have put in place programs to screen 100 percent of air cargo. Since then, however, the TSA has moved back and, more recently, postponed this deadline indefinitely. Instead, TSA is negotiating screening-abroad procedures with twenty countries that account for more than 80 percent of the cargo heading to the United States.

GOVERNMENT AGENCIES THAT TRY TO OPERATE AS CORPORATIONS: NEW YORK, LOS ANGELES, AND WIDER LESSONS FROM THEIR EXPERIENCE

As offspring of the Progressive Era, the port and airport agencies discussed in this chapter were designed to be insulated from political pressures that often undermine coherent public action—especially when long-term planning and sustained capital investment are involved. The strategies of insulation were different in important respects. In the New York region, creating a bi-state agency meant that no elected official had the ability to control its actions without agreement from across the state line; as a result, skilled entrepreneurs at the Port Authority could take initiatives and implement plans without close control from either state. In Los Angeles, the port and airport agencies were created with organizational structures that resembled those of private corporations; they were expected to develop port and airport facilities without tight control by elected officials. In addition, because they operated along the coastline, state agencies (the State Lands Commission and, later, the Coastal Commission) monitored their activities and could protect some of their actions from local interventions.

The strategies in both regions did share a few key features. All the New York and Los Angeles area agencies we discuss were constructed with multiheaded commissions at the top; the commissioners might at times interfere with staff pref-erences, but they have provided some insulation between the professional staffs and elected officials. Moreover, all the agencies have had the capacity to issue bonds and to use the proceeds from these bonds to expand their operations. Thus, they have been partly independent from the budget-review process that state and local govern-ments use to control the operations of line agencies. In the Port Authority's port and economic-development areas—where deficits are more likely than profits—profes-sional staff have given close attention to the "bottom line," lest their plans create too great a drag on the total enterprise, reducing funds for modernizing airports, maintaining bridges, and improving other facilities.

One important result of this distinctive managerial environment is that these agencies have been able to attract and hold leaders and staff members who are inter-ested in large capital projects and long-range planning, and who like to see results measured in specific, often quantitative terms. To some extent, staff motivation is also linked to a "profit-seeking" goal: projects should be designed to maximize net revenue, which means that costs should be kept under control and the needs of the customer should be given significant weight. Armed with these objectives, plus the partial insulation provided by the agencies' design, the staffs can use—and have used—managerial strategies not unlike those of a private corporation. Specific goals are set, measurable steps are identified, and progress is monitored. At the same time, agency leaders look for new directions and new projects that might help in meeting the agency's overall goals. The development of containeri-zation, led by the Port Authority and its West Coast allies, illustrates this aspect; at the time, investment in special marine facilities for these "boxes" was viewed as very risky, and so the term "entrepreneur" seems fitting for those who led that innovation. The planning, financing, and construction of the Alameda Corridor also illustrate the concrete and systematic ways in which these agencies can operate entrepreneurially.

The summary above captures what these agencies aspire to do, and what they have often been able to do. So one lesson of their activities over many decades is that it is possible to create and maintain government agencies that seek to minimize costs and maximize revenue, not unlike a private corporation. Moreover, these agencies can take a leading part in innovation, as strikingly illustrated by their key role in the "containership revolution."

As we have noted, however, insulation is often breached—at times for defensi-ble reasons (as when the mayor of Los Angeles appoints commissioners who will alter the direction of the Port of Los Angeles, or when the governor of New Jersey demands equal treatment in the Port Authority's investment choices), and some-times for dubious reasons (as when patronage appointees occupy important staff positions—a serious problem at the Port Authority under the current governors). A second lesson of this history, then, is that even when a public organization is cre-ated with substantial autonomy, political pressures may lead to policies that neither objective observers nor Port Authority executives would prefer, and to the appoint-ment of staff members of questionable competence; in addition, substantial funds may be diverted to activities desired by those with political leverage.[17]

Moreover, if the agency has been given a wide portfolio, as is the case with the Port Authority, its leaders may more readily persuade themselves to stretch their activities to the outer limits of the agency's statutory reach. In time, they—together with those who have political leverage over the agency—may allocate funds and staff energies to projects far from the agency's core mission. Much of the effort devoted to the current rebuilding of the World Trade Center might fall into this category, as do earlier projects such as the Newark Legal and Communications Center. Agencies with a narrower set of objectives, such as LAWA, are less likely to be thrown off their missions in this way.

These elements of traditional American democracy can be frustrating to those who wish the port and airport agencies could be more politically insulated and operated in ways more like a private corporation. But even with the occasional frustration, the staffs of these "semi-corporate" bodies press ahead. It is likely, for example, that among the nation's leaders in meeting more stringent environmental goals in the next several decades will be found the Port Authority of New York and New Jersey and the several port and airport agencies in the Los Angeles region.

NOTES

1. The two regions have additional gateway facilities: Newark and LaGuardia airports in New York and Ontario International Airport in Los Angeles.
2. This section draws upon Jameson W. Doig, *Empire on the Hudson: Entrepreneurial Vision and Political Power at the Port of New York Authority* (New York: Columbia University Press, 2001), chapters 2–7 and 11–13.
3. Initially each state named three commissioners; in 1930 the number was expanded to six from each state. In 1972 the agency was renamed the Port Authority of New York and New Jersey, to emphasize the equal partnership between the two states. The agency's jurisdiction extends across all of New York City and into Westchester County; west of the Hudson it includes Newark, Jersey City, and large portions of the surrounding counties.
4. At the time, about 50 percent of all US international trade flowed through marine terminals in New York City. A dozen rail lines brought goods to the New Jersey shore, where they were offloaded to barges and floated across the waterways to New York piers; the time and cost burdens for this cross-harbor trip were considerable.
5. The Port Authority also built three bridges between Staten Island and the New Jersey shore in 1927–31.
6. See Doig 2001, chapter 12.
7. On PATH and the World Trade Center, see Doig 1966, chapter 9; Doig 2001, 379–85; Dyble 2009, 237–38.
8. The common length of on-ship containers originally was 20 feet. Now, however, many containers are 40 feet long, or two TEUs.
9. Danielson and Doig 1982, 318–21.
10. The Los Angeles Department of Water and Power is the nation's largest municipally owned utility, delivering water and electricity to the city's residents.
11. By 2012 the LA-LB ports were spending $6 billion on extensive facility upgrades to maintain their long-term competitive advantage. See Ronald D. White, "Local Ports Upgrade to Build on Their Lead," *Los Angeles Times*, July 20, 2012. The airports in the

two regions are also engaged, along with other major airports, in improving their passenger terminals, at a total cost of billions. See, for example, Jad Mouawad, "Airports Focus on the Ground," *New York Times*, June 15, 2012.

12. John Schwartz, "U.S. Ports Expand, With an Eye on Panama," *New York Times*, August 21, 2012.

13. See table 4.3 above. LA-LB passed the Port Authority terminals in total TEUs during the 1980s.

14. See, for example, Joe Nocera, "9/11's White Elephant," *New York Times*, August 20, 2011, A17; also the response by the Port Authority's executive director, Christopher Ward, "Ground Zero Rebuilding," *New York Times*, August 28, 2011, A22.

15. Shawn Boburg and John Reitmeyer, "Dozens of Port Authority Jobs Go to Christie Loyalists," *The Record NorthJersey.com*, January 29, 2012; J. W. Doig, "Restore Integrity at the Port Authority," *New York Times* (online), February 21, 2012; Steve Strunsky, "Failed Christie Court Nominee Gets Port Authority Job," *The Star-Ledger*, July 27, 2012; Rob Tornoe, "Christie's Port Authority—The House That Pork Built," *NewsWorks: New Jersey*, August 6, 2012.

16. Port Authority of New York and New Jersey, Special Committee of the Board of Commissioners, with enclosure (Navigant, "Phase I Interim Report"), January 31, 2012; Navigant, "Phase II Report to the Board of Commissioners," September 2012.

17. For other examples of port authorities with substantial independence, see Peter Hendee Brown, *America's Waterfront Revival* (Philadelphia: University of Pennsylvania Press, 2009).

PART TWO

Politics and Economics

CHAPTER 5

New York City and Los Angeles

Government and Political Influence

JOHN MOLLENKOPF AND
RAPHAEL J. SONENSHEIN

This chapter compares and contrasts Los Angeles and New York City in terms of electoral demographics, political systems and structures, and local political heroes and icons. In particular, we explore how the evolution of local government and politics in the nation's two largest cities has affected the ability of various racial, ethnic, and class constituencies, including elite business interests and labor unions, to win a share of urban power and exert influence over city policies.

One striking difference between the two cities is that since 1965 Los Angeles has had a five-term African American mayor (Tom Bradley) and a two-term Latino mayor (Antonio Villaraigosa), while New York's sole African American mayor (David Dinkins) was defeated after only one term and the only Latino nominated by the Democrats (Fernando Ferrer) failed to unseat incumbent Mayor Michael Bloomberg in 2005. We are also interested in the layering of power among different political institutions, which does not always follow the same pattern: more Asian and immigrant-origin candidates have won election to lower offices in New York than in Los Angeles.

A second striking contrast is how different each city's political reaction was to the turmoil of the 1960s and 1970s, which yielded quite different notions within the majority of the electorate about what constitutes effective, even iconic, leadership. New York's massive labor and racial unrest between 1965 and 1973 under Mayor John V. Lindsay, followed by near-bankruptcy in 1975, prompted the electoral majority, centered among white ethnic Democrats but including many white liberals, to prefer a relatively conservative, fiscally cautious and proactive, mayoral leadership. By contrast, a large proportion of Los Angeles's white voters eventually developed a negative reaction to the conservative and intransigent, mayoral and police leadership under Mayor Sam Yorty and Police Chief William Parker, which they saw as exacerbating urban riots, and preferred a more liberal style of mayoral leadership under Mayor Tom Bradley. These different legacies persisted into the first decade of the twenty-first century, with the relatively conservative style of Mayor Bloomberg (albeit significantly less so than his immediate predecessor) contrasting with that of Mayor Villaraigosa.

We conclude by discussing how the slowly receding current economic and fiscal crises of the two cities have positioned various racial, ethnic, and class constituencies as we move toward open mayoral elections in 2013. Overall, New York and Los Angeles serve as ideal comparison cases for the questions discussed here because the two cities share many distinctive underlying economic and demographic qualities, even as they differ on key political dimensions.

NEW YORK CITY AND LOS ANGELES—POLITICAL SIMILARITIES AND DIFFERENCES

Electoral Demographics

New York and Los Angeles have some broad major electoral/demographic similarities. In addition to large populations spread across broad territories, both cities have unusually diverse populations with many born outside the United States (appendix table A). While non-Hispanic whites remain the largest ethno-racial group among voting age citizens, they no longer constitute a majority of potential voters in either city. And they make up barely one-third of the overall population. Both cities have large and powerful Jewish populations within this declining but still influential group of non-Hispanic whites, constituting the two largest Jewish communities outside the State of Israel. Both cities also have sizeable, long-standing African American communities, though neither has ever approached a majority of the population, much less the electorate, and both are currently declining in absolute numbers and relative proportions.

Finally, both cities have been strongly influenced by immigration, with large Latino populations—49 percent in Los Angeles and 29 percent in New York—and smaller but rapidly growing Asian populations. Despite the heightened flow of immigrants to other parts of the United States over the last several decades, both cities remain among the nation's largest immigrant destinations, drawing Latinos and Asians to live alongside and in between whites and blacks. (Both cities have white immigrants, such as Russian Jews in New York or Iranians in Los Angeles, but New York is distinct in having a large black immigrant population.) In short, both cities have diverse global populations in which non-Hispanic whites can no longer cast a majority of votes, thus requiring candidates to form cross-group coalitions to forge an electoral majority.

Despite these similarities, majority and minority populations have played quite different roles in constructing mayoral electoral majorities in the two cities. (Table 5.1 shows mayoral election outcomes since 1965.) First, Los Angeles's black community, though the largest in the West, peaked at 18 percent of the city's population in 1970 and was about 10 percent by 2010. Given this relatively small share of the population and electorate (at about 13 percent), Los Angeles's black community could never hope to exercise power through the kind of white to black racial succession that took

Table 5.1 MAYORAL ELECTION RESULTS, NEW YORK AND LOS ANGELES, 1965–PRESENT

Election Year	NEW YORK		LOS ANGELES	
	Winner	Loser	Winner	Loser
1965	John V. Lindsay (R-L)	Abe Beame (D)"	Sam Yorty (R)	James Roosevelt (D)
1969	John V. Lindsay (L)	Mario Procaccino (D)	Sam Yorty (R)	Tom Bradley (D)
1973	Abe Beame (D)"	Albert Blumenthal (L)"	Tom Bradley (D)*	Sam Yorty (R)
1977	Edward Koch (D)"	Mario Cuomo (L)	Tom Bradley (D)*	Alan Robbins (D)
1981	Edward Koch (D)"	Frank Barbaro (Unity)	Tom Bradley (D)*	Sam Yorty (R)
1985	Edward Koch (D)"	Carol Bellamy (L)	Tom Bradley (D)*	John Ferraro (D)
1989	David Dinkins (D)*	Rudolph Giuliani (R)	Tom Bradley (D)*	Nate Holden (D)
1993	Rudolph Giuliani (R)	David Dinkins (D)*	Richard Riordan (R)	Michael Woo (D)
1997	Rudolph Giuliani (R)	Ruth Messinger (D)"	Richard Riordan (R)	Tom Hayden (D)
2001	Michael Bloomberg (R)"	Mark Green (D)"	James Hahn (D)	Antonio Villaraigosa (D)^
2005	Michael Bloomberg (R)"	Fernando Ferrer (D)^	Antonio Villaraigosa (D)^	James Hahn (D)
2009	Michael Bloomberg (R-I)"	William Thompson (D)*	Antonio Villaraigosa (D)^	Walter Moore (R)

* African-American ^Latino "Jewish
Source: Compiled by Authors from Various Sources.

place in Atlanta or Detroit, but only by being part of an interracial coalition or by being a swing vote between two larger, contending coalitions.

The black population in New York City, while also far from a majority, grew rapidly after 1940, peaking at 25 percent in 2000, making it the potential nucleus of a multiracial challenging coalition in alliance with white liberals and Latinos (which was, in fact, the Dinkins coalition) (Arian et al. 1991; Mollenkopf 1993). The fact that blacks were the most Democratic in registration and voting in New York, combined with the importance of being the Democratic nominee in a city where more than two-thirds of the registered voters are Democrats, enhanced their electoral position. The difference between being the single largest and most cohesive voting bloc in a Democratic primary electorate in New York, versus being the swing vote in open, nonpartisan primaries and general elections in Los Angeles, has had important implications for the racial politics of the two cities.

The differences between the Latino populations of New York City and Los Angeles also dramatically affect their ability to form a cohesive voting block and join coalitions. New York's Latinos are much more diverse than those of Los Angeles, and New York's political system seems to reinforce their different national origins. Puerto Ricans, the largest Latino group, are not immigrants, but have US citizenship. They arrived significantly earlier than the other Latino immigrant groups and live in distinctive areas. Finally, they make up only 11 percent of the city's voting age citizens, followed by Dominicans at 4.8 percent, with those of Mexican ancestry following far behind at 1 percent. In Los Angeles, by contrast, people of Mexican ancestry alone make up 30 percent of the city's population and 21 percent of the city's voting age citizens, while all Latino groups taken together add up to 31 percent of the voting age citizens. Los Angeles's large and growing Latino electorate made it almost inevitable that Latinos would eventually hold citywide office, as evidenced by Villaraigosa's election in 2005, although non-Hispanic whites and blacks had historically not been too eager to see this happen.

The victory of a Latino mayoral candidate may well have been hastened by the fact that the mayoral primary is open to members of any party, with party affiliation forbidden on the ballot, as discussed below, so that partisan adherents of a losing primary candidate might be less likely to hold it against the winner, as they often do in New York City's partisan primaries.

In New York, by contrast, no one minority group seems to be as ascendant as Latinos in Los Angeles. While Jews and blacks have combined at points in New York to support a winning candidate—as evidenced in John Lindsay's victories in 1965 and 1969 or even Ed Koch's Democratic primary runoff victory in 1977—the racial cleavages of the late 1960s and 1970s eroded this tradition, whereas events built and sustained this relationship in Los Angeles. Indeed, the 1991 disturbances in Crown Heights, Brooklyn, in which the death of a young Haitian boy (hit by a car in a Lubavitcher Rebbe's entourage) and the murder of a Hassidic rabbinical student punctuated four days of rioting, further eroding Jewish-black relations (Halle 2003).

Until the early 1970s, conservative, business-oriented administrations governed Los Angeles (table 5.1), excluding all minorities and white liberals, and, unlike in New York, had neither the interest nor the means to provide partial incorporation. As a result, only an interracial alliance could enable white reformers to seek, win, and exercise citywide, especially mayoral, power. Just such a biracial coalition kept an African American, Tom Bradley, in office for a record twenty years from 1973 to 1993 (Sonenshein 1994). As Bradley was repeatedly reelected, he pursued a pro-development agenda (e.g., most notably the massive downtown redevelopment that began in 1975), failing to take effective steps to enhance the political representation of Latinos. Still, he increased the level of minority employment in city government and maintained good relations with minority elected officials.

In the wake of Los Angeles's riots in 1992, sentiment within the white electorate shifted in a relatively conservative direction, enabling a Republican, Richard Riordan, to win two terms in office against relatively weak candidates who appealed to the fragmented liberal coalition (see table 5.2). As the memory of the uprising faded, however, the African American portion of the former interracial coalition was able to reassert itself, first under James Hahn (supported by white conservatives and blacks) and then Antonio Villaraigosa (also supported by Latinos, blacks, and white liberals).

Black voters were crucial to the victories of both James Hahn, a non-Hispanic white, in 2001, and Antonio Villaraigosa, a Latino, in 2005. Their swing from incumbent Hahn to challenger Villaraigosa helped ensure his victory. With continued black support, alongside his Latino core and substantial white liberal support, Villaraigosa won a lopsided mayoral reelection contest in 2009. Like black empowerment before

Table 5.2 MAYORAL VOTE SHARES IN LOS ANGELES, 1993–2009

Year	Winner	Vote Share	Whites	Blacks	Latinos	Asians
1993	Richard J. Riordan (R)	54.0	67	14	43	31
1997	Richard J. Riordan (R)	61.0	71	19	60	62
2001	James K. Hahn (D)	53.5	59	80	18	65
2005	Antonio Villaraigosa (D)	58.6	50	48	84	44
2009	Antonio Villaraigosa (D)	55.6				

Source: *Los Angeles Times* exit polls (not conducted in 2009).

it, Latino empowerment has moved ahead broadly in Los Angeles, as other Latino elected officials have joined the mayor in local office (e.g., former City Attorney Rocky Delgadillo and numerous members of the city council).

Latinos had to use their rising voting strength to force their way to the center stage. Still, when the remnants of the Bradley coalition came to terms with Latino empowerment in the 2005 mayoral campaign, the result was more convincing and durable than in New York City. In 2005, Villaraigosa won office; in the same year, Mayor Bloomberg defeated former Bronx Borough President Fernando Ferrer, a Puerto Rican, by a wide margin, in part because black voters who had backed Ferrer strongly in the 2001 primary bid did not do so in the 2005 general election.

Overall, the emergence of a substantial Mexican American and Latino electorate in Los Angeles makes them a natural competitor for citywide power in a way that New York's Puerto Ricans, or even its entire Latino potential electorate, at 20 percent, cannot be. Instead, Latinos can be the swing vote between whites and blacks in New York, just as blacks can oscillate between whites and Latinos in Los Angeles. Similarly, Jewish voters in Los Angeles have always provided strong support for minority candidates, while those in New York have not. Despite the size and political history of the group, however, Los Angeles has never elected a Jewish mayor. Instead, they achieved influence through a successful coalition with African Americans to support Tom Bradley. In the late 1980s, conflict over growth issues and a visit by Louis Farrakhan created strains in the coalition, leading Councilman Zev Yaroslavsky to contemplate a challenge to Bradley in 1989 with the support of influential Congressmen Howard Berman and Henry Waxman. But Yaroslavsky did not run, while Jewish candidates in subsequent mayoral primaries split the Jewish vote, and none could make it into the general election. By the time Villaraigosa ran in 2001 and 2005, demographic change had eclipsed the Jewish moment in LA politics. Yet Jews continued to be part of the scene. One of the leading mayoral candidates for 2013 has a Jewish mother ("Eric Garcettit"); another is an African American woman who converted to Judaism (Jan Perry); and a third is married to a Jewish community activist (Wendy Greuel).

The racial polarization that was relatively contained in Los Angeles (with, of course, the dramatic exception of a massive riot in 1992) has largely framed the electoral history of New York. Racial conflict motivated white Catholic and Jewish voters and even Latinos to more consistently back relatively conservative white candidates, reduced the willingness of white liberals to support challengers favored by minority voters, and divided black, Latino, and white liberal constituencies from each other (Mollenkopf 1993, 2003). While the racial divisions of the Koch, Dinkins, and Giuliani eras are well known, they have continued to influence the elections of the last decade, which have been dominated by a more moderate and centrist mayor, Michael Bloomberg. In the 2001 general election, Latino voters were upset that their favored candidate, Fernando Ferrer, who had attracted black as well as Latino support, did not win the nomination, and so voted at lower rates than might have been expected and were open to being wooed by the white-supported Republican candidate, Michael Bloomberg (see table 5.3). Bloomberg won a considerable share of the black vote in 2005 when the Democrats nominated a Latino candidate (Fernando Ferrer), and then Bloomberg substantially increased his share of the Latino vote in 2009 when the Democrats nominated an African American (William Thompson).

Blacks fought an uphill battle not only to join other voters in enabling a black candidate to win the Democratic nomination for mayor, but to gain a majority in the general election in the face of a substantial defection of white Democrats from black nominees. They succeeded only once (David Dinkins, 1989–1993). In the most recent mayoral elections, minority-backed candidates won the Democratic primary only to lose a racially polarized general election (Ferrer, a Latino, in 2005 and Thompson, a black, in 2009). New York City exemplifies the obstacles facing a potential black-Latino-white liberal challenging coalition in urban politics, even as white ethnic voters have diminished into a mere plurality of the electorate. Since 2001, Mayor Michael Bloomberg (a Democrat turned Republican and then independent) has deployed his wealth to take durable advantage of these divisions, forming his own multiracial electoral coalitions.

While the high level of political involvement of the large Jewish communities of the two cities makes them a significant part of each city's electorate, we have explained how they operate in different ways. New York's Jewish community, at roughly 15 percent of the city's population, is larger than that of Los Angeles, at about 6 percent. At the same time, New York's Jewish communities are far more demographically, politically, and religiously heterogeneous than those of Los Angeles, ranging from the ultra-Orthodox communities of Brooklyn or Queens to the Russian-speaking

Table 5.3 MAYORAL VOTE SHARES IN NEW YORK, 1989–2009

Year	Winner	Vote Share	Whites	Blacks	Latinos	Asians
1989	David N. Dinkins (D)	48.3	26	91	64	
1993	Rudolph W. Giuliani (R)	49.2	77	5	37	
1997	Rudolph W. Giuliani (R)	55.2	76	20	43	
2001	Michael R. Bloomberg (R)	50.3	62	25	43	53
2005	Michael R. Bloomberg (R-Ind)	58.4	74	47	32	62
2009	Michael R. Bloomberg (R-Ind)	50.7	67	23	43	

Source: *New York Times* exit polls from 1989 to 2001 and 2009. Estimate by authors for 2005.

Jewish immigrant population in South Brooklyn to the secular and liberal Jews of Manhattan and Brownstone Brooklyn.

In Los Angeles, by contrast, Jewish voters are generally liberally inclined. In New York, Jewish voters have made up a large share of those normally Democratic voters who defected from Democratic mayoral nominees backed by minority voters, even when those nominees (like Ruth Messinger or Mark Green) were Jewish. Remarkably, Orthodox and Russian Jewish voters enabled a Christian Republican to defeat a Jewish Democrat in the September 2011 special election to replace Representative Anthony Weiner in a Congressional district that spans Brooklyn and Queens. The high voter participation and relative political and ideological cohesion of Los Angeles's Jewish community magnifies its impact, with Jews casting anywhere from 15 to 18 percent of the votes in city elections, just as they do in New York.

In terms of political culture, then, while both cities are considered liberal (with more than three-quarters voting Democratic in the last presidential election), have many minority local office-holders, strong labor movements, and vigorous grassroots activism, two quite different leadership models have emerged in New York and Los Angeles. The icons of reform in New York City took a conservative stance toward the politically decaying and fragmented liberal welfare state, while the heroes of Los Angeles took a liberal tack toward a previously more conservative local government. (Arguably, the conservative reformers of New York City have had a larger and more thorough impact on city policies than the liberal reformers of Los Angeles have had on their government.)

Economic Interest Groups

While racial and ethnic demographics have clear political implications in the two cities, economic similarities also create class constituencies that are important to both cities' political dynamics. In many respects, New York and Los Angeles have comparable economies. They are huge engines of creation and export (mainly of services rather than goods) that play important roles in the global economy. The global connectivity ranking (appendix table A) measures the degree to which firms headquartered in the city have offices elsewhere, the degree to which their banking resources and financial markets are large, and the extent to which the cities are linked to other cities as nodes in global transportation networks. In this ranking, New York is second after London and Chicago is slightly ahead of Los Angeles because of its role in global commodities markets, but Los Angeles is still ranked ninth out all the cities in the world. While New York has more corporate headquarters, corporate service firms, and a bigger capital market and Los Angeles has more entertainment and high technology firms, both have major concentrations in creative industries and feature world-renowned universities, hospitals, and museums. Their airports, communications infrastructure, and ports connect them with the rest of the world. Both economies employ disproportionately large numbers of university-educated professionals, many of whom migrated from elsewhere in the United States, as well as low-wage, low-skilled workers, many from immigrant backgrounds. While the labor movement has made great strides in Los Angeles in recent decades, New York still has the highest union density of any large American city. Both locales are relatively affluent, at least as measured by per capita income. At the same time, both have highly unequal income distributions. In other words, both cities are replete with powerful and well organized economic interests, from the points of view of business and labor alike, which are contending for economic position.

Despite these similarities, organized labor is differently constituted and has played different roles in the politics of the two cities. Organized labor made a real surge in Los Angeles politics during and after the 1990s. While fewer workers are union members in Los Angeles than New York, its service unions grew substantially over recent decades by organizing immigrant workers. They worked closely with rising Latino politicians, culminating in the campaigns of Villaraigosa, a former United Teachers of Los Angeles organizer. Indeed, it may not be too much to say that organized labor has now largely supplanted the business community as the main organizational force in city politics in Los Angeles. Organized labor is larger and older in New York City and has strong historical ties to Democratic Party politics, but its very institutionalization distinguishes it from the social movement orientation of its sisters and brothers in Los Angeles. Some of the most dynamic unions, such as SEIU 1199, the Hospital Workers, are more oriented to the State of New York than the city, while the city's Central Labor Council has historically been strongly influenced by relatively conservative construction trade unions, which have a stake in the public works contracting and construction business in New York City. Its public employees' unions have been weak and are careful not to challenge incumbent mayors who will sit across the bargaining table from them.

Political Structures

While demographics clearly define the terrain on which elections are contested, they do not determine their outcome. The similarities and differences in how government is structured in Los Angeles and New York have a profound effect on the political opportunity structures in each city. Although the nominal budget of the City of Los Angeles is much smaller than that of New York City, both in absolute size and relative to the population served, both cities have large public sectors, with New York being among the largest and most costly of any municipality in the United States. Indeed, as the lower rows of appendix table 5.A show, after adding together the public functions that are provided by different levels of government in Los Angeles but by the City of New York, per capita spending levels are comparable. Both cities too have wrestled with how to balance meeting citywide needs while responding to neighborhood input and wooing disaffected parts of the city. In recent decades, both Staten Island and the San Fernando Valley had strong, though now defeated, secession movements. In both cities, the stakes and prizes of local government are worth fighting over and the make-up of the governing coalition has real implications for the distribution of benefits and costs. Table 5.4 summarizes some of the key differences in institutional features between the two cities.

Table 5.4 NEW YORK CITY AND LOS ANGELES GOVERNMENTAL INSTITUTIONS

	NEW YORK CITY (charter amended 1989)	LOS ANGELES (charter amended 1999)
Council size	51	15
% Minority Members on Council (2009)	51%—14 Black, 10 Latino, 2 Asian	47%—3 Black, 4 Latino, 0 Asian
Council election	District	District
Partisanship	Partisan	Nonpartisan
Budget	Mayor creates and council may modify. Mayor can veto any items added by council, but it can override mayoral veto by two-thirds vote	Mayor prepares with help of City Administrative Officer (CAO) and council may modify. Mayor can veto any items added by council, but council can override mayoral veto by two-thirds vote
Neighborhood government	Boroughs/community boards	Neighborhood councils/area planning commissions
School board	Mayor appoints school chancellor directly as well as eight members of the thirteen-member board	Elected by district
Department heads	Commissioners serve at pleasure of mayor; no council approval required	Mayor appoints with council majority; removes unless two-thirds council overrides
Council authority	Legislative and oversight roles	Legislative and oversight roles with some administrative authority
Budgeting Process	Mayor issues a five-year revenue forecast and uses it to craft a preliminary budget. The city council cannot alter the mayor's revenue projection but holds hearings on the preliminary budget. The mayor revises the budget based on input from Borough Presidents and city council votes to approve or reject the mayor's budget.	The City Administrative Office (CAO) and Controller produce revenue projections for the coming year. Based on those binding projections, the mayor prepares a preliminary budget. The city council's five-member Budget and Finance Committee holds public hearings on the mayor's budget. The budget is then sent to the full council for a majority vote. Once approved, the mayor has five days to veto or approve any council changes.

Source. Compiled by Authors.

The two cities differ greatly in how they organize local government, what powers they grant different parts of local government, how various interests are represented within these different parts, and what main policy thrusts have been pursued by the dominant political coalition. While both cities have had many reform movements,

New York City has a much more traditional, partisan political system, while Los Angeles reflects a long history of nonpartisan reform. New York's city charter requires partisan elections, which means that a candidate can stand for the general election only if nominated by a political party, typically one of the major parties sometimes with cross-endorsement from a minor party.

The New York City charter also grants the mayor strong executive power over virtually every domain, including the capital and expense budgets. Only the Metropolitan Transportation Authority (MTA), which runs the subways, bus system, and commuter rail lines, the City University of New York (CUNY), and the bi-state Port Authority, which runs the airports and the port, are not fully under mayoral control. Even with the MTA and CUNY, the mayor appoints a minority of board members. Further, the New York City central government exercises all the powers that, in other urban places where city and county boundaries do not coincide such as Los Angeles and Chicago, are exercised by counties.

Regarding the budget, New York's 1988/89 charter revision made a strong mayor even stronger by eliminating the Board of Estimate, which had previously enabled the borough presidents and other citywide officials to offset the mayor's influence. The New York City Council had almost no role in the budget. After the US Supreme Court declared the voting scheme of the Board of Estimate to be in violation of one person one vote (e.g., the borough president of Staten Island, with half a million people had the same voting power as that of Brooklyn, with four times the population), the new charter abolished the Board of Estimate and divided its budgetary power between the mayor and the City Council. Above all, the mayor's control over setting revenue estimates and proposing the budget gives him or her crucial power in the process. (If the City Council wants to spend more, it basically has to propose tax increases to fund the increases, which its members typically do not want to do.)

The five boroughs of New York continue to have strong party organizations, at least in the sense that parties control the nominating process and "the regulars" have experience in fending off political challengers. Indeed, Max Weber's description of professional politicians in "Politics as a Calling" or Robert Merton's famous description of the functions of the urban political machine would largely apply to New York City today. This political framework has been sustained by strong mayoral authority, high levels of public employment and government contracting, partisan nominating and redistricting procedures, strong partisan attachments within the electorate, and a large city council (fifty-one members) with many districts. Active local media compete to throw light on and create heat within city hall politics. Neighborhood politics are lively and long institutionalized; Community Boards have been part of New York City government since Robert Wagner's mayoralty at the end of the 1960s, with charter reform making them permanent in 1974. (The Community School Boards created after the contentious strikes of 1968 eventually became sites for corruption and Mayor Bloomberg won their abolition when he gained control of the schools in 2002.) Many neighborhood and civic organizations have mobilized around the local land use process, which requires community board review of all projects requiring city approval.

In Los Angeles, by contrast, nonpartisan reformers who feared the immigrant-based political machines of the older Eastern cities, structured Los Angeles city government in ways designed to make it more professional and less responsive to political entanglements. City elections in Los Angeles are by law nonpartisan—a candidate's party affiliation cannot appear on the ballot. Candidates run in an open primary election, in which all registered voters can participate, and a general election then takes place between the top two if no one wins a majority in the primary. In part because elections have been nonpartisan, voting turnout has historically been low and party organizations do not play a major role in nominating candidates.

Further, the 1925 Los Angeles city charter hemmed in the mayor with a small, more powerful city council (fifteen members) representing large districts, as well as interposing commissions to supervise most administrative functions and shifting much public employment into semi-autonomous "proprietary" departments like Water and Power, or the Harbor, as well as the independently-governed Los Angeles Unified School District. A major 1999 charter revision did grant new authority to the mayor and created a system of advisory neighborhood councils, but Los Angeles's mayor still has much less direct authority than New York's and its advisory councils attained only spotty and inconsistent influence over local issues. Equally important, it is LA County rather than the city that provides many social and health service functions and the districts of the county's five-member Board of Supervisors are not coterminous with those of the city.

Today, LA government is one of the more fragmented aspects of this fragmented metropolis. The County of Los Angeles, overseen by five County Supervisors who each represent two million constituents, delivers most human and social services. The Los Angeles Unified School District is independent with its own elected board and right to levy taxes. While the mayor appoints the members of the Water and Power Board and the Airport Commission, they must be approved by the Council. Under the new charter, the mayor can remove these commissioners unilaterally, a change that has reduced the historic independence of these commissions from mayoral control. However, these departments are "entrepreneurial," have their own sources of revenue, are therefore a bit outside direct mayoral and council control and tend to operate semi-independently. The mayor of Los Angeles thus directly controls a much narrower set of service areas than does the mayor of New York, and these services are much more closely related to property services (such as zoning, housing, development, transportation, and capital construction) than human services (which are largely delivered by the county). As a result, property-related interests are much more interested in what goes on in Los Angeles's city hall than are human service advocates. Reflecting this political difference, the Los Angeles Times and other regional media, unlike their New York counterparts, give scattered attention to city hall and to the county hall of administration, in part because key service functions are in different places. City hall's range of functions is relatively limited. So with some exceptions, such as utility rates or scandals over police misconduct, the public has less awareness of what city politicians are doing than do residents of New York.

These different political arrangements have also influenced which interests try to mobilize advantages in city elections. One result is that the course of minority empowerment has differed considerably. To be sure, in the wake of the Civil Rights movement, both cities saw a gradual and steady rise in the number of black and Latino

Table 5.5 MINORITY MEMBERSHIP ON CITY COUNCILS, NYC AND LOS ANGELES,
1966–PRESENT

		NYC						LA			
Year	Total	White	Black	Latino	Asian	Year	Total	White	Black	Latino	Asian
1962	**31**	29	2	0	0	1960	**15**	14	0	1	0
	100.0%	93.5%	6.5%	0.0%	0.0%		**100%**	93%	0%	7%	0%
1972	**37**	35	2	0	0	1970	**15**	12	3	0	0
	100.0%	94.60%	5.40%	0.0%	0.0%		**100%**	80%	20%	0%	0%
1982	**35**	26	6	3	0	1980	**15**	12	3	0	0
	100.0%	74.2%	17.1%	8.5%	0.0%		**100%**	80%	20%	0%	0%
1992	**51**	30.0	12.0	9.0	0.0	1990	**15**	9	3	2	1
	100.0%	58.8%	23.5%	17.6%	0.0%		**100%**	60%	20%	13%	7%
2002	**51**	26	14	10	1	2000	**15**	9	3	3	0
	100.0%	51.0%	27.4%	19.6%	2.0%		**100%**	60%	20%	20%	0%
2012	**51**	24	14	10	2	2010	**15**	8	3	4	0
	100.0%	47.1%	27.5%	19.6%	4.0%		**100%**	53%	20%	27%	0%

Source: LA City Council; lacity.org; John L. Flateau, Ph.D.; New York City Official Directories; council.nyc.gov
Variation in the number of NYC members from 1960 to 1992 is because the number of single member
districts changed, and there were also 10 "borough at large" seats from 1964 to 1983. One member, Eric
Martin Dilan, is both black and Hispanic (Puerto Rican and African American descent according to his bio).

legislative office holders. Still, New York City has done a marginally better job than Los
Angeles in "partially incorporating" minority communities. In other words, minority
elected officials have gained a real foothold in the city's legislative system with the
result that budgets have flowed toward their constituencies, even when they are not
part of a mayoral governing coalition. As early as the Fiorello LaGuardia coalition in
1933, liberal reformers used an expanding city government to provide employment
opportunities to Jews and African Americans. The politically entrenched Democratic
county organizations typically coopted and absorbed rising minority activists, limiting
insurgent challenges and managing ethno-racial succession. Because the party organizations and their elected official allies retained considerable influence over the distribution of the rewards of local government, liberal reformers found it hard to mobilize
minority communities independent of these channels. Minority representation on
the City Council was somewhat slower to develop in Los Angeles, with the city's large
and growing Asian population still unrepresented. But with the legacy of the Bradley
coalition, as renewed by Mayors Hahn and Villaraigosa, Los Angeles's minority communities have also benefited from employment in public service positions.

Differences in the Evolution of the Liberal Tradition

Many of the differences in current liberal traditions in the two cities stem from how
each city confronted the racial and economic cauldrons of the 1960s and 1970s, which

were formative years for subsequent national and local political alignments. In Los Angeles the alliance between blacks and Jews helped both groups to rise up, while the initial black–Jewish alliance in New York—as exemplified by the early efforts to organize Brooklyn hospital workers in the early 1960s—unraveled just a few years later when blacks demanded community control over the school system, many of whose teachers were Jewish (Pritchett 2002; Rieder 1987). The intergroup dynamics of New York City moved Jews from seeking alliances with minority groups against more conservative white Catholics to a more conservative position in alliance with these white Catholics against minority empowerment. The relatively conservative bent of the Democratic County Organizations in the Bronx, Queens, and Brooklyn during these years fostered this shift (Mollenkopf 2003). While still highly Democratic in state and national elections, Jews became available for recruitment—and advancement—by relatively conservative mayoral candidates, including Republican Rudolph W. Giuliani.

Crucial in saddling liberal governance with a battered reputation in New York were the political and governing crises that beset liberal mayor John V. Lindsay (1965–1973) (Cannato 2002; Morris 1981). On his first day of office in 1965, the Transport Workers Union of America (TWU) led by Mike Quill shut down the city with a complete halt of subway and bus service. As New Yorkers endured the transit strike, Lindsay remarked, "I still think it's a fun city" and walked four miles from his hotel room to City Hall in a gesture to show it. Columnist Dick Schapp satirized the term in an article titled *Fun City*. This was the first of many labor struggles during Lindsay's mayoralty. In 1968, the teachers' union (the United Federation of Teachers (UFT)) struck over the firings of several teachers in a school in Ocean Hill-Brownsville. That same year also saw a nine-day sanitation strike. As the quality of life in New York reached a nadir, winds caused garbage to whirl through the streets. With the schools shut down, the police engaged in a slowdown, firefighters threatened job actions, and racial and religious tensions broke to the surface. Lindsay later called the last six months of 1968 "the worst of my public life."

The Lindsay years set the stage for New York's 1975 traumatic near-bankruptcy. In the aftermath of this crisis, the city adopted new budgeting procedures and other policy reforms (many imposed by the state) that had a major, positive effect on the city's ability to navigate subsequent economic downturns, including the 2008 financial crisis, as well as on its general preference for more conservative mayors. Overall, the rapidly rising spending, pro-labor contracts and racial struggles of the Lindsay era, followed by the 1975 bankruptcy crisis, broadly symbolized the failure of liberal government in New York City.

During these years, the opposite happened in Los Angeles, which was governed by conservative Sam Yorty, a Democrat who eventually became a Republican (1961–1973). While no mayor navigated this era particularly successfully, Yorty was a signal failure, as his city deteriorated into mass violence in Watts in 1965 and the mayor fanned the flames of racial polarization in subsequent years. Yorty formed an alliance with Police Chief William Parker, backing the police department's militaristic and often racist practices in minority communities. When Yorty faced police critic and council member Tom Bradley who challenged him for mayor in 1969, he accused

Bradley of wanting to turn the city over to black militants and left wing radicals. Yorty, whose governing skills were negligible at best, and who had turned down considerable federal assistance while South Central Los Angeles suffered economically, held power largely by playing on the fears of white residents of the rise of African Americans and white liberals. Yorty's race baiting in that 1969 campaign earned him a listing as one of the worst mayors in American history (Holli 1999).

In this context, Tom Bradley, Yorty's successor, became a widely popular, even revered, symbol of a sensible, moderately progressive governance, adopting a more cosmopolitan, global view of Los Angeles. Bradley's five successful terms were marked by civic calm and steady growth, at least until the April 1992 civil disturbances in the wake of the Rodney King verdict, which led to the two-term mayoralty of Richard Riordan. The subsequent liberal mayoralties of James Hahn and Antonio Villaraigosa were also marked by relative calm.

Succeeding mayors in each city have built their ability to help, even "save," the city on these contrasting examples. In New York, the business community, conservative advocacy organizations, white ethnic Democrats, and many parts of the mainstream media have at various points hailed Ed Koch, Rudolph Giuliani, and Michael Bloomberg as tough, conservative mayors who successfully tackled such difficult problems as incivility in public space, crime, welfare dependency, and a poorly performing public school system. The supposed failure of liberal government in the Lindsay era echoed in the minds of many detractors during the one-term mayoralty of David Dinkins from 1989 to 1993 as he faced the crack and crime epidemics. The Dinkins mayoralty was also marred by the Crown Heights Riot and a black boycott against a Korean grocery in Brooklyn.

In Los Angeles, only one white conservative, Richard Riordan, punctuated the series of relatively liberal mayors who have cloaked themselves in the mantle of Tom Bradley's coalition politics. After claiming a series of accomplishments such as labor concessions, rising test scores in charter schools, and lower crime rates, Antonio Villaraigosa added in his April 2012 State of the City address: "The Los Angeles of 2012 is a better city. Somewhere in the heavens Tom Bradley is smiling" (Linthicum 2012).

Occupy Wall Street and Occupy LA

The startling populist critique embodied in Occupy Wall Street during the fall of 2011 further illustrates the differences between the political cultures of the two cities. Given the locus of Wall Street and concentration of the financial industry in downtown New York City, the Occupy movement began in New York, and took on a particular intensity that attracted widespread support among rank and file New Yorkers. Supporters included several members of the City Council, where a Progressive Caucus had been seeking to pass a living wage bill against the mayor's firm opposition. While Mayor Bloomberg's administration was relatively tolerant of the encampment for the first few months, it did not particularly encourage it, and then clamped down firmly in the early hours of November 15, 2011, in a raid that arrested several hundred people and shunted the press aside. By the time the Occupy movement made it to Los Angeles, it received a quite different reception. Camped out on the lawns around City Hall, dozens of protesters ignored city ordinances, and set up their tents, their media center, and other facilities. Meanwhile, both the city council and mayor issued strongly supportive statements, and the locally influential labor movement backed Occupy LA. With few corporate headquarters in Los Angeles, and no target equivalent to Wall Street, a friendly city hall provided a comfortable setting for protest.

Still, as in New York, Los Angeles's mayor and police department ultimately lost patience with the protesters, and called on them to move on. After fruitless attempts to negotiate alternate sites, the city announced that the area would be cleared. In a cautious mission meant to counter generations of LAPD excesses, and in stark contrast to the NYPD's night-time clearing operation, the LAPD police removed the remaining Occupy residents with minimal fuss several weeks after Occupy Wall Street. Their task was eased when leaders of organized labor distanced themselves from those in the Occupy movement who pledged not to leave.

ON TO 2013

Despite the differences between the two cities, their elected officials continue to face comparably immense political and economic challenges. The policies pursued by Mayors Bloomberg and Villaraigosa are less substantively different than their divergent political coalitions and orientations might suggest. Even Mayor Koch adopted some highly "progressive" public policies—like a large-scale effort to build affordable housing. Conversely, Los Angeles's mayors have also favored growth and sought to reduce crime. Both cities also face the challenge of incorporating a broad range of new immigrant groups into the civic and political life of the city. In both cities, the active voter is far more likely to be an older, native born white person than is the resident population as a whole.

Both cities will elect new mayors in 2013 and neither race will feature an incumbent office holder. This poses the intriguing question of whether past electoral patterns and ideological orientations will continue in the two cities, or whether either will break with past patterns. In Los Angeles, the battle to succeed Villaraigosa is increasingly blurring the traditional coalition lines. Where once the race would have featured candidates clearly representing African Americans, Latinos, Jews, or white Republicans, the field for 2013 included seven candidates with overlapping constituencies. The main ones include Jan Perry, an African American woman on the city council, Controller Wendy Gruel, and Eric Garcetti, the city council president. A major Jewish candidate, County Supervisor Zev Yaraslovsky, considered an early favorite, with a strong base in the Westside and the Valley but limited appeal downtown and in the inner city, chose not to run. It will be intriguing to see how these candidates deal with the Villaraigosa legacy. The peripatetic mayor would have been recognizable in New York City, but his energetic style sometimes seemed to wear down the more politically lethargic Angelenos. Nevertheless, he clearly brought a more mayor-centered style of governance to city hall.

The field is also large in New York City. With no obvious white conservative reformer to succeed Mayor Bloomberg, and with the disgrace of Anthony Weiner, once quite popular with Jewish and white Catholic voters of his Brooklyn-Queens Congressional district, it is not clear who might fill the political space defined by Mayors Koch, Giuliani, and Bloomberg. (Republicans have urged Police Commissioner Raymond Kelly to run, but he has not indicated any willingness to do so.) The potential candidate leading the polls in the fall of 2012 is City Council Speaker Christine Quinn, a lesbian with Irish roots who represents the West Village, Chelsea, and West Midtown, and who came to her office with support from the Queens and Bronx county party organizations. She has worked closely with Mayor Bloomberg and seems likely to receive his support in the mayoral primary.

Among those who might spearhead a multiracial liberal reform coalition is an African American, former Comptroller William Thompson, who held Mayor Bloomberg to a surprisingly narrow margin in 2009, but his fund-raising is lagging. Prospects for another liberal contender, Comptroller John Liu, a Chinese-American breakthrough candidate, have been clouded by a federal indictment of several of his fund raisers in the 2009 campaign. Another strong reform contender is Public Advocate Bill DeBlasio, a progressive white former City Council member and campaign manager for Hillary Clinton's first Senate campaign who received support from black voters and the Working Families Party for his citywide win in 2009. (Notably, neither a major Latino nor a major Jewish candidate seems to be emerging in the Democratic mayoral primary.) Since the political, media, and corporate elites who are so comfortable with Mayor Bloomberg find many of these candidates unappealing, they may still attempt to put forward their own alternative if one of these liberal-leaning, neighborhood-oriented candidates wins the Democratic nomination. In December 2012 the head of the MTA, Joe Lhota, resigned so as to explore running for mayor as a Republican. As a result, the political futures of New York and Los Angeles will both be far more open to political redefinition in the 2013 elections than they have been for decades.

APPENDIX

Table 5A A COMPARISON OF NEW YORK, LOS ANGELES, AND CHICAGO, 2010

	New York	Los Angeles	Chicago
City population (2010 Census—includes group quarters)	8,175,133	3,792,621	2,695,598
Metro Area population (2010 Census—includes group quarters)	18,987,109	12,828,837	9,461,105
City Area (miles^2)	309	469	227
City density in 2010 (persons/miles^2)	26,457	8,086	11,874
City share of metro population in 2010	43.1%	29.6%	28.5%
City NH white (2010 Census)	33.3%	28.7%	31.7%
City NH black (2010 Census)	22.8%	9.6%	32.9%

(Continued)

Table 5A (CONTINUED)

	New York	Los Angeles	Chicago
City NH Asian (2010 Census)	12.6%	11.3%	5.5%
City Hispanic (2010 Census)	28.6%	48.5%	28.9%
City NH white pct of Voting Age Citizens (2010 ACS)	41.6%	42.2%	39.7%
City Foreign Born (2010 ACS)	37.2%	38.9%	20.8%
City Naturalized among Foreign Born (2010 ACS)	51.2%	40.2%	38.9%
Naturalized FB share of Voting Age Citizens (2010 ACS)	30.0%	28.0%	12.2%
Votes in last Mayoral General Election	(09) 1,178,057	(09) 285,658	(11) 590,357
Votes as share of Voting Age Citizens (2010 ACS)	23.3%	13.6%	33.7%
Democratic Share of 2008 Presidential Election Vote	78.5%	76.3%	85.4%
Global Advanced Services Connectivity ranking	2	9	7
GDP (2010 dollars)	$1,281billion	$736 billion	$532 billion
GDP per capita	$67,789	$57,370	$56,231
City Median HH income per capita (2010 ACS)	$25,000	$21,400	$22,000
City tax burden (2003–04) per $100 gross taxable resources	($4.51) $5.62	$2.87	$3.57
(NYC without medicaid local share)			
State tax burden (2003–04) per $100 gross taxable resources	$3.40	$4.01	$2.33
Total central city taxes (2003–04) per $100 in taxable resources	$9.02	$6.88	$5.89
City budget (FY 2011)	$66.4 billion	$6.7 billion	$8.3 billion
City share of County budget (39.2% in LA and 51.9% in Chicago) and 39.22% in LA)	NA	$9.1 billion	$1.2 billion
School Board/Water Board/Harbor	NA	$7.0/6.3/1.0 billion	NA
Transit Authority (Pro-rated city share)	$6.8 billion	$1.5 billion	$0.7 billion
Total City-County budget/person	$8,954	$6,302	$3,524
Miles of rail mass transit	722	73	222
Mass transit riders (millions/weekday)	7.8	1.5	1.4

Source: P. J. Taylor, G. Catalano, and D. R. F. Walker. 2002. "Measurement of the World City Network." *Urban Studies* 39(13): 2367–76; Bureau of Economic Analysis, US Department of Commerce, "GDP by Metropolitan Area, Advance 2010, and Revised 2007–2009," table 1 (September 13, 2011); Belkin and Beiseitov 2007, Independent Budget Office, City of New York. "Comparing State and Local Taxes in Large U.S. Cities." *IBO Fiscal Brief* (February).

CHAPTER 6

Financial, Economic, and Political Crises

From Subprime Loans to Dodd-Frank, Occupy Wall Street, and Beyond

DAVID HALLE AND ANDREW A. BEVERIDGE

New York and Los Angeles together helped create the 2007–08 financial crisis, though each played a different role. The Los Angeles region was a major driver of the real estate bubble. For example, seven of the top 10 US lenders making "subprime loans" in the period 2005–07 were based in Southern California, including the three largest—Countrywide Financial, Ameriquest, and New Century. New York's Wall Street firms, in turn, invented and promoted key financial instruments, especially Credit Default Swaps, that fueled the mortgage lending spree. Wall Street also pushed deregulation, which facilitated the excesses. The first part of this chapter discusses the key roles of New York and Los Angeles in the crisis.

The collapse of the resulting housing bubble triggered events leading to the world financial and economic crisis in the fall of 2008, which then morphed into multiple further issues. This interdependence of some central parts of the system, which is what above all characterizes the current stage of "globalization" in the financial world, is a second key point. Underlining this interdependence, by late 2011 problems starting in Greece, a nation with an economy no larger than Dallas, Texas, threatened to break apart the entire seventeen-country Euro monetary union.

Still, one reason Greece's problems carried such weight was the political failure of the European Community to deal adequately with sovereign debt issues. This illustrates a third key point, namely the complex but intermittently important role of public opinion in the process. For example, the European Community's failure to handle sovereign debt issues decisively was driven by the unwillingness of many German voters to help Greece, Spain, and Italy, whose citizens were seen as wedded to excessively generous government entitlement programs. Likewise in the United States the election to Congress in 2010 of a vocal group of Tea Party conservatives limited the Obama administration's options to deal with the economy. Housing debates played a key role in the very emergence of the Tea Party. In early 2009, CNBC TV commentator Rick Santelli, in a widely viewed broadcast, lashed out at the Obama administration's program to help homeowners facing foreclosure. Santelli, from the floor of the Chicago Board of Trade, claimed the program misused taxpayer dollars in order to subsidize irresponsible "losers' mortgages" and suggested a new version of the Boston Tea Party to protest.

Still, how far these currents of public opinion could have been mitigated or directed in other ways by more skillful leadership is a major question. This underlines a fourth key point of this chapter, the importance, as in any crisis, of having talented leaders who can manage complexity and channel public opinion fruitfully. So far, no major political figure has risen decisively to this occasion, which is an important reason the crises have continued at this writing for half a decade. Indeed, it is two central bankers, Ben Bernanke, US Federal Reserve chair throughout the crisis, and Mario Draghi at the European Central Bank since late 2011, who have made some of the most crucial, positive contributions, in part because they were less directly constrained by politics.

Finally, we cover various calls for reform, especially in two ongoing policy issues—managing the power of the banks and what to do about homeowners in financial trouble. These issues resonate with the respective roles of New York and Los Angeles in the original bubble and are likely to remain policy priorities for years.

In this connection the power of the banks and finance peaked in 2007 and has been in contention ever since. The initial major attempt to curtail bank power was Dodd-Frank, which if fully implemented, will likely have large ramifications for years. Congress passed Dodd-Frank in mid-2010 on a wave of public outrage over bank bonuses, which were in part funded by the taxpayer bank bailouts. This was followed by a different, but equally frontal, attack on bank power and inequality, Occupy Wall Street, the grassroots movement that burst onto the scene in September 2011.

Throughout the crisis to this writing many policy analysts and economists called for help for US homeowners facing foreclosure or whose mortgage balances now exceed their house values. Such measures were proposed not primarily for moral reasons but because the depressed housing sector, especially the number of foreclosures, was a huge drag on the US economy. Still, the Obama administration did less than numerous economists proposed, in part because of fears, highlighted by its pollsters, that political opponents would persuade Americans who had not gotten into mortgage difficulties to disapprove of using public funds to help those who had—the charge that played a key role in the Tea Party's emergence. Again, the role of public opinion and debates over leadership's ability to navigate and channel public opinion, are key.

SOUTHERN CALIFORNIA'S CONTRIBUTION: SUBPRIME LENDING AND A HOUSING BOOM

Los Angeles was, historically, built on successive waves of real estate speculation and associated booms and busts. In this tradition, financial companies in Orange and Los Angeles counties led in making subprime mortgages and in developing some of the most toxic new so-called Alt-A mortgage instruments in the years preceding the crisis (Morgenson and Rosner 2011.) Subprime loans are often defined as loans to borrowers with weak credit histories or repayment capacities or both, at high interest rates. However, during the crisis a variety of new loan instruments with low initial payments but high overall costs were developed. All the top 10 US lenders making "subprime loans" in the period 2005–07 were based in California, with seven of these in Southern California (either Orange or Los Angeles counties). (See table 6.1.)

This geographic clustering had three main contemporary causes, the first two of which are also long-standing factors driving the Los Angeles region's history of real estate speculation. First, the region has, and had, abundant farm land available for new construction, especially nowadays in the "Inland Empire" of Riverside and San Bernardino counties. Second, its population grew rapidly via immigration, providing a stream of people eager to acquire homes, which was a major reason why some observers believed the real estate boom could continue indefinitely. For these two reasons especially, Southern California was the largest real estate market in the country.

Third, California is a state (one of twenty) with "anti-deficiency" legislation, which has the effect of encouraging some borrowers to take loans they might be unable to repay, although states vary considerably in the details of how this operates.[1] Under such legislation, which is rare in other major industrial countries (Lea 2010), a borrower who defaults on a mortgage is not responsible for any "deficiency" between the price at which the lender sells the foreclosed property and any outstanding balance

Table 6.1 TOP 10 LENDERS MAKING SUBPRIME LOANS, 2005–2007

1. Countrywide Financial Corp. LA County
   Amount of Subprime Loans: At least $97.2 billion

2. Ameriquest Mortgage Co./ACC Capital Holdings Corp. Orange County
   At least $80.6 billion

3. New Century Financial Corp. Orange County
   At least $75.9 billion.

4. Long Beach Mortgage Co./Washington Mutual Northern CA
   At least $65.2 billion

5. Option One Mortgage Corp./H&R Block Inc. Orange County
   At least $64.7 billion

6. Fremont Investment & Loan/Fremont General Corp. Orange County
   At least $61.7 billion

7. Wells Fargo Financial/Wells Fargo & Co. San Francisco
   At least $51.8 billion

8. HSBC Finance Corp./HSBC Holdings plc San Francisco
   At least $50.3 billion

9. WMC Mortgage Corp./General Electric Co. LA County
   At least $49.6 billion

10. BNC Mortgage Inc./Lehman Brothers Orange County
    At least $47.6 billion

Source: NovaStar Financial Inc., in a Center for Public Integrity analysis of loans from 2005 through 2007.

of the mortgage (provided certain conditions are met, for example, the mortgage is for a dwelling occupied by the purchaser, and the borrower has not taken on additional mortgage debt after purchasing the house). By contrast, in states without anti-deficiency laws, the borrower might remain responsible for this balance and so is likely to be more cautious about incurring large mortgage debt.

But why were lenders, throughout the country, not just in Southern California, willing to make mortgage loans that conventional credit analysis would deem risky and unlikely to be repaid? There are two interrelated reasons. Almost as soon as originators made the loans, they were typically able to sell them to others, after extracting fees and commission. This gave lenders little incentive to be careful about the repayment capacity of borrowers, just incentives to make the maximum number of loans, as long as they could be sold. Meanwhile those who purchased these toxic loans from the initial lenders felt safe doing so because of instruments that Wall Street created, which will be discussed later.

In short, Southern California had a lethal combination of plentiful land on which to build new homes, a huge and growing population eager to buy these, and the ability of lenders to easily offload loans (including the riskiest) thanks to the willingness of Wall Street and others to insure and purchase almost unlimited quantities of these loans. Other states such as Nevada and Florida were also epicenters of the real estate boom. These, together with California, were dubbed "the sand states" when studies showed where foreclosures were concentrated. Further, the real estate bubble was a national phenomenon. Still Southern California provided, overall, the most hospitable location for subprime lenders.

Stated Income and "Piggy Back" Loans

At the level of individuals receiving residential mortgage loans, some abuses and recklessness were incredible. These fell into two main groups. First, borrowers were encouraged to be untruthful about their payment capacity. For example, some lenders offered "stated income" or "no documentation" loans (informally known as "liar loans"), in which individuals were not asked to prove their incomes. Ameriquest Mortgage in Orange County was a pioneer of these, which became the dominant feature of most subprime loans. By 2006 Countrywide's internal risk assessors knew that, in one-third of its stated income loans, borrowers overstated income by more than 50 percent (Nocera 2010). There were also "stated value" loans where the house's value, as claimed by individual home sellers and buyers on the loan application, was accepted by the lender with no outside appraisal.

A second series of reckless practices encouraged transactions where purchasers contributed little, if any, of their own cash, and so had little, or even negative, equity in their homes. These included "piggy back" loans, where a buyer received a first loan for the "cash" down payment, and then a second loan for the remaining sum to purchase the home. By 2006, roughly 48 percent of home purchases in the LA region involved piggy back loans, compared to 32 percent nationwide and 28 percent in New York. There were also "interest only" loans where the monthly payments covered only interest on the loan and none of the principal. Worse, there were "negative amortization" loans, where the monthly payments did not even cover the monthly interest, so the principal owed rose each month. Apocryphal stories from the period are numerous. For example, in 2011 a Newport Beach, California, banker commented:

> There were all those billboards along the freeway saying, "125 percent loans." My gardener got a $600,000 loan to buy a new house in San Bernardino. He was earning $10 an hour and I don't think he was here legally. After the crash he gave the house back to the bank.

In another case, a New York resident was approved by Wachovia for a loan to buy a second residence in 2004. On reading the approval documents, he saw the loan officer had filled out fictional figures for his income. He questioned the officer, who repeatedly insisted that it did not matter, since the loan had been approved and the closing was scheduled to happen in two days. Only after the applicant said he would forego the loan rather than sign false papers did the officer correct the data.[2]

Showing that this practice was not confined to Wachovia, seven years later in July 2011, the US Federal Reserve fined Wells Fargo $85 million based on the charge that Wells employees "falsified income information on mortgage applications" during the subprime bubble (Nocera 2011b). Likewise, Washington Mutual's CEO, Kerry Killinger, from 1990 until he was forced out in September 2008, notoriously drove his employees to make the maximum number of loans with minimal regard for borrowers' incomes and assets (Goodman 2008; Grind 2012). These processes were, of course, going on nationwide, but were especially present in California and the other "sand states."

There also seems to have been some targeting of "minority" neighborhoods. In New York City, for example, by 2006 the median down payment to purchase a one- to four-family house or condo had already fallen to just 6 percent of the total price, from roughly 20 percent in earlier decades. But in Brownsville, Brooklyn, a neighborhood then 71 percent black and 19 percent Latino, and in Jamaica, Queens, also a heavily minority neighborhood, the median down payment in 2006 was an incredible 0 percent (Ellen 2012).

The United States led the world in making subprime loans. A study (Lea 2010) of twelve major industrial countries showed that in 2006 the United States gave a huge 29 percent of all its mortgage loans as subprime, followed distantly by the United Kingdom at 8 percent. After that, Canada gave 5 percent and Australia just under 2 percent. The percentage of subprime loans was negligible in the other countries studied (Denmark, Ireland, Japan, Germany, the Netherlands, Spain, and Switzerland).

THE NEW YORK/WALL STREET CONTRIBUTION AND THE POWER OF THE BANKS

Finance and Two Types of Power

The power and significance of the US financial sector grew rapidly in the years before the crisis. From 1978 to 2007 the amount of debt it held soared from $3 to $36 trillion, more than doubling as a share of GDP. By 2006, financial sector profits constituted 27 percent of all corporate profits in the United States, up from 15 percent in 1980. Pay ballooned too. From 1945 to the mid-1970s, pay in the financial sector was at parity with the rest of the private sector, but by 2006 was 1.7 times higher, the level it had reached just before the 1929 crash (Tett 2012a).[3] There was, too, concentration. By 2005 the ten largest US commercial banks held 55 percent of the industry's assets, more than double the level held in 1990.[4] A key development during this period was a qualitative change in the risk structure, as many Wall Street firms went from relatively staid private partnerships, where the partners' money was at risk, to publicly traded corporations taking greater kinds of risk and increasingly with other people's money.

Social and political scientists typically define "power" in two main ways (Lukes 1974). On the eve of the crisis, the financial sector was preeminent in both. First, power is the "ability to make or directly affect key, relevant, decisions." Exemplifying its exercise of this kind of power, from 1998 to 2008 the financial sector spent $2.7 billion in reported federal lobbying expenses, more than any other sector, directly influencing political decision makers. Results of this lobbying included the significant weakening of the financial regulatory regime, as discussed later.

Another aspect of this "decision-making power" is that some financial sector personnel held key decision-making posts in the federal government, which raised questions about government decisions being made to benefit friends ("crony capitalism"). For example, in 2004 Henry Paulson, as CEO of Goldman Sachs, together with several other financial CEOs, successfully lobbied the Securities and Exchange Commission (SEC) to remove limits on how much debt the brokerage units of banks, including Goldman Sachs, could acquire. Paulson's argument, echoed by many finance leaders and some regulators at the time, was that financial institutions were too sophisticated and self-interested to recklessly jeopardize their own viability. Two years later Paulson became Secretary of the Treasury, in time to hand out Troubled Asset Relief Program monies and other funds in 2008 to rescue the financial institutions from the recklessness that he and many others now recognized as threatening the entire international financial system.

The second type of power that social scientists stress is the "ability to achieve one's interests," which can be done without necessarily making or directly affecting key decisions (i.e., without dealing in the first kind of power). The most striking example of finance's possession of this kind of power was the widespread belief by national policymakers during the initial crisis that it was not in the national interest for a country's major financial institutions to collapse, they were "too big to fail" and therefore had to be rescued.

Another key way that this second type of power (i.e., ability to achieve one's interests) operated before, during, and after the crisis was "regulatory arbitrage," basically the ability to move, or just threaten to move, personnel and capital to more lightly regulated locations/structures. "Regulatory arbitrage" comes in two main versions, "geographic" and "institutional." There is the ability to move geographically, for example, from New York to London or Hong Kong. Awareness of this ability operated, and still operates, as a key constraint on policymakers reluctant to risk losing their financial titans to less tightly regulated locations. The other main aspect of regulatory arbitrage is the ability, while remaining in the same geographic place, to move resources and activities into less regulated institutions, including the "shadow" financial/banking system, which included hedge funds and insurance companies, especially AIG.

The following is an account of the financial sector's contribution to the crisis, showing how its vigorous exercise of both kinds of power peaked just before the crisis. By 2011 that power was weakened in interesting ways as we discuss, especially by Dodd-Frank, which presented a massive new regulatory framework for finance, and, for about a year by Occupy Wall Street, which returned issues of the inequality and unfairness of the financial system to the central stage they have often occupied in American history.

Regulatory Arbitrage: The Race to the Bottom

Wall Street's contribution to the unfolding fiasco was basically twofold. First came a continual and successful lobbying effort to deregulate, removing rules that constrained the financial sector. For example, in 1999 Congress dismantled the Glass-Steagall Act, passed in 1933 during the Depression to separate investment banking from commercial banking. The point of the original Act was that speculative activities (investment banking) should not put an organization handling ordinary deposits insured by the federal government (commercial banking) at risk. Amid heavy Wall Street pressure, Washington, with Treasury Secretary Robert Rubin, former Co-Chairman of Goldman Sachs in the forefront, came to view Glass-Steagall as an outmoded relic of an era when banks could not be trusted.

Then in 2000, again after heavy lobbying from Wall Street, Congress banned federal and state governments from regulating Over the Counter (OTC) derivatives, of which Credit Default Swaps, key to the credit boom as discussed below, were a major type. A prime motive of the ban was to curb an outspoken regulator, Brooksley Born, who, as head of the Commodities Futures Trading Commission (CTFC), from the late 1990s repeatedly tried to regulate OTC derivatives to no avail. Appointed by Clinton in 1996, Born knew how markets could be manipulated, having represented a major Swiss bank in litigation over the Hunt family's attempt to corner the silver market in the 1980s. In April 1998 Born wrote a memo saying the CTFC should gather information about how the murky OTC derivates market actually operated. Rubin, and Federal Reserve Chair Alan Greenspan, after being lobbied heavily by the banks, tried to stop her. Greenspan, concerned about the geographic arbitrage so key to finance's power, told Born that merely inquiring about this field would drive an important, expanding, and creative financial business offshore. In testimony at a congressional hearing he repeated the common claim of deregulators, namely that there was no need for government oversight because the derivatives market involved sophisticated Wall Street "professionals" who would police it themselves and that Wall Street had built-in safety mechanisms, especially a strong desire for self-preservation, that prevented firms from behaving in financially reckless ways and also gave them greater insight into the market than "clumsy" regulators.

In December 2000, Wall Street preempted Born's ongoing efforts by promoting the Commodity Futures Modernization Act, which stripped the CFTC of its power to regulate derivatives, since they were not "futures." As a result, much of the derivatives market remained outside regulatory reach, part of the "shadow banking system" (Goodman 2008). Looking back later, one banking expert commented ruefully, "We should have listened to Brooksley."

Another key deregulation decision came in 2004 when the SEC, headed by Christopher Cox, was lobbied heavily by five major investment banks, including efforts from Henry Paulson, Goldman Sachs CEO and just two years before he became Treasury Secretary, as mentioned. As a result, the SEC exempted the banks' brokerage units from the "net capital rule" that limited the amount of debt they could take on. This exemption now freed billions of dollars that the banks had held in reserve as a cushion against losses, allowing them to invest in the growing market for mortgage-backed securities, among other areas. "We foolishly believed that the firms had a strong culture of self-preservation and responsibility and would have the discipline not to borrow excessively," explained one SEC member. "Anyway, I didn't think the SEC had the staff and wherewithal to impose its own standards. We've all learned a terrible lesson." Again, there were dissenters at the time. A software consultant, who wrote programs that financial institutions use to meet capital requirements, warned the SEC that the firms' computer models could not anticipate severe market turbulence (Labaton 2008). Still, such criticisms were swept aside as old-fashioned.

Similar changes occurred in London, often seen as New York's financial twin and major competitor. After the Labor Party took power in 1997, Gordon Brown, as Chancellor of the Exchequer, aligned Britain with the free-market, deregulatory approach of Greenspan and Rubin in order to keep London bank-friendly and in step with New York. He combined about nine different regulators into the Financial Services Authority (FSA), which then adopted "light touch regulation," as Brown called it. All this was part of what Joseph Stiglitz called an international, regulatory "race to the bottom" in the pre-crisis years, with countries competing on the "lightness" of their regulations. Stressing finance's mobility/ability to engage in geographic arbitrage, a crucial source of its power, Stiglitz (2010) commented: "Banks within any jurisdiction threaten to take their business elsewhere if tough regulations are imposed...Modern finance is a footloose industry, so the threat seems at least partially credible. If regulations are different in different jurisdictions, there is a real risk of regulatory arbitrage."

Credit Default Swaps—"Weapons of Mass Financial Destruction"

Wall Street's second major contribution to the crisis, in addition to deregulation, was inventing the instruments that enabled lenders to sell their risky mortgage loans to others almost as soon as they made them. Without these instruments, lenders would not generally have made loans with such a high risk of default. By the mid-1990s, JPMorgan Chase's books were loaded with loans to corporations and foreign governments, and by federal law it had to keep huge amounts of capital in reserve in case any of them went bad. But what if JPMorgan Chase could create a device to protect it if those loans defaulted, and thus free up that capital? The bankers hit on a sort of insurance policy, Credit Default Swaps, under which a third party would assume the risk of the debt going sour, and in exchange would receive regular payments, insurance premiums, from the banks. JPMorgan Chase could then remove the risk from its books and free up the reserves (Tett 2009).

In 1998 AIG, the country's biggest insurer became the third party insuring what were then corporate Credit Default Swaps. The original Credit Default Swaps invented by JPMorgan Chase were mostly intended for corporate debt, to insure, for example, holders of corporate bonds in the event that the company defaulted. Then in the early 2000s a small London-based unit of AIG Financial Products began to insure Mortgaged Back Securities, the collateralized debt obligations (CDOs) that packaged thousands of mortgages into a single instrument. Once insured, the packaging of mortgages in so-called tranches of risk in CDOs took off throughout Wall Street with the exception, ironically, of JPMorgan Chase, the inventor of Credit Default Swaps. Traders there felt that there was not enough historical experience with mortgages to easily evaluate the risk (Tett 2009).

In less than a year the subprime mortgage component of the loans that Wall Street firms, with Goldman Sachs in the vanguard, got AIG Financial Products to insure went from only 2 percent to 95 percent. For a few million dollars a year in insurance premiums, AIG was now responsible for $50 billion in triple B rated subprime mortgage bonds that it had insured.

Goldman's traders, hungry for financial products to market, now created an even riskier bet, a "synthetic mortgage bond backed CDO" or Collateralized Debt Obligation, sometimes called CDO squared. The original mortgage bonds insured by Credit Default Swaps consisted of thousands of loans packaged together on the (as it turned out, false) assumption that they were unlikely to all fail together, and rated by one of the major rating agencies, such as Moody's, from triple A to triple B. Goldman now created a new package composed of around 100 different, subprime triple B rated mortgage bonds extracted from the original packages. Incredibly (or perhaps not given that rating agencies were paid fees by Goldman and others for each package that they rated), the agencies now pronounced around 80 percent of the debt package triple A, even though it was composed entirely of bonds originally rated triple B. In 2006, Moody's alone stamped roughly thirty mortgage-related securities as triple A every working day. The CDO was, in Michael Lewis's words, "a credit laundering service for residents of Lower Middle Class America and for Wall Street a machine that led into gold" (Lewis 2010).

Worse, Goldman and others then purchased insurance (Credit Default Swaps) from AIG and others on these synthetic bonds, insurance which AIG was willing to issue, since the synthetic CDOs had been given a triple A rating. Even though Goldman and others were sometimes at the same time betting that these CDOs would fail, they then sold these triple A rated CDOs to their customers. Whether this was legal became a major issue for investigators after the crisis, and Goldman paid a $550 million fine to the SEC (Chan and Story 2010).

This market for "synthetics" (CDOs) removed limits on the size of the risk associated with subprime mortgage lending, and in fact made it possible for many buyers to share in the gains or losses from each mortgage instrument. Nor was AIG Financial Products required to put up more capital, since it was unregulated (i.e., part of the "shadow banking system"). Morally, and as a risk to the stability of the entire financial system, these arrangements were, as Michael Lewis (2010) put it, "obscene." The Commodity Futures Trading Commission might have stopped the riskiest transactions and queried AIG's ability to stand behind them, had it not been forbidden, as part of deregulation, from examining Credit Default Swaps.

It was not just AIG. Leading up to the crisis, many financial institutions, and households, borrowed to the hilt. For example, as of 2007 the five major investment banks, Goldman Sachs, Morgan Stanley, Merrill Lynch, Lehman Brothers, and Bear Stearns, ranked in that order, were operating with extraordinarily thin capital, facilitated by such decisions as the 2004 SEC's to exempt their brokerage firms from the "net capital rule." By one measure, their leverage ratios were 40:1 (i.e., for every \$40 in assets they had only \$1 to cover losses). So, less than a 3 percent drop in asset values could wipe out a firm. Worse, much of their borrowing was short-term, in the overnight market and needing to be renewed every day (which became a colossal problem when lending froze right after Lehman Brothers collapsed). More exposed still were Fannie Mae and Freddie Mac, the behemoth, Government Sponsored Enterprises (GSE) mortgage lenders, whose combined leverage ratios were now an incredible 75:1. In particular Fannie Mae's quest for bigger market share, profits, and bonuses for its executives had led it to ramp up its exposure to risky loans and securities just as the housing market was peaking (US Senate 2011).

The Unsustainable Housing Boom

The housing bubble fueled by this loan spree was pervasive and unsustainable in both regions. A widely recognized measure of reality in home prices is the ratio of median home price to median income. Historically in the United States it has been around 3:1. In both the Los Angeles and New York regions by 1990 the ratio was roughly between 4:1 and 6:1 for our three defined areas outside of West of Downtown and Manhattan. It was roughly 11:1 for West of Downtown. (See figure 6.1. The home price data until 2000 refer to single-family homes, too few in Manhattan for reliable data. After 2000 they also include co-ops and condos, allowing reliable Manhattan data.) By 2008–10 the ratios were substantially higher, as compared with 2000, for all the defined areas (even though the 2008–10 average figure already includes roughly two to three years of substantial price declines after 2007). In the most desirable sections of each city, West of Downtown and Manhattan, the 2008–10 ratio was roughly 13:1. In the other three defined areas in each region the ratio ranged from roughly 5:1 to just over 10:1.

This reflected the fact that house prices were shooting upward while median household incomes after 1990 (through 2008–10) were stagnating or declining for all four defined areas in each region except Manhattan where they rose steadily. (See table 2.7 and figure 2.19.) In Los Angeles, for all four of our defined areas, house values had increased from between 56 percent and 76 percent (West of Downtown) from 2000 to 2008–10. In the same period in New York, for all four areas, house

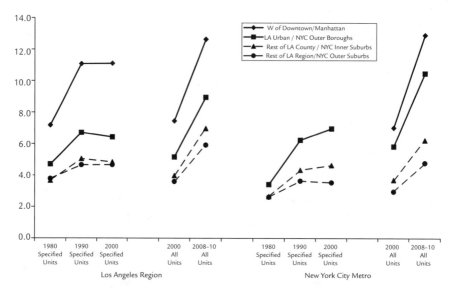

Figure 6.1
Ratio of Median House Value to Median Household Income for Los Angeles and New York
Defined Areas by Region, 1980 to 2000 and 2000 to 2008–2010
Source: Andrew A. Beveridge from figures 2.19 and 2.22.
Note: From 1980 to 2000 the Census Bureau computed house value just for single-family detached houses, which
it called "specified owner occupied units." There were not enough such units in Manhattan for a reliable estimate of
house value. Starting in 2000, the Census Bureau broadened this to all owner-occupied units, which include condos
and co-ops, producing reliable Manhattan data.

values had risen from between 55 percent and 94 percent (Manhattan). See table 2.8
and figure 2.22. Also, in all four sections of each region, rents rose between 2000 and
2008–10, from 10 to 30 percent.

Given stagnant or falling median household income in all sections of the region
except Manhattan, together with rising rents, the temptation for those who wished to
enter the housing market to take a loan allowing them to borrow above their means is
apparent. Nationally, from 2001 to 2007 mortgage debt almost doubled, and the amount
of mortgage debt per household rose over 63 percent from $91,000 to $149,000.

Subprime Loans: This Time Was Not Different

The view that "this time is different" typically precedes, and is an ingredient of, financial crises. It argues that, despite previous crises, another one is now unlikely because
the present situation has carefully avoided the circumstances that caused previous
crises (Reinhart and Rogoff, 2009). A popular version of this view in the immediate
pre-crisis years, especially in Los Angeles and New York, was the idea that immigration, flowing freely after the 1965 Hart Cellar Act, would supply an endless stream
of new customers for houses, so prices would keep rising. The main flaw in this view
was the rising tide of subprime loans, which eventually overwhelmed the supply of
qualified purchasers and collapsed home prices.

So long as US house prices increased, borrowers with difficulty meeting their payments could sell their homes and pay off the mortgage. But as the numbers and proportions of subprime loans grew, so did that of stressed borrowers needing to sell, so total houses for sale nationwide began increasing in mid-2005 and never stopped. As more of these properties came on the market, house prices leveled. In early 2006, the Case-Shiller index of house prices for the ten largest metropolitan regions started to fall, as did the indices for the New York and Los Angeles regions, though substantial declines did not occur until 2007–08 (see figure 2.25).

Since a growing proportion of homeowners in financial difficulty were now "under water," owing more than their homes were worth, the number of foreclosures began rising nationwide and in the Los Angeles region by the summer of 2006, and a year later in the New York region (see figure 10.1). A hallmark of the crisis was that the foreclosure rate then rose far higher in the Los Angeles region than in the New York region, for reasons Ellen and O'Flaherty discuss in chapter 10. Nationwide by 2011 just 4 percent of prime loans but 15 percent of subprime loans were in foreclosure (Nasiripour 2012).

EDGE OF THE ABYSS

The entire financial structure, the "House of Cards" in William Cohan's phrase, now began crumbling as the waves of mortgage defaults presented banks with huge losses and presented insurers, especially AIG, with a tide of claims they could not meet. The first companies affected were those directly involved in home construction and mortgage lending. Some of the earliest major signs of trouble came in the United Kingdom. In mid-September 2007, Northern Rock, a medium-sized bank whose business was highly leveraged with mortgages, requested help from the Bank of England, leading to a bank run. In February 2008 the British Government, having failed to find a private sector buyer, took over Northern Rock (still owning 83 percent of the bank by May 2012).

The British banking sector consisted of huge banks in a medium-size economy, especially as its banks became truly immense during the bubble. For example, Royal Bank of Scotland was the largest bank in the world by assets—$3.8 trillion—when it ran into trouble in 2007. (For comparison, Citigroup's assets were then $2.2 trillion.) The Royal Bank of Scotland was loaded with subprime mortgages and debt after leading a consortium (with Spain's Santander and Fortis, the Belgian-Dutch lender) that paid 71 billion Euros to take over the Dutch bank ABN in October 2007, in terrible timing just before the bubble burst. The Royal Bank of Scotland's assets easily exceeded the gross domestic product of all of Britain, which was $2.1 trillion, as well as the entire 2008 US federal budget ($2.8 trillion). The bank's total losses for 2008 were 24.3 billion English pounds, one of the largest annual losses in British history. (Iceland's banking sector was even more imbalanced. In the pre-crisis years, its banking sector, measured by assets, ballooned to ten times Iceland's gross domestic product.)

For the United States, Countrywide in the Los Angeles region was an early harbinger of trouble, teetering on bankruptcy by the end of 2007. In 2006 Countrywide had financed 20 percent of all mortgages in the United States, more than any other mortgage lender. In July 2008, Bank of America purchased the failing Countrywide for $4.1 billion in stock—in retrospect a disastrous deal for Bank of America as over time it became apparent how close to the epicenter of the mortgage crisis Countrywide was.

Meanwhile the financial institutions that had engaged in the securitization of mortgages fell into trouble. In March 2008 Bear Stearns was acquired by JPMorgan Chase through deliberate assistance from the US government. Bear's stock was acquired for $10 per share, compared to its 52-week high of $134. The crisis now accelerated. In August 2008, the Treasury Department reacted to the dire financial conditions of Fannie Mae and Freddie Mac and put them into federal conservatorship on September 7, 2008.

Lehman Brothers Collapse

On September 15, 2008, the teetering international financial system entered trauma as Lehman Brothers was allowed to fail by the Federal Reserve and filed for Chapter 11 bankruptcy protection, following the massive exodus of most of its clients, drastic losses in its stock, and the devaluation of its assets by credit rating agencies. This was the largest bankruptcy in US history and Lehman Brothers was at that time the fourth largest investment bank in the United States. The trauma also decisively swung the 2008 US presidential election in favor of Obama and Biden, who until then had been almost even in the polls with Republicans McCain and Palin (Abramson et al. 2011).

Until Lehman Brothers, national governments had bailed out their major, failing institutions as the crisis unfolded, concerned that the interconnectedness of institutions held the potential for serious national, and even international, economic problems. Still, in the United States each major government bailout met a rising tide of critics complaining that bailouts undermined the principle of "moral hazard" according to which those who took risks in pursuit of financial gain should suffer the financial consequences. The day Lehman failed, the *Wall Street Journal* and *New York Times* wrote editorials congratulating the Federal Reserve for finally allowing a major institution to go bankrupt and so upholding the principle of "moral hazard."

Over time, the lesson learned from Lehman was a different one, namely capital's ability to achieve its interests via mobility and geographic arbitrage, as former Treasury Secretary Larry Summers (2011) stressed:

> Teaching investors a lesson is a wish not a policy. Punishing creditors for the sake of teaching lessons or building political support is reckless in a system that depends on confidence. US policymakers were applauded for about 12 hours for their willingness to let Lehman go bankrupt. Those who let Lehman go believed that because time had passed since the Bear Stearns' bail-out, the market had learnt lessons and so was prepared. In fact, the main lessons learnt [by the markets] were how best to find the exits, so uncontrolled bankruptcies had systemic consequences that far exceeded their expectations. The maintenance of systemic confidence is essential in a financial crisis.

Credit markets froze the day after Lehman's bankruptcy. Even money market accounts, supposedly rock solid, turned out not to be, since they were dependent on short-term interbank lending which had stopped. For example, at the end of 2007 Bear Stearns had $11.8 billion in equity, $383.6 billion in liabilities, and was borrowing up to $70 billion in the overnight market. This was the core fragility of the financial system—the dependence of key parts of it on short-term financing. So when short-term credit froze, most major financial institutions were insolvent (Sorkin 2009).

Publicly, until Lehman's bankruptcy, Federal Reserve Chair Bernanke and Treasury Secretary Paulson had been saying that everything remained under control, but privately they were clearly unsure. In March 2008 they secretly drafted a version of the Troubled Asset Relief Program (though funded then at $500 billion, not the $700 billion when it passed in October) as a contingency plan. Later they justified their public calm on the standard grounds that a truthful discussion would have worsened the situation by undermining confidence. Still, partly they had just not understood how dire things were and would become; otherwise, they would not have allowed the Lehman bankruptcy.

A hallmark of the run-up to the crisis was this failure of almost all the nation's best economic minds to understand the risks of systemic instability associated with trillions of dollars in risky mortgages having become embedded throughout the global system (Levitin and Wachter 2011). This became clear when the transcripts of the 2006 Federal Reserve meetings were released in 2012, after the standard five-year delay. The Federal Reserve committee consists of the governors of the Federal Reserve and the presidents of the twelve regional banks. In 2006 the committee, meeting every six weeks to discuss the nation's economy, knew the housing market was faltering, but had no notion that this might negatively impact the broader US economy, let alone the world financial system. Instead the committee believed throughout 2006 that the greatest danger was inflation resulting from the possibility that the economy would grow too fast. Fed officials, like many other experts, were convinced that financial innovations, by distributing the risk of losses more broadly, had increased the system's resilience. The main exception was the Fed's chairman, Ben S. Bernanke, who by late 2006 was warning that problems in the housing market could have broader consequences (Appelbaum 2012).

Still, by the time of Lehman's bankruptcy in September 2008, it had become clear (at least to key players behind the scenes) that a mega financial crisis, perhaps one of the greatest in US history, was at hand. The weekend before Lehman Brothers went bankrupt, AIG was teetering after a credit rating downgrade triggered margin calls. Treasury and Federal Reserve officials were privately told by their economic forecasters that if AIG was not saved, Morgan Stanley would likely fail on Monday, Goldman Sachs on Wednesday, followed by General Electric with its 287,000 employees, dragged down by its financing arm, GE Capital. They also heard that Bank of America was preparing to tell McDonalds it lacked cash to meet the company's payrolls. Federal forecasters privately predicted 24 percent unemployment in the United States two years after an AIG failure.

So the day after Lehman Brothers declared bankruptcy, the US Federal Reserve created an $85 billion credit facility for AIG to meet increased collateral obligations it owed consequent to the credit rating downgrade. AIG had already defaulted on $14 billion worth of Credit Default Swaps it had made to investment banks, insurance companies, and scores of other entities. In exchange, the Federal Reserve received stock for 79.9 percent of the equity of AIG. The deal, using taxpayer dollars, enabled AIG to reimburse 100 percent of what it owed to Goldman Sachs, again raising allegations of "crony capitalism," since Treasury Secretary Paulson had a few years earlier headed Goldman Sachs when it linked its fate with AIG's.

Troubled Asset Relief Program (TARP)

Two weeks later, Congress went much further, passing the Emergency Economic Stabilization Act, signed by Bush on October 3, 2008, which created the Troubled Asset Relief Program (TARP) to bail out banks and homeowners. The program had $700 billion available, an amount equal to 25 percent of the entire Federal budget for 2008 and exceeding the whole Defense Department budget of $607 billion.

In addition, the Federal Reserve provided $7.7 trillion in emergency credit during the crisis (December 2007–April 2010), acting through several special financing programs starting in 2007, including the Primary Dealer Credit Facility for overnight funding of investment banks and the Term Auction Facility for one- to three-month loans (Ivry et al. 2011). Underlining the interconnectedness of US and Western European financial institutions, foreign banks were among the biggest beneficiaries (though this only became public knowledge later, as a result of a Dodd-Frank transparency requirement). For example, of the ten largest Term Auction Facility recipients, seven were Western European banks.[5]

Over the next two-and-a half years, TARP funds and other measures gradually stabilized the US financial system, and for a while contributed, together with efforts by other major national financial systems, to doing the same for the world system. The Obama administration, eager to stress the program's careful use of taxpayer dollars, for a while even suggested that as a result of banks repaying their TARP loans with interest, the program would make a profit, though by April 2012 TARP's Inspector General estimated that, over its lifetime, the program would make a net loss of $68 billion, largely because of bailouts to General Motors and Chrysler, as well as mortgage assistance programs (Puzzanghera 2012).

BAILING OUT THE BANKS/NEW YORK, NOT INTERVENING DIRECTLY

In the period right after the collapse of Lehman Brothers, the Treasury Department and Federal Reserve made two other key decisions, both of which meant that help to homeowners in distress was minimal. First, they recapitalized ("bailed out") the banks by loaning funds to them rather than intervening more directly as they had in the savings and loan crisis of the 1980s, the US's last financial crisis. During that crisis the federal government set up the Resolution Trust Corporation (RTC), a US-government-owned company, charged with liquidating assets (primarily real estate related, such as mortgage loans) that had been in the hands of savings and loan associations declared insolvent by the Office of Thrift Supervision. Between 1989 and mid-1995, the RTC closed or otherwise resolved savings and loan associations with total assets of $394 billion, using funding provided for by the 1989 Financial Institutions Reform Recovery and Enforcement Act.

The RTC pioneered the use of equity partnerships to help liquidate real estate and financial assets inherited from the insolvent thrift institutions. These partnerships all involved a private sector partner acquiring a partial interest in a pool of assets, controlling the management and sale of the assets, and making distributions to the RTC based on the RTC's retained interest, so the RTC participated in any gains from the portfolios. Had this been done in 2008, a government agency (an RTC equivalent) would have taken over the major, nonperforming real estate assets of the banks, albeit at some cost to taxpayers. The banks, in turn, would have been relieved of these assets and, presumably after the old management had been removed, would have been freed to make new loans to creditworthy businesses. Another problem in the 2008 crisis was massive uncertainty over the legality of a significant proportion of the mortgage loans made and foreclosures carried out. This was rooted in banks' inadequate practices such as "nondocumentation" loans and "robo-signing" foreclosures (whereby bank officials signed foreclosure documents without reading them). For example, by mid-2012 Fannie Mae and Freddie Mac still held large numbers of such loans they had originally purchased from banks even though the loans were written so as to legally require banks to repurchase any that turned out not to have been made following properly agreed procedures. Bank of America, for example, was arguing with these government agencies over such loans, which it was reluctant to repurchase.

Instead of an RTC-type solution, the banks, almost all of whom were technically insolvent by the end of 2008, were given loans that saved them from failing, but they retained masses of nonperforming loans on their books. This acted as a major drag on banks' willingness to lend, slowing the economic revival especially the real estate sector, since very tight lending standards made it hard for even creditworthy buyers to obtain mortgages, as policymakers increasingly realized by 2011 with unemployment persisting around 9 percent and dropping only slowly to 7.8 percent in September 2012. Summers, Paulson, and Geithner said the financial system in 2008 was too fragile for an RTC approach. They might have been right, though others at the time disagreed.

BAILING OUT THE BANKS/NEW YORK, NOT HOMEOWNERS/LOS ANGELES/REST OF THE COUNTRY

A second consequential decision in the period after Lehman's collapse involved using TARP funds to bail out banks but not also to help homeowners in distress. In March

2011, Neil Barofsky, TARP's Inspector General, resigned in disgust over the discrepancy between the massive assistance the federal government gave to Wall Street and what he considered the feeble effort government made to help homeowners at risk of losing their homes through foreclosure. In a *New York Times* op-ed piece published just after his resignation, Barofsky (2011) stressed that when Congress passed the Emergency Economic Stabilization Act in October 2008, creating TARP, it had only done so with the understanding that the program would help homeowners, as well as banks. This was because several members of Congress had balked at passing a bill that only bailed out banks, especially with a fund that size.

At that time Congress was told that TARP would be used to purchase up to $700 billion of mortgages, and the Treasury Department, which administered the program, promised to modify those mortgages to assist struggling homeowners, which the Act directed the department to do. For mortgages involved in assets purchased by the Treasury Department, the Act required the Treasury Secretary to (1) implement a plan seeking to maximize assistance for homeowners, and (2) encourage the servicers of the underlying mortgages to take advantage of the HOPE for Homeowners Program of the Housing and Economic Recovery Act or other available programs to minimize foreclosures. Also, the Treasury Secretary was allowed to use loan guarantees and credit enhancements to encourage loan modifications to avert foreclosure.[6] An early warning that TARP might not be used also to help homeowners as intended by Congress was that Treasury Secretary Paulson, in testimony at the time to the House Financial Services Committee, insisted "The primary purpose of the bill was to protect our financial system from collapse. The rescue package is not intended to be an economic stimulus or an economic recovery package." Helping homeowners was not Paulson's priority.

Almost immediately after the Act was passed, the Treasury's plan for TARP shifted from purchasing mortgages to infusing billions of dollars into the nation's largest financial institutions, basically recapitalizing them by making capital injections (buying stock in) the banks. That use of TARP was highly successful and was permitted by the broad language with which TARP was written. A total of $380 billion was spent on the banks, AIG, and auto groups (by the end of 2011 the loans paid to the big banks, though not all the smaller ones, had been repaid with interest) (Puzzanghera and Lazo 2012; Nocera 2011a; Tett 2009). Barofsky agreed that using TARP funds to bail out the banks was the right thing to do, since a collapsed bank system would have been a general economic catastrophe. His complaint was that almost nothing was done to help homeowners too, despite promises to Congress. Instead, the Treasury basically gave TARP capital injections to the banks with no requirements or incentive to increase lending to homebuyers. Only in April 2010, did the Treasury even ask banks to report how they used TARP funds, and only in response to recommendations from Barofsky's office to the Treasury Department.

The Act's goal of helping struggling homeowners was basically shelved until February 2009, when the newly elected Obama administration passed its Home Affordable Modification Program (HAMP), promising to help "3–4 million at-risk homeowners avoid foreclosure" by assisting them with mortgage modifications. HAMP included provisions to use federal funds to pay roughly $1,200 to servicers and mortgage holders (basically the banks) for each qualifying loan modification they made. That program, Barofsky and others complained, has failed, with far fewer permanent modifications (540,000) than modifications that have not worked and been canceled (over 800,000). Indeed, the banks during this period showed scant interest in mortgage modification and were under little public pressure to do so. Instead, much of the public pressure on banks at this time and until the end of 2011 was over the bonuses they were handing out, discussed below.

HAMP's relative failure resulted also from several program design flaws, above all the absence of a mechanism to change the "win-win" or "Pareto optimum" provision according to which the terms of a mortgage could not be altered without the consent of a company holding a stake in that mortgage (i.e., basically the bank). This was a huge stumbling block. A related problem was the failure to remedy the fact that it was often in the economic interests of mortgage servicers to foreclose rather than to put borrowers into a HAMP loan modification. For example, in the case of principal forgiveness, Barofsky complained, "one of the problems is that servicers are paid based on a percentage of the active principal. Principal reduction eats right into their bottom line" (Nasiripour 2012). A related problem was that the banks were keeping the $1,200 given to them by the government for every loan modified, instead of giving part of it, as an incentive, to the bank employee down in the hierarchy handling loan modifications. Also, servicers would have needed to hire many additional employees to handle loan modifications, which were far more complex matters than just processing mortgage payments, which they were set up to handle. A crucial further problem was the prevalence of junior/second mortgages, estimated to be linked to half of all loans at risk of delinquency. Such second liens significantly complicate modifications because first lien holders may lose their senior status upon modification and so usually will not modify unless second lien holders agree to resubordinate their claims, which often does not happen (Been, Vicki, Chan et al. 2011).

HAMP continued to "woefully underperform," in the judgment of government auditors, by January 2012 having helped fewer than 763,000 homeowners permanently cut their monthly payments, far short of the 3–4 million it was supposed to have helped. The basic design flaws remained, especially leaving it to mortgage servicers (basically the banks) to decide if it was in their financial interests to make a loan modification, which typically it seemed not to be.

Finally HAMP suffered a major blow when the US Senate in April 2009 defeated the bankruptcy reform bill known as the "mortgage cram-down" bill, which would have allowed bankruptcy judges to order mortgages on a primary residence to be written-down to the property's current fair-market price (the bill had passed the House a month earlier). When Obama was running for president he had promised to support such bankruptcy reform. "I will change our bankruptcy laws to make it easier for families to stay in their homes," he told voters in September 2008, lambasting the exclusion of mortgages from debts that could be written off in a bankruptcy filing as "the kind of out-of-touch Washington loophole that makes no sense" (Ulam 2011). The bill's supporters believed that often homeowners in difficulty would not have needed to actually file for bankruptcy, since the cram-down provision gave homeowners a bargaining chip to negotiate sustainable loan modifications from the banks

(Ulam 2011). HAMP's designers had, likewise, counted on the "mortgage cram-down" bill to push servicers to modify more loans especially via principal reduction (Been, Vicki, Chan et al. 2011).

Instead, the banks lobbied heavily against the bankruptcy reform bill, saying they would have to raise interest rates to account for the risk of underwater homeowners having their mortgages modified in a bankruptcy. They also argued that bankruptcy reform would create a "moral hazard" by rewarding irresponsible borrowers who took out mortgages they could not afford.

As mentioned, CNBC host Rick Santelli, on February 19, 2009, attacked the mortgage cram-down bill in an episode that played a part in, some argue even launched, the Tea Party. In a live broadcast Santelli asked cheering traders on the floor of the Chicago Mercantile Exchange, "How many of you people want to pay for your neighbor's mortgage that has an extra bathroom and can't pay their bills?" Santelli accused the government of "promoting bad behavior," raised the possibility of a "Chicago Tea Party," and added, "Let's have a referendum on the web to see if we really want to subsidize the losers' mortgages." Ironically, some of the cheering traders probably worked for bailed out banks.

The bankruptcy reform bill's defeat is one of the moments on which turns the ongoing debate over the quality of Obama's leadership. Those sympathetic to Obama argue that events such as the bill's defeat hampered a well-intentioned administration (Been et al. 2011). Critics, by contrast, fault the administration for not lobbying harder for the bill. Georgetown Law School professor Adam Levitin (2011), an expert on legislation, claimed: "Had Obama put his weight into [the bill] it would have passed...but he was too chicken to have the fight." Critics added that, unlike the Obama administration's HAMP under which the taxpayer partially foots the bill, court-ordered mortgage cram-downs would have cost the federal government nothing.

Underlining the complexity of the debate, some observers added that the Obama administration, like the Bush administration before, was concerned the bill might economically undermine the banks. Democratic Representative Brad Miller of North Carolina who sponsored the cram-down bill commented: "The bankruptcy law change...would have required the banks to recognize a lot of losses immediately and might very well have revealed some of them to be very nearly insolvent or actually insolvent." Further, the banks were holding a substantial amount of the outstanding unsecured debt on underwater homes in the form of second loans and home equity lines of credit. Given their second-lien status, the drop in housing prices meant that many of these loans had become partially or completely unsecured, and if passed the cram-down legislation would have led many of them to be written off completely.

In early 2011, Treasury Secretary Timothy Geithner, who was clearly not inclined to push the banks to the brink, probably both because of concerns about the system's stability and because he was more sympathetic to them than were the major critics, acknowledged that the HAMP program "won't come close" to fulfilling its original expectations, and that the mortgage servicers are "still doing a terribly inadequate job."

THE "HOUSING DEATH SPIRAL" AND REMEDIES

Lending continued declining and foreclosures mounting, major reasons the recovery had stalled or moved so slowly. During the rest of 2011 a rising chorus of distinguished economists called for radical measures to assist homeowners, not just out of a sense of fairness but because, despite mortgage rates being historically low, the housing sector was a major drag on the economy. In November 2011, Laurie Goodman, an expert on mortgage-backed securities, warned of a "housing death spiral" as lower house prices meant more borrowers under water and so likely to default, producing even lower prices. She argued that of the 55 million mortgages in America, roughly 20 percent were reasonably likely to default in the next few years, mainly because so many were on properties worth less than the mortgage owed. She stressed too that house prices were being pulled down by a developing glut of unneeded homes, perhaps 6.2 million over the next six years, above all because the recession meant that so many young adults were living with their parents instead of moving into their own homes.[7]

In August 2011, Kenneth Rogoff (2011), coauthor of the definitive historical study showing that recovery, especially in employment, after a major financial crisis often took a decade, likewise argued that the economy's major problem was a huge overhang of household (and government) debt. So Rogoff advocated directly addressing the problem, for example, with programs to reduce the principal of mortgage debt, as well as via Keynesian stimulus of aggregate consumer demand. Likewise in December 2011, the economist Robert Shiller (2011) commented: "We used to talk a lot about helping homeowners in trouble. Instead, the bankers were bailed out—and now we hardly talk at all about aiding ordinary Americans. Yet the problems facing homeowners today are even bigger than they were in the dark days of the financial crisis... more homeowners are underwater on their mortgages—and more Americans are out of work. And home prices are still falling." Shiller favored replacing the current mortgage interest deduction program, which is only open to those who itemize their returns and who tend to be relatively wealthier, with a refundable tax credit as a percentage of mortgage interest payments that could be used even by those who take the standard deduction.

One of the most detailed sets of proposed remedies came in October 2011, from a trio including economist Nouriel Roubini and law Professor Robert Hockett (Alpert et al. 2011). Trying to get away from "one size fits all solutions," they offered a package of suggestions—temporary "bridge" loans, refinancing at lower rates, loan principal reduction, and allowing foreclosed homeowners to stay in their homes paying rent. These suggestions were tailored to suit the following three different categories of distressed homeowners, classified by the gravity of their situation.

Helping the Temporarily Distressed

The first, and least distressed, category of homeowners were those who were, probably just temporarily, having difficulty remaining current on mortgage debt payments simply because of being underemployed in the current recession. Their mortgages were not under water and their capacities to pay were not permanently impaired. The suggested solution for this group was a bridge loan for no more than 24 to 36 months, probably from a federal or state program. As a model, Pennsylvania's Home Emergency Mortgage Assistance Program, on the books since 1983, had performed fairly well.

A related plan would help homeowners who were underwater but current on their payments take advantage of low interest rates by refinancing into cheaper loans, as mortgage rates were so low. The current obstacle was that neither private lenders nor the now-government controlled Fannie Mae and Freddie Mac would allow these homeowners to refinance if their current loans were underwater. The remedy, which could be implemented without going through a difficult Congress, would have the Federal Housing Finance Agency tell Fannie and Freddie, of which it was custodian, to allow refinancing in these circumstances. This was the only major proposal the Obama administration had actually adopted by November 2012.

Helping Homeowners Substantially Underwater but Current on Payments

A second group of homeowners were substantially underwater with their mortgages. For this group, the only sustainable solution would be principal reductions large enough to bring the loan amounts to a level at or near the current value of the home. Regarding the potential for moral hazard that might result from apparently giving borrowers "something for nothing," Roubini and colleagues argued that lender debt forgiveness should be "earned" by being "contingent" on debtor behavior during a trial period. The programs, whether government enhanced (e.g., the Home Affordable Refinance Program (HARP) or the Home Affordable Modification Program Home (HAMP)) or otherwise, should mandate a 12-month test period during which borrowers' payments were at their original level. Borrowers would be required to execute so-called confessions of judgment in favor of the most senior mortgage lender, which enabled the lender to repossess and liquidate the home on an expedited basis, if more than two payments were missed by the borrower during the test period, after which the principal reduction would become automatic. Also, there might be a "shared appreciation" structure, with creditors who accepted principal reduction of a mortgage receiving a "warrant" giving them a capital gain if the home securing the mortgage was eventually sold for more than the restructured mortgage amount (the excess would be shared between debtor and creditor until the creditor is made whole).[8]

Helping Homeowners Who Cannot Afford Homeownership

Finally, a third subclass of borrowers are those in so much economic difficulty and/ or whose homes have fallen so far in value that they cannot qualify for the above measures. Many of this subclass probably should not have attempted to own, rather than rent, in the first place. Still, the authors argued it was important to eliminate the downward price pressure these houses were having as they were repossessed and put up for sale in order to help a recovery in the housing market. The proposed solution for this group involved shifting from mortgage to rental payments. They would voluntarily surrender the deed to their house in return for cancellation of existing mortgage debt. They would then have the right to a five-year market rate lease for what was formerly their home, with all of the normal services provided by the new landlord, as would be typical for renters in that region. Meanwhile the former lender, now landlord, would have the right to sell the home, either subject to the lease during the term thereof, or "free and clear" at the expiration of the term. The former owner, in turn, would have the right to reacquire the home—at fair market value—before the home is put up for sale free and clear of the lease. In effect, this amounted to a variation on the "statutory redemption right" that many states confer upon foreclosed mortgagors.

In November 2011, former President Clinton (2011), in a book that quickly became a bestseller, joined those calling for radical measures, mostly similar to those of Roubini and colleagues, to deal with the housing debt. Again his central argument was that this debt was a major reason the US economy was stuck at unemployment levels of around 8 to 9 percent. Although Clinton suggested forty-six remedial measures for high unemployment, tackling housing debt was top of his list.

Clinton, as always the practical politician, suggested three main reasons why his housing debt proposals were not so far being implemented. One problem was the absence of a single authority to institute and accelerate these proposals. Another was Edward DeMarco, interim director of the Federal Housing Finance Agency, which was created on September 7, 2008, to supervise Fannie Mae and Freddie Mac, which were now technically insolvent and dependent on taxpayer loans (by now over $140 billion) for survival. Although Freddie and Fannie hold over 50 percent of all delinquent mortgages, DeMarco sees his mission, Clinton complained, as conserving Fannie and Freddie, not writing down the mortgages they hold.

Public opinion was the third obstacle that Clinton identified, with many Americans who are making their payments being opposed to the idea of modifying the mortgages of those who got into trouble. As mentioned, the Obama administration was deeply reluctant to run afoul of public opinion here. Its pollsters had warned all along, but especially after the 2010 midterm congressional election fiasco for the Democratic Party, that if the administration moved aggressively to use public funds to help homeowners in difficulty, then conservatives would likely pit better-off people against the struggling by depicting the administration as using public funds ("taxes") to bail out those who had irresponsibly taken mortgages they could not repay. As one observer commented, while Obama's economic advisers stressed the need to revive the housing market, his political team has long argued that most Americans oppose bold government action to stem home foreclosures, like forcing lenders to reduce borrowers' principal, seeing it as rewarding those who had bought houses they could not afford (Calmes 2012).

Clinton's response to this public opinion argument was that, while these objections were reasonable in normal times, in the current situation the housing market collapse was hurting the entire economy including many people who did not behave imprudently. Anyway, if principal reduction was done in a way that required the owner to share future profits with the lender if the house rises in value, then the so-called "moral hazard" argument had less validity.

Underlining his reluctance to go in that direction, the Federal Housing Finance Agency's acting director, DeMarco, told Congress in January 2012, in reaction to strong urgings for Fannie Mae and Freddie Mac to apply principle reduction so as to return loan-to-value rates to 100 percent (e.g., a homeowner owing $400,000 on a house now only worth $300,000 would have the loan balance reduced to $300,000) that it "could cost taxpayers $100 billion" to reduce the loan balances of the roughly 3 million Americans with currently "underwater" loans from Fannie Mae and Freddie Mac to the point where they had equity in their homes. By May 2012 DeMarco still opposed a principal reduction program, protesting that "moral hazard" and "strategic defaults" would be a huge problem since under such a program at least 5 percent of those holding Fannie and Freddie mortgages would likely decide to stop making monthly payments and default in order to benefit from principal reduction. This would be enough, he argued, to destabilize Fannie and Freddie again. Instead, DeMarco favored a program of "principal forbearance," according to which homeowners' monthly mortgage payments would be adjusted to no more than 30 percent of their monthly income by such devices as extending the life of the mortgage (e.g., to forty years), rather than reducing the principle.

By October 2012, the only new major proposal adopted by the administration was the plan targeted at the least troubled class of homeowners, those current on their payments but under water so that they were not being allowed to refinance at currently lower rates. So in February 2012 the Federal Housing Finance Agency (FHFA) instructed Fannie Mae and Freddie Mac to allow this class of homeowners whose mortgages it held to refinance through HARP. Still the FHFA expected only 1 million homeowners to benefit, with analysts predicting that another 10.4 million homeowners (roughly 20 percent of all homeowners with mortgages) would default in coming years.

Meanwhile, downward home assessments as a result of price declines in the previous years were now eating into local government revenues, heavily dependent on property taxes, leading to layoffs of local government employees, especially teachers, and further hampering improvements in employment. Desperate, by fall of 2012, San Bernardino County and its largest cities, including the City of San Bernardino which had filed for bankruptcy in August, were considering a hugely radical plan to allow cities to exercise eminent domain. They would seize the mortgages (not the homes) of underwater borrowers who were still current on their payments, pay the investors that owned the mortgages a fraction of what they were owed, forgive all the homeowners' debt in excess of what the house was worth, and then help homeowners refinance at a new, lower value. Supporters said the plan would send a bolt of energy into the local housing market, but the mortgage industry, predictably, hated the plan and warned it would raise local borrowing costs sky high. The plan's future remains unclear.

Behind the scenes the Obama administration supported a plan by several state attorneys general, led by Iowa's, to make a deal with the nation's five largest mortgage servicers—Bank of America, JPMorgan Chase, Citigroup, Wells Fargo, and Ally Financial—whereby in exchange for settling claims of bank misbehavior (e.g., improper foreclosure), the banks would provide a fund large enough to reduce the mortgages of about 1 million homeowners by about $20,000 each. The advantage to the Obama administration here was that it was less politically exposed, since it was not itself orchestrating the deal or using taxpayer funds, yet there would clearly be a boost to the flagging housing market.

By June 2012 some observers were arguing that the housing market might be close to stabilizing. For example, while median home prices had fallen in Southern California from their peak of $505,000 in 2007 to $280,000 in March 2012, prices in Los Angeles City leveled off between February and March 2012 (Lazo 2012). By the end of 2012, it seemed clear that the housing market had stabilized and was even rising slowly. Still, the best estimates predicted a long, slow recovery in the absence of any aggressive measures to help the market.

THE STRUGGLE OVER BANK POWER: POPULISM, BONUS SCANDALS, AND REGULATORY REFORM (THE 2010 DODD-FRANK ACT)

The Bonus Scandals

The second drama likely to continue for years, in addition to the fate of struggling homeowners, was the fight over bank power. Although polls showed that popular anger at the banks was high throughout the crisis, it erupted in late 2008 over bonus scandals. These involved financial institutions that had been bailed out by the federal government but still paid multimillion dollar bonuses to their top personnel (e.g., figure 7.2 shows the data on bonuses). A stream of well-publicized scandals began in late 2008 just months after some of the major bailouts, and continued for at least two years, providing constant, new inflammatory material which helped ensure passage in mid-2010 of the Dodd-Frank Act.

The "bonus culture," in the hyper form into which it had developed, was fairly recent, dating from the early 1990s. At that time the IRS declared that any salary over $1 million could no longer be classified as part of a corporation's costs. So corporations moved to make increasingly large proportions of executive pay strictly "performance based" using measurable criteria. These could be included as part of the corporation's costs on the grounds that they were "bonuses" for adding extra value to the organization.

It was during the bonus-triggered frenzy of anti-bank sentiment in 2009 that President Obama, who had not been anti-banks or corporations during his candidacy but who was certainly following the polls, tapped into public outrage, famously calling bankers "fat cats," and in an Oval Office meeting with some of America's thirteen top bankers warning that his administration was "the only thing [standing] between you and the pitch forks" (Johnson and Kwak 2010). By January 2010, it was further clear to Obama's pollsters that to bolster his flagging political standing in the country he needed proposals to curb "Wall Street greed," which set the momentum for Dodd-Frank. Likewise during the same period New York State Attorney General Andrew Cuomo made growing outrage over the huge bonuses, combined with salvos against corrupt New York State politicians, the basis for his successful election as New York Governor in November 2010 (he had made an unsuccessful attempt in 2002). For example, in January 2010, he sent letters to eight of the nation's biggest banks—which were also TARP recipients—asking why they were giving bonuses and how their bonus structure related pay to performance. "Wall Street says we had a very profitable year," Cuomo wrote, "but that's not what 10 percent unemployment says.... Housing values are down and housing values are everything to the American economy. So where's the return on the taxpayer's dollar?" Stressing that New York State's Comptroller had found that Wall Street firms paid out $18.4 billion in cash bonuses in 2008 right after the financial system nearly collapsed, Cuomo proclaimed: "Compensation became un-moored from the financial performance of the banks. This year it's expected to be even higher, with some predicting bonuses approaching, if not eclipsing, boom-year levels." (See chapter 7 and figure 7.2, which shows that bonuses were paid even when banks made no profits and had been bailed out.)

Likewise in Washington, Phil Angelides, Chairman of the Congressional Financial Crisis Inquiry Commission, during testimony from the heads of Goldman Sachs, JPMorgan Chase, Morgan Stanley, and Bank of America in January 2010 criticized the bonuses: "People are angry. They have a right to be. Acts of God will happen. These were acts of men." Similarly, British Chancellor of the Exchequer, George Osborne, referring to Britain's comparable bonus scandals, commented in January 2012: "I always thought it was incredibly short-sighted, even stupid, of banks to pay bonuses in 2009 when taxpayers had only months earlier spent vast sums bailing them out and propping up the whole system" (Osborne 2012).

The bonus scandal facilitated Dodd-Frank in somewhat the same way as in the 1930s the Pecora hearings had facilitated Glass-Steagall. Glass-Steagall sailed through Congress in 1933 because during the entire time it was under consideration, Ferdinand Pecora, chief counsel of the Senate Banking Committee, was calling well-known bankers before the committee and exposing how they had abused their investment banking roles, sometimes to the point of criminality. Those hearings infuriated the country.[9] Glass-Steagall was hugely radical, ordering banks to get out of the securities/investment banking business, then their chief activity, and creating the Federal Deposit Insurance Corporation, which insured customer deposits for the first time (and which Republicans tended to view as "socialism," though after a sound defeat in the 1932 elections, they could not prevent it). As noted, Glass-Steagall had been repealed (finally) just a few years before the financial crisis and many commentators blame that repeal and other deregulation of banks and near or shadow banks for helping to bring on the crisis.

Dodd-Frank

Subtitled the "Wall Street Reform and Consumer Protection Act," the Dodd-Frank bill's 2,319 pages, passed by Congress in 2010, constituted the most sweeping change to financial regulation in the United States since the Great Depression. The bill's provisions were basically an attempt to deal with what its advocates believed were the main causes of the 2007–08 financial crisis and to remedy the perceived deficiencies of some solutions applied at that time. The Act was a massive victory for the financial industry's critics, with major measures to rein in the sector. Its array of powerful measures included:

- A Consumer Financial Protection Bureau that could autonomously write rules for consumer protections governing all financial institutions—banks and nonbanks.
- A requirement that regulators prohibit banks that have retail customers whose deposits are insured by the federal government from "proprietary trading" (i.e., investment banking), which deals in the bank's own money. The justification was that an institution with government-insured retail accounts/customers should not be put at risk if its investments fail. This was informally called "the Volcker Rule," after the former Federal Reserve Chairman who had strongly advocated for it.
- A requirement that large financial companies periodically submit plans ("living wills") for their orderly shutdown should they go under.
- A mechanism for the FDIC to liquidate failing, systemically significant financial companies, in an orderly process. Shareholders and unsecured creditors would bear the losses, management and culpable directors would be removed, taxpayers would bear no cost, and the government was first in line for repayment.
- A Financial Stability Oversight Council charged with identifying and responding to emerging risks throughout the financial system, including the monitoring of institutions deemed large enough to pose "systemic" risks should they fail.
- Authority for the SEC and CFTC to regulate over-the-counter derivatives, requiring central clearing and exchange trading for derivatives that can be cleared.
- Curtailing the "shadow" financial system by requiring hedge funds and private equity advisors to register with the SEC as investment advisers and provide information about their trades and portfolios.
- Creation of an Office of Credit Ratings at the SEC to examine Credit Rating Agencies at least once a year, and require them to disclose their methodologies, their use of third parties for due diligence efforts, and their ratings track record. Also, investors could bring private rights of action against ratings agencies for a knowing or reckless failure to conduct a reasonable investigation of the facts or to obtain analysis from an independent source.
- Regarding executive compensation, public companies are obliged to set policies to take back executive compensation if it was based on inaccurate financial statements that do not comply with accounting standards. Companies are also required to put proposed executive compensation levels to an (advisory) shareholder vote.

- Creation of a whistleblower program within the SEC to encourage people to report securities violations, with rewards of up to 30 percent of funds recovered for information provided.[10]

Minsky versus Greenspan on Stability

These measures more than reversed decades of deregulation and a core belief held by Greenspan and others that a modern capitalist economy is inherently stable, provided there is a competitive economy and a central bank that anchors inflation expectations, which are seen as the main risk to stability. The financial crisis had clearly disproved this view and instead vindicated Hyman Minsky (2008) who, in *Stabilizing an Unstable Economy*, argued that a modern capitalist economy is inherently unstable. Minsky claimed that periods of stability and prosperity sow the seeds of their downfall because leveraging of returns, principally by borrowing, gets to be viewed as a certain route to wealth. Those engaged in the financial system create, and profit greatly from, such leverage as people underestimate perils in good times, and leverage explodes. In the run-up to collapse, finance goes through three stages, from stable arrangements (which Minsky called "hedge"), in which interest and principal is repaid out of expected cash flow, to "speculative," in which interest is paid out of cash flow but debt needs to be rolled over, and finally to "Ponzi" in which both interest and principal need paying from capital gains.

Executive Compensation, the "Looting Problem," and Instability

The Dodd-Frank provision obliging corporations to set policies to take back executive compensation if based on inaccurate financial statements was an attempt, albeit modest, to address what has emerged as a key failing of contemporary capitalism's core institution, the limited liability corporation. Companies are vulnerable to the "looting problem" (as economists George Akerloff and Paul Romer have called it), whereby incentives such as share options and "bonus" payments, allegedly provided to align the interests of top employees with those of shareholders, create incentives to manipulate short-run corporate earnings at the expense of the long-term health, and even financial stability, of the company (Leonhardt 2009). Looking back Martin Taylor, the former chief executive of Barclays Bank, argued it was the bonus system that drove executives to "search for higher remuneration pools that led banks to expand their balance sheets, running risks with results from which we have all suffered" (Taylor 2012).

A related criticism argued that many investment strategies have the characteristics of a "Taleb distribution," which for any period or year has a high probability of a modest to large gain and a low probability of huge losses (Taleb 2007). In this context, if fund managers are paid a percentage of the annual profits, they will likely reap continual benefits for a considerable number of years until the low-probability event occurs, which it may eventually. At that point the huge losses will be borne by the bank and/or investors if this is a financial fund, or, far better from the latter's point of view, by taxpayers if the bank needs to be rescued by the government. The managers will have pocketed their steady previous gains already anyway (Wolf 2012).[11] In 2009 Federal Reserve chair Bernanke called for tougher regulation to deal with the "looting problem," stressing that, because the government is unwilling to let big, interconnected financial firms fail and people at those firms knew it, they engaged in "excessive risk-taking" (Leonhardt 2009). Harvard Law professor Lucian Bebchuk has gone much further than Dodd-Frank, arguing that bonuses should not be cashed right away, but placed in a company account for several years and adjusted downward if it turns out that the reasons for the bonus no longer hold up.

Others cautioned that no such simple remedy exists (Wolf 2012).[12] The corporation is the best institution we know of for running large, complex, and dynamic businesses. Clearly it is vital to encourage the creation of genuinely independent, diverse, and well-informed boards, and sensible to ensure that pay packages are transparent and incentives for destructive forms of remuneration are removed. But except in banks, where the public interest demands intervention in the incentives of management, governments should not intervene directly, by insisting on measures such as Bebchuk's.

Finance Briefly Reasserts Itself

Still, by the end of 2010 and six months after Dodd-Frank, virulent anti-bank talk had faded from the Obama administration's discourse. There were several reasons for this. Arguably, Dodd-Frank had partially leashed the banks that were, in turn, behaving less provocatively on salary and bonus issues—for a while CEO's of pivotal financial institutions took well-publicized salary cuts.

Also, the Democrats lost control of the House in the 2010 mid-term elections, and the Republicans were inclined to protect the banks prerogatives, so Washington's public attitude to the banks became far less hostile. The Obama administration, which had only turned anti-bank to keep in step with public outrage over the bonus scandals, now feared losing Wall Street financing for its political campaigns, especially for the 2012 presidential campaign. In a move clearly intended to signal conciliation, in January 2011, Obama appointed former JPMorgan Chase executive Bill Daley as his chief of staff.

Also, doubts and uncertainties emerged among experts and professionals about some key measures in Dodd-Frank. These measures were not discredited but it was unclear exactly how they would be implemented—Dodd-Frank set roughly a year for most of the details of the new legislation to be worked out by regulatory agencies, but some were set to take longer and by mid-2012 were still unfinished. In this context, the financial industry, especially the largest institutions, began to try to water down Dodd-Frank in a process that basically repeated the tactics applied in the first deregulation wave, drawing on the same two sources of power. First, direct lobbying of decision makers, accompanied by judicious use of campaign contributions. Second, talk of "regulatory arbitrage," especially the standard threat of taking the industry's jobs and status abroad.

A bevy of bank CEOs lectured the administration on "bank-bashing," with implicit threats to find and fund politicians less hostile to finance. By early 2010 bankers such as Jamie Dimon, the chief executive of JPMorgan Chase & Co., were publicly complaining about bashing banks for having caused the Great Recession. "Not all banks are the same and I just think that this constant refrain 'bankers, bankers, bankers' is unproductive and unfair," Dimon told a panel at the World Economic Forum, in Davos, in January 2010 (Cohan 2011).

When Obama came to New York in June 2011 to host a $33,000 per person fundraising dinner to court and reassure Wall Street that his administration was on its side, the heads or presidents of JPMorgan Chase (Jamie Dimon), Citigroup (Vikram Pandit), Blackstone, Morgan Stanley, and Goldman Sachs declined to attend. Dimon was also now publicly lobbying against the Federal Reserve's plan to raise capital requirements for major banks from 7 to 10 percent. In September 2010, the International Basel Committee on Banking Supervision—Basel III—set minimum capital ratios of 7 percent high-quality capital (common equity) to risk-weighted assets, with talk of a capital surcharge for the biggest banks.

Still, key parts of Dodd-Frank, if not most of it, seemed likely to take effect. For example, although opponents lobbied successfully to stop Elizabeth Warren from heading the new Consumer Financial Protection Agency, instead the White House nominated her capable deputy, Richard Cordray, and when Republicans in Congress tried to stall the nomination, Obama implemented it with a "recess" appointment while Congress was technically adjourned. By early 2012 the Consumer Financial Protection Agency was hard at work, for example, starting an inquiry into how banks levy penalty fees on customers who overdraw their accounts. Here the Agency was looking into whether, if customers made several financial commitments, some large and some small but which together constituted a negative balance, the banks first processed the larger transactions so as to maximize the number of subsequent transactions that carried overdraft penalties (Wyatt 2012).

Regarding the ban on proprietary trading by retail banks (the "Volcker Rule"), already by mid-2012 many banks had spun off their proprietary trading desks, that is, short-term gambling (though they can retain most "principal investments"—longer term investments in property or companies). US regulators had until mid-2012 to complete writing the details of the Volcker Rule and gave the banks an extension until 2014 to fully comply (Protess and Eavis 2012). The main lobbying by banks was confined, for now, to trying to modify parts of the Volcker Rule but not to repeal it. For example, at the World Economic Forum in Davos in January 2012, banks and foreign finance ministers complained repeatedly to Treasury Secretary Timothy Geithner about a Volcker Rule provision that said that US banks—and possibly certain foreign banks that do business in America—would be restricted in trading foreign government bonds (although not US government securities). The foreign finance ministers and bankers, led by the Japanese, Canadians, and Europeans, complained that this restriction would hamper the ability of their governments to sell bonds at favorable prices and would exacerbate the sovereign debt crisis in Europe by increasing borrowing costs of countries like Italy, Portugal, Spain, and even the United Kingdom and Canada.

Supporters of the rule, including Volcker himself, countered by pointing out that the outsize bet on foreign government bonds that the scandal-ridden MF Global took (see below) showed why the rule was needed. Volcker also expressed surprise at the opposition, given the well-known hostility by some European governments (especially the Germans and French) to speculative trading in the Eurozone. As he said: "What I've heard repeatedly out of European governments in the past is their concern about all this speculative activity in financial markets by hedge funds taking proprietary positions and destroying our own currency. Now...they want more speculative activity in their currencies" (Mackenzie 2012).

Some supporters of the Volcker Rule worried that it contained easily exploitable loopholes, such as a "market-making" rule that allowed commercial banks to purchase (risky) investments, provided they were doing so at the request of, and for, their customers; or provisions allowing banks to "hedge" their portfolios. How could banks be prevented from using these to actually engage in proprietary trading for their own accounts? The answer, as in so much of Dodd-Frank, was that much would depend on the quality of enforcement.

Back in September 2011, the United Kingdom's Independent Commission on Banking (the Vickers report), set up to recommend measures to prevent another crisis, had likewise made as its main proposal ringfencing retail banking from investment banking. Again the goal was to ensure that banks did not make bets with their own money but instead separated the "risky casino element of Wall Street from the utility role of helping finance the economy" (Sorkin 2012).

After Citi's stock had sunk by 20 percent in 2011, the following April, shareholders of Citigroup exercised their Dodd-Frank granted opportunity to cast an advisory vote on executive pay at least every three years and rejected a $15 million pay package for CEO Vikram Pandit as unmerited. The vote was widely publicized amid much speculation over the likely course of shareholder votes for other companies' CEOs. Other parts of Dodd-Frank were also having effects. George Soros, perhaps the best known hedge fund manager, closed his fund, unwilling to have it subject to Dodd-Frank required regulation. At least 60 percent of the current "over-the-counter" derivatives market was set to be centrally cleared. Banks with more than $50 billion of assets were deemed "systemically important" and were required to face more supervision and higher capital requirements.

Among the key Dodd-Frank related issues still unsettled by late 2012, perhaps the largest was whether authorities would, in the future, really wind down, in an orderly bankruptcy, a systemically important, failing institution as Dodd-Frank prescribed, rather than bail it out. The credit rating agency Standard & Poor's claimed there was still a good chance the government would choose a bail out. A senior Treasury official responded that it might take the failure of a financial institution to convince the skeptics.

A more general criticism was that Dodd-Frank changed so much of the structure of banking regulation that implementation risks were formidable. While true, there was not much to be done about that.

Another indicator of the difficulty of financial reform was that by the summer of 2011, mega financial crises in the United States and Europe had brewed whose proximate causes were political deadlock of the kind that few of Dodd-Frank's measures could avert. In the United States, Republicans (led by "Tea Party" types) who insisted that the growing public debt should be tackled by massive spending cuts and no tax increases, threatened not to raise the debt ceiling, a move which would have precipitated a government default and an unimaginable financial crisis. In Europe the German government of Chancellor Merkel, reflecting an important strand of German public opinion as mentioned, determined that Greece's debt crisis should only be resolved by imposing austerity on the Greeks for overspending and on investors for speculating. So for 22 months she stopped decisive intervention, permitting only minor measures. As a result, what started as a national debt crisis, morphed into a mega threat to the Eurozone and even the entire European Union by November 2011 and continues to be so at this writing.

Still, Dodd-Frank's reform momentum was helped by periodic financial scandals, which reminded the public and policymakers of the need for remedial measures, especially for the Volcker Rule separating commercial from investment/speculative banking. For example, in mid-September 2011, it emerged that a "rogue" trader at UBS, the giant Swiss Bank that almost collapsed during the 2008 crisis, had engaged in unauthorized trades, mostly in the last few months, causing $2.3 billion of losses to UBS. Martin Wolf (2011), chief economist of the *Financial Times* and member of the United Kingdom's Independent Commission on Banking that had a few days earlier, in the Vickers report, proposed ringfencing retail banking from investment banking, wrote: "Thank you UBS ... I could not have asked for a better illustration of the unregulatable risks to which investment banks are exposed.... No sane country can allow taxpayers to stand behind such risks. That is the kernel of the case for ring fencing of retail banking from investment banking."

A month later a US-based, widely publicized, financial scandal broke, replete with many of the worst features of those immediately preceding the 2007–08 crisis, such as crony capitalism, making money by assuming governments would bail out institutions "too big to fail," risk taking with other people's money, and engaging in behavior that looked plain illegal. This involved Jon Corzine, who had been cochair of Goldman Sachs from 1994 to 1999 and New Jersey Governor from 2005 to 2009. In 2010 Corzine became head of the brokerage firm MF Global and quickly drove it to a scandal-ridden collapse in October 2011, amid the disappearance of masses of clients' money (variously estimated from $600 million to $1.2 billion) after making huge bets on European sovereign debt and in particular that the governments of Italy, Spain, Portugal, and Ireland would not allow their bonds to default.

Then in May 2012 JPMorgan Chase's chief executive Jamie Dimon, who had been leading the criticism of key aspects of Dodd-Frank, especially the Volcker Rule, revealed that a trader at the UK-based unit of the bank, which others had long dubbed "the London whale" because of the size of his trades, had lost at least $2 billion in a debacle. The unit was supposedly not engaged in proprietary trading but in hedging the bank's portfolio against risk, and it was working with a mathematical model suggesting that 95 percent of the time the hedging activities could lose no more than $67 million. (So the Volcker Rule might not even have applied here.) Dimon had little choice amidst the uproar but to admit he had been "dead wrong" in denying the risk. Critics seized on the matter to reiterate the case for the Volcker Rule and even argue for tougher regulation (Partnoy 2012).

Then in June 2012 the Libor (London Interbank Offered Rate) scandal, the biggest of all, broke. Libor is a set of rates used to price hundreds of trillions of dollars of financial instruments worldwide. It is based on self-reported borrowing costs for unsecured loans between banks. It turned out that banks had been manipulating the rates that they reported, in order to gain financially. Barclays bank agreed to pay US and UK authorities $450 million to settle allegations that it had fixed Libor over several years, and a slew of government investigations threatened over twenty banks and inter-broker dealers. Also, aggrieved investors and individuals started to sue the banks. For example, in October 2012, five US homeowners filed a class action, whose plaintiffs could number 10,000, against traders at twelve of the largest banks in Europe and North America, including Bank of America, UBS, and Barclays. The plaintiffs claimed that the banks had manipulated Libor to set at a higher rate on the dates on which the homeowners' Libor Plus adjustable-rate mortgages were reset, complaining that Libor rose consistently on the first day of each month from 2000 to 2009 (Binham 2012). Overall, the Libor scandal assures a slew of lawsuits and huge costs for the banks over the next several years.

OCCUPY WALL STREET: SOCIAL AND POLITICAL INSTABILITY AND THE UNEXPECTED

By the fall of 2011 the struggle over bank power had again swung toward reform, as during the bank bonus scandal. As unemployment remained extremely high (9.1 percent nationwide, with unemployment far higher at 15.5 percent for those age 20–24), concern about social and political stability mounted, especially in the US's two largest cities. Riots in London, New York's financial twin, began on August 6, 2011, were a harbinger. Triggered by a march to protest the fatal shooting of a young man two days earlier by London police, the riots included not just protest but also looting, thuggish destruction, and arson at unprecedented levels for twentieth century Britain. They lasted for six days and occurred in several London districts, and spread to several cities in the Midlands and Northwest of the country. About 3,100 people were arrested, amid five deaths and an estimated £200 million in property damage.

Mayor Bloomberg in New York sensibly warned that similar trouble might occur in major US cities, given their high rates of youth unemployment. He did not elaborate, but was certainly aware that high levels of inequality added dangerously to the mix, with inequality in New York City the second highest among the twenty-five largest US cities (table 1.3). Trouble, when it came, did so in an unexpected form. The Occupy Wall Street protest was started by a Canadian online magazine, *Adbusters*, which mixed highly radical aims with more reformist ones. *Adbusters'* general aim was to "topple existing power structures and forge a major shift in the way we will live in the 21st century." Inspired by the Arab Spring movements and in particular by the occupation of Cairo's Tahrir Square that eventually led to the fall of Egyptian President Mubarak, *Adbusters* on July 13, 2011, urged its followers to likewise:

> ...use the tactic of seizing a public square of singular symbolic significance and put our asses on the line to make it happen. The time has come to deploy this emerging stratagem against the greatest corrupter of our democracy: **Wall Street, the**

financial Gomorrah of America, [with the goal of] propelling us toward the radical democracy of the future. On September 17, we want to see 20,000 people flood into lower Manhattan, set up tents, kitchens, peaceful barricades and occupy Wall Street for a few months.

Still, *Adbusters* combined this highly radical claim with a far more reformist one:

Once there [in Wall Street], we shall incessantly repeat one simple demand in a plurality of voices. We demand that Barack Obama ordain a Presidential Commission tasked with ending the influence money has over our representatives in Washington. It's time for **DEMOCRACY NOT CORPORATOCRACY**, we're doomed without it.

Presciently, *Adbusters* added:

This demand seems to capture the current national mood because cleaning up corruption in Washington is something all Americans, right and left, yearn for and can stand behind. If we hang in there, 20,000-strong, week after week...it would be impossible for Obama to ignore us. Our government would be forced to choose publicly between the will of the people and the lucre of the corporation.

This could be the beginning of a whole new social dynamic in America, a step beyond the Tea Party movement, where...we the people start getting what we want whether it be the dismantling of half the 1,000 military bases America has around the world to the reinstatement of the Glass-Steagall Act or a three strikes and you're out law for corporate criminals.

This initial call for action was spread via Twitter and Facebook. The protestors camped in downtown Manhattan for two weeks, attracting only minor attention until the unexpected intervened again: 700 Occupy Wall Street protestors marching across the Brooklyn Bridge. The police claimed the protestors had illegally taken to the road rather that sticking to the public footpath.

The mass arrests produced huge publicity that set the Occupy protest on the path to become a mass movement. Two weeks after the Brooklyn Bridge arrests, Occupy had spread to dozens of cities across the country, with protesters camped out in Los Angeles near City Hall, assembled before the Federal Reserve Bank in Chicago, and marching through downtown Boston to rally against corporate greed and unemployment. Within two months by mid-November the movement had expanded into over 1,500 towns and cities around the world.

A number of factors, both substantive and publicity-driven, explain Occupy's success. On the marketing side, "Occupy" was an effective instance of what is known as an umbrella brand name (Rawsthorn 2011). The key slogan "We are the 99 percent" was originally a reference to the growing concentration of personal wealth in the United States among the richest 1 percent of the population, but is applicable to any other country, too. The phrase also explains a complex economic concept clearly and persuasively. By christening its first camp "Occupy Wall Street," Adbusters adopted a customizable name whereby diverse other groups could instantly invent their own versions of "Occupy" in different locations—Occupy Paris, Occupy Poughkeepsie, and so on—still linking to the global movement with the first part of its name.[13] On the objective conditions side of Occupy's success, key issues in the original New York version—corporate greed, high student debt, ecological concerns, and the lack of jobs—resonated with actual problems in the city and around the nation (and world).

In New York, the protestors' camp in Zuccotti Park for two months was accepted by the city as more or less legal, since the park's owner and manager, Brookfield Office Management, had at the time of construction agreed with the city to make the park publicly accessible 24-hours a day (unlike a public park, which closes at night) in return for the right to construct taller buildings on the adjoining site. Then, after several mayors of other US cities had forcibly acted against the protestors in their cities, at 1:00 A.M. in the morning of November 15, 2011, the NYPD and NYC Sanitation Department, under Mayor Bloomberg's orders, forcibly removed the protestors and their tents and other belongings, claiming that the park needed cleaning. The protestors would be allowed to return later in the day, but not with tents, since the city was now arguing that camping in the park was illegal. So concerned was the city about popular sympathy for the protestors that almost no one in the police or sanitation department except those at the very top were told about the eviction plan until orders went out to implement it.

Although the Occupy Los Angeles counterparts were, by contrast, illegally camping outside City Hall in a park supposed to close to the public each night, reflecting the City of Los Angeles's more liberal political proclivities (as documented in chapter 4), Mayor Villaraigosa not only welcomed them but sometimes served the demonstrators breakfast. He also purchased 100 raincoats for them when the weather turned. Likewise the LA City Council passed a motion welcoming the protestors, and the City Council head told them they could stay as long as they wished.

Still, a week after Bloomberg had forcibly acted against the New York protestors, LA City officials also told its protestors they could not stay indefinitely. Yet, again reflecting LA mayors' generally liberal proclivities compared to New York's, the city offered the protestors a generous package of incentives to move, including a $1-a-year lease on a 10,000 square-foot office space near City Hall, land elsewhere for those who wished to farm, and additional housing for the homeless who had joined the camp (Linthicum 2011).

Carried-Interest Income, Mitt Romney, and the Tax Code Debate

Despite losing its physical camps, the Occupy movement had a clear impact on the mainstream political environment.[14] For example, in November Mayor Bloomberg went to Washington, DC, and told the liberal Center for American Progress that he believed, in this general economic climate, "All sides have to be willing to give on something." In that spirit he joined those proposing to correct the "carried-interest" tax provision, which benefits finance fund managers apparently unfairly.

"Carried-interest" works as follows. Under current IRS rules, fund managers get paid in two main ways. First, they receive a management fee, which is a percentage (often 2 percent) of the total assets under management. This is usually taxed at regular income tax rates for wages and salaries, which for the highest brackets is 35 percent. Second, fund managers are paid "carried-interest" or "deal-carry," which is a percentage, usually 20 percent, of the fund's annual profits and is taxed lightly as long-term capital gains at 15 percent, and it is the main way that hedge fund and other financial fund managers amass great wealth. For example, if a fund goes from $100 million to $200 million in a year, then management get usually 20 percent of the increase (and by agreement with clients), which would amount to $20 million and just $3 million in taxes.

Bloomberg echoing many commentators and economists said that "carried-interest" income should instead be subjected to the regular income-tax rate. While this view clearly had merit as a move toward greater fairness and even support among many financial people, it is unlikely that Bloomberg would have publicly taken this view before Occupy Wall Street began.

The unfairness of taxing "carried-interest" income reached the center-stage of American politics in January 2012 during Mitt Romney's campaign for the Republican nomination. His party rivals stressed that most of Romney's income, originally derived from Bain Capital, the private equity firm he left in 1999 but from which he still derived income, was lightly taxed at just 15 percent. Public discussion also now turned to wondering why the capital gains tax, at 15 percent, was so low. It had dropped considerably since under Reagan in 1986, when it was set at the same level as the rates on ordinary income like salaries and wages, with a maximum of 28 percent for both. But the link was dropped under George Bush Sr. and then the rates on capital gains and dividends under Clinton were lowered to a maximum of 15 percent, less than half the now 35 percent top rate on ordinary income. Some economists claimed the cuts stimulated economic growth and were necessary to keep capital from fleeing the United States to lower-tax countries. But the nonpartisan Congressional Research Service issued a report in 2011 arguing that tax cuts on capital gains did little for job creation and just reduce federal revenue (Kocieniewski 2012).

The Obama administration, now tacking to the left again, announced the departure of his chief of staff and former JPMorgan Chase executive, Bill Daley (Luce 2011). By January 2012 a poll by the Pew Research Center showed that 66 percent of all respondents believed there were "strong conflicts between rich and poor" in the United States, a 19 percent increase compared with 2009 and higher than the 62 percent who believed there were "strong conflicts between immigrants and native-born," and the 38 percent who believed there were "strong conflicts between blacks and whites." This too seemed a clear sign that the Occupy Wall Street's concern about income inequality was spreading (Tavernise 2012). Likewise a survey of attendees at the January 2012 Davos World Economic Forum showed that "income disparity" topped the list of issues they thought would most threaten global stability in the coming year, a startling change since income disparity had never even appeared on the list before (Tett 2012b). Overall, while Occupy Wall Street has made a major impact, by late 2012 it had petered out as an ongoing movement.

CONCLUSION

What is certain about the aftermath of the financial crisis is the persistence of several major uncertainties, especially regarding two key policy themes stressed here—helping the housing market and struggling homeowners, and trying to rein in and reform the banks. The fate of homeowners in danger of losing their residences remains bleak. As the housing market continues to be sluggish, an economic case for stronger measures to help remains. The two major themes—bank power and the plight of homeowners—converge here since a major obstacle to mortgage principal reduction is the unwillingness to apply it without the agreement of the banks holding and servicing the loan in each case, with the banks lobbying heavily against many such attempts. Important too is a third major theme—the role of public opinion. Fear of being criticized for misusing tax payer funds has clearly for several years constrained the Obama administration from strongly advocating widespread principal reduction. That raises the fourth theme of whether more skillful leadership could creatively handle public opinion here.

On the bank/financial side, Dodd-Frank is likely here to stay although details of many key rules for implementing it are unsettled at this writing. Dodd-Frank does address the realization that capitalist economies are inherently unstable (tending to excessive leverage in apparently good times), and the related problem that politicians and regulators tend to act pro-cyclically (e.g., increasing government spending in good times without setting aside "rainy day" funds). Dodd-Frank does this with measures such as the Financial Stability Oversight Council, "the Volcker Rule," the requirement that large financial companies periodically submit their own "living wills," authority for the SEC and CFTC to regulate over-the-counter derivatives, measures curtailing the "shadow" financial system by requiring hedge funds and private equity advisors to register with the SEC, and the creation of an Office of Credit Ratings at the SEC to examine credit rating agencies at least once a year. Still, how the rules are implemented will be particularly important for Dodd-Frank.

Also, many problems still remain, especially those that came to the forefront in the second wave of criticism in late 2011 and 2012. These include inequality and the tax system, job creation, issues regarding the current phase of "globalization," public goods, and the role of money in politics.

Inequality

On inequality, as the Organisation for Economic Co-operation and Development showed in a recent report, high-income countries have seen large rises in inequality over the past three decades. The rise in inequality is the result of complex forces: globalization and the increasing mobility of capital, technological change, changes in social norms over pay, shifts in taxation, and especially in the United States, the reduced bargaining power of labor resulting from lower unionization of the labor force exacerbated by high unemployment (Hacker and Pierson 2010).

Many of these changes, perhaps, were irresistible and irreversible. But the level and increase in inequality does vary across countries, which suggests that economic structures and policies do alter outcomes. The United States and United Kingdom, for example, have seen far faster rises in the real incomes of the top decile than of the bottom decile of household income distribution since the 1980s. In France, income growth followed the opposite pattern. The United States and United Kingdom, of course, have very large financial sectors—The City in London and New York's Wall Street.

To the claims of some that inequality is not important, there are two powerful responses. The first is that it is politically salient. Second, inequality of outcome has a strong bearing on equality of opportunity, about which many more do care. It is harder for children who grow up in deprivation to obtain a decent start in life than those brought up in happier conditions, especially if parents cannot find remunerative jobs and young people cannot hope to do so in the future. Stiglitz's (2012) *The Price of Inequality: How Today's Divided Society Endangers Our Future,* sees inequality as crippling to society in these very ways.

What are the answers? Among them should be major efforts to improve the quality of education and childcare for all, including public financing of access to higher education; a determination to sustain demand more effectively in severe downturns; some subsidization or direct provision of jobs; some fiscal redistribution from the winners to the losers and particularly to the children of the losers; and at least the maintenance of current limits on the ability to pass massive amounts of resources from generation to generation (recent changes to the tax code are making such transfers easier[15]).

Plutocracy and Super-PACs

Finally, a long-standing concern is protecting democratic politics from plutocracy and the ability of the wealthy to unduly influence and corrupt the political process. The solution, long known, is to regulate the use of money in elections. Yet in 2010 the US Supreme Court dealt reform efforts a huge setback with its decision in the Citizens United Case, which upended campaign finance laws that limited the amount of money that could be spent in political campaigns. Ruling that unions and corporations have a right to "free speech," the Court allowed the creation of "'super-Political action committees," which can raise and spend unlimited amounts of money so long as they do not formally coordinate their activities with the candidates' campaigns. This gives huge potential power to individual rich donors, as well as to large organizations like unions. By early 2012 the Republican presidential primaries had shown the power of super-PACs to sway voters, as massive injections of their money into negative advertising within days erased candidate leads in particular elections (McGregor and Dunbar 2012). Despite Super PAC money, Republican presidential candidate Romney failed to unseat President Obama. In part that was because Obama too raised and spent comparably huge funds, helping to make the 2012 presidential campaign the most expensive race ever for both political parties.

NOTES

1. The other "anti-deficiency" states are Alaska, Arizona, Arkansas, Colorado, District of Columbia (Washington, DC), Georgia, Hawaii, Idaho, Mississippi, Missouri, Montana, Nevada, New Hampshire, Oregon, Tennessee, Texas, Virginia, Washington, and West Virginia. There are variations among these states over exactly how "anti-deficiency" legislation works.
2. Both these stories were told to Halle, and such anecdotes and examples became rife throughout the media coverage of the crisis.
3. The data are based on studies by economists Thomas Philippon and Ariell Reshef.
4. This section draws on several accounts including Lewis (2010), Financial Crisis Inquiry Commission (2011), Sorkin (2009), and Reinhart and Rogoff (2009).
5. The entire ten, in size order, were: Barclays (UK) $232 billion, Bank of America $212 billion, Bank of Scotland (UK) $181 billion, Wells Fargo $154 billion, Wachovia $147 billion, SocGen (France) $124 billion, Dresdner (Germany) $123 billion, Royal Bank of Scotland (UK) $117 billion, Bayern (Germany) $108 billion, and Dexia (Belgium) $105 billion (Harding and Braithwaite 2010).
6. This $24 billion asset detoxification plan was requested by Federal Deposit Insurance Corporation Chair Sheila Bair, but, as mentioned, the Treasury did not use the provision.
7. The New York Partnership (a business trade group formerly the New York Chamber of Commerce), was telling the Obama administration in late 2008 to fix housing, for example, by offering principal reduction. HAMP aims to reduce payments by paying mortgage servicers, homeowners, and investors for successful loan modifications. The initiative has been dogged by inadequate servicing practices by the companies that dominate the US mortgage market. In response, the Treasury recently began withholding payments to Wells Fargo, Bank of America (BofA), and JPMorgan Chase, the three biggest servicers who collectively process nearly half of all home loans. All three needed "substantial improvement," the agency said in June. Wells Fargo has since improved its practices and will receive about $21 million in withheld payments, the Treasury said. But BofA and JPMorgan Chase again failed to meet benchmarks and the department will continue to withhold about $18 million from BofA and $28 million from JPMorgan Chase.
8. Roubini said these "Contingent Principal-Reductions" should only be available for homes with mortgages that cumulatively—that is, with first and second mortgages combined—exceed 110 percent of the home's market value.
9. The House and Senate did not even bother with a roll-call vote for final passage of Glass-Steagall, which flew through on a voice vote (Nocera 2011a).
10. For a discussion of the Whistleblower provision in Dodd-Frank, see Hornblower (2011).
11. Wolf cites work by economists Dean Foster, the Wharton School, and Peyton Young, Oxford University.
12. The text discussion of reforms draws heavily from Wolf (2012).
13. Occupy activists in the feisty Scottish city of Glasgow opted for a sentimental series of symbols for their site, including flowers, a heart, a rainbow, and the slogan "Occupy Glasgow Nicely."
14. The best demographic study of supporters of the Occupy movement was based on an online survey, conducted in four waves, of 18,500 visitors to the occupy Wall Street site—occupywallstreet.org—conducted by Hector Cordero between October 9 and November 17, 2011. It turned out that site visitors were, compared with the

population overall, somewhat younger, better educated, and, for their level of educa-tion, underpaid or underemployed (Cordero 2011).

15. Former *New York Times* reporter and now journalism professor, David Cay Johnson's (2005) *Perfectly Legal: The Covert Campaign to Rig Our Tax System to Benefit the Super Rich—and Cheat Everybody Else* argues that many of the changes in the tax code are setting the stage for an inherited class system, which would transform the society in ways that would institutionalize inherited inequality.

CHAPTER 7

New York City and Los Angeles

Taxes, Budgets, and Managing the Financial Crisis

GEORGE SWEETING AND ANDREA DINNEEN

NEW YORK CITY AND LOS ANGELES: HANDLING THE 2008 GREAT RECESSION

The Great Recession seriously exacerbated the long-running fiscal difficulties faced by many American state and local governments, including in these two cities. While state governments play an important role in how crises are addressed, ultimately each local political system must find its own way to keep the lights on, the streets safe, and city services functioning. Given the differences between New York City and Los Angeles in electoral demographics, government institutions, and local political cultures, it is perhaps no surprise that the two cities have experienced and dealt with their fiscal crises somewhat differently.

Both New York City Mayor Michael Bloomberg and Los Angeles Mayor Antonio Villaraigosa have been creative and effective leaders during the crisis. Still, New York City has, so far, fared somewhat better than the City of Los Angeles for several reasons, which we detail in this chapter. Here we mention just two. First, historical legacy: Proposition 13, which passed in 1978, saddled the State of California and its localities with a restricted ability to tax, which had major, negative ramifications for Los Angeles. By contrast, New York City's 1975 near-bankruptcy experience left, as part of its legacy, a cautious fiscal orientation involving not only the attitudes of key policy leaders but also some legally mandated budgetary practices, which served the city well in the recent economic climate. A second key reason New York has fared better than Los Angeles is how the federal government responded to the financial crisis. The Federal Reserve's monetary policy and various asset purchase programs have kept costs in the financial industry, New York's leading industry, low and helped to clean up balance sheets. In addition, the Treasury's $700 billion Troubled Asset

Relief Program (TARP) helped stabilize the financial sector by injecting capital into banks and other financial firms, including AIG, which had made disastrous bets on credit default swaps for mortgage-backed securities. By contrast, the federal government has given only modest help to the struggling housing market, which has been a drag on the economy of Los Angeles, as well as much of the United States.

FISCAL STRUCTURE MATTERS

There are important differences in the scope of the budgets directly under the control of the Mayor of Los Angeles and the Mayor of New York. In turn, these differences influence the types of taxes used by the two cities, their overlapping jurisdictions, and the state governments. Given these differences, comparisons of budget politics by the elected leadership of the two cities need to consider the differences in the institutional scope of the two municipalities. The Los Angeles City government proper is responsible for public safety, sanitation, and other local public services. Social services and much of transportation policy are financed at the county level. There is also a separate school district with its own taxing power and independent board and budget. In contrast, New York City government encompasses all local services including education, social services, and transportation other than mass transit. In both cities there are also overlapping regional transportation authorities, again with independent boards and budgets, which have primary responsibility for public transportation. Another difference is that New York City and all other localities in New York State bear a much larger share of the nonfederal cost of Medicaid and public assistance than in other states. California requires the second highest local share of these costs after New York, but the difference is wide: 16 percent of the total cost in New York and 2.5 percent in California (Citizens Budget Commission 2011).

A study comparing overall tax effort in the nine largest cities in the United States, taking into account the differences in fiscal responsibilities of overlapping governments using data from 2003–04, found that tax effort in New York City was higher than in any of the other cities, and 70 percent higher than the average of the other eight. Los Angeles ranked third (Belkin and Beiseitov 2007). There have been important changes in state fiscal policies in both New York and California in the intervening years. Nevertheless, the results provide a means of comparing the fiscal regimes that the two cities operate under.

The extent of the differences in government structure between the two cities can be gleaned from table 7.1, which compares the tax effort extracted by each level of government (taxes per $100 of "gross taxable resources," which measures the earnings of households and businesses in each of the cities). Taxes not exported are those that fall on local households and businesses. The exported taxes are those such as hotel taxes and commuter taxes that are directly imposed on households and businesses outside the city. Note that whether we look at the city-only level, the combined local level (which takes overlapping jurisdictions into account), or the total for all levels of government, the tax effort in New York City is much higher than in Los Angeles, with the overall effort roughly one-third higher in Gotham.

Table 7.1 TAXES PER $100 GROSS TAXABLE RESOURCES OF DIRECT AND OVERLAPPING GOVERNMENTS, 2003–2004

Level of Government	Los Angeles			New York		
	Non Exported	Exported	Total	Non Exported	Exported	Total
City	0.92	0.06	0.98	5.46	0.07	5.53
County	1.83	0.01	1.84	0.00	0.00	0.00
School	0.11	0.00	0.11	0.00	0.00	0.00
Other Local	0.01	0.00	0.01	0.14	0.00	0.14
Total Local	2.87	0.07	2.94	5.60	0.07	5.67
State	4.00	0.16	4.16	3.39	0.40	3.80
Total	6.87	0.23	7.10	9.00	0.47	9.47

Source: Belkin and Beiseitov 2007.

In New York City, where the counties and school district are part of the municipal government, the city government commands about 61 percent of nonexported effort and 58 percent of the total effort supporting state and local services. By comparison, the Los Angeles City government is responsible for a much smaller share of the total tax effort extracted from the city (13 percent nonexported and 14 percent total), while the County of Los Angeles extracts 27 percent of the nonexported and 26 percent of the total. Thus, even when combining the effort by all of the local levels of government, New York's local share of the total local plus state effort is 60 percent, compared to only 41 percent in Los Angeles. Sacramento and Albany account for the balance, with Sacramento's share of the total higher than Albany's (59 percent versus 40 percent).

These differences suggest that municipal fiscal policy plays a larger role in local politics in New York. With a much higher tax effort supporting a more expensive, and arguably more extensive, set of government services, decisions about what to tax, how much to tax, and what areas should be spending priorities often generate battles at the local level that are more commonly waged at the state level in other jurisdictions where local government is more diffuse and taxing power is relatively weak. It also means that perceived fiscal competence matters a great deal in mayoral politics in New York.

Table 7.2 compares the mix of taxes each of the cities used in the 2006–07 fiscal year before the financial crisis. The revenue amounts in the table exclude state and federal grants so that we are only looking at revenues raised by the cities using taxes, fees, fines, permits, charges, and so on. Los Angeles is able to use transfers from various reserve funds, which are reported on the transfer line in the table. New York is required to use different accounting rules that prevent the use of such transfers. Another difference in the accounting between the two cities is Los Angeles's heavy reliance on dedicated fees to fund specific services, reported as "Special Receipts" in the table. New York provides virtually all of its services directly from the general fund.

Table 7.2 LOS ANGELES AND NEW YORK CITY REVENUE SOURCES (EXCLUDING STATE AND FEDERAL GRANTS), 2006–2007 (DOLLARS IN MILLIONS)

Revenue Source	Los Angeles			New York		
	Revenue	% of Taxes	% of City Revenue	Revenue	% of Taxes	% of City Revenue
Property Tax	$1,334.2	42.4%	21.2%	$13,122.8	34.7%	31.2%
Sales Tax	333.9	10.6%	5.3%	4,644.5	12.3%	11.0%
Business Income Tax	464.3	14.8%	7.4%	6,994.2	18.5%	16.6%
Transfer Tax	188.1	6.0%	3.0%	1,726.2	4.6%	4.1%
Hotel Tax	134.6	4.3%	2.1%	330.1	0.9%	0.8%
Personal Income Tax	0.0	0.0%	0.0%	8,052.1	21.3%	19.1%
Utility Users Tax	605.3	19.3%	9.6%	0.0	0.0%	0.0%
Utility Gross Receipts	0.0	0.0%	0.0%	368.1	1.0%	0.9%
Other Taxes	82.7	2.6%	1.3%	2,603.7	6.9%	6.2%
Total Taxes	**$3,143.0**		**49.9%**	**$37,841.9**		**89.8%**
Miscellaneous Revenues	814.1		12.9%	4,278.4		10.2%
Transfers from other Funds	425.8		6.8%			0.0%
Special Receipts	1,913.9		30.4%			0.0%
Total City Revenue	**$6,296.8**			**$42,120.2**		

Sources: Comptroller of the City of Los Angeles, Annual Financial Report for Fiscal Year 2006–07; Comptroller of the City of New York, Comprehensive Financial Report for Fiscal Year 2006–07.

Because of the accounting differences, the "Total City Revenues" amount reported for each city may not be exactly comparable, although they should be pretty close.

The property tax is traditionally the main tax source used to finance K–12 education and other local services. Not only is it stable, but with property values correlated with the quality of local services, there is logic in relying on the tax to fund them. In the case of Los Angeles and the rest of California, Proposition 13 (see below) has broken that relationship and the tax is now largely controlled by the state. Although Los Angeles, like other local governments in California, is constrained in determining property tax policy, the tax is still the city's largest tax source. In 2006–07, property tax revenue was 42.4 percent of tax revenues and 21.2 percent of all city revenues.

In New York City, with county and school district functions folded into the general city budget, the property tax is also the single largest revenue source for the city. It accounted for 34.7 percent of tax revenue in 2006–07 (31.2 percent of all city revenues), although the share varies significantly year to year, depending on how other, more volatile taxes are doing.

Among the nine large cities in the 2003–04 tax effort comparison study, New York and Los Angeles ranked second and third lowest in their reliance on the property tax. Only Philadelphia, which relies heavily on a wage tax for local revenues, was less reliant on the property tax.

The sales tax is usually another source of significant revenue for state and local governments other than school districts. For Los Angeles, it was about 5.3 percent of the city's revenues in 2006–07, compared to 11.0 percent in New York. Because the county and state governments also make heavy use of the sales tax, the share of total tax effort attributable to the sales tax in Los Angeles is probably higher—measured by tax effort in 2003–04, the total was nearly 24 percent, compared to 16 percent in New York. While less volatile than income taxes, sales tax revenues are still strongly correlated with the state of the economy.

Business income taxes are a highly volatile revenue source used by both cities, although Los Angeles's reliance on these taxes has been diminishing as the city has enacted a number of business tax cuts. In 2006–07, business income taxes accounted for 7.4 percent of LA city revenues, while they amounted to 16.6 percent in New York City (18.5 percent of tax revenue alone). In both cities, the state governments impose their own business taxes as well so that the burden on local businesses is quite high.

New York City is an outlier among large cities in having a personal income tax; Los Angeles does not use it. In most years it is New York's second largest single revenue source, although its share varies widely in some years due to the high volatility of the tax base (personal income). In 2006–07 as incomes were still soaring, particularly on Wall Street, New York City received 19.1 percent of city revenues from the income tax (21.3 percent of tax revenues). New York State is also extremely dependent on its own statewide income tax. Measured by tax effort, over 50 percent of total state tax effort extracted from New York City in 2003–04 is attributable to this tax (a higher share of state tax effort than California extracted in Los Angeles with its income tax).

Los Angeles relies heavily on the Utility Users Tax, which accounted for 14 percent of general fund revenues in 2006–07. The tax is an excise tax levied on phone, gas, and electricity bills. Utility usage can vary in response to economic conditions, particularly by business customers who may cut back or simply go out of business. New York has a far smaller utility tax that is a gross receipts tax on utility companies themselves. It accounted for less than 1 percent of city revenues.

Two other taxes that are used by both cities are also quite sensitive to the business cycle. Each imposes an extra excise tax on hotel stays (the Transient Occupancy Tax in Los Angeles and the Hotel Occupancy Tax in New York City). With most hotel guests coming from outside the city, the burden of hotel taxes is largely exported to nonresidents. With tourism affected not only by the state of the US economy but also by economic conditions in potential foreign visitors' home countries, there can be great variability in revenue from such taxes. The Document Transfer Tax in Los Angeles and the Real Property Transfer Tax in New York City depend on the volume and value of real estate transactions. During the real estate boom, these taxes grew greatly in their significance; in 2006–07 they accounted for 3.0 percent of LA city revenues and 4.1 percent in New York City. With the collapse of the real estate bubble after 2006, revenue from these tax sources has also shriveled.

Thus, when these cities experienced the economic downturn, the impacts on the city budgets differed because of the taxes each city employs and how sensitive those taxes are to the business cycle. As these cities have complex relationships with other levels of governments, the differences in tax mix for those other governments also matter.

LOS ANGELES

In Los Angeles, the fiscal crisis hit the city early, toward the end of 2007. The local housing market peaked in 2006 and construction employment in Los Angeles County started to fall on a year-over-year basis in August 2007; as the drag increased, overall employment began to decline (again on a year-over-year basis) in January 2008. When the City Administrative Office released its mid-year fiscal report, Los Angeles found itself facing a $154.9 million budget gap for the current 2007–08 budget, almost 2.3 percent of the total budget at adoption and three times larger than the gap the city had covered in the 2006–07 fiscal year (see table 7.3). In fact, the 2007–08 budget gap approached the size of the city's entire "rainy day" reserves of $192 million built up for fiscal emergencies. Los Angeles's budget immediately spiraled out of control as the national recession worsened, whereas New York City did not experience significant fiscal stress until the 2008–09 fiscal year, when the national recession and housing market collapse finally undermined the financial markets,

Three main factors drove this quick descent into crisis. For one, when the housing bubble burst, the LA economy was heavily tied to related industries like real estate, construction, and mortgage lending. For example, seven of the top 10 US lenders making "subprime loans" between 2005 and 2007 were located in Orange or Los Angeles County, as detailed in chapter 6, and nearly 4 percent of the LA metropolitan labor force was employed in construction (Employment Development Department 2012).

Any city similarly concentrated in the housing industry would have experienced fiscal strain but Los Angeles's problems were worsened by the relatively small share of the city's revenues coming from the property tax, usually the stalwart of local government finances, leaving the city relatively more reliant on more volatile tax sources. (Note that the Los Angeles School District and Los Angeles County rely heavily on the property tax to finance their services.) The LA city government had drawn 54.9 percent of its tax revenue and 27.4 percent of its city revenue from the general sales, utility user, business income, hotel, and transfer taxes in 2007—five sources that are highly "pro-cyclical" (i.e., sensitive to downturns). In contrast to property values, which often take time to change, people in a recession tend to reduce their consumption, business spending and profits fall, and tourism drops. With the downturn centered in real estate, the collapse also brought a decline in transfer tax revenue. By 2011, when the recession's impact on tax revenues was at its deepest in Los Angeles, these five taxes had fallen by a collective $148 million (8.6 percent) and their share of total city revenues were down to 24.3 percent. Over the same period, the property tax had grown by 7.5 percent. (Because New York City

Table 7.3 CITY OF LOS ANGELES YEARLY ADOPTED OPERATING BUDGET AND MID-YEAR
SURPLUS OR DEFICIT, FY2001–11 (DOLLARS IN MILLIONS)

	Total General City Adopted Budget	Mid-Year City Wide (Deficit)/ Surplus	Mid-Year Gap as percent of total budget
2001–02	$4,854.10		
2002–03	$4,827.10		
2003–04	$5,163.40	Data not available	
2004–05	$5,388.10		
2005–06	$5,985.27		
2006–07	$6,673.21	$(41.30)	–0.62%
2007–08	$6,817.68	$(154.90)	–2.27%
2008–09	$7,113.12	$(100.60)	–1.41%
2009–10	$6,884.80	$(208.50)	–3.03%
2010–11	$6,749.23	$(62.70)	–0.93%
2011–12	$6,871.56	$(72.00)	–1.05%

Source: LA City Administrative Office, Annual Budget Summary, 2012.

also relies on the even more pro-cyclical personal income tax, Gotham's tax system has an even greater exposure to pro-cyclical taxes, which accounted for 51.6 percent of city revenues in 2006–07.)

A key reason why local governments in California have been forced to rely on more volatile taxes rather than the property tax, is Proposition 13, the ballot initiative sponsored by anti-tax crusader Howard Jarvis and passed in 1978 that capped local property tax rates for existing owners, undermined localities' fiscal autonomy, and prevented them from reaping the full fiscal benefits of California's real property boom—at least through the property tax. The local property tax is traditionally cited as the least popular and least fair tax. In part this is due to how it is collected. Rather than withheld throughout the year like the income tax or collected in modest amounts with individual retail transactions, property owners are presented with a significant, annual bill directly from the government. It is commonly referred to—incorrectly—as regressive, although poorly administered property taxes can be quite uneven and discriminatory in their application. One problem that plagues the property tax is when rapid appreciation drives up assessments, threatening existing homeowners with significant tax increases even if their incomes have not seen corresponding gains. Of course, localities have the option to lower rates in such situations and thereby hold down increases in the tax burden, but few governments can resist the alternative of using the higher revenues to support increased spending. Proposition 13 emerged from a period of rapid price appreciation and corresponding tax increases, and anxious homeowners responded to the appeal of capping the increases. Proposition 13 not only reduced property taxes—a central issue for voters then—but it also made California's property tax much less fair. Property would be taxed based on how long someone had owned their home, rather than simply by its market value. As a result, two similar, adjacent houses could have vastly different tax bills.

New York City's property tax was not subject to an across the board cap as in Proposition 13, but there was a major overhaul of the city's property tax system at about the same time in 1981. While the NYC system includes provisions that phase in annual changes in assessments over a number of years, there is still room for revenues to grow significantly. With a pipeline of deferred assessment increases waiting to be phased-in, the NYC property tax is even more stable than others, helping to smooth out downturns.

Los Angeles's early budget tailspin as the financial crisis worsened was also driven by the inability of the California state government to overcome political and constitutional limitations on its budget process and resolve its own fiscal problems. For the state and its local governments, Proposition 13 shifted control over the remaining property tax to Sacramento, transferring more governing power and financial burden to the state. Another major challenge imposed by Proposition13 is the requirement of a two-thirds majority vote for legislative passage of a tax increase.

With Republicans in California, as nationwide, becoming united in opposition to higher taxes, the state was unable to raise substantial new revenue to balance its budget. In fact, in 2009, facing billion dollar deficits, California even redirected an estimated $113 million in city property tax revenues to cover its own operating costs and has yet to repay localities for these foregone revenues (Los Angeles City Administrative Officer 2009). Hence, not only did city governments like Los Angeles see a reduction in state aid, but they actually saw some of their revenues redirected to fix state-level budget problems. By the end of 2011, a frustrated Governor Brown decided that Republicans in the State Legislature would never agree to any budget with higher taxes, and he organized a campaign for a measure to that effect on the November 2012 ballot.

Californians then approved two tax proposals to address the State's $15.7 billion budget shortfall, a quarter-cent sales tax increase and a tax increase for high income households, creating new tax brackets and higher rates at thresholds of $350,000, $500,000, and $1,000,000. Further, voters gave Democrats in the State legislature a two-thirds majority, the "super-majority" needed to enact tax increases under Proposition 13. These changes have the potential to ease fiscal pressures on local governments across California, although they offered no immediate direct help to the City of Los Angeles, which continues to face budget difficulties.

In addition to budgeting limits due to Proposition 13, California as a state must deal with two other major structural problems (Kogan 2011). First, it has a pro-cyclical revenue system. Its income tax is highly progressive, and (unlike the federal government) it taxes capital gains and dividends at the same rate as earned income. So when the economy is doing well, wealthy people pay a lot; in some years the top 1 percent of California taxpayers contribute half the state's income tax revenue. The New York City income tax and New York State income tax also share these features. In New York City, during the boom year of 2007, the top 1 percent of taxpayers accounted for 58 percent of the city's income tax liability (Jacobs 2011). When the economy and stock market are doing poorly, capital gains realizations and bonus income fall rapidly, so that high-income households owe less tax—often a lot less. Broad-based job losses add to the income tax shortfall, leaving the state facing deficits that can be a billion dollars or more. Unless California chooses a less progressive income tax (which polls show the vast majority of voters do not want), broadens its array of tax sources to include less cyclically sensitive revenues, establishes effective spending limits, or develops a more comprehensive "rainy day" mechanism, this will continue to be a problem. In practice, these options are very difficult to implement due to the time inconsistency problem. In good times there is little sense of urgency to spend less. During bad years, the two-thirds vote requirement for raising taxes (and, until recently, passing budgets) makes it very hard to take corrective action.

A second key exacerbating issue in California and to a lesser extent in New York is public pension financing. Since the 1980s, pension fund assets have been increasingly invested in the stock market, making earnings more volatile. During good years, the rapid growth in fund values can tempt government to cut back on employer contributions (which some local governments, like San Diego, did) or to give retroactive benefit increases (which is what both state legislatures have done at times). During bad years, investment earnings shrink, and the employer contribution needed to maintain the actuarial balance goes up, leaving some governments unable or unwilling to pay the full amount due, which increases the unfunded liability. Even though the actuarially determined employer contribution is usually calculated with lags to help smooth out year-to-year swings in valuations, the system has a pro-cyclical bias: during good years, when the state/local governments have more revenue, they often pay the least into pensions, and during bad years, when the state and local governments have less revenue, they often face a call for greater employer contributions.

Villaraigosa has been inventive in the face of LA budget issues, as the previous chapter mentioned. He has also involved himself actively in budget and planning for the broader region. The City of Los Angeles has little fiscal responsibility for public transportation, which lies instead with a regional Metropolitan Transportation Authority (MTA). However, the Mayor of Los Angeles exercises considerable sway over the MTA in his role on the board. Villaraigosa has used this role to advocate effectively for transit development and the financing to help make it possible. In 2008, Villaraigosa led a countywide campaign to pass a half-cent sales tax increase to pay for mass transportation ("Measure R" transit tax). He then developed a "30–10" plan to make use of a federal bridge loan—this proposal calls for borrowing from the federal government over ten years the total amount expected to be raised and repaid over thirty years from the sales tax authorized by LA County voters in 2008. With this money the MTA could complete transit and highway projects (such as the Westside subway and the Green Line/LAX extension) in ten years instead of thirty. The proposal was widely heralded by transportation experts. (See figure 7.1.)

In contrast, the Mayor of New York City has little power over the regional public transportation entity (as in California, it is known as the Metropolitan Transportation Authority), which is dominated by the Governor. Nevertheless, Bloomberg did find a way to pay for a subway expansion that was important to one of his major development initiatives (Hudson Yards)—the project was not initially a priority of the

—— **Existing lines**   ---- **Lines under construction or in the planning stages**

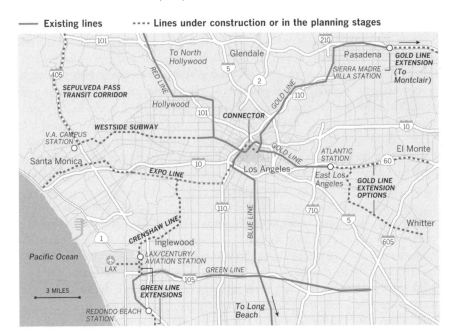

Figure 7.1
Map of Current and Proposed Rapid Transit Lines
Source: Matt Moody Copyright© 2012. Los Angeles Times. Reprinted with Permission.

transportation authority in its own capital plan. The city government, through an off-budget development arm, effectively controls the financing for the subway extension, using a mechanism that resembles California's tax increment financing model. Having arranged the financing, the city will essentially turn the new track and station over to the MTA to operate.

Local development forces and political leaders in Los Angeles also coalesced around an ambitious plan to build a National Football League stadium downtown and to lure an NFL team there. In 2011 they won support from the city council, the state legislature, and the governor to accelerate any appeals of the plan based on environmental considerations, although at present there are no specific plans for an NFL team to relocate. The most recent possible candidate was reportedly the Minnesota Vikings, but they won backing for public assistance to build a new stadium in Minneapolis and will remain in place.

Bloomberg, too, has been a strong proponent of sports-centered development, first with his attempt to build a stadium on the West Side of Manhattan (Hudson Yards) that was part of the city's failed bid for the 2012 Olympics and would have doubled as the home for the New York Jets football team. The stadium plan, which was backed by developers and the construction unions, was eventually blocked in Albany after much opposition from community groups and others who wanted the resources spent elsewhere. However, Bloomberg was able to guide the construction of new baseball stadiums for the Yankees and Mets, offering substantial public financial support (the teams also made major financial contributions), as well as institutional leverage. Working with state development officials, he has also been able to overcome fierce opposition to development of a new basketball arena in downtown Brooklyn (Atlantic Yards), which, according to plans, will eventually be surrounded by a major new mixed-use development. In this case there was also support for the plan from some community groups who welcomed the promised affordable housing and jobs, while others objected to the scale of the development and the use of eminent domain. The residential and commercial development beyond the arena has been stalled by financing difficulties.

The fiscal crisis in Los Angeles remained a challenge for Villaraigosa. Tax revenues continued to fall, offsetting much of the effort to control spending. In 2009–10, there were declines in all of the major taxes, totaling $160 million (–5.2 percent), and the 2010–11 fiscal year had similar, albeit somewhat smaller, declines. Revenues from both the property tax and the more cyclically sensitive taxes fell, reflecting the depth of the local recession.

Given his strong base in the labor-dominated city council, Mayor Villaraigosa was also able to negotiate a series of public employee union givebacks that allowed the city to largely close its budget gap in 2011 without much fanfare (at least compared to the daily drama of the state budget crisis), in particular, a series of raises in return for larger contributions toward their retirement. While there was considerable angst among local unions about being pushed so hard by a pro-labor mayor, partisan budgetary conflict and Republican attacks on public workers in states like Wisconsin convinced them of the value of a relatively harmonious relationship that yielded budgetary solutions within the framework of collective bargaining. The importance of public employee unions in the city's budget is huge (Zahniser 2012). In 2011–12, police and fire constituted 70 percent of the city's expenditures from unrestricted revenues, and 37 percent of its total budget. (See table 7.4.)

Still, by April 2012 the city's fiscal outlook remained troubled. The budget for the upcoming 2012–13 fiscal year had a shortfall of $222 million, 3.2 percent of the city's

Table 7.4 LOS ANGELES 2011–2012 EXPENDITURES (DOLLARS IN MILLIONS)

Unrestricted Revenues	Expenditures	% of Total
Police	$1,940.5	53.1%
Fire	621.2	17.0%
Public Works	303.3	8.3%
City Attorney	113.3	3.1%
Recreation and Parks	219.3	6.0%
Library	135.2	3.7%
Other	321.6	8.8%
Subtotal	3,654.4	53.2%
Restricted Revenues		
Sewer revenues, gas tax, grants, and fees for special Services	3,217.2	46.8%
Total Expenditures	6,871.6	

Source: City of Los Angeles, City Administrative Office, April 2012

$6.8 billion budget. The gaps were projected to widen in the following years to nearly $500 million (Los Angeles City Administrative Officer 2012). Despite budget cuts and concessions from the unions, expenses were still projected to outpace revenues, with the former expected to grow at an annual rate of 3.8 percent (the forecast for worker-related costs is 4.7 percent), while the latter are expected to grow by only 2.3 percent annually.

In the context of this new budget uncertainty, the city's relationship with its unions came under further pressure. In 2007, before the financial crisis started cutting into the city's tax base, the mayor and other city leaders had approved a five-year package that promised 5 percent raises each year to the coalition of unions representing most civilian city workers, who had helped Villaraigosa win election. Fairly soon afterwards, in response to the 2008 downturn and to help pay for raises given, the city had to cut labor costs. Villaraigosa and other city leaders tried to minimize the impact by shifting city workers from jobs paid for by the general fund to jobs, as they became vacant, supported by their own revenue streams (e.g. sanitation paid by sanitation fees). The aim was to lighten the burden on the general fund without casting employees aside. The problem was that by early 2012 the bulk of city employees now worked in "safe" jobs supported by their own revenue streams and were unwilling to forego raises to help avoid layoffs among workers supported by the general fund. Villaraigosa has a talented budget team, and in the past has proved willing to make hard choices. Still, by 2012 the wage increase commitments made in 2007 were clearly burdensome (Newton 2012).

In response, Villaraigosa proposed in his 2012 budget speech to eliminate 669 city jobs—231 through layoffs—mostly civilian employees in the LAPD. He also called for a rollback in the retirement benefits offered to newly hired civilian city employees, limiting their pensions to no more than 75 percent of their salaries, as well as increasing the retirement age to 67. City union leaders, who earlier in the year rebuffed a city request that employees give up pay raises negotiated in years past, attacked Villaraigosa as out of touch with average workers. "If you're the mayor and living a jet-setting lifestyle, it's easy to imagine living that lifestyle until age 67," said Lowell Goodman, spokesman for Service Employees International Union Local 721. "That's not the case of a tree surgeon who's carrying a chain saw up into a tree or a street services worker who's operating heavy machinery to fix our potholes" (Linthicum and Zahniser 2012).

In mid-November, 2012, the LA City Council voted to place a half-cent sales tax rise on the March 2013 ballot (the same day voters would select a new mayor), to help close a looming budget shortfall for 2012–13, estimated at around $216 million. Villaraigosa opposed the measure, arguing instead for cutting city jobs.

There were difficulties on the broader fiscal front as well. A key, new problem was that in March 2012 the mayor's "30–10" transportation plan was thrown into doubt as the Republican-led Congress, in no mood to help Los Angeles's Democratic and liberal mayor, extended federal transportation spending for only 90 days—the ninth such action since 2009—to avoid a complete shutdown of Washington-funded highway work, but funds for the mayor's proposal were not part of these interim bills. It is unclear whether the Congress elected in November 2012, with its somewhat larger Democratic (and urban) caucus, will be more receptive to the Villaraigosa proposal.

Rather than wait for Washington to act, Villaraigosa turned again to LA County voters, placing an initiative on the November 2012 ballot asking voters to extend the 2008 half-cent sales tax increase beyond its 2039 expiration date. The move would have allowed officials to borrow against nearly 50 years of future tax revenue and quickly raise an additional $8 billion for highway and transit projects, with the latter clearly now seen by Villaraigosa as one of his key legacies (Zahniser 2012). The initiative narrowly failed to get the two-thirds majority needed to pass (a far higher bar than the simple majority required by the successful State-wide Proposition 30).

Alternative funding plans have been suggested too in order to bypass Washington (Schweitzer 2012). These included borrowing from the California Infrastructure and Development Bank, which has been around since 1994 and has a triple A rating. Another possibility is to borrow in the private global capital market. These options would probably require Villaraigosa to break his 30–10 plan into smaller, less ambitious financing proposals. Still, the fiscal benefits, as well as new construction jobs and more transit options, might make it worth it.

NEW YORK

In New York City, the locus of the meltdown of the national financial services industry, the timing of the fiscal crisis played out quite differently. As previously mentioned, New York City's budget did not really show the effects of the nationwide fiscal crisis until mid-2008 and early 2009 after the recession had first spread from the housing and construction sectors to the broader economy, before finally threatening financial markets and the firms participating in them. In fact, the city posted two of its largest budget surpluses since 1999–2000, in 2006–07 and 2007–08, $2.0 billion and $1.6 billion, respectively (table 7.5). However, employment in the city peaked in mid-2008 at 3,807,400 jobs, and then fell precipitously in the last months of the year for a fourth quarter loss of 27,110 jobs. Employment continued to fall through late 2009, with a total loss of 135,000 jobs (seasonally adjusted) over five quarters. Furthermore, Wall Street firms lost $11.3 billion in 2007 and $42.6 in 2008 (figure 7.2), leading the city to expect huge drops in its business income taxes, personal income tax, and transfer taxes, which are three of its biggest revenue sources (OMB 2009). The administration's preliminary budget for 2009–10 identified a gap of $4.3 billion to be closed (10.4 percent of city-funded revenues) and $7 billion in 2010–11 .

Still, New York City has more than weathered the budgetary storm. By the first quarter of 2012, it had regained all of the jobs it had lost since 2008 and although the city predicted in May 2012 an operating budget deficit for the 2012–13 fiscal year of $1.6 billion—2.3 percent of the total budget—it ended the 2011–12 fiscal year with a cumulative budget surplus of $2.4 billion (OMB 2012b).

New York City has been able to weather the fiscal crisis better than expected, and better than Los Angeles, for several reasons. First, federal actions including TARP,

Table 7.5 NEW YORK CITY YEARLY OPERATING BUDGET AND PROJECTED SURPLUS OR
DEFICIT, FISCAL YEARS 2001–02 TO 2011–12 (DOLLARS IN MILLIONS)

	Total General City Budget	Operating (Deficit)/ Surplus	Surplus/Deficit as Percent of Total Budget	Cumulative (Deficit)/ Surplus (End of Year)
2001–02	$40,860	($2,200)	–5.38%	$700
2002–03	44,340	700	1,58%	1,400
2003–04	47,292	700	1.48%	2,100
2004–05	52,789	1,900	3.60%	4,000
2005–06	53,999	400	0.74%	4,400
2006–07	58,768	2,000	3.40%	6,400
2007–08	61,971	1,600	2.58%	8,000
2008–09	60,166	(2,500)	–4.16%	5,500
2009–10	62,808	(1,900)	–3.03%	3,600
2010–11	65,315	100	0.15%	3,700
2011–12	68,039	(1,300)	–1.91%	2,400

Source: New York City Office of Management and Budget, 2013 Executive Budget Summary, May 2012; 2013
Adopted Budget, June 2012; Independent Budget Office, 2012c Revenue and Spending Since 1980.

which helped to recapitalize the financial sector by buying about $245 billion of
shares (generally nonvoting) in commercial and investment banks, as well as $40 bil-
lion of AIG shares, and the Federal Reserve's policy of lending against sub-par financial assets to inject liquidity into financial markets, helped to prop up some of the
city's largest and (usually) most profitable businesses. The Federal Reserve's very easy
monetary policy has also saved financial firms tens of billions of dollars by dramatically lowering their interest costs. Second, the city was in good fiscal shape before the
housing bubble popped. At the beginning of the 2007–08 fiscal year, New York City
had a cumulative budget surplus of nearly $6.4 billion (OMB 2012a) and continued to
add to the cumulative surplus until reaching a peak of $8 billion by the end that year
(see table 7.5). Despite having to cover major operating deficits in 2008–09, 2009–10,
and 2011–12, the city still had an estimated $2.4 billion cumulative surplus by the
end of the 2011–12 fiscal year. While the milder than expected local downturn meant
that tax revenues rebounded faster than originally anticipated, the relatively small
fiscal impact on the city was also helped by proactive budget actions under Mayor
Bloomberg beginning early in 2008, even before local employment had turned down.
This response was consistent with the fiscally conservative policies that have helped
guide city budget policy for more than a quarter of a century.

The 1975 Near-Bankruptcy and Its Lessons

New York City's fiscal management is still shaped by measures put in place after it nearly went bankrupt in 1975, measures intended to ensure that city budgeting was careful and conservative (Fuchs 1992). Crucial are the requirements, outlined in chapter 5, that the city must make its budget forecasts with four-year projections with quarterly updates to take account of new circumstances, and must follow generally accepted accounting principles (GAAP), which require the city to balance its budget every year, leaving no surplus or deficit. This requirement was originally in the Financial Emergency Act (FEA) passed in response to the city's near-bankruptcy described below and was later added to the city charter by referendum in 2005 as the FEA was due to expire.

Indeed, the 1975 fiscal crisis left a whole generation of policymakers with a strong commitment that the city should never lose control of its budget again, and left the city with institutions such as the Financial Control Board, a State Deputy Comptroller for New York City, and the Independent Budget Office that look over the mayor's shoulder and contribute to an aversion to fiscal risk. There are also respected private budget watchdog groups such as the Citizens Budget Commission whose analysis frequently influences policy.

In 1975, after years of fiscal gimmicks and questionable borrowing practices that hid a growing structural deficit, the city had literally run out of money and could not pay for normal operating expenses. Only state and federal action, along with concessions from labor and the banks, saved the city from defaulting on its obligations and possible bankruptcy. However, the cost was the loss of fiscal autonomy for nearly a decade.

At the end of the 1974–75 fiscal year, New York City had $11.4 billion of debt outstanding, of which almost $6 billion was short-term. That spring, the city was faced with the need to rollover each month an average of $750 million in short-term notes, with much of those proceeds needed to service long-term debt coming due. By May 1975, the wheel stopped spinning and the city found itself shut out of credit markets.

The accumulation of short-term debt was a result of the city running chronic budget deficits obscured by financial gimmicks such as overly optimistic forecasts of revenues, underfunding of pensions, using funds raised for capital expenditures for operating costs, and writing checks late. Compounding the problem was an ineffective accounting and financial control system, which left officials with little sense of the city's true fiscal condition (Dunstan 1995). The city was already running operating budget deficits during the 1961–65 mayoral term of Robert Wagner, who increased municipal expenditures to maintain his political support. Under Wagner overall revenues did rise because of higher taxes, but not as fast as expenditures.

John Lindsay had criticized Wagner's deficits during the 1965 mayoral campaign and in his first term largely avoided adding to the problem even as city services were expanded, thanks in part to new taxes and growing federal aid. State aid was also generous, partly because of Governor Nelson Rockefeller's ambitions for national office. Reflecting the changing demographics of the city, welfare rolls were growing too, a cost that the city shared with the state and federal governments. In 1969, the mayor granted very generous contracts to the public employee unions to avoid labor unrest (Cannato 2002). Local employment also peaked in 1969 when it reached 3.8 million before beginning a steady decline that saw over 750,000 jobs lost by 1977. In Lindsay's second term, operating deficits grew larger, although much of the gap each year was hidden through fiscal gimmicks and borrowing even as taxes were raised again.

Lindsay left office at the end of 1973 with the city budget just barely holding together, but his successor, the former City Comptroller Abraham Beame was not so lucky. Local employment was continuing its free-fall and the US economy was suffering through a bad recession sparked by the 1973 oil shock, slowing tax collections. The market began to sour on New York municipal debt and by July 1974 the city was being forced to pay higher interest rates to rollover its notes. Beame adopted measures that he hoped would allow the city to access credit markets on reasonable terms but the access did not improve.

By April 1975, the city was essentially out of money to meet its normal obligations, including payroll. Bankruptcy or default had become very real options, but such outcomes threatened a broad array of institutions and interests with such prohibitive costs that they were eventually forced to work together (Shefter 1985). The city's banks and underwriters held a significant amount of city debt, particularly short-term notes. Nonpayment either as the result of default or ordered by a bankruptcy judge threatened their balance sheets. The threat to confidence in the broader municipal financing market was also of grave concern for banks and bondholders. City workers were threatened with wholesale abrogation of labor contracts and the erosion of hard-earned collectively bargained rights under a bankruptcy proceeding. The state government had to be concerned that city default would damage its own credit rating (the state's economic development agency had recently defaulted on some bonds in late 1974). The state and federal governments both had to consider the risk if the city government stopped delivering services.

In the spring of 1975 New York Governor Hugh Carey stepped in to help. Not only would the state's own debt rating probably have been adversely affected, but chaos loomed, especially if public employees were unwilling to work if paychecks were missed. Carey, who was a Democrat, had the backing of the Republican leader of the state Senate in Albany. Carey relied heavily on the advice of investment banker Felix Rohatyn and other business leaders who helped engineer a plan that enabled New York City to regain access to the credit markets but not before more than three years of painful adjustments to city fiscal priorities and procedures. Ultimately, the reason bankruptcy was avoided was political leadership (Baum 2009).

Governor Carey appointed an advisory committee, which led to state legislation in June 1975 creating the Municipal Assistance Corporation (MAC), an independent corporation authorized to sell bonds to help refinance the city's maturing short-term notes. The majority of appointees on the corporation's board were made by the governor. As part of the creation of MAC, the state passed legislation that converted the city's sales and stock transfer taxes into state taxes, which were then used as security for the MAC bonds. The MAC legislation also required accounting reforms and limits on the city's use of short-term debt (Shalala and Bellamy 1977).

Some MAC bonds were placed privately, but public markets remained unimpressed and in August 1975, Carey asked MAC to develop a new program to rescue the city. The MAC board recommended that the city institute a wage freeze, lay off employees, reduce its subsidy to the subway system (which led to an increase in subway fares), and begin charging tuition at the city university. To bring some order to the budgeting and management of New York City, Carey's advisors on the MAC board recommended the establishment of a new board that would have the authority to review the city's budgetary decisions and overturn those which did not conform with the goal of balancing the city budget and restoring market access. Following these recommendations, the state legislature passed the Financial Emergency Act (FEA), which created the Emergency Financial Control Board (EFCB) in September, essentially putting the city into state receivership. The EFCB had authority over the finances of the city, could control the city's bank accounts, issue orders to city officials, remove them from office (Beame was forced to fire his First Deputy Mayor, the Deputy Mayor for Finance, and his budget director), and press charges against city officials. The governor made the majority of appointments to the EFCB. The FEA required the city to balance its budget within three years, change its accounting to conform to GAAP, and submit a three-year financial plan. The EFCB had the power to review and reject the city's financial plan, operating and capital budgets, contracts negotiated with the public employees' unions, and all municipal borrowing.

The federal government also agreed to assist the city although the help came with a high price. In November 1975, federal legislation extending up to $2.3 billion of short-term loans to the city passed the House of Representatives by just a ten-vote margin. Federal involvement was motivated by concerns over the impact of a bankruptcy on the city, state, other public agencies, and abroad. Both President Giscard of France and Chancellor Schmidt of West Germany told President Ford they were worried about a possible bankruptcy's effect on the international banking system (Herbert 2008). The recent hike in oil prices had pushed the oil-consuming countries into a harsh recession and the banking system had yet to recover.

Still, the Ford administration, especially Treasury Secretary William Simon who took the lead in negotiating an agreement, was concerned about setting a precedent whereby other public agencies would seek federal assistance, and so wanted to make New York an example to the rest of the country. Ron Nessen, Ford's spokesman, even compared New York to a "wayward daughter on Heroin" (Tolchin 1975). As a result, conditions were set to discourage other municipalities from coming to the federal government for help. In addition, the major stakeholders—banks, employees, and state taxpayers—had to provide additional assistance. Assets of the city pension funds were to be invested in MAC securities. The state pension fund also invested in MAC securities. A total of $2.7 billion of city debt was bought by the pension funds. The banks who had served as the underwriters for New York's securities agreed to purchase additional securities and/or lengthen the maturity or lower the interest rate on the securities that they held. Finally, the city and state were required to raise taxes by an additional $200 million. At this point, New York City was again able to borrow, but only from the institutions that had a stake in its survival, namely the banks holding its notes, the state and federal government, and the employees' pension funds. The city was still unable to borrow in the municipal bond market.

The city kept its part of the bargain in dealing with public employees. City employment fell by 20 percent and work rules were loosened. Wages were reduced and eventual raises were held below the level of inflation. By 1977–78, the city had no short-term debt. As part of its obligation imposed by the federal government, the state assumed most of the cost of financing the city university system and a portion of the welfare and court systems. The state also tightened controls over Medicaid reimbursements to healthcare providers.

By 1983 the city had retired its federal obligations and the Financial Control Board (FCB), which was the successor to the EFCB, determined that the city was able to operate without the active supervision of the board. The FCB officially entered a sunset mode where it reported on the city's budget performance without daily control. Until 2008, the FCB was empowered to reimpose a control period if it determined that the city was not complying with the requirements of the FEA, but when the authority granted to the board under the FEA ended in 2008, the threat of a control period is no longer available, absent new state legislation.

One later development further altered the city's budget process. As a result of New York City's 1988–89 charter revision, the mayor's power over the budget has been expanded through his control of the revenue estimates for all taxes other than the property tax. With the FEA's balanced budget requirement and its prohibition of borrowing to pay for operating expenses this means the mayor also largely controls the overall level of city services. If the City Council wants to increase total city spending above what the mayor will agree to put in the budget, its only tool is to raise the property tax rate, which its members do not typically want to do. As a result, at the end of the day the mayor controls most of the budgetary process, with the City Council typically negotiating with the mayor over how to spend a few hundred million dollars (the city's overall budget in 2011–12 was $68 billion). The Council is forced to spend much of its political capital during the budgetary process fighting to restore mayoral cuts to popular programs such as libraries, cultural institutions, and childcare.

Wall Street

After Wall Street firms had their two worst years on record in terms of net losses in 2007 and 2008, the firms who are members of the New York Stock Exchange saw record profits in 2009 of $61.4 billion, more than three times their most profitable pre-crisis year (New York State Comptroller 2011). (See figure 7.2.)

Employment in the securities industry fell by over 27,000 from the last quarter of 2007 to the first quarter of 2010, a decline of 14.4 percent, with most of the losses occurring in 2009. Average wages and aggregate earnings fell by even greater amounts (Belkin 2010). Still, throughout the crisis, those Wall Street employees who remained pulled in large bonuses even when their employers registered losses (though the bonuses were substantially less than the record bonuses in the boom

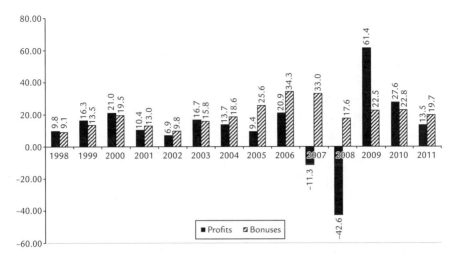

Figure 7.2
Wall Street Profits and Bonuses, 1998–2011
Source: NYS Comptroller, The Securities Industry in New York City, October 2011.

years of 2005 to 2007 leading up to the crisis). The related income tax revenues have helped buffer New York City through much of the crisis.

Still, the future of Wall Street remains uncertain, especially as regulations under the Dodd-Frank reform legislation begin to take effect. One change already roiling the industry is the so-called Volcker rule that aims to force banks to shed their proprietary trading business, which accounted for much of their profits in recent years, surpassing such traditional profit centers as investment banking and underwriting. As firms spin off their proprietary trading units or restructure to segregate that activity from the rest of the business that benefits from implicit and explicit promises of government protection, the question from the city's fiscal perspective is whether the new firms settle in New York or elsewhere.

Bloomberg

Under Mayor Bloomberg, New York has continued to distinguish itself as a fiscally savvy city. Bloomberg was elected mayor two months after the 9/11 attacks. As he took office, the city was already facing looming deficits caused by the aftershock of the attacks and a mild recession that began earlier in the year. Never having served in office before, he had won the election partly on the claim that the city needed a businessman in such economically challenging times.

His first budget proposal addressed an anticipated deficit of $4.8 billion in the upcoming 2002–03 fiscal year. He planned to deal with it using state and federal emergency recovery assistance, $727 million in agency savings (the majority of which came from actions other than direct service reductions), and most notably $1.75 billion in borrowing for operating expenses, which had been outlawed since 1978 under the FEA, but thanks to legislation passed two days after the Trade Center attack was authorized on a one-time emergency basis.

By November 2002, tax collections in the current year were falling short and the mayor now projected a budget deficit of $6.4 billion (24 percent of city revenues) for the fiscal year that would start the following July. He argued that if New York City wanted to continue attracting business and get people to stay, it needed to maintain, not cut, services, and that therefore tax increases would have to be part of the solution. He proposed raising the property tax by 25 percent and offered a personal income tax reform that would increase revenue even while lowering rates for residents by making commuters subject to the city income tax. (A separate commuter tax had been repealed by the state legislature in 1997.) The property tax rate is the only rate that the city can raise without state approval, and after negotiations with the City Council a scaled back increase of 18.5 percent was passed, effective January 2003. The mayor's income tax proposal went nowhere in Albany. Still looking for additional tax revenue, the mayor settled for three-year increases in the city's personal income tax (commuters would continue to be exempt) and the sales tax, which were authorized by the state legislature in June.

One of the Bloomberg administration's hallmarks has been its development of new ways of dealing with budget surpluses while retaining substantial control over spending. Following in the steps of his predecessors, Bloomberg and his budget staff have generally been conservative in their tax revenue forecasts, with collections often exceeding initial projections, resulting in a surplus in the current year. This is a notable change from the pre-1975 practice when the city would present budgets with wildly optimistic revenue forecasts to hide operating deficits. By hoarding or hiding surpluses during the current year, Mayors can prevent them from being used for new spending on services or increasing employee salaries. But this strategy requires a means of rolling surpluses forward while still complying with GAAP rules.

If the city could maintain the kind of rainy day fund that Los Angeles and many other states and municipalities employ, there would be a much more transparent and useful means of assessing the city's structural fiscal balance. Instead, because under GAAP the city must balance its budget every year, revenue collected in a given fiscal year can only be used for expenses accrued to that year.

Yet in many fiscal years beginning in the mid-1980s the city has collected more money than it spends. Starting in the Koch years, the city developed methods for "rolling" these surpluses while not running afoul of GAAP. The most frequently used method was to prepay debt service that was not scheduled to be paid until the next year with surplus dollars from the current fiscal year. The city was also allowed to prepay some annual subsidies to entities that are technically separate from the city's books, such as the Metropolitan Transportation Authority (which runs the subways, buses, and commuter rail), the Health and Hospitals Corporation (which runs the public hospital system), the public library systems (there are three which are private charitable organizations with independent boards), and major cultural institutions operating in city buildings, such as the Metropolitan Museum of Art.

The city's fiscal system began to once again generate operating surpluses starting in 2002–03, which quickly grew in size so that budget managers faced a state constitutional constraint on the amount of surplus that could be rolled through pre-paying debt service. The Bloomberg administration found creative new ways to lock up surpluses for future use while preserving the executive's control on new spending and when surpluses are used. These moves have effectively given the city a counter-cyclical reserve (some would call it a "rainy day" fund) while maintaining compliance with GAAP, and these reserves were critical in avoiding deeper service cuts once the post-2008 fiscal crisis hit.

One new method was to essentially retire or "economically defease" some soon to expire debt. For instance, in 2007, $536 million in bonds were defeased, in 2008 another $1.986 billion, and in 2009 $718 million more, resulting in substantial debt service savings in 2008, 2009, and 2010, which provided budget relief particularly in 2010 (Independent Budget Office 2012a). A second method used by Bloomberg was to begin funding a Retiree Health Benefit Trust Fund to pay current health insurance obligations for retired city workers and also to begin to accumulate assets to defray future obligations. Under accounting rules introduced in 2004, governments are now required to report their projected post-employment benefit commitments on an actuarial basis, although there is no requirement at present to fund such obligations as there is with pensions. The initial deposits into the trust fund all came from operating surpluses and amounted to $2.5 billion, although the 2011 estimate of the obligations on an actuarial basis is $86 billion. With the city running operating deficits for the last three years, Bloomberg stopped making new contributions to the trust fund and then began to withdraw money to provide current budget relief. The Retiree Health Trust Fund is now projected to be depleted in the next fiscal year.

Early in 2008, before the financial market crisis had affected the city budget, the Bloomberg administration revised its tax revenue forecasts downward so that 2008–09 and 2009–10 were projected to result in consecutive years of declining revenue. Thanks to the large surplus that had been rolled into 2007–08 it remained in balance—still, the administration began to rein in spending growth, and Bloomberg moved to cut current year spending by 2.7 percent to help build up a cushion. The cuts included a $99 million reduction to the Education Department, which marked the first time since 2003 that education had not been exempted from budget actions. He also proposed rescinding a 7 percent property tax reduction that had only taken effect in the 2007–08 fiscal year, bringing in $590 million in 2008–09 and $1.3 billion in 2009–10. A few months later when presenting his executive budget for the upcoming fiscal year (2008–09) the revenue picture appeared to have brightened in the near term, although the projections for 2009–10 through 2011–12 had worsened modestly. The spending cuts largely remained intact.

By January 2009, a year after Bloomberg first warned of the likely budgetary impact of the financial crisis and three rounds of budget cuts, 2008–09 agency spending was $1.4 billion less than originally planned. Police spending was down by $163 million as the hiring of a new class of cadets had been cancelled, resulting in declining patrol strength as retirees were not replaced. The education budget was $479 million lower than had been anticipated. Having implemented the property tax hike, the mayor now proposed a package of sales tax changes, the centerpiece of which was a permanent 0.5 percentage point increase in the rate, which is generating over $600 million annually. Notably, the mayor has resisted calls for raising the income tax burden, either through an across the board rate increase or an increase aimed at high income taxpayers (the millionaires tax).

Unlike Villaraigosa in Los Angeles, Bloomberg has not been able to reach significant compromises with the city's municipal labor force since the 2008 crisis began. After signing contracts earlier in his term that granted many workers annual raises of 4 percent, there have been no new agreements and at present most city workers are working without contracts. (Under New York State municipal labor law, expired contracts remain in place while negotiations continue, including any contracted step increases for seniority, which allows teachers and many uniformed workers to continue receiving annual raises.) The Bloomberg administration's current position is that any contracts signed now would include raises only if they were paid for through productivity; nor would any raises be retroactive. Some of the budget actions that the mayor has taken in response to the financial crisis have been to withdraw money from the budget that had been previously set aside for retroactive raises.

Nor has Bloomberg had much success in negotiating savings in worker health insurance costs—most city workers make no contribution to the basic insurance plan—or until recently, in reducing pensions for newly hired workers, which requires action by the state legislature, which is traditionally quite responsive to public employee unions. However, Andrew Cuomo, who was elected governor in 2010, succeeded in passing a new pension tier for public workers in early 2012 (see below).

Over the five years since the Bloomberg administration first began taking steps to address the budget pressure expected to emerge with the onset of the financial crisis, the city slowed or reduced spending in eleven different rounds of retrenchment that have contributed a total of $5.4 billion toward balancing the 2012–13 budget (Office of Management and Budget 2012a), although the budget also depended on a number of large one-time transactions. Four months into the fiscal year, the Bloomberg administration conceded that $635 million of one-shot revenue from the anticipated sale of tax medallions would not become available, at least for the 2012–13 fiscal year and in November 2012 ordered another round of budget cuts totaling $555 million for the current year and $1 billion for 2013–14 (OMB 2012b).

Although the November 2012 budget revision was released a few days after Hurricane Sandy slammed into the New York region, no impacts from the storm were reflected in the budget projections. The storm took scores of lives, destroyed hundreds of homes, flooded many low-lying neighborhoods, and severely disrupted the region's transportation network (seven subway tunnels under the East River, the PATH tunnel connecting New Jersey and lower Manhattan, and two major trans-river car tunnels were flooded). Flooding was also severe on the New Jersey coast. Early estimates of the recovery and rebuilding costs exceeded $50 billion for the region, with a significant portion of the initial outlays expected to come from New York City and other local governments in the region, although some or all of the local and state expenditures are likely to be reimbursed by the federal government. Depending on the how much is covered by the federal government (under existing law 75 percent of recovery and rebuilding costs would be covered) and whether the lost business activity depresses tax revenues, the city's budget could face additional challenges in 2012–13 and 2013–14.

By moving quickly to adjust the budget, drawing down the accumulated surpluses from the boom years, and benefiting from a faster than anticipated recovery in the local economy, the Bloomberg administration has avoided some of the budget brinksmanship that has occurred in a number of municipalities and states.

In responding to the post-2008 fiscal crisis, Bloomberg largely did as his predecessors have done since the 1970s fiscal crisis when an economic slowdown or recession looms. Yet this episode has largely occurred after the FCB's power to install a control period had expired. The city took the steps needed to balance the budget even though the legislation waving the "big stick" of a state takeover if the budget spun out of balance was no longer in effect, reflecting how the lessons of the 1970s crisis remain part of the city's budget culture.

New York City has also experienced a milder financial crisis because parts of its overall tax structure do not react as quickly to economic downturns as Los Angeles's. In particular, it relies on the property tax to a greater degree than Los Angeles. Hence, New York City has created a somewhat more stable tax base for itself in which its personal income tax will bring in a lot of local tax revenue when economic times are good and incomes are high, while the city's property tax continues to grow during economically difficult times. This is especially true because the city's property tax system phases in assessment increases over several years so that total assessed value continues to grow even if market values start to decline.

Nor has New York City been subjected to a prolonged and nasty state budget crisis, as in California. Although state budget cuts (mostly to education funding) resulted in a $1.4 billion state revenue decrease to the city in 2009–10, the state government has taken steps toward fiscal solvency. Governor Cuomo negotiated a series of budgetary compromises with major stakeholders, particularly the hospital workers union, giving them a place on a panel charged with reforming (constraining the growth) of Medicaid. At the same time, he has pushed through a 2 percent cap on property tax increases (excluding New York City) while putting in place a gradual increase in the share of Medicaid paid by the state, thereby reducing one of the localities' largest budget items. In 2012, the governor overcame the opposition of state employee unions while working out a compromise with the legislature to create a new pension tier with significantly reduced benefits for many new hires (benefits for new police and fire workers had already been reduced under Cuomo's predecessor). This too will eventually result in significant savings for local governments, including New York City.

In late 2011, the governor and legislative leaders also finessed a resolution to an income tax change that threatened to knock at least $2 billion out of the state budget. The governor had publicly stated his opposition to extending the temporary income tax on high-income households (a "millionaires tax") that had been passed under the previous governor. The Democratic majority in the Assembly pushed hard for retaining the tax and using the revenue to avoid threatened budget cuts, particularly to education aid. By devising a new set of tax rates that left the top rate close to what it was under the millionaires tax while adjusting some others to make the tax slightly more progressive, the governor and legislative leaders came to an agreement that preserved most of the revenue from the expiring surcharge while avoiding a straight extension.

CONCLUSION

Both Los Angeles and New York felt the impact of the financial crisis and its deep recession, but the effects were not the same due to structural, political, and cultural differences. Legacies of 1970s fiscal policy that are embedded in state and local law still affect the options available to each of these cities in terms of tax policy and budget-making. The allocation of fiscal responsibility between state, county, and local government shapes the mix of taxes each city relies on, and the mix can determine how quickly tax revenues fall as the economy enters a recession. Los Angeles descended faster in part because it relied more heavily on sales tax and business income taxes, whereas New York benefited from the stability of its property tax. In this crisis, federal policy also mattered greatly, particularly given how much New York City benefited from Federal Reserve policy and federal bailouts of many of its large banks. The budget-making tradition of New York also helped as budget-makers were still spooked by the brush with bankruptcy in the 1970s and observed both law and tradition to take the steps necessary to avoid a repeat. In Los Angeles, the ability of the mayor to appeal to progressive forces while also following a generally prudent course on fiscal policy has helped avoid the blowups that have occurred in other states and cities.

PART THREE

Social and Urban Problems

CHAPTER 8

Policing, Crime, and Legitimacy in New York and Los Angeles

The Social and Political Contexts of Two Historic Crime Declines

JEFFREY FAGAN AND JOHN MACDONALD

The relationship between citizens and police occupies a central place both in urban politics and in the political economy of cities. In this respect, for nearly fifty years, New York and Los Angeles have been bellwethers for many of the nation's larger cities. In each city, as in cities across the world, citizens look to police to protect them from crime, maintain social order, respond to a variety of extralegal community concerns, and reinforce the moral order of the law by apprehending offenders and helping bring them to justice (Reiss 1971; Black 1980; Skogan and Frydl 2004). Beyond enforcing social and political order, the police are the front line representatives of a variety of social service needs in communities (Walker 1993). Accordingly, policing is an amenity of urban places that shapes how citizens regard their neighborhood and their city, and in turn, the extent to which citizens see their local institutions as responsive and reliable (Skogan 2006). Effective and sustainable governance, especially when it comes to public safety, depends on the capacity of criminal justice institutions to provide "value" that leverages legitimacy and cooperation among its citizens (Moore et al. 2002; Skogan and Frydl 2004; Tyler and Fagan 2008; Tyler 2010).

How the police exercise their legal authority is an aspect of policing that is particularly salient in larger urban areas and often competes with performance-based evaluations of police. Their legal authority has fundamental implications for public sentiments about the quality of police services and trust in political institutions more generally (Moore et al. 2002; Tyler and Fagan 2008). There is an expressive function in the way that police exercise their authority that signals their regard for the dignity and rights of citizens (Smith 2008). These signs of respect leverage the cooperation of citizens with police and engage citizens as partners in security (Fagan and Meares 2008). When these expressions are absent, though, trouble follows when citizens depend on the police for their safety and at the same time harbor resentments over the omnipresence of police in their lives.

For nearly five decades, tension between citizens and police in Los Angeles and New York City has pervaded relations and fouled the polity. Throughout this time, the institutions of policing occupied a special place in the political and social cultures of each city for at least four reasons. First, Los Angeles and New York City each suffered a crime epidemic from the late 1960s to the early 1990s that is visible in each city's homicide and robbery trends. These epidemics placed unprecedented demands on the police and on each city's political institutions, and created recurring conflicts between police and the most crime-ridden and heavily policed minority communities. The mix of crime, race, and policing placed intense political pressures on the police.[1]

Next, a series of police scandals and crises focused unwelcome attention on the police, threatening to undermine their perceived legitimacy and corrode citizen confidence in the police as effective agents of crime control. Third, the scandals of the police were also confounded with racial politics of cities, as a number of high-profile police abuse of force cases deepened historical minority distrust of the police in both Los Angeles and New York City. Both the scandals and patterns of civil rights violations by police landed each city in federal court and resulted in legal interventions that attempted—and as we show later, largely failed—to reshape the institutions of policing.

Fourth, in response more to different forms of corruption scandals than to racial upheavals or conflicts, police in both Los Angeles and New York City underwent significant institutional transformations in their policing architectures. The tipping point in this transformation in each city was the intervention and administrative reforms brought about by (twice) former commissioner William J. Bratton. At the outset, these reforms fundamentally changed the strategies and tactics of policing. In both cities crime rates dropped significantly after these reforms, lending credence to the argument that the police have a material impact in influencing crime rates (Kelling and Cole 1996; Bratton and Knobler 1998).

These seeming "victories" over crime changed the discourse on the politics of the police in Los Angeles and New York City from one of scandal and reforms to control corruption, to managing the conflicts between aggressive police tactics and disparities in their application toward minorities (Alpert et al. 2006; Ayres and Borowsky 2008; Gelman, Fagan, and Kiss 2007; Ridgeway 2007; Fagan et al. 2010). Nevertheless, policing in each city in the last decade was colored and shadowed by the attention of the federal courts who responded to investigate, assess, and monitor both police agencies' responses to controlling crime and maintaining civil rights.[2] Beyond the acute periods of crime decline, as each city transitioned to a low(er) crime era, the two cities took sharply divergent paths in police–citizen relations and also policing tactics. Litigation bore very different kinds of fruit in each city, and the current atmosphere in the two cities reflects sharply divergent institutional postures toward crime and community.[3] Those divergent paths form the core of this chapter and forecast very different futures for policing in the two cities.

In this chapter, we tell the story of policing, crime, and the search for legitimacy over the past two decades in Los Angeles and New York City. Throughout this complex political, normative, and legal landscape, crime rates dropped dramatically in each city to levels not seen since the early 1960s. Accordingly, a full understanding of the natural history of crime and policing in each city has to start at a much earlier point in time for two reasons. First, criminologists tend to forget history, especially history that pre-dates the sharp rise in crime that began in the United States in the mid-1960s, and the nationwide decline starting in 1993. There is a tendency in the criminology literature to decouple periods of rising crime from periods of falling crime, without viewing the two movements as a single social and historical process.[4]

So, to understand the present, we look to the period before the crime rates began a steep rise in each place, at the moment when the smoldering tensions between citizens—especially racial and ethnic minorities—and the police exploded into open conflict. One part of this chapter, then, is a modest effort to construct a "history of the present" to explain how two cities took different but intertwined paths from low to high crime and back again.[5]

Second, crime itself has undergone historic transformations, both in its substance and its trends. While crime in each city has shown patterns typical of recurring and closely spaced epidemics, the longer view shows that its rise and fall over five decades seems to reflect a historic step and transformation that itself may have defied the best efforts of police, police reformers, and courts to effect short-term change. Rather, the trends over a longer interval seem to point to profound political, economic, and structural transformations in the two cities into eras of relative safety and calm.

The chapter tells this story in four sections. We begin with a discussion of the evolution of policing in the two cities, assessing reciprocal and dynamic changes that reflected both the crises of crime epidemics and crises within the police. Next, we examine the role of litigation on the evolution of policing. Policing regimes in each city were challenged in federal courts, as well as by elected officials in local investigations. The outcomes of litigation in the two cities were starkly different, a reflection in part of the structure of the litigation itself, as well as the posture of each city toward the links between scandal and reform. While Los Angeles linked a major policing scandal with reform, the NYPD compartmentalized the origins of its scandal to specific forms of police corruption and use of force, while ignoring the need to regulate the constitutional parameters of routine police–citizen interactions.

Third, we examine the historic transformations in crime itself. Criminologists, as we noted, tend to take a shorter view of crime trends that expand for one or perhaps two decades. Shorter-term crime trends are important in their social, political, and personal consequences. But short-term boom-or-bust explanations provide limited perspective for the longer historical trends that we observe for each of the two cities. Crime rates today in both New York and Los Angeles have returned to the same levels as fifty years ago, before the upheavals in policing in the midst of that cycle, eras that spanned significant changes in the social and political order of the cities. By stepping back, we show that what may be meaningful and consequential in the short-term may be less important when contextualized from longer and larger historical processes.

In the fourth section, we broaden our focus to examine basic changes in the structures of the cities, looking closely at factors that were implicated in the boom-and-bust cycles of crime that characterize the past half century. We locate crime trends in these larger structural transformations of the cities, and contextualize policing in what seems to be a historic and evolutionary cycle. We conclude with a brief look at the past and the future.

POLICING IN THE CITY

The Legacies of the Riots

The scars of riots in New York City and Los Angeles, events that took place nearly fifty years ago, were part of the historical process that shook the police departments in each city, and perhaps intensified the fifty-year cycle of crime and its decline that followed.

By 1967, riots erupted in more than 250 both large and small cities across the country (Kerner Commission Report 1968). The 1965 Watts Riot in Los Angeles received closer scholarly and popular attention than the Harlem riots in New York City a year earlier (Cohen and Murphy 1966; Perlstein 2008). Nevertheless, the two events had much in common. In each case, tensions between black citizens and police ignited sustained violence and property damage. The riots revealed a breach of trust between minority citizens and the police that lasted for decades.

Harlem, in northern Manhattan, was the scene of one of the nation's first riots. The riot erupted in July 1964, when police shot and killed a 15-year-old African American teenager following a dispute with a local white building superintendent. When a police officer intervened, the teenager attacked him with a knife and was shot by the officer. Riots followed in neighborhoods across the city, often beginning with protest marches that ignited into violence when police attempted to control them (Walker 2012).

Within days, the Harlem Riots spread across the country, including to several cities with multiple episodes of riots. More than 325 riots in 257 cities broke out between 1964 and 1968 (National Commission on the Causes and Prevention of Violence 1969). For police in New York City, the Harlem Riots were a turning point not only in their relationships to the minority communities, but in the stance of the city and its political leadership toward crime and the underlying social conditions. While the US Supreme Court had sought to curb the police tactics that led to many of the riots at the outset of the 1960s, the Harlem Riots exposed fractures in the Court's dual campaign of improving police procedure and supporting civil rights in the 1960s (Stuntz 2011). The election of liberal mayor John Lindsay in 1965 represented the face of social reform in response to the riots, while the battle over civilian oversight of the police brought forward a quite different face that sought deregulation of the police and a pullback from the procedural reforms earlier in the decade (Perlstein 2008).

The spark for the 1965 riots in the Watts section of Los Angeles illustrates this triggering mechanism. Marquette Frye, a 21-year-old African American, was pulled over for running a red light by a California Highway Patrol officer. Mr. Frye had allegedly been drinking alcohol and could not produce a driver's license. It was a hot night, and many people were outside to witness the event, including Mr. Frye's mother. An altercation began between Mr. Frye, his mother, and the police and ended with Mr. Frye, his brother, and his mother under arrest. The crowd became rowdier when the LA police (LAPD) arrived in response to a highway patrol officer's distress call, and more general violence in the Watts ghetto broke out as the crowd "stoned passing automobiles, assaulted white motorists, and threatened a police command post" (Oberschall 1968). The six-day Watts Riot spread throughout Los Angeles and resulted in 3,927 arrests, more than 1,000 injuries, 600 buildings damaged, and 34 deaths.[6]

Governor Pat Brown appointed a commission of six whites and two African Americans to prepare "an objective and dispassionate study" of the Watts Riots. The commission interviewed seventy-nine witnesses and questioned around 10,000 people about the events. Three months after the commission began, it produced its report "Violence in the City—and End of a Beginning?" The report was short, only 88 pages, and the description of the riots was only about 15 pages.

"Violence in the City," also known as the McCone Commission report, presented what might be read as the "Riffraff Theory" of the Watts Riots. Police Chief Parker was blamed by many South LA residents for exacerbating tensions with the African American community by disregarding widespread claims of police abuse—including claims of excessive force and routine use of abusive language. Yet the McCone report exculpated whites, including the police, from blame, focusing instead on "social, economic and psychological conditions" that faced rioters, but it still placed blame on the Watts residents. The commission found that (1) less than 3 percent of the ghetto population participated in the riots; (2) that rioters were "riffraff" meaning unemployed, young, criminals, and outsiders; and (3) that the majority of the black population opposed the riots.

The McCone Commission and Chief Parker were not alone in hurling racial invective at the rioters. Future California governor Ronald Reagan referred to the rioters as "law-breakers and mad dogs," and Parker insisted that the riots were the work of "a gang of Negro Hoodlums" (Cohen and Murphy 1966; Perlstein 2008) and "monkeys in the zoo" (Oberschall 1968). LA Mayor Sam Yorty insisted that a small portion of the ghetto community had instigated the riots and had expertise in areas such as making Molotov cocktails, a fact that was rejected by the McCone Commission.

The national reaction to the riots was quite different. The Kerner Commission, named after its chairman Illinois Governor Otto Kerner, Jr., delivered a report starkly in contrast to the McCone Commission. The riots that produced a nationwide disturbance in 1967 created a space in which to challenge the riffraff theory that was advanced by the McCone Commission (1965). The Kerner report saw the violence as criminal, but also as a response to oppression, and something that could only be cured by a change in the actions of white America.

The riots were the product both of increasing crime and disorder in inner cities and increasing tension and conflict between citizens and police in those same neighborhoods. Surveys in that era showed that "nonwhites were more apprehensive than whites" (Weiner and Wolfgang 1989). They had reason to be, as the number of index crimes in the cities ("homicide, forcible rape, aggravated assault, robbery, burglary, grand larceny and auto theft") in proportion to the population, was nearly three times higher than in the surrounding suburbs. Most of the victims of crimes were other city residents, meaning that nonwhites were far more likely, in some instances 78 percent more likely, to be the victims of crimes.

The scars of the riots remain visible today in two ways. First, the scars are painfully visible in the physical landscape of a few stubbornly poor cities, as well as those where poverty and crime have abated. In both gentrifying Harlem and chronically poor Newark, vacant lots and abandoned buildings or factories are visceral physical reminders of the struggles of that era. But the scars also remain visible in a philosophy and jurisprudence of criminal law that has instantiated the disparate fates of racial minorities in the criminal justice system (Stuntz 2011). A sign of the legacy of the close connection between race, police, and riots could be seen in the police posture toward rioters in the Rodney King riots in Los Angeles that erupted in 1992. There, the police were known to use the term NHI—"No Humans Involved"—when issuing radio calls to patrolling officers who were being sent to homes in black sections of the city (Independent Commission on the Los Angeles Police Department 1998).

Scandals

Los Angeles

The history of corruption within the LAPD ranks during the first half of the twentieth century led the organization under police Chief William H. Parker and his successors to separate itself from the political establishment. The LAPD was managed from 1950 to 1966 by Chief Parker, who—despite the Watts Riots—was celebrated within the police profession for innovation in civil service protections of officers and command staff, professional development and training, and vice enforcement.[7] Parker's innovations came after a previous half-century of repeated corruption scandals and frequent turnover of police chiefs.[8]

While the McCone Commission report offers very little in the way of direct criticism of the LAPD, the report does note the problems between the LAPD and the African American community. It suggested that they "place greater emphasis on their responsibilities for crime prevention as an essential element of the law enforcement task, and that they institute improved means for handling citizen complaints and community relationships" (McCone 1965, part 5). In particular, the report offers suggestions for revamping the citizen complaint process to increase the transparency of the system and prevent conflicts of interests, that emerged when police commanders were required to review complaints against their own subordinate officers (see Abu-Lughod 2007).

The LAPD, through the history of police chiefs Parker, Davis, and Gates, was focused on professional police administration and not known for its community relations. It also became politically insulated from both democratic regulation and administrative accountability. The Los Angeles City Council, at the urging of Chief Parker, enacted an appointment process for its chief of police that guaranteed virtual lifetime tenure (Greene 1998). These three chiefs moved toward a strong centralized command and control structure that emphasized full enforcement of the law and limited officer discretion. The eclipse of political control and external accountability over the LAPD insulated it and fostered its own cultural norms (Independent Commission on the Los Angeles Police Department 1991; Greene 1998). Partnership with the community was simply not paramount in this design of police professionalism.

At the same time, communities in South Los Angeles near Watts were still very much attuned to the legacy of the Watts Riots. Full and formal enforcement of the law was not what residents of South LA neighborhoods had in mind for police reform when they complained in 1965 about police abuse, entrenched poverty, inadequate access to housing and schools, and crime. Despite the structural problems noted in the McCone Commission report, concentrated poverty, racial segregation, and poor police–community relations remained endemic of Los Angeles through the 1970s and 1980s. Formal, militarized policing embraced by Chief Gates in zones that are best portrayed as "poverty traps" (Bowles, Durlauf, and Hoff 2006) was a prescription for tensions and a breach in trust between minority citizens and the police.

It was in this context of twenty-five years of a politically isolated police force and a socially and economically isolated and impoverished minority community that two scandals emerged within a decade. Both shook the LAPD from its closed posture and launched the processes of reform. On March 3, 1991, an African American resident named Rodney King attempted to evade a traffic stop by the LAPD. His arrest and beating were caught on videotape and "went viral" long before there was *YouTube*, much less a widely accessible Internet.[9] The subsequent acquittal of LAPD police officers charged with the beating sparked the 1992 LA urban riots. Like the 1965 Watts Riots, police abuse of authority (Independent Commission on the Los Angeles Police Department 1991) was again the touchstone event that triggered massive riots. The fact that the King incident led to such violent protests was indicative of the deep tensions that existed in South LA neighborhoods, and in particular the poor relations with the African American community.[10]

Mayor Tom Bradley appointed a commission headed by Warren Christopher to investigate the King beating and the riots; its 1991 report provided the catalyst for change in the LAPD. The Commission found the LAPD had created a "crime fighter" and "warrior" culture among its officers that rewarded high arrest rates and overwhelming force when civilians resisted arrest. The department rejected the moves to community policing that had become an important innovation in policing elsewhere in the nation (Independent Commission on the Los Angeles Police Department 1991).

In June 1992, LA City Council followed the Christopher Commission's recommendations and replaced Daryl Gates with former Philadelphia Police Commissioner Willie L. Williams, who was the first African American police chief of Los Angeles.[11] Two years later, the LAPD issued a strategic plan, "Commitment to Action," which called for partnerships between the police, community, and other branches of local government. The plan involved a revamping of the Basic Car Strategy, which set up a defined neighborhood area for a dedicated patrol car all under the guide of one of eighteen community police divisions (as defined by police with community input), and increased training of

RAMPART COMMUNITY POLICE STATION

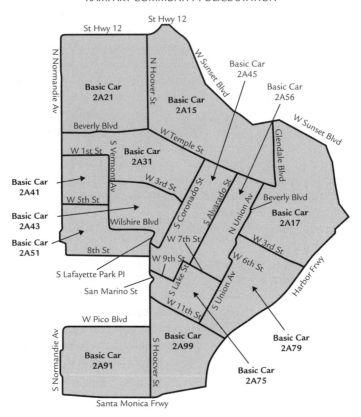

Figure 8.1
Map of the Rampart Police Division in LA
Source: Los Angeles Police Department.

senior officers and new recruits on community and problem-solving policing strategies (Glenn et al. 2003).[12] These were the first halting steps by the LAPD toward a community policing model. Figure 8.1 shows an example of the Rampart Community Police Division and corresponding basic car areas. (The Rampart police division, as we discuss later, becomes an important part of the story of scandal and reform.)

Still, there was intense resistance to community policing within the LAPD middle and upper management ranks (Glenn et al. 2003), eventually costing Williams his job. He was replaced in August 1997 by Deputy Chief Bernard C. Parks, the city's second African American chief. Parks, even while attempting to build community ties, focused his efforts on tactical units to combat crime. Crime dropped significantly under Chief Williams, and rose again under Chief Parks.

It was on Parks's watch that the Rampart scandal was uncovered, the second deep scandal in the LAPD within a decade. On September 21, 1999, Parks formed a Board of Inquiry (BOI) of LAPD command staff to examine the depth of the alleged corruption in the Rampart police division and the celebrated CRASH (Community Resources Against Street Hoodlums) program. The BOI report focused almost exclusively on the problem of a few corrupt officers and not the systemic problems within the LAPD (Board of Inquiry into the Rampart Corruption Incident, Public Report 2000).[13] A subsequent report commissioned by the LA Police Commission criticized the LAPD for its failure to address larger problems in the department's internal culture that rewarded the *ends-justify-the-means* approach to crime fighting (Report of the Independent Review Panel 2000). The fallout from the LA Police Commission review panel was apparent. By 2005 the California courts overturned 100 falsely obtained convictions, 20 officers were removed or left duty, and just over $70 million was paid in civil settlements as a result of this corruption scandal.

The Rampart scandal set the stage for the two measures that led to major changes in the internal operation of the LAPD and its relationship to the community: federal civil rights litigation that produced nine years of federal oversight under a Consent Decree negotiated with the US Department of Justice, and the hiring of Commissioner William Bratton to oversee the transformation of the LAPD.

New York

One of the legacies of the riots in New York City was the ascension of a new class of political leaders from the city's African American and Latino communities. Adam Clayton Powell, Jr. was elected to Congress representing Harlem in 1960 and immediately raised issues of civil rights, including police misconduct, both on the floor of the House and also in Harlem and across the city's minority neighborhoods. Powell was especially hard on the NYPD, accusing police in Harlem of corruption that included providing protection to drug sellers in return for lucrative payoffs. Powell had some history to draw on, including a scandal involving a gambler, Harry Gross, who made payoffs regularly to every precinct in Brooklyn (English 2011). The Gross scandal led to hundreds of arrests and convictions. The trail of payoffs eventually led to City Hall and forced the resignation of Mayor William O'Dwyer.

Powell's accusations, made in 1960, before the riots, presaged the corruption scandal of 1964 involving the NYPD's elite forty-eight-person "Watchdog" group. The most volatile scandal was dramatized by the revelations of Detective Frank Serpico and became public news in 1971. His disclosures of pandemic corruption and cover-ups led to the appointment of the Knapp Commission in 1970. The antecedents of this scandal lie in the ashes of the 1960s and could be traced to three narratives. First, in the wake of the riots, a heroin epidemic spread through New York City's minority neighborhoods (Preble and Casey 1969). Drug distribution organizations profited heavily, as did secondary markets in prostitution, gambling, and fencing goods stolen by addicts. These networks depended on police protection. Testimony before the Knapp Commission revealed how, fueled by the new economics of heroin distribution, the residual system of low-level routine payoffs and minor acts of corruption among police suddenly became big business, reaching from the lowest ranks of patrol officers through the detective branches, and into some corners of the command ranks (Knapp Commission Report 1972).[14]

Second, the late 1960s was a period of political violence in New York City. Both in New York City and elsewhere, revolutionary groups including the Black Panther

Party, the Weather Underground, and smaller groups all engaged in either shoot-
ings of police officers or conspiracies to bomb public places. Although the ambitions
of these groups outstripped their impacts, they were seen by NYPD officers as an
imminent threat to their lives. In addition to a conspiracy indictment against the
Panthers, the shooting of a police officer at a Harlem Mosque in 1972 set off sparks
of conflict not only between the police and the Nation of Islam community in Harlem
but also between the police union, police commanders, and city leaders over blame
for the officer's death. Blame was at first placed on then Lieutenant Benjamin Ward,
who a decade later went on to become the city's first African American police commissioner. The conflicts with community and the external threats against police officers
shielded public attention from the spreading knowledge of corruption in the NYPD.

The third narrative was the political hangover from the battle over civilian review
of the NYPD. In 1966, Mayor John Lindsay created a Civilian Complaint Review
Board (CCRB) to address citizen grievances of excessive force, false arrest, and other
forms of police misconduct. The move came at a time of racial polarization in New
York City over citizen control of schools, a conflict that played out both publicly
and bitterly in the predominantly African American Brownsville neighborhood of
Brooklyn. The police union, the Patrolman's Benevolent Association (PBA), pledged
to empty its treasury to defeat Lindsay's creation (Perlstein 2008). After a 1966 riot
in Brownsville, the PBA qualified a referendum on the November ballot to dissolve
the CCRB. The CCRB was defeated in a 55–40 landslide.

One of the sites of the scandals that led to the Knapp Commission Report was
the 30th Precinct in Harlem, which twenty years later became the site of another
NYPD drug corruption scandal, known as the "Dirty 30." The Knapp Commission
was formed in 1970 to investigate police corruption, based in no small part on
Serpico's 1971 whistle-blowing testimony and that of fellow officer Sergeant David
Durk. The Commission, officially known as the *Commission to Investigate Alleged Police
Corruption,* in fact did not begin its hearings until after Serpico's revelations to the
commission's investigators. The commission produced criminal indictments against
corrupt police officials and officers, and led to the replacement of Commissioner
Howard Leary (a Lindsay appointee) with Commissioner Patrick V. Murphy. Murphy
was tasked with cleaning up the department rather than redesigning its strategies
and tactics. Murphy implemented proactive integrity checks, oversaw massive transfers of senior personnel, implemented mandatory job rotation in key areas, and provided funds to pay informants. He also went after citizens who were complicit in
attempts to bribe police officers.

Within two decades, a second corruption scandal erupted, with the drug trade
again central to the narrative. Mayor David Dinkins appointed former judge Milton
Mollen in July 1992 to head *The City of New York Commission to Investigate Allegations
of Police Corruption and the Anti-Corruption Procedures of the Police Department,* popularly referred to as the Mollen Commission. The Mollen Commission was tasked to
investigate "the nature and extent of corruption in the Department; evaluate the
departments procedures for preventing and detecting that corruption; and recommend changes and improvements to those procedures" (Mollen Commission Report
1994). Mollen carefully drew lines to distinguish the corruption patterns uncovered

by the Knapp Commission from the corruption of the Mollen era. Corruption during the Knapp investigation was systemic: a pattern of monetary exchanges between criminals and police, with an unspoken agreement to conceal other forms of police misconduct including brutality and other constitutional violations. In other words, Knapp revealed a culture and practice where criminals and police officers gave and took bribes, and bought and sold protection.

Mollen's investigation revealed deeply ingrained patterns of brutality, theft, abuse of authority, and active police criminality (Mollen Commission 1994). The commission report described a nexus between corruption and brutality, which essentially doubled down on the Knapp era scandals. One testifying officer, Michael Dowd, discussed the deep place of this nexus in the culture of the NYPD, "[Brutality] is a form of acceptance. It's not just simply giving a beating. It's the other officers begin to accept you more" (Mollen Commission 1994). Officer Dowd and others described hundreds of acts of brutality they had engaged in; yet, apparently no fellow officer had filed a complaint about either one of them. Officers primarily from the 30th, 9th, 46th, 75th, and 73rd precincts were caught selling drugs and beating suspects.[15] The "Dirty 30" scandal resulted in nearly one hundred convictions against seventy defendants being thrown out due to police perjury (Human Rights Watch 1998). By 1988, with approximately fifteen lawsuits still pending, the city has already paid $2 million in civil settlements to perjury victims (Kocieniewski 1998).

The scandal bled into the regime of the next police commissioner, William Bratton, who was appointed in 1994, shortly before the Mollen Commission report was published. In his efforts to reform the department, Bratton stated that if officers behaved properly, he would back them absolutely, but if they used unnecessary force, "all bets are off" (*New York Times* 1994a, b). Yet, when a civilian deputy commissioner in charge of internal affairs pushed for the creation of a special anti-brutality unit that would be available twenty-four hours a day to investigate allegations promptly, he was forced out of the department in 1995 (Kraus 1995; Human Rights Watch 1998). Although most of the reforms recommended by the Mollen Commission—improvements in recruiting, scrutiny during probation, integrity training, and improved supervision—were implemented by 1998 (Herbert 1998b), the tensions from as far back as the 1960s and the struggle for police oversight were a constant in the culture of the NYPD. The PBA continued to oppose Bratton's stricter disciplinary measures, and the Mollen Commission's call for changes in the police union's response to allegations of corruption. Indeed, litigation surrounding the Abner Louima assault by NYPD officers in 1997 (BBC News 1999) implicated the police union in the cover-up of that infamous incident.

Reform

The common thread in the stories of police reform in Los Angeles and New York City is not just the presence of William Bratton, but rather the critical role of scandal as a launching pad for reform. In Los Angeles, Commissioner Bratton used the platform of scandal and an external commission to achieve reforms in accountability of individual officers, while also pursuing the types of strategic and tactical reforms that have been influential across the country. In New York City, Bratton also benefited from a scandal—the "Dirty 30"—that created a political space in which he could implement both management and tactical reforms in the political slipstream of the Mollen Commission's findings without the external constraint of litigation. In a similar pattern, Bratton used both scandal and litigation as a rationale for departmental reform in Los Angeles, where he relied on both his own instincts and the reform insights gained in New York City.

The Rampart scandal, the review, and the subsequent consent decree set the stage for a new era of management reform in LAPD. In October 2002, William J. Bratton was appointed as LAPD's police chief. Having served as Chief of NYPD and instituting its COMPSTAT program, Bratton brought a similar management philosophy to the LAPD. COMPSTAT was a method of policing that focused upon mapping and statistically analyzing crime and crime "hotspots" and deploying police based upon that analysis. Since 1996, Bratton had worked in the private sector, including serving as a consultant for Kroll Associates monitoring team that oversaw the implementation of the Federal Consent Decree with the LAPD.[16]

Bratton's primary focus was on implementing steps of the consent decree and instituting COMPSTAT within the LAPD command staff. His management philosophy was to use COMPSTAT to make strategic decisions about officer deployment and to set police division benchmarks for crime reductions. In contrast to previous efforts to reduce crime, this new LAPD approach did not rely exclusively on specialized units and tactical responses. Instead, each division captain was going to be responsible for crime trends and formulating a response in his or her police area. The LAPD instituted this approach under the title of COMPSTAT Plus, under the direction of George Gascón, LAPD Assistant Chief of Police and Director of Operations.

In contrast to the NYPD COMPSTAT model where performance was benchmarked in monthly command staff meetings, COMPSTAT Plus involved detailed inspections of underperforming police divisions. For police divisions that were underperforming, Gascón assigned an audit team of LAPD commanders who would inspect the current patrol, investigation, analysis, management, and supervision of these areas. After a thorough review, the audit team would work with the police division to develop its own strategic plan to meet the crime reduction goals.[17] It is notable that this approach to policing was a sea change in the LAPD. Never before had efforts to reduce crime focused on a community-wide approach that relied primarily on line officers and command staff. Gone was the sole focus on tactical units that had been the staple LAPD approach dating back to the Parker administration. The model of COMPSTAT Plus, however, was based on police accountability to the crime rates and not improving community relations. Although one can reasonably argue that the LAPD was mindful that reducing crime could in turn improve public sentiment, even in the African American areas, community policing was not a central player in the department's organizational change. Interestingly, the LAPD continued to direct its field services through its community policing plan, and the use of the Basic Car Strategy remained part of the LAPD organization, but the actual benchmarks of the organization were not strictly on community-relationship building.

Like New York City, Los Angeles witnessed a significant reduction in crime rates after the implementation of Bratton's COMPSTAT approach. But in contrast to the NYPD model, the COMPSTAT Plus approach did not result in the rapid reallocation of line officers to impact zones or the deployment of aggressive stop and frisk polices (Alpert et al. 2006; Ayres and Borowsky 2008). By the time Bratton resigned as police chief in October 2009, he oversaw a six-year decline in crime, the lifting of the Federal Consent Decree, and no major corruption scandals. At present it is unclear whether his replacement LAPD Chief Charlie Beck will continue to focus resources on the COMPSTAT model or develop other strategies instead. It is notable that Charlie Beck was appointed, in part, because of his reputation for community collaboration, including overseeing relationships with the business improvement districts and nonprofit services groups in MacArthur Park, located in the Rampart Division, and Downtown Los Angeles.

LITIGATION

In each city, litigation formed the legacy of the crime declines and scandals of the 1990s. It also was a background drama in the consolidation of crime declines through the following decades. Litigation was an essential intervention that complemented the internal management reforms of Chief Bratton and was part of the fabric of policing during most of his tenure in Los Angeles. In New York City, the threat of litigation was raised in 1999 by an investigation by the New York State Attorney General of alleged civil rights violations, including racial profiling, by the NYPD. Litigation has been a constant in the political and policing environment since 2001, but with seemingly little effect (Fagan et al. 2010). The case studies of each city show the stark differences in the responses to litigation by each city and its police, and raise important questions about what litigation can achieve as an intervention in police reform.

Los Angeles

The next phase of LAPD reform came through outside intervention. In November 2000, the city of Los Angeles entered into a consent decree with the US Department of Justice to oversee the operations of the LAPD, in part responding to the specific Rampart scandal, as well as a concern with widespread police abuse of authority that violated constitutional guarantees of citizens under the Fourth and Fourteenth Amendments. This five-year term of the Consent Decree dedicated a large share of oversight to the review of procedures of management and supervision of officers to promote civil rights integrity, as well as the conduct of general police activity, including the use of stop, search, and arrest powers. Included in the consent were specific provisions that indicated "LAPD officers may not use race, color, ethnicity, or national origin (to any extent or degree) in conducting stops or detentions, or activities following stops or detentions, except when engaging in appropriate suspect-specific activity to identify a particular person or group." And, the Consent Decree also required that LAPD officers complete an "electronic report each time an officer conducts a motor vehicle stop" (Consent Decree, p. 40).

The Consent Decree was helpful to Commissioner Bratton in his program of reform, both internally and externally. Many of the requirements of the Consent Decree worked reciprocally but in parallel to the strategic, tactical, and cultural innovations that he pursued. Whether the litigation was successful, however, was sharply contested. An analysis of the reforms of the LAPD under the Consent Decree was sought by the Los Angeles Police Foundation, an independent organization that supports the activities of the LAPD (Stone et al. 2009). The report found that the LAPD was in substantial compliance with the terms of the Consent Decree, and it was a factor in the decision by the US District Court Judge Gary A. Fress to terminate the Consent Decree in July 2009. In his order, Judge Fress noted that: "When the Decree was entered; LAPD was a troubled department whose reputation had been severely damaged by a series of crises.... In 2008, as noted by the Monitor, 'LAPD has become the national and international policing standard for activities that range from audits to handling of the mentally ill to many aspects of training to risk assessment of police officers and more'" (Rubin 2009).

The conditions cited in the report that suggest substantial reform are in fact a curious mixture of increases in policing coupled with reports of citizen approval of police effectiveness in the heavily policed African American and Hispanic communities. The report describes a declining rate of use of force at the same time that both pedestrian and motor vehicle stops doubled over the seven years of the Consent Decree. Arrests rose in the period of the Consent Decree, as did arrests per stop, while prosecutorial declinations declined (Stone et al. 2009). These increases were seen as successes, despite the general view that arrest should be a last resort when policing crime and disorder, a notion endorsed in the "Broken Windows" framework (Wilson and Kelling 1982) that informed the NYPD reforms under Commissioner Bratton (Bratton and Knobler 1998; Maple and Mitchell 1999). The increased police activity was seen as a positive sign that litigation did not inevitably lead to a withdrawal from policing, or de-policing, by officers fearing increased departmental oversight and scrutiny.

Two other indicia suggest that the reforms left substantial room for improvement. According to the Stone et al. (2009) report, more than two-thirds of Hispanic and African American residents rated the LAPD as doing a "good" or "excellent" job at controlling crime and calling offenders to account. But other indicia suggest that a substantial minority within each of these groups was dissatisfied with the LAPD. One in ten African American residents reported that almost "none" of the LAPD officers they encounter treat them and their friends and families with "courtesy or respect." Others cited the persistence of racial disparities in police–citizen contacts.

It is surprising that approval of the LAPD is so strong given the demography of police–citizen contacts in Los Angeles (Ayres and Borowsky 2008) and the increase in the incidence of both nonarrest and arrest contacts between citizens and police. Analyzing stop data from 2004, the only year made available to them, Ayres and Borowsky reported statistically significant higher rates of police stops, searches, citations, and arrests of African American and Hispanic persons compared to whites, even after controlling for differences by location in crime and other social conditions. They also report that "hit rates" from stops, frisks, and searches were significantly lower for nonwhites compared to white suspects. Ayres and Borowsky (2008) reject a claim that these rates reflect higher rates of criminality among minority citizens, citing the lower rates of seizure of weapons, drugs, or other contraband, and arrests on outstanding warrants.

The two pictures of the Consent Decree mirror the experiences of other cities that were placed under federal court supervision through court-appointed monitors (Schwartz 2010; Fagan et al. 2010). One reason for the gap in these narratives about consent decrees is the difference in emphasis on which factors matter to which communities. To a court, or perhaps to a public seeking a more accountable and professional police regime, the reforms in the inner workings of the department were good news. But to those who sought relief from policing excesses or constitutional violations in decisions on whom to stop and search for suspicious behaviors, the failure to curtail racial disparities suggests that the policing biases of the pre-litigation era remain unabated. Accountability, then, has two different faces—internal accountability for professionalism and good management, and external reforms for accountable and performance-based policing. One might reasonably ask whether the achieved reforms, however welcomed and needed they may be, are the right reforms when the racial disparities in police conduct that motivated the litigation remain persistent realities of policing.

New York

The cycles of scandal and reform that have burdened the NYPD for nearly fifty years led to litigation against the City of New York and the NYPD in the late 1990s. And since that time, class action litigation (as opposed to individual civil actions) has multiplied. Two incidents in particular motivated an investigation of the NYPD by the New York State Attorney General, and subsequent litigation based on the investigation reports. One was the 1997 assault on Abner Louima in a NYPD precinct station, and the other was the 1999 killing of an unarmed citizen, Amadou Diallo, by officers who were part of an elite Street Crime Unit (SCU) that conducted aggressive stops and searches in the hunt for guns. The SCU was formed early in the Bratton police administration and was expanded following Commissioner Bratton's resignation in 1996.

The Spitzer Report, as the Attorney General investigation was known, cited evidence that the NYPD engaged in racially biased police practices in decisions on whom to stop and frisk (Spitzer 1999; Gelman, Fagan, and Kiss 2007). About one stop in six lacked a clearly articulated justification on forms filled out by the NYPD, and nearly one in four lacked sufficient documentation to render a judgment of its constitutionality. The racial disproportionality was stark: black New Yorkers were nearly three times more likely to be stopped relative to their crime rate than were white New Yorkers; the comparable rate for Hispanics was about half the disparity for blacks. While there has been some debate about the causes of these disparities (Ridgeway 2007), no one can deny that blacks and Hispanics were feeling the brunt of the

NYPD's stop and frisk tactics, and that these disparities are not a simple artifact of differences in crime rates between areas that different groups inhabit.

The Center for Constitutional Rights filed the lawsuit *Kelvin Daniels v. City of New York* in 2001, relying on the Spitzer report as evidence, coupled with the testimony of a class of plaintiffs. The litigation was settled in an agreement in December 2003 that—unlike the Los Angeles Consent Decree—did not include court oversight. New York City promised to reduce racial disparities in police stops, to improve documentation, and to reject racial profiling as a basis for conducting street stops. Training on constitutional requirements for street stops and other reforms designed to increase constitutional compliance were also put in place. Assorted other reforms were promised, including the conduct of citizen forums and community surveys. Documentation of street stops, thought to be spotty at best by the Spitzer investigation, was integrated into the COMPSTAT system of crime accounting.

Daniels was, however, a failure. There was no internal report comparable to the Stone et al. (2009) assessment of the LAPD to determine whether there were significant or effective institutional reforms that resulted from *Daniels*. Even so, lawyers for the *Daniels* plaintiffs reported that there was little compliance with the terms of the settlement. And, there was an exponential growth in street stops during the interval of the *Daniels* settlement. Fagan et al. (2010) showed that stops increased 600 percent between 1998, the year preceding the Spitzer Report, and 2006, a year before the December 2007 expiration of the *Daniels* Consent Decree. Almost all of the increase during that time was in districts that were predominantly populated by African Americans. Fagan et al. (2010) observed that the increases were present even after controlling for race-specific crime rates in each police precinct. Similar patterns, though smaller in magnitude but still statistically significant, were found for areas with concentrations of Hispanic residents. The "yield" from these stops was low—about one gun seized for every thousand stops and arrests in about one stop in twenty. Figure 8.2 shows the growth in racial disparity throughout this period. While the NYPD claims that the growth in stops has kept crime rates low (Smith and Purtell 2007), figure 8.2 suggests that in fact, crime rates were declining since long before the run-up in stops and have in fact been declining in New York City since 1991 (Zimring 2011).

Daniels failed for four reasons. First, there was the absence of any external oversight or enforcement of reforms. Essentially, the NYPD and the City promised to reform, but faced no incentive to do so in a timely fashion. Second, the NYPD firmly believed that these tactics were essential to keep the crime rate low and maintain its slow decline through the decade following the appointment of Raymond Kelly as Police Commissioner. Third, there was public support to continue these tactics, though the public has been split on this question for over a decade. The support was equivocal in the minority communities, where stops were most heavily concentrated and was strong in predominantly white sectors of New York City.[18] Accordingly, there was no sense of urgency among community or political leaders to hold the NYPD accountable for compliance with the terms of the settlement that largely impacted minority communities. Perhaps most important was the timing of the litigation: *Daniels* was filed in 2001, before the 9/11 terror attacks, and shortly afterward, the Police Commissioner Bernard Kerik—in his final year in office—very publicly renounced racial profiling. And within a few months, the 9/11 attacks generated widespread support if not admiration for the NYPD. In that climate, there was no political will or even attention to the issues raised by *Daniels* and Spitzer before that.

But the most significant reason for the failure of *Daniels* was the structure of the stipulated settlement agreement. The terms did not include an external or court-appointed monitor, a departure from other consent decrees or collaborative agreements negotiated around the same time, including the Los Angeles Consent Decree. There were no stated performance benchmarks to assess changes in racial disparities in stops and frisks. There was no requirement for public release of data. Rather, the NYPD were required to produce reports to plaintiffs and later, to the City Council, a requirement they ignored until the shooting death of Sean Bell during a botched undercover operation in November 2006, a year before the scheduled expiration of the *Daniels* settlement. There were no requirements for evaluation of training or other personnel management systems. There was no external auditing of the data or of the routine reports on the reasons for citizen stops to determine if they were consistent with Fourth Amendment requirements. When violations were detected, as in the case of the 600 percent increase in stops from 2003 to 2006 that exacerbated racial disparities (Fagan et al. 2010), there was no enforcement mechanism for reversing these practices. The NYC settlement agreement stands in sharp contrast to the Consent Decree in Los Angeles that required active monitoring of racial disparities in stop, arrests, and use of force behaviors by the LAPD. One can only imagine what reforms and changes in transparency might have occurred if the NYPD had been subject to similar oversight.

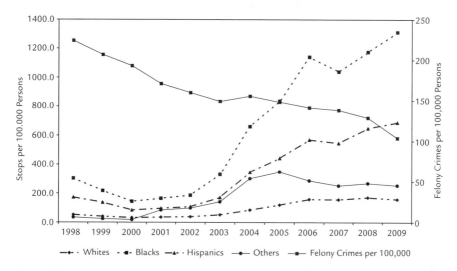

Figure 8.2
Terry Stops and Felony Crimes per 100,000 Persons, New York City, 1998–2009
Source: New York City Police Department, Various Years; Fagan et al., 2010; Uniform Crime Reports, various years.

The growing disparities led to a second lawsuit, filed immediately upon the expiration of the *Daniels* settlement, by the same civil rights organization that had filed *Daniels*: the Center for Constitutional Rights. The litigation continues through this writing with the case *Floyd et al. v. City of New York*.[19] In addition, two other lawsuits have been filed, *Davis et al. v. City of New York* in 2010, and *Ligon et al. v. City of New York* in 2012. Each alleges both racial discrimination and Fourth Amendment (search and seizure) violations in the conduct of police operations in the apartment buildings that characterize much of the city's housing stock. Plaintiffs in *Davis* allege discrimination in the conduct of stops and the enforcement of trespass laws in public housing complexes. Plaintiffs in *Ligon* allege similar claims in the enforcement of these laws in privately owned buildings. In *Ligon*, the litigation cites abuses under the NYPD's *Operation Clean Halls* program, where officers conduct patrols in the lobbies and stairwells of privately owned buildings—with the consent of the landlords—searching for persons who are illegally in the buildings.[20] The City says these tactics are essential to eliminating long-standing problems of drug dealing and related violence in these buildings. However, residents are mixed on these tactics, and the plaintiffs complain not only of illegal searches but also of often being arrested in their own buildings that they are legally allowed to be in.

The persistence of litigation in New York City suggests both the animating power of scandal to provoke litigation but also the limitations of political regulation and accountability in policing in the post-*Mollen* era. It is not just class action litigation that characterizes this climate, but private litigation as well: according to the City Comptroller, New York City has paid out over $570 million in settlements of individual private law suits in the past decade (Liu 2012).

Litigation in New York City and the disagreements over the impacts of the litigation in Los Angeles suggest a further and difficult question: Will the aggressive and proactive policing tactics that characterize both cities inevitably lead to racial conflict and litigation? Perhaps the absence of meaningful regulation of the police in New York City, dating back at least fifty years, creates a political climate where accountability and lawfulness is secondary to both the norms of the police culture and the demands for security at all costs. The scandals dating back to the 1960s and before suggest that this is not simply a matter of high crime eras, for as we show below, that era ended both in New York City and Los Angeles a decade ago. Rather, the persistence of litigation and the allegations that these lawsuits seek to address may suggest a more disturbing notion of the endogeneity of such norms in the modern policing institution when unabated by outside intervention. In New York City, the bitter war over these three lawsuits suggests a dark vision of a permanent divide between the minority citizens of the city and the institutions that exist to protect them. Los Angeles seems to be on a very different path.

CRIME AND POLICING

The connection between the crime reductions in New York and Los Angeles since the height of the crack epidemic in each city in 1990, with the cycles of scandal and reform, is not a simple calculation. While notable reforms in policing occurred in each city following urban unrest, corruption scandals, internal reforms, and new models of policing, it remains unclear how much these cascading dramas shaped the crime trends we observe in each city. In this section we analyze the changes in crime rates between 1960 and 2010 in the two cities, using the broader historical lens that captures the eras of unrest, rising crime, scandal, and reform. We focus on only robbery and homicide rates because these crimes are less likely to be influenced by changes in police reporting practices over this time period. Homicide in particular has not changed by definition. And, there are reasons to expect that the police generally do not underreport homicides.[21]

The Fifty-Year Arc

The trends over the fifty-year period in robbery and homicide rates in the two cities are very similar in both timing and the shape of increase and decline. Both cities experienced a massive increase in crime between the mid-1960s and the early 1980s, despite different trajectories in internal governance and reforms. In Los Angeles, the various efforts of the professional model of law enforcement under police chiefs Parker, Davis, and Gates had little discernible effect on crime, as measured by robbery or homicide rates through the 1980s. Crime rates also rose in New York City under several police commissioners through the same eras. The crime increase in New York City and Los Angeles mirrored the crime increase seen in the majority of large US cities across this period (FBI Uniform Crime Reports, various years), suggesting that large secular processes were animating crime trends through forces that were beyond the control of local police in any single city.

Bad Things Come in Threes

From the 1960s through the early 1990s, violent crime increased in three waves, each one closely tied to an epidemic of drugs—heroin in the late 1960s, cocaine and the emergence of street drug markets in the late 1970s, and crack cocaine and the rapid expansion of retail drug selling predominantly in American inner cities by the 1990s (Johnson et al. 1990). In each city, starting in the mid-1980s, the increase was best described as an epidemic of violence, especially among adolescents and young adults ages 13–24 (Cook and Laub 1998). The coupling of the temporal phasing of crime in each city with concurrent drug epidemics has been the key source of theoretical speculation and empirical analyses (Blumstein 1995; Fagan 1990, 1992). In these renderings of the causes of a violence epidemic, the connection was through drug selling in open-air markets (Zimmer 1984; Goldstein 1985, 1989; Fagan 1990) and the proliferation of high caliber firearms (Blumstein and Wallman 2000). In each city, drug-selling organizations animated forms of group violence that were tied to the economic instrumentality. In Los Angeles, these groups emerged from, and sometimes coincided with, the rise of street gangs in the late 1970s. In New York, drug-selling organizations dominated territories and markets (Fagan 1990, 1994; Johnson et al. 1990).

Drugs were hardly the only crime correlate that was co-morbidly tied to the three-stage run-up in crime. By the mid-1970s, guns became the weapon of choice in homicide

(Zimring and Hawkins 1997). We cannot know whether the proliferation of gun homicides was the result of excess gun manufacture and faulty marketing controls that put
guns into the hands of young offenders (Hemenway 2004) or a by-product of the rapid
expansion of inherently violent street drug markets (Johnson et al. 1990; Fagan 1992)
in each city. But the fact remains that nearly all of the increase and the entire decline in
homicides across the fifty-year window was due to changes in gun-related deaths (Fagan,
Zimring, and Kim 1998; Cook and Laub 2002; Zimring 2006, 2011; Hemenway 2004).

The Crime Declines

Figures 8.3 and 8.4 shows the trends for homicide rates and robbery rates between
1960 and 2010 for New York and Los Angeles, and begins the discussion of the crime
declines. In these figures, we placed lines marking years where major police issues
occurred, including the 1965 Watts Riots, the 1991 Safe Streets Act of New York, the
1992 Los Angeles riots, the 1994 advent of COMPSTAT in New York and the LAPD
community policing plan, and the 2002 COMPSTAT Plus program launched by LAPD
police chief Bratton.

The similarity in the patterns of increase and decline are remarkable. The rates rose
and declined in both cities in the same decades, despite public perception that the cities
are distinct from each other with regard to both crime and its correlates. The trends show
with clarity that policing crises and reforms are correlated with general secular trends.
When we examine any year as a point of departure from the decade-specific trends in
homicide and robbery for both cities, it suggests that a police reform contributed to a
lower rate of crime. Still, the effects of reforms are best viewed as nested in the longer fifty-year secular trends in these and other major cities (Rosenfeld, Fornango, and Baumer
2005; Harcourt and Ludwig 2006). Crime rates began declining in each city in 1992,
despite starkly different political, social, and policing environments. In other words, the
shared onset and shape of the decline could suggest that policing had a modest effect.

So, for example, we could attribute the decline in Los Angeles to the Rodney King
riots, the appointment of Chief Williams in 1992 to lead the LAPD, the work of the
Christopher Commission in revealing systemic problems in the LAPD and in the communities most heavily policed, and/or to Williams's community policing plan that
began in 1994 (and that was fiercely resisted by the patrol force). In New York City, we
could claim that the onset of the crime decline began with police reform resulting from
the 1991 Safe Streets Act, the implementation of COMPSTAT initiatives and other
policy reforms in 1994, and/or the work of the Mollen Commission that investigated
police corruption beginning in 1993. In other words, no matter what the political landscape or the specific local crime conditions, a secular decline in crime began in the two
cities at almost exactly the same time, and by the year 1993, this trend was seen in
cities across the nation (Blumstein and Wallman 2000).

Perhaps the most remarkable trend within the larger arc is the sharp decline in
each city's crime rate between 1990 and 2000. Within this shorter period, almost any
year that we estimate as a parameter in the decade of the 1990s after 1992 in either
New York City or Los Angeles shows a significant downward trend that dominates
any reform occurring in the following decade, including both the appointment of

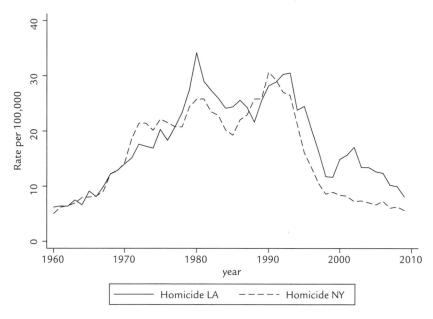

Figure 8.3
Homicide Rates per 100,000 Persons, New York and Los Angeles, 1960–2010
Source: Uniform Crime Reports, various years.

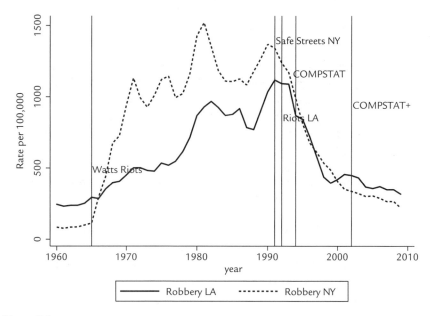

Figure 8.4
Robbery Rates per 100,000 Persons, New York and Los Angeles, 1960–2010
Source: Uniform Crime Reports, various years.

Chief Bratton in Los Angeles and the Consent Decree that went into effect in 2000. Even when we adjust for the full series of observations going back to 1960 for robbery and homicide, the trend in the near decade from 1992 to 2000 shows that declines in each city were steep and systematic, even under starkly different conditions.[22]

So, while Bratton's reforms in New York City in the 1990s and in Los Angeles a decade later showed some promise in reducing crime, one should also point to Chief Willie Williams as the great crime drop leader in Los Angles through his effort to institute community policing and transform the culture of the LAPD. The successes of Chief Williams were interrupted (and cost him his job) in the trend in Los Angeles in the years surrounding the Rampart Scandal. Between 1999 and 2001 both homicide and robbery rates in Los Angeles reversed course and increased for the first time since the early 1990s. After 2001, with the Rampart Scandal resolved and new management in place under Bratton, the decline in LA robbery and homicide resumed. The salient point here is that in both Los Angeles and New York City, in very different policing regimes and political and social contexts, a crime decline began that has—with the interruption of the Rampart years—sustained itself for nearly two decades into 2010.

The COMPSTAT Effect

The COMPSTAT innovation used spatial analysis of crime patterns with constant updating to drive the allocation of police resources to crime "hot spots." It is an innovation first developed by William Bratton in New York City when he headed the NYPD's Transit Bureau, and he brought it to departmental scale when he was appointed Police Commissioner in 1994 (Bratton and Knobler 1998). Since then, it has been adopted by law enforcement agencies across the country and in several cities in Europe and Latin America (Weisburd et al. 2004). Arguably, its effects have been most deeply felt in Los Angeles and New York City, where Bratton was the police executive during the implementation of the management design.[23]

If we were to focus on only examining the effect of the COMPSTAT program in New York City that started in 1994, we would see a clear influence of this program in reducing robberies and homicides. Figure 8.5 shows the linear trends in homicide rates for New York City and Los Angeles in the years after each city adopted its version of COMPSTAT under chief Bratton. In New York City, the linear trend was 14.5 fewer homicides per 100,000 residents after 1994. In Los Angeles, the linear trend was 11.5 fewer homicides per 100,000 residents after 2002. These trends suggest that COMPSTAT efforts provided a meaningful contribution to the crime decline in each place. But, if we look back to the date of the onset of the crime decline in Los Angeles in 1994, the linear trend would be similar to New York City's—including the three-year spike in crime between 1999 and 2001 in Los Angeles.

Street Tactics

In both Los Angeles and New York City, *Terry* stops were the hallmark of the policing regimes in the past decade. Street stops of pedestrians under *Terry v. Ohio* (1968)[24] permit officers to engage, question, then possibly frisk suspects for weapons based

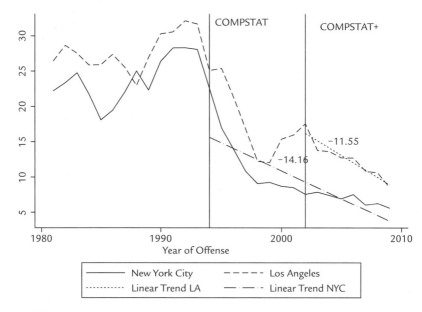

Figure 8.5
Homicide Rates with Linear Trends in New York and Los Angeles following COMPSTAT,
1980–2010
Source: Uniform Crime Reports, various years.

on reasonable suspicions that "crime is afoot." Officers can search a suspect based on probable cause that the suspect is either armed or has contraband in his possession or has committed a crime. In New York City, with its high volume of pedestrian traffic, most stops have been street stops. In Los Angeles, with a lower population density and far greater use of automobiles, stops are a combination of street stops and motor vehicle stops. The stops, whether in a car or on the street, are invasive, often unpleasant, and usually did not result in an arrest. The apparent racial disparity of street stops and car stops was, in each city, a driver of litigation.

Table 8.1 shows data on *Terry* stops in each city for two years in the past decade. At first glance, it seems that "street" policing in New York in the past decade has not only grown substantially, but the number of involuntary police–citizen contacts also rose by nearly 500 percent within five years. The years in table 8.1 were chosen for ease of comparison based on available data. In the four years from 2008 to 2011, the rate of involuntary citizen stops in New York rose to 686,724, an increase of 45.5 percent from 2007. The rate in Los Angeles rose by 100 percent, a far higher increase. But the LAPD made a total of 875,204 stops including vehicle stops, so the focus on pedestrian stops vastly understates the extent of LAPD citizen interdictions. The percent black or Hispanic in New York was 86.6 percent in 2011, a rate that has been rising slowly since the first analysis of these data in 1998 (Spitzer 1999).

Blacks and Hispanics in both cities remain the primary recipients of proactive police actions and attention. Data on pedestrian stops in both cities for years 2002 and 2007 presented in table 8.1 show that the majority of stops in each place are of

Table 8.1 PEDESTRIAN STOPS PER 100,000 PERSONS, NEW YORK AND LOS
ANGELES, 2002 AND 2007

	New York		Los Angeles	
	2002	2007	2002	2007
Total	97,830	472,096	76,615	135,263
Rate per 100,000	1,210.1	5,705.4	2,010.8	3,384.9
% Black or Hispanic	73.4	81.7	78.5	81.0

Source: Source: Stop and Frisk data for New York 2002 and 2007 provided to Fagan in *Floyd v City of New York*, 08 Civ 1034 (SAS) (2008). Stop and Frisk data for Los Angeles available from LAPD at http://www.lapdonline.org/search_results/content_basic_view/9016.

Hispanic and black suspects. Although the LAPD has been subject to less scrutiny than NYPD on disparities in police stops, the stop proportions by race in both cities are quite similar. Ayres and Borowsky (2008) showed stark racial disparities in Los Angeles in 2004, after controlling for crime rates. Fagan et al. (2010) showed the same in New York for 2006.

Our data in table 8.1 most likely understate race- or ethnic-specific disparities. We combine black and Hispanics, but one should recognize that this masks the stark disparity borne by blacks in Los Angeles (Ayres and Borowsky 2008). Over time, blacks have been a far smaller percentage of the LA population (9.6 percent in 2010) than are blacks in New York (25.5 percent in 2010). Conversely, the Latino population in Los Angeles is a far greater share of the city's population (48.5 percent in 2010) compared to New York (28.6 percent in 2010). A separate analysis of stops per capita by race would show a far higher rate of pedestrian stops for blacks in Los Angeles that is comparable to NYC's rate.

The higher per capita stop rates in New York City may reflect more than simply tactics, but rather the size of human resources devoted to stopping citizens. The number of officers in uniform at the NYPD was 34,060 in June 2012, well below the peak force of 41,000 in 2001, and the lowest since the 34,825 officers on the force in 1992 when crime rates began their decline (New York City Independent Budget Office 2011). In contrast, the LAPD had 9,927 officers from 2009 to 2012 (KPCC 2010; Heaton 2010; Berk and MacDonald 2010; Villancourt 2012). So, the disparity in personnel—a ratio of 3.5 to 1—between the two cities does not explain the 1.7 to 1 disparity in *per capita* stop rates. When we include motor vehicle stops and pedestrian stops, the LAPD appears to be stopping far more citizens relative to the size of its police force.

Pedestrian or "street" stops are hardly the only policing story in each city. The totality of policing over the past decade in each place has been substantial. Several specific enforcement priorities, consistent with its Order Maintenance Policing strategy, have produced significant numbers of arrests for several types of low-level misdemeanors and violations. The NYPD has averaged over 45,000 marijuana possession arrests since 2000 (Geller and Fagan 2010) and an additional 16,000 criminal trespass arrests each year since 2007. More than one in three of those arrests were resolved in favor of the defendant (NYCLU 2012). In 2011, prosecutors did not charge 13 percent of people arrested for trespassing in the city (Bowers 2010). NYPD officers also issue numerous citations for a variety of "quality of life" violations that are not criminal offenses, but carry criminal liability if the citation is not answered. Comparable data in Los Angeles are difficult to obtain, though the combination of pedestrian and motor vehicle stops suggests a rate of involuntary contact with police—whether through stops or citation of other enforcement initiatives—that is comparable to that in New York.

The move over the past decade to a policing regime in each city that emphasizes proactive contacts with citizens, whether at the moment of an offense or before it occurs, has produced a thick net of social control that envelopes each city's minority neighborhoods. For adolescents and young adults, the frequent police contacts have become a part of the normal process of adolescent development, a form of anticipatory socialization that internalizes the stigma of police contact, whether founded or not by the detection of crime. If the contacts themselves are harsh and unpleasant, the negative aftermath generates not just ill will but also a withdrawal of citizens from cooperation with the police (Tyler 1990). In an era of steeply declining crime rates in each city, the theoretical and empirical basis for the escalation of police contact may be questionable and has the potential to strain public confidence in the police, especially among minorities most likely to experience police contact.

THE POLITICAL ECONOMY OF POLICING AND CRIME

The shared temporal shifts in patterns of bellwether crimes in Los Angeles and New York are remarkable given the distinct political trajectories and institutional structures of policing in each city over this fifty-year period. One might assume that, given the influence of William Bratton as the commissioner of the NYPD and later chief of the LAPD, a remarkable figure in policing in each city and within the profession, the developmental teleology of policing would be similar. But it is not. The forces that shape policing are a combination of both the unique social and demographic circumstances of the two cities, as well as their responses institutionally and politically to parallel pressures of crime, scandal, and reform. The two cities were each undergoing rapid and profound transformations, not just since the peak of the crime decline, but for many years before. The twin patterns of ecological change and the teleology of policing and crime raise important questions about the ordering of these influences in the broader transformation of the city.

Housing and Gentrification

The physical space of each city has transformed dramatically in the past two decades. Gentrification in the central core of each city, as well as in selected neighborhoods, has both displaced populations from poor, high crime areas and reconfigured the built environment in dramatic ways. In each city, the process of transforming both the residential and commercial built environments has required the police to engage in more "order maintenance" styles of policing in the central business districts.

New York

In the midtown business core of New York, between the Theater District and office towers to the east, the gentrification of the Times Square area was a process designed and implemented in the 1990s. Together with zoning changes, tax incentives to spur development helped replace the licentious carnival atmosphere of Times Square with retail stores, hotels, and restaurants that draw from mainstream American culture.[25] Physical disorder was replaced by the construction of several office towers housing professional workers.

As part of the development effort, the shift in policing strategy beginning in 1994 facilitated the removal of the signs of social disorder. This meant using zoning laws to force the closing of destinations for "undesirables" including pornography shops and cheap eateries. The aggressive policing strategy focused on prostitution, vagrancy and loitering, and other petty misdemeanors to remove prostitutes, homeless persons, street card games, and groups of persons loitering around X-rated movie houses. The result was the replacement of old visible signs of disorder with businesses and buildings that reassured tourists, merchants, and consumers that the area was safe. The local business community encouraged the creation of new forms of court services to reduce the recurring nature of much of this crime by providing remedial services to those who formerly occupied the streets rather than only fines or incarceration (Briffault 1999).

Although this is an appealing story, consistent with the "broken windows" theories of policing (Kelling and Cole 1996) and its impact on disorder (Skogan 1990), whether crime dropped due to policing or due to changes in the environment or both is hard to disentangle. In other words, the two faces of "broken windows" were remediated simultaneously, with perhaps unique, additive, or even multiplicative effects.

Development in the neighborhoods outside New York City's business districts was based less on commercial development than on the transformation of housing and other faces of the built environment. Much of the development was driven by gentrification, but its forms varied by neighborhood. Gentrification in Harlem, Red Hook, Washington Heights, and the South Bronx brought about extreme transformations in housing and population composition, as well as reductions in crime. Gentrification in Chelsea, largely by gay populations, converted a working-class residential and rough area into a wealthy enclave. But the economic and cultural dislocations caused by this displacement were dramatic. New businesses in those areas were created to serve the new residents, but the jobs they brought demanded skills that the remaining local residents did not have, increasing economic tensions and inequality within neighborhoods.

Police responses in these places, where the crime rate is now low, are no different now than they were during the era of dramatic crime reduction in the 1990s. Aggressive enforcement of low-level crimes, and aggressive interdiction of those who are "out of place," helped drive more than 500,000 citizen stops every year since 2003. Harlem, a relatively safe neighborhood today, still has a very high concentration of police activity, including *Terry* stops, marijuana enforcement, trespass enforcement

(Operation Clean Halls), and bans on public drinking. Gentrification inevitably led to the displacement of older residents by wealthier (and whiter) newcomers. There is some evidence that those who left took crime with them and have adversely affected the areas to which they have dispersed.[26]

The relationship between housing and crime in New York is complicated not only by real estate booms over the period since the mid-1980s but also by strategic investments in housing for poor people. Since crime in New York, as elsewhere, was concentrated in the poorest neighborhoods, we might expect those neighborhoods to be the most crime-sensitive to both housing development and crime. Figure 8.6 shows the distribution of $5.8 billion in housing construction and rehabilitation programs for the poor across three mayoralties, starting in 1987, under a program known as the "10-Year Plan" (Van Ryzin and Genn 1999). Figure 8.6 shows that these investments were made in the New York City's poorest neighborhoods, which were those with the highest homicide and other violence rates during the peak violence years in the late 1980s and early 1990s.

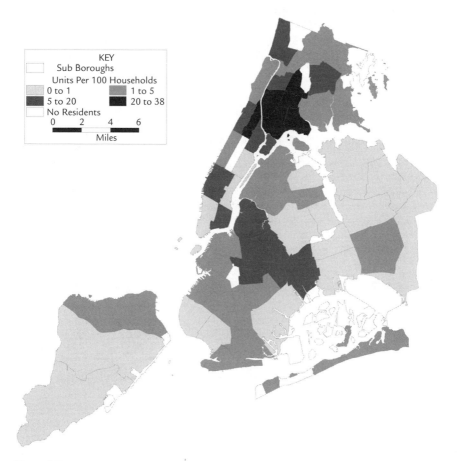

Figure 8.6
Concentration of Ten-Year Plan Units in New York City, 1985–1995
Source: Greg Van Ryzin and Andrew Genn, 1999.

The decline in crime mirrors these investments. Figure 8.7 shows homicide "trajectories" for the city's 275 neighborhoods from 1985 to 2002 using boundary definitions of neighborhoods generated by the Department of City Planning.[27] Both raw and smoothed trends are shown for each neighborhood trajectory group. The trajectories were identified using trajectory modeling methods based on Poisson mixture models (Nagin 2005). Fagan and Davies (2007) identified four crime trajectories that grossly describe crime trends across NYC neighborhoods, with Group 4 comprising the most dangerous and the others showing a more gradual decline that began in 1991. These were not only the most heavily policed places in the city (Fagan et al. 2010), but they also were the beneficiaries of the Ten-Year Plan investments. To illustrate this, figure 8.8 shows that homicide declines were greatest in the same neighborhoods where housing investments for the poor were the highest.

There are good reasons why people in poor neighborhoods may be more responsive to housing investments. First, housing imparts stake in one's community (Toby 1957). Homeowners are more likely to exercise guardianship over their homes and neighborhoods when they have such stakes. Second, housing is a critical pathway to wealth and an escape route from the poverty traps that characterize many poor and high crime neighborhoods (Massey and Denton 1993; Sampson and Morenoff 2006). Housing ownership reduces transience and mobility, in turn promoting the kinds of strong social ties that can inoculate neighborhoods against crime through collective social actions (Sampson, Raudenbush, and Earls 1997).

Of course, policing throughout this period was concentrated in the areas with the highest homicide rates and most active drug markets (Letwin 1990; Karmen 2000; Fagan et al. 2010). Accordingly, the simultaneity of policing and the economic

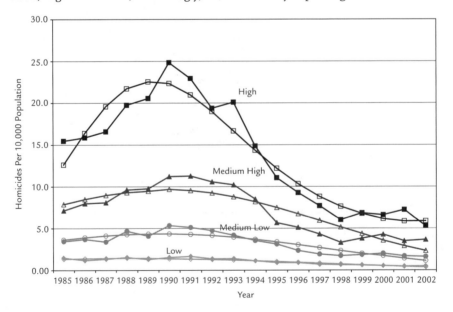

Figure 8.7
Homicide Trajectories, New York City Neighborhoods, 1985–2002
Source: Adapted from Fagan and Davis, 2007.

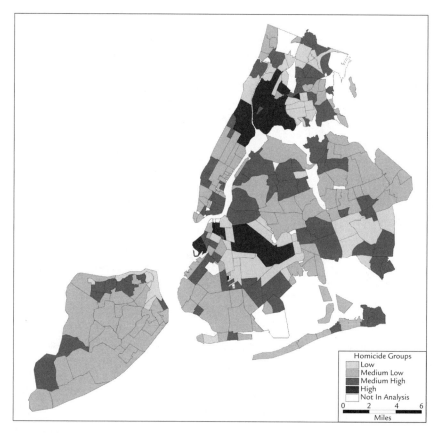

Figure 8.8
Map of Homicide Trajectories by Neighborhood, New York City, 1985–2002
Source: Adapted from Fagan and Davis, 2007.

transformation of housing complicate efforts to sort out the temporal sequence of changes between crime rates shaped directly by the police from those influenced by changes in the built environment. Empirical arguments depend in part on the starting point for measuring change, on the lens—whether borough, neighborhood, census tract, or police precinct—and how one conceptualizes housing and physical disorder (Schwartz, Susin, and Voicu 2003; Fagan and Davies 2007).

Los Angeles

The same tension in causal mechanisms is evident in the story of housing and crime in Los Angeles during the same era. Was the drop in central Los Angeles caused by gentrification in downtown neighborhoods and areas near the University of Southern California? This is a complex picture because crime rates do not easily reconstitute themselves in areas settled by displaced residents. In fact, when we examine the data on Los Angeles, it is clear that across all police divisions crime rates dropped significantly after 2002—the period in which Bratton instituted COMPSTAT Plus (Gascón 2005). Yet, the crime drop in the central business district area (Central

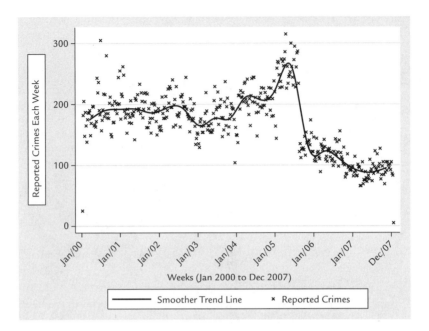

Figure 8.9
Crime Trends in Los Angeles Central Police Division, January 1, 2000, to December 31, 2007
Source: Los Angeles Police Department.

Police Division) of Los Angeles occurred during this period of police reform, while crime rates in South Los Angeles did not enjoy a similar decline.

In Los Angeles, the redevelopment of neighborhoods like Skid Row in the downtown area and Bunker Hill adjacent to downtown, have fueled similar conflicts and tensions over how to appropriately police homeless populations when areas become prime targets for real estate investment and urban renewal (Blasi 2007; Harcourt 2005). Figure 8.9 shows the decline in total violent, property, and nuisance reported crimes in the Central Police Division of Los Angeles (where Skid Row is located) between January 1, 2000, and December 31, 2007 (Berk and MacDonald 2010). Like New York, there is empirical evidence that the LAPD's efforts through its Safer Cities Initiative to crackdown on misdemeanor crimes and enforce vagrancy laws that ban the formation of large homeless encampments led to meaningful reductions in crime (Berk and MacDonald 2010). Further information on how this played out in Skid Row is in chapter 14.

Whether a greater investment in LA County Mental Health and Health and Human Services agencies could have been equally effective as the LAPD's approach to reducing crime and disorder in Skid Row is an open question. But in both cities a focus on crime reduction through getting tough on vagrancy always brought out tensions between those concerned with crime control and those concerned with the plight of homeless.

We can expect this to continue through the coming decade as neighborhoods develop, populations change, and older residents are dislocated. Gentrification will always bring about tensions for police as community expectations about the police response shift in response to changing dynamics of neighborhood property owners and residents.

Immigration

The second major transformation of the city during the past sixty years has been the increase in both size and neighborhood concentration of immigrants. The relationship between immigration and crime has been a topic of policy interest at different times in twentieth century, and the current era is no different. The 1931 report by the National Committee on Law Observation and Enforcement, popularly called the Wickersham Commission (National Commission on Law Observance and Enforcement 1931), observed no evidence linking immigration to increased crime patterns (Tonry 1997).

Despite the Wickersham Commission's observations, sociology was dominated by the thinking that immigration was linked to crime through neighborhood social disadvantage. Sociologists studied immigration as a central feature of the social structure of neighborhoods in the first half of the twentieth century. Most concluded that immigrants themselves had relatively low rates of criminal offending, but that immigrants settled into disadvantaged areas that exposed their children to higher rates of offending. Several notable sociologists theorized that any evidence of higher crime rates in immigrant neighborhoods was a result of the exposure of second-generation immigrants to economic disadvantage, a culture of conflict, and underclass norms that were more favorable to violations of the law in the presence of relative economic disadvantage (see Reckless and Smith 1932; Sutherland 1934; Sellin 1938; Shaw and McKay 1942).

But recent empirical research on the immigration–crime nexus suggests that the earlier links between immigrant settlements and neighborhood crime rates have changed, suggesting a new and different interpretation of the social disorganization theories of the first generation of immigration–crime studies (Morenoff and Astor 2006; Martinez, Stowell, and Lee 2010). During the 1990s, a number of US cities, including both New York and Los Angeles, experienced substantial growth of immigrant settlement into inner-city poverty-stricken neighborhoods (Malone et al. 2003; Passel and Suro 2005; Davies and Fagan 2012). Neighborhood patterns of poverty and residential segregation in New York and Los Angeles, like many other large cities, shifted the demographic makeup of high poverty neighborhoods that had been the areas of standing racial or ethnic disparities in income and housing segregation since the 1960s (Cutler, Glaeser, and Vigdor 1999; Glaeser and James 2011). The New York neighborhoods of Harlem and the South Bronx that had been settled by African Americans and Puerto Ricans for decades became areas of concentrated poverty that were emblematic of crime in the city (Davies and Fagan 2012). In the Los Angeles neighborhoods of East Los Angeles, South Central, and Watts, African Americans and Mexican Americans had been living in entrenched poverty since the 1960s. These neighborhoods were considered hotbeds of crime and violence; Watts, as we mentioned earlier, was the center of an apocalyptic riot.

For reasons perhaps owing to both economics and race or ethnicity, these areas of entrenched poverty became destinations for new immigrants. Immigrants tended to settle in places they could afford and places where people looked like them (Davies and Fagan 2012). In Los Angeles, this meant that areas of both Mexican American and African American poverty became increasingly concentrated with foreign-born residents. In New York, the neighborhood of Washington Heights became a reception zone for immigrants from the Dominican Republic in the 1970s, while American residents of Puerto Rico in-migrated to the neighborhoods of the South Bronx and East Harlem in the 1960s. Haitian and other Caribbean immigrants settled in the East Flatbush area of Brooklyn in the 1970s, accelerating an outmigration of whites to the suburbs that began two decades earlier.

These were neighborhoods with high crime and violence for decades, but as we show for each city, that is no longer the case. As crime rates declined in each city, we show that the decline in crime in the new immigrant neighborhoods was greater than in other parts of the respective cities. Below we show evidence in both New York and Los Angeles that neighborhoods with high concentrations of immigrants have experienced larger crime declines than similarly situated neighborhoods without heavy influxes of immigrants. As with housing, the worst places in each city became safer, and the evidence suggests that this marginal gain in public safety was attributable to immigrants.

Los Angeles

Figure 8.10 shows the distribution of foreign-born residents and Latinos (predominately Mexican American) in LA census tracts in 1990 and 2000. What is striking from this figure is how immigrant enclaves became more concentrated in Los Angeles, even in areas previously not considered immigrant enclaves.

MacDonald and colleagues (MacDonald, Hipp, and Gill 2012) showed that these areas with high expected probabilities of immigrant settlement[28] had greater reductions in crime between 2000 and 2005 than other similarly situated areas.[29] Figure 8.11 shows the average change in neighborhood crime rates as measured by the total number of serious crimes[30] declined substantially more in neighborhoods with higher expected immigrant settlement patterns. What these findings suggest is that part of the crime decline in Los Angeles is a story of immigrant concentration. But there are several immigration stories in Los Angeles, owing to the multiple countries of origin of various immigrant groups, especially from Central and South America. Identifying unique sending-country effects is complicated by the absence of country of origin measures prior to the 2000 census. Even with those data, parsing the unique country-of-origin effects would be complicated by the high percentage of Mexican immigration and the residential integration of all immigrant groups in neighborhoods where Spanish is the first language.

New York

In New York, immigration rose steadily beginning in the 1970s, with settlements of Caribbeans in East Flatbush and Dominicans in Washington Heights. Two decades before, Puerto Ricans in-migrated to New York City and settled primarily in East Harlem and the South Bronx, spreading out from there to other neighborhoods across the city. Figure 8.12 shows maps of immigrant concentration in 1990 and again in 2000. Immigration since 1990, primarily South Asians, Mexicans, and other

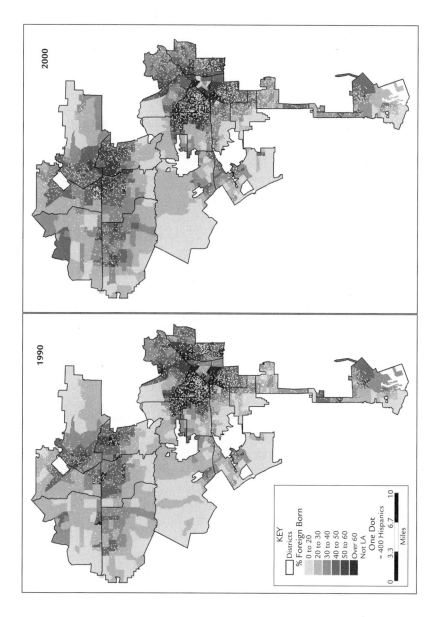

Figure 8.10
Distribution of Foreign-Born and Hispanics in Los Angeles Neighborhoods (1990 and 2000)
Source: Adapted from MacDonald, Hipp, and Gill, 2012.

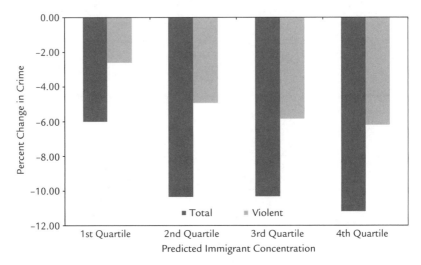

Figure 8.11
Average Change in Crime by Quartiles of Predicted Immigrant Concentration, Los Angeles
Census Tracts, 2000–2005
Source: Adapted from MacDonald, Hipp, and Gill, 2012.

Central Americans, and several East Asian groups, has been concentrated in several
neighborhoods in Queens and Brooklyn, with smaller concentrations in Manhattan
and the Bronx.

As in Los Angeles, immigration has been a protective factor in the natural history
of crime in the city's neighborhoods. Figure 8.13 shows the effects of immigrant concentration on specific types of crime in New York during the same period, as reported
by Davies and Fagan (2012). To assess potential cohort effects, immigrant neighborhoods were measured both as the percentage of all foreign-born residents and then
as the percentage of foreign-born residents who had lived there for less than five
years. In each case, there were strong significant effects for the total immigrant population on all crimes, plus three specific crime types. But the effects were more muted
for recent immigrants, owing perhaps to the fact that by 1997, they had arrived in
neighborhoods that already had experienced strong crime declines, and that realized
significant improvements in housing (Fagan and Davies 2007).

Davies and Fagan (2012) also showed differences by ethnicity and race in the effects
of immigrant concentration on neighborhood crime. Figure 8.14 shows the effects of
immigrant concentration on both total and violent crime were greatest in neighborhoods where white (mainly Russian and other Eastern Europeans) and black (mainly
Caribbean) immigrants settled. Concentrations of Latino immigrants showed little effect
on crime rates, perhaps for different reasons. One was the generally lower concentration
of Latino immigrants and their entry into a heterogeneous set of neighborhoods, with
both low and high crime rates. Asian immigrants tended to settle in stable, low-crime
areas, muting any effects of either long-standing or more recent immigrant status.

In both cities, generational effects are evident, though they seem to work in opposing directions. In New York, neighborhoods with newer immigrants had smaller crime

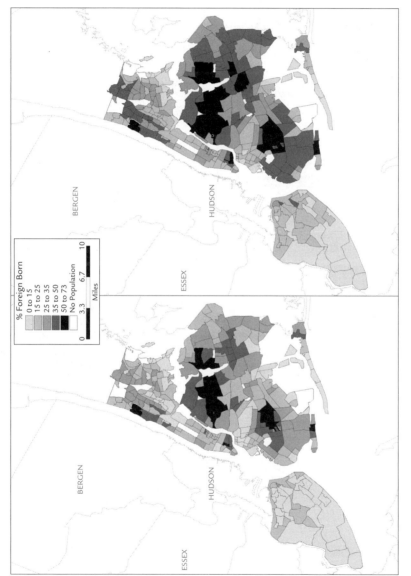

Figure 8.12
Distribution of Foreign-Born Population in New York Neighborhoods (1990–2000)
Source: Created by authors from Neighborhood Boundaries and Census Data 1990 and 2000.

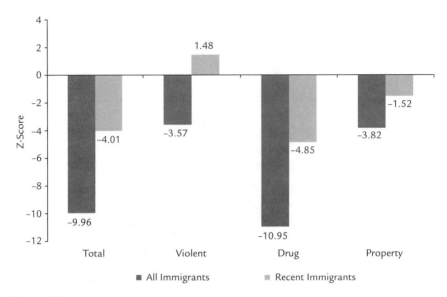

Figure 8.13
Effects of Immigrant Concentration on Crime by Type of Crime (Z Scores), New York City
Census Tracts, 1990–2002
Source: Davies and Fagan, 2012.

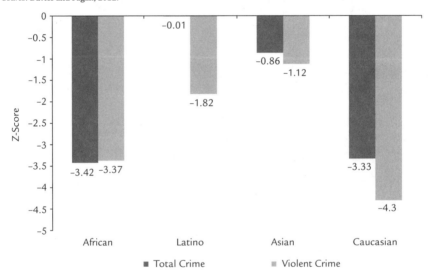

Figure 8.14
Effects of Immigrant Concentration on Crime by Ethnicity (Z Scores), New York City Census
Tracts, 1990–2002
Source: Davies and Fagan, 2012.

declines than the more settled immigrant areas. While this may be an effect specific
to the ethnic group, it may also suggest that the effects of immigrant generation
covary with preexisting crime and other social conditions in the neighborhoods.

But the story is somewhat different in Los Angeles. Areas settled by more recent
Central American immigrants have had lower crime rates through the late 1990s

than areas settled several generations ago by Mexican immigrants (MacDonald, Hipp, and Gill 2012). Boyle Heights, for example, had a smaller crime rate drop than Southeast Los Angeles, where newer generations of immigrants had arrived since 1990. Although both areas had similar percentages of Hispanic residents, Southeast Los Angeles became an area of greater immigrant concentration over the decade of the 1990s. These trends suggest that acculturation by the second generation accompanied by poverty trapped neighborhoods reduces any generational effect of immigration on lowering crime (MacDonald, Hipp, and Gill 2012). In short, by the third generation the rates of crime climb back to what would be expected if a neighborhood had concentrated poverty and few immigrants.

This suggests that the benefits of immigrant concentration on reducing crime may be transitory and can be affected by immigrant social mobility to diffuse and assimilate into the city (and regional) social structure and economy. In other words, racial and ethnic segregation might erode the gains in crime reduction and social control that are produced by new immigrants. In the first generation, segmented assimilation of self-selected immigrants into new ethnic enclaves may produce social capital benefits that help control crime and even provide some protection for second-generation residents during adolescence (MacDonald, Hipp ,and Gill 2012). But, as time goes by, neighborhoods entrenched in poverty regardless of the historical ethnic heritage will have crime rates that return to normal states. The South Central and Southeast neighborhoods of Los Angeles are not only central to this story of crime decline in Los Angeles but also to the immigration story. The crime declines in these places were strongly correlated with the arrival of new immigrant residents. So, while Los Angeles as a whole was growing safer between 1994 and 2005, the dominant trend was in the areas that were undergoing significant immigrant arrival and gentrification.

Policing Immigration and Crime

One might expect that the potential benefit of immigration for reducing crime rates in neighborhoods has not been lost on the police and public officials in either city. But on this question, the two cities differ. In Los Angeles, for example, former police chief Daryl Gates helped to establish an LAPD departmental policy in 1979 to not initiate "police action with the objective of discovering the alien status of a person" and to not arrest or book a person for "illegal entry" into the United States (Rampart Independent Review Panel 2000). The LAPD have been vigilant about not enforcing federal immigration laws so that they can encourage immigrants to actively report crimes.

How do police patrol these neighborhoods, and what is the nature of police–citizen interactions? Crime and arrests are endogenous, so it is difficult to sort out whether the lower crime rates in immigrant neighborhoods are externalities of immigration, or whether the police alter their strategies in areas that they may believe to be different and (more importantly) less problematic. While there is no direct data on police patrol strength in Los Angeles and immigrant enclaves, it is noteworthy that the LAPD has had a friendly immigrant policy on the books since 1979.

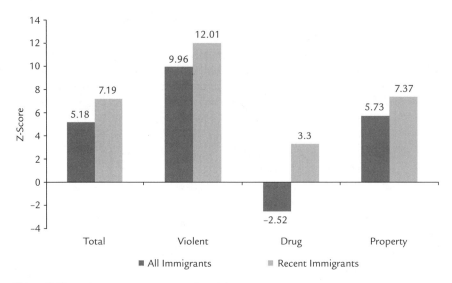

Figure 8.15
Effects of Immigrant Concentration on Enforcement by Type of Crime (Z Scores), New York
City Census Tracts, 1990–2002
Source: Davies and Fagan, 2012.

In New York City, there is no specific policy on policing immigrant neighborhoods.
However, there is evidence that police in New York City more aggressively patrol
neighborhoods with poor and African American populations, after controlling for
crime, but they are less aggressive in areas settled by immigrants from Latin America
generally. Figure 8.15 shows that enforcement for total, violent, and property crimes
is significantly higher in places with greater proportions of immigrants, after controlling for any differences in crime. Only for drug crimes does there appear to be
less enforcement in immigrant neighborhoods. And enforcement here, defined as the
sum of *Terry* stops (stops and frisks) plus misdemeanor arrests, is greater in neighborhoods with higher concentrations of recent immigrants. This effect is especially
strong for newer immigrants who have been in the country for less than five years.
Although crime is on balance lower in neighborhoods with higher immigrant concentrations, the ratio of stops and arrests to crime is higher in these same places.

These enforcement patterns vary by the race and ethnicity of the immigrant group,
especially for immigrants of African descent. Figure 8.16 shows that enforcement,
controlling for crime, is slightly higher for recent immigrants of Latino origin, but
lower for both whites (again, primarily Eastern Europeans) and significantly lower
for immigrants of African descent. Evidently, while African immigration protects
neighborhoods from crime, it also protects them from the excesses of racially tinged
enforcement that characterizes the NYC neighborhoods where native born African
Americans reside (Fagan and Davies 2000; Fagan et al. 2010).

Immigration in Los Angeles and New York City will continue throughout the
coming decade (contingent on national political considerations) but at a pace that
may not equal what we saw in the past decade. And as second- and third-generation

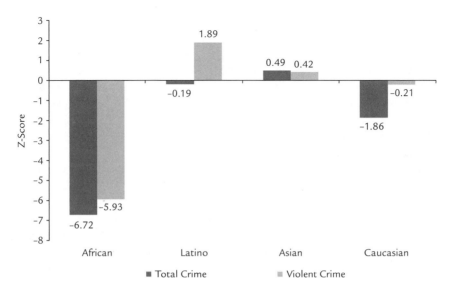

Figure 8.16
Effects of Immigrant Concentration on Enforcement by Ethnicity (Z Scores), New York City
Census Tracts, 1990–2002
Source: Davies and Fagan, 2012.

immigrants occupy the neighborhoods where their parents landed, their immersion
into the (nonwhite) American culture suggests the possibility that crime problems
will emerge. How the intergenerational path from immigration to crime patterns
emerges in each city is difficult to predict.

The interaction of immigration and gentrification is also a cautionary tale.
Tensions and conflicts between African American and Latino groups in Los Angeles
and Northern Manhattan suggest the possibility of a return to the social dynamics of
a century ago in Chicago, where immigrant groups clashed, organized into gangs, and
crime and conflict were prevalent. Finally, the role of police in enforcing immigration
laws is complex and changing. Most police agencies see this as outside of their mission and jurisdiction, and they also see it as a procedure that could risk dissuading
citizens from voluntary cooperation with police in investigating everyday crimes.

Sampson (2008) suggests that there is a link between rising immigration patterns
in cities and the declines in crime rates that occurred during the 1990s. More recent
work by Stowell et al. (2009) and Martinez, Stowell, and Lee (2010) suggests these
trends are true across cities and within San Diego. Our review of the data suggests
a similar pattern in Los Angeles and New York City. Immigrant settlement has not
played a central role in explanations of neighborhood patterns of crime. But, our
research in both cities suggests a link between neighborhood changes in crime and
immigrant settlement patterns, holding constant the effects of population and housing characteristics traditionally correlated with crime. Thus, immigrant settlement
patterns are associated with appreciable reductions in crime for neighborhoods in
both cities.

THE FUTURE

For a half century, policing in the two cities has gone through a cycle of crime booms and more recent busts that have oscillated around periods of scandal and reform. Crime has declined for nine consecutive years in Los Angeles, including a 9.6 percent decline in 2010. While crime has also declined throughout the past decade in New York, the pace of change has been slower than during the first decade of the unprecedented decline that started around 1992. Los Angeles is slowly catching up to the low crime rates that now characterize New York. The connection between the two phenomena is part of a larger and more complex evolution in each city: the trends in crime and the episodes of policing scandal and reform have also coincided with changes in the social fabric of New York and Los Angeles.

The past decade has been a time of battles with civil litigation in Los Angeles and New York over accusations of unconstitutional police practices. In 2009, Los Angeles emerged from nine years under a consent decree. In lifting the consent decree, the US District Court Judge Gary A. Fees overseeing the decree noted that "LAPD has become the national and international policing standard for activities that range from audits to handling of the mentally ill to many aspects of training to risk assessment of police officers and more" (Rubin 2009). The LAPD has entered into new partnerships with various community organizations (Nagourney 2011), and nearly 80 percent of LA residents expressed strong approval for the performance of the department. This approval included 76 percent of the black and 68 percent of the Latino respondents to the poll. These signs show that the LAPD has recovered, both in reputation and in performance, following what was perhaps the biggest police corruption scandal in the United States.

While Los Angeles has emerged from civil rights litigation in 2009 following a lengthy period of intensive federal court monitoring, New York City emerged from the *Daniels* litigation in 2007 only to become immediately mired in three new separate lawsuits alleging both racial discrimination and a pattern of unconstitutional street stops. The NYPD has intensified its spectrum of Order Maintenance Policing tactics, including trespass enforcement in public housing, street stops, and misdemeanor marijuana enforcement. All three prongs of this strategy have led to litigation and their wisdom and benefits continue to be hotly contested. The divided response of New York City's diverse communities to the Stop and Frisk program, the centerpiece of the NYPD strategy, shows the depth of the racial breach between citizens and police: white voters approve 59 to 36 percent, while disapproval is 68 to 27 percent among black voters and 52 to 43 percent among Hispanic voters.

In Los Angeles, the future of the LAPD and its ties to the diverse communities of the city was set in motion by the changes brought about through both the external pressures of the litigation and the internal push for reform and responsiveness by Chief Bratton. The LAPD has become more diverse in the past decade, including a plurality of minority officers, a compositional change that has been linked to the positive response by the diverse communities of Los Angeles. There has been an active effort in the LAPD to diversify its department and find ways to enhance its recruitment efforts, including using a new recruiting system developed by researchers at the RAND Corporation (Lim et al. 2009).

Like New York, racial disparities in police contacts remained in Los Angeles through 2004, even after controlling for differences in crime rates between locations (Ayres and Borowsky 2008; Fagan et al. 2010). Still, the structural and cultural reforms in the LAPD suggest that Los Angeles has entered a new era, marked by collaboration between the LAPD and the community, built on a platform of accountability, transparency, and positive performance in maintaining safety and order. What is perhaps most important for the future are the signs of the community investment in this collaboration (Nagourney 2011). Whether this future will hold, and for how long, is uncertain. But it is notable that there has not been a similar period in the past 50 years where the LAPD was viewed in such a favorable light by a wide cross section of racial and ethnic minorities in the city.

The future in New York is not quite as bright. High profile scandals continue to surround the policing of racial and ethnic minorities, including, allegations of falsification of victim reports to suppress crime statistics (Rayman 2012; Eterno and Silverman 2012), monetary damage settlements of more than $57 million per year over the past decade in police misconduct litigation (Hennelley 2012), allegations of arrest and "stop" quotas and illegal arrests (Powell 2012), extensive targeted surveillance of Muslim groups in madrassas and mosques both inside the city and in neighboring cities (Gold and Apuzzo 2012), constitutional violations in the handling of political demonstrations in 2004 and in the recent Occupy Wall Street movement, and chronic conflicts with the press over reporting of crime and political demonstrations. Even as crime rates decline in a period where the NYPD force has shrunk by over 6,000 officers (Zimring 2011), the tension between ethnic minorities and the NYPD remains front-and-center.

While the LAPD has emerged from a period of crisis and deep institutional reform to build an umbrella of legitimacy through close ties to the varied communities of Los Angeles, the current posture of the NYPD and its resistance to outside monitoring and internal reforms suggests a less clear future. The LAPD has harmonized, to the extent possible given its recent past, with the future of the social fabric of Los Angeles. The same cannot be said in New York City. Many citizens in New York City, including those most heavily policed, await the next mayor and police commissioner to see whether a new era of reform can begin that includes citizen trust and satisfaction as an outcome as equally worthy of addressing as the crime rate.

NOTES

1. The *New York Post*, as only the *New York Post* can, published a front-page headline on September 7, 1990, that screamed "Crime-ravaged City Cries Out for Help: Dave, Do Something." The headline was aimed at Mayor David Dinkins, demanding that he take strong measures to stop crime after a particularly gruesome few days of lethal violence in New York City. Dinkins did just that, collaborating with then-Speaker Peter Vallone of the New York City Council to pass the Safe Streets, Safe Cities Act in the state legislature, funding 5,000 new police officers who were deployed a year later in 1991. By 1992, crime had begun to fall, dropping 10 percent in two years (Fagan, Zimring, and Kim 1998; Karmen 2000; Zimring 2011). Crime continued to fall for the next twenty years.

2. Litigation in New York was filed by the Center for Constitutional Rights in 2001, following an investigation of the NYPD Stop and Frisk tactics by the New York State Attorney General (Spitzer 1999). The 2001 litigation resulted in a Stipulated Settlement in *Kelvin Daniels et al. v. City of New York et al.*, 99 Civ. 1695 (SAS) (2003). Subsequent litigation was filed by the Center for Constitutional Rights in January 2008 following the expiration of the Daniels settlement. The current case, *David Floyd et al. v. City of New York et al.*, 08 Civ 1034 (SAS) (2008), will proceed to trial later this year. In Los Angeles, the United States Department of Justice (DOJ) filed a civil suit alleging that the department was engaging in a pattern or practice of excessive force, false arrests, and unreasonable searches and seizures. The litigation produced a Consent Decree in *United States of America v. City of Los Angeles et al.*, Civil No. 00–11769 (C.D. Cal.) (GAF) that was signed in 2001.

3. Compare Stone et al.'s 2009 report on Los Angeles to Fagan et al. 2010's report on New York City.

4. David Garland points out in *Culture of Control* (2001) that two entire generations of Americans and Britains have knowledge only of insecurity, and either lack knowledge of or cannot remember low crime eras. This tends to make criminology a distinctly ahistorical discipline. Most active criminologists were born after 1960 and received their advanced degrees after 1980. As a cohort, they have no memory of low crime eras or the theory and discourse on crime in the lower crime eras that pre-date the Presidents Commission on Law Enforcement and Criminal Justice (1967) or the Kerner Commission Report (1968). There also are some difficulties in accessing reliable data on those eras. Current theory on crime is framed by the limitations of our data sources, which too often began after 1975 for crime victimization or 1976 for homicide incidents.

5. For illustrations of this Foucaultian idea, see Garland (2001). See also Garton Ash (1999).

6. During the riot, the incomparable baseball pitcher Sandy Koufax pitched a no-hitter for the team, the Dodgers, in a game that was witnessed by less than one-fifth of those who had bought tickets.

7. http://www.lapdonline.org/history_of_the_lapd/content_basic_view/1110.

8. Chief Parker died within a year of the Watts Riots. He was replaced in by Ed Davis, who instituted several reforms that sought closer ties to the minority community. One innovation was the Basic Car Plan, which assigned officers to specific geographic boundaries, an early version of local—if not community—policing. Davis also increased the number of specialized units (Encyclopedia of Police Science). Aside from these marginal changes though, the LAPD remained focused on police efficiency and administration while rebuilding community relations damaged by the riots (Greene 2007). Daryl Gates succeeded Parker in 1978, an internal hire. He focused primarily on budget-driven reductions in hiring during massive population growth, the emergence of dense networks of street gangs, and the first of two waves of rising crime rates. Gates served as LAPD chief of police until he retired under pressure in 1992 after the riots set off by the Rodney King incident.

9. King had previously been convicted of driving while intoxicated and was currently driving under a suspended license. He led the LAPD on a high-speed chase for approximately 10 minutes. In total twelve cars were involved in the pursuit. Upon exiting the car, King allegedly refused to lie down, was shot with a Taser, and then was repeatedly hit with batons and kicked while on the ground (Independent Commission on the Los Angeles Police Department 1991). This may have been a routine police–citizen use of force case had it not been captured on videotape from a nearby resident.

10. A poll taken by the *LA Times* newspaper shortly after the incident found that 87 percent of African American and 80 percent of Hispanic respondents thought that police brutality in the LAPD was common (Independent Commission on the Los Angeles Police Department 1991, 16). Tuch and Weitzer's (1997) examination of *LA Times* public opinion poll data over periods before and after highly publicized incidents of police brutality (e.g., January 3, 1979, shooting of Eulia Love; March 3, 1991, beating of Rodney King) found dramatic reductions in public approval of the LAPD among African American and Hispanic respondents. Studies in other cities also show that high-profile media cases of police abuse increase minority distrust of the police (Jefferies et al. 1997; Weitzer 2002). The trends of declining opinion appear to last in Los Angeles until 1995 (Tuch and Weitzer 1997), years after the LAPD had instituted its first series of reforms.

11. Williams's five-year term effectively removed the life tenure status of the police chief and made the LAPD executive more accountable to the political constituents. Williams was known for his ability to form tight bonds with the public in Philadelphia. However, Williams experience in the LAPD was short-lived, as his powers as a chief were circumscribed in many ways, including limiting his ability to bring in outside command staff. The LAPD did, however, under Chief Williams's direction form a strategic plan for change that fully embraced the goals of community policing, as well as the mission.

12. See http://www.lapdonline.org/search_results/content_basic_view/6528.

13. The BOI noted numerous problems with the recruitment screening and supervision of CRASH officers in the field and downplayed wider problems of routine illegality by CRASH officers.

14. For example, the Knapp Report identified two particular classes of corrupt police officer, which it called "Grass Eaters" and "Meat Eaters." Each was endemic to the culture of the department, and the sustaining norms were passed on from the older generations of police to the new recruits. The classification itself refers to petty corruption under peer pressure ("eating grass") and aggressive premeditated major corruption ("eating meat"). "Grass Eaters" were police officers who routinely took five, ten, twenty dollar payments from contractors, tow-truck operators, gamblers, and others working both inside and outside the law. "Grass eating" was a way of life for many cops, normalized in the police culture, and was considered part of the "pay" for being a cop. The Knapp Commission found that "grass eating" was used by police officers to prove their loyalty to the "brotherhood" of cops and was essential to sustaining the police culture. "Meat Eaters" were officers who "spend a good deal of time aggressively looking for larger paydays," such as shaking down pimps and drug dealers for money. The Commission noted that these officers justified this extortion by marginalizing their victims as criminals and undeserving of police protection.

15. The Mollen Commission heard from officers who admitted pouring ammonia on the face of a detainee in a holding cell and from another who threw garbage and boiling water on someone hiding in a dumbwaiter shaft. Another officer allegedly doctored an "escape rope" used by drug dealers so they would plunge to the ground if they used it, and the same group also raided a brothel while in uniform, ordered the customers to leave, and terrorized and raped the women there.

16. See background at: http://www.lapdonline.org/history_of_the_lapd/content_basic_view/1120.

17. http://policechiefmagazine.org/magazine/index.cfm?fuseaction=print_display&article_id=593&issue_id=52005.

18. According to the latest Quinnipiac University Poll, New Yorkers were narrowly split in their approval of the Stop and Frisk tactic, with 50 percent disapproving the practice. The rate of disapproval has hovered between 45 and 50 percent since Quinnipiac began asking this question. See Quinnipiac University Polling Institute, "Cutting Stop and Frisk Won't Increase Crime, More New Yorkers Tell Quinnipiac University Poll," August 12, 2012. Available at: http://www.quinnipiac.edu/institutes-centers/polling-institute/new-york-city/release-detail?ReleaseID=1788.

19. One of us (Fagan) was a consultant to the New York State Attorney General and assisted in the analysis that was published in the Spitzer (1999) report on racial disparities and Fourth Amendment concerns in the NYPD Stop and Frisk Program. This review focuses on the larger social and political contexts of policing in New York before and after that era.

20. See *Ligon et al. v. City of New York*, 12 Civ. 2274 (SAS) (2012), for a description of how Operation Clean Halls operates. According to data provided by the City of New York in the *Davis et al. v. City of New York*, 10 Civ. 0699 (S.D.N.Y.) (SAS) (2010), litigation, police conduct approximately 25,000 "vertical patrols" each month where they patrol the halls and stairwells of these buildings, as well as buildings in New York City Housing Authority developments.

21. To control for the potential underreporting of robberies over time, we adjust robbery rates by subtracting the ratio of robberies to homicides in each year. This in effect reduces the influence that changes in the reporting of robbery will have on the robbery rate. A big ratio will result in down-weighting the rate or robberies. The results we display with or without this adjustment have no material effect.

22. Adjusting robbery rates for changes in reporting practices relative to homicide does not change the story of the 1990s.

23. The statistical analysis was not the only component of Bratton's reforms. He developed new models of accountability for field commanders, also instituted new tactics including aggressive street stops as part of his response in crime "hot spots" (see, e.g., Maple and Mitchell 2000; Dickey 2009).

24. *Terry v. Ohio*, 392 U.S. 1 (1968)

25. Chain stores (e.g., Gap, Levi Straus, Disney, Toys "R" Us), hotels (e.g., Marriott, W, Hilton, Crowne Plaza), and entertainment (e.g., ESPN Zone, MTV), all with nationwide identity, proliferate in Times Square today.

26. Incarceration rates in the upstate counties contiguous to New York City have risen sharply since 2000, in part because of the social shock to quiet and homogeneously white upstate areas of newly transplanted former New York City residents. See, for example, Carrie Johnson, "As Gangs Move to Upstate New York, So Too Does Crime," National Public Radio, Morning Edition, March 14, 2009, available at: http://www.npr.org/2012/03/14/148160372/as-gangs-move-to-new-york-suburbs-so-does-crime.

27. Boundary maps for these neighborhoods of approximately 15,000 population are available at: http://www.nyc.gov/html/dcp/html/bytes/meta_nynta.shtml.

28. Measured by a standardized value of percentage of foreign-born residents and percentage of Hispanic/Latino residents.

29. Immigrant enclaves were matched with other neighborhoods based on local poverty index, a measure of residential stability, the number of males under age 25, and the regional patterns of immigration in Los Angeles.

30. FBI index offenses, which include murder, rape, robbery, assault, burglary, theft-person, theft-vehicle, kidnap, arson of a dwelling, and motor vehicle theft.

CHAPTER 9

Los Angeles and New York City Schools

JULIA WRIGLEY

The huge public school systems of New York City and Los Angeles rank first and second in the nation in size, with New York City serving just under a million students and Los Angeles counting close to 700,000 (NCES 2010). The districts face similar problems of students living with poverty (Trounson and Poindexter 2012; Roberts 2012), racial segregation (Orfield, Kucsera, and Siegel-Hawley 2012, 45), and low achievement levels (National Center for Education Statistics 2011a, b). The two districts' political paths differed in the early twenty-first century, with Los Angeles operating on a more inchoate level, while Mayor Michael Bloomberg established firm control over the New York City school system. By 2011, their paths began to converge, with each under leadership strongly influenced by a national school reform movement supercharged by private wealth, federal power, and an ascendant ideology of accountability, school choice, and reliance on standardized tests. In New York City and Los Angeles, Washington, DC, and many state capitals, reformers battled teachers unions over how teachers would be evaluated, how bonuses would be assigned, and how teachers would be fired. Reformers blamed poorly trained and ineffective teachers for low levels of student achievement and fought for teachers to be assessed on the basis of value-added models of student test score gains. The number of charter schools, mainly nonunionized, multiplied in both Los Angeles and New York City. The popular documentary, *Waiting for Superman*, captured the moment, portraying teachers unions as enforcing ossified work rules while charter schools operated nimbly and creatively.

In New York City, mayoral control of the schools paved the way for attempts to implement a school reform agenda. Lack of mayoral control, except in a limited and indirect form, in Los Angeles, helped slow implementation of a similar school reform agenda supported by the mayor and by wealthy individuals, such as Eli Broad. To the extent such an agenda was implemented in Los Angeles, it occurred in an erratic form that increased the fragmentation and contentiousness of the district. Even in New York City, with a high level of mayoral control, school reform has not always proceeded smoothly. In 2009, public satisfaction with Mayor Bloomberg's control of the schools reached a peak level of 57 percent, according to a Quinnipiac University poll, but after a number of setbacks, including the recalibration of students' test scores and the brief interregnum of an unpopular superintendent, that number fell to 34 percent in a 2011 *New York Times* survey (Otterman and Kopicki 2011). Those surveyed registered dissatisfaction with school closings, services for students with disabilities, and the focus on testing. More parents said the teachers were the best thing about their children's school than had done so seven years earlier in 2004, despite attacks on teachers and unions in the intervening years (Otterman and Kopicki 2011).

The national school reform agenda might be more popular among elites than parents in urban districts, but mayoral control usually follows from years of dysfunction in urban districts when power is split among the chief school officer, the school board, unions, and local political leaders. This was the case in New York City. In response to the pressure for community control, the state legislature created thirty-two decentralized districts in 1969. Teachers union lobbying helped limit the power of the local bodies. They were given control over elementary and intermediate schools, but high schools and special education remained under the control of the central administration. The best of the thirty-two local school districts, including the famous District 4, which seeded Debbie Meier's Central Park East, allowed innovations to flourish, but for the most part they became vehicles for intensely local politics. Tiny bands of politicians on the make rounded up votes to install themselves in power; with turnouts in the range of 5 percent, it was not hard for candidates to gain control of a local district, and then direct patronage and supply money as desired. The New York City school district was battered by charges of corruption issued by a full-time investigator, who documented fraud at both piddling and grand levels, ranging from theft of supplies to one local district's diversion of $6 million to private schools.

With the legislature's authorization of mayoral control in 2002, the sclerotic board of education was swept away. The mayor gained the power to appoint the chancellor and the school board was replaced by an advisory body, the Panel for Educational Policy, eight of whose thirteen members were appointed by the mayor and could be removed by him at will. In a later rendition of the law, community school boards were abolished and replaced by weak advisory boards. While this was part of a national shift toward mayoral control in cities where school systems were viewed as victims of patronage politics, corruption, and incompetence (Moscovitch et al. 2010; Wong et al. 2007), in New York mayoral control might have reached its apogee. Mayor Michael Bloomberg gained almost unchecked authority over the schools, with no competing bodies to offer checks and balances (Fruchter 2008, 95).

Mayor Bloomberg made clear his low regard for traditional school chiefs by successively picking three chancellors whose appointments required waivers from the New York State Education Department because they lacked the required professional credentials. The first two appointees, Joel Klein and Cathie Black, had extensive (Klein) or exclusive (Black) experience in the corporate world. Saying that, "It's not an education job," Bloomberg appointed Joel Klein Chancellor in 2002 (Meyer 2008). This was the first time in the city's history that a school head had been appointed by a mayor and not a board. Klein came from the worlds of law and business. He had served as head of the Antitrust Division of the Department of Justice, leading the prosecution of Microsoft, followed by appointment as CEO of Bertelsmann. For eight years, Klein exercised vigorous control over the schools, emphasizing assessment, accountability, and competition, and claiming major test score gains. Critics claimed gains were illusory and decried lack of parental or community input (Haimson and Kjellberg 2009).

In December 2010, Klein resigned as chancellor to become an executive vice president at Rupert Murdoch's News Corporation in charge of digital education initiatives; he also emerged as a key Murdoch advisor when the News Corporation was buffeted by a British phone hacking scandal. In a controversial move, Mayor Bloomberg appointed Cathie Black, a magazine publisher and media mogul, to succeed Klein, despite her lack of background in education. After an outcry by critics, State Education Commissioner David Steiner approved a waiver that allowed Black to take the position despite lacking the required credentials on the condition that a deputy with educational qualifications be appointed (Halbfinger, Barbaro, and Santos 2010). Shael Polakow-Suransky, a former teacher and principal before he joined Klein's administration as deputy chancellor of performance and accountability, was promoted to the new position of chief academic officer.

After three months, Bloomberg, despite famous loyalty to his appointees, asked Black to resign. At the time she had a public approval rating of 17 percent, having displayed little facility at operating in the public arena. Bloomberg then opted for a less controversial choice, appointing a member of his inner circle, Deputy Mayor Dennis Walcott. He too needed a state waiver, but he and his family had attended public schools, he had briefly taught in a preschool, and he had played a major City Hall role in developing school policy. It is notable that despite the varying fortunes of his appointees, in each case Mayor Bloomberg had made his choices without public discussion or vetting of candidates, in contrast to the public searches usually conducted in urban districts. Chancellors were appointed, as were other agency heads.

Los Angeles underwent no such centralizing dynamic. Mayor Antonio Villaraigosa, first elected in 2005, struggled for mayoral control (Maxwell 2007) but achieved only a limited victory from the state legislature and in 2006 had even that overturned by the courts. Power remained with a seven-member school board elected by districts, although Mayor Villaraigosa achieved indirect control by backing successful board candidates. In 2004 the school board appointed retired navy admiral David L. Brewer III as superintendent. He was soon criticized for being ineffectual at managing the sprawling district and was ousted in 2008. He was succeeded by his deputy, Ramon C. Cortines, who had headed five school districts, including serving briefly as New York City's school chancellor. In mid-2010, Cortines appointed a deputy and heir apparent, John Deasy, to whom he ceded his office and much of his power. Deasy officially replaced Cortines in April 2011.

Mayors Bloomberg and Villaraigosa both aimed for mayoral control, but one gained a far higher level of power than the other. Bloomberg achieved authority over the whole district. He renamed the school system the New York City Department of Education and turned it into a city agency under his direct command in the same mode as the police, fire, and parks departments. He argued that his control rein-forced, rather than undermined, democracy, "The Mayor should have sole control over the appointment of the Schools Chancellor, and the Chancellor should report directly to the Mayor. That establishes democratic accountability—and if democracy can be trusted to safeguard our social services, police forces and other essential ser-vices, why wouldn't it work to protect our most precious resource, our children?" (Wong et al. 2007, 6).

In Los Angeles, Mayor Villaraigosa struggled for mayoral control, arguing that the district's political fragmentation took an educational toll (Weintraub 2007, 50), but was blocked by the courts. He tried to create indirect control of the schools through supporting school board candidates, but his own personal authority over the dis-trict extended only to running what became a group of fifteen schools with nearly 20,000 students, in the same way numerous other charter and independent opera-tors assumed authority for blocks of schools. Dubbed the mayor's "consolation prize" (Fuller 2010, 12), this left him to cope with disgruntled teachers, high dropout rates, and low levels of student performance in his own small educational sector, rather than assuming unquestioned command of the whole (Ferrell 2009).

While Bloomberg and Villaraigosa had differing levels of political authority, they both had to cope with increased federal control of schools. The 2001 No Child Left Behind Act set a new context for framing the problems of urban schools. Its focus on testing, accountability, and privatization for failing schools reverberated in districts across the country. The Act required states to test all students annually (with the tests chosen by the states themselves). All schools receiving federal funding had to participate in the high stakes tests. The schools were required to demonstrate Annual Yearly Progress (improvement over the prior year's testing) in core subjects, with each racially defined subgroup (whites, Blacks, Hispanics, and Asian Americans) required to demonstrate 10 percent progress each year. Failure to reach these tar-gets resulted in increasingly severe outcomes, ranging from being labeled "in need of improvement" in the second consecutive year of failure, to being required to offer tutoring in the third year, to facing "corrective action" (such as staff replacement or redesign of school curriculum) in the fourth year. In Year Five, plans had to be devel-oped for restructuring failing schools, which were to be implemented in Year Six. The restructuring could include closing the school or turning it into a charter school.

Los Angeles and New York City responded to these new pressures in ways con-sonant with their urban political cultures and the forces that shaped their local regimes. Each district struggled to improve students' results on high stakes tests and to develop strategies for managing their giant school systems. Despite differ-ences in their initial paths, their goals converged around those advanced by national school reformers exemplified by the Bill and Melinda Gates Foundation and asso-ciated philanthropists and policymakers, who favored greater competition from charter schools, the evaluation of teachers based on their students' test score gains, and policy changes that reduced the power of teachers unions to protect teachers deemed poor performers. By the summer of 2011, their leaders, John Deasy and Dennis Walcott, had very similar policy goals, though they drew on somewhat differ-ent political resources.

MAYORAL CONTROL: BLOOMBERG TAKES CHARGE IN NEW YORK CITY

America's cities could be considered one giant experimental laboratory after another, where ideas that gain traction in one place can spread to others. Mayoral control of schools represents a striking example of the spread of one such idea (Wong et al. 2007). In the early twentieth century, Progressive reformers struggled to keep mayors and other politicians out of schools, upholding a professional ideal as a counterweight to the corruption and patronage they associated with political control (Wrigley 1982; Kerchner, Menefee-Lieby, and Mulfinger 2008). Professionals gradually assumed control in most big cities and mayors exerted influence only indirectly, which allowed them to avoid the often messy racial and ethnic politics associated with the schools (Henig and Rich 2004a).

The wheel turned in the 1990s when mayoral control began to seem a positive alternative to the political gridlock and fractiousness of big city school politics (Payne 2008, 126). Mayors argued that giving control to them was the only way to assure accountability. To reformers of the late twentieth century, this had appeal as a bold way to end wrangling over the schools by boards, mayors, teachers unions, and community leaders. In each city where mayoral control has been tried, corporate elites have been prime backers (Henig and Rich 2004b, 250). The idea was first implemented in Boston in 1992, a city whose school governing body had long been disdained as parochial and ineffective. Mayoral control got an even bigger boost after it was adopted in Chicago in 1995. The Chicago schools had acquired unwanted attention in 1987 when Education Secretary William Bennett declared them the worst in the nation ("Schools in Chicago are Called the Worst by Education Chief" 1987). Chicago first tried a radical form of school decentralization, with each school having substantial budget power and the right to choose its own principal. This was a more radical plan than New York City's earlier version of decentralization, under which the state legislature gave power to thirty-two local school districts in 1970. In Chicago, each individual school operated with considerable autonomy. While the decentralization plan inspired enormous early enthusiasm, parent participation soon fell off and many schools floundered.

Mayoral control beckoned as a way to avoid endless strife over the schools and to impose a clear sense of direction. Chicago's unified business elite had the clout to push the plan and the city had a strong mayor willing to embrace it (Shipps 2008). In 1995 the state legislature handed control of the schools to Mayor Richard M. Daley, known for his long tenure and iron control of the city. He appointed Paul Vallas, a close adviser who had served for the preceding five years as the city's budget director, as school system CEO (Russo 2003). With Daley's backing, Vallas brought the school budget under control, took over failing schools, secured state legislative approval for a school construction program, and began an intensive program of student testing. His willingness to tackle seemingly intractable problems led policymakers across the country to hail Chicago's dramatic new school reform model, although later critics, including former supporters in the city's business elite, have questioned Chicago's gains (Commercial Club of Chicago 2009). They have pointed out that Chicago continues to have low graduation rates and that many students who do graduate are unprepared for college work.

In many cities, mayors with less strength, confidence, and political support than Mayor Richard M. Daley of Chicago had no desire to add schools to their portfolios. Schools were seen as truly messy institutions, often rife with racial conflicts and not likely to yield gains for those who tried to remake them. Only a minority of cities adopted the new model of mayoral control, but they were important cities, with Cleveland, Hartford, Philadelphia, Washington, DC, and, in 2002, New York joining early leaders Boston and Chicago (Moscovitch et al. 2010).

Four successive New York City mayors (Beame, Koch, Dinkins, and Giuliani) advocated for mayoral control before Michael Bloomberg achieved it. Mayor Rudy Giuliani had declared that the "board system makes no sense" (Lueck 2000), and on leaving office in January 2002 he said that his biggest regret had been his inability to secure control of the schools. His successor, Michael Bloomberg, fared better. In his inaugural speech when first elected, he announced he wanted control of the schools. The state legislature, tired of endemic corruption in New York's scandal-ridden community boards, wrangling on the citywide board, and jousting between mayors and superintendents, voted in 2002 to abolish the city's central school board and to give the mayor sweeping new powers over the schools. As in Chicago, in New York it was not just any mayor who acquired these powers, but one with the political chops to try to redirect the school system, with billionaire Mayor Michael Bloomberg declaring that school reform would be his legacy. Mayoral control comes in many variants, but Boston, Chicago, and New York have had the highest level of mayoral influence over the schools (Moscovitch et al. 2010, 12). The mayoral control law was slated to sunset in 2009, but Bloomberg and supporters secured legislative reauthorization.

The switch to mayoral control represented a governance change and, on the surface at least, did not entail any particular educational agenda (Henig and Rich 2004a, 4). However, in practice, mayoral control across the country was associated with a focus on market-oriented solutions to educational problems and on increased assessment and accountability (Wong et al. 2007, 2). Bloomberg and Chancellor Joel Klein went through several changes of direction, but throughout welcomed expansion of charter schools and focused on quantitative assessment of students and of schools, with the system centralized around those numerical assessments (Pasanen 2010).

In Klein's first reorganization, in 2003 he replaced thirty-two elected community school boards, which had been created by the state legislature in 1969 after the bitter Ocean Hill-Brownsville decentralization battle that pitted the United Federation of Teachers (UFT) against black and Latino activists, with ten administrative regions, each with 100 to 150 schools of varying levels of success (Hemphill et al. 2010). The thirty-two decentralized school boards, which administered elementary and middle schools while the central board set overall policy and administered the city's high schools, had lost public support due to revelations of cronyism and corruption on many of the nine-member bodies (Buder 1989). Even without malfeasance, board members were plunged into complex budgeting tasks without training or oversight by the central board, leading to frequent fiscal overruns. Board elections drew few voters, with turnout generally in the range of 6 percent, and investigators charged that elections were often poorly and incompetently run (Stancik 1993). In 1996, the State Legislature had responded to scandals involving the boards by stripping them of most of their powers to hire and fire (Goodnough 2002). Klein's elimination of the local boards ended what many considered to have been a failed experiment but also replaced bodies rooted in local communities with more distant administrative regions that covered far larger areas.

Klein also moved quickly to establish a mandatory school curriculum, create a centralized Leadership Academy to train principals, and intensify the police presence at schools deemed unsafe (Fruchter 2008). Most importantly, Klein's administration adopted the small schools model that had grown out of efforts to counteract the bureaucracy and impersonality of New York City's schools with more intimate and communal schools, with Deborah Meier's famous Central Park East as the iconic version of a small school as a caring and intellectually lively community (Meier 2002). With support from major foundations, including the Bill and Melinda Gates Foundation and the Carnegie Corporation, by 2007 the Department of Education had closed, or slated to close, twenty-three comprehensive zoned high schools with consistent records of low performance, including graduation rates of less than 45 percent (Quint et al. 2010). They were replaced by almost 200 new small high schools. As part of this change, New York also instituted a new system of school choice. Students applied to up to twelve high school programs and even if they wanted to attend the local school zoned for their neighborhoods, had to apply through the citywide selection process.

The new schools were much smaller than their predecessors. Large academically unselective high schools in New York City typically enrolled about 3,000 students, while the new small schools usually had around 400 students (Quint et al. 2010, 42). The small high schools had widely varying styles and academic orientations but were designed to focus on three principles: academic rigor (high standards and preparation for college and life); personalization (each student would be known by at least one adult at the school); and community partnerships (linkages with outside organizations, including community groups and cultural institutions) (Bloom, Thompson, and Unterman 2010, 8–9).

The Gates Foundation funded intermediary organizations to help establish and support new schools, but they struggled to get them on a sound footing (Foley 2010). The schools had many practical problems to deal with, including finding decent physical facilities. Many were placed in wings or halls of existing schools, where disputes often arose over shared cafeterias, gyms, or auditoriums. The early idealistic creators of small schools in New York City had carefully nurtured them, slowly building cohesive teaching forces and developing common understandings of how to proceed (Meier 2002; Fliegel 1993). The new crash course for small schools strained the institutional resources for overseeing them or insuring adequate professional development for teachers.

By 2009, evaluations of student achievement in small schools had convinced Bill Gates that they were not the answer (Gates 2008), despite his national investment of $2 billion to promote them. The small schools often had higher attendance and graduation rates than their peers, but academic achievement remained low (especially in math) and graduates were often not ready for college work. Gates noted that the most successful of the small schools were often charter schools (publicly funded but privately run schools freed from most regulations imposed on traditional public schools). This led Gates to announce a new strategy of trying to increase the number of charter schools. As a first step, the foundation committed to lobbying states to lift or remove caps on the number of charter schools they would authorize. He also announced that the foundation would focus on improving teaching, aiming to do so through rigorous teacher evaluations followed by retraining or dismissal for those found to be weak.

After Gates shifted funding away from the creation of small schools, New York City's Department of Education also toned down support for the schools but continued to see them as safer, more manageable, and more likely to graduate students than large, unselective high schools. Between 2002 and 2012, the Department of Education opened 528 new schools (New York City, Department of Education 2012). Small schools got a boost when a rigorous analysis found that they raised graduation rates by 6.8 percent (Bloom, Thompson, and Unterman 2010), but this was not enough to move them back to center stage. Increasingly, small schools seemed like transitional organizations, vehicles for breaking up the large high schools that had dominated the city's secondary school landscape for decades. They also opened the door for a shift of energy to charter schools, as they helped sever the link between communities and zoned schools, accustoming students and parents to choose schools rather than rely on traditional attendance patterns. The small schools also created a new model of how multiple schools could share physical spaces. These new ways of thinking about schools had much application to the rise of charter schools in the city.

After a slow start, charter schools have gained ground in New York. The State Legislature authorized charter schools in 1998 but placed a cap of 200 on them across the state. Charter schools represented a more radical step away from traditional public schools than small schools. The small schools were designed as an antidote to the anonymity students experienced in high schools with thousands of students, but they operated according to the same basic rules as the traditional schools. By contrast, charter schools are governed by outside entities. Charter schools can determine their own curriculum, their own requirements for student behavior, and their own schedules. Since the charters are publicly funded, students pay no tuition. When more students want to attend than there are seats, students are selected by lottery. In New York, and other states, charters require state approval, with applications vetted by designated agents of the state; in New York, these agents have been SUNY, the State Board of Regents, and the New York City Department of Education (Robinson 2005). Charter schools are intended to have high levels of accountability to their chartering agencies in return for their freedom to operate from restrictions. In practice, charter schools have hardly ever been closed, but New York City and Los Angeles are among the districts that have taken this step (although rarely).

Charter schools usually operate without unions, although there are exceptions, including a New York City charter school from the national Green Dot network, which is cosponsored by the UFT. The UFT also operates two charter schools of its own and is also engaged in organizing the faculty and staff at thirteen other charter schools in the district.

Charter schools have replaced school vouchers as the most widely endorsed alternatives to traditional public schools. By 2012, forty-two states and the District of Columbia had passed laws authorizing charter schools (National Alliance for Public Charter Schools 2012). Several national charter school networks, such as the Knowledge is Power Program (KIPP), have established a wide reach, with KIPP operating 109 schools in twenty states. The founders of these nationally branded school models promise consistency and an ability to replicate themselves to produce success across sites. KIPP has received extensive funding from foundations and wealthy donors. New York also boasts such famous homegrown products as the Harlem Children's Zone, made famous by the film *Waiting for Superman,* with its focus on wraparound services for children from cradle to college, such as afterschool programs, an extended school year, health programs, improved parks and recreation facilities, and social services. Parents of young children are offered workshops on parenting in the zone's Baby College. The Harlem Children's Zone also works to strengthen community life in the almost 100 blocks served by the organization (Otterman 2010a). Charter schools are predominantly found in areas serving disadvantaged students; in New York, they are concentrated in Harlem, Central Brooklyn, and the South Bronx.

New York City's charter schools disproportionately enroll black students (who comprise 60 percent of the students in charter schools but only 30 percent in the school system), with Latino students relatively underrepresented (Medina and Gebeloff 2010). A number of reasons have been advanced for this: charter schools got an early start in Harlem, where they won support from black politicians and ministers; Hispanic families looking for educational alternatives might turn first to Catholic schools; and Harlem's location is attractive to founders, teachers, and donors from nearby but more affluent areas of Manhattan (Medina and Gebeloff 2010). Harlem's charter schools have been very generously supported by donors, often including those from the financial industry and hedge funds (Otterman 2010a).

Charter schools have been enthusiastically endorsed by many philanthropists and school leaders, but research shows they cover a wide quality range. A rigorous study conducted by the Center for Research on Education Outcomes (CREDO) at Stanford University found that 17 percent of a national sample of charter schools provided superior performance, roughly half did not differ from traditional public schools in their outcomes, and over a third (37 percent) had educational outcomes that were significantly worse than those in traditional public schools (CREDO 2009). The charter schools of New York City fared significantly better in a subsequent CREDO analysis. Charter school students in grades three through eight (the grades for which standardized test scores were available) had better outcomes than a matched virtual comparison group, with charter students having better outcomes in math than in English. Black and Latino students did significantly better than their peers in a virtual comparison group (CREDO 2010). The UFT has raised cautions about relying on test scores to measure charter school success. It contends that charter schools enroll very few special education students who need the most intensive services (United Federation of Teachers 2010a) and that they also limit the number of the economically neediest students they enroll (United Federation of Teachers 2010b).

Charter schools have been a focus of national conflict between teachers unions and charter advocates (Hill, Rainey, and Rotherham 2006). Unions have contended that charter schools exemplify managerial control and threaten teachers' professional rights, including their right to have a voice within schools. Charter advocates, for their part, have viewed teachers unions as protectionist preservers of the status quo. They blame unions for allowing bad teachers to stay on the job and for creating work rules that hamstring reforms. Charter supporters have directed particular fire at union seniority rules. When asked about seniority rules, Bill Gates replied, "Is there any other part of the economy where someone says, 'Hey, how long have you been mowing lawns? I want to pay you more for that reason alone'" (Alter 2010). Like many charter supporters, Gates argues that master's degrees and seniority have little correlation with teacher quality, setting up a battle with unions that have long fought for salary systems that leave little room for principal intervention or possible favoritism. In charter schools, teacher salary systems and seniority rights are not entrenched features of the environment, with their absence representing both a threat to unions and freedom to charter operators.

Conflicts over charter schools have demonstrated the power of foundations to set educational agendas, and when combined with governmental authority, to force through changes to established ways of running schools. Teachers unions have been major players in the politics of many states, including New York, but lost ground in charter battles during the Race to the Top grant competition sponsored by President Barack Obama's administration. US Secretary of Education Arne Duncan structured the competition to reward states that raised charter caps and included student test score gains as elements of teacher performance reviews. Many states complied to have a shot at the funds; after a bitter battle between teachers unions and their allies and Mayor Michael Bloomberg's administration and his supporters, New York joined them, increasing the charter cap from 200 to 460 schools, with 214 of the slots allocated to New York City (Medina 2010b; Martinez 2010). The teachers unions also got some things it wanted in the bill, as New York State banned for-profit operators, made charter schools more subject to state audits, and increased pressure for charter schools to accept English language learners and students with disabilities. With the State Legislature also approving a bill to factor students' test score gains into teacher evaluation, ultimately New York State was awarded $700 million in Race to the Top funds.

By 2011, New York City had 124 charter schools, with two-thirds of these co-located in public school buildings shared with traditional schools. As the charter movement built up steam, Chancellor Joel Klein placed dozens of charters into existing schools (Medina 2010b). The small schools movement had paved the way for shared buildings, but co-location with charters spurred more intense disputes. Charters predominated in neighborhoods serving low-income black and Latino students, and Harlem, in particular, soon attracted a large number, intensifying space battles. It was anticipated that if charter schools continued their growth rate, up to 10 percent of New York City's students could be enrolled in charters by the time the new cap on charters was reached (Martinez 2010).

The battles over charter schools and teacher evaluation systems rested on different visions of public education, with the long-standing vision of the teachers unions strongly contested by those who thought they had a better model. On a less visible level, Chancellor Joel Klein brought many other changes to the New York City schools. In a second reorganization in 2007, middle managers were removed and principals were given significant autonomy in exchange for increased accountability (Fruchter 2008). They gained meaningful control over their own curricula, budgets, and hiring, and no longer answered to local superintendents. In school year 2010–2011, district principals collectively had discretion over $9.4 billion (Independent Budget Office 2011d, 11).

While charter schools received greater autonomy, on the flip side accountability demands increased from school district headquarters at the Tweed building (Hemphill et al. 2010, 15). Principals were evaluated according to a grading system initiated in 2006. Their schools received annual Progress Reports, with letter grades from A to F. The grades were based on student performance on state standardized tests, student attendance, the progress of English language learners and students with disabilities, and the results of surveys of teachers, students, and parents (DOE 2010). Starting in 2010, high school Progress Reports also included data on graduates' college readiness. School grades are consequential for principals and teachers, as bonuses for those in high-needs schools are tied to meeting performance goals. Even more importantly, failing grades help define the pool of schools eligible for closure or transformation. In 2009–10, the year in which school grades reached their peak, only 53 schools fell into this pool, while 109 schools did a year later (Phillips 2011).

The Progress Reports could themselves be considered to be a work in progress, as the DOE did not find it easy to settle on a consistent method of ranking and evaluating schools. In many cases, schools' grades fluctuated greatly from year to year. In 2009–10, 97 percent of schools received A's or B's (due in part to students' test scores also peaking during the year, before the state recalibrated the tests). In the following year, the DOE established a wider spread of scores and also tried to create greater score stability. A *New York Times* commenter wrote, "City education officials sought to emphasize that while scores in previous years sometimes swung wildly from top of the class to a danger zone that could lead to closing, many schools' grades did not change from last year. That fluctuation had befuddled parents and school staff members for years as they tried to understand how the grades related to their own experiences with the schools" (Phillips 2011). District leaders seemed sensitive to the need to create a less volatile system that would inspire more confidence.

With their focus on accountability, competition, and testing, Bloomberg and Klein undertook an ambitious agenda that involved many challenges to established prerogatives. While they faced protests from parent groups and from the UFT, the New York City Department of Education under mayoral control was insulated to a remarkable extent from challenges by competing bodies. In many cities with mayoral control, mayors selected some or all members of the school board (Wong et al. 2007), but in New York City, the central school board was abolished. It was replaced by an advisory body called the Panel for Educational Policy (PEP), with no authority over the budget, hiring, or curriculum of the school system. Eight of its members are appointed by the mayor and five by the borough presidents. In 2004, three members of the PEP announced their intention to vote against Mayor Bloomberg and

Superintendent Klein's plan to enforce strict promotion standards for third graders. Bloomberg promptly removed the dissenters from the panel and replaced them with new members who voted according to the mayor's wishes. Bloomberg declared that: "This is what mayoral control is all about. . . . Mayoral control means mayoral control, thank you very much. They are my representatives and they are going to vote for things I believe in" (Herszenhorn 2004).

Under the old system, New York City parents had never found it easy to make their voices heard in the giant district, but mayoral control brought an end to most channels for parent and community representation (Fruchter 2008, 98). New York University education policy professor Pedro Noguera commented that "no one thought that mayoral control would mean that the mayor would be the only person who makes decisions" (Otterman 2010b, 2). Bloomberg and Klein argued, however, that boldness was necessary to improve the city's schools. On the eve of Chancellor Klein's departure in December 2010, he said that his greatest regret was that he had not been bold enough in restructuring the school system (Hernandez 2010).

Even in Chicago, with its mayors with legendary powers, there are more alternative power centers than in New York. When the schools were put under mayoral control, City Hall's reach extended over the district. Chicago mayoral appointee Paul Vallas ran the schools with an iron hand, but parents used a variety of civic institutions to help learn about the schools and engage with them. Local school councils, a carryover from the district's earlier decentralization initiative, still existed in the Vallas era and provided a forum for parents. On the citywide level, a well-established monthly publication, *Catalyst*, established in 1990, provided exceptional reporting on Chicago school issues, creating a broad base of community knowledge about the schools. An independent research group, the Consortium on Chicago School Research at the University of Chicago, also established in 1990 as Chicago's schools underwent their first major restructuring, has provided extensive data on school performance, offering an outside check on leadership claims of performance gains. Most dramatically, in September 2012, the Chicago Teachers Union staged a bold, seven-day strike and succeeded in at least fighting Mayor Rahm Emanuel to a draw (Davey and Yaccino 2012).

Such resources are not entirely lacking in New York City, but they are not as well institutionalized. New York has no parallel to *Catalyst* or to Chicago's independent research consortium, although some of the gap has been taken up in recent years by lively and iconoclastic bloggers and by researchers from university institutes including, particularly, the New School's Center for New York City Affairs. Klein recognized the disaffection and alienation of many parents but saw the issue as a public relations failure rather than a reflection of a major power imbalance (Hernandez 2010). Polls showed that public satisfaction with the schools peaked in 2009, when 57 percent of respondents said they approved of the mayor's handling of the school system, but then declined, with 34 percent expressing approval in 2011 (Otterman and Kopicki 2011). Roughly two-thirds of the 2011 respondents said they thought the school system had struggled or declined since the mayor had gained control of it, compared to 54 percent expressing disapproval of the mayor. In response to follow-up questions, many said they were unhappy about the school choice system, services for disabled children, and the emphasis on standardized testing. These are specific sources of dissatisfaction and perhaps reflect concrete experiences or attitudes not easily changed by better outreach.

COMPETING POWER CENTERS IN LOS ANGELES

Antonio Villaraigosa, who won a runoff election to become mayor of Los Angeles in 2005, supported a bill for mayoral control of the school system "modeled after Mayor Bloomberg's history and example" (Partnership for Los Angeles Schools 2008). Bloomberg appeared with him to help win support for the governance change. In Los Angeles, however, the teachers union, local political leaders, and school board members fiercely opposed mayoral control. They were joined by the leaders of twenty-six localities whose cities were encompassed in the Los Angeles school district, a complication never faced by the New York City school district, which is conterminous with the city. The California state legislature passed a bill that provided only a weak form of mayoral control; the *New York Times* summed up the situation by saying that the legislation "gives little real power to the mayor, spreading it instead among myriad officials. Further, it leaves many important decisions in the hands of the very school board that such legislation usually seeks to marginalize" (Steinhauer 2006). The Los Angeles mayor was to share control with a "council of mayors" from the twenty-six other cities included in the school district, although he could dominate the council, as voting was made proportional to student enrollment. Unlike in New York City, the school board was not abolished. It retained the power to decide on the curriculum and to appoint superintendents, although appointments were subject to veto from the council of mayors. Even this modest version of mayoral control proved unrealizable, with the courts striking it down as unconstitutional after a two-year battle.

After the courts disallowed mayoral control, Mayor Villaraigosa created a non-profit organization, the Partnership for Los Angeles Schools, which set out to reform three low-performing high schools and their feeder schools as a pilot project. The schools had the right to decide if they wanted to join the partnership, requiring the mayor to campaign to secure their assent. While Bloomberg had won control over the 1,400 or so schools in the New York district at a legislative stroke, Villaraigosa faced numerous delays and obstacles in trying to attain even a pale shadow of Bloomberg's control. Eventually he secured control over schools serving roughly 18,000 students (Blume 2008e), but *The Economist* commented that, "in a district that serves some 708,000 pupils, it was hardly a power grab" ("Villaraigosa's Frustration" 2007).

Mayor Villaraigosa tried a variety of means to secure greater control over the schools, but each involved costs and left him still contending with fractious groups. These included the teachers union, which actively ran candidates in school board elections and whose members often challenged principals' authority at local schools. In New York City, Bloomberg also battled with the UFT, but with decisive power over the district (and with no elected school board) he did not have to wage electoral war with them.

In Los Angeles the superintendent also had trouble establishing firm control over the schools. In 2006, the LAUSD school board appointed David L. Brewer III, a retired admiral with no educational experience, as superintendent. Vallas in Chicago and Klein in New York also lacked educational backgrounds, but each had strong backing from a powerful mayor. Brewer had less political capital at his disposal. He confessed that he had not anticipated how hard it would be to bring change. "The captain of a ship is a god," he said. "I want[ed] the principals to be captains of their ships.... Then I found out about all the union issues." Brewer ran up against teacher seniority rights and the difficulty of removing weak teachers. He asked board members and civic leaders to "Give me political cover to kick some ass and make some changes" (Blume 2008b). Instead, the board reduced his authority. Less than two years into his term, the board appointed Ray Cortines as Brewer's deputy. Cortines had a long educational resume, having served as school chief in San Francisco, San Jose, Pasadena, and New York City, as well as serving as the interim head of the LAUSD in 2000 and as Mayor Villaraigosa's chief school advisor. It soon became clear that Cortines was the real authority in the district, as the top administrators reported to him and not to Brewer ("Editorial: Too Many Chiefs" 2008), leading a governance expert to declare him to be the "de facto superintendent" (Jaime Regalado, quoted in Boghossian 2008). Then on January 1, 2009, Cortines assumed the superintendency in name, as well as in practice.

The weak governance of the Los Angeles schools reflected a broader truth, the district's increasing inability to control its fiscal, political, or organizational environment, with observers commenting that "the district has lost power over its revenues, the allocation of many of its expenses, many of its personnel decisions, its curriculum, the standards to which it educates children, and the means by which they are assessed" (Kerchner, Menefee-Libey, and Mulfinger 2008, 130). Proposition 13, passed in 1978, had long since removed fiscal power from local authorities, with the state supplying the bulk of school funding. In the intervening years, political incoherence had become a feature of the state government, intensified by mounting fiscal challenges (Schrag 2004). With its influx of children from impoverished immigrant families, the Los Angeles district would have faced major challenges even if run by a steady hand, but with its own administrative weaknesses, lack of resource control, and erratic educational decision-making, combined with the growing instability of California's larger political system, the district entered a state of "permanent crisis" (Kerchner, Menefee-Libey, and Mulfinger 2008, 1331).

While Los Angeles remained a cacophony of competing groups, in New York Bloomberg exercised his authority to the full and repeatedly declared that mayoral control over the schools would be the standard by which his mayoralty should be judged. Although the Los Angeles district struggled to adopt reforms similar to those enacted in New York, the districts had different governance structures and authority relations, which affected their ability to enact reform strategies.

CREATING NEW TYPES OF SCHOOLS

New York City has experienced conflicts around charter schools, but in Los Angeles the spread of charter schools has caused greater fears, including concern that they will lead to further fragmentation of the district. Many conflicts have arisen over charter schools' use of public space, and the district has had trouble adjudicating resource demands. Charter schools now enroll 7 percent of the district's pupils and have fought for resources. Proposition 39, passed in 2000, requires school districts to provide space for charter schools (Bradley 2008). Charter school advocates and parents of children in existing schools have squared off in conflicts over whether charters would be allowed to take over heavily used school space. In one dispute that occurred during Superintendent Brewer's administration, he agreed to turn over seven schools to charter organizations, only to have the order rescinded when Ramon Cortines was appointed as his deputy (Blume 2008d). The district eventually provided space after charter organizations filed lawsuits.

Even at the beginning of the charter school expansion, then-Superintendent Roy Romer (the former governor of Colorado) expressed concern about the effects on the district, saying that: "Nobody has worked out what it's going to look like if you take this district and checkerboard it with 15 to 35 charter high schools. I would like to find a way to maintain some coherence about how you operate public schools" (Hendrie 2003). He argued that the conversion of existing schools to charters posed a "very serious threat" to the whole district. The later administration of Ramon Cortines did not share Romer's doubts, instead declaring charter schools to be "part of the District's family and as an asset from which we can learn" (LAUSD 2012).

Los Angeles has more charter schools than any other district in the nation, with 183 in 2010, serving 78,000 students. Although the Los Angeles Unified School District is significantly smaller than the New York City district, it has fifty-nine more charter schools and they enroll 48,000 more students than the charter schools of New York City. In 2008 billionaire philanthropist Eli Broad gave $23.3 million to fund charter schools organized by the KIPP and Aspire networks, with the new funding bringing his foundation's total spending on Los Angeles charter schools to $55 million (Maxwell 2008). He declared that he would not have gone the charter route if mayoral control had been instituted, but failing that, charters appeared the best option (Blume 2008a). As Broad put it, "We haven't had reform from the top here, so instead we're seeing change from the bottom up" ("The Untidy Revolution" 2007). Some charter advocates declared they had the explicit goal of creating a "shadow" public school system within the district, aiming to establish a "brand-name network of high-quality charter schools" that could become very large (Hendrie 2002). Steve Barr, head of the Green Dot charter network, said that "we want systemic change, not to create oases in a desert" (quoted in Dillon 2007).

Although New York's charter schools have precipitated conflicts, they have operated under more constrained conditions than those in California. The UFT has had less tense relations with local charters than has its counterpart in Los Angeles. Instead, the more intense disputes in New York City have occurred over assessment and accountability, perhaps because charter schools still serve only 30,000 students, a tiny number in a district of 1.1 million students.

The Los Angeles district has operated within a volatile state political context, with California politics often roiled by battles over ballot initiatives (Schrag 2004). The impulse toward direct democracy extended to the schools, when, as part of California's effort to bolster its chances in competing for federal Race to the Top school funding, the state legislature passed a law authorizing a direct form of parental empowerment.

The law enabled a majority of parents at a low-performing school, or parents of children in feeder schools, to force the local school district to take any of four options specified in the No Child Left Behind law. The options are to bring in a charter school to replace the failing school, with the district no longer having governance rights over the school but with it still serving the original school population; to require the school district to bring in a new staff and provide the local community with more control over the school's budget; to transform the school through bringing in a new principal; or to close the school, with the students transferred to higher-performing schools. A maximum of seventy-five schools in the state could be subject to parental triggers. The law attracted national attention, winning praise from the Obama administration and fierce denunciation by the teachers union. McKinley Elementary School in Compton became the first site of an organizing effort to bring in a charter operator (Medina 2010a). The effort precipitated a bitter battle, with charges and countercharges over which side was intimidating the other. California's tradition of direct democracy was brought to the most local of levels, the operation of an individual school, and at least in the first attempt to implement it, produced a local shock that echoed the statewide shocks of California's many controversies over ballot initiatives. In New York City, in contrast, a parent trigger law on the books for more than twenty years attracted little attention (Decker 2012).

Political controversies over the parent trigger helped drive a further wedge between Mayor Antonio Villaraigosa and the United Teachers of Los Angeles (UTLA), even though Villaraigosa had once been an organizer for the union. He declared that there had been "one, unwavering roadblock to reform: UTLA union leadership. While not the biggest problem facing our schools, they have consistently been the most powerful defenders of the status quo" (Villaraigosa 2010b). He criticized the UTLA for opposing his efforts to increase the number of charter schools and for their hostility toward the parental empowerment act. Villaraigosa also demanded changes in the teacher tenure system, including extending the probationary time from two to four years and making it easier to dismiss poor teachers.

Pressure on the union increased when the *Los Angeles Times* published the performance rankings of the district's teachers in August 2010, with individual teachers identified by name (Felch, Song, and Smith 2010). In May 2011, the *Los Angeles Times* followed up with a still more extensive list of teacher rankings; the updated list covered 11,500 teachers who taught third through fifth grades and also included overall value added rankings for 470 schools (Song and Felch 2011). The newspaper acquired the data through a Freedom of Information Act request and hired a researcher to do the analyses. Some teachers were not just listed, but were named in the articles as poor teachers, with their performance contrasted with that of more effective teachers in their schools and grades. One of the teachers labeled as "less effective" in the list, 39-year-old Rigoberto Ruelas, committed suicide and his family told union officials that he had been depressed about his ranking.

The UTLA decried the public display of individual teachers' rankings and charged that the analysis was faulty and rested on weak and unreliable test score data, a charge supported by some academic critics (Corcoran 2010). The union's ineffectuality was highlighted a few months later when the *Los Angeles Times* ran an article questioning whether teachers had lost their clout (Landsberg 2010). It noted that teachers had collided with the school reform movement over three issues: the growth of charter schools, merit pay for teachers, and the use of value-added scores in teacher evaluations. On each, unions were a step behind in framing discussions. Despite state and federal campaign expenditures of more than $56 million in 2008, the National Education Association faced a negative political environment, from the president and Arne Duncan on down. The California Teachers Association had spent $211 million on state political campaigns over the preceding ten years and had turned out armies of disciplined volunteers to make phone calls, but teachers unions were on the defensive. A UTLA vice president told union members that "to say we're under attack is an understatement" (Landsberg 2010).

The Los Angeles schools entered a new phase when deputy superintendent John Deasy was named to the top job in January 2011, which he officially took over in June. The announcement was not a surprise, as Deasy had been effectively acting in the role from the time Superintendent Ramon Cortines had hired him in August 2010. At that time, Cortines vacated his office and gave it to Deasy (Samuels 2011). Deasy was not brought in to the schools from outside, as Bloomberg's three chancellor's appointees had been; he was steeped in the world of urban school districts and deeply integrated into school reform networks. Arne Duncan praised his appointment and Mayor Villaraigosa had helped engineer it behind the scenes (Llanos 2010). Deasy had served as deputy director of education for the Bill and Melinda Gates Foundation and also had been a resident at a management development program funded by the Eli and Edythe Broad Foundation; to complete the connections, the Gates Foundation gave the Broad Center $3.6 million for its residency program. Broad Residents are selected from among a large pool of applicants, whose qualifications include advanced degrees and at least ten years of experience in Fortune 500 companies or the equivalent in the public sector. Residents are selected on the basis of their potential to take on top jobs in school districts, state education departments, or charter management organizations (Broad Foundation 2012). In his work as superintendent of three school districts before taking the Broad Residency, Deasy had shown a strong affinity for the reform agenda, including creating small schools, endorsing merit pay, and implementing new teacher evaluation systems.

Deasy's appointment brought Los Angeles to the forefront of districts with leaders committed to the changes endorsed by the school reformers. It remains to be seen whether his pragmatic personal style will help him achieve greater cohesion and create a more coherent strategy in the sprawling Los Angeles district, even as his agenda is almost certain to involve goals the teachers union will find problematic.

HAVE REFORMS WORKED?

In 2011 both the New York and Los Angeles districts acquired new leaders. Dennis Walcott promised to continue the reform agenda of Joel Klein, and John Deasy clearly planned to follow the key tenets of the national school reform model. With all the changes the districts had gone through in the first decade or so of the twenty-first century, had much changed in students' actual learning? This is a hard question to answer, despite reams of data. In New York City, Chancellor Klein and Mayor Bloomberg made accountability the cornerstone of their educational policy. When Bloomberg took control of the schools, he applied the concept to himself, saying, "I want to be held accountable for the results, and I will be" (Williams 2005). The mayor and chancellor initiated sweeping changes in the schools. They encouraged the growth of charter schools, closed failing schools, and limited children's social promotion. Focusing on school choice, they created a citywide high school admissions process, with parents choosing among more than 600 programs at 400 schools. Many large high schools were closed, with multiple small schools opening in their buildings. Police presence was increased in a dozen of the remaining large high schools that had poor safety records. They also introduced new systems rewarding district personnel, with both principals and teachers given bonuses if their schools exceeded performance targets (Fruchter 2008).

These extensive changes yielded results in improved climates in many schools, including those in tough neighborhoods. An experienced school observer who visited thirty schools in the South Bronx, part of the poorest congressional district in the nation, found a marked improvement between 2002 and 2009 (Hemphill et al. 2010). Schools where she saw many students wandering the halls on her first visit, with teachers talking with students in half-empty classrooms, were far more orderly on her second visit. Where books and supplies were once scarce, the schools were well supplied by 2009. Students no longer spent years in Spanish-only classes but were taught in either bilingual or English classes. Principals no longer secured their jobs through patronage but were appointed from lists supplied by the Department of Education. However, not all was well, with instruction often dry, rote, and heavily geared to test prep. Students registered test score gains but continued to lag academically compared with others in the district. Yet, the schools at least had the preconditions for effective education in terms of improved focus and more orderly environments. This encouraging development suggests that change down to the classroom level is possible with clear plans and leadership. Along the same lines, a careful MDRC study found that small high schools have significantly higher attendance rates and graduation rates on average than their larger peers (Bloom, Thompson, and Unterman 2010). More research is needed to understand the dynamics of how schools in the South Bronx improved and to identify the specific policies and practices that yielded better attendance and graduation rates in the city's small schools of choice. Qualitative research could make a critical contribution, in addition to the more common reliance on test score analysis to understand school successes and failures.

Klein changed educational strategies during his time in office, starting with a uniform curriculum and eventually abandoning that in favor of increased autonomy for successful principals. What remained constant, however, was his and Bloomberg's insistence that they be judged on the two prime metrics of student test scores and high school graduation rates; they were confident that they had achieved significant gains on each. Critics objected that state exams had become easier and more predictable over time. This made New York City's scores on federal National Assessment of

Education Progress (NAEP) exams critical as a point of comparison. NAEP exams are considered the gold standard of educational testing, as they are low-stakes for children and teachers, reducing or eliminating problems of teaching to the test or cheating. NAEP exams have been given to samples of fourth and eighth grade students in urban districts since 2002. Review of NAEP scores led some analysts to conclude that state scores were inflated, as NAEP scores were largely flat (Medina 2010c; Pallas 2011). NAEP scores, however, show some areas of improvement. Gains were registered in fourth grade reading scores and in fourth grade and eighth grade math over the years from 2005 to 2009 (Independent Budget Office 2011d, 31; see also Klein 2011).

Student scores on state exams attracted much more attention than those on NAEP exams since high stakes exams counted not only for children but also for adults, with district leaders, teachers, and principals judged by them. High stakes tests are intended to modify behavior, as well as provide assessment, and there is much evidence that they do just that (Marsh, Pane, and Hamilton 2006, 8). In New York critics decried increasing amounts of class time devoted to test prep, and parents worried that their children no longer had time for art, music, or physical education (Stern 2009).

The discussion took a new turn in July 2010, when state education officials said that state test standards had become too lax (NYSED 2010). They recalibrated state exams, with the result that the proportion of New York City students passing the state reading tests fell by more than 25 percent. The recalibration also wiped away the city's progress in reducing racial gaps in test results (Otterman and Gebeloff 2010), which had once been hailed (Jennings and Pallas 2009). On a broader level, testing was criticized as being subject to various sorts of manipulation, such as the exclusion of students who might perform poorly (Jennings and Beveridge 2009).

New York was hardly the only state to have made its state exams easier over time. In many states, disparities had become increasingly evident between results on state exams and on NAEP. The recalibration still came as a blow to the Bloomberg and Klein team, which rebounded by pointing to areas of improvement on state exams and to higher graduation rates (Medina 2010c). The four-year graduation rate rose to 60.7 percent in 2008, marking the first time in the city's history it had risen above 60 percent. Critics attributed some of the gain in graduation rates to a process known as "credit recovery," by which students who failed classes could make them up with modest effort, and to increased numbers of students "discharged" from schools for various reasons and thus not included in tabulations (Stern 2009; Jennings 2008; Jennings and Haimson 2009). The gain was quite significant, however, and came after graduation rates in the district had been flat for more than a decade.

The new mayoral regime also attracted critics who saw the basic educational policies of Bloomberg and Klein as misguided. They included one-time supporters, such as Diane Ravitch and Sol Stern, who concluded that the Bloomberg/Klein reforms were not built on a sound instructional core. Ravitch, in particular, became a tireless adversary of school reform leaders at both the national and local levels. She argued that teachers had been demonized for not being able to solve problems arising from poverty and racial isolation, and that school reformers were on a quest for a quick fix for the schools. While focusing on test scores, reformers lost sight of the need for connection in schools, for students to be encouraged and exposed to a broad curriculum of history and the arts and literature. Ravitch and Stern did not see reform leaders as offering a clear educational plan; they saw a business model of accountability, competition, and privatization imposed on schools without thought for the fabric of the institutions (Ravitch 2008; Stern 2009). They also believed many gains were illusory, a product of the need of those being held accountable to show results at all costs.

The Los Angeles district did not experience a major test score adjustment, and thus was not subjected to the controversy that greeted assertions of major progress in New York City's schools. Its students' NAEP scores improved significantly from 2002 to 2007, but, as in New York, students' scores were largely flat between 2007 and 2009. In Los Angeles, however, students began from a much lower base than in New York; in 2009, only 46 percent of eighth grade students in Los Angeles scored above the Basic level, compared to 60 percent in New York City. The district faced very challenging instructional problems, but its leaders were not able to adhere to a consistent reform plan. It has veered from one strategy to another, abandoning each as it becomes an evident failure (Kerchner, Menefee-Libey, and Mulfinger 2008). Its record led Marshall Tuck, chief executive of Mayor Villaraigosa's Partnership for Los Angeles Schools, to comment that: "Frankly, a lot of the schools are suffering from reform fatigue. There have been new superintendents and new programs almost every year, so nothing gets changed" (Orlov 2008).

Convinced that the district had done a poor job running the schools, philanthropists asserted that they could do better if given authority over individual schools. Associates of Eli Broad, who helped fund the new $230 million School for the Visual and Performing Arts, floated the idea of his taking direct control of the school, while former Mayor Richard Riordan suggested that he take over Dorsey High School, a floundering school in the heart of Los Angeles's black community. Riordan stated that "I'm offering my heart, my soul, my reputation, my pocketbook and everything to the students of Dorsey High School," but the offer was rejected (Blume 2008c). Mayor Villaraigosa continued to run the schools in his partnership. Individual schools have occasionally been plucked from obscurity in the system and selected for attention by the wealthy or powerful, but many flounder with little direction.

The district's 2007 strategic plan started on a grim note, stating that almost 100,000 students in the district attended thirty-four secondary schools that had failed by the standards of both the State of California and No Child Left Behind. Another 309 Los Angeles schools serving nearly 400,000 students were at risk of falling into failure status. In New York City, leadership priorities, even if controversial or changeable, have been clear, while in Los Angeles the district offers a profusion of ideas. The strategic plan could not be said to be highly strategic; the district reported that its plan provided "seven strategies and hundreds of tactics" to address the schools' failures. It called upon each school to develop its own plan, worked out with all stakeholders, and integrating "all of the other plans that might exist (e.g., SAIT, QEIA, Program Improvement plans, WASC, etc.)" (Brewer 2008, v).

In August 2009, the school board voted to open the management of up to 250 schools to bidders, with charter operators and nonprofits allowed to compete with teachers and principals in LAUSD to run new and underperforming schools (Maxwell 2010, 10). In the absence of a clear agenda, the district opted to parcel out the schools to different operators, including charter schools, the mayor's office, community groups, and the teachers union. After UTLA won its March 2010 bid to manage twenty-four schools (out of the thirty whose management was up for grabs in the first round of decisions), its president said he wished they had had more time to prepare their proposals, "so we could have captured 100 percent of these schools" (Maxwell 2010, 10).

A focus on assessment and accountability in both Los Angeles and New York led not only to new schools and increased competition from charter schools but also to strong drives to evaluate teachers based on value-added analyses of their students' test scores. Seniority rules came under attack, with political leaders and school officials demanding the right to take teacher performance into account when laying off teachers (Villaraigosa 2010b). Teachers unions were increasingly seen as barriers to change, with their power used to enforce restrictive rules (Strunk and Grissom 2010). The Obama administration strongly supported the focus on teacher performance and tried to induce states to move in this direction through the competition for Race to the Top funds. Critics decried the public display of individual teachers' rankings and charged that the analysis rested on weak and unreliable test score data (Pallas 2010; Corcoran 2010). It was clear, however, that teachers unions were operating in a new environment, one in which long-standing protections and modes of operation were forcefully challenged by school system leaders who claimed the mantle of reform.

CONCLUSIONS

School reformers have strategies they want to implement, money, a large network of well-placed supporters, and the power of the federal government behind them. This is an unusual combination of forces to bring to bear on what have historically been locally focused school systems. In the past the political context has mattered for the New York and Los Angeles school districts, but it may matter less in the future as local factors become secondary to more powerful national forces. The districts' differences may diminish as they follow, or try to follow, common paths in dealing with teacher accountability, the growth of charter schools, and the drive for improved test scores within a reform framework that operates at every level, including local, state, and federal.

Philanthropists have long played a role in shaping schools, but in the past, according to educational historian Maris Vinovskis, they seldom came with such specific ideas of what they wanted. In the current context, philanthropists come bearing ideas developed by their own foundation staffs or by people in their circles, which they share with those in governmental power. The Gates Foundation and Education Secretary Duncan "move in apparent lockstep" ("Bill Gates' School Crusade" 2010).

The Gates Foundation can take political risks, such as antagonizing the teachers unions by pressing for value-added evaluations, and the federal government can build on that groundwork to develop plans and policies that districts and states cannot afford to reject. This happened in the Race to the Top grant competition when many states scrambled to change their laws to increase their chances of winning an award. The distribution of $4.3 billion, less than 1 percent of total public spending on education, led states to change teacher evaluation systems to include student gain scores and to raise caps on charter schools—all for an uncertain result. Brenda Welburn, the executive director of the National Association of State Boards of Education, said, "States were willing to change their policies based on a gamble" (quoted in Yadron 2010). Diane Ravitch, an opponent of Arne Duncan's policies, nonetheless concedes their effectiveness, writing that "Duncan's Race to the Top competition has had an enormous effect on American education," with states rushing to create value-added systems for judging teachers and also raising charter caps to further educational privatization in the hope of securing federal funds in a time of scarcity (Ravitch 2010).

The same dynamic is set to occur when states apply to the US Department of Education for waivers of the No Child Left Behind Act's harsh provisions (with whole schools declared failures) for school systems whose students do not reach 100 percent proficiency by 2014. In exchange for providing waivers, the Obama administration has required states to focus on revamping their lowest-achieving schools and to create teacher evaluation systems based on value-added measures (US Department of Education 2012).

Federal pressure on the states to adopt elements of school reformers' agendas comes with potential costs. States may make promises they cannot meet. The states that triumphed in the Race to the Top Competition made a bevy of promises that are now coming due. Many of the winners have already requested extensions (Cavanagh 2011). New York promised that 40 percent of a teacher's evaluation would be based on student test score gains, with 20 percent to come from local test measures and 20 percent from state tests or the equivalent. The New York State teachers union accepted the evaluation plan, but went to court to block a later revamped state version that based 40 percent of the teacher evaluation on student gains on state tests. Other states are faltering as they try to figure out how to measure student gains in subjects like art, music, or science in which there are no state-level tests.

Presumably states can solve their implementation problems, and they have great incentive to do so, but the history of reform efforts in New York and Los Angeles suggests that in school reform, coming up with ideas is important, but making the ideas work is equally important. Los Angeles had trouble with both parts of this equation, while New York fared somewhat better on both. Its rewards were modest gains on NAEP exams and progress in increasing graduation rates. These are not the great victories that had been hoped for, but represent improvements nonetheless.

What remains to be seen is how these districts, each with its own complex political dynamics, develop workable strategies to deliver quality instruction in many hundreds of schools. Each district's history shows the difficulty of extending change down into the heart of the enterprise, the actual teaching in classrooms. In neither

New York nor Los Angeles was there a clear instructional plan. In New York, teachers and principals were incentivized by bonuses, but were mainly left to work out their own teaching strategies (Hemphill et al. 2010). Some fared well under this version of accountability, while others floundered.

In Los Angeles, several much-publicized educational reform plans of the 1990s fizzled and were abandoned, replaced in the new century by struggles over the political control of the schools. A focus on changes in school governance can, however, bring its own problems, with political leaders anxious for quick results (Payne 2008, 174). Disillusionment often follows early claims of radical improvements, as occurred with Paul Vallas's tenure in Chicago and also with Arne Duncan's (Commercial Club of Chicago 2009). Improving schools is hard, slow work, and the very different political cultures of New York and Los Angeles demonstrate its difficulty, suggesting that claims of silver bullets should be viewed with skepticism, despite pressure from the combined forces of philanthropists and the federal government to adopt their chosen strategies.

CHAPTER 10

How New York and Los Angeles Housing Policies Are Different—and Maybe Why

INGRID GOULD ELLEN AND BRENDAN
O'FLAHERTY

Almost everyone says New York City is exceptional, and many people think that housing is one of the most exceptional aspects of New York life.* But New York's housing conditions are not so different from those in other large US cities, or at least not in the ways that are commonly believed. Policies, not conditions, are what truly set New York's housing market apart.

New York City had the nation's first tenement laws, its first notorious slum, its first comprehensive zoning ordinance, and its first public housing project. Its present policies continue to make the city unique within the United States. Practically nowhere else has rent control persisted so long, or do public housing developments house so many residents so happily, or do local governments spend so much money to house the poor, the homeless, and the middle class (who would be considered rich in many parts of the country). The city's capital expenditures for housing, meanwhile, were more than three times the housing expenditures of the next thirty-two largest cities combined during the late 1980s and 1990s (Schwartz 1999).

Our aim in this chapter is to describe New York City's policies, to explore how and why they differ from those in Los Angeles and other large cities, and whether they have shaped how New York City's housing market has weathered the recent downturn. The policies we consider are public housing, *in rem* properties, other subsidized housing, rent regulation, housing allowances, city capital subsidies for construction and rehabilitation, special needs housing, local tax structures, and building codes. Do unusual housing market conditions lead to these unusual policies? Do some common

*We thank Frank Braconi, Irv Garfinkel, Marcia Meyers, Ed Olsen, and Max Weselcouch for their excellent comments on an earlier draft and Marilyn Sinkewitz and Samantha Wright for their careful research assistance. Finally, we thank the Russell Sage Foundation for financial support.

factors cause both unusual policies and conditions? Naturally, we cannot answer these questions definitively. But we can offer some alternative explanations.

The chapter is organized as follows. The first section describes the city's housing policies and contrasts them with those in Los Angeles and other large cities in the United States. The second section compares how the housing markets in New York and Los Angeles have fared during the recent downturn and considers whether differences in policies have shaped differences in outcomes. The third section explores some likely explanations for New York City's set of housing policies. It compares and contrasts housing and economic conditions in New York City with those in other cities to explore if conditions in the city explain its unusual set of policies. The line between policies and conditions or outcomes is not sharp and bright because ideally we would like to think of both as endogenous. Still, we try to separate those aspects of New York City housing that could be changed immediately and directly by a (possibly politically suicidal) mayor and city council (or governor and legislature) from those that could not. The former we call policies; the latter, outcomes. The final section concludes.

POLICIES

Over the past century, New York City proved to be a pioneer in many areas of housing policy (even though its example has not always been followed), and today, its institutional infrastructure for housing is more extensive than that in any other city in the United States. In this section, we summarize New York City's major housing policies and find out how they compare to those of other large cities.

Rent Regulation

Both New York City and Los Angeles regulate rents on most apartments; they are the only two large US cities (cities with more than a million people) to do so. During the late 1970s, rent control laws regulated rents in as many as 170 municipalities in the Northeast and California. Today, a dwindling number of housing units in the United States are governed by rent regulation, and they are concentrated in New York City, Washington, DC, and selected cities in New Jersey and California, including Los Angeles (Keating and Kahn 2001).

Rent regulation in these cities is complex and nuanced, since the rules cover not only many contingencies in rent-setting but also conditions of tenancy, like grounds for eviction and security deposit maintenance. New Yorkers—and others—often think that rent regulation in New York is more stringent than anywhere else (only New York City rent control has its own Wikipedia entry), but the comparison of New York's system with that in Los Angeles is by no means unambiguous. In some respects, rent regulation is clearly softer in Los Angeles. Los Angeles has strict vacancy decontrol: whenever a tenant vacates a covered apartment, the landlord can raise the initial rent on the incoming tenant to any desired level. Los Angeles also permits landlords to raise rents by 10 percent when a tenant household adds a member (Los Angeles Housing Department 2012).

But rent regulation in Los Angeles is stricter than that in New York in other dimensions. (Note that the vast majority of regulated units in New York City fall under the less strict rent stabilization regime, rather than under traditional rent control.) In New York City, rent-stabilized units can sometimes leave rent regulation altogether: as of 2011, this happens if the permitted rent rises above $2,500 a month for other reasons, and if either the tenant vacates the apartment or the tenant's household income remains above $200,000 for two consecutive years (Buckley 2011). Los Angeles has no comparable escape clause: once regulated, an apartment stays regulated as long as it is an apartment.

New York's vacancy provisions under rent stabilization are also fairly generous. The landlord can raise the rent by 20 percent (when the new tenant opts for a two-year initial lease; or slightly less with a one-year initial lease), plus an additional amount if the previous tenancy lasted eight or more years—0.6 percent times the number of years (New York State Division of Housing and Community Renewal 2011a). This is in addition to the annual or biennial increases that are permitted within a tenancy. These increases are set every year by the Rent Guidelines Board and are about the same as the within-tenancy increases permitted in Los Angeles. For instance, for 2011 New York allowed a 2.25 percent increase on rent-stabilized apartments where the tenant pays utilities and Los Angeles allowed an increase of 3 percent; New York also allows rent increases for rent-controlled apartments.

Moreover, the reach of Los Angeles rent regulation appears to be somewhat wider than that of New York rent regulation. In Los Angeles, rent regulation applies to all units with two or more apartments. With minor exceptions, New York covers only buildings with six or more apartments. Rent regulation in Los Angeles covers all apartments built before October 1, 1978, as measured by issuance of the certificate of occupancy (Los Angeles Housing Department 2012). Meanwhile, rent regulation in New York covers apartments built before January 1, 1974, together with most units subsidized under the J-51 and 421a tax abatement programs, which put such units under rent stabilization for certain periods (New York State Division of Housing and Community Renewal 2011b).

The real measure of stringency, of course, is in the actual application of the laws, not in abstract contemplation of their provisions. In New York, the regulated rents are not binding in many neighborhoods in the city, as the rents allowable under stabilization are in fact higher than market rents. Pollakowski (2003) estimates that the median subsidy for the more than 200,000 regulated units in Queens and Staten Island was effectively zero at the turn of the century. In other neighborhoods, however, rent regulation has kept rents well below market levels. The estimated median subsidy enjoyed by regulated apartments on the Upper West Side, for instance, was $485 per month. No follow-up has yet estimated the effect in New York of the bubble and the bust, and no comparable study has yet been completed for Los Angeles. Bhakta (2011) shows that on average rent control makes little difference for rents or rent burdens in Los Angeles County, but does not have data on apartment characteristics or location and so cannot estimate whether rent control is binding.

Interestingly, the data in table 10.1 show that more renters in New York report that they live in rent-regulated units, perhaps because regulated rents are more binding or

Table 10.1 PROPORTION OF RENTAL HOUSING UNITS RECEIVING SUBSIDIES OR UNDER
RENT REGULATION, TEN LARGEST CITIES

	Public Housing	Other Subsidized	Rent Regulated	Unregulated
New York City	8.65%	5.73%	49.62%	36.00%
Los Angeles	2.82%	5.47%	22.81%	68.90%
Chicago	6.83%	4.54%	0.00%	88.63%
Houston	1.83%	6.22%	0.00%	91.95%
Philadelphia	9.11%	3.60%	0.00%	87.29%
Phoenix	2.49%	4.77%	0.00%	92.75%
San Diego	2.69%	6.82%	0.46%	90.03%
Dallas	0.94%	5.15%	0.00%	93.90%
San Antonio	6.56%	5.11%	0.00%	88.33%
Detroit	4.43%	8.62%	0.00%	86.95%

Source: American Housing Survey, Metropolitan Data, various years compiled by the authors. For New
York City, data are taken from 2008 NYC Housing and Vacancy Survey because it includes more reliable
rent regulation information. For Houston and San Antonio, the data are taken from the 2007 and 2004
metropolitan AHS surveys respectively (using the city sub-area). For Los Angeles, Chicago, Philadelphia and
Detroit, the most recent data are from the 2003 metropolitan AHS for that area (using the city sub-area). For
Phoenix, San Diego and Dallas, the most recent data are from 2002 (and we also rely on city sub-area).

because rent regulation is simply talked about more often. As shown in table 10.1, half of
New York City's renters report that they live in rent-regulated units. By comparison, just
23 percent of renters in Los Angeles report that they do.

Because of rent regulation, a much greater share of units in New York City is
shielded from the market than in other large cities (see table 10.1). San Francisco
appears to be the only large city with a stated proportion of protected rental units
that comes close to that of New York City (67.6 percent). Due to rent regulation, the
share is relatively high in Los Angeles too, but not as large as in New York City, at
least according to the available data.

Rental Subsidies

Another notable difference between New York City and other large cities is the much
greater share of New York's housing units that are explicitly publicly subsidized
through federal, state, and local programs. As shown in table 10.1, about 14.4 percent
of New York's rental housing units are subsidized, compared with 8.3 percent in Los
Angeles. Moreover, because a higher proportion of units in New York are rental than
in Los Angeles and other large cities (see table 10.3), the differences in the proportion of total units that are subsidized are even greater. For instance, 10.1 percent of
all housing units in New York City are subsidized rental units, compared to only 5.1
percent of units in Los Angeles. In Philadelphia and Detroit, the proportion of rental
units that are subsidized is almost as high as it is in New York City (12.7 percent and
13.1 percent, respectively) but the proportion of all units that are subsidized is considerably lower (5.2 percent and 5.9 percent, respectively).

The sections below provide information on the particular subsidies used in New York City.

Federal Public Housing

Public housing is owned and operated by local public housing authorities established by local governments. The federal government paid for the initial construction, provides some funding for rehabilitation needs, and since 1970, also provides ongoing subsidies for operation. Tenants pay 30 percent of their income for rent. To be eligible for public housing in the United States, households must earn less than 80 percent of the local area median income (AMI), but most tenants earn far less, due to policy preferences for lower income households. In 2008, 71 percent of all households living in public housing had incomes that were under 30 percent of their local area median (HUD USER 2008).

There are approximately 1.2 million public housing units in the United States, 15 percent of which are in New York City. The New York City Housing Authority (NYCHA) currently maintains approximately 180,000 units of public housing. NYCHA is by far the largest housing authority of any city in the country; the next largest is Chicago, which managed 21,442 units of public housing in 2008 (HUD USER 2008). New York has almost twice as many public housing units as the next nine largest cities combined. This is partly because more traditional public housing units were originally built in New York City but also because fewer have been demolished. The number of public housing units has been shrinking nationally as no new traditional public housing units are being built and many are being demolished, at least in some cities. Chicago's "Plan for Transformation" calls for the demolition of over 20,000 units of public housing, and a net reduction in public housing stock in the city of 13,000 units (Goetz 2011). In New York, in part because public housing is viewed more positively than in other cities, virtually no units have been torn down. Rather than demolishing units to create mixed income communities, the NYCHA is in the process of creating mixed income communities by selling land on a few public housing sites (such as Harborview Terrace) to private developers (Vitullo-Martin 2008). Even in the wake of Hurricane Sandy, when many NYCHA apartment buildings were heavily damaged, there has been no serious discussion about the long-term viability of these coastal developments in the first three weeks after the storm.

Public housing also represents a relatively large share of New York's total stock of housing. NYCHA's public housing units represent 9 percent of the city's total rental housing stock and 5 percent of its total housing stock. As table 10.1 shows, this is the highest proportion among the ten largest cities, other than Philadelphia. In Los Angeles, public housing comprised just 2.8 percent of the rental housing stock.

Public housing in New York City has historically had a reputation for being better managed and more properly maintained than public housing in most other large cities (Thompson 1999). NYCHA has not undertaken any of the major demolitions of public housing that have occurred in other large cities, and unlike many large public housing authorities, NYCHA has never been placed on the US Department of Housing and Urban Development (HUD)'s list of troubled housing authorities.

By contrast, four of the housing authorities in the ten largest cities (Los Angeles, Chicago, Philadelphia, and Detroit) have spent time on HUD's troubled list for cities that fail to manage public housing properly. Some credit NYCHA's commitment to keeping working families in developments; others argue that NYCHA's large developments are a better match with New York City's housing stock, which has a very large share of large, multifamily buildings (Thompson 1999; Been et al. 2011).

Private, Project-Based Subsidized Housing

According to the New York City Housing and Vacancy Survey (HVS), approximately 6 percent of rental housing units (or roughly 120,000 units) in New York City are privately owned (by both for-profit and nonprofit entities), but subsidized through a variety of federal, state, and local programs. (These units are counted in the "other subsidized" column in table 10.1.) These projects date from the mid-1950s when the federal government began to subsidize private developers to provide housing for low-income households. Developers were required to keep rents affordable for a specified number of years. Income limits in the project-based Section 8 program are comparable to those in public housing, but the limits in other federal subsidy programs, like Section 221(d)(3), are typically higher. Launched at about the same time, the Mitchell Lama Housing Program was a state program that aimed to provide affordable housing for moderate and middle-income families. Developers received low-interest mortgages and property tax abatements in return for accepting limits on profits and tenant incomes for either twenty or thirty-five years. Although many of these projects are now becoming eligible for buyout, the HVS reports that there were still just over 60,000 Mitchell Lama units in New York City in 2008.[1]

The Low Income Housing Tax Credit Program is the most recent of these sorts of programs. Created by the federal Tax Reform Act of 1986, the Low Income Housing Tax Credit Program allocates tax credits to states and localities that can be used to leverage capital for the construction or rehabilitation of affordable housing. A project can qualify for tax credits in two ways: either 20 percent of its tenants must earn less than 50 percent of local area median income or 40 percent must earn less than 60 percent of the local area median. In reality, most projects receiving credits house an even greater share of low-income tenants, since most states give preference to projects including a larger share of affordable units. Tax credit projects are required to meet these income requirements for a period of fifteen years. By the end of 2010, New York City and State had allocated millions of dollars in tax credits to over 1,585 different projects, comprising of 80,395 low income units (Furman Center 2011). (Note that these units are not included in the total number of subsidized units shown in table 10.1. Many are probably included in the total number of rent-stabilized units, however, since many of the tax credit projects are governed by rent stabilization.)

Rental Vouchers

In addition to the supply-side programs outlined above, some tenants also receive Section 8 rental subsidies to protect them from rent increases. Funded through the federal government, Section 8 vouchers permit eligible households to rent private market units and generally pay only 30 percent of their income for housing.[2] (Voucher holders can live either in rent-regulated units or unregulated units.) New York City's voucher program is the largest in the country; nearly 125,000 households in New York City receive housing vouchers (HUD USER 2008).[3] The next largest program exists in the city of Chicago, where the local housing authority administers 48,000 vouchers (HUD USER 2008). The Housing Authority of the City of Los Angeles administers 38,000 housing vouchers (HUD USER 2008).

Section 8 vouchers are now restricted to households earning less than 50 percent of the area median income, and 75 percent of a housing authority's vouchers must go to households earning less than 30 percent of AMI. In New York City, voucher holders have historically had lower incomes than households living in public housing, given that the city's voucher program gives stronger preference to households who are formerly homeless, living in substandard housing, or paying more than 50 percent of their income for rent.

New York City also innovated in the wake of Superstorm Sandy by partnering with Airbnb to encourage households that were not affected to offer spare rooms for free to displaced households (NYC Mayor's Office, 2012). Almost 1,100 households participated in this program in the first three weeks after the storm (Airbnb. com, 2012). This compares with about 800 people in city shelters for Sandy victims. Airbnb waived their typical fees, and the City provided advertising and held back on enforcement of standard restrictions governing temporary rentals.

Capital Budget Expenditures

The City of New York has also spent an unprecedented amount of its capital budget to support housing construction and repair. Indeed, between 1987 and 2000, New York City engaged in the largest municipally supported housing production program in the history of the United States. Announced in 1985 by former Mayor Edward I. Koch, the Ten Year Plan originally committed the city to invest over $4 billion to build or renovate more than 100,000 housing units over a period of five years (Schill et al. 2002). A key goal was to renovate and, in some cases completely rebuild, the roughly 100,000 units that the city then owned and return them to for-profit and not-for-profit owners (Schill et al. 2002). The commitment later grew, and by the end of fiscal year 2000, New York City had spent $5.1 billion on the Ten Year Plan, 81.7 percent of which came from the city's capital budget (Niblack 2001). The remaining funds were from state and federal sources, like the federal HOME and Community Development Block Grant programs. During the peak years of the plan, about 6 percent of the city's capital budget was dedicated to housing (New York City Independent Budget Office 2000).

Average capital subsidies across all programs amounted to $28,000 per unit in the 1990s (Schill et al. 2002). In addition, the city typically provided land or buildings at a nominal cost to developers, and most of the housing assisted through the program also qualified for property tax abatements and/or exemptions (see below). Units do not receive ongoing operating subsidies from the city, though many tenants receive Section 8 rental subsidies, and properties are typically governed by rent stabilization. In addition to the vouchers, the city also channeled many of its low-income housing tax credits to projects that were supported through the Ten Year Plan.

The scale of the plan was remarkable. A total of 115,000 occupied housing units received subsidies for renovation and repair (approximately 100,000 of which were rental apartments). In addition, the city capital dollars supported the creation of 66,000 new units, of which 70 percent were in rental buildings (Schill et al. 2002). In total, roughly 6 percent of all housing units in New York City received assistance through the plan.

Because the initiative involved so many distinct programs, it is difficult to get reliable data on tenant incomes. But program guidelines indicate that the vast majority of units have been occupied by households earning less than 80 percent of the city's median income (Schwartz 1999). Still, approximately one-fifth of the 66,000 new units created through the program were homeownership units, targeted to households earning up to or beyond the area median income (Ellen et al. 2001).[4]

Mayor Bloomberg made another substantial commitment to subsidized housing through his new Housing Marketplace Plan, launched in 2003. As of July 2011, 124,510 units of affordable housing had been started under the plan, putting the City on track to achieving the Mayor's goal of creating and preserving 165,000 affordable housing units. Because the stock of housing units and land owned by the city had dwindled down to almost nothing by the time Mayor Bloomberg came to office, his plan had to find new ways of identifying land for affordable housing creation. The programs did so through inclusionary zoning, rezoning of former manufacturing land, and the creation of an acquisition fund, which blends foundation and public funds to provide low-interest loans for the purchase of buildings and land for affordable housing. The plan projected that 68 percent of the units created and preserved would be affordable to those earning less than 80 percent of Area Median Income (a HUD determined level that is based upon the number of persons in the household and the median income for that size household), 11 percent of the units were to be for households earning between 80 percent and 120 percent of AMI (up to $85,080 for a family of four), and the remaining 21 percent would be reserved for middle-income households, earning up to 250 percent of AMI (New York City 2005).

Tax Incentives

The New York City government also offers a more extensive set of property tax abatement programs than most other cities. (Los Angeles uses tax increment financing to fund urban redevelopment.[5]) For multifamily housing, the city offers two chief incentive programs: the 421-a program and the J-51 program. Aimed at new construction, the 421-a program offers fifteen-year property tax exemptions to all new multifamily housing built outside of a "geographic exclusion area," which was originally defined as certain prime neighborhoods in Manhattan and was expanded considerably in 2007 to all of Manhattan and select neighborhoods in the outer boroughs, such as

Brooklyn Heights, Park Slope, and Williamsburg/Greenpoint. The exemption can be extended to twenty-five years if 20 percent of the units in a project are set aside for families earning no more than 80 percent of the city's median income.[6] Residential buildings located in the exclusion zone can receive tax exemptions too, but only if at least 20 percent of the units are set aside for low-income tenants. Rental units in all buildings receiving these tax incentives are placed under rent stabilization during the benefit period (New York City Department of Finance 2007; Citizens Housing and Planning Council 2002; Schultz, Perine, and Feibusch 2011).

The J-51 program offers similar incentives for rehabilitating multifamily buildings. In that program, all neighborhoods are eligible, but the benefits awarded to projects south of 110th Street in Manhattan are more modest. Rental units in buildings receiving J-51 tax incentives are subject to rent stabilization for the duration of the benefits.

The New York City Department of Finance estimates that in 2007, the 421-a program provided $500 million in tax benefits to approximately 76,000 units, while the J-51 program provided $220 million in tax benefits to 740,000 housing units, approximately 62 percent of which were in rental buildings (New York City Department of Finance 2007). Despite these seemingly large benefits, analysts agree that city property tax burdens remain higher for owners of multifamily buildings than they are for owners of single-family homes. The differences in the ratio of what one pays for a given assessment is part of the way taxes are levied in New York City (Sweeting 1998).[7]

First, the city also offers tax incentives for the construction of single and two-family homes, through the 421-b program, which provided $32 million in tax benefits to just over 24,000 units in 2007. Second, and perhaps even more fundamental, properties in New York City are not assessed at their full market value, but only at some proportion of that market value. The assessment ratio applied to the fair market value of a class one property (1–3 family home) is currently just 6 percent, while that applied to larger buildings is 45 percent. There are also caps on the rate of growth of assessments for smaller properties. Increases in assessments for class one properties are limited to 6 percent per year and 20 percent over five years (New York City Department of Finance 2011).

Summary

In short, New York City has invested far more heavily in subsidized housing and done far more to protect tenants from market forces than the City of Los Angeles and other large cities. Note that the rental housing benefits provided by New York City do not appear to be highly redistributive toward poor people, largely due to rent regulation. Because rent-regulated apartments are not means-tested, some of the households living in housing units with below-market rents often have relatively high incomes. (On average, however, renters in rent-stabilized apartments have lower incomes than renters in unregulated apartments.) In addition, while its rental subsidies are clearly aimed at lower income households, New York City probably targets a somewhat greater share of its subsidy dollars to moderate and middle-income households than other large cities. Consider that the city oversees 60,000 Mitchell Lama rental units that are aimed at moderate- and middle-income households, offers tax breaks for rental housing for moderate- and middle-income households, and compared to other cities, has traditionally reserved a greater share of its public housing units for families with working adults. In addition, as discussed below, New York City has invested considerable funds in creating homeownership opportunities for moderate and middle-income households through its Ten Year Capital Plan for housing.

WEATHERING THE DOWNTURN

While few parts of the country were completely untouched by this recent economic downturn, the extent of housing price declines and foreclosures varied considerably among cities. Arguably, New York City has weathered the storm better than other cities. In the Los Angeles metropolitan area, for example, the number of foreclosure starts rose from 38,987 in 2006 to 175,810 in 2009 (RealtyTrac). In the New York City metropolitan area, the increase has been far less dramatic, with annual foreclosure starts rising from 65,292 to 84,054 over the same period. Similarly, in New York City itself, the number of foreclosure notices has risen from 14,000 in 2006 to about 20,000 in 2009 (see figures 10.1 and 1.26).[8]

Several factors explain the differences between New York and Los Angeles. For one thing, a far higher share of borrowers in Los Angeles turned to high-cost loans during the subprime lending boom in 2005 and 2006.[9] Home Mortgage Disclosure

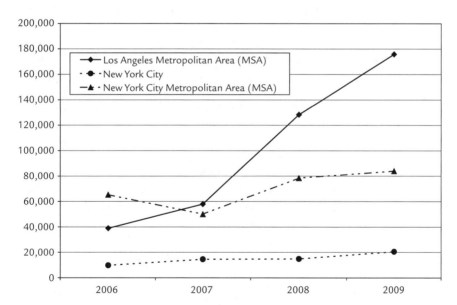

Figure 10.1
Foreclosures in New York City and Los Angeles, 2006–2009
Source: RealtyTrac foreclosure data.
Note: The Los Angeles Metropolitan Statistical Area (MSA) consists of Los Angeles and Orange Counties, the New York City MSA consists of 22 counties in New York and New Jersey. The MSA in both regions is smaller than the Consolidated Statistical Area (CSA), which is used in chapters 1, 2, and 11 to define the two regions. The MSA is used in other chapters.

Act (HMDA) data indicate that about one-third of borrowers in Los Angeles received high-cost mortgages in these peak years, compared to around one-fifth in New York City. Similarly, close to half of the borrowers in Los Angeles turned to second liens, or piggyback loans, in 2006, compared to just over one-quarter in New York City.[10] So it does seem as though borrowers had higher-priced loans and were more highly leveraged in Los Angeles. They were more at risk of foreclosure as a result.

In addition, as noted in chapter 3, the labor market conditions have been worse in Los Angeles than in New York City (see figure 3.1). While the unemployment rates in the two cities largely follow the same trends until the summer of 2007, in the years since then, the unemployment rate in Los Angeles has been about two percentage points higher than that in New York City. So borrowers in Los Angeles were much more at risk of losing their jobs and thus being unable to make their mortgage payments.

Finally, house price trends have also diverged in the two cities. Figure 2.25 shows repeat sales housing price indices for the Los Angeles metropolitan area and for the New York City metropolitan area.[11] As illustrated, both metropolitan areas experienced a substantial boom in house prices from the mid-1990s through about 2006. With this steady and dramatic house price appreciation, there was little downside to risky loans, since borrowers could easily resell their homes for more than their mortgages if they could not afford their mortgages. But prices rose and fell more dramatically in Los Angeles. Between the middle of 2006 and the start of 2009, prices fell by 40 percent in Los Angeles on average. In the New York City metropolitan area, the decline has been more gradual and gentler. So lending and market conditions surely led to a more dramatic crisis in Los Angeles. But in addition, policies—and the structure of the housing stock—may have played a part in moderating the crisis in New York City.

First, New York City is the only major metropolitan area in which a majority of the housing units are located in buildings with five or more units. In 2009, 44 percent of New Yorkers, or nearly 3.7 million individuals, lived in a rental property with at least five units. This compared to 34 percent of the population in Los Angeles, 19 percent in Chicago, 16 percent in Phoenix, and 10 percent in Philadelphia (Been et al. 2011). Multifamily buildings transact less often[12]—and thus fewer were sold at the height of the market. So residents of larger buildings are more protected against risk.

Plus, the homeownership rate is lower in New York than in Los Angeles (30 vs. 39 percent, see table 10.3), which means that households were less apt to stretch to borrow to buy expensive homes. To the extent that ownership is correlated with wealth, New York's low ownership rate means that its least wealthy homeowners are higher in the wealth distribution than the least wealthy homeowners in Los Angeles. And to the extent that New Yorkers own their units in multifamily structures, they are much more likely to be cooperatives than condominiums; in 2000, cooperative units outnumbered condominiums in New York by a factor of four (Schill et al. 2007). Coop boards scrutinize households' financing arrangements and commonly insist that purchasers put down much larger down payments than are required by lenders. They typically require prospective owners to apply to and interview with the Board of Directors and to submit detailed financial statements and letters of recommendation (Schill et al. 2007). Thus, fewer borrowers in New York City were likely to have loans with high Loan-to-Value ratios.

In terms of policies, as noted already, more New Yorkers live in subsidized housing and a far greater share live in rent-regulated units. This in combination with the larger buildings may have meant it was less attractive—and more difficult—for inexperienced speculators to jump into the market and buy up homes at inflated prices. Because of the prevalence of subsidies and rent regulation, households are also less mobile in New York City, opening up fewer opportunities for transactions. And because of the city's efforts, and the rich network of nonprofits, a larger share of the housing stock in New York is likely controlled by nonprofit organizations, which may be less likely to take out risky loans. The experience of the downturn suggests that the policy differences across cities may have significant impacts and may help to shape how cities are affected by national economic cycles. Of course, there are other cultural and historical differences that explain why Los Angeles was hit harder than New York City, such as the fact that some lenders specializing in subprime started in California and targeted the market there, or that there has historically been less of a push for homeownership in New York City, or that New Yorkers simply tend to be less mobile (perhaps even independent of rent regulation).

WHY ARE NEW YORK'S HOUSING POLICIES DIFFERENT?

Clearly, then, New York City's housing policies are distinct from those in Los Angeles and continue to be unusual within the United States. The difficult question is "why?" While we do not purport to provide a definitive answer, in this section we explore a few alternative possibilities for why city policymakers have chosen these policies. Are hardships simply greater in New York City, calling for greater investments in turn? Alternatively, is the difference political—is the city's population more liberal and inclined toward redistribution? Or finally, are the objectives of housing policy in New York City simply different, calling for different policies? We explore each of these possibilities in turn. We generally focus our analysis on data from the 2000 Census as we are trying to explain why differences in housing policies have emerged.

Greater Needs

One possible reason for New York's greater investments in housing is that needs in New York are simply greater than those in other large cities in the United States. But it turns out that while housing is surely expensive in New York, New York is not an outlier among large cities.

Housing Costs and Burdens

A simple comparison of rent levels (with no adjustments for size or quality), shown in table 10.2, suggests that rents in New York City are among the highest in the country, but not that different from those in Los Angeles and other large California cities.

In 2000, the median rent for a housing unit in New York City was $705. By comparison the median rent for a housing unit in Los Angeles was $672. In 2000, the median renter household paid 26.6 percent of its income on rent in New York City, while the median rent burden was 29.1 percent in Los Angeles. Indeed, the median rent burden was higher than New York's in four of the ten largest cities. As for the median value of owner-occupied homes, New York emerges as the third most expensive of the ten largest cities (behind San Diego and Los Angeles).

Naturally, we do not know what rent levels would be in New York if subsidies and controls were not so pervasive. Moreover, these simple comparisons of prices and rents fail to control for the characteristics of the housing stock in each area and do not control for the fact that the marginal renter in New York (the household right on the margin between renting and homeownership) is probably richer than the marginal renter in most other cities. (This is because a higher proportion of New Yorkers are renters.) Creating quality-controlled comparisons is difficult, since it is hard to control for the idiosyncratic features of each housing unit and its neighborhood. Many researchers have attempted to create constant quality housing price indices, using data on structural characteristics. However, the geographic unit has typically been the metropolitan area and not the city. In these indices, New York rent typically falls near the top of list, but once again, not the very top. Malpezzi, Chun, and Green (1998) attempt to estimate constant quality housing price indices for US metropolitan areas using the 1990 Census. While the New York metropolitan area does not appear to be the most expensive, its rents and home values are typically within the top ten or fifteen most expensive metropolitan areas. Together with New York, Los Angeles, several other metropolitan areas in California, Honolulu, Boston, and Stamford, Connecticut, appear to be consistently more expensive than other large metropolitan areas (Malpezzi, Chun, and Green 1998; Thibodeau 1995).

Table 10.2 MEDIAN RENT, RENT-TO-INCOME RATIO, AND HOME VALUE, 2000, TEN LARGEST CITIES

City	Median Gross Rent	Median Gross Rent to Income Ratio	Median Value of Owner-Occupied units (thousands)
New York City	$705	26.6	$211.9
Los Angeles	$672	29.1	$221.6
Chicago	$616	25.3	$132.4
Houston	$575	24.1	$79.3
Philadelphia	$569	28.4	$59.7
Phoenix	$622	26.5	$112.6
San Diego	$763	28.3	$233.1
Dallas	$623	24.4	$89.8
San Antonio	$549	24.9	$68.8
Detroit	$486	26.9	$63.6

Note: Rents refer to gross rents here. Home values are self-reported values.
Source: US Census Bureau 2003. Census 2000.

Glaeser and Gyourko (2003) provide estimates of the proportion of owner-occupied houses in different central cities that are worth more than 140 percent of their construction cost. New York City is one of the more expensive cities on this measure, but far from the most expensive. Using this measure, housing in Los Angeles is considerably more expensive than it is in New York.

Ultimately, New York's housing prices, while high, do not appear to be out of line with those in Los Angeles and other large, coastal cities. We do not maintain, of course, that the data on rent burdens or hardships are uncontaminated by policies. Housing costs in New York would be different if the city's regulation and subsidy policies were different, but it is not at all obvious that adopting more standard policies in either arena would make New York's outcomes greater outliers. Our point is not to give a precise estimate of the force of hardship on the determination of New York's policies. We just maintain that there is no reason to believe that if New York had more standard policies it would be by far the most horrible place in the United States, measured by these hardships.

Taste for Redistribution

Another possible explanation for New York's large investments in housing is a political one. Are New Yorkers simply more interested in redistribution than citizens elsewhere in the United States?

One plausible argument is that because New York City has so many renters, New Yorkers are more inclined to pass laws (like rent control) that redistribute income to existing renters. New Yorkers are indeed much less likely than other Americans to own the housing they occupy. In 2000, the Census reported that just 30.2 percent of New York households owned the units they occupied. The comparable figure for the United States was 66.2 percent.

New York does not appear as unusual, however, when it is compared with other large and dense cities. Table 10.3 performs this exercise. To be sure, New York has

Table 10.3 PERCENT OF HOUSING UNITS OCCUPIED BY THEIR OWNERS, 2000, TEN LARGEST CITIES

1. New York	30.2
2. Los Angeles	38.6
3. Chicago	43.8
4. Houston	45.8
5. Philadelphia	59.3
6. Phoenix	60.7
7. San Diego	49.5
8. Dallas	43.2
9. San Antonio	58.1
10. Detroit	54.9

Source: US Census Bureau 2002. 2000 Census.

a lower proportion of homeowners than the other nine largest cities, but the homeownership rate was relatively low in all of these cities, and the rate in Los Angeles
was almost as low as that in New York.

While the predominance of renters probably helps to explain some of the regulations in New York City (in particular the persistence of rent control), it seems
unlikely to explain all the oddities of New York's housing policies. For one thing,
the city's high proportion of renters certainly does not explain the general bias
discussed earlier in the city's tax policies toward single-family homes. Another
possibility is that New Yorkers are simply wealthier than residents in other cities.
As a result, they can afford to redistribute more and make greater investments
in the housing stock. But as shown in table 10.4, which compares the proportion
of households earning more than $150,000 and $100,000 for the ten largest cities in 1999, New Yorkers are not the most affluent. In 1999, 5.9 percent of New
York's households had incomes of $150,000 or greater, while in Los Angeles, the
proportion was 6.2 percent. The proportion of households earning more than
$150,000 a year was higher in San Diego than it was in New York, and the pro-
portion earning more than $200,000 a year was higher in Los Angeles and Dallas
than New York.

A more sophisticated version of the wealth story emphasizes inequality. Rich New
Yorkers are generous, in this story, because they see poverty around them. This story
has more support from the data than the pure wealth story, but it still does not seem
to be a good explanation of New York's exceptionalism. The final column in table
10.4 shows the proportion of persons in each city in 2000 who were poor in 1999.
Los Angeles has both greater proportions of poor people and greater proportions of
rich households than New York. And Chicago and Houston do not differ substantially
from New York on either measure.[13]

Table 10.4 EXTREMES OF THE INCOME DISTRIBUTION: 1999 INCOME RECEIVED BY RESIDENTS, TEN LARGEST CITIES

	% of Households Earning >= $150,000	% of Households Earning >= $200,000	% of Households in Poverty
New York City	5.9%	3.4%	21.2%
Los Angeles	6.2%	3.7%	22.1%
Chicago	4.5%	2.5%	19.6%
Houston	4.9%	2.6%	19.2%
Philadelphia	2.0%	1.0%	22.9%
Phoenix	4.3%	2.2%	15.8%
San Diego	6.0%	3.0%	14.6%
Dallas	5.9%	3.5%	17.8%
San Antonio	2.9%	1.5%	17.3%
Detroit	1.8%	0.9%	26.1%

Source: US Census Bureau 2000 census data. For the first two columns the observations are households; for the last column, persons.

Finally, New Yorkers may simply have more liberal political attitudes. This seems an odd claim about a city in which the last five mayoral elections have been won by Republicans. If we measure liberalism by the Americans for Democratic Action (ADA) score of a city's congressional delegation, New York is less liberal than the four large cities (Los Angeles, Philadelphia, San Diego, and Detroit)[14] that passed resolutions opposing the Iraq war before New York did.[15]

Perhaps the strongest reason to doubt that New York's housing policies are driven by a desire for redistribution is simply that they do not redistribute very well. To be sure, low-income households in New York City are more likely to receive housing subsidies than wealthier households. Yet, as we have shown, the nominal beneficiaries of many of the city's housing policies are not poor, and in most the poorest of the poor do not receive the majority of nominal benefits. Even more telling is the extensive evidence that the beneficiaries of these housing programs would have been quite a bit better off if they had received cash instead of either the subsidized apartment or the right to rent control, and landlords and taxpayers would have been no worse off. For instance, see Olsen (2001), for evidence on housing subsidy programs and Glaeser and Luttmer (1997), for evidence on New York rent control. Surely a city intent on redistributing resources to the poor could have found more effective means of doing so.

Other Objectives

While we believe that both politics and needs have played some role in driving New York's distinctiveness, we also believe that the goals of housing policy in New York City differ from those in other cities. In particular, we argue that much of what is different about New York City's housing policies can be explained by the city's greater attention to externality-related goals.

The objectives of housing policy typically fall into three general categories. The first is redistribution. Although not all housing subsidies seek to transfer income from higher to lower income households (consider the generous tax code provisions favoring homeowners), this is probably the most frequent justification offered for rental housing programs.

The second objective is to address externalities in the housing market, which are likely to be particularly large in cities. The more people crowded together in a small space, the more likely they are to affect one another. Thus, urban housing policies have long tried to keep people from spreading disease, raising immoral children, disposing of waste in an unsanitary manner, interfering in the normal flow of business, or presenting unsightly spectacles. Similarly, they have tried to subsidize construction and repairs in distressed neighborhoods, in the hope of generating positive spillovers. We call this the inter-household externality story. (Inter-household externalities are also one reason why New York City has a low homeownership rate. When lots of people live in close proximity to each other and share many common facilities, common ownership—or rental housing—is efficient.)

The final objective is more subtle. Economies of scale mean that higher population increases output per worker. In the absence of congestion and negative externalities, everyone gains when more people live and work in a city—firms are more productive, specialization offers better goods and services, recreation is more abundant, and learning opportunities are better. Thus, another goal of housing policy may be to pack a greater number of people into a city. We call this the production externality story.

We believe that as compared to other cities, New York placed more weight on these latter two, externality-related goals. This is what may make New York City's policies look so different from those in other large cities. New York's leaders have repeatedly stressed these kinds of externalities. The mission of the Housing Development Corporation (HDC) is perhaps the most succinct statement, "HDC seeks to increase the supply of multi-family housing, stimulate economic growth, and revitalize neighborhoods" (New York City Housing Development Corporation 2011). Mayor Bloomberg's ambitious 2002 housing plan begins by emphasizing production externalities, "In order for New York City to remain competitive and to ensure that its record growth can continue, significant housing issues must be addressed" (New York City Department of Housing Preservation and Development 2002).

This rhetoric is not confined to the Bloomberg administration. The Koch administration made similar arguments when the municipally supported housing push first began, although with slightly more emphasis on inter-household externalities. According to the Mayor: "First, we intend to undertake a major effort to rebuild entire neighborhoods of, perhaps 15 to 25 square blocks throughout the City.... It is anticipated that such concentrated revitalization would provide the hub for further development" (Koch 1985, 11). And, a document from the city's Department of Housing Preservation and Development on the city's ten-year plan for housing stated: "We're creating more than just apartments—we're re-creating neighborhoods. We're revitalizing parts of the city that over the past two decades had been decimated by disinvestment, abandonment, and arson" (New York City Department of Housing Preservation and Development 1989.)

But production externalities also played a major role, especially in more high-level discussions. Abraham Biderman, a senior city official when the plan was conceived, recalled the arguments for housing at the crucial early stages, "At that time, the city population was growing, the jobs were growing, but there was no housing being created for all sorts of reasons, and this was the critical linchpin to the whole city economy" (Soffer 2010). Then Deputy Mayor Stanley Brezenoff responded to critics who wanted a more redistributive program by invoking production externalities again, "We cannot preserve the city's long-term health if we do not address the needs of the middle class by putting public resources into creating housing for this group. If we don't, who will be there to fill the jobs and pay the taxes that support services and housing creation for the poor?" (Soffer 2010). Consider that while policymakers discussed reducing density or abandoning parts of New Orleans and the Jersey shore after they were hit by hurricanes, discussion of exposed sections of New York City after Superstorm Sandy focused almost entirely on measures to strengthen protection from future storms, not abandonment.

We could find no record of Los Angeles mayors or city officials making similar statements about how crucial new housing is to the city's well-being. The mission statement of the Community Redevelopment Administration (CRA), which handles business development as well as housing, is merely, "We make strategic investments to create economic opportunity and improve the quality of life for people who live and work in our neighborhoods" (Los Angeles Community Redevelopment Administration 2011). Inter-household externalities matter, but production externalities are not the life-or-death issue that is portrayed in official New York City rhetoric.

Inter-household Externalities

Let us start with inter-household externalities. New York City policymakers might pay more attention to such externalities for the simple reason that New York City is much more densely populated than other US cities around the rest of the country. Indeed, if the rest of the country were as densely populated as New York, the current US population would fit into Maryland. Table 10.5 shows the standard measure of population density—recorded population per square mile—for the ten largest cities.

New York City dominates the list. Not one of the other cities has even half New York's density. Indeed, except for Staten Island, every borough of New York City is more densely populated than every other city on the list.[16] Even Staten Island, though sometimes depicted as a semi-rural enclave, is more densely populated than Detroit and Cleveland, almost as dense as Los Angeles, and almost twice as dense as Denver.

To some extent, then, housing market externalities will be larger in New York City, and thus demand greater government involvement. The more people crowded together in a small space, after all, the greater the payoff from reducing the harm that they cause each other. Certainly, its stringent building code is related to some

Table 10.5 CITY POPULATION DENSITY, 2000, TEN LARGEST CITIES (PERSONS PER SQUARE MILE)

1. New York	26,402
2. Los Angeles	7,877
3. Chicago	12,750
4. Houston	3,372
5. Philadelphia	11,233
6. Phoenix	2,782
7. San Diego	3,772
8. Dallas	3,470
9. San Antonio	2,809
10. Detroit	6,855

Source: 2000 Census, from United States Census Bureau, 2001. Statistical Abstract of the United States, table 34.

degree to the city's high density of development. But its massive capital investment in the city's private housing stock can also be understood in light of New York's high density (Schill et al. 2002). At higher levels of density, a greater number of housing units will benefit from the improvement of a given property.

As for empirical support, there is growing evidence that New York's housing production programs have, in fact, delivered substantial external benefits to surrounding properties. Schwartz, Ellen, Schill, and Voicu (2006) find that prices of properties surrounding city housing investment sites are significantly lower than those of comparable properties prior to project construction. After construction, the gap narrows considerably—price appreciation in the vicinity of new housing exceeds that found outside the area. The magnitudes of the external effects are found to increase with project size and to decrease with the proportion of units in multifamily, rental buildings. Consistent with expectations, the authors find that spillover effects diminish with distance from the housing investment sites.

Inter-household externalities may also play a role in the form of subsidies that New York City uses. We have seen that the ratio of supply-side to demand-side programs is unusually high. Supply-side programs (or programs that provide subsidies to develop housing) give the government much tighter control over where people live and the physical conditions under which they live. A government intent on using housing policy to manage inter-household externalities would be much more inclined to use supply-side rather than demand-side programs (or programs that provide housing assistance directly to tenants).[17]

New York City officials might also try harder than officials in other cities to promote residential stability. The development of trust and social capital among neighbors seems more critical, after all, in dense residential environments. (And households who leave their units may impose greater external costs when they are living close to a larger number of neighbors.) Both rent control and subsidies to single-family owners help to further population stability. Perhaps partly because of these policies, New Yorkers appear to be less likely to move than their counterparts in other cities.

Admittedly, measuring stability is not easy. Ideally, we want to estimate the proportion of people who lived in a given city in year t who remained in their housing unit x years later. Table 10.6 explores this issue, using 1990 as the comparison year. For each city, we find the number of occupied units in 1990 (from the 1990 census) and divide this into the number of 2000 occupants who said they moved in before 1990 (from the 2000 census). This measure has weaknesses: it misallocates move-ins between January and March 1990; it relies on faulty recall; it does not correct for mortality; and it deals only with a specific pair of years.

According to the table, 35.2 percent of New York renting households in 1990 remained in the same unit in 2000; no large city even comes close. Nationally, only 13.6 percent of 1990 renting households remained in their units until 2000, and in several large cities the proportion of 1990 renters staying until 2000 is under 10 percent. Part of the reason for greater stability in New York may be the presence of rent regulation. Rent regulation appears to promote stability, although empirical studies are not unanimous on this point.[18] New York homeowners were also more likely to remain in place than homeowners in Los Angeles and in most of the other large cities.

Table 10.6 PROPORTION OF 1990 HOUSEHOLDERS
REMAINING IN THE SAME UNIT UNTIL 2000, TEN
LARGEST CITIES

	Owners	Renters
1. New York	63%	35%
2. Los Angeles	55	14
3. Chicago	57	17
4. Houston	48	10
5. Philadelphia	60	18
6. Phoenix	45	6
7. San Diego	53	9
8. Dallas	53	7
9. San Antonio	65	5
10. Detroit	58	16

Source: Authors' calculations from 1990 and 2000 Census.

Stability is also associated with another kind of externality: it may make citizens better voters. To the extent that rent control and rent subsidies mean that tenants realize consumer surplus from their apartments in New York, they have a stake in the outcome of local political decisions, and so are more likely to participate intelligently in the development of those policies. This argument is usually made for homeownership (see, for instance, DiPasquale and Glaeser 1999 and Glaeser and Shapiro 2002), but if it is true, then rent control and rent subsidies provide the same sort of advantages. New York's housing programs, in this view, are the city's substitute for homeownership.[19]

Density and externalities also matter for how New York City rebuilds from natural disasters like Superstorm Sandy and the Great Blizzard of 1888. Consider electrical wires. A city can reduce storm-related outages either by hardening the transmission network from centralized generating facilities, or by moving to decentralized, distributed generation—generators for everybody, in the current day. (Good ways of using solar cells in a power outage have not yet been popularized.) Hardening transmission is expensive, and the ratio of benefits to costs depends on the value of the electricity used per mile of transmission line that has to be hardened. A mile of transmission line that serves 10,000 customers including hospitals and Fortune 500 companies is a better prospect for hardening than two miles of transmission line that serves a pair of farm households. Generators are noisy, polluting, and can cause fires; the damage they do is greater the more dense the neighborhood they are operating in. So hardening works relatively better in denser areas.

It should not be surprising, then, that New York City hardened infrastructure by moving it underground after the Great Blizzard of 1888, and most of the city did not experience the power outages from downed wires that were ubiquitous in the rest of the metropolitan area after Sandy. Power failed in many places when utility tunnels flooded, but this was a simple case of "fighting the last war"—just putting the wires underground protects them from blizzards and windstorms, but not from flooding.

Production Externalities

The existence of production externalities may also help to explain New York's policies. New York's unusual productivity, the argument goes, is due in large part to the economies of scale which have made the city unusually productive in making goods, in providing services, and in producing entertainment, recreation, and education. People work better, play better, and learn better in large cities like New York. The presence of so much activity, the continuous and spontaneous exchange of ideas, and the diversity of activity enable workers to hone their skills and become more productive. From this perspective, housing investments can help further economic development, perhaps especially for cities that are already quite dense.

If true, then it may make sense for the city to provide housing subsidies to as many households as possible, which sounds a lot like what New York has done. The production externality is an added benefit to housing programs that makes them relatively more attractive in New York than in other cities.[20] It also increases the benefits to New York of receiving federal funds.[21]

The political strength of the production externality argument for more housing will be an important factor in how beach communities in New York City rebuild after Sandy.

They will be rebuilt. They will not be like the Lower Ninth Ward in New Orleans where many lots are vacant and unused seven years after Katrina. The land is too valuable for that. While vacant land assessments and sales at under $10 per square foot are common today in New Orleans (Zillow 2012 and Orleans Parish Assessor 2012), Haughwout et al. (2008) report vacant land sales in the Rockaways at over $100 per square foot, with prices even after Sandy likely far above New Orleans.

But like New Orleans, the old, cheap, small houses—converted bungalows—that were common in these areas before Sandy will not return. Buildable land in these communities is considerably more valuable now than it was when the original bungalows went up, and so standard urban economics predicts that rebuilding will increase density. Economies of scale in storm protection—building on stilts, for instance, or raising the elevation of the entire neighborhood—may also make greater density more attractive. So in a regime where citywide production externalities matter, the converted bungalows get replaced by reinforced apartment buildings built on stilts, platforms, or hills.

On the other hand, some political forces may push in the opposite direction. On Staten Island, zoning for lower density has been popular for decades; it was a major rallying cry for secession in the 1990s, for instance. Pre-Sandy residents of the beach communities may also want to return to the bucolic *status quo ante*. And since the national flood insurance program's lower than actuarially fair premiums encourage inefficiently high levels of building in flood-prone areas, there are solid efficiency arguments on a national level for not rebuilding to the density that may be optimal for New York City as a whole.

The city government is now using FEMA funds to start up ferry service to Manhattan from Rockaway and the South Shore of Staten Island (Gothamist, 2012). It will be interesting to see whether these ferries continue.

CONCLUSION

Housing policies in New York are clearly different from those in Los Angeles and from those in other large cities in the United States. New York has more subsidized housing, more rent regulation, more extensive efforts to alleviate homelessness, and more local spending to produce housing. Some of the expenditure comparisons are astounding. The housing market in New York City is also more heavily regulated than in most other cities. These generous policies arguably helped to buffer New York from the effects of the Great Recession.

Los Angeles has a fairly extensive program of housing support too, though not as vast as that in New York. The programs in Los Angeles have also been more targeted to lower income households than those in New York.

Although needs are great in New York, they do not appear to be different enough from those in other cities to fully explain New York's unusual set of policies. Most households in New York are renters, but so are most households in Los Angeles. The city's politics are liberal, but again, we think this explanation falls short. We argue that because of the extreme density of population, employment, and recreation in New York City, policymakers have used housing policy tools toward different ends than in many other cities. We believe that city policymakers have used housing investment as a tool not simply to build more housing for needy families, but also to revitalize and restore the city's neighborhoods and to enhance its overall economic health. We do not maintain that traditional motivations are absent in decision-making about housing in New York City—they are just very far from being the complete story.

NOTES

1. Furman Center estimates suggest that the program had 43,000 units at the end of 2008, but there were a few large developments that opted out of the program and converted to market-rate in 2007 and 2008, conversions which the HVS might not have captured. For consistency sake, we rely on the HVS estimates. If we used the Furman Center estimates, the share of rental housing that was privately owned but publicly subsidized would fall to 5 percent.
2. The Section 8 voucher program allows participants to live in units that rent for more than the specified fair market rent and to pay up to 40 percent of their income toward rent.
3. There are in fact two separate and very large Section 8 voucher programs in New York City. NYCHA runs the largest program (98,000 units); HPD administers another 27,325 vouchers.

4. New York City launched two programs, the Nehemiah Plan and the New Homes Program of the New York City Housing Partnership, which subsidize the construction of affordable, owner-occupied homes for moderate and middle-income households. Together, these two programs have produced over 15,000 affordable homes (Ellen et al. 2001).
5. Under tax increment financing, the city or state pays for a portion of a development, sells tax-exempt bonds to pay for it, and then dedicates a portion of the increase in property taxes that follows the development to paying off the bonds. To the extent that a private party would otherwise have financed this portion of the development itself, this effectively lowers the private party's cost of development.
6. The income limits vary depending on location of project and what other subsidies, if any, it is receiving. See Schultz, Perine, and Feibusch, 2011.
7. Many observers have criticized these tax disparities between multifamily and smaller properties as unfair and charge that political considerations dissuade lawmakers from meaningful reforms (Scanlon and Cohen 2009).
8. There are some neighborhoods in New York City, which have been hit extremely hard by high-cost lending and subsequent foreclosures, especially those in Southeastern Queens (e.g., Jamaica and Queens Village), and Northern Brooklyn (e.g., Bedford Stuyvesant).
9. "High cost" is a measure of subprime lending. Loans are classified as high cost if they have an interest rate more than some specified threshold above the Federal Treasury rate of like maturity. This commonly used definition of subprime lending is more dependable than identifying loans made by subprime lenders (using the HUD Subprime Lender list), as prime lenders can make subprime loans, and lenders labeled as subprime can originate prime loans.
10. A piggyback loan is basically a subordinate, second mortgage, often taken out at the time of a home purchase or a refinance. Piggyback loans allow borrowers to avoid having to purchase private mortgage insurance when they acquire or refinance a home while borrowing more than 80 percent of the value of the home.
11. A repeat sales price index measures average changes in prices of homes that transact more than once. Unlike comparisons of average or median sales prices, repeat sales indices control for changes in the quality and characteristics of the homes sold. As noted in chapter 2, the repeat sale price index of Case-Shiller Housing Price Index for New York City and Los Angeles metros seasonally and inflation adjusted provides a good measure of housing price changes.
12. In New York City in 2004, buildings with five or more apartments were sold 65 percent less frequently than those with four units or fewer.
13. Ideally we should have corrected table 10.4 for differences in city costs of living. Such a correction, however, would not have changed our conclusions to any great degree. The Texas and Arizona cities would have appeared richer, and so New York would have been even less of an outlier on wealth, and New York's poverty would have increased.
14. We define a city's congressional delegation as the members of Congress in 2003 who listed that city as their "hometown" in the directory published by the clerk of the Congress (http://clerk.house.gov/members/index.php). This is an imperfect measure because congressional districts are not coterminous with cities. We use the 2002 liberalism score provided by Americans for Democratic Action (http://www.adaction.org/2002voting.html). Except for those from Dallas and Houston, all members with city hometowns in 2003 were also members in 2002, although their districts may have been different. We were unable to use this procedure for Dallas and Houston, but it is unlikely that they were more liberal than New York.

15. New York was one of 160 jurisdictions passing resolutions opposing a unilateral war against Iraq, but the resolution passed only after four of the other top 10 largest cities (Los Angeles, Chicago, Philadelphia, and Detroit) had already passed similar resolutions. The Los Angeles resolution was adopted by a vote of 9–4 on February 21, 2003, and the New York resolution was adopted 31–17 on March 11, 2003. (See Common Dreams 2003 and Whitaker 2003.)

16. The population densities of New York City's boroughs in 2000 ranged from 66,940 people per square mile in Manhattan to 7,588 people per square mile in Staten Island. Densities in Brooklyn and the Bronx were both above 30,000 people per square mile, while the density of Queens was above 20,000 people per square mile (New York City Department of City Planning 2004).

17. Another factor that may have inclined New York to invest more heavily than other cities in supply-side housing programs is the concentration of financial expertise. In the 1997 economic census, 46 percent of the national payroll in the "securities intermediation and related activities" industry (NAICS code 523) was earned in the New York metropolitan area. Most debt issuances generate some rents and quasi-rents for various financial middlemen (bond counsels, underwriters, sales people). To the extent that these rents and quasi-rents accrue to firms and workers outside the city arranging to have the debt issued, they are losses to that city. Because these losses were probably smaller for New York than for any other US city, supply-side housing programs were more attractive for New York.

18. Nagy (1995) finds that while rent-controlled tenants in New York are less mobile than other tenants, the difference is entirely explained by the characteristics of those tenants. But Gyourko and Linneman (1989) for New York and Munch and Svarer (2002) for Denmark find that rent regulation has an independent effect.

19. Of course, simple subsidies for length of tenure would also promote stability with far fewer deadweight losses. We are not arguing that New York's housing policies are the optimal way to promote stability—only that promoting stability is one of the benefits that these programs have. The same argument can be made against homeowners' tax preferences.

20. The inter-household externality motive also interacts with the production externality motive. Policies that reduce inter-household externalities efficiently also reduce deadweight losses, and so allow more people, in the long run, to live and work in New York City, without raising wages to attract them.

21. We acknowledge that the production externalities story has not been fully explored yet. Even the most basic question—do supply-side subsidies and rent control increase New York City's employment density?—has no empirical answer. Several papers— Murray (1983), Murray (1999), Sinai and Waldfogel (2005), and Malpezzi and Vandell (2002)—suggest that publicly subsidized housing crowds out private housing at a very high rate, but those studies do not rule out the possibility that supply-side housing programs can increase the population of a central city. For all of these studies, the units of observation are metropolitan areas or states, and so they provide no information on how these programs affect where people live and work within metropolitan areas. The latter two papers, moreover, control explicitly for population size—their dependent variable is housing units per thousand people—and so cannot answer, even on a state or metropolitan basis, the question we are interested in.

CHAPTER 11

Residential Diversity and Division

Separation and Segregation among
Whites, Blacks, Hispanics, Asians,
Affluent, and Poor

ANDREW A. BEVERIDGE, DAVID HALLE,
EDWARD TELLES, AND
BETH LEAVENWORTH DUFAULT

The Los Angeles and New York City region areas are strikingly diverse. Civic leaders often point to diversity as a major asset. As seen in chapter 2, each area is home to members of the major racial and Hispanic groups, including whites, blacks, Asians, and a small number of Native Americans and Hawaiian and other Pacific Islanders. Although both areas are very diverse, as we will see in this chapter, both are also quite segregated in certain ways, with members of the groups living apart (at least to some extent) from one another. The discussion here will focus mainly on the "official" racial and Hispanic groups, but one should remember that each of these large and "pan ethnic" groups—non-Hispanic white, black, and Asian, as well as Hispanic—includes people of very diverse origins.

There are also very affluent households in the New York City and Los Angeles regions. It is also well known that much of the income gains over the past thirty years have not gone to those in the middle, but rather to those in the top one percent of earners (Congressional Budget Office 2011; Krugman 2011). However, there is a higher percentage of highly affluent households in the New York City region than in Los Angeles. We will examine the extent to which the primary residences of the very affluent are now more and more geographically remote from those of the rest of the residents in each region. Some researchers have found this to be true for various areas in the United States. At the same time, in both regions there are also those living in poverty, and we will also examine the extent to which poverty has become more or less concentrated in each region. Researchers have found that concentrated poverty leads to a wide variety of social problems, and so the extent to which poverty is concentrated becomes an important indicator of the health and well-being of a city and its residents.

Finally, we will examine the interaction between affluence and race and Hispanic status in terms of segregation. Are rich blacks, Asians, and Hispanics separated from rich non-Hispanic whites? What about those in poverty? The answers to these questions begin to get at the extent to which the Los Angeles and New York City regions are "one community" or rather a series of ethnically and economically separate places.

In both regions, the residential patterns are driven, at least in part, by racial and Hispanic segregation, as well as by divisions of economic status. Although both regions are becoming somewhat less segregated in terms of race and Hispanic status, it appears that there now is more segregation of the affluent from the rest. Furthermore, areas that become identified as occupied by one race can change over time and become less concentrated, but whether changes in Harlem or southeastern Queens in New York City, or changes in South Central or Ladera Heights in Los Angeles imply a diminution in segregation or simply a reshuffling of population requires further analysis.

THE MYTH OF THE NONSEGREGATED SOCIETY: RACIAL AND HISPANIC SEGREGATION IN THE NEW YORK CITY AND LOS ANGELES REGIONS

Before the Civil Rights Act of 1964, the state of race relations in the United States could be summed up by Big Bill Broonzy's famous blues song "Black, Brown and White," recorded in 1951: "If you was white, should be all right, if you was brown, stick around, but as you's black, hmm brother, get back, get back, get back." During President Obama's inauguration, Reverend Joseph Lowery recited his own update of those lyrics: "We ask you to help us work for that day when black will not be asked to get back, when brown can stick around, when yellow will be mellow, when the red man can get ahead, man, and when white will embrace what is right."

The analysis of segregation in the United States is often controversial. When the 2000 Census was released, Milwaukee was deemed to be among the most segregated regions in the United States by a Census Bureau study (Weinberg and Iceland 2002). The researchers were interrogated by the local congressman, and a local foundation funded a study by a faculty member of the University of Wisconsin Milwaukee using a "new approach" to measuring segregation that put Milwaukee more in the middle of the ranking. This study, comments upon it, and its unusual measure of segregation were then investigated by the *Milwaukee Journal*, which eventually published about thirty articles, editorials, and commentary on the controversy (Goering 2004; Quinn 2004).

One reason that segregation is controversial is that some, such as in Milwaukee, consider that it is at least implicitly seen as an index of the degree of prejudice in a given locale. In fact, historic housing patterns in the United States reflect both past legal segregation as well as current de facto segregation in the housing market. Indeed, the many studies of housing discrimination and preference for residential settings do seem to indicate that though both blacks and whites may claim to prefer living in integrated neighborhoods, what that means to each group is quite different—for whites it generally means some sprinkling of blacks throughout an area, while for blacks it means something more like parity (Farley et al. 1978; Farley et al. 1993).

Furthermore, all of the Department of Housing and Urban Development studies of housing discrimination and recent scholarly work show that when given only small cues about a neighborhood's racial composition, many non-Hispanic whites will classify neighborhoods with non-white residents as much less desirable (Krysan et al. 2009). In short, there is still much prejudice within the white population with regard to housing for blacks. Beyond this, much work shows that if one expects others to shun a neighborhood with black residents, then one may not welcome blacks in one's own neighborhood. However, how these preferences led and lead to segregation is more complex (Bruch and Mare 2006). The patterns for Hispanics and Asians seem to be different and are mediated by color, affluence, and immigrant status (Iceland 2009).

The study of segregation in the United States grew hand in hand with the development of urban sociology and the availability of Census tract data. In the United States, urban studies and certain types of demography were heavily influenced by the so-called "Chicago School." Developed after the founding of the University of Chicago sociology department in the 1920s, it featured one of the earliest models designed to explain the spatial organization of urban areas, and it was associated with sociologists Robert Park and Ernest Burgess. The so-called "Concentric Ring" model assumed that members of similar racial and economic groups would live in close proximity to one another. Once the Census tract system was put into place with the censuses of 1940 and 1950, researchers began to measure segregation explicitly.[1] Nowadays, while most sociologists analyzing patterns of segregation over time see some decreases in the past decade (Farley 2011), a recent study claims that segregation has all but ended (Glaeser and Vigdor 2012). The reason for this discrepancy will be discussed below. Different approaches to measuring segregation yield different, even contradictory, results. Suffice it to say, segregation continues, even if it has diminished somewhat, and as we will show, it is still prevalent in both regions.

OUR STUDY

For this analysis we will use the following basic units of analysis, which were discussed, in part, in chapter 2:

(1) CSAs: The combined statistical area (CSA) in New York is a thirty-county area. The LA CSA includes Los Angeles, Riverside, Orange, San Bernardino, and Ventura Counties. The NYC CSA encompasses over 22 million people, the LA CSA nearly 18 million.

(2) Counties and cities: New York City, Los Angeles City, and Los Angeles County. New York City includes five counties: the Bronx, New York (Manhattan), Kings (Brooklyn), Queens, and Richmond (Staten Island). Los Angeles County is far larger than Los Angeles City (it is the largest county by population in the United

States) and includes an additional 87 cities and unincorporated territories like East Los Angeles. The City of Los Angeles contains incorporated cities fully encircled by the city but not formally part of it, such as Beverly Hills, Santa Monica, and San Fernando. Here we will use the portion that is officially in the city limits of Los Angeles, so the embedded municipalities and East Los Angeles are not included.

As noted in chapter 2, over the past decades, Los Angeles has grown rapidly, but the Los Angeles region has become proportionately less and less non-Hispanic white and increasingly Latino and Asian. The New York City region and New York City have also experienced major increases in the proportions of Latinos and Asians. So no one would doubt that the city, the county, and the region of Los Angeles, or the city and region of New York City are now more diverse. The question is to what extent are these areas segregated, and how has that changed, if at all, for the various populations?

Chapter 2, figures 2.7 and 2.10 for the Los Angeles region, and figures 2.8 and 2.11 for the New York City region, maps the distribution of non-Hispanic whites and non-Hispanic African Americans in the two regions. Although useful, such maps do not quantify segregation. The most basic and widely used measure of segregation is the *Dissimilarity Index*. It is computed based upon the concentration of a group across geographic areas. Let's suppose that 10 percent of people residing in a given county were members of a minority group. Then, if every single census tract had 10 percent of that group, one could say that there is no (0.0) segregation. If, on the other hand, the entire minority group lived in one set of census blocks or census tracts, and every one of those tracts was only inhabited by the minority while all of the other tracts or blocks were only occupied by the nonminority, one could say that there is total (1.0) segregation. Technically, the *Dissimilarity Index* is the proportion of a minority group that would need to move to make the distribution of that group the same over all geographic units. It thus can vary from 0.0, representing no segregation at all, to 1.0, representing total segregation.

We also use the *Isolation Index*, which is another standard and useful measure. It gives the proportion of one's own group (e.g., non-Hispanic black or non-Hispanic white) that live in the neighborhood (e.g., Census tract or block). If a group has an Isolation Index value of 0.90, then on average a member of that group would find that in his or her tract 90 percent of the population would be from the same group as him or her self. Both of these measures have a very simple interpretation, and both go from 0.0 (no segregation) to 1.0 (total segregation). Social scientists have developed a large number of measures of segregation, but Massey and Denton (1988) clarified the relationships among the various measures proposed and reaffirmed the utility of these fundamental measures.[2]

The patterns of segregation in the Los Angeles and New York City regions are presented in table 11.1. All these measures are computed with the reference category being the non-Hispanic white population. Since segregation indexes measure the separation of two groups, here the separation is measured between each minority group (non-Hispanic African Americans, non-Hispanic Asian and Pacific Islanders,

Table 11.1 SEGREGATION INDEXES FOR LOS ANGLES AND NEW YORK CITY REGIONS, 1980 THROUGH 2010

	Los Angeles Combined Statistical Area				New York City Combined Statistical Area			
	1980	1990	2000	2010	1980	1990	2000	2010
Dissimilarity NH Black/NH White	0.78	0.67	0.65	0.62	0.80	0.79	0.79	0.76
Rank	16	37	37	33	11	7	4	2
Dissimilarity Hispanic/NH White	0.55	0.56	0.58	0.57	0.67	0.66	0.65	0.61
Rank	7	7	6	5	1	1	1	1
Dissimilarity NH Asian/NH White	0.41	0.45	0.50	0.49	0.48	0.49	0.52	0.52
Rank	16	44	22	24	4	26	10	12
Isolation NH White/NH Black	0.70	0.59	0.56	0.53	0.72	0.74	0.74	0.72
Rank	9	26	27	30	5	3	3	2
Isolation NH White/Hispanic	0.54	0.64	0.71	0.74	0.52	0.57	0.61	0.61
Rank	4	4	2	2	5	6	6	7
Isolation NH White/Asian	0.22	0.33	0.43	0.48	0.17	0.24	0.32	0.39
Rank	3	2	2	2	6	4	3	3
Isolation NH Black/NH White	0.96	0.93	0.92	0.91	0.94	0.94	0.93	0.92
Rank	60	82	86	84	78	81	80	77
Isolation Hispanic/NH White	0.82	0.76	0.70	0.65	0.93	0.90	0.88	0.84
Rank	119	121	121	119	109	110	107	107
Isolation NH Asian/NH White	0.93	0.88	0.85	0.81	0.98	0.95	0.92	0.89
Rank	122	124	124	124	111	120	120	118

	Los Angeles County				Los Angeles City			
	1980	1990	2000	2010	1980	1990	2000	2010
Dissimilarity NH Black/NH White	0.81	0.73	0.69	0.67	0.85	0.78	0.73	0.69
Rank	29	48	55	41	3	7	9	11
Dissimilarity Hispanic/NH White	0.46	0.61	0.63	0.63	0.62	0.65	0.66	0.65
Rank	18	20	13	7	3	4	3	3
Dissimilarity NH Asian/NH White	0.47	0.46	0.50	0.50	0.50	0.47	0.47	0.45
Rank	30	84	26	25	6	18	19	17
Isolation NH White/NH Black	0.76	0.69	0.66	0.64	0.83	0.77	0.73	0.68
Rank	23	41	47	50	12	15	21	21
Isolation NH White/Hispanic	0.26	0.71	0.78	0.80	0.66	0.76	0.81	0.81
Rank	13	8	18	8	4	4	4	4
Isolation NH White/Asian	0.28	0.40	0.50	0.55	0.33	0.41	0.46	0.47
Rank	9	10	8	9	4	8	8	11
Isolation NH Black/NH White	0.94	0.92	0.90	0.89	0.94	0.92	0.90	0.90
Rank	422	598	526	496	12	17	20	19
Isolation Hispanic/NH White	0.85	0.74	0.69	0.66	0.80	0.74	0.70	0.68
Rank	648	815	688	687	51	54	56	56
Isolation NH Asian/NH White	0.92	0.85	0.81	0.78	0.91	0.86	0.82	0.79
Rank	657	833	717	712	51	57	58	64

Table 11.1 SEGREGATION INDEXES (CONTINUED)

	New York City			
	1980	1990	2000	2010
Dissimilarity NH Black/NH White	0.83	0.84	0.84	0.82
Rank	6	3	2	2
Dissimilarity Hispanic/NH White	0.64	0.66	0.67	0.66
Rank	2	2	2	2
Dissimilarity NH Asian/NH White	0.49	0.48	0.50	0.52
Rank	7	17	9	7
Isolation NH White/NH Black	0.82	0.84	0.85	0.84
Rank	13	11	10	10
Isolation NH White/Hispanic	0.62	0.69	0.73	0.73
Rank	5	7	8	11
Isolation NH White/Asian	0.25	0.34	0.44	0.52
Rank	7	12	10	9
Isolation NH Black/NH White	0.91	0.91	0.90	0.89
Rank	26	24	21	24
Isolation Hispanic/NH White	0.86	0.82	0.79	0.77
Rank	41	44	41	43
Isolation NH Asian/NH White	0.95	0.90	0.84	0.82
Rank	46	52	56	61

Source: Andrew A. Beveridge, computed from Census data, 1980, 1990, 2000 and 2010.

and Hispanics) and non-Hispanic whites. The first part of the table gives information on the whole area for both Los Angeles and New York City. It also includes the rank of both the LA and NYC CSAs compared to the other 123 CSAs in the United States. The first set lists the Dissimilarity Index values with respect to non-Hispanic blacks. The index dropped from 0.78 in 1980, when the LA CSA was the 16th most segregated out of 125, to 0.62 in 2010, dropping to the 33rd most segregated. In the NYC CSA the pattern is very different. The index barely budged from 0.80 in 1980 to 0.76 in 2010. The NYC CSA rose from the 11th most segregated to the 2nd most segregated with respect to African Americans. Further, segregation levels in the other CSAs around the country declined substantially during the decades—the average went from 0.63 to 0.54. Therefore, the level of the Los Angeles region's segregation declined by nearly twice the average for the United States, while the New York City region's level hardly changed.

The pattern for Hispanic/non-Hispanic white segregation follows a different trend in both CSAs. In Los Angeles, it stays almost flat, going from 0.55 to 0.57 over the four decades, with its national rank as 7th out of 125 in 1980 inching up to 5th in 2010. In the NYC CSA, the index goes from 0.67 to 0.61, with New York having the highest level of Hispanic/non-Hispanic white segregation in the nation for all four decades examined. Over the same period, the overall average Hispanic/Non-Hispanic white segregation in all 125 regions went from 0.34 to 0.38.

Segregation with respect to non-Hispanic Asians from non-Hispanic whites increased in both regions from 0.41 to 0.49 in Los Angeles, and from 0.48 to 0.52 in New York. In 2010 Los Angeles ranked 24th out of all 125 regions, while New York ranked 12th. As with Hispanic segregation, non-Hispanic Asian segregation increased overall during the four decades in the large regions from 0.31 to 0.42. Nonetheless, in both regions non-Hispanic blacks are substantially more segregated from non-Hispanic whites than are either Hispanics or Asians.

When one compares New York City to Los Angeles City and Los Angeles County, quite similar patterns are found to those in the regions generally. Here the ranks are computed for cities larger than 250,000 and for counties that were larger than 50,000 in 1980. The City of Los Angeles is more segregated than the LA CSA for all three groups. New York City is highly segregated compared to other cities.

It is also interesting to look at segregation with respect to the counties in both regions. This is a somewhat complex undertaking, because the spatial organization of each region is so different. Appendix table 11.A1 shows Dissimilarity Index scores for all the counties in the two regions, as well as their ranks with respect to all counties that had at least 50,000 population in 1980. The data underscore the continuing high level of black/non-Hispanic white segregation in New York City and Nassau County in New York, and Essex County in New Jersey. Indeed, Brooklyn (Kings County) is the most segregated county in the country with respect to non-Hispanic black segregation from non-Hispanic whites. Queens is second, Nassau County is seventh, and Essex County is fifth. The five Los Angeles metro counties have much lower levels of segregation with respect to non-Hispanic black—indeed the highest is LA County with a Dissimilarity Index of 0.67, which ranks 41st. So it is not surprising, given these patterns in some of the larger counties in the New York City CSA, that the whole region is the second most segregated with respect to African Americans. With respect to Hispanic segregation, NYC counties once again are among the highest, with the Bronx ranking fifth at 0.65 and Manhattan (New York County) ranking fourth at 0.66. LA County, however, ranks seventh at 0.63. Remember that for the whole region, the New York City metro ranks first for Hispanic segregation, while the Los Angeles metro ranks fifth.

What accounts for the large differences in segregation in the New York City and Los Angeles regions, as well as the relatively high levels of segregation with respect to the Hispanic population in both regions? One explanation advanced by Farley and Frey (1994) is that with the advent of the Civil Rights Acts, and the Fair Housing Act of 1968 as amended in 1988, most developers of new housing chose not to discriminate explicitly. However, such acts did little or nothing to disturb the patterns that had developed for decades. In the early part of the twentieth century many developments had restrictive covenants on deeds that made it illegal to sell property to "members of Negro race." Although formally struck down by a Supreme Court case in 1948, such patterns continued well into the twenty-first century. For example, Levittown, New York, the well-known Long Island suburban development that provided housing for returning veterans, had restrictive covenants in its deeds and leases when it opened in 1947 (Lambert 1997). In 1960, the first year for which official figures exist, the population was 65,276. There were 57 blacks, 158 Asians, and two residents of other races, so Levittown was 0.09 percent black. Fifty years later, the 2010 Census found 470 blacks among the population of 51,881 or 0.91 percent. Although the number of blacks had increased, Levittown was still predominantly nonblack. It was 88.9 percent white, including Hispanics. So the segregation pattern after World War II, when Levittown was founded, persists and affects the composition of the community today.

The Isolation Index is computed for all three groups with respect to non-Hispanic whites. The isolation of the three groups from non-Hispanic whites is quite high in nominal terms. For instance, in 2010 for the two CSAs the isolation of non-Hispanic blacks from non-Hispanic whites is 0.91 in Los Angeles and 0.92 in New York. So a typical non-Hispanic African American would have on average (just considering non-Hispanic white and black categories) less than 10 percent non-Hispanic white residents in his or her tract. The figures for Hispanics are 0.65 for the LA CSA and 0.84 for the NYC CSA. The figures for Asians are 0.81 for Los Angeles and 0.89 for New York. Remember that these indexes do not take into account the size of the two groups in any way. The figures are similar for LA County, LA City, and New York City. Although the Isolation Index values are quite high in the Los Angeles and New York City regions, while generally lower in the Los Angeles region, it is also the case that the isolation index declined over the decades, as shown in table 11.1. In summary then, segregation remains relatively high in both the Los Angeles and New York City regions, though it has declined in both, but much more so in Los Angeles. The New York City region has emerged as the second most segregated region in the United States.

How then did Glaeser and Vigdor (2012) conclude that segregation had ended in the United States? The reason is simple: they used everyone else in the area (regardless of race or ethnicity) as the contrast group, which violates a fundamental principle of the analysis of segregation. Instead of computing segregation of the various minorities groups from the traditional majority group, non-Hispanic whites, they computed index values using as the comparison *all other groups*. By using this method, they do not report how the level of segregation between groups changed, but rather how segregation of each group from all other groups has changed, a very different measure that tells us little or nothing about segregation of the minority groups from the majority. Using these methods, they published their findings with the title "The End of the Segregated Century," as a report for the Manhattan Institute.

But following the usual literature regarding segregation and the most common measure of segregation, the Dissimilarity Index for all three groups with respect to non-Hispanic whites is quite high for the New York region and New York City, while for the Los Angeles region it is quite high with respect to Hispanic segregation. This is also the case for LA City and County. Nonetheless, the New York region is much more segregated than Los Angeles at every level and by every measure. New York, which developed much of its housing long before the Fair Housing Act and had a long history and heritage of segregation and restrictive covenants, seems to have perpetuated that tradition well into the twenty-first century. Without massive housing turnover, it seems unlikely that the pattern will be reversed soon.

THE DECLINE OF AFRICAN AMERICANS IN HARLEM AND SOUTH LOS ANGELES

As seen in chapter 2, both cities have registered decreases in the black population, and this trend is now affecting black settlement patterns in both regions, including the once iconically black neighborhoods of Harlem in New York and Watts and South Central in Los Angeles. These areas now face a decline of the black population and an increase in residents of other minority groups.

Harlem: Demographic Changes from 1910 to 2010

Harlem, often seen as synonymous with many positive aspects of black life in the United States, is a prime example of this transition. Major changes in Central Harlem and New York City from 1910 to 2010 are shown in table 11.2. "Central Harlem," defined by Gilbert Osofsky in his 1966 book *Harlem: The Making of a Ghetto*, is basically the area north of Central Park and east of Morningside and St. Nicholas Avenues. The southern edge starts at 96th Street on the East Side at Fifth Avenue and Central Park. It goes up to 110th, and then cuts over to 106th Street on the West Side. The northern boundary in most places is 155th Street, though it extends a bit further up on the East Side. Greater Harlem goes river to river and includes both East Harlem and West Harlem.

In 1910, Central Harlem was about 10 percent black, Greater Harlem was a little more than four percent black, and the rest of New York City was less than two percent black. Just twenty years later during the Harlem Renaissance, Central Harlem had become a definably black area in a largely white city. Central Harlem was over 70

Table 11.2 POPULATION AND RACIAL COMPOSITION OF HARLEM AND NEW YORK CITY, 1910 TO 2010

	Central Harlem	Greater Harlem	Rest of NYC		Central Harlem	Greater Harlem	Rest of NYC
1910				**1970**			
Black	9.89%	4.28%	1.73%	Black	95.42%	63.53%	18.48%
White	90.01%	95.64%	98.12%	White	4.28%	34.44%	79.82%
Other	0.10%	0.08%	0.15%	Other	0.29%	2.02%	1.70%
Total	181,949	593,598	3,191,962	Total	157,178	430,567	7,083,455
1920				**1980**			
Black	32.43%	12.28%	1.46%	Black -NH	94.17%	58.76%	22.20%
White	67.47%	87.60%	98.39%	Hispanic	4.32%	28.46%	19.45%
Other	0.15%	0.14%	0.15%	White-NH	0.62%	10.29%	53.98%
Total	216,026	652,529	4,767,727	Other-NH	0.89%	2.49%	4.37%
1930				Total	108,236	339,490	6,732,149
Black	70.18%	34.82%	1.99%	**1990**			
White	29.43%	64.78%	97.80%	Black -NH	87.55%	52.37%	23.93%
Other	0.39%	0.40%	0.21%	Hispanic	10.14%	33.94%	23.90%
Total	209,663	580,277	6,168,984	White-NH	1.50%	10.85%	44.74%
1940				Other-NH	0.80%	2.85%	7.43%
Black	89.31%	48.32%	2.65%	Total	101,026	334,076	6,988,199
White	10.48%	51.38%	97.10%	**2000**			
Other	0.21%	0.31%	0.25%	Black -NH	77.49%	46.03%	23.67%
Total	221,974	576,846	6,677,187	Hispanic	16.82%	38.02%	26.47%
1950				White-NH	2.07%	10.45%	36.11%
Black	98.07%	57.52%	5.64%	Other-NH	3.62%	5.50%	13.75%
White	1.76%	41.89%	94.03%	Total	109,091	354,057	7,654,221
Other	0.17%	0.60%	0.33%	**2010**			
Total	237,468	593,246	7,078,650	Black -NH	58.64%	36.61%	22.20%
1960				Hispanic	23.61%	36.62%	28.29%
Black	96.71%	58.53%	10.71%	White-NH	11.76%	17.95%	33.92%
White	2.94%	40.55%	88.62%	Other-NH	5.99%	8.82%	15.59%
Other	0.35%	0.92%	0.67%	Total	126,558	379,131	7,805,768
Total	163,632	467,634	6,829,199				

Sources: 1910 to 1940, Census tract data from National Historical Geographical Information System, compiled by Andrew A. Beveridge and co-workers; 1950, Ellen M. Bogue File, as edited by Andrew A. Beveridge and co-workers; 1960 through 2000, Tabulated Census Data from National Historical Geographic Information System; 2010 Data from American Community Survey, US Bureau of the Census. Boundary Files from National Historical Geographic Information System 1910 to 2000, US Bureau of the Census, 2010. Since results are tabulated from the sources indicated, they may not necessarily exactly match Census published figures for population and race.

percent black and Greater Harlem was about 35 percent black, but the rest of New York City was still less than two percent black. By 1950, Central Harlem was about 98 percent black, while Greater Harlem was 58 percent black. Central Harlem remained almost entirely black through 1980, with the black population never dropping below 94 percent.

In the early days of Harlem, the black community there was quite diverse economically, especially when African Americans in Harlem are compared to those who lived elsewhere in the city. However, as the "great migration" of blacks from the American South continued, and the size of the black population expanded, an area of concentrated poverty developed. The period from 1950 to 1980 was a period of sharp demographic decline for Harlem. Central Harlem lost more than half of its population, dropping from roughly 237,000 to 101,000, and Greater Harlem also saw its population drop, from roughly 593,000 to 339,000. This came during an era of urban renewal when many older housing units were razed, either for public housing projects or for other apartment developments, and the new developments did not come close to housing the same number of people. At the same time, areas further from the city center, such as southeastern Queens, attracted affluent black families.

This period from 1950 to 1980 was arguably the "classic" period of the American urban ghetto. In order to understand fully why this was so, it is necessary to look briefly at the usage of the term "ghetto." In writings and discourse, it has been used primarily to describe two situations: that of Jews in many European cities from the late middle ages until World War II and that of blacks in American cities, especially in the period from the 1960s until the 1980s. In each case, a core set of characteristics made the term "ghetto" seem an appropriate designation to most observers (though there was never unanimity about use of the term for blacks in American cities).[3]

In the European case, the "ghetto" was used to refer to a situation that had three main features. It was a spatially bounded residence that was basically involuntary, and the inhabitants were all Jewish. The Venetian ghetto from the early fifteenth century on was a prototype of the European Jewish ghetto. It was a gated community whose residents were locked in each night by the city. Being locked in was not typical of most Jewish ghettos, but they were more or less involuntary residences imposed by law, physical force, or both.

By the 1960s, "ghetto" was routinely being used to refer to the situation of blacks in many American inner cities. In this US context, the "ghetto" was generally viewed as having three main features. It was spatially bounded, residence there was viewed by many observers as basically involuntary, and the inhabitants were predominantly black. These features seem to more or less replicate the use of the term for European ghettos (with blacks switched for Jews), which is clearly why many people thought the term was appropriate for the US case.

Actually, the nature of the "involuntariness" associated by observers with the US case is somewhat different from the Jewish ghetto. Residence in the US ghetto was not formally imposed legally or by physical force though it was difficult for African Americans to find housing outside black neighborhoods until the passage of the Fair Housing Act as amended in 1988, and even then challenges remained. Thus, it makes sense to add four corollary features of the US case, which flesh out the character of the "involuntariness" ascribed to urban "ghetto" life. First, the vast majorities of residents were poor, and hence for economic reasons would have had difficulty leaving. Second, the outside environment was hostile, in particular with prejudice in the external housing market, and this made it hard for residents to move elsewhere even if they could afford it. Third, the ghetto was dangerous (high crime) and not heavily policed, with the implication that people might prefer to leave if only they could. Fourth, the ghetto had meager day to day economic resources; for example, few medium-level (let alone high-end) retail outlets operated in the area, again with the implication that people with choices would probably not remain. All these features together clearly made a compelling case, to outsiders at least, that residence in the ghetto was typically involuntary.

That said, the concept of "involuntariness," though central to the idea of the ghetto as applied by observers to the US case, is complex, and the appropriateness of its applicability should not be overstated. There is no doubt that many urban black residents felt some sense of community and solidarity in their neighborhoods and probably would not have moved elsewhere even if given a real choice. Still, most such choices were not realistically afforded to blacks until the end of legal residential segregation, which came with the first Civil Rights Act of 1964. For instance, as mentioned previously, black servicemen were not allowed to purchase homes in the new suburban development of Levittown, despite the 1948 abolition of racial convenants, whose effects still lingered.

It is now clear why, in the heyday of the use of the term "ghetto," the term seemed appropriate, at least to outside observers. Looking at the Harlem case in the 1950–80 period, all the characteristics associated with the ghetto as outlined above basically held true.

The Whitening of Harlem

A review of recent demographic changes in Harlem also makes it clear why the term "ghetto" is now used far less often for Harlem. First, since 1980, Central Harlem has become less black. By 2010, the percentage of the population that was black had dropped to 58.6 percent, well below the 1930 level of 70.2 percent. Meanwhile, the Hispanic and white populations rose. Hispanics accounted for 4.3 percent of Central Harlem residents in 1980 (the first year they were classified separately in the US Census). In 2010 that number reached 23.6 percent. The movement of Latinos into areas of Harlem raises the question of whether sections with significant numbers of Latinos are "ghettos." Latinos, of course, refer to their urban areas not as "ghettos" but as "barrios," a term that translates exactly as "neighborhood" with none of the negative connotations of "ghetto." The in-movement of non-Hispanic whites to Harlem has compounded the problem of calling Harlem a "ghetto." In 1980, there were just 672 non-Hispanic whites in Central Harlem, constituting about 0.6 percent of the population. By 2010, there were 14,484, or about 11.8 percent. Furthermore, the non-Hispanic white population that had moved to Harlem by 2010 was distributed in many different places throughout Harlem.

Additionally, areas of Harlem are clearly once again sought after places to live. By 2010, there were some areas of highly affluent black and white residents. Median household income in Central Harlem rose from about $13,765 in 1950 to over $35,335 in 2010 (in 2010 dollars). However, this figure is still well below the median of $48,743 for New York City. The traditional townhouse areas around Strivers Row, Sugar Hill, and Marcus Garvey Park have undergone a rebirth. At the height of the housing boom in 2006, some sold for one to three million dollars. Stores and restaurants catering to the affluent have opened in West Harlem, while Magic Johnson opened a Starbucks and a Multiplex on 125th Street, near where former President Bill Clinton has his office suite and where James Beard award-winning chef Marcus Samuelsson opened his popular upscale Red Rooster Harlem restaurant. Columbia University's planned campus expansion will bring more change and real estate development to West Harlem in the coming years. The plans include a 17-acre $6.3 billion campus expansion and the right of eminent domain to condemn property in the area for new development (Bagli 2010).

Figure 11.1 compares the concentration of the black population in 1980 and 2010 at the tract level. As that makes plain, the deconcentration of the black population

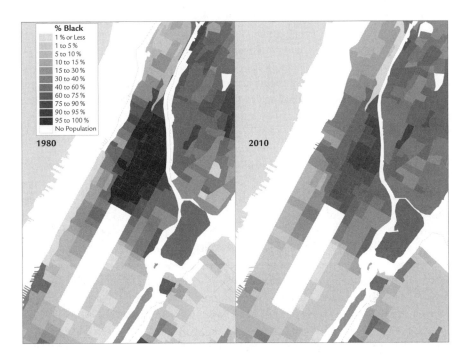

Figure 11.1
Percent African American in Harlem by Census Tract, 1980 and 2010
Source: Andrew A. Beveridge based upon Census 1980 and 2010, data and boundaries.

in Harlem is happening in many different areas. Central Harlem may soon follow greater Harlem and lose its black majority.

For Harlem, all of this has seriously clouded the "involuntariness" traditionally ascribed to life in the ghetto. The well-publicized existence of some middle-class (by income) blacks and the sale of townhouses in excess of one million dollars, some reduction of crime, and the well-publicized appearance of retail chain stores means that it is no longer clear to outsiders that those who live in Harlem are there on an "involuntary" basis in the sense that they would (and should) leave if they could. Still, the large stock of public housing and the relatively low income of many residents ensure that high levels of poverty will continue to be a feature of Harlem.

THE RETREAT OF AFRICAN AMERICANS FROM WATTS, SOUTH CENTRAL, AND SOUTH LOS ANGELES

As with New York City, Los Angeles also developed some highly concentrated areas of black population, and several of these have become famous in part because of the riots that began there and became associated with the areas. In 1965 the five-day Watts Riot erupted after an attempted arrest was thwarted by a crowd of Watts' residents that then led to five days of rioting in Watts and elsewhere (Oberschall 1968). In 1992, Rodney King was beaten by members of the Los Angeles Police Department, and a riot ensued in South Central after the police officers involved were acquitted, although many areas in Los Angeles outside of South Central were affected in subsequent days (Medina 2012). These and nearby areas with high concentrations of black population have undergone a more massive transition than that found in Harlem from 1910 to 2010. In Los Angeles, usable neighborhood data do not exist before 1940, but most growth in Los Angeles occurred after World War II, and the consolidation of an African American area clearly did not occur until well after the war, unlike in New York City.

In 1940 the two areas that would become well-known as African American bastions had developed some concentration of African American population, over 21 percent in South Central and nearly 30 percent in Watts.[4] However, as data in table 11.3 show, by 1960 African Americans had become a majority in South Los Angeles; they constituted five of six residents in Watts and two of three in South Central Historic. By 1970, the year of the first map in figure 11.2, the percentage of blacks in the entire South Los Angeles area had reached its peak at over 77 percent. In every succeeding decade the proportion of blacks fell in each of the areas discussed here. By 2010, the percentage of black residents in South Central had fallen to 30.9 percent, and by then Watts had an African American population of slightly more than one-quarter, while South Central did not even have one-tenth. However, as figure 11.2 shows, there are parts of South Los Angeles, especially on the western edge, that are still predominately black like the neighborhoods of Ladera Heights, View Park, and around Crenshaw Blvd that are middle or upper middle class.

Unlike Harlem, where there has been a substantial increase in the non-Hispanic white population, this growth did not seem to occur in South Los Angeles. Rather,

Table 11.3 POPULATION AND RACIAL COMPOSITION OF SOUTH LOS ANGELES, WATTS, SOUTH CENTRAL HISTORIC, LA CITY, AND LA COUNTY, 1940 TO 2010

	Watts	Historic South Central	South LA	Los Angeles City	Los Angeles County
1940					
Black	29.55%	21.13%	11.59%	2.30%	2.70%
White	69.19%	75.54%	87.05%	93.49%	95.50%
Other	1.26%	3.33%	1.36%	4.21%	1.80%
Total	21,604	40,345	468,828	1,504,227	2,785,643
1960					
Black	86.03%	67.79%	50.65%	13.51%	7.60%
White	13.36%	27.74%	44.79%	83.17%	90.30%
Other	0.62%	4.48%	4.56%	3.31%	2.00%
Total	41,091	32,753	557,662	2,479,015	6,038,771
1970					
Black	91.13%	66.45%	77.19%	17.88%	18.48%
White	7.97%	28.98%	18.58%	77.18%	79.82%
Other	0.91%	4.57%	4.24%	4.94%	1.70%
Total	34,760	28,399	572,314	2,816,061	7,083,455
1980					
Black-NH	83.90%	31.81%	70.10%	16.70%	22.20%
Hispanic	15.08%	64.01%	22.86%	27.50%	19.45%
White-NH	0.46%	2.10%	4.19%	47.80%	53.98%
Other-NH	0.56%	2.08%	2.86%	8.00%	4.37%
Total	32,923	34,222	569,665	2,966,850	6,732,149
1990					
Black-NH	53.94%	14.68%	49.26%	13.00%	23.93%
Hispanic	45.05%	82.84%	45.84%	39.90%	23.90%
White-NH	0.53%	0.89%	2.61%	37.30%	44.74%
Other-NH	0.48%	1.58%	2.28%	9.80%	7.43%
Total	39,153	44,242	671,376	3,485,398	6,988,199
2000					
Black-NH	35.42%	9.70%	38.46%	10.90%	23.67%
Hispanic	63.48%	87.77%	57.02%	46.50%	26.47%
White-NH	0.65%	1.36%	2.30%	29.80%	36.11%
Other-NH	0.45%	1.18%	2.21%	12.80%	13.75%
Total	43,233	44,803	692,768	3,694,820	7,654,221
2010					
Black-NH	26.21%	8.69%	30.87%	9.20%	22.20%
Hispanic	72.32%	88.98%	64.21%	48.50%	28.29%
White-NH	0.85%	1.29%	2.40%	28.70%	33.92%
Other-NH	0.63%	1.04%	2.53%	13.60%	15.59%
Total	48,908	43,572	731,905	3,792,621	7,805,768

Source: Published Census tables for the areas noted, 1940 through 2010, compiled by Andrew A. Beveridge and co-workers. Race not tabulated in 1950.

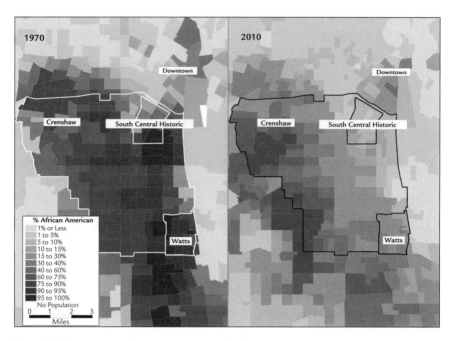

Figure 11.2
Percent African American in South Los Angeles, Watts, and South Central Historic by Census
Tract, 1970 and 2010
Source: Andrew A. Beveridge based upon Census 1970 and 2010, data and boundaries.

what has happened in South Los Angeles is really very similar to the classic pattern
elucidated by Park and Burgess (Burgess 1925), where the African American population first "invades" an area and displaces the population living there (here the white
population in the 1940s to 1970s). This is then followed by the black population moving elsewhere, to be replaced by the next group of newcomers—here largely Hispanics
(mostly Mexicans). This pattern does not at all follow that found in Harlem, nor is it
reminiscent of a "ghetto." Rather, as the older immigrant group (here the blacks, who
emigrated from the southern United States) moves up and out, it is replaced by the
next poor immigrant group.

POVERTY, AFFLUENCE, AND RESIDENTIAL ISOLATION

The quality of neighborhoods can affect the lives and life chances of their residents.
Beyond the simple distribution of members of various racial and ethnic groups in
neighborhoods are the concentrations of the poor and the affluent, and the allocation of various amenities and services in the urban context. Various methods of
neighborhood exclusion and selection have an effect on racial and ethnic segregation, and have also led to the clustering of residents based upon income, education,
and the like (Bishop and Cushing 2008). Among the common practices are gated

communities (Vesselinov 2012), where members need to have a pass or a visitor must vouch for them to come into the neighborhood; exclusionary zoning, which makes it impossible to build multifamily housing or even single family houses on relatively small lots; and, in New York City and its suburbs, the emergence of cooperative apartments, where a purchase gives the buyer stock in the corporation that owns the whole building and a proprietary lease to a specific apartment. It is well known that many coops have stringent financial qualifications that enforce minimum income and wealth requirements.

At the same time, the concentration of poverty is well known to have a variety of negative effects on individual welfare, as well as social development. As outlined in chapter 2, there is growing inequality in the United States with respect to income and wealth.

For this analysis, two measures from the Census will be used—percent of households having more than $200,000 of annual income, and percent of persons in poverty—to assess the geographic concentration of the rich and poor. We will use the Dissimilarity Index, which is the basic and most common index used for analyzing racial and ethnic segregation, as we have seen earlier in the chapter. It is completely suitable for this sort of analysis of affluence and poverty, as well as race, and can give us a general idea of the extent to which the affluent live apart from everyone else and those who are in

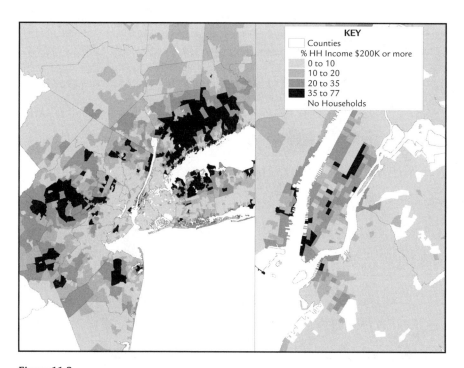

Figure 11.3
Percent Households with Incomes $200,000 or more by Census Tract, New York City Region, 2006 to 2010
Source: Andrew A. Beveridge based upon American Community Survey, 2006 to 2010 data and boundaries.

poverty live apart from others. It is obvious from examining the maps of where the affluent live in the two regions that there are areas with high concentrations of the affluent, defined here as those with incomes of $200,000 or more. Figure 11.3 shows that highly affluent residents live in a strip that goes up Fifth Avenue in Manhattan, as well as areas on Central Park South and Central Park West. Some other areas in Midtown are notable, as well as a large area in Downtown. In the suburbs, areas in Westchester County and Connecticut along the shore, as well as in Nassau County along the shore and in Central New Jersey are all inhabited by a high proportion of affluent households.

The Los Angeles pattern is presented in figure 11.4. It is similar to New York in some ways and different in others. Affluent communities include the well-known west-side areas of Malibu, Brentwood, Beverly Hills, and northern Santa Monica, as well as scattered coastal communities such as Palos Verdes Estates and Laguna Beach or the hillside community of San Marino. However, unlike New York City, there are no highly affluent areas near downtown or in highly urbanized areas. Also, Los Angeles has a lower proportion of affluent residents, and they live in fewer concentrated areas than in the New York City region.

The distribution of poverty shown in figure 11.5 for the New York City region follows a very different pattern from that of affluence. There are areas with high concentrations of poverty in the Bronx, Northern Manhattan including Central and Greater Harlem, and Brooklyn. There are very few poor areas in Queens and Staten Island,

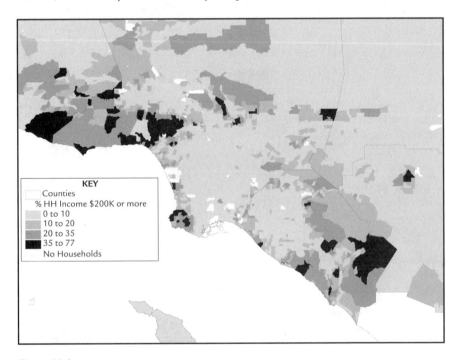

Figure 11.4
Percent Households with Incomes $200,000 or more by Census Tract, Los Angeles Region, 2006 to 2010
Source: Andrew A. Beveridge based upon American Community Survey, 2006 to 2010 data and boundaries.

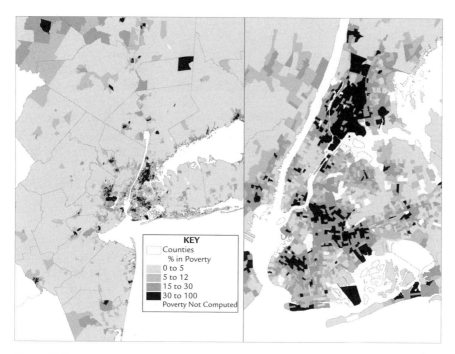

Figure 11.5
Percent of Persons in Poverty by Census Tract, New York City Region, 2006 to 2010
Source: Andrew A. Beveridge based upon American Community Survey, 2006 to 2010 data and boundaries.

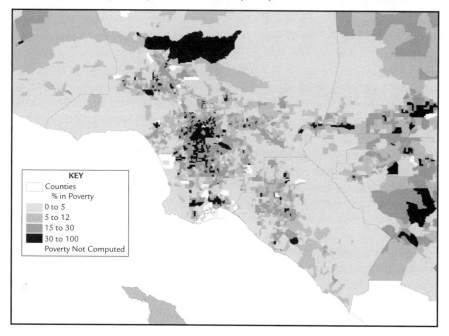

Figure 11.6
Percent of Persons in Poverty by Census Tract, Los Angeles Region, 2006 to 2010
Source: Andrew A. Beveridge based upon American Community Survey, 2006 to 2010 data and boundaries.

but there are pockets of poverty in Newark and Paterson, NJ, as well as in Yonkers, NY, and Bridgeport and New Haven, CT. In short, poverty is concentrated in the urban core for the most part. As illustrated in figure 11.6, the pattern in Los Angeles also shows a heavy concentration in the area around downtown that includes Skid Row (see chapter 14) and in outlying neighborhoods and cities. The largest concentration seems to be in or near East Los Angeles, which has a high concentration of Hispanics, as well as a significant section of South Los Angeles, including Watts and South Central. There are also concentrations in outlying cities including Long Beach, Oxnard, San Clarita, and San Bernardino. Poverty seems to coincide with concentrations of Latinos and African Americans in both regions.

How segregated then are households and residents with respect to affluence and poverty? Table 11.4 presents the results. Four conclusions can be drawn:

1. The Dissimilarity Index, measuring the levels of separation between the affluent and all other households is 0.51 across the whole Los Angeles region and 0.49 across the New York City region. These levels are much lower than those with respect to the separation of blacks from non-Hispanic whites, lower than the separation between Hispanics and non-Hispanic whites, and about comparable to the separation between Asians and non-Hispanic whites (table 11.1).
2. Segregation of the affluent from the nonaffluent increased during the last decade, which is counter to the trend for racial segregation.
3. The degree of segregation of the poverty population from the nonpoverty population is much lower than the level of segregation of the affluent from all other households. So the poverty population is more dispersed among the general population than are the affluent.
4. Poverty has declined a small amount in the past decade.

One way that the segregation of the affluent is maintained can be seen by examining the situation in Westchester County that resulted in a court challenge. Because of zoning rules and the unavailability of moderate income housing in many areas, the ability of the nonaffluent (including members of minority groups) to move into some of the very wealthy and very white hamlets in Westchester was thwarted. The judge set forth a consent decree intended to overcome this segregation of the affluent from the middle class (Roberts 2009). Despite a legal settlement that called for building moderate income housing in affluent white communities, the prospect of introducing significant amounts of affordable housing in such communities is dim (Applebome 2012).[5]

Despite a number of other demographic shifts, poverty areas seem not to have changed much in the past decade. While Harlem has become less poor as whites and other affluent individuals moved in and Columbia University continues to develop the western portion of Harlem, other areas continue to have very high concentrations of residents in poverty. Little change in the income profile has occurred in South Los Angeles either, even with massive demographic shifts in the composition of the population.

Table 11.4 PERCENT AND INDEXES OF SEGREGATION FOR HOUSEHOLDS WITH INCOME $200K OR MORE AND THOSE IN POVERTY, NEW YORK CITY AND LOS ANGELES REGIONS, 2000 AND 2006–2010

	Los Angeles Combined Statistical Area		New York City Combined Statistical Area	
	2000	2010	2000	2010
% of Households with Income $200K or more	6.24%	6.16%	8.50%	8.59%
Dissimilarity Index of HH Income Above $200k to All Other Households	0.48	0.51	0.47	0.49
Isolation of Lower Income Households from Affluent Households	0.95	0.95	0.93	0.93
Isolation of Higher Income Households from Lower Income Households	0.17	0.17	0.21	0.21
% of Persons with Income in Poverty	15.62%	14.10%	12.90%	12.33%
Dissimilarity Index of Those in Poverty to All Other Households	0.35	0.35	0.44	0.43
Isolation of those in Poverty	0.24	0.22	0.25	0.24
Isolation of those not in Poverty	0.86	0.87	0.89	0.89

	Los Angeles County		Los Angeles City		New York City	
	2000	2010	2000	2010	2000	2010
% of Household with Income $200K or more	6.11%	5.98%	6.07%	5.97%	5.79%	6.25%
Dissimilarity Index of HH Income Above $200k to All Other Households	0.49	0.53	0.52	0.56	0.50	0.55
Isolation of Lower Income Households from Affluent Households	0.95	0.95	0.95	0.95	0.95	0.95
Isolation of Higher Income Households from Lower Income Households	0.18	0.19	0.20	0.20	0.17	0.19
% of Persons with Income in Poverty	17.91%	15.71%	22.11%	19.45%	21.25%	19.11%
Dissimilarity Index of Those in Poverty to All Other Households	0.34	0.34	0.32	0.33	0.34	0.35
Isolation of those in Poverty	0.26	0.24	0.30	0.28	0.30	0.28
Isolation of those not in Poverty	0.84	0.86	0.80	0.83	0.81	0.83

Source: Andrew A. Beveridge, computed from Census Data, 2000 and American Community Survey Data, 2006–2010.

SEGREGATION BY RACE, HISPANIC STATUS, AND INCOME: WHAT MATTERS MOST?

Often local commentators and even some scholars attribute racial and Hispanic segregation to differences in income between various groups or the operation of self-selected, neighborhood preferences of members of various groups. However, as we have seen historically, the United States had a highly segregated housing market with rampant discrimination against African Americans. In the case in Westchester discussed above, the county government claimed that the exclusion of minorities from any part of the county was due only to differences in income, but the judge ruled otherwise. For these reasons, it is important to know to what extent segregation by race (as well as Hispanic status) is related to income level in these two large regions.

To be able to assess the degree to which segregation is driven by affluence, race and Hispanic status, or a combination of both, the same methods used to assess racial and economic segregation can be employed. We simply apply these measures to groups that include both a race or Hispanic status and levels of affluence. So we computed ten different measures of segregation of each minority group from non-Hispanic white households, with different combinations of affluence considered. These are presented in table 11.5. Here we present the highlights.

Affluent minority households are highly segregated from both all non-Hispanic households and from affluent non-Hispanic white households. For instance, in the New York City CSA, all black households are segregated from all non-Hispanic white households at 0.76, while all affluent black households are even more segregated from all non-Hispanic white households, at a level of 0.82. Affluent black households are segregated from affluent non-Hispanic white households at 0.77. In short, affluent minority households are segregaed at comparable or higher levels from all non-minority households, and often are more segregated from all non-Hispanic white households than are minority households in general. Thus, despite commentaries and views to the contrary, affluence does not mitigate segregation, and sometimes it even compounds it.

CONCLUSION

From this examination of the residential patterns in the New York City and Los Angeles regions, the following conclusions can be drawn:

1. Segregation is more pronounced among African Americans with respect to non-Hispanic whites than it is for other groups. In general, the New York City region is much more segregated than the Los Angeles region, and the New York City region has some of the most segregated counties in the United States with respect to non-Hispanic blacks and Hispanics.
2. The changes in Harlem, a once black neighborhood that is becoming more diverse and more upscale, and in South Los Angeles, an area known as being a black neighborhood that is now predominantly occupied by Hispanics, exemplify two

Table 11.5 SEGREGATION INDEXES FOR RACE AND HISPANIC STATUS AND AFFLUENCE FOR LOS ANGELES AND NEW YORK CITY REGIONS, 2006–2010

	Los Angeles CSA	New York City CSA
% All Households with $200K or more income	6.16%	8.59%
% Non-Hispanic White Households with $200K or more income	9.70%	11.91%
% Black Households with $200K or more income	2.58%	2.28%
% Hispanic Households with $200K or more income	1.82%	2.32%
% Asian Households with $200K or more income	6.99%	10.32%
Dissimilarity Index of HH Income Above $200K to All Other Households	0.51	0.49
Dissimilarity Index of HH Income Above $200K for Non-Hispanic White Households for All Non-Hispanic White Households	0.44	0.43
Dissimilarity Index of HH Income Above $200K for Black Households for All Black Households	0.76	0.64
Dissimilarity Index of HH Income Above $200K for Hispanic Households for All Hispanic Households	0.71	0.74
Dissimilarity Index of HH Income Above $200K for Asian Households for All Asian Households	0.54	0.58
Dissimilarity Index for Black Households with respect to Non-Hispanic White Households	0.64	0.76
Dissimilarity Index for Black Households with respect to Non-Hispanic White Households with Income of $200K or more	0.80	0.86
Dissimilarity Index for Black Households with respect to Non-Hispanic White Households with Income of less than $200K	0.63	0.76
Dissimilarity Index for Black Households with Income of $200K or more with respect to Non-Hispanic White Households	0.85	0.82
Dissimilarity Index for Black Households with Income of $200K or more with respect to Non-Hispanic White Households with Income of $200K or more	0.64	0.77
Dissimilarity Index for Black Households with Income of $200K or more with respect to Non-Hispanic White Households with Income of less than $200K	0.82	0.82
Dissimilarity Index for Black Households with Income of less than $200K with respect to Non-Hispanic White Households with Income of less than $200K	0.80	0.86

(Continued)

Table 11.5 (CONTINUED)

	Los Angeles CSA	New York City CSA
Dissimilarity Index for Black Households with Income of less than $200K with respect to Non-Hispanic White Households with Income of $200K or more	0.85	0.83
Dissimilarity Index for Black Households with Income of less than $200K with respect to Non-Hispanic White Households with Income of less than $200K	0.63	0.76
Dissimilarity Index for Hispanic Households with respect to Non-Hispanic White Households	0.55	0.61
Dissimilarity Index for Hispanic Households with respect to Non-Hispanic White Households with Income of $200K or more	0.76	0.76
Dissimilarity Index for Hispanic Households with respect to Non-Hispanic White Households with Income of less than $200K	0.54	0.60
Dissimilarity Index for Hispanic Households with Income of $200K or more with respect to Non-Hispanic White Households	0.61	0.65
Dissimilarity Index for Hispanic Households with Income of $200K or more with respect to Non-Hispanic White Households with Income of $200K or more	0.56	0.62
Dissimilarity Index for Hispanic Households with Income of $200K or more with respect to Non-Hispanic White Households with Income of less than $200K	0.62	0.61
Dissimilarity Index for Hispanic Households with Income of less than $200K with respect to Non-Hispanic White Households with Income of less than $200K	0.77	0.77
Dissimilarity Index for Hispanic Households with Income of less than $200K with respect to Non-Hispanic White Households with Income of $200K or more	0.63	0.67
Dissimilarity Index for Hispanic Households with Income of less than $200K with respect to Non-Hispanic White Households with Income of less than $200K	0.54	0.61
Dissimilarity Index for Asian Households with respect to Non-Hispanic White Households	0.48	0.52
Dissimilarity Index for Asian Households with respect to Non-Hispanic White Households with Income of $200K or more	0.64	0.63
Dissimilarity Index for Asian Households with respect to Non-Hispanic White Households with Income of less than $200K	0.48	0.52

(Continued)

Table 11.5 (CONTINUED)

	Los Angeles CSA	New York City CSA
Dissimilarity Index for Asian Households with Income of $200K or more with respect to Non-Hispanic White Households	0.59	0.60
Dissimilarity Index for Asian Households with Income of $200K or more with respect to Non-Hispanic White Households with Income of $200K or more	0.49	0.54
Dissimilarity Index for Asian Households with Income of $200K or more with respect to Non-Hispanic White Households with Income of less than $200K	0.56	0.53
Dissimilarity Index for Asian Households with Income of less than $200K with respect to Non-Hispanic White Households with Income of less than $200K	0.66	0.66
Dissimilarity Index for Asian Households with Income of less than $200K with respect to Non-Hispanic White Households with Income of $200K or more	0.61	0.62
Dissimilarity Index for Asian Households with Income of less than $200K with respect to Non-Hispanic White Households with Income of less than $200K	0.49	0.53

Source: Andrew A. Beveridge, computed from American Community Survey Data 2006–2010.

kinds of large population shifts. The first includes some gentrification, while the other is a simple exchange of one disadvantaged group for another as the first group becomes more affluent and leaves.
3. Aside from the concentration of the minority groups and the non-Hispanic white population, it is also the case that affluent households and those in poverty are very concentrated in both areas. Furthermore, while most minority groups have become somewhat less segregated from non-Hispanic white households, affluent households are becoming more segregated from nonaffluent households.
4. Increased affluence within a minority group does not reduce segregation from the majority group, and can sometimes even compound it.

Although diverse and rapidly changing in composition, both the New York City and Los Angeles regions suffer from very large residential divisions between racial and Hispanic groups, as well as the affluent and the poor. As the data analyses show, minority group status and affluence both affect segregation levels. In some cases, these factors compound one another, leading to even higher levels of segregation between certain populations. Since the sources of these divisions go back for decades, efforts to ameliorate them in any significant way are daunting, especially when very few residents or policymakers seem interested in remedying these gaps, while others are downright hostile toward such endeavors.

APPENDIX

Table 11.A DISSIMILARITY INDEX VALUES 1980 TO 2010 COUNTIES IN LOS ANGELES AND NEW YORK CITY REGIONS FOR NON-HISPANIC BLACK, HISPANIC, AND NON-HISPANIC ASIAN AND PACIFIC ISLANDERS AND RANKS FOR ALL COUNTIES GREATER THAN 50,000 IN 1980

Los Angeles Region-Counties	Dissimilarity Non-Hispanic Black/ Non-Hispanic White				Dissimilarity Hispanic/ Non-Hispanic White				Dissimilarity Non-Hispanic Asian and Pacific Islander/ Non-Hispanic White			
California	1980	1990	2000	2010	1980	1990	2000	2010	1980	1990	2000	2010
Los Angeles	0.81	0.73	0.69	0.67	0.46	0.61	0.63	0.63	0.47	0.46	0.50	0.50
Rank	29	48	55	41	18	20	13	7	30	84	26	25
Orange	0.45	0.37	0.38	0.38	0.37	0.50	0.55	0.54	0.27	0.33	0.42	0.44
Rank	477	633	506	454	96	66	45	40	513	393	117	81
Riverside	0.53	0.47	0.49	0.42	0.36	0.35	0.41	0.41	0.31	0.35	0.38	0.38
Rank	345	454	331	372	100	217	191	197	378	335	193	178
San Bernardino	0.52	0.40	0.42	0.45	0.34	0.36	0.43	0.43	0.26	0.32	0.40	0.43
Rank	357	589	438	328	140	195	173	156	545	445	164	94
Ventura	0.56	0.48	0.49	0.40	0.37	0.52	0.56	0.55	0.37	0.30	0.31	0.31
Rank	309	435	329	420	85	52	40	37	184	520	447	408

NYC Region-Counties	Dissimilarity Non-Hispanic Black/ Non-Hispanic White				Dissimilarity Hispanic/ Non-Hispanic White				Dissimilarity Non-Hispanic Asian and Pacific Islander/ Non-Hispanic White			
New York City	1980	1990	2000	2010	1980	1990	2000	2010	1980	1990	2000	2010
Bronx	0.72	0.74	0.74	0.73	0.49	0.69	0.67	0.65	0.43	0.50	0.50	0.50
Rank	105	44	27	19	8	5	6	5	72	37	27	24
Kings	0.88	0.87	0.86	0.84	0.47	0.68	0.67	0.61	0.45	0.43	0.46	0.51
Rank	7	3	2	1	12	10	7	13	57	133	62	22
New York	0.77	0.76	0.77	0.72	0.45	0.69	0.72	0.66	0.56	0.52	0.46	0.37
Rank	49	30	21	22	19	6	1	4	4	31	59	205
Queens	0.84	0.83	0.83	0.82	0.39	0.49	0.52	0.53	0.46	0.44	0.44	0.50
Rank	16	9	4	2	63	72	74	47	39	102	83	28
Richmond	0.74	0.74	0.75	0.74	0.29	0.36	0.42	0.44	0.31	0.28	0.33	0.36
Rank	79	45	24	13	231	204	181	137	367	574	351	253
New York Other												
Dutchess	0.54	0.56	0.55	0.50	0.30	0.40	0.33	0.30	0.38	0.31	0.29	0.30
Rank	331	279	224	239	220	148	331	416	150	501	490	450
Nassau	0.83	0.83	0.81	0.78	0.28	0.42	0.47	0.49	0.28	0.31	0.35	0.41

(Continued)

Table 11.A (CONTINUED)

NYC Region-Counties	Dissimilarity Non-Hispanic Black/ Non-Hispanic White				Dissimilarity Hispanic/ Non-Hispanic White				Dissimilarity Non-Hispanic Asian and Pacific Islander/ Non-Hispanic White			
New York City	1980	1990	2000	2010	1980	1990	2000	2010	1980	1990	2000	2010
Rank	*23*	*12*	*8*	*7*	*262*	*124*	*115*	*88*	*498*	*489*	*283*	*128*
Orange	0.54	0.54	0.51	0.46	0.32	0.39	0.39	0.37	0.30	0.26	0.28	0.29
Rank	*339*	*320*	*296*	*320*	*178*	*165*	*232*	*252*	*425*	*659*	*528*	*480*
Putnam	0.25	0.24	0.20	0.19	0.12	0.14	0.15	0.17	0.28	0.17	0.14	0.09
Rank	*660*	*815*	*715*	*713*	*661*	*798*	*697*	*683*	*493*	*824*	*720*	*724*
Rockland	0.56	0.56	0.61	0.60	0.34	0.39	0.43	0.47	0.24	0.30	0.32	0.34
Rank	*308*	*282*	*135*	*94*	*142*	*157*	*169*	*112*	*592*	*514*	*420*	*332*
Suffolk	0.70	0.69	0.67	0.62	0.33	0.42	0.46	0.48	0.32	0.30	0.33	0.31
Rank	*130*	*91*	*66*	*78*	*159*	*125*	*126*	*98*	*352*	*517*	*358*	*422*
Sullivan	0.43	0.48	0.48	0.46	0.29	0.37	0.35	0.35	0.42	0.30	0.24	0.23
Rank	*497*	*423*	*355*	*310*	*240*	*186*	*297*	*296*	*85*	*522*	*624*	*639*
New York Other	1980	1990	2000	2010	1980	1990	2000	2010	1980	1990	2000	2010
Ulster	0.41	0.46	0.44	0.41	0.35	0.41	0.36	0.30	0.30	0.30	0.28	0.25
Rank	*541*	*473*	*415*	*397*	*113*	*139*	*272*	*424*	*403*	*504*	*527*	*607*
Westchester	0.67	0.67	0.67	0.66	0.39	0.52	0.54	0.53	0.32	0.29	0.28	0.28
Rank	*175*	*107*	*75*	*49*	*62*	*51*	*50*	*52*	*342*	*548*	*521*	*522*
Connecticut	1980	1990	2000	2010	1980	1990	2000	2010	1980	1990	2000	2010
Fairfield	0.70	0.69	0.70	0.68	0.47	0.60	0.61	0.59	0.28	0.28	0.32	0.31
Rank	*125*	*84*	*48*	*39*	*11*	*21*	*18*	*20*	*481*	*575*	*384*	*402*
Litchfield	0.30	0.32	0.29	0.30	0.19	0.22	0.24	0.31	0.28	0.25	0.25	0.25
Rank	*628*	*739*	*637*	*606*	*532*	*565*	*527*	*388*	*474*	*692*	*613*	*610*
New Haven	0.69	0.68	0.67	0.64	0.43	0.57	0.58	0.54	0.37	0.36	0.34	0.30
Rank	*155*	*96*	*76*	*62*	*36*	*28*	*31*	*38*	*167*	*300*	*332*	*452*
New Jersey												
Bergen	0.74	0.68	0.66	0.60	0.25	0.32	0.39	0.41	0.30	0.30	0.35	0.37
Rank	*69*	*105*	*83*	*101*	*325*	*268*	*225*	*199*	*409*	*510*	*294*	*215*

(*Continued*)

Table 11.A (CONTINUED)

NYC Region-Counties	Dissimilarity Non-Hispanic Black/ Non-Hispanic White				Dissimilarity Hispanic/ Non-Hispanic White				Dissimilarity Non-Hispanic Asian and Pacific Islander/ Non-Hispanic White			
Essex	0.81	0.83	0.81	0.80	0.49	0.68	0.64	0.64	0.29	0.25	0.30	0.33
Rank	*31*	*13*	*6*	*5*	*7*	*8*	*10*	*6*	*442*	*690*	*467*	*338*
Hudson	0.77	0.72	0.67	0.64	0.43	0.43	0.45	0.49	0.48	0.42	0.45	0.46
Rank	*53*	*60*	*71*	*56*	*31*	*120*	*146*	*87*	*24*	*135*	*66*	*52*
Hunterdon	0.55	0.55	0.54	0.43	0.16	0.22	0.26	0.24	0.24	0.29	0.26	0.27
Rank	*313*	*301*	*243*	*367*	*626*	*572*	*499*	*548*	*593*	*565*	*585*	*536*
Mercer	0.70	0.68	0.64	0.64	0.41	0.55	0.53	0.56	0.35	0.37	0.39	0.45
Rank	*124*	*97*	*106*	*61*	*40*	*41*	*63*	*30*	*247*	*261*	*175*	*73*
Middlesex	0.57	0.50	0.46	0.42	0.46	0.52	0.52	0.49	0.35	0.35	0.41	0.42
Rank	*287*	*387*	*375*	*371*	*17*	*57*	*70*	*91*	*243*	*350*	*139*	*109*
Monmouth	0.67	0.66	0.66	0.60	0.29	0.35	0.40	0.41	0.33	0.34	0.38	0.37
Rank	*180*	*125*	*80*	*99*	*239*	*223*	*219*	*190*	*305*	*380*	*207*	*211*
Morris	0.59	0.51	0.46	0.42	0.41	0.44	0.48	0.43	0.27	0.29	0.35	0.36
Rank	*265*	*384*	*370*	*386*	*43*	*109*	*110*	*165*	*528*	*545*	*295*	*236*
Ocean	0.63	0.57	0.55	0.42	0.31	0.32	0.34	0.31	0.34	0.32	0.32	0.32
Rank	*224*	*253*	*227*	*390*	*199*	*277*	*317*	*398*	*251*	*425*	*378*	*392*
Passaic	0.82	0.81	0.79	0.78	0.53	0.72	0.69	0.68	0.39	0.39	0.36	0.38
Rank	*27*	*16*	*11*	*8*	*2*	*2*	*5*	*2*	*122*	*193*	*276*	*196*
Somerset	0.72	0.59	0.61	0.60	0.33	0.39	0.51	0.49	0.27	0.25	0.27	0.33
Rank	*95*	*226*	*137*	*98*	*160*	*164*	*77*	*85*	*526*	*684*	*573*	*370*
Sussex	0.29	0.37	0.32	0.27	0.18	0.17	0.16	0.18	0.22	0.28	0.23	0.25
Rank	*638*	*643*	*616*	*650*	*571*	*727*	*685*	*667*	*625*	*584*	*647*	*595*
Union	0.72	0.71	0.67	0.66	0.52	0.61	0.60	0.59	0.28	0.26	0.27	0.25
Rank	*104*	*68*	*70*	*48*	*4*	*19*	*19*	*23*	*480*	*668*	*574*	*594*

Source: Andrew A. Beveridge, computed from Census Data, 1980, 1990, 2000 and 2010.

NOTES

1. The classic work in this area is *Negroes in Cities: Residential Segregation and Neighborhood Change* by Karl E. Taueber and Alma F. Taueber. It was originally published in 1965 and summarized the patterns of segregation using the Dissimilarity Index (see later in chapter), which is still one of the fundamental indices for measuring segregation.
2. The other measures and their uses are discussed in Massey and Denton (1988). More recently so-called entropy measures have become popular (Fischer et al. 2004). These will not be used since the effort here is to have simple comparisons of overall levels of segregations by specific groups using standard measures. Entropy measures are helpful to measure multigroup segregation and to measure the degree of segregation that is due to differences within and between sets of geographic units.

3. For an excellent discussion of the ghetto, including the history of the use of the term, see the online discussion by members of the American Sociological Association Community and Urban section which later was the basis of a forum on the Ghetto published in *City & Community* (Haynes and Hutchison 2008).

4. The areas used for South Los Angeles, South Central, and Watts are based upon neighborhoods classified by the *Los Angeles Times*. See the following URL for information: http://projects.latimes.com/mapping-la/neighborhoods/. The areas were used to define Census tract based areas for the years noted in table 11.3. Slight changes in tract boundaries decade to decade were ignored.

5. Beveridge was a plaintiffs' expert in this case.

PART FOUR

Immigration and Ethnic Communities

CHAPTER 12

New York and Los Angeles as Immigrant Destinations

Contrasts and Convergence

NANCY FONER AND ROGER WALDINGER

Los Angeles and New York City are the two major immigrant centers in the country. Despite the growing dispersal of the immigrant population to new destinations in the South and Midwest in the last decade, Los Angeles and New York City remain the nation's immigrant behemoths; the two metropolitan areas contain almost one-quarter of the US foreign-born population. In 2008, 18 percent of the nation's immigrants lived in New York City and Los Angeles County alone (only a slight decline from the 20 percent figure in 2000).[1] As of 2009, a little over one-third of the population in metropolitan Los Angeles, and almost 30 percent of the population in metropolitan New York, was foreign-born.

If Los Angeles and New York City are the nation's premier immigrant areas, there are also marked differences between them in the origins and characteristics of the immigrants who have moved there, their immigrant histories, and their economic, social, and political institutions, which have a wide-ranging effect on the foreign-born. Earlier comparisons of New York and Los Angeles, including work by the authors of this chapter and George Sabagh and Mehdi Bozorgmehr (2003) have emphasized the contrasts (Foner 2005, 2007; Sabagh and Borzorgmehr 2003; Waldinger 1996b). The contrasts remain significant, and they are the subject of the first part of this chapter.

But another theme in this chapter is convergence and parallels between Los Angeles and New York. There has been a surprising degree of convergence between New York City and Los Angeles as immigrant centers, which has become more prominent since 2000, particularly when we compare the two metropolitan areas rather than simply focus on the two major cities within them. This is the case, not only in terms of characteristics of the two regions' immigrant populations but also relating to features of the regions' social and political contexts and responses to newcomers. To a large degree, this convergence, as we will argue, is due to the declining impact of geography and history. By now, both Los Angeles and New York have been receiving massive numbers of immigrants for nearly half a century so that large-scale immigration is not a new phenomenon in either region, as it was for Los Angeles a few decades ago. While geography continues to play a role in attracting different immigrant flows to the two regions, it has become less significant in the context of a large population of settled immigrants.

In our comparison, the primary focus is on the Los Angeles and New York metropolitan areas, the first containing almost 13 million people, the second containing almost 19 million people, as of 2009. These areas—and our tables—refer to the Los Angeles and New York Metropolitan Statistical Areas (MSAs), meaning Los Angeles and Orange counties on the West Coast, and, on the East Coast, New York City, the older, inner suburbs of Bergen, Hudson, Passaic, Westchester, and Rockland counties, as well as the Newark-Union, Edison, and Suffolk-Nassau MSAs.

While comparing the two regions is not ideal, it is preferable to the alternative of just comparing New York and Los Angeles cities. Looking only at the two cities is problematic for reasons that mainly have to do with Los Angeles's peculiar geography, which straddles areas that are sociologically and topographically suburban, as well as urban, in character and leave out much of what would normally be considered core urban functions. As a political unit, the City of Los Angeles is far less self-contained than New York City, receiving services from the county and sharing a school district with other municipalities. Moreover, immigrants in Los Angeles have never been as concentrated within the area's biggest city's boundaries, in contrast to New York area settlement patterns; much of the Asian population, for example, has settled in a series of small municipalities east of the City of Los Angeles. And the area's long-established, largest Latino concentration—East Los Angeles—is an unincorporated section of Los Angeles County, left out of the City of Los Angeles in the earlier twentieth century precisely because the city fathers preferred to keep Latinos living in East Los Angeles outside of municipal boundaries.

CONTRASTS

Los Angeles and New York are remarkably different in many ways, and at the end of the first decade of the twenty-first century, the contrasts in their immigrant populations and the effects of immigration remain striking.

Characteristics of Immigrants

The differences in the immigrant flows and characteristics of immigrants are immediately apparent in the following tables for the New York and Los Angeles metropolitan areas, which use census data for 1980, 1990, and 2000, and merged 2007–09 American Community Survey data to document changes that have occurred in recent years. What they point to is the role of geography in influencing the different origins in immigrant populations, with proximity accounting, in part, for the flow of

Caribbean migrants to New York and of Mexicans (and later Central Americans) to Los Angeles, and location accounting for the relative differences in trans-Atlantic vs. trans-Pacific flows. Because migration is a path-dependent process, the historical experience of immigration increases the likelihood that current newcomers will resemble their predecessors. Once immigrants establish a beachhead in a particular location, friends and relatives tend to follow. For example, New York City had a significant wave of West Indian migration in the first few decades of the twentieth century, which helps explain why West Indians headed there when mass migration again became possible after 1965 US immigration legislation changes; in the current period, one reason West Indians continue to flock to New York is owing to its large and vibrant West Indian community. Los Angeles has long had a substantial Mexican population—indeed, it was once part of Mexico!

In a continuation of a pattern prominent in the last few decades, the tables show the much greater diversity of the New York metropolitan area's immigrant population—and the overwhelming preponderance of Mexicans and other Latin Americans in Los Angeles.

In Los Angeles, from 1980 through 2007–09, Mexicans have been consistently—and by far—the largest immigrant group, representing 40 percent or more of the foreign-born throughout this period, and a little over 40 percent as of the present. No other group comes close. The next largest national foreign-born group is Salvadorans, who, in 2007–09, comprised 6 percent of Los Angeles's immigrants. Altogether Mexicans and immigrants from the "Other Americas" comprised almost three-fifths of the Los Angeles metropolitan area's foreign-born population.

While in Los Angeles the top five immigrant source countries in 1980 are the same as those in 2007–09, this is not the case in the New York area. Reflecting the New York area's longer history of large-scale immigration, in 1980 three European groups (Italy, Germany, and Poland) were top source countries—mostly made up of older

Table 12.1 REGION OF BIRTH OF FOREIGN-BORN

Los Angeles Region	1980	1990	2000	2007–09	New York Region	1980	1990	2000	2007–09
Mexico	40%	40%	44%	41%	Mexico	0%	2%	4%	5%
Other Americas	12%	16%	16%	16%	Other Americas	33%	41%	45%	44%
Canada/ Europe/ Australia	20%	11%	9%	7%	Canada/ Europe/ Australia	47%	30%	23%	20%
Asia	21%	27%	30%	33%	Asia	12%	20%	24%	26%
Other	6%	6%	1%	3%	Other	8%	8%	3%	50%

Source: Authors' Analysis from 1970 to 2007–2009 Integrated Public Use Micro-Data Samples. Ruggles et al. 2010.

Table 12.2 AVERAGE NUMBER OF YEARS IN UNITED STATES

Los Angeles Region	1980	1990	2000	2007–09	New York Region	1980	1990	2000	2007–09
Mexico	9.8	11.8	15.5	21.2	Mexico	11.5	8.4	8.9	12.8
Other Americas	10.0	11.1	16.2	21.1	Other Americas	10.9	13.1	15.7	20.2
Canada/ Europe/ Australia	20.4	22.3	24.2	25.2	Canada/ Europe/ Australia	21.8	24.7	24.7	27.6
Asia	8.0	10.7	15.4	20.0	Asia	9.7	11.0	13.6	17.7
All immigrants	11.7	12.5	16.3	22.0	All immigrants	16.2	16.1	16.9	21.8

Source: Authors' Analysis from 1970 to 2007–2009 Integrated Public Use Micro-Data Samples. Ruggles et al. 2010.

Table 12.3 PERCENT LESS THAN HIGH SCHOOL EDUCATED AMONG FOREIGN-BORN

Los Angeles Region	1980	1990	2000	2007–09	New York Region	1980	1990	2000	2007–09
Mexico	78%	69%	63%	60%	Mexico	55%	56%	56%	55%
Other Americas	43%	45%	44%	42%	Other Americas	44%	30%	27%	27%
Canada/ Europe/ Australia	21%	11%	6%	5%	Canada/ Europe/ Australia	41%	27%	15%	12%
Asia	18%	14%	11%	10%	Asia	24%	17%	15%	15%
All immigrants	46%	41%	39%	36%	All immigrants	40%	26%	22%	22%

Source: Authors' Analysis from 1970 to 2007–2009 Integrated Public Use Micro-Data Samples. Ruggles et al. 2010.

immigrants from the massive waves earlier in the twentieth century. By 2007–09, the European groups were no longer in the top five. Nor were Cubans, a sizeable group as of 1980, owing to large numbers who came to live in New Jersey after the huge influx of refugees from the Cuban revolution. Mexicans, who were practically invisible in New York in 1980, were 5 percent of the New York region's foreign born in 2007–09.

What stands out is that no one sending country—or even two or three—dominates in the New York area the way Mexico does in Los Angeles. In 2007–09, the

Table 12.4 PERCENT COLLEGE EDUCATED OR MORE AMONG FOREIGN-BORN

Los Angeles Region	1980	1990	2000	2007–09	New York Region	1980	1990	2000	2007–09
Mexico	2%	3%	3%	5%	Mexico	12%	11%	6%	6%
Other Americas	13%	10%	10%	13%	Other Americas	10%	12%	14%	18%
Canada/ Europe/ Australia	22%	29%	41%	49%	Canada/ Europe/ Australia	17%	24%	36%	44%
Asia	39%	40%	44%	51%	Asia	43%	45%	48%	47%
All immigrants	17%	19%	21%	25%	All immigrants	18%	24%	28%	33%

Source: Authors' Analysis from 1970 to 2007–2009 Integrated Public Use Micro-Data Samples. Ruggles et al. 2010.

Table 12.5 PERCENT CITIZENS AMONG FOREIGN-BORN

Los Angeles Region	1980	1990	2000	2007–09	New York Region	1980	1990	2000	2007–09
Mexico	15%	18%	23%	28%	Mexico	30%	18%	10%	11%
Other Americas	22%	21%	33%	40%	Other Americas	34%	33%	43%	51%
Canada/ Europe/ Australia	62%	53%	55%	61%	Canada/ Europe/ Australia	73%	66%	57%	66%
Asia	27%	37%	56%	64%	Asia	37%	38%	45%	54%
All immigrants	30%	28%	38%	45%	All immigrants	54%	44%	45%	52%

Source: Authors' Analysis from 1970 to 2007–2009 Integrated Public Use Micro-Data Samples. Ruggles et al. 2010.

top two groups in the New York area—Dominicans and Chinese—made up 15 percent of the region's foreign-born. No other country accounted for more than 5 percent. Altogether Mexicans and immigrants from the "Other Americas" represented about 50 percent of the New York area's foreign-born, but the composition of the "Other Americas" group was very different from its makeup in Los Angeles. Many in the "Other Americas" category in the New York area are from the English-speaking Caribbean and Haiti who immigrated in huge numbers in recent decades. In Los Angeles, these groups are tiny in number.

Table 12.6 TOP SENDING COUNTRIES: PERCENT FOREIGN-BORN BY 2007–09 RANK
ORDER

Los Angeles Region	1980	1990	2000	2007–09	New York Region	1980	1990	2000	2007–09
Mexico	40%	40%	44%	41%	Dominican Republic	5%	8%	10%	9%
El Salvador	3%	6%	6%	6%	China	3%	4%	5%	6%
Philippines	4%	5%	6%	6%	India	2%	3%	4%	5%
Korea	3%	4%	4%	5%	Mexico	0%	2%	4%	5%
Vietnam	2%	4%	5%	5%	Ecuador	2%	3%	4%	5%

Source: Authors' Analysis from 1970 to 2007–2009 Integrated Public Use Micro-Data Samples. Ruggles et al. 2010.

Table 12.7 TOP SENDING COUNTRIES: PERCENT FOREIGN-BORN BY 1980 RANK
ORDER (NEW YORK REGION ONLY)

	1980	1990	2000	2007–09
Italy	11%	2%	2%	3%
Poland	5%	6%	4%	2%
Cuba	5%	3%	2%	1%
West Germany	5%	3%	3%	1%

Source: Authors' Analysis from 1970 to 2007–2009 Integrated Public Use Micro-Data Samples. Ruggles et al. 2010.

In 2007–09, the New York and Los Angeles metropolitan areas had fairly similar proportions of Asian immigrants—a little over 30 percent in Los Angeles and 26 percent in New York—although the percentage growth between 1980 and 2007–09 was a good deal greater in New York. The main Asian groups differ as well, as the table on the top five source countries indicates. In 2007–09, Koreans, Vietnamese, and Filipinos were the Asian groups in the top five in Los Angeles, while in the New York area; the Asian groups who had this rank were Chinese and Indians.

Origins are not destinies, but they are influential because of their strong association with social class. Los Angeles's preponderance of Mexicans and other Latin Americans has tilted the immigrant profile there toward those with lower skills and training, more so than in the New York area. Altogether in 2007–09, just over one-fifth of immigrants in the New York area had less than a high school education compared to 36 percent for Los Angeles.

The same pattern shows up at the higher ends of the scale too. In 2007–09, one-third of immigrant adults in the New York area had a college degree or more, as opposed to one-quarter in Los Angeles. In both places, Asians were at the top of the scale—on both coasts about half of the Asian immigrants had a college degree or more.

The preponderance of Mexicans in Los Angeles has another consequence and that has to do with the unauthorized population. The large Mexican and Central American presence in Los Angeles has meant there are a far greater number and a higher proportion of undocumented immigrants there than in the New York area. In 2004, Los Angeles County's undocumented population was an estimated one million, which was almost twice the size of New York City's, the heart of the metropolitan area with the next highest number of undocumented immigrants in the United States. To put it another way, more than one-third of Los Angeles County's foreign-born population was undocumented compared to about one-sixth in New York City (Fix et al. 2008; Hinojosa-Ojeda and Fitz 2011; Lobo and Salvo 2013).[2]

Other Differences

The data in the tables do not, of course, tell the whole story of New York and Los Angeles contrasts. A combination of broader demographics, history, and institutional contexts also help to account for the different immigrant experiences—and reactions to immigrants—in New York and Los Angeles.

In general, historical responses to earlier waves of migration affect the circumstances under which later migrants are received, as well as the opportunity structures they encounter. Here the contrast between the two major cities in each region is relevant. (New York City with 8.2 million people in 2010 was home to less than half of the New York metropolitan area's population; the City of Los Angeles with 3.8 million people had about one-third of the metropolitan area's total.) New York is America's quintessential immigrant city and has been shaped by successive, large waves of immigration, including a massive inflow of Italian and Eastern European Jewish immigrants at the turn of the twentieth century (Foner 2000). By contrast, the City of Los Angeles in the early and mid-twentieth century was populated by internal, mostly white, migrants who were trying to get away from the type of racially diverse city exemplified by New York, producing a political culture and structure that made for lower receptivity to the newcomers of the past four to five decades.

New York's history has defined it as an immigrant city, generating a popular self-identity and political culture that is one source of its "immigrant friendliness." New York City's political culture bears the stamp of earlier European immigration, and sanctions, indeed encourages, newcomers to engage in ethnic politics. Indeed, ethnic politics is sometimes said to be the lifeblood of the city's politics, with no group finding "challenge unexpected or outrageous" (Glazer and Moynihan 1970: xxx). For many years, politicians made ritual visits to the "three I's"—Israel, Italy, and Ireland—the touchstones for so many Jewish and Catholic voters. By 2003, after two years in office, Mayor Michael Bloomberg had already visited the Dominican Republic three times.

As compared to the City of Los Angeles, New York's political structure has been more open to aspiring immigrant politicians, as well as recognizing claims from immigrants. Among other things, New York City has a larger number of political positions up for grabs (including a fifty-one-member New York City Council and numerous state legislative offices), a more traditional, partisan political system, and a long history of balancing ethnic interests and managing ethnic competition. Paradoxically, however, political and cultural factors that have provided opportunities for immigrant political incorporation in New York City, especially on the City Council, have also made it hard for immigrant groups (and indeed native minorities) to attain political success at the citywide level, most notably the position of mayor. Los Angeles was able to elect an African American mayor, Tom Bradley, for a record twenty years (1973–93) and a Mexican American mayor in 2005, while New York City had only a one-term African American mayor, David Dinkins (1989–93) and, so far, no Latino or Asian. Among other things, John Mollenkopf and Raphael Sonenshein (2009) argue that the greater strength of New York City's mayor in relation to other officeholders has increased concerns of non-Hispanic white voters (still a plurality in both cities) about the ethno-racial background of the mayor and contributed to greater white unity against immigrant minority empowerment than in Los Angeles. At the same time, non-Hispanic white voters in Los Angeles are divided more by ideology than ethnicity, and thus more likely to back a minority mayoral candidate whose ideology they support than are voters in New York, where strong ethnic divisions among whites, rooted in the city's immigration history, can cut into support for aspiring minority mayors.

The legacy of the past operates in another way. New York City, unlike Los Angeles, is home to many social service organizations and institutions that were founded a hundred years ago during the huge wave of Eastern and Southern European immigration, including settlement houses and Jewish social welfare agencies that in their modern guise provide services and assistance to many new arrivals (Foner, forthcoming). Owing in good part to union organizing efforts by earlier European immigrants and their children, contemporary immigrants in New York City have benefited from living in a more consistently strong union town (at least since the mid-twentieth century) than have those in Los Angeles.

Another contrast has a lot to do with demographics. The City and County of Los Angeles have seen a rise in African American-Latino competition and conflict as Latinos have grown to far outnumber African Americans in the population (especially in areas of historic African-American concentration, such as Compton in South Los Angeles) and Latinos have become the important minority group; in 1970 the City of Los Angeles was 17 percent black and 18 percent Hispanic, whereas in 2000, blacks had declined to about 10 percent while Hispanics were up to 47 percent. Several studies of Compton describe how the public schools became a setting for conflict, as blacks felt their core educational institutions threatened and Latinos resented that a heavily non-Latino black teaching and counseling staff was not meeting their children's needs (Mindiola, Neimann, and Rodriguez 2002, 115; Camarillo 2004; Johnson et al. 1999). In New York City, African American–Latino tensions have been reduced in salience and seriousness for three main reasons: (1) a large black, as well as Latino, immigration has created a demographic balance between the two groups (in 2009, non-Hispanic blacks were 24 percent of New York City's population, Hispanics, 28 percent); (2) no one Latino group dominates in New York City the way Mexicans do in Los Angeles and the different Latino groups (including Puerto Ricans, who had earlier access to political power and political clout) are sometimes at odds with each other rather than in conflict with native blacks; and (3) owing to the large number of dark-skinned Puerto Ricans and Dominicans with some African heritage, many Hispanic New Yorkers identify themselves as black, at least in some contexts.

Finally, it is worth mentioning the different built-environments in Los Angeles and New York City, which have implications for established residents' comfort with immigrants—and newcomers' comfort with people in other immigrant groups. Compared to car-dependent and sprawling Los Angeles, New York City is a place, as a *New York Times* editorial put it, "where the world rubs shoulders on subways, stoops and sidewalks, where gruff tolerance prevails and understanding thrives" (*New York Times* 2010). New Yorkers may simply bump into each other on the street and subway, yet even this fleeting and superficial contact exposes them to people of different racial groups and cultures on a regular, often daily, basis in a way that is much less likely to happen in Los Angeles.

PARALLELS AND CONVERGENCE

The immigrant story in Los Angeles and New York is not just a case of contrasts that have persisted throughout the last forty years. There are also parallels and some trends toward convergence. Changing demographics and the recent historical experience of the past few decades are among the factors involved in understanding these trends.

In both Los Angeles and New York, the historical experiences of the late nineteenth and early to mid-twentieth centuries now seem less important the further these periods recede into the past. At the same time, the impact of recent—post-1960s history—is of great significance. At the beginning of the second decade of the twenty-first century, the so-called "new" immigration in Los Angeles and New York is relatively old, with its impact first detected by the late 1960s, if not earlier. New York and Los Angeles now share a relatively long history of ongoing immigration for more than four decades—inflows that are likely to continue for the foreseeable future and appear to have produced quite similar responses.

As table 12.2 shows, immigrants make up an increasingly settled population in both the Los Angeles and New York metropolitan areas: by 2007–09 the average number of years in the United States for all immigrants in both places was about the same, a little over twenty years.

The table on naturalization shows a similar kind of convergence, no doubt reflecting the settlement trends. The proportion of the Los Angeles area's naturalized immigrants rose from 28 percent in 1990 and 38 percent in 2000 to 45 percent in 2007–09, approaching the proportion in the New York area, which has hovered around the 50 percent line for the past thirty years. The growing proportion of naturalized immigrants in the Los Angeles metropolitan area suggests that the area's historically greater attraction for undocumented immigrants is of diminishing impact, as many recent arrivals have headed elsewhere and the earlier settled immigrants have found a route to citizenship. (Naturalization rates are lower among Mexicans in New York than Los Angeles, undoubtedly because most Mexicans in New York are very recent arrivals compared to Los Angeles's longer-settled Mexican population.) Geography, in short, has become less important in both places as the immigrant population has put down roots, thereby not only continuing to attract compatriots from the same countries in a network-driven process but also providing the material, social, cultural, and political resources needed for movement beyond these two capitals of immigrant America.

There is another trend toward convergence as Los Angeles has become a more immigrant-hospitable environment, and the stark dichotomy of an immigrant-friendly New York vs. an immigrant-unfriendly Los Angeles becomes increasingly dated. By now, Angelenos have become used to immigration, much like New Yorkers, and the growing immigrant population and increasing political clout of Latinos in Los Angeles have also had decided effects.

In the political realm, the City of Los Angeles elected a Mexican-American mayor in 2005, a time when New York City's mayor was Michael Bloomberg (a third-generation Jewish American). Indeed, the size of the Latino (largely Mexican) community in the City of Los Angeles means, as Mollenkopf and Sonenshein observe in their chapter, that the rise of Latino office holding there was "almost inevitable" even if it was long delayed.

New York City's political structure may present fewer barriers of entry to immigrant political entrepreneurs than the City of Los Angeles, but a regional focus highlights that the smaller cities in the Los Angeles region into which so many immigrants have moved—whether east of Los Angeles City, as among Asians, or south of Los Angeles City, as among Latinos—have provided relatively easy entry points to a variety of municipal positions. The best known of these cases is Monterey Park, where Chinese immigrants have been politically influential for over two decades. In the New York area, too, it should be noted, immigrant politicians have won electoral office in cities, towns, and villages outside the five boroughs—for example, a Jamaican-born mayor of Mount Vernon (in Westchester) in the 1980s and 1990s and, more recently, a Dominican mayor of Passaic and a Korean mayor of Edison (both in New Jersey).

Scholars, including one of the authors of this chapter, have pointed to the City University of New York (CUNY), the largest urban public university system in the nation, as an example of an exceptional New York institution—rooted in the city's immigrant history—that has long provided an avenue of mobility for first- and second-generation immigrants (Foner 2007). In 2010, CUNY had about 262,000 students, including full-time and part-time enrolled undergraduate and graduate students; 43 percent of the undergraduates at CUNY's eleven senior and six community colleges were born outside the United States mainland, and CUNY boasts that its undergraduates can trace their ancestries to 205 countries. Yet, there may be more parallels than differences between the Los Angeles and New York areas when it comes to opportunities for college and university education. It is not clear that CUNY (and the State University of New York and equivalent New Jersey systems with campuses in the New York metropolitan area) really provide superior access to higher education than do their counterparts on the West Coast. The Los Angeles metropolitan area includes two campuses of the University of California (UC) system (enrolling about 50,000 students), six California State University (CSU) campuses, and a large number of community colleges. In many respects, the UC system has become an immigrant university: as of the mid-2000s, over one-quarter of the undergraduates at UCLA were themselves immigrants; and another 40 percent had at least one immigrant parent (Brint et al. 2007, 10). While the immigrant-origin student body is itself highly diverse with respect to national and social class origins, many are of very modest backgrounds, as reflected in the large proportion of UCLA undergraduates (35 percent in 2009–10) receiving federal Pell grants provided to low-income students.[3] Ever since 2008, the California financial crisis has had a severe negative impact on public higher education, yielding significant tuition increases in the UC and CSU systems with slightly later, somewhat less drastic, increases in the community colleges. Nonetheless, as both the UC and CSU systems have sought to offset tuition increases with greater financial support for low-income students, it seems likely that public higher education in California remains an important ladder of upward mobility for today's immigrants and their children.

Immigrants and labor unions are also an area of convergence as Los Angeles emerges as a center of labor movement dynamism and innovation to rival New York—and older patterns in Los Angeles are of steadily diminishing importance. Immigrants in New York City profit from the fact that labor unions have been consistently strong and politically influential for many decades. Indeed, in 2009–10, 25 percent of all wage and salary workers in New York City were union members, a proportion higher than any other major US city; among the foreign-born in New York City, the unionization rates of those who had become US citizens and entered the United States before 1990 were comparable to or higher than those of US-born workers (Milkman and Braslow 2010). This is also the case in the Los Angeles metropolitan area, but the overall unionization rates there are significantly lower than in New York City—15 percent for all wage and salary workers in 2006 (Milkman and Kye 2006). Despite these lower unionization rates, Los Angeles is moving, one might say, in a New York City direction. Once known as an anti-union town, in recent years Los Angeles has emerged as a "crucible of labor movement revitalization," in large part because of the huge Latino immigrant influx (Milkman 2006, 3).

Union membership in Los Angeles went into steep decline starting in the late 1950s, but organizing drives since the 1990s have begun to reverse this downward trend (Milkman 2006). By one account, the city's labor movement has been adding workers at a remarkable rate by focusing on immigrant workers—with unions organizing part-time school aides, home-care workers, food service workers, park and recreation workers, and, most famously, office janitors after a strike in 2000 in which the public donated more than $2 million for food and the city's Roman Catholic archbishop embraced the janitors' cause (Greenhouse 2001). Highly publicized marches of chanting Latino janitors drew attention to the maintenance workers' low wages, which were called unjust in a city with such high living costs. In the end, the janitors, nearly all of whom were Latino immigrants, won a 25 percent salary increase over three years. The *New York Times*'s Steven Greenhouse (2001) writes that in general, Los Angeles's union movement is now looked to as a model for labor movements in other American cities and in 2001, the national AFL-CIO "arranged for Los Angeles labor leaders to hold what was essentially a tutorial for New York labor leaders." Or as sociologist Ruth Milkman puts it, Los Angeles is one of the few bright spots for the beleaguered US labor movement and a proving ground for strategic organizing innovation (Milkman 2006, ix).

Less happily, evidence from media reports indicates that the growing Mexican presence in New York City has created tensions with black residents in at least one neighborhood that is new to immigration and in which such tensions have developed in a manner that has similarities to strains reported in formerly African American-dominated communities in Los Angeles that have become heavily Latino. The summer of 2010 witnessed a series of attacks on Mexican immigrants by young black men in Staten Island's Port Richmond neighborhood. A predominantly black area in the 1980s and early 1990s, Port Richmond has recently seen a sharp rise in the Mexican population. By 2008, 8,400 people of Mexican descent lived in the police precinct that includes Port Richmond, up from 950 in 1990, and the student body at the local elementary school, once mostly black, had become largely Latino and heavily Mexican. In a time of high black unemployment, blacks complained that Mexicans and other Latinos took jobs that should have been theirs (Semple 2010).

Los Angeles is often thought of as a cauldron of anti-immigrant sentiment, dating to the early 1990s when 56 percent of the voters in Los Angeles County supported the statewide Proposition 187; had it been implemented, Proposition 187 would have made undocumented immigrants ineligible for government-funded social and health services. (The law was found to be unconstitutional in federal court.) New York, by contrast, has a reputation as a city that is relatively welcoming to the undocumented. Around the same time that Proposition 187 was passed in California, New York City Mayor Rudolph Giuliani issued an executive order protecting undocumented immigrants from being reported when they used city services.

Yet, since the early 1990s, the City and County of Los Angeles have become more New York-like in the warmth of their welcome to immigrants. In the City of Los Angeles, as in New York, immigrant-friendly politics is good politics, especially at the citywide level. This is not surprising given the large number of first- and second-generation immigrants who represent a growing proportion of the electorate. Right after Arizona enacted a harsh law against undocumented immigrants in 2010 (which, had certain provisions not been blocked by the courts, would have allowed police to detain people on the suspicion that they were in the country illegally and made the failure to carry immigration documents a crime), New York City's Mayor Bloomberg was quick to attack it, saying that with this law "we are committing national suicide.... This is not good for the country. We love immigrants here" (Sherman and Lisberg 2010). In Los Angeles, Mayor Antonio Villaraigosa went even further, backing a boycott of Arizona in response to the immigration crackdown (Villaraigosa 2010a).

Beyond electoral politics, Los Angeles churches, civic agencies, and trade unions have sought to remedy poverty among Latino immigrants through organized action. In 2006, the demonstrations for the rights of undocumented workers were much larger and played a more significant role in Los Angeles than in New York City. According to some estimates, the March 2006 protests over US immigration policy reforms drew half a million people in Los Angeles, as compared to 10,000 in New York City a few days later in a march across the Brooklyn Bridge to Foley Square, and 70,000–125,000 in an April demonstration in front of New York's City Hall. This difference is partly linked to the much larger proportion of undocumented immigrants in Los Angeles than in New York. Also, organizing efforts in Los Angeles may have been more effective because they were mainly pitched to one group—Mexicans, who make up the overwhelming majority of the undocumented there. In New York City, one reason the mobilization was slower to develop is that the undocumented population (like the immigrant population generally) is so incredibly diverse, with large numbers of West Indians, Central and South Americans, and Asians, as well as Mexicans, making it more difficult to mobilize across cultural, racial, ethnic, and linguistic lines (see Zepeda-Millan 2011).

There is still another way that the New York and Los Angeles regions appear to be converging as immigrant destinations. New York City continues to be a relatively welcoming city for immigrants; at the turn of the twenty-first century, the City of Los Angeles largely resembles New York in this respect. However, in both regions, the environment in many towns and cities with a more recent immigration history is aversive, if not more hostile—in many ways, reminiscent of the City of Los Angeles in the early days of the post-1960s inflow. As in Los Angeles in this earlier period, recent immigration, since the early 1990s, in many New York towns and cities represents a sharp growth spurt. (This is in contrast to New York City, where the post-1965 inflow was a gradual increase, since the proportion of foreign-born was already substantial there throughout the twentieth century.) The presence of large numbers of nonwhite, often low-skilled, Latino immigrants in many formerly all or nearly all white suburban and outer-rim New York communities has been a radical change—and a jolt. Many of the new arrivals outside of New York City are Mexican—indeed, the advent of Mexican immigrants as a major immigrant group in the New York area is an additional sign of convergence between the two regions.

Not only is the dispersal of immigrants to native white suburban regions in the New York metropolitan area a dramatic change, but established residents often moved there precisely to flee the problems and ethnoracial diversity of the inner city. Tensions are frequently rife between established white residents and newcomers, particularly when the new arrivals are low-skilled, poorly educated, and often undocumented Latinos who have come in search of low-level work. Bitter conflicts have arisen over day-labor sites and overcrowded immigrant housing in towns in Westchester County and on Long Island. Two hate crimes on Long Island in Farmingville, a largely white community in Suffolk County about fifty miles from New York City, attracted national attention; in 2000, two Mexican day laborers were beaten nearly to death by two men from nearby towns, and three years later, four Farmingville teenagers burned down the house of a Mexican family who barely escaped alive.

Eight years later, in 2008, a stabbing attack of an Ecuadorian immigrant nearby in Suffolk County by a gang known as the "Caucasian Crew" also indicated the animosity of many white long-established residents toward Latino newcomers. The teenagers on trial for murdering the Ecuadorian spoke of getting together to hunt down and hurt Hispanic men—what they called "beaner hopping," a reference to the staple Hispanic dish of rice and beans. One teenager told a reporter: "These guys, these Mexicans, everyone has a hatred for them. Downtown Patchogue used to be nice, and now they make it all dirt baggish" (Algar, Crowley, and Alport 2008). While these crimes are extreme, they are indicative of a deep anti-immigrant and anti-Latino sentiment and reaction that have not occurred (or at least been sharply curtailed and contained) in New York City.

Before he fell from political grace and anti-immigrant politics became a liability in California, former California Governor Pete Wilson's support for Proposition 187 helped give him a landslide win in his reelection campaign in 1994. More than ten years later in the New York area—outside of New York City—some politicians have taken up the anti-undocumented banner. Most prominent has been Steve Levy, a two-term County Executive of Suffolk County, the fast-growing eastern half of Long Island with some 1.5 million residents that has witnessed a dramatic growth in its foreign-born, heavily Latino, population in recent years. Levy's crusade against undocumented immigrants helped make him virtually unbeatable in the mid-2000s. Elected as a Democrat in 2003 in a county dominated for years by Republicans, Levy won re-election four years later with cross-party endorsement, receiving 96 percent of the vote.[4] Among other things, he lent county police officers to town building inspectors for raids to shut down rooming houses, and he increased arrests of unlicensed contractors and immigrant checks on prisoners in the county jail. In 2007, he supported a bill, dubbed "Standing While Latino," which, had it passed the county legislature, would have banned day laborers from seeking employment along county roadways.

CONCLUSION

At the beginning of the second decade of the twenty-first century, after nearly fifty years of large-scale immigration, New York and Los Angeles have come to resemble each other as immigrant destinations in many ways, owing, in good part, to the very fact that they are both now major, long-term immigrant centers. The historical legacy of the early twentieth century remains important in understanding the institutions that greet the new arrivals, especially in New York City, but what is increasingly relevant is the weight of the more recent past that has led to large settled populations of immigrants.

Predicting the future is a risky business, yet it seems likely that convergent trends will become more prominent in the years ahead in the context of continued immigrant inflows, while at the same time, huge numbers of the children of post-1965 arrivals will come of age. As long as the United States keeps on receiving hundreds of thousands of immigrants each year, the New York and Los Angeles metropolitan areas will continue to attract large numbers if only, as we have mentioned, because of the networks that link newcomers to settlers. Some longer-term immigrants, as well as many in the US-born second generation, will move elsewhere; yet, sizable numbers will remain in the Los Angeles and New York areas. By dint of their number—and the social and economic successes of a substantial proportion—first- and second-generation immigrants in the two regions are bound to have a greater influence on a broad range of institutions in the coming years, an impact that is also likely to be similar in many ways.

This does not mean that differences between the New York and Los Angeles areas will fade away—far from it. The characteristics of immigrants who move there in combination with distinctive institutional contexts (themselves shaped by the historical experience of immigration) will undoubtedly sustain and reinforce contrasts between the regions as immigrant centers. The particular contexts of the Los Angeles and New York metropolitan areas will, in short, continue to matter. We have identified some of the contrasts and convergences that have already developed, but more research is clearly needed to deepen our understanding of these dynamics in the present period. Moreover, as we look ahead, one of the challenges of the future will be to explore the parallels and differences that persist or emerge in the years to come.

NOTES

1. Our estimate for 2008 is an average based on pooled samples from the 2007–09 American Community Survey.
2. In 2004, an estimated 583,000 undocumented immigrants lived in New York City, in 2010, 499,000 (Lobo and Salvo 2013).
3. Data on Pell grants from http://www.aim.ucla.edu/publications/main.asp, accessed November 19, 2012.
4. Under fire for corruption charges regarding fundraising, Levy announced in March 2011 that he would not seek a third term.

CHAPTER 13

The Transformation of Chinese American Communities

New York vs. Los Angeles

MIN ZHOU, MARGARET M. CHIN,
AND REBECCA Y. KIM

Classic theories of assimilation have long stressed the transitory nature of ethnically distinct urban enclaves as springboards facilitating immigrants' eventual integration into the host society's mainstream. New York's Little Italy and
Los Angeles's Little Tokyo are perhaps two of the best known classic examples of
such enclaves. The general belief was that new immigrants first clustered in ethnic enclaves and toiled to pave a path for their children or grandchildren to "melt"
into middle-class suburbia and to become "indistinguishably" American, or white.
Since the 1970s, however, this classical inner city-to-suburbia residential mobility
model has been challenged. America's largest metropolitan regions have witnessed
the direct insertion of large numbers of new immigrants into middle-class suburbs,
which does not seem to follow the patterns predicted by classical theories. Many
neighborhoods in cities and suburbs that whites once dominated have now evolved
into "global" neighborhoods where native-born groups live side-by-side with new
immigrants of diverse national or ethnic origins. Some of these neighborhoods have
been rapidly transformed into "ethnoburbs" (or middle-class suburban communities
concentrated by ethnic minorities and ethnic businesses) (Li 1998a) by newcomers
possessing higher than average levels of education, occupation, and incomes, as well
as social capital networks that branch out to tap financial resources and markets
offshore in creating their own ethnic economies.

The study was partially supported by research grants from the Academic Senate, the
Asian American Studies Center, and the Walter and Shirley Wang Endowed Chair's fund,
University of California, Los Angeles, and the PSC-CUNY award program of The City
University of New York. The authors thank David Halle, Andrew A. Beveridge, Nancy
Foner, and John Logan for their insightful comments, and Omar Montana, Stella Xingin
Li, and Ada Lingjun Peng for their assistance.

In this chapter, we reexamine the formation and development of sprawling Chinese urban enclaves and ethnoburbs in New York and Los Angeles to raise critical questions about residential assimilation. How have Chinese immigrants of diverse origins and socioeconomic backgrounds negotiated their way into American metropolises and suburbia since the turn of the twenty-first century? How have new Chinese urban enclaves and ethnoburbs differed from old Chinatowns and from typical suburban American communities? What are the implications of twenty-first-century ethnic community development for our understanding of the socioeconomic and political incorporation of contemporary immigrants? In New York, we focus on two outer-borough relatively affluent urban Chinese enclaves (Flushing in Queens and Sunset Park in Brooklyn). In Los Angeles, we focus on the sprawling ethnoburbs in the San Gabriel Valley, which is a vast suburbia to the east of the city of Los Angeles.

THE CHANGING CONTEXTS OF EXIT AND RECEPTION OF CHINESE IMMIGRATION

Global economic restructuring has moved people and capital, leading to sweeping changes in local economies of both sending and receiving countries. In many of the sending countries, globalization has significantly altered the structures of local economies and opportunities for social mobility, causing people and capital to move and cross borders in ways that render neoclassical economic theories of international migration inadequate. Wage differentials and access to better employment opportunities are no longer the main forces that push people to move. Other compelling causes include access to formal and informal migration networks, access to well-established institutionalized credit and insurance markets, educational opportunities for children, and family's risk diversification, as well as extreme hardships arising from war, political and religious persecutions, (de)colonization, and military involvement (Portes and Rumbaut 1990; Sassen 1994).

As a result, the contexts of exit for contemporary international migrations have been substantially reshaped. Since the 1960s, international migrants to the United States constitute not only the poor and huddled masses but also the affluent and highly skilled groups. For example, contemporary immigrants from China and the greater Chinese Diaspora include not only low-skilled urban workers, uneducated peasants, and penniless refugees, but also urban workers and highly skilled professionals, most of whom received advanced degrees from universities in the United States or elsewhere in the Western world (Zhou 2009; Zhou and Gatewood 2000, 5–29). Globalization has also changed the contexts of reception. In the United States, economic restructuring divides urban labor markets into a dominant core sector characterized by knowledge-intensive or capital-intensive jobs that offer high salaries with fringe benefits, fair working conditions, and good opportunities for upward social mobility, as well as a marginal but sizeable sector characterized by low-skill, labor-intensive jobs that offer minimum wages with no benefits, poor working conditions, and few opportunities for upward social mobility (Edwards 1979; Tolbert et al. 1980, 1095–1116). The urban employment base of unionized, blue-collar manufacturing jobs that used to facilitate intergenerational mobility of the working class is shrinking. Consequently, local labor markets consist of jobs that either require advanced education and skills or pay minimum wages. Less skilled natives or immigrants living in the central city are trapped in the ranks of the underemployed, unemployed, or working poor (Waldinger 1996a, 445–70). On the other hand, the United States has become one of the most attractive places for highly skilled professionals, as well as for investment from overseas Chinese, as fueled by the rapid economic developments in mainland China, Hong Kong, Taiwan, and the rest of the Chinese Diaspora. Wealthy, skilled immigrants stimulate entrepreneurial development in the Chinese American community (Fong 1994; Horton 1995; Lin 1998; Saito 1998; Tseng 1994; Wong 1989; Zhou 1996; and Zhou et al. 2008).

Parallel to this economic restructuring is the trend of accelerating suburbanization. Most of the country's large metropolises have witnessed a massive growth of developments away from the central cities. Much of this has been fueled by immigrant and minority growth. In Los Angeles, for example, non-Hispanic whites as a proportion of the metropolitan population declined from over 85 percent in 1970 to about one-third in 2010. In the New York Metro the figures are from about 85 percent to just over half. Now many of the country's major urban centers have a racial nonwhite group as the majority—made up of both native and foreign-born alike (Pollard and Mather 2011). Further, because of increasing numbers and increasing class variations of contemporary international migration, many immigrants have settled directly into the suburbs that used to be exclusively white middle class. Moreover, new Chinese immigrants are more likely than their predecessors to take a variety of pathways to assimilation instead of following one linear path.

CONTEMPORARY CHINESE IMMIGRATION
Rapid Demographic Change and Diversification

Chinese immigration to the United States occurred several decades before the mass migration from southern and eastern Europe. But unlike earlier European immigrants at the turn of the twentieth century, who were expected to assimilate into mainstream American society as quickly as possible and who succeeded in doing so in the course of one to three generations, earlier Chinese immigrants were barred from immigration, naturalization, and assimilation by law, most notably the Chinese Exclusion Act (1882–1943). Over sixty years of legal exclusion confined Chinese immigrants to Chinatowns. The old-timers created their own means of survival via ethnic economies and organizations in order to avoid direct competition with native workers while also keeping alive their sojourner's dream that one day they would return to China with gold and glory (Zhou 1992). Such segregated living reinforced their ethnic difference and unassimilability.

At the turn of the new millennium, Chinese America remained a predominantly immigrant community despite its long history. Between 1960 and 2010, the number

of Chinese Americans grew exponentially from 237,292 to 3.8 million. The first generation comprises the overwhelming majority (over two-thirds) with more than
one-third (37 percent) of them entering after 2000 (Terrazas and Batalova 2010;
Zhou and Gatewood 2000).

Unlike the old-timers who were mostly unskilled laborers from the southern
region of Guangdong Province, new Chinese immigrants come from diverse origins
and socioeconomic backgrounds. The three main sources of Chinese immigration
are mainland China, Taiwan, and Hong Kong. Since 1980, Chinese immigrants from
Southeast Asia and the Americas have also grown in number. Immigrant Chinese from
different origins or different regions of the same origin do not necessarily share the
same culture or lived experiences. Language is perhaps the most significant cultural
barrier, creating a subtle social distance to separate coethnics who speak Cantonese
or other southern regional dialects from those who speak Mandarin. The new Chinese
immigrants have also been disproportionately drawn from highly educated and professional segments of the sending societies. The 2010 American Community Survey
(ACS) data showed that 66 percent of young foreign-born Chinese (aged 25 to 34)
had four or more years of college education.

Neighborhood Transitions

These developments have drastically changed the Chinese American community from
a few homogeneous inner-city Chinatowns to often relatively affluent urban Asian
enclaves and global ethnoburbs. Residential patterns of the Chinese are now characterized by dispersion away from the inner city, as well as regional concentration.
The latter to some extent follows a historical pattern: Chinese Americans continue to
concentrate in the West and in urban areas. As of 2010, California by itself accounted
for 37 percent of all Chinese Americans. New York accounted for 17 percent, second only to California, and Texas accounted for 5 percent. Other states that historically received fewer Chinese immigrants also witnessed phenomenal growth. These
include New Jersey, Massachusetts, Illinois, Washington, Pennsylvania, Florida, and
Maryland. New York City (486,463), San Francisco City (171,974), and Los Angeles
City (66,509) had the largest number of Chinese Americans of all major cities.

At the local level, traditional Chinatowns continue to receive newcomers and
attract economic investments from coethnics, but they no longer serve as primary
centers of initial settlement. Today, less than 10 percent of Chinese in Los Angeles
City and New York City live in old Chinatowns. However, demographic changes
caused by international migration do not appear to be associated with the disappearance of old Chinatowns (Lin 1998; Zhou 1992). As of 2010, seven out of fourteen of
the census tracts in New York City's old Chinatown (in downtown Manhattan) had
a Chinese majority. Likewise, four out of seven of the census tracts in Los Angeles's
Chinatown had a Chinese majority. Even so, New York City's old Chinatown was
dealt a blow after the 9/11 terrorism attack on the World Trade Center (Chin 2005a;
Chin 2005b). The neighborhood was still mostly Asian/Chinese (at 55 percent) in
the 2006–2010 ACS, but there was a 15 percent drop in the Asian population and a

42 percent increase in the white population in the ten-year period. The number of Chinese increased in New York City, but the rapid growth occurred in Queens and Brooklyn (American Community Survey 2005–09).

As of 2010, more than half of all Chinese Americans in the United States live in suburbs. Others (such as those in New York City) live in enclaves away from the conventional central cities. Some of these areas have become Chinese dominant. For example, in New York City's Flushing, sometimes known as the "second [urban] Chinatown," ten out of the neighborhood's eleven census tracts had a Chinese majority as of 2010. In Los Angeles's Monterey Park, sometimes known as "the first suburban Chinatown" (Fong 1994), eleven out of the neighborhood's fifteen census tracts had a Chinese majority as of 2010. Small suburban cities in Los Angeles and the San Francisco Bay Area have witnessed extraordinarily high proportions of Chinese Americans in the general population and the emergence of a new and distinct phenomenon—"ethnoburbs."

The current trend of Chinese immigrant settlement suggests that residential reconcentration of an immigrant group in suburban communities may not necessarily be accompanied by complete assimilation.

NEW YORK: URBAN ENCLAVES IN TRANSITION

Demographic Shifts beyond Old Chinatown

Flushing, Queens, and Sunset Park, Brooklyn, are both suburblike neighborhoods located in an outlying area of a major city. Since the 1980s, these neighborhoods have grown into visible Chinese communities, each with its own distinctive flavor.[1] In the 1970s, two demographic trends—accelerated white flight and rapid Asian influx—contributed to the areas' demographic transformations. Both Flushing and Sunset Park emerged as multiethnic neighborhoods when native-born whites either moved out or "aged" out and new immigrants began to pour in, though residents in Flushing were generally of higher socioeconomic standing than those in Sunset Park, and the neighborhood's residents were predominantly non-Hispanic white until 1980 (98 percent in 1960 and nearly 80 percent in 1970). Between 1980 and 2010, the proportion of the non-Hispanic white population of Flushing fell dramatically from 42 percent to less than 20 percent.

The rate of Flushing's white flight far exceeded what was occurring at the same time in the borough of Queens and in New York City as a whole. In most parts of central Flushing, Asians became the majority group by 1990 and remained at 55 percent in 2010. Likewise, non-Hispanic whites in the Sunset Park area of Brooklyn decreased from 51 percent in 1980 to 22 percent in 2010. Immigrants from mainland China and Hong Kong tend to settle in Manhattan and Brooklyn, while Taiwanese immigrants mostly concentrate in Queens. Our fieldwork at the sites indicates a further nuance to these settlement patterns—Fujianese (from the province of Fujian in Southeast China), known for their undocumented status, are concentrated in old Chinatown and Sunset Park, rather than in Flushing.

As for commonalities, Flushing and Sunset Park are both easily accessible by sub-way lines that connect to Manhattan's historic Chinatown. Both neighborhoods have relatively good housing stock including single-family units, as well as numerous mid- and high-rise apartment buildings. Flushing has pockets of affluence with old homes on large grounds. Sunset Park has many more two- or three-family homes built for the working class. Both have become full service communities offering an array of retail and services for the Chinese. The growth of both of these satellite Chinatowns can be traced to the increase of Chinese immigration during the 1980s.

The Chinese immigrant community in Flushing was initially built by foreign capi-tal from Taiwan and Taiwanese immigrants (Zhou 1992). Many Taiwanese came to Flushing because they had few ties to Manhattan's old Chinatown and did not identify with the old-timers and their family-sponsored immigrants, who were predominantly Cantonese speaking. Their better educational backgrounds and greater economic resources enabled them to build their own enclave away from the existing center of Chinese settlement. Once the movement to Flushing began, other coethnic Chinese soon followed; some moved in from old Chinatown as a step up the socioeconomic lad-der while others came directly from abroad. Thus, Chinese immigrants in Flushing are more diverse in their places of origin and class backgrounds than those in Manhattan's Chinatown. Figure 13.1 shows the Chinese concentration in New York City in 2010.

Prior to the Chinese influx, Sunset Park was once a thriving industrial waterfront with thousands of entry-level jobs in the American Can Company, Bethlehem Steel, and many other maritime occupations. The construction of the Gowanus Expressway and its expansion in the 1960s created a physical barrier that severed the water-front and its industries from the community. As is typical of many urban neighbor-hoods, Sunset Park experienced rapid deindustrialization, and with it came a loss of industrial and manufacturing jobs, as well as population. The decline in shipping and manufacturing, accompanied by white flight, led to the designation of Sunset Part as a federal poverty area (Hum 2003). Ninety percent of the storefronts on 8th Avenue were vacant during those times.

By the late 1980s, Asian and Latino (Puerto Rican and later Mexican) immigrants began moving into the area because of affordable housing. Initially, Chinese immi-grants who depended on jobs in Chinatown were drawn to Sunset Park for its easy access by subway to old Chinatown where many still worked. The N train goes from Chinatown to Sunset Park with the "blue sky" stop easily recognizable as the first stop after the subway train leaves the tunnel. Besides the trains, Chinese-operated vans started to pop up to drive workers to their jobs at cheap rates.

In addition to good transit, this neighborhood appealed to Chinese immi-grants because it had significantly lower home prices. Many of the early Chinese who lived in Sunset Park remarked on the lucky symbolism behind 8th Avenue (as the number "8" is a euphemism for prosperity), the identifiable "blue sky" sub-way stop, and of course, the easy commute to and from old Chinatown. According to the 2010 Census, more than one-third of the neighborhood was Chinese, up from a tiny 4 percent in 1980. Sunset Park's Chinese are mostly from mainland China and increasingly from the Fujian Province in the Southeast. Today, Sunset Park is known as the third Chinatown (after Flushing, the second), and it is anchored

Figure 13.1

Percent Chinese in New York City Region and in Areas of High Concentration (All Chinese or Taiwanese)

Source: Andrew A. Beveridge based upon 2010 Census Data and Boundaries.

by 8th Avenue and runs from 39th Street to 68th Street. The new Chinese immigrants opened numerous retail, service, and manufacturing firms where they and their coethnics work and/or shop, and developed and remodeled older buildings for newcomer coethnics to live.

Ethnic Enclave Economies and Neighborhood Revitalization

Before the urban transformation, the retail scene in Flushing and Sunset Park was dominated by an amalgam of small specialty shops and services, most of which were operated as typical "mom and pop" stores. New York City's overall economic recession in the early 1970s hit the business community in the outer boroughs hard, causing many small shops and commercial enterprises to close, commercial vacancy rates to increase, and property values to drop. White flight and the loss of manufacturing jobs in the city during the late 1960s and early 1970s exacerbated the deterioration and economic downturn at the neighborhood level.

However, this trend dramatically reversed with the arrival of immigrants from different parts of Asia since the 1970s. With the injection of massive amounts of immigrant capital and entrepreneurship from Taiwan, and to a lesser extent from Korea and India, Flushing experienced economic revival in the service, commercial, and consumption sectors. Since 1975, new retail and office development has sprung up regularly in Flushing's downtown area. Property values in Flushing increased 50 percent to 100 percent during the 1980s, and commercial vacancy rates plummeted from 7 percent in the late 1970s to less than 1 percent in the early 1990s (Parvin 1991). Flushing's commercial development today is extraordinarily active with new businesses. In the very heart of the downtown commercial and transportation hub, the multilingual signs of several mainstream bank branches and Chinese-owned banks are on display (Korean and Indian businesses are also quite visible). Near the subway station, upscale Chinese restaurants and full-service supermarkets, interspersed with small cafes, green groceries, drug stores, and fast food restaurants, owned by the Chinese, give the area the unmistakable look and feel of Chinatown.

The visibility of Chinese faces, the economic diversity of the Chinese population, and business signage turned Flushing into a relatively affluent Chinese enclave. It has some features of Chinatown and some of ethnoburbs. It is like Chinatown because of its urban location and density of ethnic businesses; unlike Chinatown because of its ethnic diversity and the socioeconomic statuses of residents. There are modern office complexes that house banks and service-oriented firms owned by Taiwanese immigrants and transnational Taiwanese, as well as subsidiary firms from the Asian Pacific. The commercial core is also filled with Korean, Indian, Pakistani, and Bangladeshi restaurants and stores, packed into the shop fronts along the main streets.

The expanded downtown is now a bustling, vibrant commercial area attracting suburban Chinese to return on a regular basis. For example, many Chinese families come in from the outer suburbs to bring their children to the Chinese Cultural Center for Saturday afternoon language classes, academic tutoring, college prep programs, and recreational activities. While children engage in these activities, parents usually shop at the local grocery and specialty shops or get ethnic-specific services such as a haircut or hair coloring, facial, or foot massage. Others come to Flushing to study or browse at the crowded public library that has books, magazines, and newspapers in different Asian languages, and stay afterward for shopping and dining. The development of Flushing as a comprehensive ethnic business center means that suburban Chinese residents no longer have to go into the Manhattan Chinatown to visit an authentic restaurant, to do their shopping, or to satisfy their cultural needs.

Initially, Sunset Park was something in between the Chinatowns and new ethnoburbs. Sunset Park served as a bedroom community for old Manhattan Chinatown. Chinese-owned businesses and ethnic nonprofit organizations went there to offer basic services to the Chinese who lived there. There were few, if any, souvenir stores to attract visitors. Nor were there many upscale or luxury stores or Chinese Language and Culture after school programs for children. They were not necessary because many families still had connections to, and preferred, Manhattan's Chinatown for these services. As immigrants moved into Sunset Park in large numbers to escape rising rents in Manhattan's Chinatown, retail, garment shops, and services followed.

The ethnic enclave economy developed along 8th Avenue between 39th and 68th streets, which traces its origin to the opening of Fung Wong Supermarket owned by a Hong Kong immigrant, Tsang Sun (Sunny) Mui, in 1986 (Aloff 1997; Mustain 1997). Just when the Chinese started to move into the neighborhood, the local economy was devastated by the closing of the Brooklyn waterfront, the main source of employment for the mostly European immigrant residents. Rapid white flight accelerated the neighborhood's further decline. Real estate values plummeted, the crime rate went up, and close to 90 percent of the storefronts on 8th Avenue were vacant—making them affordable for the Chinese willing to invest (Brooklyn Chinese-American Association 2011). Walking down the avenue today, there is an unmistakable scene of thriving Chinese-owned commerce supported with investments from wealthier newer immigrants. Chinese businesses cater to the growing ethnic population's basic needs and include low-priced groceries, hair salons, herbal medicine stores, home appliance stores, as well as accounting, real estate, insurance, travel agencies, and restaurants. The neighborhood reminds many of a "place called home."

As the ethnic enclave took root in Sunset Park, nonprofit community-based organizations also emerged to serve the newcomers. The Brooklyn Chinese-American Association (BCA) was founded in 1987 as a small storefront service organization located in the heart of Sunset Park Chinatown on 50th Street and 8th Avenue. It has now become an essential support organization for the Sunset Park's Chinese. Staff members of the BCA explained that the Chinese community in Sunset Park changed over time from those who were originally from southern China and Hong Kong to the newer immigrant group from Fujian Province. The Chinese living in Brooklyn, while also able to speak Mandarin, are distinct from those of Flushing. Whereas Flushing Chinese are mostly Taiwanese or mainlanders with relatively high socioeconomic status, the coethnics in Sunset Park were primarily Cantonese and Fujianese, some of whom have the lowest income levels in the city. Fujianese immigrants who settled in Sunset Park have the least education, English proficiency, job skills, and financial resources of any of the Chinese immigrants in New York City. Furthermore, many of the early Fujianese settlers were undocumented and often arrived with heavy debt. The BCA became a crucial source of support for these immigrants who in turn were very appreciative of the BCA and other similar community organizations for understanding their complicated immigration histories and the challenges of settlement.

The Chinese-American Planning Council Brooklyn (CPC) is one of the oldest Chinese community organizations in New York City. It was established in 1966 in Manhattan's Chinatown with the Head Start program for the children of Chinese immigrants in Manhattan's old Chinatown. Only in the past twenty years has the organization branched into Flushing and Sunset Park. It opened in Sunset Park after the BCA established its presence. Like the BCA, CPC Brooklyn caters to a variety of age groups and provides essential job training, as well as children, youth, and senior services. Unlike the BCA, CPC has name recognition and an excellent reputation among many of the earlier Chinese immigrants from southern China and Taiwan, as well as from national funders. The CPC is not only better able to tap into funding sources from grant organizations or donors throughout the nation than the BCA, it is also more capable of persuading earlier immigrants who are bilingual to give back by volunteering at CPC.

Local institutions serving families and children in Sunset Park have also become increasingly Chinese. For example, 39 percent of the student population at PS 169, also known as the Sunset Park School, was Asian in the late 2000s. The Lutheran Medical Center on 55th Street and 2nd Avenue, about 15 minutes away from central Chinese Sunset Park has special language, food, and cultural services available to the Chinese community. Last but not least, Sunset Park's churches have been welcoming Chinese into their congregations. The Chinese are often the mainstays for the churches, providing membership and funds.

By the mid-1990s, housing prices started to increase in Sunset Park, but were still relatively more affordable than in Manhattan and Queens. Residents say that rents and even housing prices were half that of Queens and Manhattan in the late 1980s and early 1990s. Since the 1990s, larger scale developments have taken place in the area, including hotels and luxury apartment complexes built by Chinese developers. This type of development—not always aimed at the ethnic communities—provokes the ire of the longtime non-Hispanic white population out of the fear that their community, already changing, will also be gentrified. Speculators (including Chinese real estate developers) continue to buy land because of the development of the Bush Terminal Waterfront Park Area, making Sunset Park attractive and very livable for young non-Chinese city dwellers. Young white non-Hispanic urbanites who are being priced out of more established Brooklyn communities are the target buyers and renters, furthering the gentrification process.

Political Participation

Historically, Chinese immigrants were denied the right to become naturalized citizens and were thus indifferent to politics. Much of the political activity in Chinatowns across the nation was oriented either toward homeland politics or local neighborhood ethnic Chinese interests—such as garbage pickup, parking, and after-school and weekend Chinese language school for children. New York City had a segmented political system that was organized along ethnic lines and was used as a vehicle for the expression of ethnic interests (Waldinger and Tseng 1992). Because of their small numbers and lack of citizenship status, early immigrant Chinese were not only economically marginalized and socially isolated, they were hardly visible in local politics. In recent years, more immigrant Chinese have become naturalized citizens and have become more active in local politics than ever before.

In Flushing, immigrant Chinese formed various civic organizations serving multiethnic interests in the local community, rather than narrowly defined ethnic interests. These new ethnic organizations work with other ethnic organizations in the neighborhood to mediate intergroup misunderstandings and conflicts. They also routinely mobilize local business owners and residents to participate in productive activities such as street-cleaning campaigns, voter registration drives and lobbying the Community Board and City Hall on urgent neighborhood issues. However, the scale and the effectiveness of Chinese immigrants' participation in local politics remained limited until the new millennium. For example, in 1990, Asians made up almost one-third of Flushing's population but only 7 percent of registered voters. Councilwoman Julia Harrison was twice challenged by Asian American candidates. But, she won both elections in the 1990s, even though she was depicted as an "anti-Asian bigot," publicly referring to the influx of Asian immigrants and Asian-owned businesses as "invasion" and making a calculated effort to gather white voter support by attacking the Asian immigrant community (Dugger 1996; Lii 1996). However, the tide turned in the next few elections in the 2000s when Chinese candidates were formidable. John Liu, who was born in Taiwan and immigrated to the United States as a child won with Harrison's endorsement in 2001 after she had to give up her seat because of term limits. He became the first Asian American elected to the New York City Council. Liu joined the black caucus and the Hispanic caucus in the Council, in some ways pulled together the old Dinkins coalition and won the New York City Comptroller seat in 2009, becoming the first Asian American to win a citywide election. Until a recent campaign finance scandal broke, Liu was expected to be a leading candidate for mayor when Bloomberg's term ends. Liu was succeeded in the council by Peter Koo, who won the seat in 2010. Koo, who started his life in America working at Kentucky Fried Chicken, was an active member of Community Board 7, which represents Flushing and a few other neighborhoods. He has been called the "Mayor" of Flushing because of his active involvement in civic organizations, his accessibility to the public and philanthropic endeavors, and his leadership role in the business community, serving as the President of the Flushing Chinese Business Association. In 2008, Grace Meng, an attorney who grew up in Flushing, became the youngest Asian American ever elected to the New York State Legislature. In 2012, Meng became the first Asian American from New York to be elected to Congress.

Chinese Americans in old Chinatown have also made inroad into politics. Another Asian American "first" in the New York City political scene was the election of Hong Kong-born Margaret S. Chin (similar name but not related to the author). In 2009 she became the first Chinese American woman elected to the City Council, representing

District 1, which includes old Chinatown, where she grew up. However, in Sunset Park the actual number of Asian American voters decreased during the last two elections in the 2000s despite the fact that the Chinese population increased. Even though there are more new immigrants, they have yet to become naturalized citizens. With time Chinese Americans in Sunset Park will likely play a more active role in politics as has happened in Flushing and in old Chinatown. Overall, the growth of Chinese communities (often along with other Asian or other ethnic groups) in the outer boroughs of New York City implies a new kind of acculturation across economic, residential, community, and political spectrums.

LOS ANGELES: THE RISE OF CHINESE ETHNOBURBS

The Demographic Transformation of the San Gabriel Valley, California

The San Gabriel Valley is part of metropolitan Los Angeles. Located to the east of the City of Los Angeles, to the north of the Puente Hills, to the south of the San Gabriel Mountains, and to the west of the Inland Empire, this vast suburbia encompasses thirty-one municipalities and fourteen unincorporated communities of Los Angeles County (Conway 2003). Chinese ethnoburbs that we describe in this chapter are defined rather loosely to refer to the emerging immigrant Chinese community in the region. At the core of the development of San Gabriel Valley's Chinese ethnoburbs is Monterey Park (Fong 1994; Horton 1995). Monterey Park is an incorporated municipality with its own elected city council. From the beginning of World War II until 1960, Monterey Park prospered as the wartime economy brought new people from across the country to Southern California (Fong 1994; Horton 1995). In the decade immediately after the war, Monterey Park was one of the most affordable suburban bedroom communities—a cozy town with various single-family homes, tree-lined streets, and spacious green lawns. In the 1960s, about 85 percent of housing consisted of detached single-family homes, and 4 percent consisted of ten or more units. About two-thirds of the housing was owner-occupied and vacancy rates were about 5 percent.

Postwar Monterey Park was predominantly non-Hispanic white. But due to its suburban atmosphere and proximity to downtown Los Angeles, it began to draw upwardly mobile Mexican Americans from neighboring East Los Angeles, Japanese Americans from the Westside, and Chinese Americans from Chinatown (Fong 1994; Horton 1995). By 1960, Monterey Park's ethnic makeup was 85 percent non-Hispanic white (down from 99.9 percent in 1950), 12 percent Hispanic, 3 percent Asian, and 0.1 percent black; by 1970, it was 51 percent non-Hispanic white, 34 percent Hispanic, and 15 percent Asian (two-thirds Japanese American and one-third Chinese). Many of the Hispanic and Asian Americans arriving in Monterey Park during the 1950s and 1960s were educated, acculturated, and middle-class second- or third-generation immigrants who were driven by the American dream of upward mobility and suburban life. By 1970, Monterey Park became the first and perhaps one of the very few middle-class suburbs that were ethnically diverse, with non-Hispanic whites holding a slight majority. The process of ethnic integration was fairly smooth, since it very much conformed to the conventional model of residential assimilation. Most of the new residents were acculturated second- or third-generation members of ethnic minorities and were not perceived as a threat to existing Anglo political and institutional dominance (Horton 1995).

The arrival of immigrants and investors from Taiwan and the Pacific Rim and the influx of foreign capital that started in the 1970s and accelerated since then set off a dramatic demographic transformation in Monterey Park. By the mid-1980s, the city had been transformed from an Anglo bedroom town into a community with an Asian majority and a visible presence of immigrant Chinese. Non-Hispanic white residents declined from 51 percent in 1970 to 26 percent in 1980 and to a tiny 5 percent in 2010. In contrast, the proportion of Asian residents increased from less than 15 percent in 1970 to 56 percent in 1990, making it the first and only Asian-majority city in the United States of the time. As of 2010, Monterey Park's racial composition was 48 percent Chinese, 19 percent other Asian, 27 percent Hispanic, 5 percent white, and 0.3 percent African American. Those in the other Asian category included Japanese Americans (mostly US-born), Vietnamese, Filipinos, and other Southeast Asians. In 1980, less than one-third of the Monterey Park population was foreign-born; but the proportion increased to 54 percent by 2000 and a decade later stayed consistent. Not surprisingly, more than three-quarters (77 percent) of those in Monterey Park spoke a language other than English at home, according to the 2006–10 ACS data. Clearly, this suburban city has been transformed into an immigrant-dominant ethnoburb.

Unlike earlier Chinese immigrants who were mainly from rural regions in South China, Monterey Park's Chinese immigrants of the early 1980s were mostly from Taiwan either as investors and entrepreneurs or as professionals (Tseng 1994). Once the Chinese community took shape, family migration and migration from mainland China, Hong Kong, and Southeast Asia followed. By the mid-1980s, the number of mainland Chinese immigrants surpassed that of the Taiwanese. Yet, the visibility of Taiwanese money, Taiwanese-owned businesses, and Taiwanese involvement in local politics earned Monterey Park the nickname, "Little Taipei," with which both Taiwanese and mainlanders were identified.

What made Taiwanese immigrants in Monterey Park distinct was that they were disproportionately high skilled and capital-rich, and many of them obtained immigration visas through direct investment or employment either by Chinese-owned businesses or mainstream American businesses. According to 2006–10 ACS data, the Chinese were more highly skilled than Los Angeles County's population: nearly half of the adult Chinese population completed at least four years of college (31 percent bachelor's degree and 18 percent advanced graduate degrees), compared to 29 percent countywide; and 40 percent of them held professional occupations, compared to 35 percent countywide. A telephone survey of Chinese business owners in Los Angeles also showed that Chinese immigrant entrepreneurs had much higher levels of educational attainment than other immigrant entrepreneurs—88 percent respondents reported having earned four years or more of college education, compared to 35 percent of white male business owners. Moreover, Chinese immigrant business owners were nearly twice as likely as Korean business owners (who are known for their propensity for entrepreneurship) to be members of the business-owner class prior to migration

(43 percent versus 24 percent), and some of these entrepreneurs continued to run their businesses in the homeland after migration, or became transnational (Li 1998b; Tseng 1994; Yoon 1991, 303–31). This selective group of entrepreneurs were not only highly educated with entrepreneurial expertise and skills but also had extensive homeland and transnational business ties that had been established prior to their arrival in the United States, which were further strengthened through their homeland or transnational businesses and their frequent visits to the homeland (Tseng 1994).

Another distinct characteristic of Monterey Park's Chinese immigrants was the visibility of transnational migrants. In contrast to the traditional male sojourner who left his family behind to find riches in America, a new group of Chinese transnationals—"spacemen" as the media calls them—settled their wives and children in Monterey Park while shuttling back and forth between both sides of the Pacific Ocean. And in other cases, the children—known as "parachute kids"—were left in the United States alone to attain education in the United States while both their parents remained in Asia (Fong 1994; M. Zhou 1998; Zhou 2009). Instead of moving from immigrant enclaves like other native-born Latino or Asian Americans, the new Chinese immigrants inserted themselves directly into the middle-class suburb without much acculturation.

As more Chinese immigrants put down their roots in Monterey Park, newer arrivals started to settle in adjacent suburban communities, such as Alhambra, Rosemead, San Gabriel, and Temple City, and branched out north to more affluent suburbs such as Arcadia and San Marino, and southeast to Diamond Bar. Figure 13.2 maps the spatial distribution of Chinese Americans for Los Angeles County at the census tract level. Patterns of Chinese American settlement generally reflect the duality of concentration and dispersal. These patterns are distinct insofar as the ethnic population has grown beyond the boundaries of the central city and has become increasingly concentrated in multiple locations that expand eastward into the San Gabriel Valley. As table 13.1 shows, Chinese settlement is most concentrated in Monterey Park, San Marino, Arcadia, San Gabriel, Alhambra, Rosemead, Temple City, and as far southeast as Hacienda Heights, Rowland Heights, Walnut, and Diamond Bar.

Comprising less than 4 percent of Los Angeles County's total population, Chinese Americans are overrepresented in many suburban cities in the San Gabriel Valley even though none of these cities have a Chinese majority. As shown in table 13.1, there are thirteen cities with over 10,000 people in the United States in which the share of the ethnic Chinese population is 20 percent or more. All these cities are in California and all but two are in Los Angeles's San Gabriel Valley.[2] Except for Los Angeles and San Francisco, all the cities listed in table 13.1 can be considered typical ethnoburbs, which were barely visible before 1980. Another marked characteristic of the ethnoburb is its ethnic plurality, in which non-Hispanic whites are a numerical minority.[3]

The Development of the Ethnic Enclave Economy in the San Gabriel Valley

Contemporary Chinese immigration has driven much of the demographic transformation in these Los Angeles suburbs. Prior to 1970, only a few small specialty

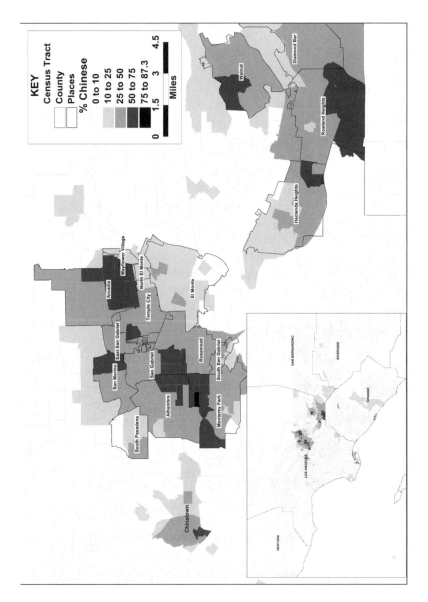

Figure 13.2

Percent Chinese in Los Angeles Region and in Areas of High Concentration (All Chinese or Taiwanese)

Source: Andrew A. Beveridge based upon 2010 Census Data and Boundaries.

Table 13.1 ALL CITIES/PLACES IN THE UNITED STATES WITH OVER 10,000 PEOPLE
WHERE THE CHINESE POPULATION IS 20% OR MORE

Census Places	Total Population N	Non-Hispanic White %	Asian %	Chinese %	Median Household Income ($)[a]
Los Angeles County[b]	9,758,256	28	14	4	55,476
Los Angeles City[b]	3,772,486	29	11	2	49,138
San Francisco	789,172	42	33	21	71,304
Monterey Park	60,176	5	66	44	52,159
San Marino	13,114	38	51	35	154,962
Arcadia	55,704	27	57	41	77,024
San Gabriel	39,670	12	58	39	56,720
Alhambra	83,389	11	52	37	51,527
Rosemead	53,670	6	60	34	46,706
Temple City	35,222	22	56	40	65,668
Rowland Heights[c]	51,566	11	57	33	68,645
Walnut	29,327	14	62	33	100,182
Hacienda Heights	53,639	18	37	24	69,501
Diamond Bar	55,701	24	52	23	87,216
Cupertino	56,498	33	58	26	120,201

Source: Andrew Beveridge, from 2006–2010 American Community Survey.
[a] In 2010 inflation adjusted dollars.
[b] Included for comparison.
[c] Rowland Heights is not a city but a Census-designated "Place."

shops, supermarkets, and restaurants dominated commercial activities in Monterey Park. At night, streets were quiet as residents retired into their comfortable homes. A former police chief recalled, "You could shoot a cannon off at Atlantic and Garvey [one of the main intersections], and it could fly through the air and roll to a stop without hitting a soul" (quoted in Arax 1987). Today, Chinese-owned office buildings and mini-malls have replaced this bedroom community's commercial core with a cosmopolitan hub of the Asian Pacific. Various Chinese-owned businesses line up along the main streets with Chinese language signs. The vibrant commercial center expands block after block and is active from early morning until late at night, seven days a week. As a resident recalled, "at 3:30 in the morning … I counted 34 cars stopped at a red light at Atlantic and Garvey. It looked like rush hour" (Arax 1987). While many Chinese-owned businesses still resemble those in Chinatowns—such as "mom and pop" or "husband-wife" family-run restaurants, gift shops, and food stores, newly sprung-up business establishments are bigger, more diverse, and modern, much like those in mainstream economies in the United States and in Asia.

During the early period of economic transformation, real estate development was perhaps the most significant economic activity in Monterey Park. In the 1980s, rampant and speculative land development all over Southern California turned many small bedroom towns into cities with high-density commercial and residential overdevelopment. Monterey Park was simply part of the trend. What made it different, however, was that the economic boom had an Asian face and responded mainly to the demands of coethnic transnationals and immigrants.

The arrival of many Taiwanese investors, realtors, developers, and entrepreneurs, and later the mainland Chinese "nouveau riche," played a crucial role in reinvigorating a formerly inactive economy and boosting real estate values. In the 1970s, transnational investors and immigrant entrepreneurs from Taiwan invested in Monterey Park because of its growth potential and its convenient location—accessibility to Chinatown and to the Pacific Rim. By the late 1970s, 30 percent of the city's business licenses were registered under Asian names (Fong 1994, 50). The pace of foreign capital flows accelerated in the following decade as Hong Kong, China, and Southeast Asia started to transfer capital to the United States. Lots that were vacant in the 1970s were built up and old bungalows were torn down to make room for commercial or mixed-use real estate developments. By the 1980s, the price of land skyrocketed. Many lots for commercial development sold at $40 to $50 per square foot, much higher than $8 to $10 a square foot that supermarkets or department stores could afford to pay during that time. With these inflated prices, developers had to recoup their costs through intensive development—huge, luxurious single-family homes were built on joint lots alongside multiple-family apartments, condominiums, high-density office buildings, and mini-malls. The number of housing units in Monterey Park jumped from 12,833 in 1960 to 19,331 in 1980 and 20,209 in 2000, and again to 20,549 in 2009, representing a 60 percent increase from 1960 to 2009. The proportion of multiunit apartments (ten units or more) also jumped from 5 percent in 1960 to 16 percent in 2009. According to reports from a leading business real estate company in the region, 60 percent of 1989's shopping and retailing property transactions in the San Gabriel Valley was by Chinese investors, and 50 percent of the warehouse purchases in the San Gabriel Valley in 1991 were Chinese-related. Upscale strip malls now line the main streets of Monterey Park.

The newest project is the Atlantic Times Square in Monterey Park developed by Arcadia-based Kam Sang Company, Inc. It rose on seven acres of land at the heart of Monterey Park just off the Interstate 10 and was completed in 2010. This multiuse complex includes 210 condo units (selling for $350–400 per square foot), a fourteen-screen movie theater, a 24-hour fitness center, and 200,000 square feet of retail, offering a variety of cosmopolitan choices in shopping, dining, and entertainment in a relaxing Mediterranean style atmosphere (City of Monterey Park 2011; LA Curbed 2010).

The constant flow of foreign capital toward real estate and land development stimulated tremendous demand for residential and commercial space, not only from Chinese immigrants already in the United States but also from potential immigrants abroad. In the 1980s, local real estate brokers and developers rushed to capitalize on the highly specialized immigrant market and promoted Monterey Park as the "Chinese Beverly Hills" and "a Mecca for Chinese businesses" in Asia (Eljera 1996; Tseng 1994). For example, a brochure promoting Monterey Park in Taiwan read: "In Monterey Park, you can enjoy the American life quality and Taipei's convenience at the same time" (Tseng 1994, 44). Soon after the establishment of the "Little Taipei" in Monterey Park, the Taiwanese quickly dispersed to neighboring cities. Referred to as the "Taiwan Syndrome," enterprising Taiwanese investors purchased commercial properties and homes in the San Gabriel Valley in order to sell them later to wealthy newcomers from Taiwan (Wong 1989).

Since the mid-1990s, foreign capital from mainland China began pouring into the region, helping to jumpstart California out of a recession. According to the US Citizenship and Immigration Services, China ranked number one in 2010 in EB-5 visas, which are for immigrant investors who invest at least $500,000 and create at least ten jobs. A 2010 survey conducted in China showed that among individuals who had over $15 million investable funds in mainland China, 27 percent had secured investor visas from developed countries, and 47 percent were considering doing so. In addition to the growing number of import-export businesses and real estate investments from mainland China, economic development in the region also attracts tourist dollars from China. Thousands of business people, government officials, and students of all ages from China visit the area: some snap pictures of Monterey Park officials on the steps of City Hall, others check out local industrial sites and swap business cards while spending money at stores, restaurants, hotels, and local tour companies, and still others use Monterey Park as a base to explore schools and educational opportunities for their children.

Foreign investments in real estate and local businesses are evidence of a willingness to participate in US life and thus help in the immigration process. Many investors and entrepreneurs were even willing to take losses to attain immigrant visas, or nonimmigrant visas that could later be adjusted to permanent residency (Tseng 1994). Consequently, Monterey Park evolved into a commercial and banking hub for transnational businesses and an economic center for producer, retail, and professional services for local Chinese businesses from an even bigger Chinese community that has rapidly spilled over into San Marino, Arcadia, South Pasadena, and throughout the San Gabriel Valley (Li 1998a; Li et al. 2002; Y. Zhou 1998). Potential emigrants in Taiwan, Hong Kong, and mainland China were attracted to Monterey Park and its neighboring areas due to the availability of new and affordable homes and a business environment favorable for local development, as well as transnational ventures.

The proliferation of real estate and commercial developments in Monterey Park and other suburbs in the San Gabriel Valley mirror a new trend of sprawling Chinese immigrant settlement in Los Angeles. In the early 1980s, about one-third of all Chinese businesses in the Los Angeles metropolitan area listed in the Chinese language telephone directories were located in Chinatown and another third in the San Gabriel Valley. As of 1992, there were more than 11,000 Chinese-owned firms in Los Angeles listed in the Chinese language telephone directories; only 6 percent were located in Chinatown, whereas about 12 percent were located in Monterey Park and another third in neighboring cities in the San Gabriel Valley (Light 2006; Tseng 1994). Now in Los Angeles, two main Chinese telephone directories—the *Southern California Chinese Consumer Yellow Pages* (four-inch thick, 2,700 pages) and the *Chinese Yellow Pages, Southern California* (two-inch thick, 1,500 pages)—are updated annually and circulated in Chinatown and the sprawling Chinese ethnoburbs in the San Gabriel Valley.

Like businesses in Chinatown, many businesses in the Chinese ethnoburb continue to concentrate in niches characterized by low entry barriers or those markets left-over by the larger economy. Unlike Chinatown, however, the Chinese ethnoburb also concentrates a wider and more diverse range of businesses of much larger sizes and scales, and creates new economic niches that are not commonly found in Chinatown. Typical Chinatown businesses—restaurants, eateries, groceries, gift shops, herbal stores, and garment factories—have been replaced by a large spectrum of upscale restaurants, trendy cafes and coffee houses, huge supermarkets, multifunction shopping centers, and professional parks. New economic niches emerge that require either much larger startup capital or much higher human capital, such as in printing and publishing, high-tech manufacturing in computer hardware and software and in biotechnology; commercial equipment wholesale, real estate, banking, security and commodity brokerage, hotels and motels, data processing; and financial, account-ing, advertising, medical, and engineering services. To a varying degree, the Chinese enclave economy in San Gabriel Valley resembles some of the key characteristics of both primary and secondary sectors of the mainstream economy.

Social Development in the Chinese Ethnoburb

The ethnic enclave economy requires not only a sizeable coethnic entrepreneurial class but also a geographical core. San Gabriel's Chinese ethnoburb, despite its sprawl, serves to anchor the community where a wide variety of ethnic social organizations emerge side by side with ethnic businesses.

Nonprofit social service organizations are the most visible of these new ethnic organizations. Run by educated immigrants for the children of immigrants, these organizations provide community cultural centers, cultural programs in public librar-ies, history projects, English classes, job training centers, employment referral ser-vices, health clinics, youth programs, daycare centers, as well as welfare, housing, legal, and family counseling services. Unlike the traditional organizational structure of old Chinatown, which was hierarchical and paternalistic, these new ethnic social organizations tend to be horizontal and democratic and serve specialized functions (Zhou and Kim 2001). Unlike members of the old ethnic elite, who, as "cultural man-agers," supported traditional Chinese culture, ethnic identity, self-determination, and the status quo in Chinatown (Fong 1994), the leaders of the new social service organizations are more concerned about the general well-being of the large, ethni-cally diverse community. The latter group of leaders is interested in interethnic rela-tions, citizen and immigrant rights, civic duties, and equality.

Also visible in Los Angeles's Chinese ethnoburbs are Chinese language schools and ethnic institutions serving young children and youth (Zhou and Kim 2006). Chinese schools have been an integral part of the organizational structure of the immigrant Chinese community in the United States, as well as in the Chinese Diaspora world-wide. In much of the pre–World War II era, Chinese schools aimed to preserve lan-guage and cultural heritage in the second and succeeding generations. Since the 1980s, these ethnic language schools have evolved, serving a much broader range of functions. In addition to language and cultural classes, contemporary Chinese schools offer K–12 children a variety of academic and enrichment courses and extracurricular activities, ranging from Chinese music, folk dance, calligraphy, calculation with an abacus, ping-pong, SAT-II (Chinese) preparation courses to academic tutoring (Fong 2003). Most schools are registered as nonprofit organizations and rely on parental volunteerism and fundraising from the ethnic community. Parental involvement is much more intense than that in public schools; many parents volunteer to serve as principals and/or administrative officials and teaching assistants (Fong 2003; Wang 1996; Zhou and Li 2003).

The development of Chinese schools has also paralleled the development of private supplementary educational institutions since the late 1980s, such as *buxiban* (academic tutoring), early childhood educational programs, and college preparatory centers. For example, driving through the commercial corridor on Valley Boulevard from Monterey Park to Rosemead, a visitor may easily see flashy bilingual signs of establishments such as "Little Harvard," "Ivy League School," "Little Ph.D.," "Early Learning Center," "Brain Child" (a math and English pre-school), "Stanford-to-Be Prep School," "IQ180," and "Hope *Buxiban*." The core curricula of these various ethnic institutions supplement, rather than compete with, public school education. The *2010 Southern California Chinese Consumer Yellow Pages* listed ninety Chinese schools (sixty-four were located in the San Gabriel Valley's Chinese ethnoburbs).

Other spatially rooted new ethnic organizations include religious organizations of all sorts, from Protestant and Catholic churches to Buddhist, Taoist, and other folk religious temples and houses of worship. For example, Hsi Lai Temple, a grandiose temple in classical Chinese architectural style, was built in 1988 by a Taiwanese Buddhist organization. Situated in the foothills of Hacienda Heights, the temple is the largest Buddhist temple in North America, offering Dharma services and performing Dharma functions and rituals regularly. But the temple is much more than a religious center. It houses a university with academic degree programs—Bachelor of Arts and Master of Arts in Buddhist studies and in comparative religious studies, and a Master of Business Administration program, as well as secular programs, on a wide range of topics, including education, immigration, marriage and family, taxation, and legal issues. It serves as a popular site for school field trips, business trips, organization meetings, and interreligious dialogue and visitors of all kinds.

Last but not least, ethnic political and civil rights organizations can be found in the Chinese ethnoburbs. Most of these organizations are run by second-generation Chinese immigrants who came of age in the late 1960s and formed the core of the Asian American movement on college campuses on the West Coast. Inspired by the civil rights movements, these political organizations are concerned primarily with civil rights issues, particularly those relating to minority and immigrant rights, representation in the mainstream economy and politics, and intergroup relations. In effect, these ethnic political organizations have brought ethnic group members to the norms and standards of the mainstream civil society and further strengthened Chinese Americans' political power base (Toyota 2009).

Political Participation

Because many suburban communities are independent municipalities, the concentration of ethnic populations makes it possible for powerful voting blocs to form and for coethnic members or those who are sensitive to immigrant and ethnic minority issues to get elected. These possibilities, in turn, promote meaningful political participation, even among first-generation immigrants.

Monterey Park is a case in point. Monterey Park is an independent municipality. From the 1940s to the mid-1970s, politics in Monterey Park was dominated by an "old-boy network"—a local power structure consisting of predominantly white Republican professionals and businessmen. This power structure was challenged by the arrival of Japanese Americans and Mexican Americans in the 1950s and 1960s and the unprecedented arrival of Asian immigrants, mainly Chinese, during the mid-1970s and 1980s (Horton 1995). While some Democrats were willing to adapt the previously white institutions to suit new immigrants and minorities, others sided with conservatives against the Chinese newcomers and their ethnic community development. When immigrants with strong economic resources form a numerical majority, however, city politicians cannot ignore them. The growth of Chinese immigrants and the dominance of Chinese businesses tipped the power balance and transformed local politics into the politics of diversity (Horton 1995).

The shrinking non-Hispanic white population, along with the decreasing influence of the old white conservative elite, has created an opportunity for young multiethnic businesspersons, minorities, immigrants, women, multiculturalists, and nativists to engage in politics, opening up a new political order in Monterey Park (Horton 1995). In 1983 when Lily Lee Chen, a Chinese American, was inaugurated as the first Chinese American mayor, Monterey Park's five-member city council became truly multiethnic with one white member, two Mexican Americans, one Filipino American, and one Chinese American.[4] *Time Magazine* featured this "majority minority" city council as representative of multiculturalism and as a "successful suburban melting pot." However, growing resentment against demographic, cultural, and economic changes relating to the Chinese newcomers soon swept the minority incumbents out of office. In 1986, three of the city council members were replaced by long-established white residents, returning the city council to white control in pursuit of anti-immigrant campaigns and the defense of Americanism under the slogan: "English, the family, God, the nation, and the neighborhood" (Horton 1995, 108).

Backlash against the ethnic politics in Monterey Park of the mid-1980s, however, was short-lived as more immigrant Chinese became naturalized citizens and mobilized politically. Since 1988, Monterey Park's City Council has had a Chinese American presence. Judy Chu, a second-generation Chinese American, was elected to the city council from 1988 to 2001. Others such as Samuel Kiang, David Lau, Betty Tom Chu, and Mike Eng have served or are currently serving as city council members. Betty Tom Chu served as mayor in 2006, followed by David Lau (2007–08), Mitchell Ing (2009–10); and Anthony Wong is serving as the current mayor. The election of these candidates indicates the greater political maturity of this community's Chinese immigrants, who have used their increasing demographic presence and economic power to challenge traditional Anglo domination of the city council.

The electoral success of the Chinese immigrant community reaffirms the democratic message that every vote counts, which in turn empowers Chinese immigrants, nurtures a greater sense of civic duty, and facilitates their incorporation into the American polity. Today, the Asian constituency extends beyond Monterey Park to other cities in the San Gabriel Valley. In 1995, Joaquin Lim was elected to the Walnut City Council in 1995 and became mayor of the city in 1999. In 1997, Wen P. Chang, a Taiwan-born businessman, became the first person of Chinese descent to be elected to the Diamond Bar City Council, served as mayor the following year, and was reelected for two consecutive terms. In 2001, Ben Wong became mayor of West Covina. In 2002, John Wuo was elected to the Arcadia City Council and served as mayor in 2005. In 2003, Judy S. Wong, a Taiwan-born community activist, was elected to the city council of Temple City, and is the first Chinese American member to be elected to that body. In 2004, Mike Ten became mayor of South Pasadena. In 2005, Matthew Lin, became the first Chinese American mayor of San Marino. In 2006, Chi Mui, a China-born businesswoman, was sworn in as San Gabriel City's first Asian and first Chinese American mayor. In the same year, Joaquin Lim was reelected as mayor of Walnut City and Mary W. Su was elected to the Walnut City Council. At present, Chinese Americans have been elected to boards of Alhambra Unified School District (USD), Arcadia USD, Garvey USD, Hacienda-La Puente USD, Montebello USD, Rowland USD, San Marino USD, and South Pasadena USD. Most significantly, Judy Chu was elected in 2001 to the California legislature's 49th Assembly District by multiethnic support, representing Monterey Park, Alhambra, Rosemead, San Gabriel, San Marino, El Monte, and South El Monte in the San Gabriel Valley. Mike Eng was elected to succeed Chu in representing the 49th Assembly District in 2006.[5] In July 2009, Judy Chu was elected to the US House of Representatives for California's 32nd District, becoming the first Asian American Congresswoman.

GROWING CLASS DIVERSITY

Another demographic change is starting in these ethnoburbs. Over time, the pioneer settlers send for their relatives, who may not be as resourceful or wealthy. Many family-sponsored immigrants, especially from mainland China, are of urban working class or rural backgrounds and most lack English language proficiency and transferable job skills. For example, the new immigrants who have come to Monterey Park to join their families include many uneducated, low-skilled workers; they are drawn to Monterey Park because they can easily find housing through relatives and friends and because their labor is needed by the expanding ethnic community. As a result of intertwined ethnic ties, the Chinese populations in the outer boroughs of New York City and the San Gabriel Valley have become more socioeconomically diverse.

Intraethnic class diversity has implications for both immigrants and natives. For Chinese immigrants, it means greater social service burdens and a high risk of bearing a dual stigma—foreigner and poor. As a way to avoid association with working-class coethnics, the more affluent Chinese immigrants follow the pattern of outmigration, a phenomenon resembling white flight. Several immigrant Chinese business owners told us in interviews that they had moved out of Monterey Park to avoid "overcrowd-ing," "gangs in schools," and "unsafe streets." Some newcomers express a reluctance even to settle in Monterey Park. In both Flushing and Monterey Park some estab-lished Chinese voice the fear that these places are turning into traditional Chinatowns or microcosms of Taipei, Shanghai, or Hong Kong—overcrowded and congested.

In New York City, some well-off Chinese homebuyers are avoiding Sunset Park to move into another area in Brooklyn that is a bit more upscale without too many vis-ible signs of an ethnic community. Interestingly, these antipathies toward congestion and too many poor Chinese mirror those of established non-Chinese residents. For natives, the influx of working-class immigrants would mean a disruption of middle-class lifestyles and the threat of importing inner-city social problems.

CONCLUSIONS

Often middle-class immigrant Chinese communities are growing very rapidly and vis-ibly not only in New York and Los Angeles but also in other immigrant destinations in the United States and Canada. In Flushing, Sunset Park, and Monterey Park, resi-dential patterns of ethnic succession are quite distinct from those of the past. Rather than a racial/ethnic minority group that brings down the average economic level of the local populace, they involve an incoming ethnic group with often strong human capital and ample economic resources that has the capability of creating its own eth-nic economy and investing in the community. Like old Chinatowns, new middle-class immigrant communities serve the unmet needs of new arrivals. They provide oppor-tunities for self-employment and employment. But unlike old Chinatowns, they are better connected to the outside world, globally linked on economic, social, and polit-ical terms. Newer Chinese communities tend to maintain extensive cultural, social, and economic ties to the homelands. However, transnational ties no longer facilitate eventual return to the homeland but emerge as an alternative mode of incorporation into mainstream American society.

Flushing, Sunset Park, and Monterey Park can all be referred to as global enclaves—multiethnic and transnational—but they nonetheless show some signifi-cant differences. Flushing is global in terms of diverse Asian and immigrant origins, as well as the presence of all major racial minority groups. Sunset Park is global in the number of Chinese from all around China and the Chinese Diaspora, and for foreign-born Hispanics of diverse national origins. The natives are either whites or blacks. Monterey Park is diverse in a different sense. The immigrants are overwhelm-ingly Chinese from different sending sources.

Interestingly, Flushing, and Monterey Park differ in the kind of residential mobility that each stimulates. Monterey Park originally served as a relatively permanent place of settlement for middle-class immigrant Chinese. Even though secondary migra-tion is occurring, the community still serves as the most important center for the ethnic economy and for settling immigrants. Most of the residential out-movement from Monterey Park does not seem to be associated with the quest for significant improvement in socioeconomic status. Flushing, by contrast, has always served as a staging place, channeling the out-movement of socioeconomically mobile Chinese immigrants to more affluent suburbs.

These newer Chinese communities in New York and Los Angeles have become increasingly multiethnic, unlikely to be dominated by a single national-origin group. Diversity at the local level has made intraethnic and interethnic relations key community issues. Among coethnic members, the mixing of coethnics from different class backgrounds gives the community the power and vitality to combat social problems associated with ghettoization and social isolation plaguing the inner city, but simultaneously turns the place into another type of "staging place" for the more affluent immigrants. Living side by side with other ethnic group members not only provides an opportunity for intimate social contact but also garners potential tension. Flushing has not witnessed any explosive ethnic tensions. But when conflicts do surface, Flushing and Sunset Park's multiethnic immigrant groups may have relatively little solidarity to mobilize politically because the power of ethnic immigrants is fragmented in New York's municipal politics. In contrast, conflicts are much more overt in Monterey Park, often focusing on growth control movements and pro-official English resolutions, but ethnic mobilization seems more effective because native-born Latino and Asian Americans tend to align with immigrant Chinese to act on racial issues in a city where minority groups form the numerical majority.

What will be the pattern of assimilation for those Chinese immigrants who enjoy suburban living and associated middle-class privileges—will they assimilate into the host society or change American suburbs and suburban cities to accommodate their cultural needs? Tracing the development of Chinese immigrant settlement, we have seen that long-standing immigrant enclaves in the inner city absorbed the sheer numbers and successive waves of immigrants fairly smoothly, and with largely salutary results and that there are few substantive regional variations. In suburbia (or the outer boroughs in the case of New York), however, complacent "bedroom" communities have experienced widespread in-migration and rapid economic growth, tipping the suburban balance of power and raising nativist anxiety. In Flushing, Sunset Park, and Monterey Park, immigrants from Asia can cause uneasiness and anxiety among natives or long-established residents of different ethnicities. Despite their often high socioeconomic standing, contribution to the local economy, and adaptive attitude to the host society, they can pose a different kind of threat, one that undermines natives' sense of place, identity, and the notion of "Americanness." As immigration continues into the twenty-first century with its long-lasting impacts on American cities, a reconceptualization of neighborhood change and residential mobility is much needed.

NOTES

1. The term "satellite Chinatowns" originally referred to new Chinese enclaves in outer boroughs of New York City in the 1980s. The term "ethnoburb," coined by Wei Li (1998), was widely used to refer to the development suburban ethnic enclaves.

2. Diamond Bar is adjacent to San Gabriel Valley and may be more appropriately considered to be a Pomona Valley city.
3. All cities in table 13.1 are Asian-majority cities except for Los Angeles City, San Francisco, and Hacienda Heights. Not listed in table 13.1 are four other Asian-majority cities in the United States—Cerritos (58 percent) in LA County, Daly City (51 percent) and Milpitas (52 percent) in the San Francisco Bay Area, and Honolulu City (56 percent) in Hawaii. In 1990, only Monterey Park and Daly City had an Asian majority in the United States.
4. Mayors are not elected in Monterey Park. Instead, council members become mayors for nine months on a rotating basis. So the Chinese American council member is also Lily Lee Chen.
5. Dr. Judy Chu stepped down as California Assemblywoman in 2006 because of the term limit. She was elected as a board member, representing California Board of Equalization's Fourth District afterward.

PART FIVE

Planning and Environmentalism

CHAPTER 14

Planning Los Angeles

The Changing Politics of Neighborhood
and Downtown Development

ANDREW DEENER, STEVEN P. ERIE,
VLADIMIR KOGAN, AND
FORREST STUART

For most of the twentieth century, the central plotlines of growth and development policy in Los Angeles were shaped by two sets of actors—the city's business leaders and its entrepreneurial public sector bureaucrats. The region's business
elites—in particular, powerful land developers, business organizations, and the owners of the *Los Angeles Times*—provided the impetus for expansionary development.
However, it was the local public sector, with access to key governmental powers and
plentiful public capital and bonding capacity, that produced and directed the transformation of Los Angeles into the second most populous city in the country and
one of the world's leading trade hubs. By offering outlying areas access to subsidized
water, for example, the city's Department of Water and Power catalyzed continued
geographic expansion of the city's territorial boundaries through annexation (Erie
2006). Equally powerful proprietary departments overseeing Los Angeles's ports and
airports built one of the world's greatest trade-transportation complexes (Erie 2004).
Together, the partnership between the business sector and the city's bureaucratic
machines served as the basis for a strong pro-growth regime that has dominated city
politics during most of the modern era.

Beginning in the 1960s, the growth coalition turned its gaze inward, focusing
on efforts to revitalize Los Angeles's urban core that had been devastated by the
social and economic forces that continued to push white middle-class families to the
suburbs. To oversee the revival of downtown, the city called on another potent and
largely autonomous bureaucracy, the Community Redevelopment Agency (CRA),
which took the lead in coordinating and financing urban renewal efforts downtown.
Despite the CRA's record of accomplishments—including agency efforts to revitalize

the Bunker Hill area that resulted in a fortyfold increase in property values over the course of four decades, and its successful investment in the broader downtown commercial district (Marks 2004)—the political consensus in favor of urban growth began to fray by the mid-1980s.

Increasingly, middle-class homeowners came to resent the indifference of public officials toward growing congestion, environmental degradation, and general quality-of-life concerns that accompanied the continued intensification of land-use, particularly dense residential and commercial development (Fulton 2001; Purcell 1997, 2000). By teaming up with environmentalists and suburban business owners, well-organized homeowners' associations formed the basis for a new slow-growth political coalition that eventually succeeded in displacing the growth machine as the dominant force in city politics (Davis 1990; Fulton 2001; Sonenshein 1994). In one of its first acts, the slow-growth coalition and supportive elected officials took steps to neuter the CRA, which had come to embody the increasingly unpopular forces of development. Using the threat of San Fernando Valley secession, growth opponents pushed for greater public oversight and input in development decisions, leading to the creation of new local participatory bodies as part of the late-1990s city charter reforms.

In this chapter, we survey the political, institutional, and economic evolution that has accompanied the dramatic changes in Los Angeles's planning and development policy over the past two decades, both in the neighborhood periphery and the downtown core. The creation of neighborhood councils in 2000 as part of a new voter-approved city charter provided an institutional mechanism for local groups to participate in shaping their communities. Although neighborhood councils received few formal powers and were designed primarily to serve in an advisory capacity, the councils came to serve as effective institutional focal points and "fire alarms" for mobilizing constituencies that opposed continued development in their neighborhoods. While homeowners' associations saw neighborhood councils as vehicles to limit development and preserve quality of life, liberal activists saw them as a means for democratic participation involving the interests of all residents, not just homeowners, in local land-use decisions. These competing interests crystallized in vigorous and emotional battles to win control over the new councils. Nowhere was this conflict between competing visions of local participation more evident than in the racially, ethnically, and socioeconomically diverse beach community of Venice, which has a strong progressive tradition. We examine the Venice Neighborhood Council's experience in the historical context of shifting battles between local groups with different visions of community, development, and public space.

Perhaps most surprisingly, the dramatic weakening of the CRA has done little to slow downtown's economic revival. Filling the void, private developers have spearheaded the $12.2 billion building boom known as the Downtown Renaissance that has, by one estimate, produced 174,000 new jobs and tens of millions of dollars in new tax revenues (Downtown Center Business Improvement District 2006). Indeed, since the late 1990s, the three-mile downtown core—bounded by the Santa Ana Freeway (Route 101) on the north and east, the Harbor Freeway (Route 110) on the west, and the Santa Monica Freeway (Interstate 10) on the south—has been flooded by new development anchored by more than thirty largely privately-financed civic and cultural projects, including the iconic Staples Center, Los Angeles Cathedral, and Disney Concert Hall.

Despite continued downtown revitalization, the political dynamics of Los Angeles's redevelopment have been fundamentally altered. The city's once-powerful public bureaucracy has clearly become a junior partner in the growth coalition, ceding leadership and initiative to the private sector. For example, in 2010, when the Anschutz Entertainment Group, a large sporting and music entertainment conglomerate, announced plans to build another major sports complex consisting of a new retractable-roof football stadium on 15 acres of city-owned land next to the LA Live entertainment complex and the Staples Center, it was the company rather than the city that began to solicit design proposals and pick the architect for the project (Hawthorne 2010). The emerging dominance of private developers in setting the agenda for downtown redevelopment has been one of the great ironies produced by Los Angeles's recent era of political and institutional reforms. Designed to increase the responsiveness of previously insulated bureaucrats and to encourage participation among residents, efforts to increase political oversight of the CRA and decentralize responsibility over land-use and planning functions have worked to limit the discretion of democratically accountable municipal leaders over major decisions shaping downtown.

We examine the Downtown Renaissance and megaprojects in the context of the changing politics and institutions of Los Angeles's planning and development. We also consider the use of police power in the arsenal of pro-growth public policies. As part of downtown revitalization, there has been a major effort to clean up Skid Row, widely known as the "Homeless Capital of America" (Zavis 2010). Here, the Los Angeles Police Department (LAPD), rather than the CRA, has been the major public actor involved in a containment strategy for the city's large homeless population.

THE CHANGING POLITICS OF PLANNING AND DEVELOPMENT

In 1900, the City of Los Angeles was home to just over 102,000 residents, making it the 36th largest city in the country. Yet by 1960, it had grown more than twenty-four-fold to just under 2.5 million residents, a number behind only New York and Chicago. The population explosion was accompanied by continued geographic expansion. As developers constructed more and more houses to accommodate the growing numbers of Angelenos, the city's physical boundaries continued to stretch outward. Between 1910 and 1920, the municipality's total land area grew from 99 square miles to nearly 366 square miles, making it the geographically largest city in the United States. By 1960, Los Angeles's land area exceeded 450 square miles.

As in many other cities, the rise of the suburbs—aided by federal subsidies for highway construction and mortgage interest deductions and accelerated by the 1965 Watts Riot—had a devastating effect on downtown (Frieden and Sagalyn 1991).

With people, businesses, and investments fleeing the city's commercial core, downtown became increasingly shabby. Mounting urban decay attracted attention from the city's business and political leaders, who established the CRA in 1948 for the purpose of reversing the decline of Bunker Hill, a previously upscale neighborhood in the heart of Los Angeles's downtown business district that by the 1940s had become one of the most dangerous and rundown areas in the city.

Under California's redevelopment law, the agency received unusually expansive public powers, making it an ideal public-sector partner to oversee a revitalization of downtown (Marks 2004). First, the law gave the agency the power to acquire property forcefully, if necessary, through eminent domain. Once acquired, the property could be developed by the CRA or sold to private developers through private negotiations, with the agency exempted from the city's competitive-bidding requirements. Finally, the CRA was also vested with authority to regulate land use and development within geographically defined project areas and to allow developers to exceed existing density limits, usurping discretion previously exercised by the City Council.

Most importantly, in the mid-1970s, amendments to state law gave the CRA the power to collect property taxes, freeing the agency from the rough and tumble of the annual budget process. Under the new tax-increment financing system, property tax receipts within a redevelopment area were frozen at their current levels at the time of the creation of the project area. Over time, as public investments brought about urban renewal, growing property values would lead to increased property taxes. Most of these new tax proceeds above the amount collected when the area was created would be diverted to the CRA. Securitizing these expected future earnings, the agency could sell bonds to provide the initial capital needed to invest in decrepit areas. Armed with broad land-use powers and a dedicated revenue stream, and governed by an appointed board of commissioners, the CRA was, by design, insulated from direct control by elected officials and thus freed from burdensome political meddling (Marks 2004).

The 1973 mayoral election brought a strong supporter of downtown redevelopment to the city's most visible public office. Although business leaders were initially wary of the new black mayor, Tom Bradley, the former city councilman who unseated incumbent Sam Yorty and was elected with strong support from blacks and liberal Jewish voters, they quickly embraced him as one of their own (Sonenshein 1994). Over the course of the next decade, Bradley, the CRA, and business elites would form the three pillars of a strong pro-growth regime. In 1975, Bradley began to implement one of the nation's most ambitious downtown redevelopment programs. To supplement agency efforts in Bunker Hill, Bradley pushed through the creation of a second project area in the broader Central Business District. The efforts proved extremely successful, with office space downtown growing more than 50 percent between 1972 and 1982 (Saltzstein and Sonenshein 1991). Overall, redevelopment in Bunker Hill and the Central Business District would produce nearly 35 million square feet of retail, office, and industrial space (Marks 2004).

By the mid-1980s, however, Los Angeles's growth machine was facing the first phase of popular revolt brought about by changing economic and social conditions. Growing immigration and globalization, combined with deindustrialization, flooded the city with an increasing number of low-skilled, poor, and minority group residents. Like white, middle-class Angelenos, these new denizens too dreamed about leaving the central city for the tranquil suburbs. Unfortunately, many of them could not afford the detached single-family houses the region has become famous for. To satisfy this emerging segment of the housing market, land developers began to build apartment complexes in previously upscale neighborhoods. Increasing intensification of land-use was aided by Los Angeles's loose regulations, largely unchanged from the 1940s, that imposed few limits on the density of new construction and allowed developers to obtain building permits without public notice or hearings (Fulton 2001).

These new developments brought increased traffic, pollution, and an influx of lower-income Latinos into previously white neighborhoods, sowing the seeds of mass discontent (Davis 1990; Fulton 2001). Politically active and mobilized through their membership in homeowners' associations, homeowners pushed for limits on continued development, demanded greater say in local land-use decisions, and opposed further construction of multifamily housing near their homes. Social justice activists also spoke out against the CRA and the forceful relocation of downtown's poor and homeless to clear the way for redevelopment. However, with most city departments covered by civil service provisions that protected workers from politically motivated retribution and the CRA further insulated from political pressure by an independent board, city government remained largely unresponsive to the growing backlash.

In 1986, opponents of continued development scored a major victory with the overwhelming passage of Proposition U, a local voter initiative that placed strict caps on further commercial development. The initiative, described by the *Los Angeles Times* as "the most extensive one-shot effort to limit future development in the city's history" (Connell 1986), cut the size of new buildings permitted on most commercially and industrially zoned land by more than half. Developers seeking to exceed the new limits would need to obtain special dispensation from the city as part of a public process that would allow greater community input. Homeowners' association leadership was instrumental to the measure's success (Hogen-Esch 2001). Proposition U had been authored by City Councilmen Marvin Braude and Zev Yaroslavsky. Sensing the changing political tides, Yaroslavsky, a former Bradley ally, had become a born-again slow-growth advocate and the mayor's chief political adversary. Shortly after the election, Braude and Yaroslavsky unveiled a ten-point plan proposing even tighter limits on development and increased public participation and review of new projects (Braude and Yaroslavsky 1987).

To rein in the CRA, opponents of the mayor and his growth-minded allies had to find a way to pierce the agency's political shield. In 1988, critics succeeded in pushing out the CRA's longtime executive director, Edward Helfeld. Two years later, his successor, John Tuite, was also fired. As slow-growth activists scored additional electoral upsets, their influence on the City Council continued to grow. In the wake of redevelopment abuses in other cities, publicized by the statewide media, Yaroslavsky pushed ahead with a measure to dissolve the CRA board of commissioners and give the City Council direct control over redevelopment functions. The proposal failed by just one vote. In February 1991, the council adopted a far-reaching reform plan, broadening city council oversight over CRA policy, administration, and functions. Although the new ordinance affected almost every level of agency operations, its most important provisions gave the City Council power to review major agency decisions, giving elected officials final say over staff compensation and the awarding of all loans and grants over $250,000 (Marks 2004). Facing growing unpopularity, Bradley chose not to run for reelection in 1993, depriving the CRA of its leading public advocate. Once a powerful and autonomous city agency, the CRA had been reduced to "asking for City Council permission each time it needs to sharpen a pencil," according to one recent CRA official (quoted in Marks 2004). In early 2012, the City Council moved to effectively dismantle the CRA after the state legislature voted to dissolve local redevelopment agencies and redirect some of their tax increment dollars to close harrowing deficits in the state budget.

ERA OF INSTITUTIONAL CHANGE: VALLEY SECESSION AND CHARTER REFORM

Not all redevelopment agency critics were opponents of continued growth and development. In the San Fernando Valley, homeowners and environmental activists were joined by business owners who had come to resent the downtown business establishment's seemingly firm grip over city government. Organized into smaller regional chambers of commerce, Valley business owners often broke ranks with the downtown-dominated Los Angeles Area Chamber of Commerce on key issues. These business groups opposed the continued focus on downtown, believed that their tax dollars were subsidizing downtown redevelopment, and demanded increased economic investment in outlying areas of the city, including policies that would help the suburbs attract high-end retail stores (Hogen-Esch 2001).

Indeed, San Fernando Valley interests had opposed the city's downtown redevelopment efforts for decades. As chair of the City Council Planning Committee, Valley Councilman Ernani Bernardi blocked the approval of a 1972 plan calling for the creation of a redevelopment area in the city's Central Business District. In particular, Bernardi opposed the plan's reliance on tax-increment financing, which he argued would drain funds from other parts of the city and provide downtown projects an unfair advantage over development elsewhere in the city (Marks 2004). After Bradley's mayoral victory, Bernardi was replaced by Councilwoman Pat Russell, a liberal Bradley ally, as the head of the planning committee. When the Central Business District project was approved by the City Council over his objections in 1975, Bernardi filed a lawsuit in court charging that the plan had violated state environmental laws by failing to disclose its costs to taxpayers living in other parts of Los Angeles. The city eventually settled the lawsuit by agreeing to cap the amount of tax increment that could be spent downtown.

Two decades later, the new political coalition of Valley home and business owners had broader objectives than just limiting the influence and independence of the CRA. Instead, convinced that Valley residents were paying a disproportionate amount of taxes without receiving their fair share of city services, Valley interests formed the group Valley Voters Organized Toward Empowerment (Valley VOTE) and issued a declaration of independence, laying the groundwork for secession. In 1997, Valley VOTE succeeded in securing state legislation eliminating a city council veto over any secession measure (Sonenshein and Hogen-Esch 2006).

Within a year, San Fernando Valley residents submitted more than 200,000 signatures on a petition to require an initial study on the consequences of breaking away from the rest of the city. With their backs against the wall, elected city officials announced proposals to reform the Los Angeles City Charter to address Valley concerns and diffuse the growing secession movement. While the City Council made appointments to a charter reform commission, Mayor Richard Riordan pushed a competing plan with an elected commission, although the two commissions would eventually work together on a consensus document that secured voter approval in 1999 (Sonenshein 2004).

While the city charter changes did not substantively shift the balance of power between the city's elected branches, the new document laid out a drastically different approach to growth. To encourage broader community participation, the charter created a Department of Neighborhood Empowerment to oversee a new citywide system of neighborhood councils. The charter specified that the councils were to include representation of the "many diverse interests in communities" and to play an advisory role on issues of neighborhood concern. Although the councils were not given any specific public powers, the charter envisioned that they would serve as an "early warning system," creating opportunities for resident input prior to controversial decisions being made by the City Council and other city boards and commissions. This offered a formal coordination device for anti-growth interests.[1]

Without requiring that neighborhood council officers be chosen through elections, the charter specified that their membership had to be open to all "stakeholders"—those living, working, or owning property in the relevant neighborhoods. Aside from noting that the councils would be self-organized by these stakeholders, the document did not spell out how the new system would function, giving the Department of Neighborhood Empowerment the power to promulgate necessary regulations and oversee neighborhood council formation.

To encourage greater responsiveness to local interests in land-use decisions, the new charter also created a system of seven area planning commissions to supplement the previous citywide body, whose jurisdiction was now to be limited to projects with broader geographic impact.[2] Each area planning commission was to be composed of five members, all required to reside within the body's area of jurisdiction, and was given important authority over local land-use policy, including jurisdiction over local planning decisions and zoning appeals, power to grant limited exemptions from zoning rules, and ability to make land-use recommendations to the City Council. Together, the neighborhood councils and area planning commissions created additional venues for public participation in the city's planning process and gave neighborhoods new opportunities to veto undesirable projects—two key demands put forward by slow-growth advocates since the 1980s.

CONTESTATION OVER DEVELOPMENT AND PUBLIC
SPACE: VENICE'S NEIGHBORHOOD COUNCIL

By 2008, the Department of Neighborhood Empowerment had certified more than ninety neighborhood councils, each covering an area with an average of roughly 40,000 residents (Department of Neighborhood Empowerment 2008).[3] Homeowners have played a dominant role in organizing the creation of these councils, and in some circumstances, have come to control their boards, using the councils as a focal point for mobilizing like-minded groups and forming coalitions with others in different parts of the city (Musso et al. 2006). Recent studies have found that communities with more long-term residents and higher levels of ethnic homogeneity are more successful in forming neighborhood councils (Jun 2007), and that neighborhood council board members are significantly more likely to cite transportation and land-use as major city problems than regular LA residents (Musso, Weare, and Jun 2009). An analysis of council agendas has found that land-use issues represent one of the primary loci of attention during neighborhood council deliberations (Musso et al. 2007).

Yet in communities with competing groups and higher levels of racial, ethnic, and socioeconomic diversity, it has proven more difficult to unite community interests around a common purpose. In such settings, participants often label the neighborhood council system as a broken political structure that brings competing groups together in a cycle of neighborhood discord (Greene 2004). For these areas, changes to the city charter laid the groundwork for new political struggles to control local participatory bodies.

In Venice, for example, the formation of the Venice Neighborhood Council reignited a long-standing conflict between progressive activists and middle- and upper-class homeowner interests. A coastal community within the LA city boundaries, Venice is located between the independent municipality of Santa Monica and the unincorporated, county-controlled area of Marina del Rey. African American residents, left-wing political activists, homeless men and women, artists selling paintings on its famed boardwalk, and newer and wealthier homeowners, retailers, and developers have all taken part in a battle over the control of the neighborhood council.

By 1950, after decades of disinvestment, Venice's housing and commercial infrastructure was in decline. Commonly labeled as an urban slum, it was a central focus of new urban renewal and code enforcement programs along the coast. The CRA, Haynes Foundation, and Los Angeles City Planning Department all conducted studies about renewal potential and reached similar conclusions about "sub-standard" housing, "narrow lots," "poor street layout," and "under-use in relation to its potentiality for beach rental property" (Cunningham 1976, 182–83).

Just south of Venice, Marina del Rey was constructed in the 1960s out of barren marshes as an affluent residential/leisure enclave for young professionals with the largest manmade leisure boat harbor in the world (Sherman and Pipkin 2005). Interest grew in revitalizing the most rundown section of Venice, the remaining six canals located on the border of Venice and Marina del Rey. Los Angeles city officials, developers, and property speculators wanted to redesign and connect the stagnant

waterways to the marina, ultimately pushing out the bohemian culture that had settled there and transforming the area into a middle-class residential neighborhood.
In addition, new building code enforcement programs targeted beatnik cafes and the
declining housing infrastructure lining the beach (Maynard 1991).

Yet, a major progressive movement emerged in the 1960s and 1970s to promote
socioeconomic diversity and effectively stall rapid economic transition. Initially created by Councilwoman Russell in 1973, the Venice Town Council provided residents
with a voice in the process of coastal development.[4] Left-wing activists, including
members of the Peace and Freedom Party, which was formed in Venice during the previous decade, took control of the organization, championing an anti-development/
affordable housing platform. In the same decade, the state created the California
Coastal Commission; its mission was to protect coastal access to land up to one mile
inland from the coastline. Local progressive activists fought successfully for over a
decade to halt large-scale development projects and make economic diversity, affordable housing, and small-scale development central priorities. They blocked efforts
to construct luxury high-rise buildings on the northern end of the beach that many
worried would resemble a Miami waterfront (Stanton 2005).

Both progressives and middle-class homeowners feared a tidal wave of development in the 1970s and 1980s, and they influenced the framing of the Los Angeles
Planning Department's Venice Specific Plan. The plan adopted further limits on
development, including tighter restrictions on height, density, setbacks, transportation, parking, and other land-use issues in Venice. Although it did not completely
stop development, the plan changed its pace and overall design.

At the same time that luxury developments were stalled, affordable housing advocates secured major victories and social service organizations expanded, demonstrating the complexity of Los Angeles's coastal growth machine. Many of the progressive
activists and state environmentalists supported projects that could maintain socioeconomic diversity. During the 1970s, an African American community organization
called Project Action received economic backing to construct and manage fourteen
housing projects in a one-square-mile area in the center of Venice. Another nonprofit
community housing developer, the Venice Community Housing Corporation, constructed additional affordable housing units over the next decade.

Although downtown Los Angeles was the center of services for a quickly growing
homeless population, Venice emerged as another homeless mecca. Existing social service agencies expanded their programs to assist the new street population. Moreover,
the Venice Boardwalk, a vibrant public spectacle with carnival performers, artists,
and vendors, provided many homeless individuals with new economic opportunities
and turned the beachfront into another enclave for the destitute, further complicat-
ing waterfront development.

While progressive activists and middle-class homeowners were strange bedfel-
lows in efforts to stall plans for beachfront development, growing demand for coastal
property led to gradual changes in Venice's demographic composition over the next
four decades. Development interests largely failed in their ongoing efforts to amend
the Venice Specific Plan (Hathaway 2007), but developers slowly transformed the
community through condominium conversions and larger single-family dwellings

for wealthier residents. The growing proximity between classes and cultures led to a new focus on quality-of-life politics and a debate about the acceptable uses of public spaces, challenging the progressive tradition that had prevailed during previous decades.

The Venice Neighborhood Council was created in this context of changing political tides. Extensive interviews and field observations showed that its formation was marked by a strident debate between "quality-of-life" and "progressive" interest groups.[5] Like many neighborhood councils throughout Los Angeles, early coordinators of the Venice Neighborhood Council were members of a local homeowner association. They were opposed to the clustering of social services in their Rose Avenue neighborhood, where agencies had refocused much of their efforts on the growing homeless population in the 1980s and 1990s. The Rose Avenue activists slowly branched out and mobilized other homeowners from different areas of Venice around a common quality-of-life platform. To build a broader coalition, the group made an early decision to create an inclusive community-wide dialogue that was mindful of Venice's diversity.

In 2002, the Department of Neighborhood Empowerment, the new city body responsible for overseeing the neighborhood council system, formally certified the Venice Neighborhood Council. With the first election, the council devolved from its initial goal of open dialogue into intense interest group competition between the 1960s-era progressives and those interested in pursuing a quality-of-life agenda. The progressives called upon narratives about "community control of community affairs," seeking to include African American and homeless activists in their opposition to gentrification. The quality-of-life activists were comparatively more conservative residents. While most of them espoused a liberal political ideology and were Democratic Party supporters, they had become weary of increasing threats to their quality of life, including homeless residents leaving feces, urine, and garbage on streets, people dealing and using drugs in public spaces, graffiti on private property, and ongoing gang violence.

The quality-of-life faction won a clear majority on the initial council board. As the early coordinators of the certification process, their email and phone lists ultimately turned into a widespread neighborhood newsletter with thousands of subscribers and quickly facilitated voter mobilization. After serving as a minority faction on the board, progressives expanded their platform. They canvassed the neighborhood for new voters, held open forums, distributed leaflets, developed their own email lists, and published articles criticizing the board majority in the *Free Venice Beachhead*, a radical free paper dating back to the late 1960s. In the 2003 election, the Venice Progressives won every open seat.

Disturbed by the outcome, quality-of-life activists challenged the validity of the election. The president resigned from her position while she still had another year of eligibility. The board had allowed unchecked use of absentee ballots, and quality-of-life activists accused the progressives of fraud by encouraging participation from people not proven to be Venice residents. They argued that many of the voters were homeless with no formal ties to Venice. The new city charter and related implementation ordinances provided few guidelines about who was eligible to participate in the neighborhood council elections (Newton 2010) and similar confrontations took place in many Los Angeles communities. In the Venice case, the Department of Neighborhood Empowerment intervened and ruled that the Progressives had fairly won the election.

As a central venue for neighborhood politics, council meetings remained combative. Quality-of-life activists accused the progressive board members of being "Marxists" who facilitated criminal activity by making Venice hospitable to the homeless, or "low-lives and dangerous thugs," as one member described the homeless. Progressive board members labeled their opponents as "rich developers" and "racists," although there was little evidence that quality-of-life issues were about race or development. Widespread attention was brought to an increasingly fractious Venice when the *Los Angeles Times* reported in a front-page story, "As housing prices soar amid homelessness, factions feud about the community's character" (Garrison 2004).

In following years, election results were challenged, accusations of spending fraud surfaced, disputes over the definition of "stakeholder" were commonplace, and significant political issues about the right to influence neighborhood space often turned into interpersonal rivalries. With the local council embroiled in so much conflict and controversy, the Department of Neighborhood Empowerment has intervened several times and threatened decertification, which would have taken away city funding. After one fierce battle over election legitimacy in 2004, the Department of Neighborhood Empowerment rejected the council election results, accused continuing board members of going "rogue" by operating without an official quorum, and forced the community to create a new council and bylaws from scratch. The stigma of past conflicts—arguments, accusations, and process-related blunders—confronts current board members still opposed by rival groups.

Prolonged neighborhood council political tension is not unique to Venice. In Lincoln Heights, east of downtown, a conflict over whether the neighborhood council should support an AIDS memorial turned into an enduring controversy over the use of money and accusations of fraud. In Westchester, a West LA community where the Los Angeles International Airport is located, residents accused a major developer of paying for pizza parties in return for voters supporting a sympathetic faction vying for seats on the council. Existing neighborhood council board members were so concerned about losing their seats that they then illegally required voters to show income tax statements or property tax bills at the election site in order to hamper voters' ability to cast their ballots. In South Central Los Angeles, where an influential and successful community empowerment district operated for years, the creation of a neighborhood council transformed local politics into frequent and hostile battles over procedure and process (Greene 2004).

The Department of Neighborhood Empowerment has either decertified or threatened to decertify a wide range of neighborhood councils due to similar controversies. In many parts of the city, neighborhood councils have confronted difficult and divisive questions over who has the right to speak for the community, thus stalling any semblance of local unity or the emergence of consensus around shared community interests. In more homogeneous community settings, however, residents have succeeded in using neighborhood councils and area planning commissions to their advantage by blocking major developments. This has encouraged developers to seek out new opportunities in places with less community participation and greater development potential. As a result, downtown Los Angeles has become a major growth node.

A PRIVATE VISION FOR DOWNTOWN, 1990–2010

The neighborhood councils and area planning commissions opened policy decisions over local land-use to greater public scrutiny and provided venues to mobilize and institutionalize opposition to major growth. As a result, they both significantly increased the transaction costs for pursuing development in suburban parts of Los Angeles, areas where homeowner groups are most likely to be active. Increasingly, downtown has come to be seen as an attractive and politically viable site for continued development. With a large minority population and an area filled almost exclusively by multifamily residences—according to the 2000 Census, fewer than 3 percent of the roughly 13,000 housing units downtown were single-family homes—it is an area that is unlikely to produce a strong political movement opposed to major projects.[6] Although a Downtown Los Angeles Neighborhood Council was officially created in 2002, the bylaws set aside nearly half of the seats on its board of directors for business interests, cultural organizations, and local employees, leaving just eleven of twenty-eight directorships for residents and homeowners.[7]

In 1999, the City Council adopted new rules lowering the requirements for the adaptive reuse of underutilized commercial and industrial properties downtown, encouraging further growth. Between 2000 and 2009, the population of downtown grew nearly 40 percent, to 35,000 residents. Table 14.1 tracks the issuance of building permits for new construction in Los Angeles over the course of the past decade. As the table makes clear, growing hostility to construction in other parts of the city and the adoption of policies that encourage development downtown have made the area one of the leading centers of growth. With less than 1 percent of the city's total land area and population, the downtown community planning area has been the site of more than 10 percent of all new office space built since 2000 in the city and, strikingly, more than 20 percent of new retail floor space. The broader region that falls under the jurisdiction of the Central Area Planning Commission, including downtown and areas immediately west of the Harbor Freeway (see figure 14.1), has absorbed close to 30 percent of new multifamily construction, almost a quarter of all new office space, and nearly half of all new retail floor space built in Los Angeles since the start of the new millennium, which is significantly greater than its share of the total city land area (9.9 percent) and its share of the total population (18.3 percent).

Perhaps most striking is that this growth has occurred even as the CRA, subject to greater political control by the City Council, has shifted its attention away from downtown. During the late 1980s, more than 70 percent of all funds spent by the redevelopment agency flowed to project areas downtown. As figure 14.2 shows,

Table 14.1 NEW CONSTRUCTION PERMITS IN DOWNTOWN LOS ANGELES, 2000–2009

	Downtown Planning Area[a]	Central Area Planning Commission Jurisdiction[b]
Share of Citywide Population, 2009	0.9%	18.3%
Share of Citywide New Residents, since 2000	3.1%	24.1%
Share of Citywide Land Area, 2009	0.6%	9.9%
Share of New Single Family Dwelling Units, 2000–2009	0.0%	4.7%
Share of New Multi-Family Dwelling Units, 2000–2009	3.9%	28.2%
Share of New Office Floor Space (square feet), 2000–2009	10.1%	23.3%
Share of New Industrial Floor Space (s.f.), 2000–2009	2.6%	5.4%
Share of New Retail Floor Space (s.f.), 2000–2009	21.8%	47.2%

Source: Los Angeles Department of City Planning, Demographics Research Unit, "Annual Building Permit Activity," various years.
[a] This refers to Los Angeles's Central City Community Plan area, an administrative boundary that stretches from the Harbor Freeway on the west to Alameda Street on the east and covers most of downtown. See figure 14.1.
[b] Includes Hollywood, Wilshire, Westlake, Central City, and Central City North community plan areas.

beginning in the 1990s, the CRA shifted focus to other parts of the city as spending downtown continued to fall. By the middle of the first decade of the twenty-first century, less than one-third of all LA redevelopment spending was invested in the city's commercial center. Growing scarcity of public dollars and the CRA's waning commitment to downtown redevelopment has helped transform the nature of the downtown revival, giving an outsized role to the private sector.

IN THE SHADOW OF THE STAPLES CENTER: THE NEW MEGAPROJECTS

During the Bradley era, downtown redevelopment efforts focused primarily on the construction of office space to create jobs for suburban dwellers living in other parts of the city. Indeed, despite the rise of other major job centers in quickly growing parts of Southern California—Riverside, San Bernardino, and, to a smaller extent, Orange counties—central Los Angeles has remained one of the leading employment centers in the five-county region during the past three decades (Giuliano et al. 2007). However, by the 1990s, the anonymous office towers that left downtown a virtual ghost town after dark had fallen out of favor. Following the lead of many other American central cities, Los Angeles embraced what urbanist Peter Eisinger has called "the politics of bread and circuses"—redevelopment efforts centered on entertainment, sports, and high-end retail designed to attract out-of-town visitors and the money of middle-class shoppers (Eisinger 2000).

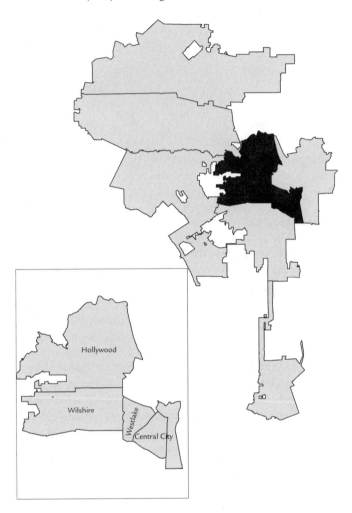

Figure 14.1
Central Area Planning Commission Jurisdiction
Source: Adapted by Steve Erie from materials from Los Angeles Department of City Planning.

Since the mid-1990s, major construction projects in downtown Los Angeles have centered around two competing megaproject development clusters, each championed by a major private-sector booster. Figure 14.3 displays the location of these two clusters in the Central City Community Plan area, and their proximity to Skid Row. In the south, adjacent to the city's convention center that first opened in 1971, Denver entertainment mogul Philip Anschutz has overseen the construction of a massive sports and entertainment complex anchored by the Staples Center sports arena and the Nokia Theater. Just over a mile to the north, wealthy housing developer and philanthropist Eli Broad has focused his efforts on promoting the Grand Avenue project, a major private development on city- and county-owned land next to the Walt Disney Concert Hall.

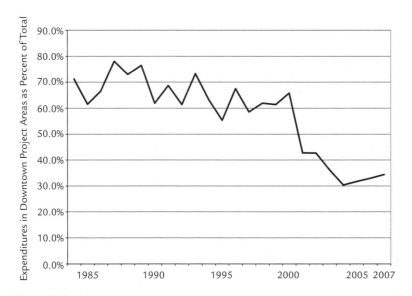

Figure 14.2
Los Angeles Community Redevelopment Agency Expenditures
Source: Compiled from California State Controller, *Community Redevelopment Agencies Annual Report*, various years.

Staples Center

In 1997, the city entered into an agreement with the Anschutz-owned LA Arena Development Company to build a major sports complex downtown. For the city, the project had two primary purposes. First, the development could help to revitalize the neighborhood of South Park, a seventy-block industrial area filled with empty parking lots, boarded-up buildings, and vacant offices. In addition, the new arena promised to lure the Lakers basketball team from their home in nearby Inglewood, and to provide a new stadium for the city's other NBA team, the Clippers, as well as its professional hockey team, the Kings. Under an initial agreement signed between the City Council and the developer, the city pledged $70.5 million in public funds toward the estimated $200 million cost of the construction (the final cost of the Staples Center would actually be close to $375 million), to be paid off over the next three decades using new tax dollars expected to be generated by the project.

Despite overwhelming city council support, the project was opposed by San Fernando Valley Councilman Joel Wachs, who objected to the subsidies being offered to the wealthy private developer. Although on the losing side of the council vote, Wachs moved to qualify a citywide ballot referendum to give LA voters final say over the future of the project. Coming at the height of the Valley secession movement, it was a vote other city leaders were eager to avoid. Using the threat of the referendum as leverage, the city reopened negotiations with the developer to address Wachs's concerns, winning additional concessions from the developer. In addition to reducing the public contribution to the project, the city won a guarantee from the Arena

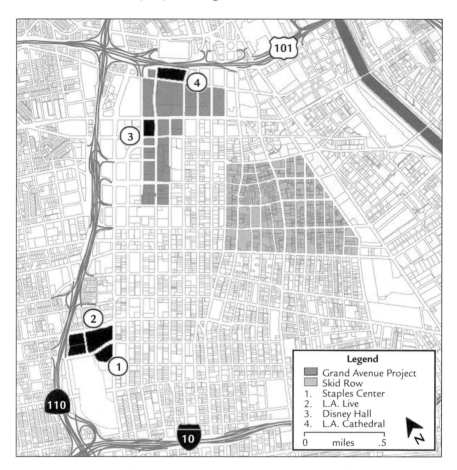

Figure 14.3
Downtown Megaproject Clusters and Skid Row
Source: Forrest Stuart.

Development Company to cover the cost of the city's annual payment needed to service the bonds from the project if the revenue generated by the development fell
short, shifting the financial risk from the city to the Anschutz-owned company.

The final agreement, which Wachs called "the best arena proposal ever negotiated in the United States" (quoted in Parlow 2002), largely set the parameters for
future development downtown. By capping the city's expected contribution and
making public subsidies contingent on the creation of new city revenues, the Staples
Center project significantly limited taxpayer costs and financial risk. In contrast to
earlier redevelopment projects, the developer, rather than the city, would provide the
primary financing. In addition, the CRA, the city's historic champion of downtown
renewal, largely played a small supporting role. Although the redevelopment agency
agreed to contribute $12 million toward the cost of public improvements in the area,
the project was negotiated directly by the City Council, and the city's contribution was

to be funded directly out of Los Angeles's general budget. Overall, despite the public subsidies, the project appears to have produced a net positive impact on the city budget, with the benefits from the Staples Center construction exceeding the economic impacts of many other stadium construction projects in other cities (Baade 2003).

LA Live

Immediately after the opening of the Staples Center, the Anschutz Entertainment Group announced plans for the construction of a major entertainment complex on 27 acres of nearby commercial land. Anchored by the arena and a new 7,100-seat theater, the $2.5 billion project sought to make downtown the city's entertainment destination. In addition to more than a dozen upscale restaurants, bars, and nightclubs, the construction included a 54-story hotel-condo tower to house a new five-star hotel and more than 1,000 hotel rooms (Reynolds 2010).

As with the Staples Center, the city's redevelopment agency played a marginal role in the LA Live project, although the plans relied heavily on public dollars. The California Public Employees Retirement System, an independent agency charged with managing the pensions of state- and local-government employees, provided key financing. In 2007, a controversial bill passed by state lawmakers also gave the Anschutz Entertainment Group access to $30 million from a recently approved statewide affordable housing bond (McGreevy and Hymon 2007). Finally, in a controversial decision, the city agreed to give the Anschutz Entertainment Group the revenues from the hotel taxes to be collected on rooms built as part of the project for the next twenty-five years, representing a subsidy of almost $250 million.

In 2012, the Anschutz Entertainment Group moved ahead with plans to build a $1 billion football stadium adjacent to the LA Live complex. Structured much like the Staples Arena project, the city has agreed to provide upfront public financing for the new stadium in exchange for the developer's commitment to cover any shortfall if new revenue generated from the project proves insufficient to repay the city's costs. However, the announcement in late 2012 that Philip Anschutz had put the Anschutz Entertainment Group up for sale raised new doubts about the viability of the project and the financial commitments made by the company to the city.

Los Angeles Cathedral and Walt Disney Concert Hall

Even as Anschutz focused on his efforts in South Park, two privately financed projects were changing the face of the northern part of downtown. In the mid-1990s, the Roman Catholic Archdiocese of Los Angeles hired world-renowned Spanish architect Rafael Moneo to design a replacement for the Saint Vibiana Cathedral, which had been seriously damaged by the 1994 Northridge earthquake. Moneo's unusual postmodern design, marked by the absence of right angles, won wide acclaim, and the

Figure 14.4
Cathedral of Our Lady of Angels
Source: Photo by Kevin Kay.

new Cathedral of Our Lady of Angels opened in 2002. Figure 14.4 shows the new cathedral.

Just down the street, another famous architect, Guggenheim Museum designer Frank Gehry, had begun work on a new facility to house the Los Angeles Philharmonic Orchestra. The project was the brainchild of Walt Disney's widow Lillian, who donated $50 million in 1987 for the effort. In the early 1990s, Los Angeles County spent more than $100 million on a new parking garage atop which the new Walt Disney Concert Hall would be built. However, the project remained dormant for years as its supporters struggled to raise the necessary private funds. In 1996, then-Mayor Richard Riordan drafted billionaire Eli Broad to spearhead a new fundraising campaign. Both Riordan and Broad, along with supermarket mogul Ronald Burkle, would eventually become the biggest personal funders of the project, with the remaining money coming from local foundations, banks, oil companies, and a donation from the Walt Disney Company. With a final cost of more than $270 million, the Walt Disney Concert Hall opened in 2003. In 2007, the nonprofit corporation responsible for building the facility transferred the title over to the county. Figure 14.5 shows the Walt Disney Concert Hall.

Figure 14.5
Walt Disney Concert Hall
Source: Library of Congress (Photo by Carol Highsmith).

Grand Avenue Project

Shortly after the completion of the new music venue, Broad spearheaded the creation of the Grand Avenue Committee, a private organization focused on developing
the 25 acres of public land surrounding the Walt Disney Concert Hall. Under Broad's
leadership, the group hired Gehry to design a major upscale residential and commercial center with more than 3.2 million square feet of housing, office, and retail space,
including a new museum to house Broad's extensive art collection (Ouroussoff 2004).
Broad also took the lead in selecting the developer for the project. With an estimated
cost of $3 billion, Gehry's final design for the Grand Avenue Project included four
high-rise residential towers, a boutique hotel, and a new 16-acre public park. Figure
14.6 displays plans for the proposed megaproject.

To oversee the development, the city and county of Los Angeles—owners of the
land on which it would be built—created a joint powers authority that has taken the
primary lead in representing the public sector in the negotiations. Under an unusual
public–private partnership, the city and the county agreed to turn the land over to
the developer on a 99-year lease and use the lease proceeds to pay the cost of necessary road improvements and of the new park construction. Although the redevelopment agency agreed to finance the construction of approximately 500 affordable

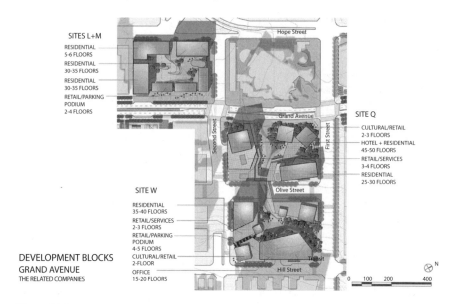

Figure 14.6
Proposed Grand Avenue Development Project
Source: Grand Avenue Committee.

housing units, the City Council again provided the primary source of public subsidies. In a deal similar to the LA Live revenue-sharing agreement, the council agreed to divert new hotel tax revenues to be generated by the project to the developer, a transfer estimated to cost the city $60 million (DiMassa 2007).

However, the collapse of the Southern California housing market in the wake of the global financial crisis has raised new questions about the viability of the Grand Avenue project, which has suffered a series of construction delays. In 2008, the state pension system pulled out its investment from the project, citing its heavy exposure to the downtown real estate market, leaving the developer significantly short of financing. In late 2010, the project's developers announced that the groundbreaking would be delayed until at least 2013, six years after work was originally scheduled to begin, due in large part to difficulty securing financing (Linthicum 2010). The elimination of all local redevelopment agencies by the state legislature in 2011 also threatened roughly $5 million in public dollars promised by the CRA to pay for affordable housing in the Grand Avenue project. Although a new public park included in the project opened in 2012, the developer has suggested that the commercial and retail portions of the project will need to be scaled back substantially to reflect slower economic growth and new market realities after the 2008 financial crisis.

CONTAINING SKID ROW

The quickened pace of development associated with the Downtown Renaissance, including the influx of new residents and shoppers flocking to the area's new retail establishments, has lent added urgency to city efforts to clean up Skid Row, Los Angeles's most concentrated site for the homeless and the social services they rely on. While land-use authority and access to public dollars have been the primary tools through which the CRA has historically influenced the development of downtown, the LAPD, under an ambitious new police chief William Bratton, has become a primary policy lever guiding the trajectory of change in the area. This section traces the development of Skid Row, focusing on its regulation throughout the last half century under what is locally referred to as the "policy of containment"—a collective effort to cordon off the area's associated populations and behaviors to approved downtown spaces. To many observers, including much of the impoverished and homeless population now residing in Skid Row, the policy represents a darker, more coercive side of downtown revival, as the LAPD has joined private developers in filling the vacuum left by the weakening of CRA powers.

Los Angeles's Skid Row was forged by an early history similar to that found in other urban centers at the beginning of the twentieth century (Anderson 1923; Rossi 1989). Proximity to the Los Angeles River and a flat topography made the fifty-block area—between 3rd and 7th Streets, bounded by Main Street on the west and Alameda Street on the east—ideal for the development of the packing and shipping industry (Spivack 1998). As the final stop of the transcontinental railroad, Skid Row housed much of the swelling migrant labor force and was the point of entry into the city for those heading westward during the Depression of the 1930s, the Dust Bowl, and World War II. Over time, single room occupancy hotels, shelters, and inexpensive retail stores developed to accommodate the influx of inhabitants. By the 1960s, however, much of the migratory labor force had given way to those more stereotypically associated with Skid Row districts—homeless men, who were often dependent on alcohol and unemployed.

For downtown' development interests, images of wayward and drunken homeless men in the doorways of skyscrapers lingered as a continual threat to development potential. In response, private developers represented by the Central City Association formed a Committee for Central City Planning made up of twenty-two executives and property owners from downtown's largest businesses. In 1972, the committee completed its "Silverbook" plan—a strategy paralleling those taken up at the same time by other major urban centers, including Chicago and New York, that were similarly wrestling with blighted areas, social service hubs, and low-cost housing near central business districts (Hoch and Slayton 1989). According to the plan, much of Skid Row's physical infrastructure would be bulldozed to make way for a university complex, police center, central library, and parking garages. However, as it circulated among interested parties, the Silverbook plan generated significant controversy. Similar to the case of Venice, a conflict between progressive and quality-of-life interests surfaced in downtown.

Skid Row's long-standing homeless advocates anticipated that the area's traditional population would be forced to other areas of the city that lacked the social services facilities serving Skid Row residents. Fearing that their own areas would become the "new" Skid Row, representatives from several communities bordering downtown joined with advocates to challenge the demolition of Skid Row. Poised against downtown business interests, this unlikely coalition pressured City Hall to devise an alternate plan for dealing with Skid Row.

In 1976, the Los Angeles Community Design Center, an advocacy planning agency charged with the design, presented a plan that called on the city to take steps to contain Skid Row physically. Rather than disperse the population, the proposal sought to essentially quarantine inhabitants within an acceptable geographic area. According to the planning document, the area would be redeveloped to act as a magnet to "Skid Row types" residing in downtown and the rest of the region (Los Angeles Community Design Center 1976). Only by doing so, its authors argued, could they hope to reduce Skid Row's influence on the rest of the central city.

This would be accomplished through a series of measures. First, "inducements" would "cause the Skid Row resident to stay within the area of containment rather than wander about the Central City" (Los Angeles Community Design Center 1976, 7). Through deliberate control of the allocation and location of housing stock, low-cost housing within Skid Row was slated for improvement, while similar housing outside of the area would be discouraged. Additionally, the plan called for the gradual elimination of those businesses—most notably liquor stores and bars—traditionally associated with Skid Row. Social services (including shelters, rescue missions, and soup kitchens) and amenities (including benches, restrooms, and parks) would also be relocated from other areas of downtown to the confines of Skid Row.

The second component of the containment plan involved the construction of "buffers" to "reinforce the edges existing between Skid Row and other land uses" (Los Angeles Community Design Center 1976, 7). Light industrial development would be encouraged along Skid Row's borders, while the physical environment would be "hardened" (Jeffery 1977) through measures such as the locking of trashcans or increasing the brightness of streetlights in areas used by homeless individuals for sleeping. If designed successfully, the plan's architects argued, "When the Skid Row resident enters the buffer, the psychological comfort of the familiar Skid Row environment will be lost; he will not be inclined to travel far from the area of containment" (Los Angeles Community Design Center 1976, 12). In this manner, Skid Row's "area of influence" would be significantly decreased.

While never formalized as official policy, the CRA took a number of steps to implement the containment plan that continues to the current day. By 1987, ten years after the completion of the strategy, the agency had spent or committed $58 million for homeless assistance programs, most of which were located in the downtown area (Goetz 1992). CRA-funded agencies providing emergency shelter and transitional housing have been relocated within Skid Row's boundaries. In 1989, for instance, the CRA provided $6.5 million for the relocation of the Union Rescue Mission from elsewhere in downtown to the center of the containment area. Since that time, the Union Rescue Mission has grown to become the largest rescue mission in the country.

Today it is flanked by two additional "mega-shelters"—the Los Angeles Mission and the Midnight Mission—which, rivaling the size of the Union Rescue Mission, were also relocated from outside Skid Row. By 2000 the gradual growth, saturation, and consolidation of services under these few large facilities created a new Skid Row, home to 40 percent of all city shelter beds and 25 percent of all county shelter beds (DeVerteuil 2006).

In a move that worked to increase the pull of Skid Row on downtown's transient population, the CRA founded the Single Room Occupancy Housing Corporation (SRO Housing) in 1984, to acquire and rehabilitate the aging single-room occupancy hotels in the area. As a direct subsidiary of the CRA, SRO Housing has intentionally focused its efforts in the heart of Skid Row, rather than along its perimeter, in an effort to further shrink the presence of the population in the rest of the downtown development area.

The pull of new single-room occupancy developments in the heart of Skid Row was accompanied by a push from the elimination of affordable housing units in the rest of the downtown area. Broader urban planning policies, most notably the 1999 adaptive reuse ordinance discussed above, paved the way for the conversion of older and economically distressed buildings into new apartments, lofts, and hotels. The Los Angeles Housing Department reports that between 2000 and 2003, 982 residential hotel units were eliminated, whereas only 100 units had been lost in the four years preceding the ordinance. As "housing of last resort," these units may be the

Figure 14.7
Skid Row (San Julian and Sixth Streets)
Source: Photo by Forrest Stuart.

last stop before homelessness. With a shrinking housing stock, many low-income downtown residents were left with two options—either leave downtown altogether or migrate further into Skid Row.

The result has been a steady and constant increase in the Skid Row population. Simultaneously, as figure 14.7 shows, the traditional image of the aged, white, alcohol-dependent "bum" has been replaced by a demographic make-up dominated by working-age African Americans seeking employment opportunities, affordable housing, and social services that were lost or removed from other areas.

As Goetz (1992) notes, while Skid Row has been manufactured in large part through urban planning policy, the everyday task of containing and regulating Skid Row has fallen primarily to the LAPD. By creating a space where the behaviors typically associated with Skid Row are tolerated, the police are called upon to use the full force of the law to prevent this behavior when encountered in other downtown areas. For roughly thirty years, police attempts to regulate Skid Row largely mirrored the debate over the Silverbook plan, which was characterized by various attempts to funnel and relocate homeless populations to acceptable city blocks, but met with repeated and successful community resistance. This process was exemplified throughout the 1980s as former LAPD Chief Daryl Gates initiated a series of homeless sweeps in which officers approached individuals and ordered them to relocate, arresting those who refused. Police sweeps were often accompanied by city maintenance trucks that

Figure 14.8
LAPD Homeless Sweep in Skid Row
Source: Photo by Forrest Stuart.

swept up any possessions left behind. Figure 14.8 shows the intersection of Crocker and 5th Streets in Skid Row immediately following a homeless sweep by LAPD officers and city maintenance workers. Blocks are cordoned off at both ends by flatbed trucks that transport items collected by bulldozers.

Actions by community organizations and a suit brought by the Legal Aid Foundation of Los Angeles forced Mayor Tom Bradley to cease the efforts and develop a softer, more comprehensive policy to deal with homelessness across Los Angeles. Simultaneously, Skid Row activists forced City Hall on a number of occasions to convert parcels of land owned or leased by the city into large, outdoor "homeless encampments" to accommodate those unable to secure shelter or acquire more permanent housing arrangements. One such camp, referred to as the "Dust Bowl Hilton" was a 12-acre plot located on the outskirts of the containment area with space for roughly 500 inhabitants. With constant pressure from coalition groups, Bradley negotiated a number of extensions for the facility, preventing the Regional Transit District from evicting its residents to make room for the city's new light rail system (Goetz 1992). In sum, throughout this period Skid Row's collection of charitable and volunteer organizations was successful in not only preventing the city from eliminating the services or populations that characterized the area but also concentrating and increasing services.

However, at the beginning of the twenty-first century, the back and forth that characterized this arrangement—between the city's criminal justice institutions and Skid Row's philanthropic organizations—swung in a drastically more punitive direction, culminating in a wave of aggressive policies that even former Chief Gates might never have imagined. A number of commentators explain this shift by pointing to the 2002 hiring of former New York Police Chief William Bratton to head the LAPD. Before arriving in Los Angeles, Bratton had been a member of the monitoring team that oversaw the implementation of the Federal Consent Decree in the wake of the city's Rampart scandal of the late 1990s.[8] Even earlier, while directing the NYPD, Bratton developed, applied, and systematized a "broken windows" policing strategy that many credit for stemming crime and reducing disorder across the city.

Arguably the best-known contemporary law enforcement paradigm, the broken windows approach postulates that if left unattended, minor forms of disorder—including littering, panhandling, jaywalking, and sitting on the sidewalk—produce neighborhood decline and ultimately increase levels of serious crime (Wilson and Kelling 1982). According to the theory, the presence of disorder signals that an area is uncared for, causing law-abiding citizens to move away while signaling to criminals that their crimes will go undetected and unpunished. Viewing Skid Row through the lens of broken windows, the exact behaviors designed to be contained, and to some extent accepted, under the 1976 plan were likely to be reevaluated as a danger not only to adjacent downtown neighborhoods but also to Skid Row's own residents seeking vital social services (for a more detailed discussion, see Stuart 2011).

However, Bratton's hiring was but one piece of a puzzle tied inextricably to alterations in the institutional landscape of Skid Row itself. As described above, while the Containment Plan did in fact preserve the facilities of the area's most vocal advocates, the efforts to concentrate amenities within the boundaries of Skid Row also brought new organizations to the area. As a result, a very different set of institutions and actors came to be viewed as the true "representatives" of the downtrodden—from a coalition of progressive charitable organizations and public interest lawyers to the small-number of "mega-shelters" supported as part of CRA's funding strategy.

When Bratton announced that he would launch sweeps reminiscent of those attempted by Gates twenty years earlier (Winton and Sauerwein 2003), prominent representatives from within these newcomer organizations responded with an unprecedented level of support, forming a partnership in the new police efforts. A recent analysis of meeting minutes and internal communications shows that a year prior to the announcement, the LAPD hired George Kelling, senior fellow at the Manhattan Institute and one of the originators of the broken windows theory, to anticipate and preempt any anticipated public backlash (Blasi 2007). At a price to the city of over a half million dollars, Kelling recruited the head of the Union Rescue Mission and the leadership of several other newer facilities to, according to Kelling, "get to the moral high ground" by developing a "coordinated strategy for communication to the press regarding the forthcoming effort in Skid Row" (Blasi 2007). Together, the group prepared media statements and newspaper op-ed pieces that were designed to tap into various public sympathies, explaining the policing strategy in terms of alternate issues such as child safety and public health.

Several years of police sweeps and mega-shelter support culminated in 2006 when the city launched its Safer Cities Initiative (SCI) in Skid Row. At the annual cost of $6 million, SCI deployed an additional fifty patrol officers, and twenty-five to thirty additional narcotics and mounted officers to police the fifty blocks (Blasi 2007). Not only did the launch of SCI distinguish Skid Row as home to arguably the largest concentration of standing police forces in the country (Blasi and Stuart 2008), the LAPD made over 9,000 arrests and issued roughly 12,000 infraction citations in the initiative's first year alone. Given an estimate of the Skid Row population as between 12,000 and 15,000 inhabitants, these numbers represent an arrest/citation rate nearly 70 times higher than those in other parts of the city (Blasi 2007).

Data produced in 2009 by a homeless legal clinic, administered by the Legal Aid Foundation of Los Angeles and the Los Angeles Community Action Network, provides a more detailed look at the initiative's intensified police practices. An analysis of intakes to the clinic between January 1 and November 4 of that year demonstrates that much police contact stems from minor pedestrian infractions. Almost 90 percent of the citations handled by the clinic were written for some form of crosswalk violation, such as crossing during a flashing red hand, crossing at a red light, or jaywalking. Many of these violations were attributable to serious physical disabilities that inhibited individuals from making it fully across an intersection in the time allotted by city traffic lights. In fact, only 23 percent of those receiving citations did not report a physical disability. While the city proposed a counterbalance in the form of its Streets or Services (SOS) program, emphasizing rehabilitation and drug treatment as nonpunitive responses to misdemeanor offenses, SOS received only $100,000 in funding. This budgetary disparity was clearly evident by May 2007, only nine months into SCI policing. The LAPD reported making 7,428 misdemeanor arrests, yet only thirty-four individuals completed the SOS program during that time period (Blasi and Stuart 2008).

As the media's interest in Skid Row has increased in recent years, a number of national and international commentators have looked to these numbers to question whether the new policing strategy may actually exacerbate the conditions of poverty and homelessness. After a 2008 tour of the area, the United Nations Special Rapporteur on Contemporary Forms of Racism, Racial Discrimination, Xenophobia, and Related Intolerance condemned the disparate law enforcement in Skid Row (McGreal 2009). Largely because of Skid Row policing, Los Angeles recently was named America's "meanest city" in a study conducted by the National Law Center on Homelessness and Poverty (Anderson 2009; Dahmann 2010).

CONCLUSION

Surveying the last two decades of downtown development in the city, *Los Angeles Times* architecture critic Christopher Hawthorne has wondered, "Is this any way to build a city?" (Hawthorne 2010). Under the new institutional and political landscape that has emerged from the ashes of the once-formidable Bradley-era growth coalition, Hawthorne has lamented that the city government's commitment to the public realm "has withered to almost nothing." "Instead," he has written, "we are experimenting with a new approach that asks developers to build quasi-public space, ringed with retail, in exchange for land, streamlined approval or help with the bottom line" (Hawthorne 2006).

It is almost certainly the case that the answer to Hawthorne's concern depends on where one stands. From the point of view of the middle-class homeowners living around the city's periphery, the decentralizing and democratizing reforms embedded into Los Angeles's city charter have delivered on their demands to increase community control over local land-use policy. For Los Angeles's growing impoverished homeless population in Skid Row, the answer is certainly much more ambiguous. What is clear, however, is that the city's slow-growth movement's primary victory has been to redirect, rather than slow, the pace of growth in the city, making downtown its new epicenter. Nor, despite shifting the priorities of the CRA, have activists succeeded in eliminating public subsidies for new downtown projects, though they have significantly changed how these projects have been financed. Under new, meeker leadership, the CRA has largely surrendered the initiative to private developers, offsetting the public participatory gains made in other neighborhoods. It is a trend that is likely to continue, as the city began work to dismantle the agency under California's new post-redevelopment era.

It remains to be seen whether Los Angeles's new approach to physical and economic development can survive and recover in an era of slower economic growth. Already, dark clouds are forming. Of the approximately 110 private residential projects planned for downtown, more than one-third have been delayed or put on hold due to financing challenges, precipitously falling home prices, and broader economic troubles (DiMassa 2007). Having largely handed over the public reins of development to the private sector, Angelenos must now fully confront both the promise and the peril of reliance on the marketplace.

NOTES

1. The Department of Neighborhood Empowerment and the neighborhood council system are discussed in the Los Angeles City Charter Sec. 900, et seq.
2. Area planning commissions are discussed in City Charter Sec. 552. While the charter only specified that at least five area planning commissions would be created, the implementing ordinance provided for seven commissions.
3. A total of ninety-one neighborhood councils were certified, though three were eventually decertified.
4. In the Venice context, Councilwoman Russell, a liberal Bradley ally, was a bit controversial. While she had a pro-growth coastal agenda, she was also willing to listen to people. There was so much backlash against development that she formed the Venice Town Council. She was ultimately succeeded by a city planner/environmental activist/coastal commissioner/Venice resident, Ruth Galanter, who was much more interested in protecting the coast and the distinctiveness of Venice. But ultimately Galanter was thrust in the middle of complex development controversies too and could only do so much to favor progressives.
5. The discussion about the formation of conflict in the Venice Neighborhood Council is the result of six years of ethnographic and historical work about neighborhood formation and differentiation in Venice. One of the coauthors regularly attended neighborhood council meetings. During this period, the coauthor interviewed thirty elected board members and regular participants in the audience and had informal conversations with countless others. The open-ended interviews started by asking how individuals first became involved in Venice politics and specifically in the neighborhood council. Commonly lasting one to two hours, the discussion focused on the process of joining and forming the council, participating in interest groups, developing oppositions in Venice, the meaning of political action, and life transitions of activists over time. The interviews were supplemented with regular attendance and observations in meetings, following online discussions, reading local newspapers, and reading distributed candidate biographies and meeting minutes.
6. We use the Central City Community Plan Area as the rough boundaries for downtown.
7. The bylaws are available at http://www.dlanc.com/bylaws/#Art5.
8. In the late 1990s, evidence surfaced regarding widespread corruption in LAPD's Rampart Division. Over seventy Rampart officers, in particular members of the Community Resources Against Street Hoodlums (CRASH) Unit, were convicted of a number of offenses including planting false evidence, robbery, perjury, drug sales, and other crimes.

CHAPTER 15

A Land Ethic for the City of Water

KRISTEN VAN HOOREWEGHE, STEVE LANG, AND
WILLIAM KORNBLUM

The land ethic simply enlarges the boundaries of the community to include soils, waters, plants, and animals, or collectively: the land....In short, a land ethic changes the role of Homo sapiens from conqueror of the land-community to plain member and citizen of it. It implies respect for his [and her] fellow-members, and also respect for the community as such.

The fallacy the economic determinists have tied around our collective neck, and which we now need to cast off, is the belief that economics determines all land-use. This is simply not true. An innumerable host of actions and attitudes, comprising perhaps the bulk of all land relations, is determined by the land-users' tastes and predilections, rather than by his [or her] purse. The bulk of all land relations hinges on investments of time, forethought, skill and faith rather than on investments of cash. As a land-user thinketh, so is [s]he.

Aldo Leopold, *A Sand County Almanac* (1949)

For New Yorkers, the meaning of a "land ethic" is rather distant from the rural America Leopold had in mind in the mid-twentieth century, but is very much a strong presence on the land and water. A twenty-first-century urban land ethic necessarily involves a combination of city planning, national environmental regulations, and local citizen activism. We explore the consequences and contradictions of this hybrid approach to urban environmental policy, paying specific attention to the role of citizen activism in engendering a land ethic for a city of water.

In April 2007, New York City Mayor Michael Bloomberg and his administration published an ambitious plan for the city's future to the year 2030 (known as PlaNYC 2030). Almost every page of PlaNYC 2030 argues for "greening the city" and making it more environmentally sustainable. Announcing it as "the most sweeping plan to enhance New York's urban environment in the city's modern history," the plan proposes projects to enhance the quality of the city's land, air, water, energy, and transportation, and asserts that it "can become a model for cities in the 21st century. The combined impact of this plan would not only help ensure a higher quality of life for generations of New Yorkers to come; it would also contribute to a 30 percent reduction in global warming emissions."

The mayor's admirable plan—published before the full brunt of the global economic crash became apparent—calls for major new investments in capital projects to address issues of air and water quality, and to provide more mass transit and affordable housing for lower income New Yorkers. But the prospects of realization of these and many specific sustainability projects will require a citizenry even more mobilized to push for a greener New York than currently exists in the city. Environmental activists inevitably must meet the challenge of developing and articulating a "land ethic" that makes sense of environmentalism in the urban context. Just as Aldo Leopold was correct to criticize the national parks as unsustainable islands of preservation, one can ask of urban environmental movements and projects to what extent they seek to foster a sense of stewardship among their participants that links local environmental activism and specific projects to issues of restoration and preservation in regional estuaries and ecosystems. This stewardship depends, as Leopold taught, on a detailed understanding of the particular stresses that are experienced in our backyards, that is, in our particular ecosystems.

On all the major dimensions of environmental quality, New York City has severe challenges and has set ambitious goals to meet them. The city's desire to limit its greenhouse gas emissions along with its energy consumption—both of which are increasing dramatically, as the following charts show—and its efforts to address a variety of pressing water quality issues highlight the goals and obstacles facing its leaders and its environmental activists. Following, we use these two environmental case studies, energy usage and water quality, as a vehicle to discuss the mayor's PlaNYC 2030 agenda and to illustrate the successes and shortcomings of the urban land ethic as it is currently practiced in New York City.

NEW YORK'S ENERGY AND GREENHOUSE GAS EMISSIONS

While the city's environmental quality has improved tremendously since the passage of the Clean Air Act of 1970, it still has a very long way to go as it strives to improve the environmental terms of its energy system. With each passing year, New Yorkers set records for energy usage, consuming more and more electricity from energy-intensive appliances and personal electronics. In an average year, New Yorkers spend approximately $13.4 billion on energy (Bloomberg 2007). By 2015, it is projected that the city's annual electricity and heating cost will increase by $3 billion, excluding delivery costs. Because the city's delivery infrastructure is unreliable and outdated, high-energy costs pose a threat to economic development.

Besides being very expensive, energy consumption is responsible for 80 percent of the city's global warming emissions and more than 40 percent of all locally generated air pollution. By 2015, the city will be pumping an additional 4.6 million metric

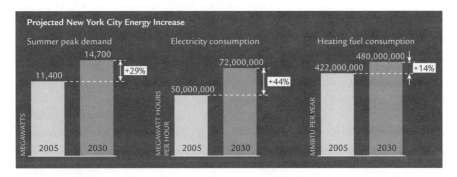

Figure 15.1
Projected New York City Energy Consumption for Year 2030
Source: Bloomberg 2007.

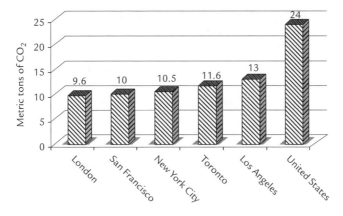

Figure 15.2
Greenhouse Gas Emissions per Capita for Major Cities
Source: Authors, compiled from Kennedy et al., 2009.

tons of carbon dioxide into the atmosphere. With population and economic growth already straining the city's energy infrastructure, many fear that energy demand and consumption will eventually outstrip supply.

To reduce the city's contributions to global climate change, the city, in conjunction with state and federal agencies, has worked to reduce its role in producing greenhouse gas emissions. New York is part of the Regional Greenhouse Gas Initiative, a program with an emission trading system that caps greenhouse gas emissions and then auctions pollution credits. In April 2003, then New York State Governor George Pataki invited governors from ten Northeastern and Mid-Atlantic States[1] to join in the nation's first market-based regulatory program to reduce carbon dioxide emissions by 10 percent from their state's power sector by 2018. Auction proceeds will help fund renewable energy and energy efficiency programs. In 2004, New York State adopted the Renewable Portfolio Standard that requires all regulated utilities to purchase at least 25 percent of their electricity from renewable sources by

2013. Launched in 2007, the program aims to develop a package of mandates and incentives that will reduce the state's energy consumption 15 percent by 2015. On April 9, 2008, Governor David Paterson signed Executive Order No. 2 (EO 2), which created a State Energy Plan charged with developing a comprehensive statewide energy plan.

In 2007, the New York City Council passed a greenhouse gas reduction bill that codifies the carbon dioxide emissions goals laid out in the mayor's long-term sustainability plan. The bill requires that heat-trapping gases from city government buildings and vehicles be cut 30 percent from current levels by 2017, and that carbon emissions from the entire city, including privately owned buildings, be reduced by 30 percent by 2030.

Improved energy efficiency and a shift to renewable energy development are the primary approaches to achieving the 30 percent carbon reduction goal laid out in the city's long-term sustainability plan. A major facet of this approach is to improve and transform the city's outdated energy infrastructure to a cleaner, more efficient energy system. Along with upgrading its energy infrastructure, the city is pushing market-based strategies to finance clean energy projects, as well as investing in new technologies to improve energy efficiency and providing financial incentives to clean energy entrepreneurs.

Bloomberg's PlaNYC 2030 calls for replacing older more polluting power plants with newer, more efficient and cleaner plants, as well as expanding distributed generation sources—relatively small, localized power sources. Many of the city's aging power plants are outdated, using 30 percent to 60 percent more fuel and producing several times the air pollution of newer plants to generate the same amount of electricity. During 2005, the New York Power Authority's newer plants emitted one-tenth of a pound of nitrogen oxide, a major source of smog and greenhouse gas, for every megawatt hour (mwh) of electricity produced. By contrast, older, inefficient plants of comparable size emitted an average of 72 times that amount (7.2 pounds of nitrogen oxide per mwh). The mayor proposes increasing natural gas usage, which fuels 80 percent of the city's power plants and a quarter of the energy used in its buildings. Newer power plants and expanded clean distributed generation will require increasing the city's natural gas infrastructure and building new pipelines and natural gas terminals. For example, early in 2012, the city endorsed a proposed natural gas pipeline that would start off the Rockaway Queens' ocean shoreline, running under Jamaica Bay, and through one of the city's largest tracts of national parkland, Floyd Bennett Field in Brooklyn. However, many local citizen groups (e.g., the Jamaica Bay Eco-Watchers, NYC Audubon) have criticized the plan both because of the environmental threats that pipeline construction and operation would pose to the sensitive ecosystem of the Jamaica Bay estuary and for the lack of public involvement in the decision-making process.

Another major component involved in updating the city's energy infrastructure involves modernizing the city's power grid—the largest underground system in the world. Designed in the 1920s, the power grid consists of almost 90,000 miles of underground cable and almost 20,000 miles of overhead cable that run throughout the city. Although the system is quite reliable, when power failures occur, the network's age and complexity often make it more difficult to identify the problem and restore power. A state-of-the art grid technology, which incorporates advances in communications, computing, and electronics, like those that exist in Tokyo, Paris, and London, would improve energy reliability and service for the city.

Automobiles and industrial agriculture[2] are the largest contributors to total carbon emissions throughout the United States. By contrast, 79 percent of New York City's total carbon emissions come from buildings, primarily older buildings burning heating oil and natural gas, whereas cars and trucks contribute roughly 17 percent of the city's carbon emissions. Greening the city building code through a system of mandates and incentives, and streamlining the process for incorporating new sustainable building technologies to improve energy efficiency are key components of the city's energy plans. While the city has been a leader in new green and sustainable building construction—many of its new buildings have LEED certification—most of its energy usage and carbon emissions come from older buildings. Conducting energy audits of older buildings and then retrofitting them with more energy efficient lighting, heating, and cooling systems is a key strategy of the plan. By 2030, approximately 85 percent of the city's energy usage will come from existing buildings that currently consume high sulfur diesel oil, the largest source of particulate matter in the city. In January 2011, the city proposed rules to phase out the dirtiest types of heating oil used in roughly 10,000 New York City buildings. The new rules would bring the city into compliance with state laws passed in 2010 mandating a 99 percent reduction in the sulfur content of common heating oils, as well as a city rule mandating 2 percent biodiesel fuel for heating buildings. If passed, the new regulations would require all new boilers to burn the low-sulfur heating oil by 2015, with modification of all boilers by 2030. Estimates for boiler conversion hover around $10,000 per building, with payment programs for those building owners facing financial hardship (Navarro 2011).

PlaNYC calls for expanding peak load management programs by installing sophisticated metering systems that would enable energy consumers to track their daily energy usage and engage in real time pricing—a system that shows when peak energy usage and costs occur. The objective of real time pricing plans is to prompt consumers to conserve energy during peak periods when the cost of energy is high. The mayor's plan calls for incentives to encourage residents and small businesses to adopt real time pricing strategies and mandates for municipal nonresidential customers.

Currently, eight different federal, state, and local agencies are involved in energy planning for the city. PlaNYC 2030 calls for the creation of an energy planning board that would coordinate and develop a broad energy vision for the city. The plan also calls for the creation of an energy efficiency authority for New York City that would streamline and coordinate energy decisions.

In addition to improving energy efficiency, the mayor's plan proposes fostering a market for renewable energies, such as solar, wind, and tidal power, through tax abatements and incentives. Additionally, the city plans to explore new technologies for producing safe and clean energy from the city's landfills and wastewater treatment plants.

NEW YORK CITY'S WATERWAYS AND WATER QUALITY

In the early 1900s, nearly 600 million gallons of raw sewage emptied into New York City waterways daily (Waldman 1999). People died from typhoid fever after handling contaminated shellfish, and bacteria levels in the Hudson River were 170 times safe limits (Waldman 1999; Bloomberg 2007). A little over a century later, Mayor Bloomberg's PlaNYC 2030 calls for opening 90 percent of the city's waterways to recreation. More advanced technology, stricter legislation, and grassroots efforts to improve the areas where people live, work, and play are largely responsible for the dramatic improvement in NYC water quality since the early 1900s.

The Metropolitan Sewerage Commission began monitoring water quality in 1909 in response to public outcry about the deteriorating quality of life near polluted waterways (NYC DEP 2006). Early reports documented sewage to water ratios of one to 20 (one part sewage to 20 parts water)—water quality levels so low they barely sustained a fish population (Waldman 1999). Despite the construction of the region's first wastewater treatment plant at Coney Island in 1886 (a system for catching floatable materials), the city closed beaches in 1914 and prohibited the consumption of oysters in 1927 (Waldman 1999; Olson 2008). In a city with nearly 600 miles of waterfront, residents were becoming increasingly landlocked.

The tides began to turn, however, in 1972 when the federal government passed the Clean Water Act requiring every US body of water be open to fishing and swimming by 1985 (Waldman 1999; Bloomberg 2007). Federal regulations in combination with improved infrastructure and sewage treatment technology brought New York City's water quality within reach of New York state standards.[3] To evaluate compliance with these standards, the Harbor Survey Program[4] now monitors NYC water quality at over sixty-two stations—thirty-five in the open harbor and twenty-seven stations in the city's tributaries. According to the Harbor Survey Program Report (2006, 22), the city's waterways generally met state standards for water quality. It stated that water quality, "for the most part retained the status quo from previous years." Despite improvements and continued monitoring, barriers to water quality persist.

The Harbor Survey Program reports on water quality using four primary indicators—fecal coliform bacteria, dissolved oxygen, chlorophyll a, and Secchi transparency. Fecal coliform is primarily found in human and animal intestines and is associated with sewage waste. It is used to indicate the possibility of disease producing bacteria in the water. Oxygen is necessary for aquatic life to survive, and levels of dissolved oxygen below 5mg/L can produce stress for aquatic life. Chlorophyll a is a plant pigment used to measure the prevalence of phytoplankton. While key to the food web and oxygen production, an overabundance of phytoplankton (over 20ug/L) indicates eutrophic conditions[5] and a decline in water quality. Secchi transparency is a measurement assessing the clarity of the water. Clean water has Secchi transparency levels above five feet, with levels below three feet indicating degraded waters (NYC DEP 2006).

The Survey Program monitors these indicators in four regions in New York harbor: the Inner Harbor; the Upper East River-Western Long Island Sound; Jamaica Bay; and the Lower NY Harbor-Raritan Bay. According to the Survey Program's latest report, while remaining below state standards, levels of fecal coliform increased throughout all regions of the harbor. In both the Inner Harbor and Jamaica Bay, fecal coliform levels rose above state standards after wet weather events, leading to the closure of beaches in the Inner Harbor region. Dissolved oxygen levels met state standards most of the time in the Inner Harbor and Lower NY Harbor-Raritan Bay areas but remained an area of concern in Jamaica Bay and the Upper-East River-Western Long Island Sound regions. The Upper-East River-Western Long Island Sound region had the lowest levels of DO throughout the harbor and failed to continually meet the state's water quality standards. Both the Inner Harbor and Jamaica Bay experienced incidents of hypoxia (oxygen deficiency) in the summer of 2006. Additionally, trends in both regions point to increased stratification between surface and bottom waters, as well as increased and prolonged algae blooms, indicating eutrophic conditions. Chlorophyll a levels in Jamaica Bay have been above state standards since 1990 and were well above those indicative of eutrophic conditions in 2006, with 64 percent of the samples failing to comply with standards. The Lower NY Harbor-Raritan Bay region failed to comply with chlorophyll a standards nearly 25 percent of the time. Average Secchi transparency levels did not meet desired depths (>5 feet = clearer water) in two of four regions in the harbor—Jamaica Bay and the Lower NY Harbor-Raritan Bay (NYC DEP 2006). See table 15.1.

New York City's wastewater infrastructure is one of the primary barriers to achieving consistently good water quality and accounts for why portions of New York Harbor failed to meet state standards in 2006. Similar to other older cities, New York City's sewer system combines street runoff and sewage in over 60 percent of the network (Waldman 1999; Bloomberg 2007). Problems occur during periods of heavy

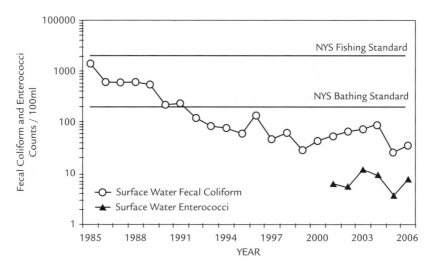

Figure 15.3
Inner Harbor Water Quality: Fecal Coliform Levels
Source: Authors, adapted from Bloomberg, 2007.

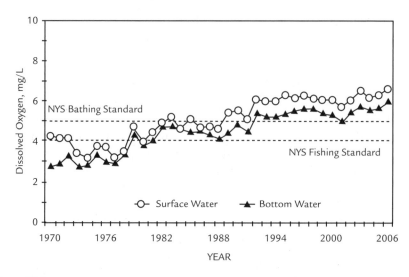

Figure 15.4
Inner Harbor Water Quality: Dissolved Oxygen Levels
Source: Authors, adapted from Bloomberg, 2007.

rain when rainwater and sewage overwhelm the holding capacity of the sewer system, resulting in an overflow of untreated wastewater into the surrounding waterways or combined sewer overflows. While treatment plants can handle nearly double their dry-weather capacity, as little as one-tenth of an inch of heavy rain can lead to combined sewer overflows (Bloomberg 2007; Murphy 2008). As a result of combined sewer overflows, 27 billion gallons of untreated wastewater enter the city's waterways each year (Murphy 2008). The overflows result in increased nutrient levels and bacteria in the water (e.g., nitrogen and fecal coliform), causing algae blooms and oxygen loss, which could cause aquatic life to die off and prohibits active recreation activities after heavy rain events.

New York City has improved its combined sewer overflows capture rate to 70 percent, up from 30 percent in 1980, and PlaNYC 2030 calls for a capture rate of 75 percent by 2030 (Bloomberg 2007; NYC DEP 2006). However, critics—such as the NY League of Conservation Voters and activist groups, including Storm Water Infrastructure Matters—demand that the city achieve higher capture rates by building storage tanks and implementing additional measures (e.g., conservation efforts and green solutions) to address the problem. Critics note that the 75 percent capture rate called for by PlaNYC 2030 is already required of the city under a 2004 consent agreement with the state and claim that the city's continued failure to meet these requirements demonstrates a lack of commitment for improving water quality (Lenzer and Murphy 2007). Critics point to the 90 percent capture rate achieved by older cities like Chicago and Boston, and the Department of Environmental Protection's elimination of half their projected storage tanks (from eight to four), as evidence that the city could move well beyond the capture rate of 75 percent; a rate that would still result in the release of 24 billion gallons of untreated wastewater per year (Bloomberg 2007: Lenzer and Murphy 2007).

Table 15.1 WATER QUALITY INDICATORS BY NEW YORK HARBOR REGION

Region	Fecal Coliform (FC)—200 cells/100mL	Dissolved Oxygen (DO)—5 mg/L	Chlorophyll a —20 ug/L	Secchi Transparency— > 5 ft clear waters; < 3 ft degraded waters
Inner Harbor	− • Fails to meet standards after wet weather events • ⇑ from 26 cells/100mL to 36 cells/100mL	+ • Average 6.6 mg/L	+ • Averages met standards	+/− • Average depths 4.6 feet
Upper East River-Western Long Island Sound	− • ⇑ from 17 cells/100mL to 55 cells/100mL	− • Noncompliance 17% for surface waters and 30% for bottom waters • hypoxia events	+ • Averages met standards	+/− • Average above 5 ft • Did not meet standards in 40% of samples
Jamaica Bay	− • Fails to meet standard after wet weather events • ⇑ from 23 cells/mL (1998) to 51 cells/100mL	− • Noncompliance for surface waters 21% of samples • hypoxia events	− • Averages did not meet standards • 64% of samples failed to comply • eutrophic conditions	− • Averages between 3.8ft-4.2 ft • Did not comply with standards
Lower NY Harbor— Raritan Bay	+ • ⇑ from 3 cells/100mL (1999) to 10 cells/100mL	+ • Average 6.1mg/L	+/− • Average value 13.7ug/L • Failed to meet standards in 23% of samples	− • Averages below 5 ft • Failed to meet standards in 31% of samples

(+): Generally meets state standards.

(−): Generally did not meet state standards.

(+/−): On average, met state standards, but a significant portion of individual samples failed to comply with standards.

Source: Compiled by Authors from data from the New York City Department of Environmental Protection (2006).

In addition to combined sewer overflows, other barriers to improving New York City's water quality exist. Besides nitrogen enrichment from overflows, nitrogen enters the waterways through atmospheric fallout associated with gasoline and oil combustion (automobiles) and from agricultural runoff (manure and fertilizer) from upstate farms (Waldman 1999). Excessive nitrogen levels can cause disease in fish populations, such as cancer and fin rot, as well as contribute to the degradation of wetlands and the creation of eutrophic conditions (Waldman 1999). New York City's heavily polluted canals and tributaries also contribute to the degradation of water quality in the city. Over 52 percent of the city's canals and creeks are unavailable for public recreation as a result of high contamination rates (Bloomberg 2007). Water quality also suffers due to the loss of crucial wetlands and open space. Nearly 90 percent of the city's wetlands have been lost over the past century and nearly 9,000 acres of permeable surfaces have been lost in the past twenty-five years—both play crucial functions in filtering water and in reducing the amount of water that enters the sewer system (Bloomberg 2007).

These functions prove all the more important when considering how global climate change will impact the city. The New York City Department of Environmental Protection (2008) expects that global climate change will produce increased rates of precipitation and an increase in the number of intense storms in the New York region. Increased precipitation and intense storms will produce more frequent overflows and result in higher levels of untreated wastewater in the city's waterways. The city already experienced such consequences in 2006, an overly wet year, when nearly 35 billion gallons of wastewater entered the waterways, up from the typical 27 billion (Murphy 2008).

The city's plans for 2030 provide a starting point for improving New York City's environmental future. However, well-intentioned plans are not enough. Citizen groups (such as the Jamaica Bay Eco-watchers, the Newtown Creek Alliance, and the Storm Water Infrastructure Matters coalition) must continually challenge city leaders to move beyond modest goals for improved water quality and continue pushing for the implementation of proven technological and best management practices. Furthermore, continued citizen action is necessary to ensure a transparent and equitable approach to improving New York City's waterways and overall environmental quality. An environmental policy that does not integrate citizen input and involvement will be neither practical nor sustainable.

ASSESSING PLANYC 2030

Mayor Bloomberg's PlaNYC 2030 must be commended for its initiatives to improve the city government's environmental impact—for its efforts to "lead by example" and its challenge to other state and federal agencies to do the same. Furthermore, in a democratic society, the mayor is, to some extent, limited in what can be "mandated" of others. However, there are several shortcomings to PlaNYC's approach to greening the city, which require local activists to take the lead in raising community awareness of environmental problems, applying political pressure for environmental solutions, and adopting voluntary citizen action (e.g., reduced resource consumption) to improve the environmental impact of New York.

PlaNYC's approach to energy consumption is largely limited to city government buildings and energy usage, which is only 6.5 percent of the city's overall energy consumption. While this is not an insignificant amount, improvements to city government alone will not solve the city's environmental problems. Furthermore, PlaNYC 2030's energy approach rarely mentions actually reducing *the amount of energy* consumed, either by government or citizens. Discussions of energy consumption are almost always couched in terms of improving energy efficiency, through power grid improvements and energy efficient lighting and appliances, and so on. While improved energy efficiency is a necessary component of green energy policy, efficiency alone will not solve our energy problems, given that New York City's energy consumption is expected to increase 44 percent by 2030. Efforts to reduce consumption, such as the real time pricing program, do not focus on *resource usage*, but rather the *time of resource consumption*, recommending a switch from peak energy periods to less expensive periods. Consequently, the rationale for conservation is economic as opposed to environmental. Moreover, with a large rental population (roughly 70 percent of New Yorkers), few residents have access to electric, gas, and heating/cooling meters necessary to monitor energy consumption through real time pricing programs. In contrast, residents of Brooklyn's Community Board 18,[6] many of whom are homeowners, have had their monitors stolen for their copper wiring. Although these examples do not indicate that real time pricing programs cannot be successful, they do illustrate the challenges of addressing energy consumption in the urban context. Finally, nearly 80 percent of the city's greenhouse gas emissions come from buildings, and residential buildings account for the largest source of the city's energy usage by building type, at 36.7 percent. As a result, citizen efforts are necessary to reduce energy consumption because reductions in consumption by government and commercial buildings will not be enough. The city's plan does not discuss this aspect of energy consumption, and in fact, promotes ideas to the contrary. "We can absorb growth while keeping our power consumption constant," later stating, "By investing in these efforts now, the city of endless energy can stay that way" (Bloomberg 2007, 106 and 115).

Similarly, PlaNYC's water quality goals of making 90 percent of the city's waters swimmable and fishable is a laudable goal considering the city's challenges to water quality. However, the Clean Water Act had already mandated the city to exceed this goal by 1985, and the city has continually failed to do so. In September 2010, the city's Department of Environmental Protection wrote the United States Environmental Protection Agency objecting to their emphasis on swimmable and fishable waters, citing excessive costs to municipalities in implementing these goals. Furthermore, the city's new wastewater infrastructure plan concedes to implementing green infrastructure solutions (such as rain barrels, street swales, green roofs, etc.), only if the state's Department of Environmental Conservation relieves the city agency from certain commitments to building other "grey" infrastructure projects (e.g., holding tanks, upgrades to treatment plants, etc.) that the city does not deem cost-effective (Storm Water Infrastructure Matters letter to Department of Environmental Conservation, November 12, 2010). Consequently, achieving swimmable/fishable waters will require continued pressure from groups, such as Storm Water Infrastructure Matters and the Jamaica Bay Eco-Watchers, to ensure that city agencies comply with federal and state mandates, as well as pushing state and federal agencies to provide adequate funding for the city to overcome the challenges to water quality that have been centuries in the making.

Local environmental advocates play a crucial role in actualizing an urban land ethic. Citizen activists are essential for holding environmental agencies accountable to current standards and regulations, for supporting legislation for more stringent environmental regulations, for pressuring all levels of government to spend limited funds on environmental improvements, for bringing environmental issues to the attention of other community members, and for taking voluntary measures to reduce their community's environmental impact.

GREENING THE GRASSROOTS: THE KEY ROLE OF CITIZEN ACTIVISM

The usual answer to this dilemma (environmental degradation) is "more conservation education." No one will debate this, but is it certain that only the volume of education needs stepping up? Is something lacking in the content as well? It is difficult to give a fair summary of its content in brief form, but, as I understand it, the content is substantially this: obey the law, vote right, join some organizations, and practice what conservation is profitable on your own land, the government will do the rest. Is not this formula too easy to accomplish anything worthwhile? It defines no right or wrong, assigns no obligation, calls for no sacrifice, and implies no change in the current philosophy of values. In respect of land use, it urges only enlightened self-interest. Just how far will such education take us?

Aldo Leopold, *A Sand County Almanac* (1949)

Absent the environmental legislation of the early 1970s, including the Clean Air and Water Acts, and the National Environmental Policy Act, which remain essential in establishing air and water quality goals, none of the progress on which New York's ambitious environmental plans are based would have been possible without an increasingly active and informed citizenry. Water quality in the extensive estuaries of New York City, for example, cannot improve appreciably without major investments in the sewage infrastructure. The massive treatment plant on Manhattan's 150th street Hudson shore, which became operative in the early 1980s at the cost then of over $2 billion in public funds, brought untold improvements in water quality in New York's upper and lower harbors. Swimming once again became possible on the beaches of Staten Island after years of closure resulting from high coliform counts.

But much remains to be accomplished and public funds will be needed, which entails a level of taxpayer support that can be difficult to mobilize. Huge underground rainwater holding tanks are needed to prevent combined sewer overflows and polluted ground water runoff after storms. These and many other environmental infrastructure investments are largely invisible to the public. In consequence, the city must rely on environmental activists who understand complex environmental situations, and who can help convince their neighbors to support these uses of their tax dollars (Greider and Garkovich 1994). But such citizens do not tend to emerge as champions of regional solutions to combined sewer overflows or wetland restoration plans before they have experienced movements to improve the quality of their local parks and natural areas.

Inspired often by the examples of Frederick Law Olmsted, William Cullen Bryant, Albert Parsons, Iphigene Sulzberger, Herbert Johnson, Jane Jacobs, Elizabeth Barlow Rogers, and many others, citizen activists have initiated most of the city's signature environmental projects, from Central Park and Prospect Park, to the Jamaica Bay Wildlife Refuge, and the Hudson River Park. New York is often thought of as a city of power brokers and "top-down" planning. Robert Moses and many other powerful figures provided grand public parks and environmental works projects but also cooperated with elite business groups to invest heavily in highway construction that destroyed wetlands and often barred New Yorkers from accessing their waterfront (e.g., the Belt Parkway completed in 1941). The ecological value of marshlands was entirely misunderstood during what Louis Mumford called the era of "insensate industrialism." Consequently, the city has lost more than half the salt marshes and brackish wetlands that once fringed its abundant shores. The reconceptualization of wetlands as in need of preservation rather than development is in large measure the result of ecologically informed citizen activism and has become a central tenet in current waterfront plans.

Now, at its best, the Bloomberg era of city planning and development represents a marriage of professional elite planning with New York style citizen-activism. What this means in practice for the city's environmental future becomes clearer by examining some contemporary examples that involve energy policy and the restoration and redevelopment of the city's waterfront. We briefly assess the strengths and limitations of some exemplary environmental movements and projects led by New York citizen activists. These include environmental justice movements around equitable energy policy, efforts to create new approaches to the urban waterfront, and efforts to preserve and protect the declining environment of Jamaica Bay. Each of these cases highlights different aspects of urban environmentalism at the level of local communities and neighborhoods. Each example represents an approach to environmental restoration and community development in areas of the city that until quite recently were urban "sacrifice zones" marked by zones of sagging piers, dilapidated industrial blocks, razor wire fences, and acres of filled or otherwise ruined wetlands.

Energy Policy, Smart Growth, and Environmental Justice

Until recently, the conservation movement, along with its offspring—the environmental movement, has had a negative view of cities. Movement participants tended to view cities as concrete jungles or environmental wastelands in contrast to pristine, "untouched" wilderness areas traditionally associated with conservation and preservation movements. Urban environmental justice activists pushed to expand traditional notions of the environment from wilderness areas devoid of people to those areas where people "live, work, and play." By reframing the environment to include people, as well as plants and animals, environmental justice activists played a large role in shifting attitudes toward urban environments. At the forefront of activist struggles has been community protection against the unequal distribution of environmental hazards associated with locally unwanted land uses, such as power plants, waste transfer stations, and incinerators (Angotti 2008; Gandy 1999; Sze 2007).

In 2001, in the wake of electricity deregulation in New York City, a citywide community-based environmental justice coalition, Communities United for Responsible Energy, emerged in response to the siting of power plants in low-income and minority communities (Sze 2007). Years of engaging in community-based participatory health research and "street science" showed a consistent link between power plant emissions and health risks. In the face of such evidence, the coalition forced state and city energy authorities to make the facility siting process more transparent and to conduct environmental health studies on the potential health risks of particulate matter.

Over time, Communities United for Responsible Energy activists became part of the city's sustainability advisory board that helped draft an influential energy report, large sections of which were incorporated into PlaNYC. Specifically, the city adopted activists' concerns about equitable energy planning and economic development into its planning documents to ensure that lower-income communities of color do not bear disproportionate risk associated with the siting of power plants and energy facilities.

In recent years, New York City, much like cities throughout the country, has seen a fusion of smart growth and environmental justice movements. Ensuring equitable distribution of potentially noxious facilities is not enough. Rather, the goal of these movements is to find environmentally clean and safe energy sources that can also create jobs and boost local economies. Environmental justice organizations such as West Harlem Environmental Action, Sustainable South Bronx, and the United Puerto Rican Organization of Sunset Park have focused on transforming environmental burdens into benefits and developing strategies for a green energy economy that could trickle down to members of impoverished communities. Similar to the NY Chapter of the Apollo Alliance, these local organizations have sought to build coalitions of labor unions, environmental justice advocates, businesses, educators, and community-based organizations to improve local living standards and promote economic growth through a modern energy policy that promotes a market for renewable energy and other green technologies.

Sustainable South Bronx and the Bronx River

During the mid-twentieth century the Bronx fell into a period of urban decay. The quality of life, particularly in the South Bronx, decreased dramatically. Neighborhoods were fragmented by the construction of numerous highways; the Sheridan and Cross-Bronx Expressways further distanced the borough's neighborhoods from each other and from the borough's outstanding environmental features—the Bronx River and its estuary at the East River. The movement to restore environmental quality and access to these ecosystems began with initiatives in the more middle-class neighborhoods

Figure 15.5
Concrete Park in the Bronx, August 27, 2010
Source: Photo by Daniel Avila, NYC Department of Parks & Recreation, used by permission.

closer to Westchester County. Now there is also a strong grassroots green movement in the lower income, minority neighborhoods of the South Bronx.

The 23-mile Bronx River winds down through southern Westchester and the Bronx. It is one of the little-known marvels of the New York City landscape. Although it never became a concrete sluiceway, as did the Los Angeles River that Martha Matsuoka and Robert Gottlieb write so eloquently about, in its most urban reaches in the South Bronx, it became more of a hard-edged channel than anything resembling a natural river. In its upper reaches, below the Kensico Reservoir, the river was trashed, polluted, and neglected.

Fed up with the dismal conditions of the Bronx River, local residents formed Bronx River Restoration Project, Inc. in 1974 with local activist Ruth Anderberg as its first director. Bronx River Restoration succeeded in removing a plethora of debris, including refrigerators, tires, and even a wine press along the shoreline in the 180th Street/West Farms area. In 2001, the Bronx River Alliance was created to build on the twenty-seven-year history of restoration work started by Bronx River Restoration Project. Today the Alliance helps coordinate efforts on behalf of the Bronx River's sixty community groups, government agencies, schools, and businesses. The river is becoming once again "a peaceful corridor of green for fishing, strolling, biking, boating and nature study amid the noise and bustle of urban life." In its southernmost section, the river passes through one of the poorest and formerly most neglected community areas of the city, Hunts Point and Soundview.

Sustainable South Bronx (SSBx) is an award-winning community organization dedicated to environmental justice solutions in this lower reach of the Bronx River. Created in 2001 under the leadership of Majora Carter, a young community organizer from the area, Sustainable South Bronx seeks to address policy and planning issues like land-use, energy, transportation, water, waste, education, and, most recently, design and manufacturing. The area it primarily serves, the Hunts Point neighborhood in the South Bronx, is one of New York City's last remaining industrial areas. The Bruckner Expressway to the north and west, and the Bronx and East Rivers to the south and east bind the one-square mile area of Hunts Point. On the one hand, the neighborhood has numerous assets, including a waterfront location on the Bronx River and East River, proximity to Manhattan, the economic engine of the Hunts Point Food Distribution Center (the second largest in the world), new city-led development projects, waterfront parks, and a strong local organizational infrastructure. Simultaneously, it exhibits one of the highest poverty and unemployment levels in the city, with poor community health, noxious industries and commercial traffic, substance abuse, and prostitution issues. Caught in the middle of these pressures are approximately 11,000 residents who have been neglected and underserved by the neighborhood's local economy.

In a relatively short time, SSBx has developed an impressive record of working for community betterment. The first issue the group took on was to develop alternatives to a city-proposed penal institution in the area, which is directly across the East River from Rikers Island, and the site of a number of existing penal facilities. After this successful protest and intervention, SSBx has moved forcefully to work with public agencies to develop green jobs and green job training programs for local residents. Ms. Carter, awarded a MacArthur Foundation "Genius" grant, has moved on to city-wide environmental leadership activities, but the organization appears to have gone through this transition well and remains a highly effective and vocal advocate for "Greening the Ghetto."

Citizen Action in Jamaica Bay

At the opposite southern extreme of the city, citizen environmental groups have played a vital role in protecting and restoring the world famous Jamaica Bay estuary. Their efforts extend from picking up trash along the beaches to lobbying public officials vigorously to address the Bay's problems of environmental quality. While the Jamaica Bay environmental groups and their constituents have varied perspectives about the causes of environmental degradation in the Bay, and about their vision for the Bay's future, they share a concern about the Bay's ecological problems, an attachment to this natural place, and an appreciation of the environmental and social benefits of the urban waterfront.

Jamaica Bay is famous for its Wildlife Refuge, the only genuine wildlife protected area accessible by subway. It is also infamous as the site of numerous landfills, of Floyd Bennett Field, and of John F. Kennedy International Airport (JFK), whose runways extend over what were once Jamaica Bay wetlands. For decades, the fate of the Bay as a natural versus industrialized estuary hung in the balance. Congress's inclusion in 1972 of most, but not all, of the Bay within the boundaries of Gateway National Recreation Area appeared to settle the issue in favor of environmental preservation. However, the reality of that federal umbrella of preservation remains complicated by continuing stresses and environmental degradation in and around the Bay's watershed, and by the immense diversity of the populations living in and around the Bay. Nonetheless, with its marshes, adjacent beaches, and upland forests, Jamaica Bay makes up approximately 26 square miles along the southeastern edge

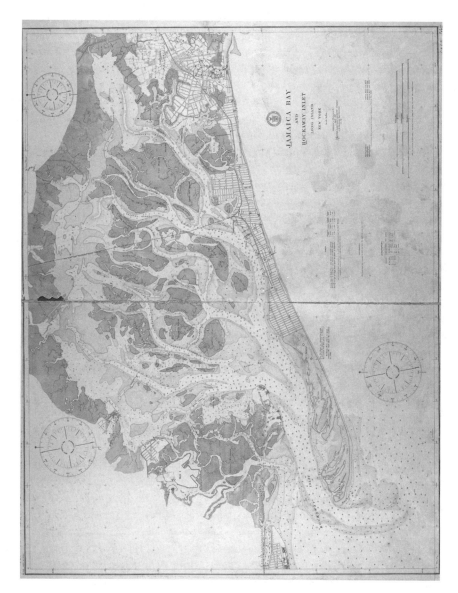

Figure 15.6
Map of Jamaica Bay, 1911
Source: New York Public Library, used by permission.

of Brooklyn and Queens, abutting JFK Airport, and is the largest natural open space in New York City.

The Jamaica Bay estuary is home to over 330 wildlife species and is a migratory bird stopover along the Atlantic Flyway, attracting 20 percent of North America's bird species. The brackish waters of the Bay and the interior marshlands play important ecological functions, including their role as nursery sites for small fish, shellfish, and crustaceans, which are key to maintaining the region's biodiversity. Moreover, the Bay and marshlands are critical for protecting the Brooklyn and Queens mainland from storm surges and floodwaters, an essential function given the roughly 1.7 million people living in the immediate boundaries of the Jamaica Bay watershed.

The loss of permeable surfaces within the Jamaica Bay watershed and the release of 40,000 pounds of nitrogen per day into the Bay from the four nearby wastewater treatment plants continue to degrade water quality and erode marshlands. Consequently, Jamaica Bay frequently fails to meet state water quality standards (see table 15.1 above) and marshlands that once covered the Bay have declined by well over 50 percent, with predictions of complete loss in less than two decades (National Park Service 2003). In response, local environmental groups struggle against the pressures of urban development that threaten the environmental integrity of the estuary.

In 1995, the Jamaica Bay Eco-Watchers, primarily based out of the Queens neighborhood of Broad Channel, formed in response to increased rates of marsh loss in the Bay. The Eco-Watchers act much as a "watchdog" group, with daily monitoring of the Bay to document threats to water quality, as well as ensuring compliance with environmental laws. The Eco-Watchers have been battling the city's Department of Environmental Protection to take the necessary and available measures to address the wastewater nitrogen problem, which they argue is responsible for marshland loss. In February 2010, the Eco-Watchers, working with the National Resources Defense Council, the NY/NJ Baykeeper, and the American Littoral Society, threatened to sue the city for failing to address the Bay's nitrogen problem. Negotiations between the various groups, the city, and the state resulted in a legal agreement wherein the city would spend $115 million over the next ten years to retrofit the wastewater treatment plants and reduce nitrogen loading into the Bay. Despite this success, group members say they must remain vigilant in their work to monitor the Bay and ensure full Department of Environmental Protection compliance. Citing state and city budgetary problems, the group recognizes that an agreement in principle will not automatically translate into action or results. Although the Eco-Watchers formed in the 1990s, many long-time residents have been fighting to protect Jamaica Bay for decades and realize that doing so is an ongoing process.

In 1968, a number of activists, including scientist René Dubos, the National Audubon Society, the Sierra Club, and local environmental groups, worked to stop a proposed JFK runway extension that would have paved over large parts of Jamaica Bay. The Sierra Club spoke out against the runway expansion, stating that the plan should be considered "ecological insanity" and offering their services to stop the project "with every means at [its] disposal" (Bryant 1968). Similarly, the President Emeritus of the National Audubon Society said, "Jamaica Bay can and must be saved.

For what good will all the enlargements of our airport and city be, if we destroy all this great area of natural beauty and the life it sustains?" (Buchheister 1969). However, in January 2011, the Port Authority of NY/NJ, via the Regional Plan Association, once again unveiled plans to extend JFK Airport into the Bay. One local resident responded to the new plan by stating, "We've been fighting this battle [to save Jamaica Bay] for over 30 years and we are already training the next generation to continue the fight. Bring it on!!!!!!!!!!" (E-mail communication, February 2011).

The Port Authority plan argues that a lack of airport capacity and increased congestion would impede regional economic development. Currently, national airport delays are about ten minutes; whereas New York City's regional delays are at least twenty minutes (Regional Plan Association 2011). The Port Authority believes these delays will deter people and goods from traveling through the region, thereby limiting economic growth. According to the Regional Plan Association's report, in 2010 roughly 104 million people flew in and out of the region's three major airports.[7] In 2009, air passengers and cargo brought approximately $16.8 billion in wages and $48.6 billion in sales to the region, as well as 415,000 jobs. Furthermore, the plan argues that failing to expand airport capacity could cost the region 125,000 jobs, $6 billion in wages, and $16 billion in sales by 2030 (Regional Plan Association 2011).

The Eco-Watchers recognize the limited capacity of local airports to meet growing demands. They also pride themselves on "commonsense environmentalism," noting that an extreme approach to protecting the Bay ultimately backfires by locking the group out of negotiations with agency officials. Rather than extending runways into Jamaica Bay, the group advocates that the federal government fully fund the Federal Aviation Administration's NexGen 1 and 2 satellite technologies to improve air traffic control and raise capacity at the region's three existing airports. Furthermore, the group advocates expanded use of outlying airports with improved ground transit to move passengers and cargo throughout the region. The group feels these options would reduce local airport delays and increase capacity without environmental harm to Jamaica Bay. In a letter to the Department of the Interior, the Eco-Watchers call on federal officials to stop the plan:

> We wanted to bring this [proposal to expand JFK into the Bay] to your attention immediately so as ensure that the Department of the Interior would be fully prepared to respond to this threat. It is ironic that your words spoken during your visit, recalling past environmentally damaging practices, would be somewhat prophetic as to the vision of what this plan would offer. When you stated that "... *It wasn't so long ago ... where we as citizens and governments turned our backs on the rivers. They were the places to dump things, the wastelands of our countries. Yet in the last 10, 15 years we've watched our society turn our faces to our rivers and embrace them for all that they can bring to us.*" It was evident that yourself, as well as this administration, would consider those past practices as the mistakes of a less enlightened generation and yet we have here in 2011, in this report, exactly that mentality. The Port Authority has put forth this proposal before, in 1970, and it was roundly denounced and rejected by residents, elected officials, and environmentalists. That they would present this proposal at this time seems so much more shocking in light of the era that we find

ourselves in with so much more awareness and regard given to the importance in preserving the environmentally sensitive areas we have for future generations. (Jamaica Bay Eco-Watchers 2011)

Another Jamaica Bay environmental group, the Fresh Creek Nature Association of Canarsie, Brooklyn, formed in 2008 to address shoreline deterioration and restore wetlands along Fresh Creek, a tributary to Jamaica Bay. After a fire started in the unmaintained Fresh Creek Nature Preserve, the group took their concerns to their local community board, the Brooklyn Borough President, park officials, and the state's Department of Environmental Conservation. The group, frustrated by the little success they had with this approach, organized neighborhood cleanups, bringing in over one hundred volunteers for each event. In early 2010, the City Parks Department took up the Fresh Creek Nature Association's cause and began a formal restoration of the preserve, removing invasive species and replanting with indigenous species. While the group views the parks department restoration as a success, the group is concerned about chemical spraying to kill off invasive plants and about the prospect that citizen input and involvement will be shutout once the two-year process begins.

Other groups along the Bay, such as Gerritsen Beach Cares of Brooklyn, the Edgemere Stewardship Group of Queens, and the Rockaway Waterfront Alliance of Queens, are also working to improve the Bay and to ensure local communities have access to it. Gerritsen Beach Cares works to maintain the shoreline park and the boat access to Gerritsen Creek, while the Edgemere Stewardship Group works to remove trash and invasive species from a small piece of marshland. The Rockaway Waterfront Alliance focuses on connecting local kids to the waterfront and raising the kids' awareness of environmental issues while providing activities to keep them off the streets.

However, the neighborhood groups are not without their limitations. In many ways they see the *ecological connections* within the Bay, for example, the connections between water quality and marshland loss, but do not see the estuary as a *social whole*. While the various groups are focused essentially on one goal—the protection and improvement of the Jamaica Bay estuary—they do not regularly work together to accomplish their goals. Many of the groups were started to preserve their quality of life on the Bay—their fishing access, their backyard preserve, and their access to a creek—but fail to see how the quality of their life on the Bay is tied up with, and contingent upon, what happens in the neighborhoods surrounding their own. Therefore, when raising environmental concerns or making demands on local, state, or federal officials, the groups do so in isolation from each other, thereby diminishing their relative power to demand environmental services. For example, the Fresh Creek Nature Association, Gerritsen Beach Cares, and the Edgemere Stewardship group have all encountered agency resistance, a lack of accountability, and agency "finger-pointing" during their efforts to improve local parks along the Bay. Although Fresh Creek Nature Association and Gerritsen Beach Cares operate out of Brooklyn and Edgemere Stewardship out of Queens, combined efforts framed in terms of Jamaica Bay watershed protection might yield more promising results. By framing their efforts to restore local parks in terms of watershed green spaces, a cross-borough coalition could then appeal to the National Park Service, local representatives and community boards, and the city Parks Department as a collective constituency, demanding official action and cooperation across political and agency boundaries.

If the city is to meet Mayor Bloomberg's environmental goals, the continued and combined efforts of these groups are essential. For, despite any limitations, the groups are important for calling attention to environmental problems or concerns that often go unnoticed by oversight agencies and other community members. The groups also provide much of the necessary labor involved in cleaning up beaches, removing invasive species, and replanting marshland and upland areas. Finally, the groups prove invaluable in holding government agencies accountable for maintaining the city's environment.

These waterfront groups recognize both the environmental benefits of the waterfront, as well as the ways the waterfront contributes to their quality of life. Therefore, in an era of environmental uncertainty where global climate change—with increasing sea levels, rates of precipitation, and severe storms—threatens the shores of New York City, citizen involvement remains an essential component to developing a sustainable urban waterfront.

Climate Change Challenges Development Plans

Global climate change will significantly impact New York City's environment and exacerbate current environmental challenges. Moreover, the "uncertainty" of how global climate change will impact the city complicates the process for addressing these environmental challenges.[8] Climate change trends (increasing temperature, precipitation levels, etc.) in New York City are largely consistent with current global trends and future predictions. See tables 15.2 and 15.3.

Modeled predictions for New York City metropolitan area and watershed (by 2080) include a 7.5 to 8 degree (Fahrenheit) increase in atmospheric temperature, a 7.5 to 10 percent increase in precipitation, and a 15.5 to 17.7 inch rise in sea level. Furthermore, climate models also predict (with less certainty) more frequent

Table 15.2 HISTORIC CHANGES IN CLIMATIC MEASURES FOR NEW YORK CITY METROPOLITAN AREA AND WATERSHED

Climatic Measure	Year
	1900–2005
Air temperature	+ 1.9°F
Precipitation	+ 10% (4.2 in.)
Sea Level	+ 12 in.

Source: Data from New York City, Department of Environmental Protection 2008.

Table 15.3 PREDICTED GLOBAL CLIMATE CHANGE CONSEQUENCES
FOR NEW YORK CITY METROPOLITAN AREA AND WATERSHED

Climatic Measure	Year		
	2020	2050	2080
Air temperature	+ 2.0°F	+ 4.0°F	+ 5.9°F
Precipitation	+ 0.7%	+ 5.7%	+ 8.6%
Sea Level	+ 3.2 in.	+ 9.0 in.	+ 16.5 in.

and extreme weather events for the region (NYC Department of Environmental
Protection 2008). In making these projections, the Columbia Center for Climate
Systems Research employed five climate models approved by the Intergovernmental
Panel on Climate Change and averaged their predictions to arrive at the climate projections for the city. The above averages are also based on "best scenario" predictions,
that is, if the city achieved greenhouse gas emissions of 550 ppm of carbon dioxide by
2100, combined with low population growth, high GDP growth, low energy use, high
land-use changes, low resource availability, and medium-paced technological development. (See table 15.3; for "worst case scenario" projections, see New York City,
Department of Environmental Protection 2008.)

Global climate change will have significant consequences for New York's waterfront unless substantial action is taken to upgrade and improve the city's environmental infrastructure. Increased severe weather events and precipitation will likely
lead to declining water quality because of more combined sewer overflows. Rising
sea levels will likely result in more frequent and intense flooding, which in severe
weather events, could cause sea water to rise above combined sewer overflow outfalls
and overwhelm the city's wastewater treatment and holding facilities.

In August 2011, Hurricane Irene threatened the city, leading to a new sense of
urgency regarding sea-level rise and flooding concerns. While the city views sustainable
waterfront development, with its emphasis on redeveloping waterfront brownfields
and dense residential settlement linked to public transportation, as a smart growth
mitigation strategy, such an approach is problematic. Indeed, there is growing concern
among city residents and public officials that there is a contradiction between the city's
push to redevelop much of its coastline and sea-level and flooding concerns. Dense and
sustainable growth and development in vulnerable waterfront areas puts thousands of
people in harm's way and raises many new political and economic questions.

In October 2012, Hurricane Sandy, the second "hundred year" hurricane to strike
the region in two years, brought the realities of climate change home to residents of
the NY-NJ metro area as never before. Storm surge flooding was more severe and
damaging than the region had ever experienced. (See figures 15.7, 15.8 and table
15.4). About 80,000 buildings, 340,000 housing units and about 770,000 households faced some sort of flooding. The city had to cope with severe massive and long-
term power outages, disruption of transportation, gasoline shortages, thousands of

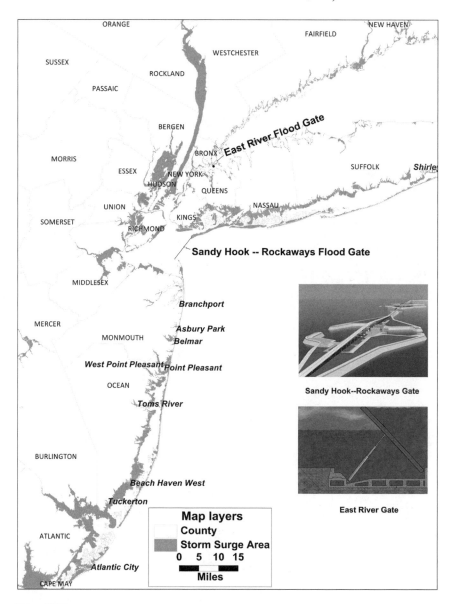

Figure 15.7
Sandy Flood Surge in Tri-State Area. Including Proposed Sandy Hook to Rockaways Storm
Barrier (in top picture) and East River Flood Gate (in bottom picture.)
Source: Created by Andrew A. Beveridge from FEMA Storm Surge Map Files. Based upon 10 Meter Grid as
of December 6, 2012. Storm Barrier Artist Rendering New Yorkers Debate Flood Protection," *Journal of Light
Construction*, November 5, 2012, and East River Flood Gate, Abrahams, 2009.

families made homeless in the city's low-lying beach communities, and all the other
consequences of a major environmental disaster in the nation's largest urban region.
One of this chapter's authors, Bill Kornblum, lives in Long Beach NY, a barrier island
community, which like the Rockaways and the beach neighborhoods of Staten Island,

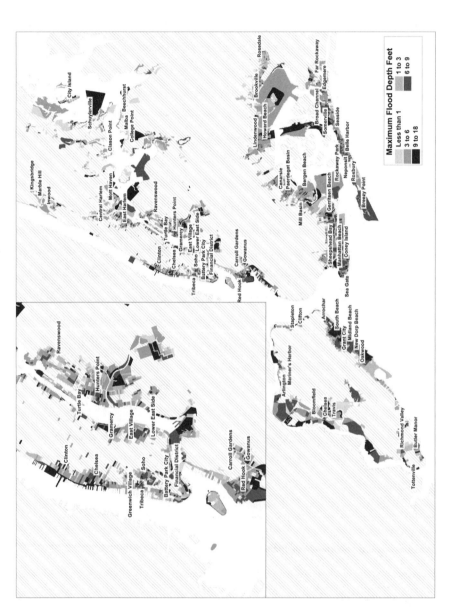

Figure 15.8

Sandy Flood Surge in New York City, Depth and Population and Housing Units Affected.

Source: Created by Andrew A. Beveridge from FEMA Flood Depth Maps 11/11/2012–3 meter and 1 meter grid processed by Archie Tse of the *New York Times*. Estimates of population and housing units created by Beveridge by allocating flood depth to census blocks.

	Population Flooded	More than 3 Feet	More than 6 Feet
NYC	775,107	48.1%	9.9%
Bronx	33,889	5.2%	0.2%
Brooklyn	251,414	54.2%	11.5%
Manhattan	281,734	44.2%	11.7%
Queens	168,242	53.4%	4.3%
Staten Island	39,827	51.8%	20.1%
	Housing Units Flooded	More than 3 Feet	More than 6 Feet
NYC	340,053	48.5%	10.6%
Bronx	13,187	5.2%	0.3%
Brooklyn	107,237	55.4%	12.2%
Manhattan	135,178	44.6%	12.1%
Queens	69,166	52.9%	5.0%
Staten Island	15,283	52.6%	19.9%

Source: Calculated from FEMA Flood Depth Maps Dated 11/11/2012 – 3 meter and 1 meter grid by Archie Tse of the *New York Times*. Estimate of population and housing units created by Andrew A. Beveridge by allocating flood depth to census blocks.

was especially devastated by the storm. Many of Kornblum's neighbors had floodwater up to their first floors and had to pile their ruined furniture and belongings on the streets. Kornblum describes the impacts of Hurricane Sandy:

> At high tide during the storm, there was five feet of water rushing over the island. That huge tree came down on my house (see figure 15.9), but right after the wind abated the city crews took it away before it could destroy the house as it fell further.

Figure 15.9
William Kornblum's House Damaged by Tree on Long Beach Island.
Source: Photo by William Kornblum.

Apartment houses along the beachfront were swept with waves. People who did not evacuate as ordered, about one third of the local population, were often without power or heat for over two weeks. The city of Long Beach, like so many others in the region, will now have to take their existing plans for storm abatement much more seriously than ever before.

Just fourteen months after Hurricane Irene, the dire predictions that highlighted the vulnerability of the New York metropolitan region as a result of rising seas were realized as Hurricane Sandy pummeled the coast. The devastating coastal flooding that wreaked havoc along large stretches of the Atlantic Seaboard raised many questions about coastal protection, sustainable development and the meaning of resiliency. For example, after Hurricane Sandy, one shorefront resident writes,

> Don't even know where to begin. No cars. Relying on friends who have cars but now they don't have gas. Some stores are opening on Brighton Beach Ave but no idea what they are selling or in what condition...Warbasse [Amalgamated Warbasse Houses] has no power. I think they always had their own power system, which was aging and balky to start with...Dozens of seniors are stuck in their apartments in this 20+ story building. Hiked up 5 flights of pitch black stairs. Lovely building, lobby completely renovated last year, looked adorable. Now no windows or doors, a muddy mess. Water came up past the first floor...But this is the craziest part. If we WANTED to evacuate, where would we go? In the 11224–11235 zip codes alone (Coney, Brighton, Sheepshead Bay/Manhattan Beach, etc.) there are something like 135,000 people. Even if half found shelter on their own, where would the rest go? And my designated shelter (FDR high school) had only space for 700. And they lost power and ran out of food and water. Only volunteers staff these shelters.

This quote illustrates the vulnerabilities of New York City's waterfront population as well as significant gaps in the city's emergency response plans.

New York City's waterfront sustainability plan, Vision 2020, which was released in 2011, lays out eight city-wide strategies for waterfront redevelopment, of which increasing climate resiliency is one.[9] Although the city does not expect to experience the greatest effects of climate change until 2020 (New York City, Department of City Planning 2011), planners have developed three primary strategies to increase climate resiliency: retreat, accommodation, and protection. For the most part, the city has dismissed the idea of retreating from coastal development, noting that this strategy has never been implemented pre-emptively at such a large scale. The administration cites the cost of shoreline retreat, and the disruptions to the city's plan to build sustainable dense waterfront development to accommodate its growing population, as reasons to down play retreat strategies. Instead, accommodation strategies primarily involve flood-proofing buildings and waterfront sites. The city champions the low costs of initial investments in these projects relative to large-scale infrastructure projects, such as levees and flood barriers. Finally, the city's protection strategies include a range of soft and hard infrastructure development projects (New York City, Department of City Planning 2011).

Protection strategies involving soft infrastructure development include wetland restoration and the development of "gradual edges." Benefits of soft solutions include decreasing speed and force of tidal action and storm surges, reduced maintenance costs, and increased intertidal zones and habitat areas (New York City, Department of City Planning 2011). During Hurricane Sandy less damage along the East River shoreline occurred in the few places where there was a gradual slope of beach into the river, notably at Brooklyn Bridge Park. The city has additional such projects under-way, e.g., working in collaboration with the National Park Service and the Army Corps of Engineers to restore wetlands in Jamaica Bay. Hard infrastructure projects include construction of breakwaters, groins and jetties, as well as levee and storm surge barrier construction. Plans for storm surge barriers, like the ones shown in figure 15.7, have been debated in New York for the past few years. At this writing, there is no consensus about which would be the most favored option. In 2009, a group of international scien-tists participated in a conference at Polytechnic of New York University titled "Against the Deluge: Storm Surge Barriers to Protect New York City." Architects and engineers presented four conceptual designs for storm surge barriers throughout the greater New York City harbor: a barrier at the south end of Arthur Kill, dividing Staten Island from New Jersey, an East River barrier, a Verrazano Narrows Barrier between Staten Island and Brooklyn, and the five-mile long New York-New Jersey Outer Harbor Gateway, a system of causeways and gates that would span the New York Bight from Sandy Hook, NJ to the Rockaways in Queens. (See figure 15.8.) The projected cost of these different plans is well into the billions, with a $5.9 billion price tag for the NY-NJ Outer Harbor Plan and a $6.9 billion cost for the Verrazano Narrows Project.

All of these proposals require additional study and refinement before they can be seriously considered. All would mitigate storm surge and protect a smaller or larger area of the metropolitan region. They also would impose heavy costs on shipping and boat traffic through the port. The Ambrose Channel, the main entry into the port from the Atlantic, requires further dredging to accommodate supertankers from the enlarged Panama Canal, scheduled to appear in 2014. The surge gates would be left open except for severe storm situations, but the passage through the massive open-ings would be treacherous. More importantly, even the largest and most ambitious of the proposals (to erect a surge barrier across the outer harbor, from Sandy Hook, NJ to Breezy Point at the tip of the Rockaways, in Queens) would potentially divert an even greater storm surge onto Staten Island and Long Island. (See figure 15.7.)

While these structures would help save much of the urban infrastructure of Manhattan and part of the outer boroughs, they cannot protect the entire coast-line of the city, to say nothing of the hundreds of miles of beaches and communities long the ocean shores of Long Island and New Jersey. For those communities on the barrier islands and low-lying former marshlands, which were so heavily urban-ized in the second half of the Twentieth-Century, there will be a long and agoniz-ing effort at rebuilding, encouraged by federal and state policies that subsidize flood insurance and by investment in rebuilding beaches and filling inlets with sand. But the thorny political questions, such as whether to concentrate efforts on hard or soft infrastructure development and whether the taxpaying public should subsidize these settlements with federally guaranteed flood insurance and favorable mortgage policies, will now be raised with ever more persuasive force. What is not yet clear at this writing is how the strategies outlined in the city's waterfront development plans will actually address the outstanding problems of the city's infrastructure, which the flooding caused by Hurricane Sandy exposed so dramatically.

With four its of its five boroughs located on islands (only the Bronx is part of the continental mainland), the city must consider costly plans to retrofit the entrances to its underground infrastructure. It will also be forced to make huge investments in seawalls and berms to protect low-lying neighborhoods and beaches. It still makes sense to set long term goals for waterfront development that enhance environmental values, increase flood protection and promote economically sound development. The experience of rising sea levels and increasing numbers of life-threatening storms, however, adds new urgency and far greater costs to the large-scale infrastructure work that will be required in the decades to come.

Uncertainty in New York City's Environmental Future

With a population of just over 8 million people, New York City constitutes 0.12 percent of the world's population, but emits 0.25 percent of the world's greenhouse gas emissions (New York City, Department of Environmental Protection 2008). New York's disproportionate environmental footprint, combined with the projected environmental consequences and the rate of environmental change (projections estimate significant environmental changes in less than 70 years) suggests the need for a swift and thorough approach to the city's climate change policy. However, the difficulty of establishing "scientific certainty" about the specific consequences of climate change (e.g., rate of precipitation increases, seasonality of changes, storm intensity) for the New York City watershed coupled with budgetary constraints ultimately handcuffs Department of Environmental Protection efforts to make major changes to the city's infrastructure.

> Despite documented changes in historical climate records and great advances in climate science, uncertainties remain. For instance, although there is broad agreement that the global climate is warming and that sea level is rising, precipitation trends are not clear. An analysis that compared the most recent 50 years of rainfall records in the New York City metropolitan area to those from the preceding 50 years showed a very small change to date in short-term rainfall intensity and duration relationships. (New York City, Department of Environmental Protection 2008, 28)

Even if climate change impacts do not meet the levels estimated in the projections, the city has already seen consequences consistent with global climate change. The need for improvements to the city's current environmental infrastructure, the scientific consensus about the probability of climate change consequences, and the city's disproportionate contributions to global greenhouse gas emissions warrant major improvements.

It seems logical to assume that the Department of Environmental Protection would strive to develop and enact efforts to achieve its "best case scenario" predictions despite some uncertainty. However, the Department of Environmental Protection says that given limited funds and high costs, "In many instances, it is unlikely that authorization would be given to spend funds on addressing a problem that is not yet very well defined, for which there is significant uncertainty that it will in fact materialize, or for which the predicted impacts are very far in the future" (New York City, Department of Environmental Protection 2008, 43). Consequently, activists' efforts to promote greater awareness of the issues in their local communities are invaluable for increasing the number of people calling on city, state, and federal governments to prioritize environmental spending, an especially difficult task given the recent economic recession.

Recently released federal and New York State budgets contain spending cuts that will likely hamper the city's immediate efforts for developing, implementing, and enforcing environmental protections and policies. In 2011, the US Environmental Protection Agency's budget was cut by $278 million to $10 billion, eliminating $200 million in spending for the Clean Water State Revolving Fund and the Drinking Water State Revolving Fund. The federal budget also reduced the North American Wetland Conservation Grants to 2009 levels. The Department of the Interior, which "protects America's natural resources and heritage, honors our cultures and tribal communities, and supplies the energy to power our future" through bureaus such as the National Park Service, the US Fish and Wildlife Service, and the Bureau of Land Management, had $750 million in reductions and terminations of "lower priority programs" taken from the 2011 budget. President Obama's proposed budget for fiscal year 2013 includes a 1.2 percent cut to the Environmental Protection Agency's budget, a loss of $1.5 million to the agency. The cuts are largely from reductions in Superfund remediation activities and the Drinking Water and Water Quality State Revolving Funds. Additionally, federal stimulus money from the American Recovery and Reinvestment Act was terminated in 2011, impacting funding to New York's environmental agencies.

New York State's Department of Environmental Conservation budget was cut 5 percent (a loss of $53 million), primarily from the loss of federal stimulus money for the Great Lakes Restoration Initiative (overall cut of $175 million), as well as a 10 percent cut to the Department of Environmental Conservation's General State Fund Operations and cuts to capital projects. The state's Environmental Protection Fund[10] will continue to receive the same $134 million as the previous year. The state's Parks Department budget was cut 6.2 percent (a loss of $17.7 million). Cuts to the Department of Environmental Conservation and Parks Department are projected to be "accomplished through administrative efficiencies in non-personal service and negotiated workforce savings to minimize layoffs to the extent possible" (http://www.governor.ny.gov/20112012ExecutiveBudget). Furthermore, state aid to New York City will be eliminated in 2011, more than $300 million, compared to 2 percent cuts for other areas of the state (Bloomberg 2011).

Despite the fiscal and environmental challenges confronting the city and the state, two new appointments appear promising for New York's environmental future. New York Governor Andrew Cuomo nominated Joseph Martens as Commissioner of the Department of Environmental Conservation. Martens, the former President of the Open Space Coalition, has a strong background in natural resource policy, with a master's degree in Resource Management from the State University of New York-Environmental Science and Forestry. He served as Assistant and then Deputy Secretary to the Governor for Energy and the Environment from 1990–94. Cuomo also nominated Rose Harvey as Commissioner of Office of Parks and Recreation and Historic Preservation. Harvey spent over twenty-five years working for the Trust for Public Land and recently served as the McCluskey Fellow and Lecturer at the Yale School of Forestry and Environmental Studies. Nominating personnel with strong environmental backgrounds and commitments to open space and preservation demonstrates the Governor's commitment to sustainability and opens up the political opportunity structure for environmental activists to push for environmental change (McAdam 1982).

The attempt to institute congestion pricing, a system for charging automobile and truck drivers extra tolls for entering the midtown commercial center, was one of Mayor Bloomberg's finest moments as an environmental leader. He managed to get the measure narrowly passed in a fractious City Council, but in 2007 it died in the disastrous New York Assembly when the Democratic conference decided not to let the bill out of committee. Nor was it clear it would have passed the Republican Senate. As his popularity began to slip in his third term, and faced with a new governor to win over, it became ever more doubtful that his administration would or could mount a new effort to revive congestion pricing.

On other environmental and health-related issues, the Bloomberg administration is forcefully engaged with highly active citizens at all levels of city life. In 2007, the mayor established the Office of the Food Policy Coordinator, responsible for convening the Food Policy Taskforce and coordinating the efforts of city agencies to improve access to healthy food. This office advances a number of cooperative efforts in the boroughs and is particularly engaged in the school lunch and school gardening initiatives. A study by the New York State Department of Agriculture and Markets found that 306 of the city's 1,600 schools have an interactive growing environment and instructional lessons. This number includes those schools that have outdoor raised bed gardens, earth boxes inside their classrooms, or relationships with nearby community gardens or larger urban farm sites. Urban farming is an increasingly active social movement in New York, as in many other cities.[11] Throughout the city's neighborhoods, a renewed urban gardening movement is likely to put more children and their parents in touch with the origins of food and with issues of its quality and its connections to the land and waters surrounding the city.

CONCLUSION

Aldo Leopold's classic *A Sand County Almanac* offered the hope that, "a land ethic changes the role of Homo sapiens from conqueror of the land-community to plain member and citizen of it." He argued that stewardship of the land and waters was an essential quality of an ecologically based idea of citizenship. In this chapter we have offered some evidence that New Yorkers are forming a version of the "land ethic" that addresses decades of misunderstanding and misuse of local resources of land and water. It is far too early to assert that this New York version of the Leopold ideal has been realized. But in the work of enlightened leaders and dedicated grassroots activists in the Bronx, the Jamaica Bay watershed, and neighborhoods and communities throughout the city, New Yorkers are finding their own versions of a land ethic in this city of water.

NOTES

1. The ten states include: Connecticut, Delaware, Maine, Maryland, Massachusetts, New Hampshire, New Jersey, New York, Rhode Island, and Vermont. The state governors signed a Memorandum of Understanding in December of 2005. Other interested states may sign the MOU and join the initiative.
2. Industrial agricultural accounts for over 30 percent of greenhouse gas emissions worldwide, through overuse of petrochemical fertilizers, enteric fermentation (part of animal digestive processes), biomass burning, manure and fertilizer production, and rice production (Food and Agricultural Organization 2009). In the United States, Concentrated Animal Feeding Operations (CAFOs), or feeding operations with more than 1,000 animals, contribute 7 percent of the nation's greenhouse gas emissions. CAFOs contribute large amounts of methane, carbon dioxide, and nitrous oxide by concentrating large amounts of animal waste (high in methane), through the use of machinery for animal food production, fertilizer use, and energy use associated with CAFO housing and maintenance, as well as in the slaughtering, processing, waste treatment, transport, and packaging processes associated with meat production. Furthermore, industrial agriculture contributes to large-scale land-use changes, such as deforestation, which might otherwise help mitigate greenhouse gas emissions by acting as carbon sinks (Cassuto 2010).
3. The New York State Department of Environmental Conservation (DEC) sets state standards.
4. The Harbor Survey Program is part of the New York City Department of Environmental Protection (DEP). The Harbor Survey Program took over monitoring water quality from the Metropolitan Sewerage Commission.
5. Eutrophic conditions occur when dissolved nutrients (e.g., phosphorus or nitrogen) enrich the water, stimulating the growth of plant life (e.g., algae blooms), which upon decay will "suffocate" the waters due to a loss of oxygen.
6. Neighborhoods in Community Board 18 include Canarsie, Bergen Beach, Mill Basin, Flatlands, Marine Park, Georgetown, and Mill Island.
7. The region's airports include John F. Kennedy Airport and LaGuardia Airport in New York and Newark International Airport in New Jersey.
8. Globally, the Intergovernmental Panel on Climate Change estimates a 99 percent probability of occurrence (virtually certain), that the Earth will experience warmer and more frequent hot days and nights over most land areas. Additionally, the Panel predicts a 90 percent probability of occurrence (very likely) that there will be more warm spells, heat waves, and heavy precipitation events over most areas of the Earth. The Panel also predicts a 66 percent probability of occurrence (likely increase) of drought-stricken areas throughout the world, as well as more intense hurricane activity and an increased incidence of extreme high sea levels (NYC Department of Environmental Protection 2008).

9. The city's strategies include: expand public access, enliven the waterfront, support the working waterfront, improve water quality, restore the natural waterfront, enhance Blue Networks, improve government oversight, and increase climate resilience (NYC Vision 2020).

10. The Environmental Protection Fund is a special revenue fund that provides monies for environmental programs. Funding is secured from the Real Estate Transfer Tax, the sale or lease of state property, and the sale of conservation license plates. For more information on the fund and its management, see a 2010 report, "Effective Management of the Environmental Protection Fund," by NY State Comptroller, Thomas DiNapoli. Available at: http://www.osc.state.ny.us/reports/environmental/epf_capstone.pdf.

11. For more information, see: http://www.fiveboroughfarm.org/urban-agriculture/.

CHAPTER 16

Environmental and Social Justice Movements and Policy Change in Los Angeles

Is an Inside-Outside Game Possible?

MARTHA M. MATSUOKA AND
ROBERT GOTTLIEB

LOS ANGELES: AN ENVIRONMENTALLY CHALLENGED CITY

For years, Los Angeles earned its reputation as the most polluted and environmentally challenged city in the country. It has long had the worst air quality in the nation (occasionally challenged by Houston in recent years). Its extensive developments at the urban edge for more than a hundred years had earned Southern California the reputation as the capital of sprawl. It gained notoriety as a "water imperialist" due to the city's (and the region's) search for new imported water supplies from the Owens Valley, Northern California, and the Colorado River. It faced numerous violations of the Clean Water Act due to contaminated runoff and bay pollution. The channelization of the Los Angeles River for flood control purposes beginning in the late 1930s transformed the river into an off-limits, barbed wired concrete channel, a place of danger and violence as noted by the scenes of movie chases (e.g., "Terminator 2" and "Repo Man") and science fiction scenarios (e.g., giant irradiated ants entering the river from the storm drains in the 1950s movie classic "Them"). Over time, the Los Angeles River became both symbol and substance of Los Angeles's degraded environment and loss of connection to urban open space (Urban & Environmental Policy Institute 2001). Along these lines, Los Angeles also emerged as among the most park poor cities in the country, most notably in the low-income neighborhoods of South, Central, and East Los Angeles. In relation to the city's demographics, as a USC study documented, "African American, Asian-Pacific Islander, and Latino dominated neighborhoods, where almost 750,000 children live, have extraordinarily low rates [of park land] (1–2 acres per 1,000 total population, and 3–6 acres per 1,000 children) compared to white dominated areas (with almost 17 and 100 acres per 1,000 total population and children, respectively) where only 235,000 children reside" (Wolch, Wilson, and Fehrenbach 2002, 20). Los Angeles encountered enormous problems of food insecurity in many of those same neighborhoods due to lack of access to fresh and healthy foods and a proliferation of fast food restaurants and liquor stores that called themselves food marts. And the Ports of Los Angeles and Long Beach, with the heaviest traffic in imported goods from places like China, along with the rail and truck distribution corridors designed to facilitate this flow of goods, created environmental and health sacrifice zones in the communities adjacent to the ports and goods movement corridors.

To bring about change in these areas seems daunting. For example, the enormous and extraordinarily rapid growth of the Los Angeles-Long Beach port complex, by 2007 accounting for 43 percent of the goods coming into the country, is touted by the shippers, the retailers like Wal-Mart, the port operators, and the policymakers as providing enormous economic benefits for the region and the country. Little if anything is said of the community, health, and environmental impacts on the communities located directly in the global trade corridor pathways, even though the air quality issues generated by the goods movement activities represents the single largest and most protracted environmental problem in the region, resulting in enormous chronic and acute health hazards like heart disease and respiratory ailments such as asthma. Food system problems also remained as intractable as ever: supermarket chains had abandoned inner-city neighborhoods, a core problem that became apparent during the 1992 civil disorders; small regional farms at the urban edge continue to disappear, exacerbating the problems of sprawl; and obesity rates have skyrocketed (e.g., from 22.2 percent to 29.4 percent for African Americans and 17.1 percent to 29.2 percent among Latinos between 1997 and 2007) (Los Angeles County Department of Public Health 2010), even as hunger has remained widespread. But the environmental and social justice movements that first emerged during the 1990s began to force a new discussion about the imperative need for environmental and social change, including the key issues of global trade-related freight traffic and food system policy change. This chapter profiles how these emerging movements confronted the question of how such change could be accomplished.

INSIDERS AND OUTSIDERS: A VALIDATING MOMENT?

In April 2001, a broad network of Los Angeles labor, environmental, housing, immigration, health, transportation, food, and community development activists, policy analysts, and academics unveiled a 21-point agenda at a mayoral debate shortly in advance of the 2001 mayoral election. The nine Task Forces had been convened through the Progressive Los Angeles Network (PLAN), which represented the latest effort to bring together an array of social movements in Los Angeles and to establish, among other goals, a progressive environmental, social, and economic community-based agenda for Los Angeles. Those efforts at networking and move-ment linkages had become particularly pronounced after the 1992 civil unrest in Los Angeles, which had an enormous impact on the city's politics. Among other con-sequences, the response to the 1992 events had led to the election of a conserva-tive businessman, Richard Riordan, on a law and order platform the following year. Nevertheless, during the Riordan years, from 1993 to 2001, progressive social move-ments had been successful in elevating important social and environmental justice goals, including passage of one of the first living wage ordinances in the country and a strong campaign to revitalize the Los Angeles River. By 2001, it appeared that this emerging set of social movements, now grouped together through the PLAN process, could have a significant impact on the politics of the region (Gottlieb et al. 2006).

One of the candidates in the 2001 election, Antonio Villaraigosa, had multiple con-nections to the various social movement activists and policy analysts. A one-time stu-dent activist and labor and community organizer, Villaraigosa had made strong links with the labor movement and with environmentalists during his tenure as California Speaker of the Assembly prior to his mayoral run. However, in the 2001 runoff election, Villaraigosa was defeated by a moderate Democrat, James Hahn, who put together a coalition of conservative white voters in the San Fernando Valley with a strong showing in African American communities, partly due to the favorable identity of his father, Kenneth Hahn, who had been the longtime supervisor representing South Los Angeles. James Hahn had also tarred Villaraigosa with drug associations that included racial overtones in a mean-spirited negative campaign (Morrison 2001).

In 2005, Villaraigosa successfully challenged Hahn in a rematch, this time making stronger inroads in the African American community combined with an overwhelm-ing margin among Latino voters and a majority of the largely Jewish and liberal vot-ers in the Westside. Although the 2005 Villaraigosa campaign lacked some of the high-intensity movement-oriented spirit of the 2001 campaign, the social move-ment groups felt validated by the Villaraigosa victory.

That sense of validation was reinforced when, on July 1, 2005, the new mayor delivered his inaugural speech that he called "Dream with Me." The speech repeated some of the major themes that had been elaborated through the PLAN process that had reflected the years of community and political organizing. One of those key themes had been the need for environmental change, and, along those lines, Villaraigosa declared that Los Angeles needed to become "the greenest big city in America" (Orlov and Barrett 2005).

In seeking to move his environmental and social justice agenda forward, Villaraigosa quickly appointed a slate of new environmental activists and policy people on powerful commissions such as the City's Department of Water and Power and the Harbor Department, which guides the nation's largest port complex. For the Harbor Commission, the mayor placed longtime renewable energy advocate S. David Freeman as Chair and environmental justice activist/lawyer Jerilyn Lopez Mendoza, formerly of Environmental Defense and architect of the sweeping community bene-fits agreement signed with the city's Airport Authority, the first Community Benefits Agreement in the country to be negotiated on a public sector project. And for the chair of the Board and Water and Power Commissioners, the new mayor tapped Mary

Nichols, a longtime environmental policy figure and onetime head of the LA office of the Natural Resources Defense Council.[1]

Four months after he took office, the mayor's themes of environment and social justice continued:

> Let's dare to imagine Los Angeles as the cleanest and greenest big city in America.... The great cities of the 21st Century will not be famous for their factories or have smokestacks in their skylines. They won't be the traditional homes of polluting or extractive industries. They'll be places where residents are at home in vibrant, clean and sustainable communities. (Villaraigosa 2005a)

The mayor's Green Vision for LA was shared by Green LA, a coalition of environmental and community-based organizations that had worked for many years on improving Los Angeles's urban environment. The Green LA coalition (originally established as the Los Angeles Working Group on the Environment) was conceived of by several longtime activists who were now mayoral commissioners, including the new LA Department of Water and Power Commission chair Mary Nichols, Paula Daniels (appointed to the Board of Public Works and who subsequently became a senior advisor to the mayor on food issues), Misty Sanford (appointed to the Environmental Affairs Commission), and new Harbor Commissioner Jerilyn Mendoza. Each of these appointees and the Green LA coalition activists, who worked with them, knew they would need to maintain their citywide activist organization to be better able to organize a base of support for these new roles on the "inside." The Green LA group also recognized the need to elevate the role of strong community-based environmental justice leaders to ensure that environmental goals and strategies addressed environmental issues in Los Angeles's low-income areas and communities of color.

The environmental appointments were not the only ones among the ranks of social justice leaders and activists to be tapped by Villaraigosa. Appointed officials also included: Regina Freer, professor of politics at Occidental College, a scholar and activist from South Los Angeles (appointed to the Planning Commission); Malcolm Carson, a Legal Aid attorney (appointed to the Board of Transportation Commissioners); and Maria Armoudian, journalist and longtime environmental advocate (appointed to the Environmental Affairs Commission). He also appointed longtime social justice activist and labor organizer Larry Frank as deputy mayor to oversee the Department of Neighborhood Services, as well as serve as a top advisor and visible go-to figure for community, environmental, and labor activists. In all, more than sixty mainstream environmental, environmental justice, housing, social justice, and labor organizations came together around the Green LA's mission and inside-outside approach. This included mainstream environmental organizations such as the Natural Resources Defense Council, Friends of the LA River, and Heal the Bay; environmental justice organizations such as Communities for a Better Environment, East Yard Communities for Environmental Justice, and Pacoima Beautiful; constituent-based advocacy organizations such as Physicians for Social Responsibility–LA; and community organizing groups such as ACORN and Union de Vecinos.

The groups on the outside and appointees on the inside needed to confront some of the most daunting environmental challenges that the new mayor said he wanted to address. Transportation represented perhaps the most protracted of those issues, given Los Angeles's massive car-centric infrastructure, auto dependence, and relative lack of alternatives, which had been a key issue, identified during the PLAN process and continued to receive prominence as a core environmental concern.[2] Groups like the Bus Riders Union had been longtime advocates for expanding bus service, a central if not exclusive means of transportation for Los Angeles's low-income population. At times, bus advocates clashed with those pushing for a major expansion of rail transit related to the issue of allocation of resources, given the cost for developing new rail lines. Both bus and rail advocates, however, came to realize the importance of shifting the focus to how the lion's share of resources were going to freeways and roads (e.g., a billion dollars to create an additional lane in 2011 over a short stretch of the 405 freeway) (Hawthorne 2011) which in turn needed to be the target for reallocating transportation funding for both bus and rail.

At the same time, those advocating for increased bike infrastructure and for more walkable neighborhoods sought to reverse their own marginalized status among transportation planners, which included the limited dollars available for bike facilities. New bike and pedestrian advocate groups became important new "green transportation" players by focusing on bike and pedestrian opportunities in a city known as the place where, as the popular Missing Persons song has it, "nobody walks" (or bikes). By shutting down one of Los Angeles's iconic freeways (the Pasadena freeway, first freeway of the West) for a bike ride and walk ON the freeway, and subsequently hosting CicLAvia, where one hundred fifty thousand bike riders enjoyed exclusive access to the surface streets of a seven-mile stretch, bike and pedestrian issues became visible players (helping convince the mayor to become one of their champions) and joined with their bus and rail advocates to become a powerful new constituency for a green transportation agenda. One of the significant moments associated with the rise of a green transportation constituency involved the series of talks in Los Angeles by New York City Transportation Commissioner Janette Sadik-Khan in March 2010. Sadik-Khan, whose innovative changes in transportation and street design in New York had established her as one of the leading national advocates for a green transportation agenda, gave talks at Occidental College (where she received an honorary degree) and at an LA "Street Summit" gathering of bike and social and environmental justice advocates, and also had meetings with top LA city officials. These events galvanized the green transportation advocates and also reinforced the idea that an inside-outside strategy was possible.[3] Villaraigosa embraced all those goals—rail, bus, bike, and walkability—though his focus remained primarily on the expansion of rail lines with his ambitious 30–10 plan to complete a thirty-year plan for a huge increase in rail infrastructure in just ten years, shown in figure 7.1.

Energy, climate change, and green job issues also figured prominently among activists and for the new mayor. Even since his tenure as State Assembly leader, Villaraigosa has been involved in issues related to renewable power and has vowed to "show the nation that we can light a city with green power" (Villaraigosa 2005b). National attention on issues of climate change fueled the debates about renewable power and greenhouse gas emissions and the impact of climate on Los Angeles's vulnerable low-income neighborhoods. The mayor rolled out a plan for renewable energy and a Climate Plan to reduce the city's greenhouse gas emissions 30 percent below its 1990 levels by the year 2030 (Dreier et al. 2006). In January 2011, the mayor announced that 20 percent of the city's power was based on renewable energy sources in 2010 (Los Angeles Department of Water and Power 2011), a goal he set when he took office. Despite turnovers on the Department of Water and Power Commission's directors, the city built the capacity of its Tehachapi wind farm so that it contributed nearly 50 percent of the city's renewable power. Although solar comprised only 1 percent, state rebates administered through the Department of Water and Power have helped catalyze solar projects throughout Los Angeles.

The energy and climate issues were also linked to the emergence of a "green jobs" agenda that the mayor sought to embrace. A key early initiative along those lines was the passage of a private sector Green Building Ordinance in 2007 that established a range of incentives and requirements for private sector builders to meet LEED standards for large-scale private development.[4] Together with Department of Water and Power's Integrated Resource Plan (passed in 2010), which provides a twenty-year plan for the city's power needs, the focus on energy, climate, and jobs identified an agenda that sought to green the nation's largest municipally owned utility combined with a focus on greening any future growth and development within the city.

The traction on green jobs was made possible in part by "outside" advocacy, notably through the Apollo Alliance–LA, a powerful community-labor-environmental coalition rooted in South Los Angeles. The Alliance, a regional affiliate of the national Apollo Alliance, includes labor unions (such as the International Brotherhood of Electrical Workers, the Service Employees International Union, and the Laborers), environmental justice organizations, and community-based organizations. In a two-year campaign, the Apollo Alliance–LA organization initiated, organized for, and won a Green Retrofit and Workforce Ordinance in 2009, the first program in the nation to create jobs, cut carbon emissions, and address employment needs in low-income inner-city neighborhoods through a green building program to remodel city buildings (Greener Buildings 2009). In 2010, the mayor appointed Teresa Sanchez, a longtime labor organizer from SEIU, to head up the city's green jobs effort through the mayor's office. In November 2011, the inaugural class of forty trainees—funded through the American Recovery and Reinvestment Act—graduated from the Los Angeles Green Retrofit Training Program to help remodel twenty-two city-owned buildings to increase energy and water efficiency.

These were just some of the key environmental issues and opportunities for change identified by the new mayor—and by environmental and social justice activists—as opportunities for change; change that could be accomplished on the inside through policy initiatives, and on the outside through community, environmental, and labor organizing. On that inaugural day on July 1, 2005, it appeared to the activists and the new mayor alike that a change agenda was clearly in the air. It was a heady moment for activists that recalled the late 1960s and early 1970s when progressive social movements led by civil rights activists had helped propel Tom Bradley's 1973 mayoral victory (after a bruising defeat four years earlier that had been marked by a type of racist backlash). Bradley's election as mayor, the first (and only) African American to hold that office, seemed then to suggest that the hard work of social movements could lead to change through the electoral and political process. The election of a progressive Latino mayor and the new agenda and themes that had emerged from Villaraigosa's victory once again suggested the possibilities for environmental, economic, and political change through an electoral and political process. For social and environmental justice activists, the 2005 election was like the 1973 election (and the preceding defeats of 2001 and 1969 that had neverthe-less laid the groundwork for subsequent victories), and the election victory was both symbol and substance of the prospects for change. At the same time, by recognizing the trajectory of the Bradley reign that had lasted from 1973 to 1993, the question also arose: would those expectations erode once the new mayor and his progressive allies confronted Los Angeles's hard environmental and political realities? During the Bradley reign, change had been uneven at best and had included setbacks and an eroding of the power of those same social movements that had helped bring Bradley to power (Sonenshein 1994).

It was clear to 2005's environmental and social justice activists, who were well aware of the mixed messages of the Bradley era, that they needed to sort out their own role in the public sphere. Were they insiders helping shape policy within gov-ernment, given the barriers to policy change, or were they outsiders, maintaining their ability to mobilize and pressure leaders to achieve their goals? Or would they be able to establish a type of hybrid approach—an inside-outside game that could use greater access to power while continuing to organize around specific issues and in the communities and among the constituencies where they were based?

This chapter explores the question of what kind of an environmental change agenda is being accomplished in Los Angeles. It looks at the question from the van-tage point of environmental and social justice activists (the outsiders) and how they have defined their role when new access to the policy process (the ability to function as insiders) becomes available. We present two case studies of environmental orga-nizing where inside-outside strategies advanced issues that represented environmen-talism linked to social justice goals, and illustrate how these issues moved through a crowded field of policy issues to gain the attention of decision makers on the inside, as well as movement actors on the outside. First, we examine the issues at the Ports of Los Angeles and Long Beach and the community, health, and environmen-tal impacts and advocacy regarding the global trade corridors, from the ships to the ports along the highways and rail transport systems to the inland warehouses in the Southern California region. Second, we examine the efforts in Los Angeles to create a more sustainable regional food system in a context where the dominant industrial and long-distance food system generates its own negative environmental, economic, health, and community impacts and disparities. We see food and global trade as sys-tems that have come to represent a set of inherent contradictions—providing many of the basics of everyday life in the form of consumer goods and food but also high levels of health and environmental risk. Both cases represent global and regional sys-tems that hold promise for the economic, social, environmental, and health future of the city and the region. At the same time, both cases represent systems that identify and highlight health, economic, and social inequities between the rich and poor in Los Angeles. The size and scale of the Southern California region and its political pre-dominance in the state policymaking and planning related to food, ports operations, and freight transport have far-reaching implications for other large cities, regions, and states in the country. To successfully address those contradictions in turn pres-ents unprecedented challenges for the environmental and social justice activists in Los Angeles and how they work with and/or criticize a mayor committed to a green agenda. Lessons and insights from how these relationships are pursued resonate for other large cities like New York, where similar challenges exist and where social and environmental justice activists in both New York and Los Angeles, have sought to develop agendas to change how those issues are framed and what changes can be accomplished.

We present these case studies as community-based participatory researchers who have been engaged through our work at the Urban & Environmental Policy Institute as observers, researchers, and participants related to these environmental and social justice issues. Through this vantage point, we witness and participate in the dynam-ics of social change as political doors open and shut.

DREAMS OF GREEN AT THE PORT OF LOS ANGELES

In 2001, scientists at the University of Southern California (USC) hosted a confer-ence on air pollution and invited a number of environmental justice groups based near the goods movement corridors in heavily impacted areas. While discussing the problem of exposure to particulate matter and diesel exhaust, several of the envi-ronmental justice activists, armed with anecdotal information, raised the concern about the ships, rail yards, trucks, and warehouses located in their communities. The activists had begun to link their own health, community, and environmental neigh-borhood issues with the regional problems represented by the global trade and goods movement corridors that the USC scientists had not directly linked to their own research agenda.

Toward the end of the conference, one of the neighborhood activists, Jesse Marquez, a resident of the low-income community of Wilmington adjacent to the Port of Los Angeles, rattled off a series of anecdotes about people in his neighborhood facing serious health problems. "The Port is not even regulated for these issues, and yet we face the consequences every day," Marquez told the assembled scientists. "Of course it's regulated," the scientists replied, also unaware that their research findings about increased air pollution exposures were so intricately bound with the phenom-enal growth of the goods movement corridors. The scientists soon learned that they were wrong and the activists were right about the source of the exposures and the failure to address them.[5] Eventually, new partnerships were formed that set about to change the nature of the debate and challenge policymakers who had failed to address community, health, and environmental issues as part of their policy agenda regarding these expanding goods movement and global trade corridors. Four years after the USC conference on air pollution, Antonio Villaraigosa took office, assuming leadership over the Port of Los Angeles and two other of the city's greatest municipal assets: the Department of Water and Power and the Los Angeles World Airports (the agency responsible for operating Los Angeles International Airport and two other regional airports). Each of these three city-owned operations represents the largest publicly owned facilities and operations in the nation, making Los Angeles City the "CEO of three major enterprises."

The Port of Los Angeles is the busiest container port in the United States. Together with its neighbor the Port of Long Beach, these two make up the San Pedro Bay Ports Complex, the largest port facility complex in the nation and the seventh largest (when combined) in the world. The Port of Los Angeles encompasses 7,500 acres, including twenty-seven cargo terminals and on-dock intermodal facilities and rail yards. Within the national landscape of freight transportation, the San Pedro Bay Ports represent a strategic hub not only for the West Coast but also for the nation. More than 40 percent of the nation's imports come through these two ports making Los Angeles and Long Beach critical to the system of trade and goods movement or freight traffic nationally and globally (Los Angeles Economic Development Corporation 2011).

In 2006, the Ports of Los Angeles and Long Beach together contributed more than 20 percent of Southern California's diesel particulate pollution and are still the single largest source of pollution in Southern California, according to the South Coast Air Quality Management District (Hricko 2008). The high level of air pollution results in negative health impacts for individuals, particularly children and communities living adjacent to the ports and goods movement facilities and infrastructure.

The California Air Resources Board estimates that there are 3,700 premature deaths per year directly attributed to ports and goods movement activity statewide and approximately 120 deaths per year associated with diesel fuel particulate matter emissions from activities at the Port of Los Angeles and Long Beach (California Air Resources Board 2008). USC scientists, through their ten-year study of children and the impact of air pollution on their development, found that children in more-polluted communities have reduced lung function growth (their lungs grow more slowly) and more school absences from acute respiratory problems (Gauderman et al. 2004). Investigators at USC, also found that children living near freeway traffic had substantial deficits in lung function development between the ages of 10 and 18 years, compared with children living farther away (Gauderman et al. 2007). Other studies have made links between traffic exposure to increased risk for low birth weight and premature birth (Wilhelm and Ritz 2005).

In addition to exposure to air toxics, residents living near rail yards, ports, and other goods movement facilities also endure high noise levels, traffic congestion, visual blight, and other community impacts. Where ports are located, other related industrial facilities—container yards, fumigation plants, truck repair, and maintenance facilities—also contribute to the overall risk and exposure to local communities, as well as workers.[6]

Given those kinds of impacts, community, environmental, and labor activists saw the opportunity with the new mayor to bring together their respective perspectives and constituencies to focus on the ports creating a nexus of economic development, labor rights, and environmental sustainability. In the first months of the new administration, the various coalitions of community groups, environmentalists, and labor began to change the nature of the debate about goods movement issues, including an insistence that issues of community, health, environment, and well-paying, secure jobs become central to the decision-making process.

The city's Harbor Department, with strong leadership from the mayor's office, launched an initiative to set a broad air quality policy framework at the Port of Los Angeles that included partnership with its adjacent competitor, the Port of Long Beach. Larry Frank, a longtime activist and bridge builder between labor and community, in his now formal role as Deputy Mayor of Neighborhood and Community Services led the effort. Frank served as the mayor's inside political go-to advisor, and he quickly reached out to labor and community groups, as well as the new coalitions forming at the port. The joint San Pedro Bay Ports Clean Air Action Plan, adopted in late 2006, set forth goals and approaches for reducing emissions from port operations over the course of five years. Importantly, it set key standards and strategies for pollution reduction, including goals and strategy for a Clean Trucks Plan that would reduce the emissions from diesel trucks serving the port; a process that led to the establishment of the Clean Trucks Program. The Clean Trucks Program's goals were straightforward: replace and retrofit approximately 16,000 trucks in order to meet the 2007 federal EPA emissions standards by 2012. To achieve these goals, the program featured a $1.6 billion concessionaire model that requires trucking companies who service the port to hire truck drivers as employees in return for securing transport contracts with the port.

The adoption of the Clean Trucks Program marked a historic and path-breaking win for truckers and members of the Coalition for Clean and Safe Ports, one of the new activist-based groups. It represented advances for each of the coalition partners—many of whom came to the coalition with specific agendas and movement backgrounds. For labor, the successful Clean Trucks Campaign, led by the Teamsters and joined by other labor unions and immigrant labor groups, directly addressed the exploitative trucking system put in place with the deregulation of the industry in the 1980s that required independent truck drivers to bear the burden of all maintenance and upkeep for trucks that cost over $100,000, along with port fees, licensure, fuel and other costs of doing business at the port. Truckers—who owned and operated their own trucks and must compete individually for hauling jobs—net less than $30,000 annually.[7]

By adopting a Clean Trucks Program that includes an employee concession model as a key aspect of its implementation, it was possible to shift the cost of doing business at the port from individual truckers to the firms that now employ them. As employers, trucking companies must now shoulder the costs of the compliance to the Clean Trucks Program instead of the individual truck drivers. In addition, as employees, truckers would have the right to organize.

The policy was immediately met with opposition from the American Trucking Associations, which filed an injunction blocking the implementation of the employee concession element of the program from moving forward. The coalition stepped up its support for the mayor and the Harbor Department's decision and organized to generate support for the program. In August 2010, a federal court judge cleared the way for full implementation of the program but an appeal filed by the American Trucking Associations put yet another stop to the implementation of the policy. The judge ruled that the program could be implemented during the appeals process except for the employee concessionaire component that continues to be held up in the legal process. By January 2012, the mayor announced that the port successfully met the program's goal of replacing 16,000 trucks and achieving 80 percent emissions reductions from truck transport activities related to the Port of Los Angeles (Mayor's Office, City of Los Angeles 2012).[8] Yet, the legal tug of war and the inability of the City of Los Angeles to implement the full program has put additional burdens on the truck drivers who are now required to retrofit their trucks but without any means to do so. As a result, port drivers are foregoing necessary maintenance on their trucks because they cannot afford the costs.

The program was also an important victory for environmentalists and public health advocates in the coalition. When the South Coast Air Quality Management District identified that the combined ports of Los Angeles and Long Beach generated more than 20 percent of Southern California's diesel particulate pollution (with diesel exhaust itself responsible for 80 percent of the total air toxics risk in the Southern California region), it reinforced the goal of longtime advocates of clean air and public health to reduce diesel exhaust as a top priority (South Coast Air Quality Management District 2008).

Meeting 2007 federal standards by replacing and retrofitting old trucks represented a significant advance in air quality policy. For coalition partners such as the Natural Resources Defense Council, the Coalition for Clean Air, and the American Lung Association, the plan met important air quality and public health needs of port communities. For the local community residents and the environmental justice organizations based in those communities (e.g. East Yard Communities for Environmental Justice and the Coalition for a Safe Environment), it was both validation for their own continuing advocacy and for their role in bringing goods movement pollution issues to the forefront. It was also a policy milestone for the mayor in helping secure a green agenda strategy focused on the needs of workers and communities by also improving air quality.

Part of the success of the Clean Trucks Campaign was also associated with the linked efforts of environmental justice and mainstream environmental groups. The two sets of groups had come together as the Los Angeles Working Group on the Environment, later called the Green LA Coalition, which also included subgroups focused on critical environmental issues in the city, including a Port Work Group. The Port Work Group brought together a number of longtime port activists and air quality advocates including the Natural Resources Defense Council, the American Lung Association–California, Physicians for Social Responsibility, and the Sierra Club-Harbor Vision Task Force, as well as grassroots, community-based organizations in the harbor and neighboring Wilmington. In addition, a number of community-based environmental justice organizations at the regional level became involved. These included community groups in such areas as Commerce (the site of a major rail yard and a string of freeways central to the goods movement corridor) and Mira Loma to the east of Los Angeles in Riverside County where huge warehouses are located and where they repackage and transfer goods to destinations throughout the United States. Such a regional approach was critical to the process: what happened at the port, the environmental justice groups understood, was also intricately tied to how and where goods were transported and the inland destinations from where they made their way to the Walmarts of the country eager to obtain imported goods.

Throughout the campaign, environmental justice coalition partners advocated—and at times struggled with other coalition partners—about the need to protect their communities from trucks and the further encroachment of port industrial facilities into neighborhoods. The place-based environmental justice framework of the environment as "where we live, work, play, pray and go to school" served as a framework that helped synthesize labor, environment, public health, and community issues in the campaign. The formation of the coalition and campaign was a natural opening and an extension of their organizing of neighbors, many of whom were truckers. This meant that environmental justice organizers engaged with truckers as community residents, focusing on issues of home, family, and children and relying on social networks (rather than only labor and worker solidarity) to link labor issues with community issues. This served as an important approach, considering that many drivers have been soured by the unsuccessful earlier organizing efforts—some led by Teamsters, other labor unions, and drivers themselves. To address some of the community concerns, the Clean Trucks Program required that trucking firms and their drivers adhere to agreed upon routes and off-street parking areas and the establishment of a community accountability system including a dial-in phone number to report complaints.

Adoption of the Clean Trucks Program in Los Angeles thus came to reflect the coming together of oft-competing social movements—labor, mainstream environmentalists, environmental justice, faith based, and civil rights—all aligned around the working conditions faced by truckers and the fight for good jobs and clean air. It also represents an example of what could happen if movements and public officials align and if movements can help public officials hold steadfast to key positions and policies. In addition, it had national implications as a policy innovation attractive to other social movements and policymakers in port and inland communities impacted by global trade and goods movement.

In New York/New Jersey, a similar labor-community-environmental coalition, the Coalition for Healthy Ports, built a campaign around the Los Angeles model and participated in the Port Authority's Truck Working Group to develop the clean trucks program. However, officials balked because of the legal challenges to the Los Angeles program. Instead, a new version, the Regional Truck Replacement Program, contained only a ban of 1994 and older trucks (Los Angeles's plan bans 2004 and older) without the attendant concession system that would require trucking firms to hire drivers as employees. With $7 million of the American Recovery and Reinvestment Act funds (a grant from the US EPA to the Port Authority) and an additional $23 million of its own funds, the Port Authority set up a loan program for drivers to make the required retrofits to get the estimated 640 old trucks off the road. According to Amy Goldsmith, from the Coalition for Healthy Ports, most drivers are not eligible for the loans due to restrictive loan criteria, and only ten have received them. The ban went into effect on January 1, 2011. One advocate argued, "There will be no diesel relief, no driver relief, and no community relief. The plan is a low-road loan model that will have an outcome far worse than what existed before" (Goldsmith interview, June 10, 2010, cited in Matsuoka et al. 2011).

The Los Angeles Clean Trucks Program nevertheless sets a precedent for other organizing such as in New York/New Jersey. The development of the Los Angeles program has ultimately provided an organizing strategy and policy objective for groups and state and local officials across the country. Yet, the ongoing opposition by the trucking industry and the huge retailers requires the clean trucks coalitions, along with progressive officials, to also consider how to scale up their efforts and seek federal policy actions to enable local governments to increase their regulatory authority over trucking. One illustration is the Clean Ports Act of 2010 (Nadler, D-NY), which was introduced in 2010, but which has not been able to advance in the wake of the 2010 congressional elections and the pro-business, anti-regulatory forces in the House.

For large cities like Los Angeles and New York, the campaign also importantly reflects how local movements can catalyze and lead broader, regional-scale movements for progressive social, economic, and environmental justice. In addition, new and growing activism focused on the health and community impacts of global trade and freight traffic continues to fuel the environmental justice movement and the movement for regional equity. By redefining the terms of the debate, by engaging in coalitions, and building power (in the face of tremendous odds), port and goods movement campaigns fuel social movement regionalism and advance the potential for new regional and more equitable economic and community development and a more progressive national politics.

Yet the Clean Air Action Plan and the Clean Trucks Program did not entirely shift the policy focus to equally consider health and community along with economic growth, as the shipping, retail, warehouse and truck and rail interests continued to push back, advocating continued expansion at the ports and the goods movement corridors. A new proposed terminal project at the Port of Los Angeles, for example, tested the new relationship between the mayor, the Harbor Department, and environmental, environmental justice, and community advocates. The proposed expansion of the TraPac terminal sought to increase the terminal acreage from 176 acres in 2003 to 243 acres by 2038, and expand the throughput of the terminal to a level that equals the current operations of the Port of Oakland, the fourth busiest container port in the United States. In 2003, the Port of Los Angeles and TraPac estimated that the terminal processed approximately 892,000 TEUs (Twenty-foot Equivalent Units, a measure of container volume). At full build out, the port predicted that the project would more than double the amount of cargo volume to approximately 2.4 million TEUs (Port of Los Angeles 2009).

The pro-development momentum around TraPac propelled the Harbor Commission (with the mayor's blessing) to approve the TraPac project in early December 2007 despite strong community criticism of an inadequate California Environmental Quality Act review in measuring the environmental and community impacts of the proposed expansion. A week later, sixteen organizations submitted a letter to the City

Council seeking to appeal the decision by the Harbor Commission. Environmental justice groups such as the Coalition for a Safe Environment (from the port community of Wilmington) and Communities for a Better Environment (Wilmington and Southeast Los Angeles), along with NRDC, the American Lung Association of California, the Los Angeles Alliance for a New Economy, Change to Win, Long Beach Alliance for Children with Asthma, Physicians for Social Responsibility–Los Angeles, San Pedro and Peninsula Homeowners Coalition, and the Sierra Club Harbor Vision Task Force were now appellants.

In April 2008, the City of Los Angeles and the Port of Los Angeles agreed to an Environmental Impact Report settlement that would create a Port Community Mitigation Trust Fund. It was an important breakthrough by the coalition. Led by Adrian Martinez and David Pettit of the Santa Monica office of NRDC, the coalition worked closely with then Council member Janice Hahn (now member of Congress and in whose district the port is located) and her staff to ensure that the port would agree to address long-term approaches to mitigating the health and community impacts of port growth and expansion. As part of the agreement, the city agreed to establish an off-port mitigation fund that would be funded by future expansion projects and would provide over $50 million in off-port property community mitigation projects. These include the installation of air purification and sound proofing systems in public elementary schools and residents' homes; public respiratory healthcare services at local community clinics and health services providers; studies of off-port property impacts on health and land use; off-port property impacts on public safety, traffic, aesthetics, light glare, recreation, and cultural resources; and potential wetlands restoration projects in Wilmington and San Pedro.

Two and a half years later in November 2010, the Harbor Commission moved to implement the historic agreement by approving a nonprofit organization, the Harbor Community Benefits Foundation, to help administer the Port Community Mitigation Trust Fund. The vote represented a second major legal milestone more than ten years after an earlier legal battle over the expansion of the China Shipping Terminal. In that case, the Harbor Department failed to adequately measure the environmental impact of the proposed expansion. NRDC along with community partners sued the city for violations under the California Environmental Quality Act and ultimately won a settlement that included electrification of the China Shipping Terminal.

The TraPac settlement, however, was important not only because it established a much needed community benefits fund, but, more broadly, because it reflected the growing legal, organizing, and advocacy capacity and influence of the environmental, environmental justice, and community organizations at the port. It also illustrated how port staff recognized the sophistication of the groups able to come up with policy solutions and generate the political influence necessary for their passage. In recognition of the significance of that shift related to the establishment of the Port Community Mitigation Trust Fund, Adrian Martinez wrote in his blog that "people would have thought pigs would fly before community, environmental and port leadership would work together to mitigate harmful impacts from port operations" (Martinez 2010).

In organizing terms, the campaigns for clean air, good jobs, and public and community health at the port have brought together unlikely partners in policy. The examples also point to the influential role of environmental justice organizing as coalitions and campaigns at the port, and reflect the historic and place-based framework of the environmental justice movement. Environmental justice organizations' community-based perspective recognizes the need for clean air and also the issues facing truck drivers as key to the quality-of-life conditions in environmental justice neighborhoods, many of which face the challenge of toxics in their air, water, and soil, and of industrial land uses adjacent to housing and other sensitive receptor sites, such as schools. Many of the truck drivers are immigrant Latino drivers who live in South Los Angeles, Wilmington, Commerce, and other communities most directly impacted by their very own occupation.

Growing activism focused on the health and community impacts of global trade, ports, and freight traffic continues to fuel and be fueled by the various movements that have come to influence port policy: the environmental justice movement; the labor movement; the environmental movement; and the health movement. By engaging in coalitions and building power in the face of powerful business interests and narrowly focused government policy, port and goods movement campaigns— along with supportive and sympathetic insiders willing to be pushed—advance the potential for such equitable regional economic and community development and a more impactful progressive politics. And those campaigns, in turn, have underlined the opportunities—and barriers—in the inside-outside game.

CHANGING THE NATURE OF THE DEBATE: FOOD SYSTEM ISSUES

If freight traffic and global trade corridor issues have forced their way onto local policy agendas, the question of food policy at the local and regional level has likewise emerged as an important new organizing focus during the Villaraigosa era. This took place nearly fifteen years after an earlier effort in the mid-1990s to bring about a new approach to local food policy in Los Angeles had withered, in part due to the lack of interest of policymakers and the relative weakness of various food-related social movements at the time. The initial effort to establish a Los Angeles food policy framework emerged in the wake of the 1992 civil disorders when problems of lack of access to fresh and affordable food underlined the protracted problems of food insecurity, hunger, and poor quality, unhealthy food in the neighborhoods most impacted by the riots. The chain supermarkets had abandoned their locations in the low-income neighborhoods of South and East Los Angeles due to mergers and a shift to lower density but a higher end clientele in more suburban locations. Liquor stores labeled as food marts and fast food restaurants proliferated in these same neighborhoods. Since the 1980s and the Reagan administration's assault on the food safety net, hunger and food insecurity had become a permanent part of the food landscape.

These issues were documented by a UCLA study that called for a new approach to food at the local level, embodied in an emerging concept called a "Food Policy Council." Released in June 1993, the UCLA study gained immediate attention, including an editorial in the *Los Angeles Times* calling for such a Food Policy Council to be established in Los Angeles. With community food and anti-hunger advocates pushing for action, a commission was established to look into how the city could develop a hunger policy. The commission held a series of hearings and meetings throughout the city on various food issues (food retail, nutrition, food assistance/safety net, community gardens, and farmers' markets) and helped generate the support for the development of one of the first Food Policy Councils in the country (Riordan 1996; Farrell 1996).[9]

In its brief three-year history from 1996 to 1999, the new commission, called the Los Angeles Food Security & Hunger Partnership, initiated several programs and policy approaches, including funding support for new farmers' markets and community gardens in three, targeted low-income council districts. However, the Los Angeles Food Security & Hunger Partnership suffered from internal conflicts and the political agendas of some of its participants, and it was never able to overcome a continuing tension over how to best define itself and its goals. This was due in part to its split personality (part movement-influenced, part political in nature). The battles over control between the food activists and the politicians eventually paralyzed the organization and led to its demise. With the community food movement in Los Angeles still limited to a handful of advocates and programs, a more comprehensive community food agenda failed to emerge (Los Angeles Community Food Security and Hunger Partnership 1999a, 1999b).

A couple of years after the Los Angeles Food Security & Hunger Partnership folded, food activists and representatives from labor and children's organizations came together at a gathering called "A Taste of Justice." Evaluating the failure of the Los Angeles Food Security & Hunger Partnership and the need for better movement facilitation and coordination, the Taste of Justice participants decided that the local food movement needed to build its capacity on several fronts—school food, food retail and supermarket issues, farmers' markets and community gardens, and a food policy working group to reexamine where and how food policy initiatives could occur at the local and regional levels. Along those lines, a Los Angeles Food Justice Network was created to help facilitate the next stages in the development of a local food movement, including pursuing city, regional, and institutional policy initiatives. The most successful of those efforts involved a series of dramatic and groundbreaking school food policies adopted by the LA Unified School District, beginning with the banning of sodas in school vending machines in 2002 (Vallianatos and Medrano 2009). While efforts to reestablish a Food Policy Council remained uneven (a 2004 initiative, following a series of meetings with then Mayor James Hahn's staff never came to fruition), a growth of community food and food justice advocacy created more possibilities, and new plans for a Los Angeles Food Policy Council reemerged, ten years after the original Los Angeles Food Security & Hunger Partnership group had dissolved (Urban & Environmental Policy Institute 2002).

These efforts were shepherded in part by Villaraigosa's Deputy Mayor Larry Frank, who also led the mayor's efforts to work with community, labor, and environmental groups around port and freight traffic issues. While Frank's efforts were initially focused on undertaking a celebration of the 30th anniversary of the reappearance of farmers' markets in Los Angeles, he was able to tap into a more mature and expansive food movement that operated at several different levels, in different communities, and with a range of programs, organizing efforts, and policy campaigns. These included successful efforts to change the school food environment at the LA Unified School District. In 2002, and again in 2004 and 2005, organizing efforts led by the Healthy School Food Coalition mobilized students, parents, and community members to bring about far-reaching policy changes by the LA Unified School District school board. These included a ban on sodas in vending machines (one of the first in the nation that helped stimulate actions in school districts around the country), a subsequent ban on junk food in schools, provisions for healthy food in the school cafeteria, and the development of farm to school programs. While the implementation of those school food policies remained contentious and uneven in some respects, the change in the LA Unified School District's school food service's approach was significant, and a growing constituency of healthy school food advocates had become an important part of the growing food movement (Vallianatos and Medrano 2009).

Los Angeles food activists also helped spawn new networks and coalitions, including the national Community Food Security Coalition, which initiated new programs that also became national in scope, such as farm to school (e.g., making local, fresh, and healthy food sourced from local and regional farmers available as part of school lunch); helped generate new linkages, such as between food and affordable housing and alternative transportation strategies; focused on an emerging "street food" constituency that involved sidewalk vendors, food trucks, and their community supporters primarily in immigrant-based neighborhoods; and played an important role in linking anti-hunger advocacy and politics with the need for broader food system and economic policy changes, such as the need for a living wage (Gottlieb and Joshi 2010). Food market issues also played an important part in the development of various campaigns, including the dramatic defeat of Wal-Mart in its effort to open a supercenter in the nearby city of Inglewood, the development of healthy corner or small store programs including an innovative "Farm to WIC" initiative, and efforts to relocate full-service supermarkets in inner-city neighborhoods (Garrison 2004; Gottlieb and Joshi 2010; Lichtenstein 2009; MacVean 2011). While these food movement developments were not unique to Los Angeles, they were significant in that food policy efforts at the local and regional levels were scattered and limited and generally off the radar screen of policymakers, including the mayor.

It was in that context that the deputy mayor began to host a series of meetings in the spring and summer of 2009 with several of the food movement activists. These were initially organized to discuss the idea of a farmers' market celebration but quickly evolved into a broader discussion of the need for more systematic food policy change. The farmers' market celebration, which took place in September 2009, also became the kickoff event for the development of a Food Policy Task Force consisting of local and regional food activists and government officials and staff. The charge for the task force was relatively vague and open-ended: develop a report on the status of food issues in the city and the southern California region; identify policy opportunities for bringing about change; and evaluate whether, how, and in what form a Food Policy Council could be established. The open-ended nature of the task force's mission was further underlined by the absence of any coherent approach toward food issues by the mayor, the county Board of Supervisors, and other local and regional government agencies, despite the heightened interest in food issues that had emerged both locally and nationally.[10]

By July 2010, the task force process, which included feedback through listening sessions involving a wide range of organizations and constituencies from labor groups to community gardeners, had resulted in a lengthy report that included a recommendation to establish a type of hybrid Food Policy Council. The proposed entity would include representatives and participation at the city and regional level, including community-based organizations and government representatives. It would not be located within government directly but would have a strong role in advising and helping facilitate government action among various departments and in conjunction with elected officials, beginning with the mayor. Policy changes were also identified, both immediate and long term, ranging from new local and healthy food-based procurement guidelines to support for the development of a regional food hub to facilitate and strengthen linkages between local growers and institutions and businesses. In a meeting with the mayor on the release of the task force report, Villaraigosa applauded the Food Policy Task Force's work and policy document and identified several areas where he pledged immediate implementation. This included adopting a "good food" procurement policy utilizing local sourcing, environmentally sustainable and worker justice criteria; increasing fresh food access opportunities in low-income communities, including establishing an Electronic Benefits Transfer (EBT) agreement at all LA farmers' markets to increase low-income participation at those markets; and advocating for farm to school and other healthy school food initiatives. These corresponded to some of the six priority areas of the Food Policy Task Force "Good Food for All" Report that ranged from broad goals to specific policy changes and programmatic developments, such as the development of a regional food hub that would facilitate the aggregating, preparing, processing, and distributing of local and regional food from multiple farmers intended for institutions such as K–12 schools, hospitals, and health clinics (Los Angeles Food Policy Task Force 2010).[11]

By the fall of 2010, a Los Angeles Food Policy Council was established and immediately set up seven working groups to develop new policy agendas and implement some of the first initiatives coming out of the mayor's office. While located outside of government, several key officials from the city, the County Public Health Department, and the LA Unified School District became members of the council, along with more than two dozen food, labor, environmental, and community participants. Villaraigosa, due largely to the organizing in this area, increased his own visibility around food issues, which once inhabited a more marginal place on the mayor's agenda. He appointed Paula Daniels, the LA Food Policy Council's chair, as his senior advisor on food issues and used his role as the 2011 President of the US Conference of Mayors to promote a "good food" agenda, notably the development of regional food hubs as a strategy to facilitate "an improved regional wholesale marketing system that addresses the major barriers and risks that limit small family farmers' ability to bring good food to market and, in turn, provide consumers and communities with access to good food" (Cech 2010, 3).

The process encouraged by the City of Los Angeles that culminated in the development of the LA Food Policy Council overlaps (but also differs in some respects) with efforts of the Bloomberg administration and other food policy advocates in New York. Bloomberg's focus along with other New York policymakers, including New York City Council Speaker Christine Quinn, has been primarily health and hunger-focused, such as initiatives around food stamp outreach, labeling (e.g., calorie counts in restaurants), limiting the size of sugar-sweetened beverages, and efforts to increase full service food markets in low-income communities (e.g., through a funding mechanism modeled after a successful program in Pennsylvania called the "Fresh Food Financing Initiative") (Quinn 2010). And while the range and capacity of grassroots activism around food issues in New York could be considered more extensive than what has developed in Los Angeles, some of Los Angeles's programs, policies, and organizing campaigns, including the development of a comprehensive food procurement approach, a more robust Food Policy Council process plus its active working groups, and changes in the school food environment, indicate an innovative and potentially deeper and more radical change agenda that has been led by community-based, grassroots groups.

What is striking about the LA Food Policy Council and its "Good Food for All" agenda is its linkage of key constituencies and food justice-related issues and goals to the policy process while at the same time developing the organizing and constituent-building efforts elaborated in the Good Food for All Agenda document. This inside-outside game includes a strong focus on health and food access disparities impacting low-income communities and communities of color, an emphasis on worker justice issues related to farm labor, food retail, and restaurant workers, and strategies to strengthen and make more sustainable the regional farm economy by, among other strategies, establishing direct links between farms and schools, as well as other institutions. The LA Food Policy Council sees its role as facilitating and strengthening the links between, on the one hand, social movements and NGOs working in neighborhoods, unions and food worker advocates, the food industries, and the farms, and, on the other hand, policy process and policymaking officials, such as the mayor. The Food Policy Council's hybrid nature of working both outside and inside government mirrored the approach of the port and freight traffic-focused environmental justice groups and their allies who are also seeking to find the right balance and approach to that outside-inside game.

The development of the Food Policy Council in Los Angeles also pointed to both the similarities and differences between the Los Angeles and New York experiences with respect to the role of the mayors as well. Unlike New York, where Mayor Bloomberg had played a more visible leadership role in identifying new health-based policies, including around food issues, and had also established a Food Policy Coordinator position within the mayor's office, LA Mayor Villaraigosa initially played more of a passive, albeit supportive role around food policy change, including identifying the need for and establishing a Food Policy Council. That passive role changed with the development of the Food Policy Council and the role of the advocate groups associated with it. What made the openings for food policy changes possible—and a structure to help facilitate those changes—was the growth and maturity of the community-based movements and the important roles of several key staff and commissioners within the Villaraigosa administration. This included his senior advisor on food issues, the deputy mayor, and a deputy counsel who also served on the Food Policy Council. It was those roles that also made possible the inside-outside connections.

CONCLUSION

In both the port and goods movement and food-related issue areas, the LA experience points to the importance of community-based organizing and policy development that has influenced and has been reinforced by a mayoral administration with roots in various social movements. In both issue areas, an inside-outside policy process took place: organizing from the *outside* made the community, environmental, labor, land use, and health issues prominent where they had largely been absent, thus changing the framework about the debate and the nature of the policy process itself. At the same time, a supportive framework *inside* government and the opportunity to establish new policies enhanced the opportunities for change. In both cases, however, counter pressures also continued to exert themselves. These included legal actions by industry against the Clean Trucks Program, pressures from the economic downturn not to launch or implement changes that involved public dollars, and pressures to generate more business-friendly measures that led to changes among mayoral appointees.

With respect to food issues, the LA Food Policy Council's approach, embedded in its Good Food for All Agenda and subsequent work to implement the document's key provisions, still faced significant barriers. These included the enormous ability of the major food system players to maintain the way food is grown and accessed, a dominant fast food culture still prevalent in schools and neighborhoods, continuing efforts by the dominant food system players to carry out their agenda, such as Walmart's efforts to establish stores in Los Angeles, and the protracted and often complementary problems of hunger and obesity, among other issues. At the same time, the modest yet important breakthroughs and innovations that have emerged around food system issues in Los Angeles, similar to a wide range of innovations in New York and other cities and counties around the country, point to how an agenda for change can be strengthened when an inside-outside strategy for accomplishing such change is effective.

The approach in Los Angeles, which to a certain extent parallels organizing work in New York around both food issues and port and goods movement impacts, was manufactured in a period of hope and tested in a subsequent period of enormous economic and political uncertainty. It can serve as a possible prototype for other large cities across the nation. A wave of progressive organizing and coalition building in Los Angeles that culminated with the election of Villaraigosa in 2005 suggests that advocates and activists playing an inside role present a continuing challenge that often yields, at best, mixed results, given the forces arrayed against such change. A more fundamental shift toward a health and equity-based policy toward global trade and goods movement and a more just and healthy food system experienced at the neighborhood and regional level would ultimately require a deeper and multilayered set of social movements, a shift in governance, and more of an alignment of the role of policymakers with the forces of change.

Leadership shifts within Los Angeles and from Los Angeles to Sacramento to Washington, DC, have presented opportunities, as well as challenges. Nancy Sutley, the mayor's appointment as Deputy Mayor for Environment, was tapped in 2009 to serve as Obama's Chair of the Council of Environmental Quality, creating a stronger opening between the city and the Obama administration. Mary Nichols, who was originally appointed as President of the Board of Water and Power, left that position after being appointed to head the powerful California Air Resources Board where she also on occasion locked horns with environmental justice groups. For many of the activists who had hoped that having allies in elected positions would facilitate action and political leadership on key issues, change has been slower than expected. Both activists and their insider allies have also been forced to deal with the economic reality of shrinking public sector budgets and a lack of staffing capacity to monitor and implement existing policies and programs, much less create new ones. The hostile political movement now arrayed against any public expenditures and any public policy role has thus made the need for organizing even more imperative. Nevertheless, the inside-outside strategies developed and implemented during the Villaraigosa years marked the continued growth and sophistication of social justice and environmental activism in Los Angeles and the capacity to influence those on the inside. At the same time, while fueling similar campaigns on ports and food issues across the country, the outsider activists and their policymaker insiders continue to face huge challenges and constant attacks from those who ultimately wish to block any agenda for change.

NOTES

1. The text of the Los Angeles Community Benefits Agreement is available at: http://communitybenefits.org/downloads/LAX%20Community%20Benefits%20Agreement.pdf.
2. See, for example, "Planning for a Livable City: Appointing the Next General Manager of the Los Angeles Department of Transportation," an open letter to the mayor by environmental and green and equitable transportation advocates, which elaborated on the original PLAN transportation and land-use agenda document, Los Angeles: Urban & Environmental Policy Institute, 2005, available at: http://departments.oxy.edu/uepi/transportationGM/letter.htm.
3. "Janette Sadik-Khan Wows L.A," Joe Linton, UEPI, March 19, 2010, available at: http://uepi.wordpress.com/2010/03/19/janette-sadik-khan-wows-los-angeles/.
4. Green Building Program ordinance, available at: http://cityplanning.lacity.org/Code_Studies/GreenLa/greenbuildingordinance.pdf.
5. Personal communication with Jesse Marquez and Andrea Hricko, July 2010.

6. See work by Rachel Morello-Frosch, Manuel Pastor, and James Sadd for literature on cumulative impacts and environmental justice communities.

7. Coalition for Clean and Safe Ports. http://www.cleanandsafeports.org. See also Block 2007

8. Mayor's Office, City of Los Angeles. January 4, 2012.

9. Personal observation and participation by one of the authors who was a member of the LAFSHP.

10. Coauthor of this article, Robert Gottlieb, has been a participant in the development of the LA Food Policy Task Force. See Gottlieb and Joshi 2010. See also, MacVean 2010.

11. The electronic benefit transfer (EBT) technology, as defined by the US Department of Agriculture, is "an electronic system that allows a recipient to authorize transfer of their government benefits from a Federal account to a retailer account to pay for products received" (available at: http://www.fns.usda.gov/snap/ebt/). This includes such benefits as Supplemental Nutrition Assistance Program (SNAP or food stamps benefits) and Women, Infant and Children (WIC) farmers' market nutrition program benefits, thereby increasing low income capacity to shop at farmers' markets.

PART SIX

Culture

CHAPTER 17

Los Angeles, Where Architecture Is At

RICK BELL

Is architecture in Los Angeles moving in one overall direction or several, and how does this answer vary between New York and Los Angeles?

New Yorkers looking at Los Angeles are blinded by the angelic light, confused by the lack of a center, and intoxicated by the sexy superficiality. The transplanted New Yorker in the LA episode of *Sex & the City*, described as a former writer for *The Observer*, may still wear a Yankee cap, but he literally spits his food out, tasting but not ingesting, seeming to eat, but starving for sustenance. How then is this writer, a native New Yorker—born in Brooklyn no less—to be objective about new architectural trends in Los Angeles? Should it be said that Los Angeles is architecturally moving in a single direction, perhaps ever-so-slowly on a congested rush-hour freeway? And, for that matter, what about the perceived limitations of architectural quality in New York—what can't we afford in Gotham when all our working cranes went to Dubai before the worldwide economic meltdown? Are designers left behind on the East Coast still dodging the trends that start in Santa Monica or Venice and are broadcast from Burbank and beamed from Los Angeles?

Rhetorical questions these, since television production has made us belligerently bicoastal and the enhanced reciprocity in the licensure of architects has made us interchangeable. While my post-earthquake yet active California architectural license has never been affixed to a building project, California dreaming has become all too real from Manhattan's Mayne streets to the Gehry spruce-ups. The Mamas & The Papas are here, *in loco parentis*, as we re-envision Manhattan's dark and dirty alleys based on a more natural and environmentally whatever model; valley girls are going by hybrid to the canyon. The cathartic loss of a never-to-be-named again bankrupt Brooklyn ballclub has left architectural nostalgia in its wake in New York that may bomb in the Bronx and be flushed out of Queens; Chavez Ravine is not, too, without its ghosts of racism, displacement, and loss. Where have you gone Sandy Koufax?

When the missions of El Pueblo de Nuestra Señora la Reina de Los Angeles de Porciuncula were new, architecture had three directives: firmness, commodity, and delight. Today there are more ways of looking at what we build and why. Do they come together in a single direction, like the merging lanes of a freeway, everyone going in the same direction but slowly and with some bending of fenders? Or is the resurgence of public transportation in both Los Angeles and New York an indication of multiple lines, transfer points, and correspondences? Separately, there are six or more trends in the practice of architects in Los Angeles and New York. Perhaps they will all end up in the same place, Manhattan Beach?

REUSE (THE STANDARD HOTEL AND THE MORGAN LIBRARY)

Jan Morris writes that "a sense of age informs the very setting of LA" and whether looking at the diverse traditions of Watts Towers and the Chateau Marmont or the tarpit bars of La Brea a lot has aged quickly, aided by architectural Botox. New York is no different, from Strivers' Row in Harlem to the Plaza, or the Red Cat hangouts in the former meat market. So what are the exceptions that set a new standard for adaptive reuse and the renovation of our coast-as-toast legacies?

The Standard Downtown in Los Angeles, a trendy big-boutique of a hotel in a former office building, sets a new level of expectation. A rooftop bar includes wee pods

Figure 17.1
Reuse Atop the Standard Hotel
Source: Photo by Rick Bell.

Figure 17.2
Reuse at the Morgan Library
Source: Photo by Rick Bell.

for hiding out next to a pool where lap-swimmers sometimes benefit from films projected on the building across the street; its *Biergarten* has new generation weighted
hula hoops. The rooms themselves have glass-walled bathrooms that reimagine our
cultural sense of privacy and security. In New York, that recast domesticity, at a
grand scale, is seen in Renzo Piano's reworking of the Morgan Library. His addition
and renovation, done in collaboration with Beyer Blinder Belle, adds glass elevators
to a new space, half-vault, half playground, that redefines the antecedent use and
circulation. The expanded building has gone from repository to gathering space, a
destination for respite and for lunch.

In Los Angeles, there is a lot to preserve and protect, from the Bradbury Building
to the Observatory. A tradition of trend-setting modern residential architecture,
from Wright's Usonian House for George Sturges to the celebrated houses by Richard
Neutra and others, happily remains. New York too, with almost a million existing buildings, offers relatively few sites for new construction. In certain quarters
the credo must be to adapt, reuse, and, most important, add on. The Landmarks
Preservation Commission in New York City has created over a hundred historic districts, and thousands of individual landmarks. Designation makes for heated discussion of the appropriateness of significant alteration of many of these structures. The
cultural and historic landmarks of Los Angeles, including modern masterpieces, are
equally valued.

SUSTAINABILITY (NRDC AND THE NEW YORK TIMES BUILDING)

There are waterless urinals in the Natural Resources Defense Council Robert Redford Building in Santa Monica, which is to Los Angeles as Coney Island was once to New York. And yes, there are accidentally waterless—call them nonfunctioning—urinals in the dismally renovated bathroom in Pennsylvania Station, near where Louis Kahn died of a heart attack. There are even some in New York's Bank of America Tower at One Bryant Park, after creative code interpretation and hardball negotiation with the plumbers union. These may not be the benchmark of sustainability, but an indication that we have to go to new ways of looking at how the greening of our buildings and communities can be accomplished.

The NRDC Building, by Moule & Polyzoides, cofounders of the Congress of New Urbanism, opened in 1993 and has 15,000 square feet of space some fifteen miles west of the Standard Hotel. The building systems, from rooftop 7.5 kilowatt solar electric arrays to gray-water retrieval, are there to be seen by visitors and the environmental activists fortunate enough to work there. One of the first LEED Platinum buildings, for a while it had more LEED points than any other building in the United States. The trademarked "Leadership in Energy and Environmental Design" Green Building Rating System was developed by the US Green Building Council. Project architect Elizabeth Moule noted that "the amount of embodied energy and pollution you save when you put your building in a place that people don't have to drive to is enormous." Another feature linking newly transit conscious Southern California with New York is the building's system of *brise soleils* shading, which helps to break the glare of the 350 day-per-year Southern California sun and anticipates the ceramic bars that do likewise at the New York Times Tower, also designed by Renzo Piano Workshop, this time collaborating with FXFOWLE Architects. The NRDC building uses almost 75 percent less energy than conventional buildings of its size and is one of the first buildings in the United States to claim net-zero production of carbon dioxide.

At the New York Times Building, other environmentally responsible features include underfloor air distribution for all of the floors occupied by the Times, though regrettably not on the floors leased to outside companies and organizations. Most importantly, the interior of the lobby and of the adjacent Times Center lecture hall benefits from a wonderful interior courtyard—a birch forest—providing light, air, and greenery. The environmental lessons for high-rise towers were learned by FXFOWLE (then Fox & Fowle, which, post-meiosis, also generated Cook + Fox) starting with the Condé Nast Building at 4 Times Square, a few blocks away from the Times. Next to Condé Nast, which with its solar panels part of its façade was labeled the "green giant" when it was new in 1999, is the One Bryant Park headquarters of the Bank of America Building by Cook + Fox. Unlike the Times Tower, the bank's building is being measured by the US Green Building Council's LEED metric. Despite the Times' bird-friendly façade (major attention was given to how to prevent fly-by deaths, if not the prevention of publicity seeking human climbers), neither of these tall towers can match LA's Audubon Society for going off-grid. Nestled in the 282-acre Ernest E. Debs Regional Park, the Audubon Center, a low-rise structure

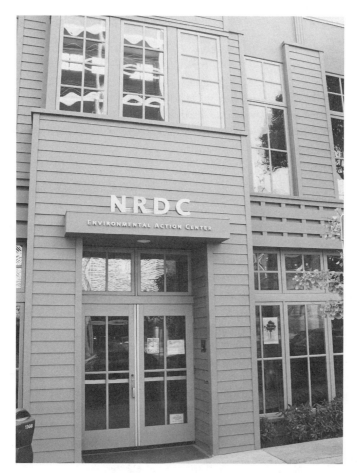

Figure 17.3
Sustainability at NRDC building in Santa Monica
Source: Photo by Rick Bell.

Figure 17.4
Sustainability at the New York Times
Source: Photo by Rick Bell.

of some 5,023 square feet, is not served by the city's electrical supply. Its electrical needs are generated by on-site solar panels. Notable for serving some 50,000 young people, predominantly Latino, within a two-mile radius, the Audubon Center was also the first US structure to receive a LEED Platinum rating with 53 out of the possible 69 points for such features as using locally produced building materials. With or without LEED, can going off-grid or providing co-generation capability become a new tradition in Los Angeles and New York?

TRANSPARENCY (CALTRANS AND THE ROSE CENTER)

Thom Mayne, FAIA, has won the Pritzker Prize and, with major commissions for public agencies such as the California Department of Transportation (Caltrans) in Los Angeles and the federal government's General Services Administration in San Francisco, may be said to have gone mainstream. This is not completely the case. His firm, Morphosis, based in Culver City and Chelsea, continues to look at all building types, including government offices, in new ways, redefining openness, accessibility, and internal movement. University work, including the new building for Cooper Union near Astor Place in New York City, does likewise. A sense of democratic purpose combines with the large scale of these structures to make a significant urban gesture. Such buildings may have been fortresses in another day, but increasingly, transparency is an appreciated quality of the structures housing those who serve the public.

Figure 17.5
Openness at Caltrans
Source: Photo by Rick Bell.

This trend can be seen in many buildings in New York, including the criminal court complex on 161st Street in the Bronx by Rafael Viñoly Architects, a stone's throw or very long home run from the new-retro Yankee Stadium. But the building in New York City that takes transparency to a global level is the Frederick Phineas & Sandra Priest Rose Center at the American Museum of Natural History, the City's planetarium. Affectionately called "a ball in a box"—the building by its use of float glass and its comprehensibly simple geometry, gives a remarkable sense of orientation to school groups and elderly stargazers alike. Designed by the Polshek Partnership (now Ennead Architects), it shares certain high-tech features with Caltrans but also more immediately with the Polshek-designed entry pavilion addition to the Brooklyn Museum. This latter project brings the *piano nobile* down to earth, just as the Rose Center explains the heavens to those venturing to the Upper West Side. Both were anticipated by the 1953 theme building at the Los Angeles International Airport, a spaceship waiting for time and technology to allow it to take off. Philip Johnson did

Figure 17.6
Openness at the Rose Center
Source: Photo by Rick Bell.

much the same for the New York State Pavilion at the 1964–65 Worlds' Fair at New York's Flushing Meadows-Corona Park. But Los Angeles was first.

FUN (DISNEY HALL AND ALICE TULLY HALL)

Gehry, one critic said, just wants to have fun. And despite the need for sunglasses inside and out (Angelenos seem to always be wearing shades), the building shimmers, glistens, bends, and turns, in more ways than the rides at the Fun Pier at Santa Monica. Acoustically the concert halls and rehearsal spaces, as well as the informal spaces scattered throughout the building, work superbly. They draw people from the region and beyond to hear the Los Angeles Philharmonic and a host of other orchestras and groups. But what makes Disney shine is the Bilbao-bulbous cladding, which is hard to pin down or draw without computer software from the aeronautical industry. Concert-goers and other visitors are brought up through the building in a variety of ways, but happily in a city that values the automobile above all other gods, some of these involve walking and climbing stairs. The sidewalk is increasingly alive with umbrella tables and pedestrians.

In a different urban context, but also a place where people go to hang out, hear and be heard, is the gut renovation of Alice Tully Hall at New York's Lincoln Center, a collaboration of Diller Scofidio + Renfro with FXFOWLE Architects & Planners. An exterior corner grandstand faces the building, whose brutal concrete walls have been replaced,

Figure 17.7
Fun at Walter E. Disney Hall
Source: Photo by Rick Bell.

Figure 17.8
Fun at Alice Tully Hall
Source: Photo by Rick Bell.

at street level, with a glazed café. A saddlebag rehearsal space adds life to the second floor Broadway frontage. With the adjacent tilted-lawn Hypar Pavillion, also by DSR, housing the Lincoln Restaurant, New York's '60s cultural Acropolis has become a fun place to savor the latest concoctions, or see the circus, film, opera, or chamber music.

Speaking of which, Elizabeth Diller debated David Byrne at the AIA New York Chapter's Center for Architecture in a program orchestrated by Chris Janney, saying that music must come before architecture, that her new design for the reworking of Alice Tully Hall required knowing, first, what type of music was to be played. David Byrne, the composer also known as a member of Talking Heads, countered that architecture comes first, that he could not write music without knowing whether it would be played in a club or sports arena. Both agreed that earphones on personal hand-held devices might make the argument moot. What does that imply for the future of performance spaces such as Frank Gehry's new hall planned for the World Trade Center site? Don't hold your breath while waiting for the answer. Go instead to classic performance spaces from the Music Box on Hollywood Boulevard and the Blue Note on West 3rd Street, to the impromptu clubs from Williamsburg to Wilshire where you will hear new sound.

CONNECTIVITY (PERSHING SQUARE AND TIMES SQUARE)

How buildings, parks, and plazas link up with each other and connect people to the urban landscape is thought of somewhat differently in New York and Los Angeles.

For example, long-term expectations for Pershing Square have been partially realized, with a seasonal ice-skating rink adding vitality. Renovated in the 1990s by Laurie Olin and the late Ricardo Legoretta, the architecture speaks of conviviality, as does the goal of creating a place of connection that can easily be accessed from other parts of Los Angeles and its metropolitan area. The Metro's Red and Purple lines are adjacent.

In New York, two different types of public space have captured the imagination. The first is the High Line, a phased linear park that stretches from the newly trendy Gansevoort market area up to Hudson Yards and the proposed redevelopment for offices and apartments that will redefine the western edge of Midtown Manhattan. The story of the preservation and reuse of the abandoned rail spur starts with the community-based activism of Robert Hammond and Joshua David, battling against economic and political forces that made retention of the industrial relic seemed unlikely at best. But, with rezoning of West Chelsea and a gradual shift of perception, the appreciation of the project's value came, as well, from real estate developers seeking opportunities in an underpopulated area a stone's throw from Penn Station. The park design, by Field Operations and Diller Scofidio + Renfro, has multiple active and static zones that recall the feeling of the wildness of the place before it became New York City's most popular destination for a leisurely stroll. Lining the High Line is some of the City's best new architecture, starting, at the south end, with the New York Standard Hotel by Todd Schliemann, FAIA of Ennead (formerly Polshek) Architects. The most remarkable residential project adjacent to the High Line is HL23, at 23rd Street. Designed by

Figure 17.9
Connectivity at Pershing Square
Source: Photo by Rick Bell.

Figure 17.10
Connectivity at Times Square
Source: Photo by Rick Bell.

Los Angeles architect Neil Denari, AIA of Neil M. Denari Architects, the angular structure speaks to the dynamism of the High Line and the connection not only of a new
neighborhood, but of the influence of LA theory on New York practice. An easy walk
from the north end of the High Line is the newly pedestrian-friendly Times Square,
which New Yorkers still think of as the crossroads of the world. With the city street
map redrawn by the Department of Transportation to create new pedestrian plazas
in the roadbed of Broadway, temporary changes are being transformed to permanent
improvements by Snøhetta. At the north end of the Times Square bowtie, the TKTS
discount ticket center's red-step bleachers are a result of a competition won by Choi
Ropiha Architects. The completed project and renovation of Father Duffy Square was
done in collaboration with Perkins Eastman and PKSB Architects.

SPIRIT (THE CATHEDRAL OF OUR LADY
OF THE ANGELS AND THE CENTER FOR
ACADEMIC AND SPIRITUAL LIFE)

It is no coincidence that Los Angeles and at least one of its baseball teams look sky-
ward with cerulean aspiration while a Broadway play too-frequently brought back
to life is called "Damn Yankees"—not to mention the success of *Wicked*. Films about
the devil, whether as fashion editor or white shoe lawyer, tend to be set in New York.

Figure 17.11
Connectivity on the High Line
Source: Photo by Rick Bell.

Spirituality goes both ways, and Los Angeles, with the construction of a new cathedral church designed to outlast earthquakes and the mortal coil, takes the high road. The mausoleum looks heavenly and has already attracted the remains of dead stars including Gregory Peck (whose father-in-law was an architect). The architecture, by Pritzker-Prize winner Rafael Moneo, collaborating with Leo A. Daly as executive architect, is writ large, even by Los Angeles standards. The site is 65 acres and the structures have over 115,000 square feet of space, including space for 600 cars. The *campanile* tower is 115 feet tall, gesturing to the LA City Hall spire of 454 feet. The plaza of the cathedral allows for many to gather for religious and social purposes, and ecumenically includes a variety of memorials. Spiritualism in the sun permits umbrella tables, and shaded arcades. The church itself provides sanctuary from the heat and glare.

In New York there are many fine churches and synagogues, some new, some wonderfully preserved, including the Eldridge Street Synagogue, recently renovated by Walter Sedovic FAIA of Walter Sedovic Architects, with Wiss Janney. This project is a winner of the Municipal Art Society MASterwork Award. And our preserved transit facilities such as Warren & Wetmore's Grand Central Terminal, restored by Beyer Blinder Belle, have a grandeur approaching that of major religious facilities, since use of public transportation, not automobiles, is the credo in New York. Grand Central's ceiling even depicts the heavens. The mezzanine level west terrace now houses the City's most open and visible Apple Store, a shrine of sorts for the Big Apple. And the 1913 Woolworth Building by Cass Gilbert, the tallest building in the world when it was completed, is still known as the "Cathedral of Commerce." But many in New York turn to Greenwich Village to find a grounding in spiritual values. The most recent addition to the Village skyline is the Center for Academic and Spiritual Life of New York University, located on the south edge of Washington Square Park, more or less on axis with Fifth Avenue. Designed by Machado and Silvetti Associates, the building is meant to evoke a "tree of life" adjacent to the park newly renovated by landscape architect George Valonikos.

The sense of spiritual sharing, not through common material connection, but through caring for others in dire need, transforms a part of both cities and should be noted as an architectural trend where the altruism and idealism of the profession shines through. My favorite project in Los Angeles is the Downtown Drop-In Center on San Julian Street by Michael B. Lehrer, FAIA of LA-based Lehrer Architects. At the Drop-In Center, thirty-five places to sleep are provided in a homeless shelter like none other I have seen. An outdoor courtyard as a noncoercive and nonthreatening space welcomes those without a home each night; social services and medical attention are available in

Figure 17.12
Spirit at the Cathedral of Our Lady of the Angels
Source: Photo by Rick Bell.

Figure 17.13
Spirit at the Downtown Drop-in Center
Source: Photo by Michael B. Lehrer (used by permission).

adjacent space. Built at an incredibly low budget of $70 per square foot and completed in 2001 when it won an AIA National Honor Award, the architectural sophistication shows respect and hope for the future. Lehrer's website relates an anecdote about how the building has changed lives. A somewhat similar project in New York, by Richard Dattner Architect, is the former New York City morgue, a somewhat lugubrious McKim Mead & White National Register landmark. It is now a Children's Center of the Administration for Children's Services, and home to the city's foster care programs. Kids by necessity torn from their homes by social workers or police officers in the middle of the night are treated with dignity in an opened-up environment enlivened by public art and influenced by the example of the prior Los Angeles Family Court project.

It is easy to note the influence of one city on another, whether through published comparable projects or through the same architects working in both places at more-or-less the same time. This begs the question of simultaneous invention—there was nothing new under the sun during our prior design penumbra. Now new design screams from the *Architects Newspaper* in Los Angeles and New York City, can be seen in *LA Architect* and *Oculus*, and even, from time-to-time informs *Architect and Architectural Record*, not to mention *Metropolis*, *Dwell* and the other design magazines that catalogue innovation. So, that said, what are the lessons from the leading cities east and west?

Do we learn from each other? Yes.

Does the economic detour mean that what we do requires more bang for the buck? Maybe.

Do environmental considerations and cultural legacies suggest that Los Angeles and New York City have come together? Time will tell.

Figure 17.14
Spirit at the Center for Academic and Spiritual Life
Source: Photo by Rick Bell.

Can we use buzzwords such as reuse, sustainability, openness, connectivity, fun, and spirit to determine if we are moving in the same direction? To answer, I would turn to Charlie Moore, much-missed architecture school dean of both UCLA and Yale. He was also the architect of the Beverly Hills Civic Center, about which he wrote in *Chambers for a Memory Palace*: "I chose an axis, the longest the site afforded, running southwest to northeast, not located so that it would ever be traversed end-to-end, or even for a major part of its length."

Take a look around, and see which way the wind blows.

CHAPTER 18

New York, Los Angeles, and Chicago as Depicted in Hit Movies

DAVID HALLE, ERIC VANSTROM,
JAN REIFF, AND TED NITSCHKE*

HIT MOVIES

There is much excellent writing on how major cities such as New York, Los Angeles, and Chicago have been depicted in the movies, yet the method used to select which movies to discuss has been somewhat arbitrary. Typically the author talks about those movies that he or she finds interesting, often heavily influenced by those movies that earlier writers found interesting. Usually the movies selected project an image of the city that the author wants to discuss and even reinforce.[1]

We adopt a different strategy here. We select hit movies—that is, the movies that interested the viewing public. We define hit movies, at least from 1947 on, as those in the top 10 for North America at the time of the movie's release, measured by reel rental until 1992 and after that by box-office receipts (see appendix 1 for details).

We focus on hit movies because we are interested in popular attitudes toward these cities, and it is plausible to assume that a hit movie resonates, at least somewhat, with the tastes and attitudes of sections of the public at the time, especially if a particular city is depicted in similar fashion in other popular movies. We also discuss the relation between the way these cities are depicted in hit movies and actual features of these cities at the time the movies were released.

We include Chicago, currently the third largest city in the United States, because it cannot be kept out of this discussion for reasons that will become apparent. For one, our account is a historical overview and until the 1970s, Chicago, not Los Angeles, was the second largest city in the United States.

Our overall conclusion is that each of these three cities is associated in public perceptions, perhaps even stereotyped, with one or more specific images or perspectives.

*We thank Laura Robinson and Alycia Cheng for their careful research assistance.

In particular, New York basically reflects whatever appears to be the dominant image(s) of city/urban life at the time the movie is made, so New York's depiction changes as those dominant image(s) change. In short, New York is a stand-in for the currently popular notion of big city life.

Still, amid this changeability, there is one constant theme. At least every few years a hit movie portrays New York as a town for business, finance, and the rich, at least some of whom are depicted critically as being one or more of the following—greedy, duplicitous, unpleasant, ruthless, sexist, and womanizing.

Chicago, by contrast, is stereotyped around four main images that have remained strikingly constant over time. These include gangsters and political corruption; ethnic groups; a vibrant urban center containing both jobs and a cutting-edge cultural life; and dull, bedroom-commuter suburbs that surround the vibrant urban core. Indeed, the Chicago portrayed in hit movies resembles the "classic" city of Burgess and Parks's famous (1925) model of urban development, which was based on Chicago, with story lines in more recent hit movies updated to capture more contemporary populations and cultural sensibilities.

Los Angeles's depictions fall midway between Chicago's thematic stability and New York's urban adaptability. The representations of Los Angeles have evolved gradually over time. From the 1930s to the early 1970s, Hollywood dominates, then fades to be replaced by auto culture, to which the theme of the ineptness of the LA Police is added. In the late 1990s, the disaster theme appears, followed more recently by an emerging motif of global institutions—corporations and/or organized crime, often with an Asian connection, operating in the region. However, neither of these last two themes—disaster and global city—are confined to Los Angeles.

METHODOLOGICAL CAVEATS

Before proceeding, some methodological issues and caveats must be addressed. There are many complexities involved in this topic. Crucial to the discussion is whether just because a city is depicted in a particular way in a hit movie, that representation can reasonably be said to resonate with contemporary public perceptions of that city. Perhaps the movies were hits primarily because of a particular star, a fine script, or studio marketing and muscle. We deal with this key question more thoroughly in our conclusion. Suffice it to say here that if a particular city is depicted in patterned ways in multiple hit movies, we believe that those patterns resonate with some sort of common public perception of that city, though other factors are surely also important in a movie's box-office success.

In our appendix, we discuss additional issues, including how we determined the list of hit movies before 1947 when neither comprehensive box-office nor reel rental data were available, and how we classified movies by city and theme depicted.

THREE SURPRISES

Our focus on hit movies produces several surprises, of which we will mention three now, one each for New York, Los Angeles, and Chicago, and which we believe validate the usefulness of our approach. We then discuss each city in detail, and in that context also suggest explanations for the Los Angeles and Chicago surprises—we explain the New York surprise right away.

New York: The Woody Allen, Spike Lee, and Martin Scorsese Surprise

Perhaps no three directors/writers have been more associated with New York in recent decades than Woody Allen, Spike Lee, and Martin Scorsese. Much has been written in scholarly and popular literature about their connection, and that of their films, to New York. But their movies are rarely major hits. Incredibly, between the three of them over their entire careers they have only two top 10 movies, both early films by Woody Allen, *What's New Pussy Cat* (1965), and the James Bond spoof *Casino Royale* (1967). Spike Lee's highest rated film was *Inside Man* (2006) which reached No. 15 on the hit movie list, and Martin Scorsese's highest rated film was the Boston-located *The Departed* (2007), which was No. 14 on the list.

This is especially surprising because a large number of New York movies have been major (i.e., top 10) hits—139 from 1920 to the present, compared with 49 for Los Angeles and 24 for Chicago. (See figure 18.1.) Indeed, for every decade the number of hit movies featuring New York has at least equaled the number featuring Los Angeles and Chicago combined, and for some decades the imbalance between New York and the other two cities has been huge (e.g., over four times as great in the 1950s and 1960s, over three times in the 1930s and 1940s). If a director wants to make a hit movie set in a city, New York is clearly a great place to try. This is also

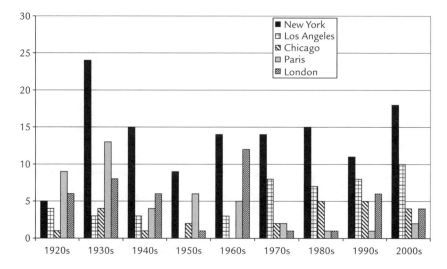

Figure 18.1
Number of Hit Movies Featuring New York, Los Angeles, Chicago, Paris, and London, 1900–2010
Source: Authors from compiled data on ticket sales as described.

true when foreign cities are included in the analysis. New York has been the setting for more hit movies than any world city for every decade except the 1920s, when Paris was featured in nine hit movies, surpassing London, featured in six, and New York in five.

The reasons for the relative lack of box-office success of New York's three most famous directors are doubtless complicated. But the most plausible is that they have famously focused on ethnic or minority groups in their movies: Allen on Jews; Scorsese on Italians; and Spike Lee on African Americans. Through their lenses, New York City is the site of racial/ethnic tension, with different parts of the city closely identified with different racial/ethnic groups. Yet the problem is that, from the mid-1970s to the present, the period when these three directors have been most active, the moviegoing public does not seem to envisage New York City primarily in this way. Earlier, particularly in the years from 1945 through the mid-1970s, there are many ethnically themed hit movies set in New York. *The Jolson Story* (1946) recounts the life of Jewish immigrant Al Johnson who became famous performing in blackface on stage and in the movie *The Jazz Singer* (1927); *Gentleman's Agreement* (1948) deals with anti-Semitism in New York society; *West Side Story* (1961) recasts Romeo and Juliet with Puerto Rican and white working class gangs; *Funny Girl* (1968) loosely depicts the life of Jewish performer Fannie Brice; and *The Godfather* (1972) features Italian mobsters.

But from 1977 to the present there is only one ethnically themed New York hit movie, the comedy *Coming to America* (1988). In it, an African aristocrat travels to New York City seeking an untraditional wife. The transition from ethnically themed films is underlined by *Staying Alive* (1983), the hit sequel to the hit *Saturday Night Fever* (1977), which featured an Italian working-class hero. In the sequel the hero, Tony, has moved from his Italian neighborhood in Brooklyn to Manhattan, and his ethnicity is scarcely mentioned. Instead, he is trying to make it in the advertising industry.

So to the extent that Allen, Lee, and Scorsese represent New York as a city of ethnic and racial groups, the potential for their films to appeal to the broad public seems limited, even handicapped, especially if, as we will argue, there is another major city—Chicago—that the public has and continues to envisage as specially associated with ethnic and racial groups. It is surely no accident that while the movies of Allen, Scorsese, and Lee, depicting New York as an ethnic and racial town failed to crack the top 10, the mega hit *My Big Fat Greek Wedding*, No. 5 in 2002, whose ethnic theme is foregrounded in its title, was set in Chicago. Here is a second reason we cannot keep Chicago out of this discussion.

Note that, to the extent that the public no longer views New York City as an "ethnic" town, the perception is accurate. While New York continues to contain a large proportion of immigrants, in recent decades no single national group dominates the city's immigrants, as Foner and Waldinger stress in their chapter in this volume. In 2007–09 the largest national group in the New York region, Dominicans, were just 9 percent of the total immigrant population, and the next largest, Chinese, were just 6 percent. The once prominent European population has shriveled, with the now largest group, Italians, representing only 3 percent of all immigrants in the New York region.

Los Angeles: The Noir Surprise

The second surprise is LA Noir. Movies in the "noir" tradition, for which Los Angeles is famous among critics and writers, are rarely major box-office hits. The "noir" tradition can be defined as films that are dark and downbeat, imbued with a large dose of fear, mistrust, bleakness, and despair.[2] The classic "noir" period is 1941–50, starting with the *Maltese Falcon* in 1941 and ending with *Sunset Boulevard* in 1950. Yet of the seventy-three movies that *VideoHound's* movie guide classified as "noir" for this period, only one, *Leave Her to Heaven* (1945), was in the top 10 during the year of its release. Such noir classics as *Murder My Sweet* (1944) and *The Postman Always Rings Twice* (1946) fell outside the top financial earners of their day. *Sunset Boulevard* (1950), perhaps the most famous LA noir film, only reached No. 29. We suggest reasons in the detailed discussion of Los Angeles.

Chicago: *The Sting* Surprise

Chicago's surprise is *The Sting* (1973). Table 18.1 lists the top 20 US box-office movies of all time, adjusted for ticket price inflation. Only two on this list are about cities, and none are the city-themed films that critics love to discuss. They are not Fritz Lang's nightmarish *Metropolis* set in early twentieth-century Berlin, or Jean-Luc Godard's 1965 *Alphaville,* depicting a Le Corbusier type landscape of gleaming high-rise buildings and long, antiseptic corridors, or *King Kong* (1933), in which the title hero meets his demise at the top of New York's Empire State Building.

Instead, they are *101 Dalmatians* (1961) No. 11 and, *The Sting* (1973) No. 17. The animated *101 Dalmatians* is set in London, leaving *The Sting* as the top movie about an American city on the list. Set in 1936 Chicago and accompanied by Scott Joplin's ragtime songs, *The Sting* features two likeable con artists played by Robert Redford and Paul Newman. Widely acknowledged as a successful movie, few people realize it surpassed every movie about New York or Los Angeles or any US city. Later, in our discussion of Chicago, we provide at least a partial explanation for *The Sting's* success. That success is a third reason we must include Chicago in this discussion.

We now turn to a direct analysis and explanation of what kinds of movies about New York, Los Angeles, and Chicago are box-office hits.

LOS ANGELES

We begin with Los Angeles. Table 18.2 presents a list of all the LA hit movies from 1920 to the present.

1920–1973: Hollywood, not "Noir"

From 1920 to 1973, the vast majority of Los Angeles hit movies, eleven of the fifteen, deal with Hollywood and the movie industry itself. (These are marked in bold on table 18.2). After 1973, the Hollywood motif practically disappears from LA hit movies.

Table 18.1 ALL TIME BOX OFFICE HITS (ADJUSTED FOR TICKET PRICE INFLATION TO 2012 PRICES[a])

Rank	Movie	Unadjusted Gross ($million)	Adjusted Gross ($million)[a]	Year
1	Gone with the Wind	198	1,582	1939
2	Star Wars	460	1,394	1977
3	The Sound of Music	158	1,115	1965
4	ET: The Extra Terrestrial	435	1,110	1982
5	Titanic	647	1,051	1997
6	The Ten Commandments	65	1,025	1956
7	Jaws	260	1,002	1975
8	Doctor Zhivago	111	971	1965
9	The Exorcist	232	865	1973
10	Snow White and the Seven Dwarfs	184	853	1937
11	101 Dalmatians[b]	144	782	1961
12	The Empire Strikes Back	290	768	1980
13	Ben-Hur	74	767	1959
14	Avatar	760	761	2009
15	Return of the Jedi	309	736	1983
16	Star Wars: Episode 1-The Phantom Menace	474	707	1999
17	The Sting[b]	156	697	1973
18	The Lion King	422	697	1994
19	Raiders of the Lost Ark	242	690	1981
20	Jurassic Park	357	674	1993

[a] Inflation adjustment is done by multiplying estimated number of admissions by the most recent average ticket price ($7.83 for 2012). Note that most pre-1980 pictures achieve their totals through multiple releases, especially Disney animated features. For example, *Snow White* (1937) made $118,328,683 of its unadjusted $184,925,486 since 1983. Note also that the data here are cumulative, unlike the rest of the hit movie data presented below which are for year of release (but also include the following year if the movie is released near the year's end).
[b] The only two movies set in cities.
Source: See the appendix "Constructing the List of Hit (Top 10) Movies."

    All the movies set in Hollywood depict it, in one way or another, as a false and corrupting place that tends to ruin personal relationships in the context of a potential star's success and, far more likely, failure. For example, one of the earliest, *Show People* (1928), features a young girl's quest to be a famous actress. As she garners attention she becomes conceited and dumps her slapstick comedian boyfriend for a higher status coactor who presents himself as a count. The count turns out to be a fake and finally she returns to her original boyfriend. Much of *The Goldwyn Follies* (1938) depicts a producer who hired his new consultant thinking her naïve innocence could give his film a "human touch," and ends up trying to protect her from Hollywood's malevolent influences. In the 1940s, two of the three hit films set in Los Angeles, *Star Spangled Rhythm* (1943) and *Hollywood Canteen* (1944) are musicals with Hollywood-oriented

Table 18.2 LOS ANGELES HIT MOVIES, 1920–2011

Safety Last (1923)	Police Academy 2 (1985)
In Hollywood with Potash & Perlmutter[a] **(1924)**	Lethal Weapon (1987)
	Beverly Hills Cop 2 (1987)
Merton of the Movies (1924)	Dragnet (1987)
Show People (1928)	**Who Framed Roger Rabbit? (1988)**
Sons of the Desert (1934)	Die Hard (1988)
A Star is Born (1937)	Lethal Weapon 2 (1989)
The Goldwyn Follies (1938)	Pretty Woman (1990)
Star Spangled Rhythm (1943)	Die Hard (1990)
Hollywood Canteen (1944)	Terminator 2 (1991)
Leave Her to Heaven (1945)	Lethal Weapon 3 (1992)
The Carpetbaggers (1964)	Speed (1994)
The Graduate (1967)	Face/Off (1997)
The Valley of the Dolls (1968)	Rush Hour (1998)
Bob, Carol, Ted and Alice (1969)	Rush Hour 2 (2001)
The Way We Were (1973)	Terminator 3 (2003)
Earthquake (1974)	The Day After Tomorrow (2004)
Shampoo (1975)	**Alvin and the Chipmunks (2007)**
Oh, God! (1977)	Transformers (2007)
Grease (1978)	Iron Man (2008)
Hooper (1978)	Hancock (2008)
California Suite (1978)	**Alvin & the Chipmunks: The Squeakquel (2009)**
Heaven Can Wait (1978)	
Beverly Hills Cop (1984)	Inception (2010)
Police Academy (1984)	Iron Man 2 (2010)

[a] Movies featuring Hollywood are in bold.
Source: The appendix ("Classifying Movies") explains, for Tables 18.2–18.7, the data source and how we determined that a film dealt with New York, Los Angeles, or Chicago.

plots that feature movie stars appearing as themselves in cameos, entertaining the many troops who passed through Los Angeles during the war. In *Star-Spangled Rhythm* (1943), the difficulty of succeeding in Hollywood again dominates, with the movie featuring a likeable, aging, silent film actor who has been demoted to studio guard.

From 1946 to 1963 there are no hit movies set in Los Angeles. This corresponds to fading popular interest in the city after World War II and a corresponding focus in America on suburbanization. Doubtless for the same reason, from 1950 to 1973 there is only one hit movie about Chicago, *Some Like it Hot* (1959), which looks back to the 1930s. By contrast, although the number of New York hit movies drops, they do not disappear—there are nine in the 1950s and fourteen in the 1960s. Further, a substantial number of these (e.g., five of the nine in the 1950s) depict the city's residents as increasingly composed of those without the economic means to leave for the suburbs. This underscores the point that New York movies tend to depict the city the way the public thinks of it at the time, as we will discuss.

In the 1960s, Los Angeles returns as a topic of major interest, with five hit movies up to 1973, all of which except *The Graduate* (1967) again deal with Hollywood. Those who work in Hollywood continue to be depicted as a vapid and spiteful bunch. For example, *The Valley of the Dolls* (1968) follows the lives of three wannabe actresses as Hollywood and the American public first build them up and then spit them out, leaving them to salvage their disappointments with liquor and drugs.

After *The Way We Were* (1973), a film that also contrasts New York with Los Angeles, the topic of Hollywood and the movie industry seems to no longer captivate the moviegoing public. It is not clear why, but the decline of the Hollywood motif is clear. The sole examples out of the thirty-four hit movies set in Los Angeles after 1973 are *Alvin and the Chipmunks* (2007) and its 2009 sequel, and *Who Framed Roger Rabbit* (1988). Interestingly, these all continue the theme of Los Angeles's entertainment industry as brutally false. For example, the animated chipmunks are forced by an exploitative music executive to lip sync even though they believed this was "cheating." Still, in an interesting sign of the possible emergence of a new Los Angeles theme of downtown as the site for mega-entertainment projects, the 2009 version opens with an elaborate concert by the chipmunks in the Staples Center, with the skyline lit at night and the surrounding area full of bright lights and activity.[3]

The Problem with "Noir" Movies

In the context of the predominance of the Hollywood motif in Los Angeles hit movies until the early 1970s, four reasons explain why LA "noir" movies of the period from 1941 to 1950 were not major hits. First, they had the difficult task of competing with movies about, and sometimes featuring, Hollywood stars.

Second, there is the demographic composition of the movie audience. It is fairly well documented that Hollywood believed women to be the primary audience for their product throughout the 1920s and 1930s (Stokes and Maltby 1999; Allen 1999). Although by the post–World War II period, research began to conclude that Hollywood films were attended equally by men and women (Sklar [1975]1994), for Hollywood and advertisers alike, women remained the primary purchasers of interest throughout the 1940s and 1950s. Yet many of the archetypical "noir" movies famously depict women unfavorably. They often feature a *femme fatale* who draws the male anti-hero into evil, whereupon he frequently ends up dead. It is plausible that this image of women did not fully resonate with many in the predominantly female audience at the time, even though it presumably intrigued the mostly male critics who wrote so much about "noir."

A third reason why noir movies were not major hits is that their dimly lit sets, which conveyed the sense of danger and shabbiness intrinsic to "noir," also made them relatively cheap to make. So they became a staple of the B movie culture—in those days movie goers as part of their admission price, were typically shown two movies, a warm-up or B movie, which was less valued and marketed by both studios and exhibitors but nevertheless important to Hollywood's total output in this period, and then the main film. Noir movies also conflicted with Los Angeles's image of sunshine and beach.

Finally, noir movies tended to highlight the older parts of the city like Bunker Hill, even as these sections were being torn down under post–World War II "slum clearance" programs on the grounds that they had outlived their usefulness. It is plausible that moviegoers were not particularly interested in seeing movies set in such doomed locations, while much of the popular focus of this period was on relocating to new suburbs.

Auto Culture

In the 1970s Los Angeles is reinvented as a site for hit movies through the auto motif. This emerging prominence of the car culture of Southern California is marked by two standout movies, *Grease* (No. 1 in 1978), which featured teenagers racing cars in the dried up but dangerous LA river, and plenty of cruising; and *The Graduate* (No. 2 in 1967), which featured a lot of freeway driving.[4]

The auto motif, a critical part of suburbanization, remains a common feature of many hit movies about Los Angeles. Consider just a few examples. In *Oh, God!* (1977) God physically appears in the protagonist's car. *Beverly Hills Cop* (1984) opens with Axel Foley driving into Beverly Hills's luxury auto culture. In *Transformers* (2007) the main characters, "Autobots," are robots transformed into cars and able to turn themselves into nicer looking and more high-tech cars. Note that *Speed* (1994) depicts those who opt for mass transit in Los Angeles, rather than the automobile, as placing themselves at risk, as Max Baumgarten (2010) has pointed out. The film depicts a criminal mastermind blowing up a bus in Santa Monica and proceeding to hold a second bus filled with innocent riders hostage. This contrasts with the way popular Hollywood films treat the perils associated with the private automobile (*Lethal Weapon* 3, *Terminator* 2, and *Judgment Day*). Instead of the public's carelessness, a terrorist's scheme, or poor driving conditions causing an accident, drivers consciously drive dangerously in an attempt to achieve some individual goal.

Inept LA Cops

In the 1980s a major new LA motif appears—inept cops—which continues well into the 1990s. The film version of *Dragnet* (1987) now mocks the dedicated LA police detective lionized in the 1950s radio and television series. Sometimes LA cops are so inept that they must be saved by a cop from another city, as in the two *Beverly Hills Cops* movies, both huge hits (No. 3 in 1984 and No. 1 in 1987). In the first, a young Detroit cop, whose best friend is murdered in Beverly Hills, comes to solve the crime himself because the local police are so incompetent. The two *Die Hard* movies (1988 and 1990) also exemplify the inept LA cops theme. In the first, foreign criminals/terrorists are thwarted by a civilian hero, whose intervention was made necessary by the bumbling LAPD that also hampered him at every turn. The two *Lethal Weapon* films (1987 and 1989) portray an atypical LAPD cop with an explosive personality who solves crimes that the bureaucratic LAPD cannot.

This image of the inept LAPD corresponds to the actuality of LA's two mega riots, Watts in 1965 and Rodney King in 1992, and in both of which the LAPD was widely perceived as having performed abysmally. In Watts, the LAPD allowed the rioting to go on for several days before intervening. In the Rodney King Riots, not only did videotaped police misbehavior precipitate the event, but the LAPD was stationed at the wrong place when the police on trial for beating Rodney King were found not-guilty. Extra police were stationed outside the Simi Valley Court House instead of in the central city neighborhoods where protest over such a verdict might have been anticipated. Note that inept cops also appear in the 1923 Los Angeles movie *Safety Last*, but are not featured.

Uncontrolled Disasters and Globalized Villains

Toward the end of the 1990s, two additional themes appear in several LA hit movies, though neither is confined to them. There is the theme of Los Angeles as a global city, usually the US headquarters of global villains in the form of corporations and organized crime, especially with an Asian connection. In *Rush Hour* (1998) the LA villains have a Hong Kong/Chinese tie, and the heroes—maverick officers, one from Hong Kong and one from Los Angeles—again solve crimes that the bureaucratic LAPD and FBI cannot. The mega hit *Iron Man* (2008) features one of Los Angeles's wealthy outer sectors, Malibu, as the headquarters of a technologically cutting edge, but sinister military-industrial corporation that is "global" in the sense that it is a command and control center for operations throughout the world (the notion of "global" stressed by Sassen 2001).

The second new theme in recent Los Angeles movies is uncontrolled disasters, as in *The Day After Tomorrow* (2004), which features worldwide climate change but with the central action in Los Angeles and New York. *Terminator 3: Rise of the Machines* (2003) traces the lead-up to "Judgment Day," where the human race is nearly wiped out by computers worldwide. Disaster movies are considered in detail in the New York discussion, where we argue that a particular type of disaster, the widespread and uncontrolled disaster that is not just a threat but actually happens, and is set in the present not the past, is increasingly common in hit movies.

To summarize, Los Angeles is coded and stereotyped rather simply in hit movies, though that coding has changed over time. This starts with movies about Hollywood, which then drop out and are replaced by auto culture, to which is added movies about inept cops, and more recently, global villains and uncontrolled disasters. It remains to be seen if the recent image of a downtown Los Angeles revitalized by mega-entertainment projects such as Staples Center, as in *Alvin & the Chipmunks: The Squeakquel* (2009), and the ever-present possibility of a NFL team, will become a new, major LA theme, and in doing so perhaps invigorate and revive the Hollywood motif.

Los Angeles: History as a Radical Break with a Non-Auto Past

A final point is that, in hit movies, Los Angeles almost always depicts the absolute present (or an imagined future), as does New York. Only 7 percent of the New

York City, and 6 percent of the LA hit movies produced since 1959 are historically themed. By contrast, around 30 percent of the Chicago hit movies produced since 1959 are historically themed, as we will discuss and explain in the next section. Actually, the sole instance of a Los Angeles hit movie set in the seriously distant past (i.e., fifty years or more before the movie's release) is the mega hit *Who Framed Roger Rabbit* (No. 2 in 1988), which is set in the 1930s. Tellingly, it points forward to Los Angeles's unfolding future as an auto-dominated society by foregrounding the corrupt deal-making in the 1930s that reshapes Los Angeles's landscape from electric trolleys to auto/freeway dominant. The only two other historically situated Los Angeles hit movies, *Grease* (1978) and *Shampoo* (1975), reference a more recent past. *Grease*, with its attention to teenagers and their car culture, likewise captures the importance of the automobile in the rapidly growing 1950s metropolis. *Shampoo* emphasizes the freer lifestyles of the 1960s enjoyed by some Angelenos. So in looking back in time, each of the few cases of historically themed Los Angeles films implicitly also looks forward, stressing what makes Los Angeles stand out as new and untraditional among American cities and regions in the middle decades of the twentieth century, including a critical fascination with Los Angeles as "the future."

CHICAGO: THE CONTINUITY OF THE CLASSIC CITY

Table 18.3 sets out Chicago hit movies from 1920 to the present.

Hit movies that depict Chicago typically have at least two of the following four themes, which are basically constants, albeit somewhat updated for recent decades.

(1) Political corruption/boss politics/gangsterism.
(2) Ethnic neighborhoods and ethnic group identifications seen as a key part of life in the city.
(3) Culture flourishing in the urban center, in the form of music, especially jazz, but also museums and other entertainment.
(4) Industry/jobs in the urban center, while dull residential suburbs are on the urban periphery. In recent movies, the theme of jobs in the urban center is updated to depict tall office buildings and sometimes condos, which is an innovation (i.e., middle-class residences in the core).

This last image resonates strongly with the city as described in the 1920s and 1930s by University of Chicago social scientists Robert Park and Ernest Burgess in their concentric ring model of urban change. The only Chicago hit movie that does not include at least one of these themes is *The Stratton Story* (1949), about a real-life Chicago White Sox pitcher who loses a leg in a hunting accident.

Chicago's Iconic Prohibition Period

Supporting the idea that Chicago is popularly viewed as having certain core, basically unchanging, characteristics is how Chicago hit movies deal with the city's history. A

Table 18.3 CHICAGO HIT MOVIES, 1920–2011

Underworld Chicago (1927)	*Ferris Bueller's Day Off (1986)*
The Public Enemy (1931)	*The Untouchables (1987)*
Little Caesar (1931)	*Uncle Buck (1989)*
The Bride Comes Home (1936)	*Dick Tracy (1990)*
In Old Chicago (1938)	*Home Alone (1990)*
Alexander's Rag Time Band (1938)	*The Fugitive (1993)*
The Stratton Story (1949)	*The Firm (1993)*
Some Like it Hot (1959)	*My Best Friend's Wedding (1997)*
The Sting 1973/1974	*Chicago (2002)*
Silver Streak (1976)	*My Big Fat Greek Wedding (2002)*
The Blue Brothers (1980)	*Transformers: Dark of the Moon (2011)*
Risky Business (1983)	

strikingly large percentage of Chicago hit movies are set in the past, as we mentioned earlier. Around 30 percent of the Chicago movies produced since 1959 that became box-office hits are historically themed, roughly four to five times more than those set in New York or Los Angeles during this time.

Furthermore, every historically themed Chicago movie since 1959 is set in the same period, the late 1920s and 1930s, basically the Prohibition period and the era of Al Capone and other gangsters, which is apparently an iconic legacy for Chicago.[5] These movies include *Some Like it Hot* (1959), *The Untouchables* (1987), *The Sting* (1973/4), *Dick Tracy* (1990), and *Chicago* (2002). This is, arguably, the period that cemented these core themes as essentially Chicago, which would also explain the propensity to look back to this period, stressing Chicago's basic continuity with that time. By contrast, neither New York nor Los Angeles has a historical period that is similarly iconic.

The following examples of hit Chicago movies drawn from the entire period under study show these thematic continuities.

The gangster/political corruption motif gets an early start in Chicago movies. In the years between the 1929 St. Valentine's Day Massacre and Al Capone's 1931 conviction for tax evasion, two of the country's most popular films provided fictional portrayals of the Capone era. These were *The Public Enemy* (1931), titled after the Chicago Crime Commission's name for Al Capone, and *Little Caesar* (1931), which also includes plenty of music and dancing. The 1938 classic *In Old Chicago* features two of the basic Chicago themes—ethnicity (the Irish) and political corruption/gangsterism/ moderate vice (a hard drinking salon and gambling), all in the central city.

The 1973 mega hit *The Sting* taps two Chicago themes, namely political corruption and jazz/cabaret. It features the (ragtime) music of Scott Joplin and depicts a gambling operation that is facilitated by payoffs to the mayor. It too is set in Chicago's iconic Prohibition era. All this does not alone explain why *The Sting* outperformed every movie set in a US city at the box office. Surely helpful was a fine script and the casting of mega stars Paul Newman and Robert Redford as the central characters, re-creating their successful pairing in *Butch Cassidy and the Sundance Kid* (1969). Still, it is clear how the movie's key themes set the stage for its box-office success and why Chicago was the logical place to site it.

As we will see, New York crime movies in the 1980s and beyond expand to include the new motif of muggings (and urban disasters that result from a criminal bent on destroying the city and its inhabitants). This is consistent with the idea that New York in hit movies changes to reflect the dominant way people think of cities at the time.

By contrast, Chicago crime films stick resolutely to gangsters and corrupt politicians, consistent with the idea that Chicago is stereotyped around a set of basically unchanging themes. For example, *The Untouchables* (1987) depicts the conflict over control of the city between Al Capone and Prohibition enforcer Eliot Ness. *Dick Tracy* (1990) foregrounds a gallery of often grotesque mobsters such as Big Boy, Pruneface, and Flattop taken from Chester Gould's comic strip of the same name. *The Fugitive* (1993), although not the classic Chicago mob or gangster film, does not stray too far. It opens with the murder of cardiologist Richard Kimball's wife, apparently by Kimball, who is convicted and sentenced to death but who escapes from custody and goes underground to clear his name. After a Federal Marshall takes over the investigation from the incompetent county and city, Kimball discovers it was a close colleague in the pay of a pharmaceutical firm who had hired a hit man to kill him (not his wife) because Kimball had found that a lucrative drug being used was harmful. In short, corruption rules Chicago and the local police are incompetent and not to be trusted, as always.

Ferris Bueller's Day Off (1986) features three core Chicago themes—dull residential suburbs, a cultured central city, and ethnic groups. Ferris Bueller, a suburban high school student, sets out to have fun, which means heading for the central city. Together with two friends, his downtown Chicago adventure includes the Art Institute of Chicago and the German von Steuben Day parade.

Boring Chicago suburbs likewise feature in *Home Alone* (1990). The McAllister family leaves for vacation to Paris, forgetting to take their youngest son, Kevin, with them. His older brother sets the familiar theme: "We live on the most boring street in the whole United States of America." Chicago does not, of course, monopolize the motif of dull suburbs. For example, *Meet the Parents* (2000) depicts the suburbs of Long Island, New York, as dull. Still, hit films set in New York usually depict the city and rarely bother showing the suburbs. By contrast, the dichotomy of dull suburbs and vibrant central city is a standard Chicago hit movie theme.

My Big Fat Greek Wedding (2002) features the stock Chicago theme of ethnicity. A Greek woman falls in love with a WASP high school English teacher as the film revolves around her family learning to accept a non-Greek. No other hit movie in recent decades set in New York as we have seen, Los Angeles, or anywhere else, revolves around tensions between WASP and white-ethnic culture. (*The Way We Were* deals with Jewish/upper-class WASP relations, but dates from 1973, *Guess Who is Coming to Dinner* dealt with WASP/black relations, but dates from 1967). For the creators of *My Big Fat Greek Wedding*, apparently Chicago remains the appropriate location nowadays to dramatize ethnic intolerance, a judgment validated by the public's favorable response to the film.

Finally, it is noteworthy that Chicago was not the setting of a hit movie from 2002 until 2011. A possible explanation is that the stock themes we have identified as associated with Chicago do not include the destruction of the current city via disaster, a theme that has now become increasingly popular, as we explore in the New York discussion. In this context it is interesting that when Chicago did finally reappear in a hit movie, it was indeed in a disaster movie, *Transformers: Dark of the Moon* (2011), which depicts evil "decepticons" laying waste to much of the city. To what extent this means the fading of Chicago's stock themes in public perception remains to be seen.

NEW YORK: CURRENT CITY LIFE

New York as depicted in hit movies reflects big city life as generally envisaged by the public around the time the movie is released. This role as carrier of current, popular images of the major city makes sense, since New York has been by far the largest city in the United States throughout the period that movies have been made. The fact that so many more hit movies have been set in New York than any other city, in the United States or abroad, also supports the idea of New York's importance in the public mind as a repository of current images of urban life. So does the rarity with which New York hit movies are set in the past—New York interests the public because of what is happening right now. Still, amidst its ability to adapt to changing images of urban life, New York does have one constant association, as a place for big business, finance, and the rich, all typically depicted as including some prominent members who are greedy, corrupt, shallow, womanizers, and so on. (We tested the theory that another constant in New York movies is that romantic relations start with a chance meeting in a public space, but it turned out the probability of such encounters was no higher than in Los Angeles or Chicago hits.)

Table 18.4 NEW YORK HIT MOVIES, 1930–1939

Anna Christie (1930)	She Married Her Boss (1935)
City Lights (1931)	Broadway Melody of 1936 (1935)
Reducing (1931)	Swing Time (1936)
Back Street (1932)	Bullets or Ballots (1936)
Golddiggers of 1933 (1933)	Mr. Deeds Goes to Town (1936)
She Done Him Wrong (1933)	The Great Ziegfeld (1936)
42nd Street (1933)	Love is News (1937)
Dinner at Eight (1933)	Artists and Models (1937)
The Bowery (1934)	Born to Dance (1937)
Chained (1934)	Holiday (1938)
Riptide (1934)	Sweethearts (1939)
Son of Kong (1934)	Angels with Dirty Faces (1939)

Because the New York material is vast, this discussion focuses on four central periods and their associated themes. These include (1) the 1930s, associated with multiple themes—social class and mobility, Broadway, the media, and gangsterism; (2) the decades after World War II associated with mass suburbanization; (3) the crime wave of the 1970s to early 1990s, especially muggings; (4) the period from 1996 to 2012, associated with a bipolar image of New York as either a place for the hedonistic pursuits of the well-to-do and wannabes, or as the site for massive disaster. Hit movies and their publics seem unsure which scenario will prevail.

The 1930s

There are twenty-four NY hit films for this period, compared with just three for Los Angeles and five for Chicago. New York clearly interests the moviegoing public far more than other big cities.

NY hits of the 1930s revolve around four identifiable and often overlapping themes. The first depicts Broadway and cabaret as avenues for success and failure. The second focuses on the dramas of social class, again stressing success and failure. The third highlights New York as a media center, especially print journalism. The last is crime. Box-office hits clearly portray New York as far more complicated than Los Angeles, whose depictions during the same period are dominated by Hollywood, as we have seen. Chicago in the 1930s is also depicted as fairly complicated, with several dominant themes (though New York's dominant themes are, in later years, changeable over time).

(1) *Broadway ("show biz").* New York is portrayed here as a city of economic (job) opportunity, especially via entertainment, above all Broadway. Examples are *Backstreet* (1932), *Gold Diggers of 1933* (1933), *42nd Street* (1933), *The Great Ziegfeld* (1936), *Swing Time* (1936), *Broadway Melody of 1936* (1936), *Born to Dance* (1937), and *Sweethearts* (1939). This theme of opportunity in show business is, as we saw, also common to LA films of this and later decades, with Hollywood substituted for Broadway. In fact, New York hit films often present Hollywood as the next level to which performers move after succeeding on Broadway. For example, *Sweethearts* (1939) depicts the most talented Broadway stars as being lured to Hollywood, an actual practice of the period which helped create the talent pool that made production there possible.

(2) *Social Class.* Dramas of Economic Success and Failure/Modernity and its Critique.

These movies deal with high society, middle-class, and poor America. Examples are *City Lights* (1931), *Reducing* (1931), *She Married Her Boss* (1935), *Mr. Deeds Goes to Town* (1936), and *Dinner at Eight* (1933). For example, *Dinner At Eight* (1933), set in Manhattan during the Depression, centers around various couples either pretending to be wealthy, trying to marry money, or with money and trying not to lose it. The main attraction of the "dinner" is that London royalty will be attending. The rich are generally depicted as shallow, duplicitous with each other (e.g., cheating on their spouses), heavy drinkers, and rude to the help (e.g., barking orders). The wealthy women have few responsibilities besides organizing parties and looking glamorous, and are prone to side liaisons. As one says to a male business protagonist, "What do you think I'm doing while you're pulling your dirty deals?"

This theme of New York as the site of business/finance/the rich, who are typically depicted critically, is one of the few constant themes in New York hit movies, as we argue. It is clearly periodically invigorated by external events (financial scandals, etc.), followed by well-publicized investigations/prosecutions, as in Ferdinand Pecora's Senate Banking Committee investigation that accompanied the 1933 the Glass-Steagall Act forbidding retail banks from engaging in speculative investment activities (as discussed in chapter 6 of this book).

(3) *Media Center.* A third 1930s theme is New York City as a center of media power especially journalism and the burgeoning world of advertising and publicity. Films such as *Love is News* (1937) set love stories against the power-laden world of mainstream journalism, while *Artists and Models* (1937) depicts Madison Avenue as a route to success and fame via advertising and marketing.

(4) *Crime.* A fourth theme of these 1930s hit movies depicts New York as corrupt and gangster/crime-ridden, overseen by often crooked politicians. Two major examples are *Bullets or Ballots* (1936) and *Angels with Dirty Faces* (1939). These themes basically mirror those of Chicago films of the 1930s. In truth, New York in the 1930s was about as gangster-ridden as Chicago. Manhattan's gang wars during Prohibition accounted for over 1,000 killings, and New York's Lucky Luciano boasted that his organization was equal to Henry Ford's. One of the most successful gangster movies of the 1930s, *Little Caesar* (1931), never specifies its urban location, and almost certainly was intended to be *either* New York or Chicago (though most of the location shots were Hollywood sets). Many people thought it was Chicago (it is here classified as a Chicago movie), but some critics placed it in New York in the world of Bugsy Goldstein of Brooklyn.

1950s and 1960s: Suburbanization and the City Where Losers Live

In the era of post–World War II suburbanization, many people lose interest in the city. The differential effect of this on movie depictions of New York versus those of Los Angeles and Chicago reflects New York's role as a repository of current images of city life. For Los Angeles and Chicago, diminished interest in the city means these two practically disappear as topics in hit movies during this period. As we have mentioned, Los Angeles had no hit movies from 1946 to 1963, and Chicago had only one for the 1950s and 1960s.

New York, by contrast, still figures in hit movies, which now however often portray a new image of the city as a place inhabited primarily by those without the economic ability to move to the suburbs, and who are often depicted explicitly as losers. In these movies, the well-to-do typically still work in the city (as do those struggling

Table 18.5 NEW YORK HIT MOVIES, 1950–1969

The Great Caruso (1951)	Lover Come Back (1961)
How to Marry a Millionaire (1953)	That Touch of Mink (1962)
The House of Wax (1953)	Thoroughly Modern Millie (1967)
Rear Window (1954)	Barefoot in the Park (1967)
The Country Girl (1955)	The Odd Couple (1968)
Guys and Dolls (1955)	Funny Girl (1968)
I'll Cry Tomorrow (1956)	Rosemary's Baby (1968)
Imitation of Life (1959)	Midnight Cowboy (1968)
North By Northwest (1959)	Planet of the Apes (1968)
From the Terrace (1960)	Hello, Dolly! (1969)
The Apartment (1960)	Goodbye Columbus (1969)
West Side Story (1961)	

in low-paying jobs), but many, though not all, of those with resources have decamped to live in the suburbs. Sometimes these movies also feature young professionals who do live, and work, in the city, though probably because they cannot yet afford a suburban residence.

A series of hit movies—*Rear Window* (1954), *The Apartment* (1960), *Westside Story* (1961), *Barefoot in the Park* (1967), and *Midnight Cowboy* (1968) make these points. Noticeable is that the losers are rarely depicted as minorities (the sole exception is *Westside Story*'s Puerto Ricans, who share the stage with poor whites—Polish and Italian Americans) and never as blacks. For the cinematic public, the urban poor of interest are basically whites who lack resources to leave.

Consider *Rear Window* (1954). A talented photographer (Jimmy Stewart) lives an economically precarious existence in his cramped apartment with a broken leg. He has nothing to do except look out the window and spy on his neighbors through their open windows across the way as they live in similarly cramped apartments. Some of these neighbors are distinctly troubled (a murderer, Miss Lonelyhearts), while others are young people trying to make it in their careers, including an aspiring dancer and an aspiring composer.

The Apartment (1960) likewise depicts the city as the residence of those in marginal jobs or those still in the early stages of a career path. A junior employee of a large New York City insurance company routinely loans his city apartment to the company's chief executive to use for liaisons with women before the executive returns to his suburban home in White Plains. Both men are attracted to the lowly female elevator operator at work, who lives in the city. Notice too the recurring New York theme of the city as a business center whose major figures are often depicted critically (e.g., here as womanizers).

Barefoot in the Park (1967) is primarily set in a tiny, fifth floor apartment in a building without an elevator in the West Village. A newlywed couple, lawyer (Robert Redford) and his wife (Jane Fonda), have just moved in. The building is full of mostly poor, often bizarre, long-time tenants. The local liquor storeowner informs Redford that "some of the biggest weirdos in the world are living in this building."

Table 18.6 NEW YORK HIT MOVIES, 1970–1995

Love Story (1970)	Fort Apache, the Bronx (1981)
Joe (1970)	Escape From New York (1981)
The French Connection (1971)	Tootsie (1982)
The Godfather (1972)	Staying Alive (1983)
The Way We Were (1973)	Trading Places (1983)
The Godfather, part II (1974)	Mr. Mom, (1983)
Dog Day Afternoon (1975)	Superman 3 (1983)
Three Days of the Condor (1975)	Ghostbusters (1984)
Funny Lady (1975)	Three Men and a Baby (1987)
King Kong (1976)	Coming to America (1988)
Saturday Night Fever (1977)	Die Hard (1988)
The Goodbye Girl (1977)	Ghostbusters 2 (1989)
Superman (1978)	Batman (1989)
Kramer vs. Kramer (1979)	Teenage Mutant Ninja Turtles (1991)
9 to 5 (1980)	Batman Returns (1992)
Superman 2 (1981)	Batman Forever (1995)
	Die Hard with a Vengeance (1995)

Midnight Cowboy (1969) broadens the loser theme to prostitution. A fresh farm boy comes to New York from a small, rural town, intent on making it big as a sexual hustler. He establishes a friendship with an impoverished, crippled man, Enrico Rizzo, from the Bronx, whose apartment in an abandoned building he shares. The movie is full of unpromising residential scenes including seedy Times Square hotels.

There are some partial exceptions to the image of the city as inhabited mainly by losers or young people in the early stages of a career. For example the three female stars of *How to Marry a Millionaire* (1953) meet plenty of wealthy and successful men, some of whom live in expensive ("Park Avenue") city apartments. But unlike, for example, *Dinner at Eight* made two decades earlier, the film does not include extensive or even brief scenes in those opulent homes.

In short, New York hit movies during the two decades after World War II offer a stream of relevant commentary on city life. Note too that this negative representation of urban centers and New York, when represented at all, is tied to Hollywood's own difficulties following the audiences to the suburbs, as most of the movie theaters remained in increasingly dwindling downtowns, and this period saw a decline in moviegoing for the first time since their invention.

Crime Especially Mugging: The 1970s to Early 1990s

New York City's murder rate climbed sharply from a low of roughly six murders per 100,000 population in the 1950s, peaking in 1990 at roughly 30 per 100,000, after which it steadily declined to about seven per 100,000 in 2000—trends basically repeated in many major American cities. A series of New York hit movies from the late 1970s to the mid-1990s depict a growing sense that the city is a dangerous place where crime is out of control. To the familiar New York mobster-gangster theme of the 1930s, New York hit movies now added a basically new type of crime, the often vicious mugging of innocent bystanders in an unorganized fashion. Chicago hit movies, by contrast, resolutely continued featuring gangsters and corrupt politicians, but not muggings, as we saw in the prior discussion.

It is true that back in the 1930s, some New York hit movies depicted petty thievery, such as stealing small change in *Swing Time* (1936) and *Mr. Deeds Goes to Town* (1936). Still, the new crime of mugging, as depicted in New York hit movies of the 1970s and later, is qualitatively more dangerous for the victims, often involving physical threats, harm, and sometimes murder. Furthermore, the mugging is commonly central to the film, not just a minor incident.

For example, as soon as Clark Kent in *Superman* (1978) arrives in New York City (to work at *The Daily Planet*), there is a mugging. The criminals are concentrated in the subway, which is viewed as an especially dangerous place. Muggers (the new criminals) and mobsters (the old criminals) now coexist, with Lex Luther, a malevolent mobster, having his lair under Park Avenue. In addition to mobsterism and mugging, there is a third kind of crime in some of these movies—an evil protagonist threatening widespread urban disaster, but it is far less prominent (especially because the disaster is typically just threats) than it became in the 1990s and beyond. For instance, in *Superman*, Lex Luther announces over a general speaker that he is about to release poison gas that will destroy everyone in the city. He also shows Superman that he has a plan to drop an enormous bomb on the San Andreas Fault, which would destroy all of California west of it, making the desert land, which he owns, extraordinarily valuable as the new West Coast. Still, these threats are not carried out, by contrast with typical scenarios of movies in the mid-1990s and beyond, where the mega disasters now usually happen.

A decade later with the first in the Batman revival series, *Batman* (1989), crime, especially street mugging, is the dominant motif and continues to be so in two successful sequels.[6] The film, the biggest hit of the year, is from the start about a city overrun by criminals, including lots of muggers. In the first shot of "Gotham City" police sirens wail while prostitutes and homeless people, some menacing, wander filthy streets. Two men viciously mug a harmless couple visiting the city. We see the mayor proclaiming: "Across our nation, the name Gotham City is synonymous with crime." It also turns out that Batman as a child saw his parents murdered by muggers in an alley, one of whom was the Joker. Joker, basically an old-style organized crime figure, takes advantage of the mayhem and fear caused by muggings to operate his criminal syndicate. As a sideline, he plans to poison the entire population of Gotham City by contaminating the water supply, but, again, this remains just a threat.

Similarly, *Teenage Mutant Ninja Turtles* (1991) depicts a chaotic city rampant with crime, especially purse snatching, pick pocketing, and shoplifting. As the movie progresses, it turns out that most of these seemingly random crimes are actually "organized" by a villain who trains young kids to fight and be criminals. Once again, the new crime of mugging is grafted onto New York's familiar, organized crime motif. The Ninja Turtles are, in turn, trained by a rat to fight criminals, recover people's

Table 18.7 NEW YORK HIT MOVIES, 1996–2012

Ransom (1996)	Spider-Man 2 (2004)
Independence Day (1996)	Batman Begins (2005)
Batman and Robin (1997)	Madagascar (2005)
Armageddon (1998)	King Kong (2005)
Deep Impact (1998)	Hitch (2005)
Godzilla, (1998)	Night at the Museum (2006)
The Matrix (1999)	Superman Returns (2006)
Meet the Parents (2000)	I am Legend (2007)
Spider-Man (2003)	Spider- Man 3 (2007)
Sweet Home Alabama (2003)	The Bourne Ultimatum (2007)
The Matrix Reloaded (2003)	Sex and the City (2008)
The Matrix Revolutions (2003)	Dark Night (2008)
The Day After Tomorrow (2004)	Marvel's The Avengers (2012)
	The Dark Knight Rises (2012)
	The Amazing Spider-Man (2012)

stolen belongings, and achieve what the New York Police Department seemed unable to do.

By 2000, organized crime and police corruption largely disappeared from New York hit movies, at least in part because of the city's dramatic and much publicized crime reduction, which started under Commissioner Raymond Kelly in 1991, continued with Bratton in 1993 under Mayor Giuliani, and then Kelly again under Mayor Bloomberg in 2002.

The Uncertain Future: 1996 to 2012

From the mid-1990s to the present (2012), New York hit movies display two radically different themes, reflecting a clear uncertainty over the city's direction. First, there is a string of disaster movies. Second, there are depictions of the city as a hedonistic place for the wealthy and their imitators/wannabes.

Disaster Movies: History and Typology

A "disaster movie" is defined here as a film that depicts major loss of life and/or physical destruction. Until the mid-1960s, and arguably even the mid-1990s, the public lacked a consistent appetite for movies that depicted actual, not just threatened, disasters set in the present (in the United States or abroad), though seemed to enjoy disasters set in previous epochs. Starting around the mid-1990s, a slew of hit movies appear that depict current, actual disasters that are increasingly set at least partly in New York and Los Angeles. Furthermore, these disasters are typically widespread in geographic scope (i.e., not limited to a small area).

By contrast, from 1920 to 1964, disaster hits are always set in the past (abroad or in the United States) instead of the present. Hit movies with a disaster component set in the past/abroad include *Ben-Hur* (1925), *Les Miserables* (1935), and *The Ten Commandments* (1956). During this period there are only three disaster hit movies set in the United States, and all feature US disasters from the past. The first was Metro-Goldwyn-Mayer's 1936 earthquake movie *San Francisco*, depicting the city's devastating 1906 earthquake and fire. Daryl Zanuck wanted a disaster movie to rival this, so his writers created *In Old Chicago* (1938) featuring the O'Leary brothers, which culminates with the Great Chicago Fire of 1871, started in the family barn. The third pre-1964 hit US disaster movie is *Gone With the Wind* (1939) that dramatized the burning of Atlanta during the Civil War.[7]

Note that *King Kong* (1933), which, following our modern appetite for disaster movies, we now tend to view mainly for the last twenty minutes when the giant ape destroys a New York subway train and is then shot off the Empire State Building, was not a major financial success, though successful enough to spawn a sequel. Tellingly, the sequel, *Son of Kong* (1934), which was a major financial success, has no New York City scenes at all. Instead, it focused entirely on exotic South Seas native locations replete with beautiful women and romantic attachments, which RKO clearly saw as the heart of the first movie's attraction, not the New York City mayhem scenes.

Before the mid-1960s, many other disaster movies that explicitly involved the contemporary United States were released, but none were box-office hits. A sampling include films about aliens from outer space, *Invasion of the Body Snatchers* (1956); hostile creatures *Them!* (1954) featuring giant, irradiated ants coming out of the LA River, and *The Birds* (1961); malicious individuals intent on mass destruction as in the first *Superman* movie (1951) whose villain is a mad scientist bent on using "death rays"; and nuclear attacks as in *The Day the Earth Caught Fire* (1961).

The mid-1960s starts a decade of disaster movies set in the present that involve the United States and in some of which the disaster actually happens, though none of these focus on America's largest cities of New York, Los Angeles, or Chicago (instead, San Francisco is a popular setting for contemporary disaster). The period starts with two hit disaster movies dealing with threatened but not actual nuclear attack, *Dr Strangelove* (1964) and *Thunderball* (1965), clearly a topic on people's minds given the Cold War. These are followed in the 1970s by *Colossus* (1970) about a computer that tries to take over the world, *Poseidon Adventure* (1972) in which a luxury liner going from New York to Athens is capsized by a huge tidal wave brought on by a submarine-induced earthquake, and *Towering Inferno* (1974), the most popular film of the year, which depicts a fire in a single, super tall building in San Francisco, and *Earthquake* (1974), also set in San Francisco. There is then a fifteen-year hiatus until *The Hunt for Red October* (1990), again about the threat of nuclear war.

In addition to the fact that the current disaster is often threatened but does not happen, another interesting feature of the hit disaster movies from the mid-1960s to the mid-1990s, which also contrasts them with later disaster hits, is that they are a mixture of three types of disasters, classified by the calamity's extent. Type 1 disasters are strictly "confined" or "container" disasters affecting a limited number of unlucky souls, as in the sinking of a ship or the burning of a high-rise building.

Titanic (1997), the 5th most popular movie of all time, is a confined/container disaster, historically themed. Type 2 disasters are more widespread, affecting a city or
region, but not beyond. In *Earthquake* (1974), the third most popular film of the year,
the disaster is limited to California, which clearly has an earthquake problem. Type 3
disasters are totally uncontained, as in those that depict nuclear threats.

Three major changes occur in disaster movies in the 1990s and beyond. First,
disaster movies become much more common. From 1990 to the end of 2011, there
have been thirty-seven hit disaster movies whose action includes the contemporary
United States and are often city-based. (By contrast, from 1965 to 1989, there were
only six hit disaster movies set in the United States.) Second, the disaster now usually actually happens, at least partially, or has happened when the movie starts.

Third, the disasters are rarely the contained, Type 1. *Titanic* is the last contained hit
disaster movie. In movies after that, at a minimum the disasters affect an entire city,
especially New York, and often a region. This series of Type 2 disaster movies include
Godzilla (1998), where a monster destroys large portions of New York City including Madison Square Garden, the Chrysler building, and the Brooklyn Bridge. *Dark
Knight* (2008) affects all of New York/Gotham City, though not beyond its borders.
The Joker is causing mayhem in a fight to the death with District Attorney Harvey
Dent, who is intent on eliminating the Joker's organized crime empire. Toward the
end, the Joker blows up "Gotham General Hospital" and causes mayhem elsewhere
throughout the city. In *Marvel's The Avengers* (2012) a battle between the villain and
the superheroes results in the destruction of large swathes of New York City.

Above all, a series of hit movies now depict uncontained, Type 3, disasters, from
which New York is almost never immune. In *Independence Day* (1996) massive space-
ships loom over the cities of the world, starting with Washington, DC. *Armageddon*
(1998) features an asteroid coming to hit the earth. It is set in several different cities
including New York, and includes blowing up the Chrysler building. *The Matrix* (1999)
depicts the aftermath of an uncontained disaster that has affected the entire United
States and in particular its largest city—not identified as New York, but the obvious candidate. The film depicts the future after machines (artificial intelligence) have
won the war for the real world, forcing all non-dominated humans underground. The
movie spawned two sequels, *The Matrix Reloaded* (2003), set in what looks like Los
Angeles, and *The Matrix Revolutions* (2003). *The Day After Tomorrow* (2004) features
a massive climate disaster. This movie is mostly set in New York and Los Angeles as
the two largest cities in the United States, but the catastrophic events affect Earth
in its entirety.

Clearly disaster movies in part reflect the threats of their time. Fires, earthquakes,
and wars in the 1930s were disasters moviegoers knew could and had happened.
After 1945 nuclear war becomes a real possibility, one that seemed even more likely
after the Cuban Missile Crisis and the United States' emphasis on civil defense. After
the 1990s there is global warming (ecological themes) and terrorism, together with
the possibility of nuclear terrorism, and also unease about the power of computers to
control our lives and of venomous foreign organisms to destroy us. Perhaps too the
urban focus, especially New York and Los Angeles, reflects the perception that people
and economic energy have returned to cities in general in a period of globalization,

with cities as command and control centers for far-flung operations, making them vulnerable targets. Still, the current appetite for widespread, actual disaster movies set in the present and near future (science-fiction) seems unprecedented. Arguably alongside unease, these also reflect almost the opposite, namely a belief that via science and technology we have mastered some of the major world threats, so that we can contemplate them playing out in movies, secure (at least fairly so) that they are unlikely to occur. Here the ability, via animated special effects, to enjoy what computer science can create, should not be underestimated. (Notice here that *United 93*, the 2006 movie about 9/11, a threat that clearly was not and has not been eliminated, was not a box-office success. Notice too that a 1953 version of *Titanic* was not a box-office hit. This was a period when such disasters at sea could still plausibly happen and trans-Atlantic sea-travel remained common. By 1997 moviegoers could flock to see a movie about the same event but now very unlikely to actually recur.)

2000s: The City as a Playground for the Rich

Alongside these disaster movies is a slew of very differently themed films that reflect the growing perception that major cities, with New York in the forefront, have become such desirable places to live that they are increasingly for the well-to-do and the rich. Notice that in these examples the rich tend not to be depicted especially critically, but as living a lifestyle to which others in the movie on the whole aspire to achieve. *Sweet Home Alabama* (2003), *Hitch* (2005), the *Pursuit of Happiness* (2006), and *Sex and the City* (2008), all New York based, are examples of this.

Sweet Home Alabama (2003) opens in New York and later switches to Alabama, and revolves around a young fashion designer (Reese Witherspoon). The New York scenes depict opulence—the fashion designer's glamorous show and the efforts by her rich boyfriend, the son of the New York's mayor, to woo her, culminating in a scene where he presents an entire room of hugely expensive wedding rings from which she can choose whichever one she wishes.

Hitch (2005) is about a man who helps other men get the women of their dreams in glamorous New York. *Sex and the City* (2008) likewise depicts New York City as a glamorous city. (The majority of the movie is set in New York City, but Malibu and Beverly Hills are briefly seen. Not coincidentally Samantha Jones, the most vacuous of the heroines, resides in Malibu but goes shopping in Beverly Hills. So this is also a Los Angeles movie, likewise depicting that city and region as a place for the wealthy.)

Clearly the 2007–08 financial crisis, followed by the 2011 Occupy Wall Street movement, has added an element of uncertainty to this picture. Tellingly, the director/producers of the 2010 *Sex and the City* sequel chose to set it in Dubai, not New York City, perhaps feeling that the latter's lifestyle no longer meshed with the latest popular perceptions of New York. Still, the movie was not a financial success, perhaps because Dubai by 2010 was also having major financial problems!

In short, hit movies set in New York in the last decade tend to depict the city as either the site of major destruction (city/region-wide, or much broader), or they depict the city as a place for the hedonistic pursuits of the rich. Hit movies, and their publics, cannot decide which, suggesting a quite uncertain perception of the future.

New York's Constant Theme as a Business and Finance Boom Town

Finally, amidst all this changeability, New York in hit movies has one constant theme, as mentioned. At least every five years throughout the entire period discussed and until the 2000s, a hit movie depicts New York as a town where avaricious and amoral business and corporate executives exploit others. This depiction clearly has affinities with the more recent (2000s) depiction of the New York a playground for the rich, but differs in tending to be more critical of the wealthy.

We have already mentioned *Dinner at Eight* (1933) and *The Apartment* (1960) as exemplifying this theme. Between those two films, *Weekend at the Waldorf* (1945) features a greedy and unscrupulous oil tycoon; *Guys and Dolls* (1955), although basically about two conmen and a Salvation Army volunteer, includes two Wall Street entrepreneurs, one of whom explains his philosophy, "It's a jungle out there, but if we all work together we can cut the throats of the opposition." The *Godfather* (1972), in its tale of New York's underworld, depicts business at its most literally cutthroat. In *9 to 5* (1980) a female lead trying to succeed in the work world tells her womanizing boss, "If you don't stop pinching and fondling me I'll cut your balls off." And in the final scenes of *Trading Places* (1983), two owners of a Wall Street firm engaged in insider trading, discuss the necessity to "always go for the throat, that's how we got rich." *Wall Street* (1987) with the stockbroker protagonist played by Michael Douglas, and his famous line "Greed is Good," is clearly in this tradition, though the film was not a top 10 box-office hit.

The Dark Knight Rises (2012) features a populist (Occupy Wall Street type) uprising of New York City's citizens, angry at the misdeeds of the financial sector.

It is, of course, possible and perhaps likely that in the context of the ongoing financial and economic crisis, this more critical perspective on New York's business/financial/rich inhabitants will reassert itself over the 2000s view of the city as increasingly a place for the rich and wannabes, depicted uncritically as models to be emulated.

CONCLUSION: AUDIENCE TASTES VERSUS STUDIO MARKETING

We have presented broad ideas about how New York, Los Angeles, and Chicago have been depicted in hit movies, and why, arguing that each of these three cities is associated in public perceptions in a particular way. New York basically picks up whatever seems to be the dominant image(s) of city/urban life at the time the movie is made. Chicago, by contrast, is stereotyped around four main images that have remained strikingly constant over time, a number of which are associated, albeit in updated form, with what seems to be Chicago's iconic period—Al Capone and the Prohibition era. Los Angeles's depictions fall midway between New York's urban adaptability and

Chicago's constancy, having evolved over time from Hollywood themed films to auto culture, and then to global institutions—corporations and/or organized crime, often with an Asian connection operating in the region.

There are, of course, many nuances and qualifications to be made, some of which we address in the appendix. Here we address one: the central question of whether, as we suggest, a movie's box-office success, if part of a pattern of similar successful movies that depict the world in a particular way, results at least partly from resonating with public perceptions and tastes, versus simply reflecting studio marketing and distribution power.

This question basically arises for hit movies released after the mid-1970s, since it was after *Jaws* (1975) that a policy of saturation release became the norm, certainly for the big films of the year, but also, increasingly, for every mainstream release (Schatz 2008, 20). Following Wasko (2003), we define a "saturation" or "wide" release pattern as a film appearing in more than 600 theaters across the US market on opening weekend. Additionally, this release pattern is usually accompanied by a national marketing campaign, especially through nationwide television advertising. By contrast, before 1975, a "roll out" or zoned system was in place, whose basic premise, which is ours too, was clearly that a successful movie would be one that resonated with public taste and perceptions organically rather than primarily by persuasion. Under the "roll out" practice, it was common to open a movie in a few influential cities and theaters across the country, build word of mouth, adjust advertising strategies to audience response, and then slowly expand to a broader audience.

Statistics showing that saturation releases now account for three-quarters of the total domestic box office (Wasko 2003, 106) have led several critics of Hollywood to suggest that a film's box-office success in recent decades has far more to do with the industrial practices of distribution and marketing than textual quality or audience choice (King 2002; Miller et al. 2005). This implies that Hollywood's distribution and marketing practices dominate the audience, and thus suggests a lack of audience agency in fueling hit movies during that period. Miller et al. (2005) make this argument explicitly. In the last decade, Miller points out, "Hollywood invests nearly twice as much money in marketing activities as do other comparable industries" (2005, 261). In fact, it is not uncommon for a big Hollywood film production to spend an additional 50 percent of its production budget to advertise, promote and market a film; during the summer months this figure often doubles or triples with studios spending more to market a film than it cost to produce (Vogel 2010, 141). According to Miller, "such costs escalate when an oligopoly of five or six companies controls the film distribution market using expensive marketing campaigns to compete with their rivals and hold back new competitors, as they collectively build and maintain ... a 'product differentiation barrier to entry' via the accumulation over time of consumer preferences" (2005, 261).

So what is the role of the audience (in this case, its tastes and existing ideas regarding the cities we discuss) in box-office success, versus the impact of studio marketing and distribution? We argue that although Hollywood's industrial structure and practices, such as saturation releases, accompanied by vast marketing campaigns are clearly an important aspect of the asymmetrical flow of media power from studios to

Table 18.8 SATURATION AND NONSATURATION RELEASES

Year	Nonsaturation releases (of top 150 box office movies)	Percentage	Nonsaturation releases in top 20
2006	14	9.3%	Borat
2005	18	12.0%	—
2004	19	12.7%	Fahrenheit 9/11
2003	20	13.3%	—
2002	21	14.0%	My Big Fat Greek Wedding; Chicago
2001	24	16.0%	—

audiences, analysis of box-office data for the period 2001–06 suggests that market-ing and distribution cannot be the only factors that contribute to a film's success. Table 18.8 shows that for most years, 10–20 percent of the films in the top 150 (by box-office) receipts were nonsaturation releases, that is, films that built an audience over time with perhaps minor "P & A" (print and advertising) spending, but never-theless achieved blockbuster status becoming part of the small percentage of films that account for much of studio revenue (e.g., in 2003, twenty-four films account for 36 percent of that year's total) (Eliashberg, Elberse, and Leenders 2006, 647).

Although for the top 20 box-office films each year, almost all had a saturation release pattern, four did not (*Borat, Fahrenheit 9/11, Chicago*, and *My Big Fat Greek Wedding*), while a fifth, *The Others* (2001), came in No. 21. Actually, a saturation release tends to produce moderate success in most cases, with blockbusters and overnight flops being the exception to the rule. Statistically, nonsaturation releases do not have as much chance of major box-office success, but that does not mean a platform or roll-out distribution strategy cannot produce a top 20 hit. In short, a saturation release does not guarantee box-office success, nor is it a necessary condi-tion for a movie to be a major box-office hit. Following Gans (1974), we believe that "popular culture" is not simply imposed on the audience from above but, rather, that it is shaped by that audience, at least in part.

Of course, a number of factors beyond interest or agency on the part of the audi-ence influences box-office success—genre, stars, rating, and so on. Also, there are, of course, a host of other factors in addition to audience agency or taste that might affect the content of movies. Skeptics, for example, might wonder whether the gen-erally favorable depiction of the NYPD in recent hit movies reflects the fact that in New York City the Mayor's Office of Film, Theatre and Broadcasting insists on reviewing scripts before giving a permit for filming, a practice arguably with echoes of local censorship boards prior to the industry-wide enactment of the Production Code of 1934. The mayor's office claims that they are "content-neutral" when review-ing scripts. An NYPD representative, in a 2011 interview, said that their only contact is providing a police detail for shooting, and suggested that the fact that no recent film has foregrounded police misbehavior (e.g., the Diallo shooting) is due to the NYPD "getting lucky." We have no evidence that these official claims are wrong, but the issue clearly needs monitoring.

Overall and when the data as a whole is taken into consideration, an argument that excludes audience agency in its account of box-office success is severely lacking. It is this lacuna that we have tried to fill in this chapter.[8]

APPENDIX

CONSTRUCTING THE LIST OF HIT (TOP 10) MOVIES

The data from 1947 onward are fairly reliable and movies can be ranked with some confidence. From 1947 to 1992 the data are based on reel rentals (fees paid by theaters to rent the movies). From 1992 onward the data are based on box-office receipts. The main compilation, based on these data sources, of the figures from 1947 to the present is *Variety*, supplemented from 1983 to 1993 by *Art Murphy's Box Office Register and Box Office Hits: Hollywood's Most Successful Movies 1939 to the Present*. Note that all our hit movie figures represent a film's domestic (US and Canadian) earnings and not its foreign earnings. This is because we are discussing here the way these key cities are depicted to, and seen by, a US audience. Note also that if a film is released late in the year (October–December) its income is reported in the following year's list, unless the film makes a particularly fast impact—in which case it may end up being reported for both years.

Before 1947, rental and box office receipts were not kept or reported and so figuring out which are the most popular movies for those earlier years is harder. The data before 1947 typically represent a best estimate that divides movies into two groups—the top money earners for a year versus the rest—but cannot reliably rank order the top money earners. From 1930 to 1946/47 the data come from *Film Facts*, which combed through the records of the *Motion Picture Herald*, *Motion Picture Daily*, and *Film Daily*. These publications estimated the top moneymakers for each year, but listed them alphabetically, since the estimates were not reliable enough to do more than that. From 1922 to 1927 the best data we have are from James Mark Purcell's estimates from an unpublished study, as reported in *Film Facts*. He put together the available figures and combined them with other data, such as exhibitors' reports appearing in the trade papers, in order to obtain an approximate ranking of the most popular films.

CLASSIFYING MOVIES

There were approximately 850 hit movies during the entire period we are discussing. In order to determine that a film dealt with New York, Los Angeles, or Chicago we started with the yearly publication *Videohounds*, a comprehensive reference volume on film, which contains a "Category Index" that groups films by genres, themes (specific city, rural America, suburban, etc.), settings, and so on. We supplemented this with the Internet Movie Database (http://www.imdb.org) and its "plot keyword" section on each film's page, which worked in a similar way to the "Category Index" in *Videohounds*. (Note that this is a user-updated website.)

After arriving at a preliminary list of movies that were about New York, Los Angeles, or Chicago using these methods, we then did a content analysis of the list in order to make sure that the references were not trivial. We set some minimal standards for deciding that a film is at least partly about a particular city. In general, a city had to appear in a movie for a significant amount of time (at least roughly fifteen minutes) and play a significant role in the plot or story for us to include it in our analysis. There might be some debate over whether particular movies should or should not have been included, but we do not believe such contentious cases affect our overall analysis.

Finally, in deciding whether a theme could be considered a major trend, we tried to stick to a rule that required that five or more hit movies in a more or less continuous time period depict that theme.

NOTES

1. For interesting studies of New York in movies, see Sanders (2003), Blake (2005), Fox (1996), and Grossvogel (2003). For New York in art, see Voorsanger and Howat (2000).
      For Los Angeles in movies, see Silver (1979), Silver and Ursini (2005), Stenger (2001), Dimendberg (2004), and Davis (1990). For Los Angeles in paintings, see McClung (2000). For studies of Chicago in movies, see note 5. For general studies of cities in movies, see Al Sayyad (2006), Barber (2002), Clarke (1997), De Vany (2004), King (1996), Shiel (2001), Sklar (1975), Wasko (1994), and Vogel (2010).
2. "Film noir" is, of course, a complex and difficult term to define. Critics debate whether the term represents a "genre," "style," or "cycle" (see Schatz 1981). But there are formal and narrative conventions of film noir—"low-key" lighting rich in shadows, voice-over narrators, crime story narratives, violent protagonists, and femmes fatales—discussed since the first essays on the genre (Franks 1946; see Naremore 1998 for detailed history of film noir concept) and present in the films themselves. Film Noir is also tied to the development of modernity and urban transformation, especially New York and Los Angeles, of the 1940s and 1950s. For Dimendberg (2004), film noir is "both a symptom and a catalyst" of the transformations of American culture in this period (p. 12).
3. This too reflects the fact that Hollywood has become representative of entertainment more broadly than the movie industry. On Hollywood's cultural and geographic diversity, see Scott (2005).
4. The Los Angeles auto motif is presaged by *Rebel Without a Cause* (No. 15 in 1956).
5. See also Ruth (1996) and Weimer (1999) for more on the emergence of the Chicago gangster motif.
6. *Batman* was actually filmed at Pinewood Studios outside of London.
7. An interesting possible exception (i.e., a pre-1964-released US-based disaster movie that is set in the present) is *House of Wax* (1953), where a madman terrorizes the women of New York City. Still, we defined a "disaster movie" as a film that depicts (actual) major loss of life and/or physical destruction, so this would not count as a disaster movie. It would have been classified at the time as a "horror movie."

8. Vogel commented on marketing costs, "In effect, the distributor must shape and create an audience with advertising and promotional campaigns (i.e. 'drivers') that have only one quick shot to succeed immediately upon theatrical release. As a result, expenditures on the marketing of films have long tended to rise considerably faster than the overall rate of inflation, and restraint in such expenditures is rarely seen. In practice, marketing decisions in filmmaking and distribution have an important effect on how a movie is initially perceived and on how it plays out in ancillary-market exposures. The notion of 'high concept' films—the underlying premises of which can be described in a sentence—is closely related to all such marketing aspects. In this regard, as De Vany and Walls (1996) note, 'the opening performance is statistically a dominant factor in revenue generation.' Yet it is also clear that audience sift the good from the bad pretty quickly and that no amount of spending or targeted promotion can save a poorly made, ill-conceived, or boring film once the information about its true quality is in circulation" (Vogel 2010, 141–42).

   De Vany wrote likewise on the influence of marketing, "Marketing can't change the odds. There is no evidence to show that marketing has much to do with a film's success. Marketing is mostly defensive anyway; a studio has to market its film just to draw attention in a field where everyone is shouting.... Nor can casting stars in movies increase the success.... Movies make stars, not the other way around.... A star movie has only a star movie has only a slightly higher chance of making a profit than a non-star movie.... Opening big and leading at the box office is a momentary success. A movie has to attain or sustain box-office dominance over many weeks to make major money. The size of the opening does not predict how the ensuing battles will evolve or how much money the film will take in" (De Vany 2004, 4–5).

CHAPTER 19

The Nonprofit Sector in New York City and Los Angeles

HELMUT K. ANHEIER, MARCUS LAM,
AND DAVID B. HOWARD

INTRODUCTION

Los Angeles and New York are often described as the social laboratory of the nation, and as "living experiments" of twenty-first-century capitalism that present us with a lens through which we can view the future of American society (Dear and Flusty 1998; Koshalek, Mayne, and Hutt 2002; Halle 2003). Like London or Paris in the past, Los Angeles and New York are at the forefront of many economic and social developments, and at the cutting edge of cultural and political trends. Los Angeles is often described as an archetype of the postmodern city, and New York as the industrial city that reinvented itself successfully as the financial capital of the world. Observers from around the world frequently look to Los Angeles and New York in search of future changes that might affect their own cities or regions.

If the future, as the popular saying goes, happens either in Los Angeles or New York, how do charities or nonprofit organizations factor into current and future scenarios? What role will nonprofits, foundations, faith-based organizations, and community associations play in fighting poverty and social disintegration, providing social services, education, or health care, or helping to create a vibrant art scene? What do recent trends suggest, and what has been the impact of the prolonged 2008–12 recession on the capacity of these organizations to meet social needs?

The purpose of this chapter is to provide a comparative analysis of the scale, scope, and role of the nonprofit sector in the New York and Los Angeles regions. As we will see, in both regions, the nonprofit sector plays important roles in health and human services, education, arts and culture, environmental protection, and many other areas of social, cultural, economic, and other needs. Yet while the nonprofit sector in both cities is in large measure a function of diverse demands for health and human services, arts and culture, and other quasi-public goods and services, both cities have developed nonprofit sectors that differ in size and composition. We argue that nonprofit sector–government relationships at the local level help account for these differences.

While research has identified some of the factors in the emergence of the nonprofit sector as a major economic force in the United States, most of this work focuses on the national (Salamon 2012; Urban Institute 2011) and international levels (Anheier and Salamon 2006). And while major theories about the role of nonprofit organizations in advanced market economies have been put forward (Powell and Steinberg 2006), few studies have systematically collected information on urban areas in that regard,[1] and fewer yet have explored within-country similarities and differences among the factors influencing the size, structure, and growth patterns of nonprofits in metropolitan centers (see Bielefeld 2000; Grønbjerg and Paarlberg 2001).

Nowhere is this neglect more apparent than in the case of Los Angeles and New York.[2] Like other world cities, Los Angeles and New York are undergoing a continued restructuring from industrial to service-based economies. International trade and commerce are becoming even more important, and migration is changing the cultural orientation and social profile of urban populations. Such trends also shift the role of how local governments can relate to increasingly diverse civil societies. At the same time, local and state governments feel the dual pressures from a retreating federal government and eroding tax bases, which both affect the amounts and patterns of public sector revenues and expenditures. What is the role and capacity of the nonprofit sector amid this shifting balance of public responsibilities?

THE NONPROFIT SECTOR IN NEW YORK CITY AND LOS ANGELES

To answer these questions, we start by looking at the local government and public sector provision in both regions.[3] Los Angeles County and New York City are comparable with respect to the number of local government employees. In terms of government expenditure, however, they differ: Los Angeles's government sector is comparatively smaller than New York City's. In 2009, there were approximately 460,000 employees in local government in Los Angeles County compared to 401,000 in New York City.[4] With government expenditure, New York City is larger with approximately $67.4 billion in expenditure compared to $35.4 billion in expenditure in Los Angeles County.[5] Per capita government spending in New York City is two times that of Los Angeles; and while the New York City public sector spends $8,000 dollars on each New Yorker, the corresponding number for Angelenos is only $1,900 by Los Angeles County and an average of $2,600 for the top 10 cities within Los Angeles County. Thus, in absolute and relative terms, New York City's public sector is larger than Los Angeles's.

But it is not only the size of government that matters and makes Los Angeles different (see Andranovich and Riposa 1998); it is also the structure of Los Angeles's public sector that stands out among major US cities like New York. There are eighty-eight cities in LA County alone. Los Angeles's government is fragmented both within and across political boundaries. The City of Los Angeles's weak mayoral system and slightly more powerful City Council are coupled with a powerful county-level Board of Supervisors.

While the City of Los Angeles (and other smaller cities in the region like Santa Monica, Culver City, or Pasadena) maintains responsibilities for certain public services, the bulk of service provision (e.g., mental health, welfare, public health, etc.) is administered through the County of Los Angeles, in particular, for unincorporated areas of the county. Some areas have considerable overlap between county and municipalities, which has frequently led to tensions and oversight conflicts among public entities. For example, coordination of regional transportation, education, and policing policies has been particularly challenging, and the creation of "intra-jurisdictional arrangements" such as neighborhood councils is largely a reaction to the difficulties of representation and service provision in the Los Angeles region (Box and Musso 2004).

While Los Angeles is a metropolis of decentralized communities with weak and shifting commitment to some form of "central" control or coordination, New York City's government, by contrast, is not only larger but also less fragmented. A stronger mayoral system and higher city-level responsibility for service provision—in addition to a smaller role for county government—lead to less jurisdictional conflict among local governments and agencies.

In New York City, a partnership between city government and nonprofit organizations was put in place early and developed over time; by contrast, in Los Angeles, such partnership remained patchy and did not evolve into a general pattern whereby public agencies and private nonprofits collaborate to address community needs of many kinds. These differences in urban government have important implications for the nonprofit sector, because community-based organizations, particularly those in the health and human services, benefit greatly from a well-functioning and supportive public sector. Frequently, nonprofit and community leaders work collaboratively with local government agencies to address social and economic issues; but they also act alone, even in opposition to city, county, state, or the federal government to protect the interest of members, users, or clients (Salamon 1995).

A Brief History

The New York region has a much longer and extensive institutional history compared to Los Angeles. That is, its business, educational, philanthropic, charitable, and religious institutions have rich and varied legacies, often with strong ties to state and local government institutions. New York has a long tradition of partnership between government and voluntary organizations, a trend which preceded the growth of federal-level social policy expansion during the New Deal. For example, as governor of New York, Franklin Delano Roosevelt experimented with various forms of nonprofit–government partnerships in human service delivery, which served as the basis for federal policies under the New Deal (Grossman, Salamon, and Altschuler 1986; Dawes and Saidel 1988). Thus, the service modalities and governance structures of many of New York's oldest charities were forged under progressive and liberal political regimes, and as a result the relationship between New York

City's charitable and philanthropic institutions and government agencies are much more developed.

More so than in Los Angeles, New York government agencies, both state and local, have made, and continue to make, more and more extensive use of nonprofit agencies. This pattern of government support for, and partnerships with, charitable organizations—be they museums, hospitals, or poverty relief agencies—extends back to the nineteenth century. For example, in the late 1880s, New York City allocated over $1 million to private institutions serving the poor (Grossman, Salamon, and Altschuler 1986). This funding complemented a growing philanthropic sector in the region, as late nineteenth-century industrialization generated enormous pockets of wealth through which John D. Rockefeller, Andrew Carnegie, and others established some of the most influential foundations in modern time (Anheier and Hammack 2010; Anheier and Howard 2012). Newly formed private foundations influenced an era of institution building in New York, influencing the founding of a diverse set of educational, cultural, and health and human service organizations (Anheier and Hammack 2010).

In fact, certain charitable organizations in New York have preceded federal agencies, including the New York Council on the Arts and Children's Aid Society. New York City is also home to some of the nation's oldest philanthropic institutions (e.g., the Ford Foundation, the Rockefeller Foundation, the Russell Sage Foundation, and the Carnegie Corporation of New York), as well as the oldest nonprofit health and educational institutions (e.g., Bellevue Hospital, founded in 1736, and Columbia University, established in 1754). Finally, agencies created to help the poor and the working class, such as the Society for the Prevention of Pauperism, which spawned the creation of the Savings Bank of New York, can be traced to the first few decades following independence (Clemens and Guthrie 2010).

Like New York City, Los Angeles's history is full of examples of how various civil society institutions have shaped important aspects of the region's development. Indeed, it would be difficult to write a history of the city without giving proper recognition of how voluntary and community-based organizations, often in close cooperation with business leaders and government, have reacted to the challenges of the times. Yet Los Angeles's nonprofit sector was less closely tied to institutional philanthropy, which was and remained relatively underdeveloped well into the twentieth century. The Los Angeles Area Chamber of Commerce, with roots dating back to 1888, became one of the most important organizations promoting business development and civic-mindedness in the nation. Not only was the Chamber part of the push to create UCLA, and a pro-business and pro-community environment generally, it also created, together with civic leaders, the Welfare Federation of Los Angeles in 1924. The Federation combined 166 separate charities at that time and worked closely with the Community Chest, which then developed into the United Way Inc. in 1964 before becoming the United Way of Greater Los Angeles in a 1980 merger with AID/United Givers (see Pitt and Pitt 1997, 516–17). A more recent example is the United Neighborhood Organization, a barrio association established in 1975, which spun off a large nonprofit, low-income housing program in South Los Angeles (Pitt and Pitt 1997, 515).

But agencies relevant to the nonprofit sector have also been created out of conflict between different levels of government, an example of the fragmented nature of Los Angeles' regional governance structure. In 1993, the Los Angeles Homeless Services Authority was born out of a lawsuit filed by the City of Los Angeles against LA County. Originally filed in response to county-imposed restrictions on general relief benefits for homeless individuals, the city–county litigation was settled in 1991. One of the results of the lawsuit was the creation of the Los Angeles Homeless Services Authority, a joint-powers authority of the city and county. The agency has experienced numerous oversight challenges (Wolch et al. 2007) and works with over one hundred nonprofit groups today. Thus, while nonprofit–government relations in New York evolved in a simpler institutional environment, they faced more complex and conflicting structures in Los Angeles.

But it is not only in the field of business promotion, welfare, and housing that nonprofit initiatives have contributed to Los Angeles's development. Think-tanks like the RAND Corporation, formed in 1946, or, more recently, the Milken Institute, have long contributed to problem-solving locally, as well as beyond. Similarly, cultural institutions like the Getty Trust, museums like the Autry Museum of Western Heritage, and numerous arts organizations and theater companies like the Actors' Gang make significant contributions to the region's cultural vitality.

What is more, local community associations like Community Coalition played a significant role in rebuilding the social fabric of neighborhoods in the aftermaths of the Watts Riots in 1965 and the civil unrest in 1992. In the aftermath of the latter, a coalition of LA-based foundations created LA Urban Funders, a partnership between the philanthropic community, the larger nonprofit service providers, and government to find better ways to reach underserved populations, especially in African American and Latino neighborhoods, but it ultimately failed to create sustainable structures.

Yet despite both the historical importance of some nonprofits, and the prominence of larger nonprofits today (e.g., the Getty Trust, the University of Southern California, the network of Catholic schools and charities, etc.) no overall pattern of nonprofit–government cooperation developed in a sustained and forward-looking way. Unlike New York City, where nonprofit–government relations, once established, provided the foundation for future policy developments, the situation in Los Angeles had more of an "on and off" pattern and remained characterized by, and subject to, the interest of particular groups at a given time due primarily to the fragmented nature of its county and municipal governments.

Scale and Composition

The nonprofit sectors of Los Angeles and New York are both vast and diverse.[6] In addition to public charities, or 501(c)(3) organizations, the nonprofit sector encompasses member serving organizations, professional associations, labor unions (i.e., 501(c)(4)–501(c)(28)), as well as grant making and operating foundations. The empirical focus in this section of the chapter, however, will be on the group of organizations classified as 501(c)(3) organizations. They are the principle providers of social, health, and human services, whereas 501(c)(4)–(28) organizations include member serving or advocacy organizations that benefit a smaller, specific group of people and do not engage in broader services provision. This approach, however, neglects the many thousands of informal neighborhood associations that are either not registered or too small to be accounted in official statistics.

The formal nonprofit organizations included here do indeed amount to a major economic force accounting for about 6 percent of Gross Metropolitan Product in Los Angeles County and 11 percent in the New York region.[7] In Los Angeles, they employ 256,000 and in New York 530,000 people (Hasenfeld et al. 2011).[8] For Los Angeles, this is equivalent to total employment in the entertainment industry and is 55 percent of local government employment. In contrast, nonprofit employment in New York is roughly 1.3 times larger than local government employment (530,000 vs. 401,000).

Gladstone and Fainstein (2003) show that the largest private employers in New York City and Los Angeles County between 2001 and 2002 were, respectively, New York Presbyterian Healthcare System and Kaiser Permanente, both nonprofit health care providers. Nonprofit institutes of higher education (e.g., University of Southern California, New York University) also rank highly. Note these rankings are by number of employees, not annual revenues as in table 3.6.

In both cities, the nonprofit sector is responsible for delivering a vast and complex range of goods and services, from health and childcare to arts and culture and educational services. The nonprofit sector in both cities, however, is not static, but has grown in recent years; this expansion, as we will show, continues to take place in both regions in similar composition but at different rates.

Table 19.1 provides a snapshot of the nonprofit sector for the Los Angeles and New York regions for 2009 and distinguishes between "registered" and "reporting" organizations. The number of reporting organizations are all charities that have been given 501(c)(3) tax status by the IRS and excludes small organizations with little or no revenue and thus not required to report their financial activities annually to the IRS (e.g., to file a Form 990). The threshold for an organization to file a Form 990 and report to the IRS is if the organization generates annual gross revenues of $25,000 or more. Thus, of the 34,261 registered nonprofits in New York and 31,486 in Los Angeles, only about one-third are required to report to the IRS annually. In other words, in both cities, the majority of nonprofits in both regions are very small organizations that operate with little revenue.

The only exceptions are organizations categorized as "religion related or spiritual development," which include churches and congregations of all denominations. The IRS does not mandate churches to file a Form 990, regardless of revenue, but rather, it allows churches to file a Form 990 on a voluntary basis (for a more thorough discussion of churches and their activities, see Chaves 2002). Thus, it is likely that the number of "registered" organizations that are religion related include large organizations, measured in terms of revenue, that choose not to file a Form 990.

For both regions, religion-related organizations are the largest category of registered nonprofits followed by educational organizations in Los Angeles and philanthropic organizations in New York. In fact, New York exceeds Los Angeles in the

Table 19.1 COMPARISON OF REGISTERED AND REPORTING 501(C)(3) ORGANIZATIONS IN NEW YORK CITY AND LOS ANGELES COUNTY, BY SUBFIELDS

	New York		Los Angeles		New York	Los Angeles
					Assets of Reporting Organizations (in $ millions)	
Sub-field	REGISTERED	REPORTING	REGISTERED	REPORTING		
Education	3,115	1,534	4,414	2,060	$46,267	$24,720
Health	876	588	782	437	$38,644	$15,857
Arts, Culture, and Humanities	4,434	2,269	3,113	1,289	$15,338	$4,447
Philanthropy, Voluntarism, and Grant making Foundations	6,625	507	3,337	430	$6,706	$3,674
International, Foreign Affairs, and National Security	1,226	655	656	259	$6,591	$311
Human Services—Multipurpose and Other	2,216	1,228	2,516	1,116	$6,358	$4,739
Housing, Shelter	947	659	887	583	$6,216	$2,846
Mutual/Membership Benefit Organizations, Other	108	41	66	15	$5,412	$31
Community Improvement, Capacity Building	1,021	526	1,037	424	$2,720	$448
Medical Research	207	134	179	114	$2,232	$1,305
Environmental Quality, Protection, and Beautification	317	143	359	134	$1,685	$161
Religion Related, Spiritual Development	8,785	823	8,306	956	$1,678	$791
Mental Health, Crisis Intervention	399	275	589	324	$1,261	$640
Animal-Related	219	84	483	204	$1,142	$184
Science and Technology Research Institutes, Services	116	43	153	62	$1,098	$889

(Continued)

Table 19.1 (CONTINUED)

Sub-field	New York		Los Angeles		New York	Los Angeles
	REGISTERED	REPORTING	REGISTERED	REPORTING	Assets of Reporting Organizations (in $ millions)	
Diseases, Disorders, Medical Disciplines	650	330	746	289	$927	$556
Civil Rights, Social Action, Advocacy	285	130	178	63	$913	$72
Public, Society Benefit—Multipurpose and Other	413	110	568	92	$865	$2,132
Recreation, Sports, Leisure, Athletics	848	372	1,271	614	$788	$334
Youth Development	407	188	707	259	$702	$420
Crime, Legal Related	315	186	391	164	$675	$142
Employment, Job Related	217	139	203	107	$586	$243
Social Science Research Institutes, Services	108	56	132	31	$239	$398
Food, Agriculture, and Nutrition	100	44	140	62	$117	$61
Public Safety	149	60	155	55	$51	$22
Other (not elsewhere classified)	158	22	118	19	$2	$10
Total	**34,261**	**11,146**	**31,486**	**10,162**	**$149,215**	**$65,434**

Source: CORE 2009; BMF 2009.

number of philanthropic organizations by about 3 to 1. New York also has a higher number of arts and culture organizations, international and foreign affairs organizations, but a smaller number of educational organizations compared to Los Angeles.

Measured in terms of assets, however, New York and Los Angeles are similar in that the two largest categories are education, which includes higher educational institutions (e.g., universities), and health (e.g., hospitals). Combined, the education and health sectors (i.e. Diseases, Disorders, Medical Disciplines; Health Care such as hospitals and health clinics; Medical Research; Mental Health, Crisis Intervention) comprise nearly $90 billion in assets (60 percent of the total) in New York and $43 billion (66 percent of the total) in Los Angeles. Thus, while the total numbers of organizations, both registered and reporting, are comparable for both regions, New York City nonprofits operate on a much larger scale with over two times the total assets of organizations in Los Angeles ($149 billion versus $65 billion).

Table 19.2 takes a closer look at the group of "registered" nonprofits in both regions. With 11,146 compared to 10,162 organizations, New York and Los Angeles are comparable. However, in terms of nonprofit activity, measured by expenditures, the nonprofit sector in New York, in the aggregate, is two and a half times higher compared to Los Angeles ($88.2 billion vs. $35.4 billion). Similarly, measured as organizations per capita, New York and Los Angeles are alike, with thirteen and twelve organizations per 10,000 persons, respectively. However, nonprofits in New York spend three times as much per person as those in Los Angeles ($10,500 vs. $3,400).

In terms of composition, the two regions are more similar in some ways but differ in others, as has already become apparent, with health organizations accounting for the largest share of expenditures, 46 percent for New York vs. 41 percent for Los Angeles. Together, the top three subfields—health, education, and human services (i.e., civil rights, legal related, employment, etc.)—account for almost 80 percent of total expenditures in New York and 87 percent in Los Angeles, and more than half of the total number of organizations for both regions. This composition is also similar to that found at the national level (Salamon 2012). Perhaps not surprisingly, New York City exceeds Los Angeles in arts and culture organizations with almost twice as many organizations and over three times the expenditures; in fact, arts and culture organizations represent the largest share of organizations in New York City (20 percent). Los Angeles, on the other hand, has a higher number of education (e.g., primary and secondary), sports and recreation, animal related, religious, and youth development organizations. However, spending, on average, by these organizations, is still far below New York nonprofits. In terms of total expenditure, Los Angeles only exceeds New York in two relatively small fields: "science and technology research institutes" and "social science research institutes."

This snapshot reveals that New York City is home to larger and more developed nonprofits, both overall and at the organizational level. This is evidenced by the average spending per organization in the largest fields (health, education, human service, and arts and culture): while New York only slightly exceeds Los Angeles in terms of the number of organizations (with the exception of arts and culture), the overall and average spending per organization in New York is nearly two to three times as much as by Los Angeles nonprofits. In the same vein, New York has more "infrastructure organizations" than Los Angeles. By this, we refer to management support and

Table 19.2 COMPARISON OF REPORTING 501(C)(3) ORGANIZATIONS' EXPENDITURE IN NEW YORK CITY AND LOS ANGELES COUNTY, BY SUBFIELDS

| | Number of Organizations | | | | Total Expenditure (in $ millions) | | | | Average Expenditure (in $ millions) | |
| | New York[a] | | Los Angeles[b] | | New York | | Los Angeles | | New York | Los Angeles |
	COUNT	% TOTAL	COUNT	% TOTAL	AMOUNT	% TOTAL	AMOUNT	% TOTAL	PER ORG	PER ORG
Health	588	5	437	4	36,663	42	12,367	35	62	28
Education	1,534	14	2,060	20	19,869	23	10,233	29	13	5
Human Services—Multipurpose and Other	1,228	11	1,116	11	6,414	7	4,046	11	5	4
Arts, Culture, and Humanities	2,269	20	1,289	13	4,591	5	1,271	4	2	1
International, Foreign Affairs, and National Security	655	6	259	3	4,281	5	469	1	7	2
Philanthropy, Voluntarism, and Grant making Foundations	507	5	430	4	2,284	3	769	2	5	2
Community Improvement, Capacity Building	526	5	424	4	2,020	2	250	1	4	1
Public, Society Benefit—Multipurpose and Other	110	1	92	1	1,586	2	227	1	14	2
Mental Health, Crisis Intervention	275	2	324	3	1,470	2	1,011	3	5	3
Housing, Shelter	659	6	583	6	1,276	1	632	2	2	1
Diseases, Disorders, Medical Disciplines	330	3	289	3	1,230	1	488	1	4	2

Medical Research	134	1	114	1	882	1	504	1	7	4
Religion Related, Spiritual Development	823	7	956	9	790	1	353	1	1	0.4
Employment, Job Related	139	1	107	1	734	1	416	1	5	4
Crime, Legal Related	186	2	164	2	635	1	127	0.4	3	1
Mutual/Membership Benefit Organizations, Other	41	0.4	15	0.1	585	1	3	0.01	14	0.2
Environmental Quality, Protection, and Beautification	143	1	134	1	495	1	86	0.2	3	1
Science and Technology Research Institutes	43	0.4	62	1	440	0.5	940	3	10	15
Animal-Related	84	1	204	2	423	0.5	110	0.3	5	1
Youth Development	188	2	259	3	398	0.5	285	1	2	1
Recreation, Sports, Leisure, Athletics	372	3	614	6	394	0.4	328	1	1	1
Civil Rights, Social Action, Advocacy	130	1	63	1	376	0.4	45	0.1	3	1
Food, Agriculture, and Nutrition	44	0.4	62	1	174	0.2	146	0.4	4	2
Social Science Research Institutes, Services	56	1	31	0.3	142	0.2	271	1	3	9
Public Safety	60	1	55	1	44	0.05	31	0.1	1	1
Other (not classified)	22	0.2	19	0.2	2	0.003	2	0.004	0.1	0.1
Total	**11,146**		**10,162**		**$88,199**		**$35,407**		**$7.9**	**$3.5**

Source: NCCS Core Files 2009.
[a] Kings, Queens, Bronx, New York, Richmond Counties (e.g., New York City).
[b] Los Angeles County.

consulting organizations that target nonprofits, lobby groups and representational bodies, and also university-based teaching and research units.[9]

Trends

In light of the tumultuous events during the first decade of the twenty-first century (e.g., the dot.com bubble burst in 2000, terrorist attacks in 2001, a mild recession from 2002 to 2003, continued government budget problems, and a severe recession from 2008 to 2012), how have the two sectors changed over the last ten years and how are they likely to change in the future? For both regions, the nonprofit sector has expanded, but at differing rates. The number of reporting organizations in Los Angeles increased 41 percent from 7,192 organizations in 2000 to 10,164 organizations in 2009. Similarly, the number of reporting nonprofits in New York also increased by about 37 percent from 8,130 in 2000 to 11,146 in 2009. Total expenditures, however, have increased at a higher rate since 2000 in New York than in Los Angeles. As figure 19.1 shows, expenditures increased by about 51 percent from 2000 to 2009 whereas in Los Angeles, expenditures increased by only 30 percent for the same period and experienced a slight 6 percent decrease between 2008 and 2009.

The composition of the nonprofit sector in both regions has remained about the same, with hospitals representing the largest share of expenditure (between 25 percent and 30 percent) since 2000. In New York, this is followed by other health organizations (excluding hospitals), education, and human services. In Los Angeles, spending by hospitals is followed by education, human service organizations, and other health organizations.

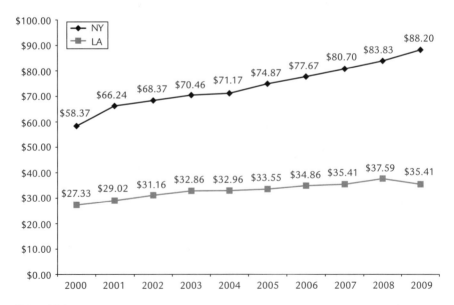

Figure 19.1
Nonprofit Expenditure 2000 to 2009, New York and Los Angeles, in $ billion
Source: National Center for Charitable Statistics, Core Files 2000 to 2009.

The overall compositions have remained relatively stable since 2000, despite an overall growth and many profound changes in the economy, politics, and society.

Government Contributions

As a measure of nonprofit reliance on government support, figure 19.2 presents the average government contributions as a percentage of total revenue across twenty-four nonprofit subfields for New York and Los Angeles in 2008.[10] Averaged across all subfields, government contributions[11] are approximately equal for both regions, 13 percent for New York and 14 percent for Los Angeles. However, parceling out and examining each subfield reveals stark contrasts. In eighteen of the twenty-three subfields, government contributions represent a larger percentage of total revenue among New York City nonprofits with the exception of five subfields (crime, legal related; youth development; human services; social science research institutions; and diseases, disorders, medical disciplines). Thus, a wider array of nonprofit organizations receive government contributions in New York than in Los Angeles, but government contributions constitute a much higher percentage of total revenue for a select group of nonprofit subfields in Los Angeles (as much as 75 percent on average for social science research institutions). Put another way, it would appear that government supports a much broader range of nonprofit organizations in New York, but in small amounts; in Los Angeles, government supports a narrower field of nonprofits in higher amounts on average.

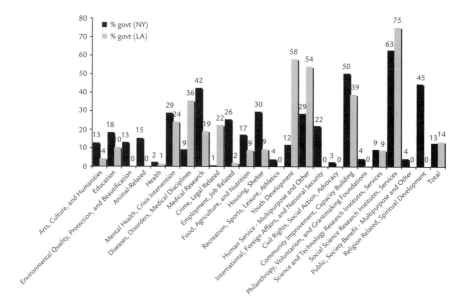

Figure 19.2
Government Grants as Proportion of Total Revenue of Nonprofits, New York and Los Angeles, 2008
Source: National Center for Charitable Statistics, Statistics of Income File 2008.

FIELDS

As previously mentioned, the nonprofit sector encompasses a wide range of public and private goods. This section highlights three key, albeit very different, segments of the nonprofit sector: health and human services, arts and culture, and foundations. The purpose of this analysis is to draw key comparisons between Los Angeles and New York and attempt to identify notable distinctions between the regions.

Health and Human Service Providers

Given that health and human service organizations (HHSOs), including hospitals, account for nearly 60 percent of all nonprofit activity (measured by expenditures), this section will explore in greater depth this subset of the nonprofit sector in terms of their geographical distribution and relationship to other regional demographic indicators. Human service organizations can be broadly defined as that set of organizations whose principal function is to protect, maintain, or enhance the personal well-being of individuals by defining, shaping, or altering their personal attributes (Hasenfeld et al. 2011), human service organizations include: Civil Rights, Social Action, Advocacy; Crime, Legal Related; Employment, Job Related; Food, Agriculture, and Nutrition; Housing, Shelter; Human Services—Multipurpose and Other; Public Safety; Recreation, Sports, Leisure, Athletics; Youth Development; see tables 19.1 and 19.2. We include health organizations—that is, Diseases, Disorders, Medical Disciplines; Health Care such as hospitals and health clinics; Medical Research; Mental Health, Crisis Intervention; see tables 19.1 and 19.2—within the broader categorization as they are also a primary resource of essential services in impoverished neighborhoods. In many underserved and marginalized communities, health and human service nonprofits are the frontline providers of basic and essential services such as shelter, food, and medical care (Allard 2009). Thus, a closer look at HHSO activity will provide a gauge of the relative well-being of these communities in both Los Angeles and New York.

In New York, HHSOs make up 39 percent of all nonprofits and represent more than half (57 percent) of all expenditures. Health-related nonprofits alone account for nearly half (46 percent) of all NY nonprofit expenditures. To illustrate the sheer size of the New York nonprofit health and human service sector, health organization spending alone (greater than $40 billion) is more than total expenditures for all Los Angeles nonprofits in 2009. Between 2000 and 2009, the number of HHSOs in New York grew by 30 percent from 3,224 to 4,191 (despite the fact that their share of all organizations decreased slightly from 40 percent to 39 percent). In contrast, HHSO activity measured in terms of organizational expenditures grew by 74 percent during that time (to over $50 billion).

In 2000, there were approximately four nonprofit HHSOs per 10,000 people in New York and HHSOs spent over $3,600 per person. In 2009, the number of HHSOs per 10,000 people increased to five (a 25 percent increase). Expenditures per capita increased to nearly $6,000 in 2009 (66 percent increase). In Los Angeles, at 41 percent of all organizations and 58 percent of total expenditures, HHSOs also make up the largest segment of the nonprofit sector. However, between 2000 and 2009, the total share of HHSOs in the Los Angeles region decreased from 45 percent to 41 percent. Like New York, LA HHSOs experienced a slight decline in their share of expenditure from 2000 (59 percent) to 2009 (58 percent).

In 2000, there were 3.4 HHSOs per 10,000 people (16 percent less than New York) and HHSOs spent nearly $1,400 per capita (just 38 percent of the New York figure). In 2009, the HHSO per 10,000 figure increased by 23 percent (slower pace than New York) to 4.2. Expenditures increased by 51 percent (lagging behind New York) to about $2,000 per person.

Arts and Culture

In addition to providing critical health and human services to a variety of populations, the nonprofit sector is also a vital source of cultural wealth and capital. In most major cities, some of the largest museums, opera houses, and music halls are nonprofit organizations. New York and Los Angeles have the two largest nonprofit arts and culture sectors in the country—with New York's tripling the size of Los Angeles's. Although New York's nonprofit arts sector is larger, and to a greater extent supported by local government, the two areas contain a similar composition of arts groups. Theater groups are the most common type of arts and culture nonprofit in both regions (13 percent in New York; 12 percent in Los Angeles), followed by cultural and ethnic awareness organizations (9 percent in New York; 11 percent in Los Angeles). New York has a slightly higher share of dance organizations (6 percent vs. 4 percent) and historical societies and historic preservation groups (6 percent vs. 4 percent).

Art museums represent the largest share of expenditures in both regions. In New York, art museums spent nearly $800 million in 2008 (16 percent of all arts and culture spending), compared to $200 million in Los Angeles (12 percent). Performing arts centers and theaters were the next largest (about 7 percent each in New York; 10 percent and 9 percent, respectively, in Los Angeles). While New York shows higher instances of opera houses, Los Angeles has a higher share of symphony orchestras. In all, there is relative congruence between the make-up of each region's nonprofit arts sector.

World renowned as the "entertainment capital of the world," the arts economy in Los Angeles provides for a substantial source of economic production and employment, in addition to critical cultural benefits to the region. The creative economy draws nearly 25 million visitors to Southern California annually; brought in an estimated $127 billion in revenue in 2009; and employs about 835,000 employees. Granted, the arts economy is comprised of a mixture of nonprofit, for profit, and public entities. Nonprofit organizations make up about 3 percent of all arts organizations in LA County and employment in these organizations represents nearly 9 percent of employment in the arts sector (Hasenfeld et al. 2011).

In terms of arts and culture's share of the local nonprofit sectors in each region, arts organizations account for 13 percent of all nonprofits in Los Angeles compared to 20 percent in New York. Aggregate nonprofit arts and culture expenditures, as a share of total nonprofit expenditures, are more even between regions. About four percent of nonprofit expenditures are for arts in Los Angeles, compared to five percent in New York.

Foundations

Private grant making foundations play an important role in supporting nonprofit organizations, advancing knowledge through funding of innovative research, and building strategic partnerships with government agencies (Anheier and Hammack 2010). While New York's private foundation sector is larger and older—on average—than Los Angeles's, foundations in Los Angeles have been growing at a faster pace than New York for many years (Anheier and Howard 2012).

Measured in assets, private foundations account for a substantial share of the total nonprofit sector; thus while small in terms of numbers compared to other nonprofit organizations, foundations have tremendous leverage given their sizable assets. Changes in foundation spending and grant making will have a direct impact on nonprofit activity, particularly those that rely heavily on foundation support. According to Foundation Center data, the New York region has nearly three times as many foundations as Los Angeles (9,551 versus 2,911). While New York has seen a larger growth in the number of foundations since 2000, increasing by about 80 percent versus 62 percent for Los Angeles, both assets of LA foundations and their total giving have grown at greater clips than in New York. In terms of total foundation giving, Los Angeles has grown by 88 percent compared to 78 percent for NY foundations. Changes in foundation assets between 2000 and 2009 reveal stark contrasts between the regions, with New York seeing a 13 percent increase in total foundation assets, and Los Angeles experiencing 36 percent growth over the same period.

In other words, and relating back to the role of government, foundations are emerging as more important actors for the local nonprofit sector in Los Angeles than they do in New York. Nonetheless, the growing capacity of LA foundations cannot make up for the continued and worsening weakness of local government funding. Foundation support is typically for new, innovative programs and start-ups, and less for supporting ongoing activities in the long run. Even if foundations were to decide to allocate significant shares of their grant-making to support core funding of local nonprofits, they would simply not have the resources to do so: total foundation grants in Los Angeles for 2009 were 0.33 percent of Gross Metropolitan Product (Anheier and Howard 2012) compared to 6 percent for the nonprofit sector as whole, as shown above. As a result, and on average, Los Angeles's nonprofit sector overall continues to be more undercapitalized and challenged in terms of sustainability than their NY counterparts.

CONCLUSION

The empirical portrait of the nonprofit sector in Los Angeles and New York has revealed both similarities and differences. Both cities are similar in that the formal nonprofit sectors provide economically, as well as socially, significant public benefits and services to a broad cross section of the population and across a wide range of fields (e.g., education, social services, health, arts and culture, housing, etc.). In terms of expenditures, nonprofits in each region have similarly experienced economic fluctuation over the past two decades and also reveal similar trends in resource concentration. One limitation of the data presented in this chapter is that it only captures formally registered nonprofits as the data is primarily based on financial reports, and little is known of the size, scale, and scope of informal organizations.

Among the major differences are: the New York City nonprofit sector is more developed compared to its LA counterpart, both in absolute as well as in relative terms (slightly higher numbers of organizations, higher overall expenditures, higher expenditures per capita, greater assets, and higher nonprofit percentage of Gross Metropolitan Product). In terms of composition, for both regions, the health and education sectors, while representing only about one-quarter of all organizations, comprise nearly 70% of all nonprofit sector expenditure. Overall, however, New York City nonprofits outspend LA organizations nearly three to one and average spending per organization is over two times higher compared to Los Angeles. Los Angeles only exceeds New York in terms of overall and average spending per organization in science and technology research and social science research institutes. With respect to government support, a broader range of nonprofits receive government contributions in New York City compared to Los Angeles, where government contribution is concentrated in only a few fields (e.g., youth development, human service, and social science institutes) but in much higher amounts.

As suggested above, variations in political context and institutional structures may help explain differences between the cities. Los Angeles's fragmented jurisdictional structure has been described as a weakness linked to poor coordination of economic and social activities, including impeded implementation of effective solutions to the area's most pressing social issues such as homelessness, transportation, or pollution (Halle 2003; Wolch and Dear 1993). The impact this has for the nonprofit sector in Los Angeles is less coordinated support as evidenced by an underdeveloped and smaller nonprofit sector in terms of size and expenditures. The LA nonprofit sector is only a little over one-third of the size of the NY nonprofit sector in terms of expenditure and less than half the size of New York in terms of total assets. It also appears that government support for nonprofit organizations is higher in New York, where eighteen of twenty-three nonprofit subfields show higher government contributions as a percentage of total revenue. In New York, where county boundaries coincide with city boundaries to a far greater extent, and service responsibilities are clearly delegated among public entities (mostly New York City), jurisdictional challenges are less commonplace, and coordination easier, both across electoral districts and sectors.[12]

Formal institutions include patterned nonprofit relationships with various levels and types of government and public agencies in terms of responsibilities, contracting, and funding. It may also include general preferences for services provided by nonprofits, as opposed to public or for profit providers of such goods as the arts, childcare, healthcare, among others. It also includes the number and density of management support organizations that offer consulting, strategic planning, and financial services to the nonprofit sector (e.g., Center for Nonprofit Management, Nonprofit Finance Fund, etc.).

Both aspects are more pronounced in New York than in Los Angeles. But differently, the relative underdevelopment of Los Angeles's nonprofit sector when compared to New York is the result of a weakness in nonprofit-government relations. Salamon's (1995) interdependence theory is instructive here. This theory begins with the fact that government and the nonprofit sector are more frequently partners rather than foes. The thrust of this argument is that government does not "supplant" or "displace" nonprofit organizations; rather, government support of the third sector is extensive and government is a "major force underwriting nonprofit operations" (Salamon 1995). The extensive government support of nonprofits can be understood if we consider what Salamon labels third-party government, the use of nongovernmental entities to carry out governmental purposes with a substantial degree of discretion over the spending of public funds (Salamon 1995).

In short, the nonprofit sector's weaknesses correspond well with government's strengths, and vice versa. The government can provide a more stable stream of resources, set priorities through a democratic process, discourage paternalism by making access to care a right and not a privilege, and improve quality of care by setting benchmarks and quality standards (Anheier 2005). In the context of this present chapter, NY government structures turned out to be more conducive to nonprofit growth and sustainability than Los Angeles's smaller and more fragmented public sector.

How can we assess the impact of the 2008–12 recession? The nonprofit sector has historically proven itself quite resilient. Despite the severe economic stress of the 2008–12 recession on the nonprofit sector, including decreases in donative income streams, loss of endowed assets, increased costs of production, and increased competition for resources (Salamon 2009), most nonprofit organizations seem to survive and even grow.

There is evidence to suggest that nonprofit organizations fared relatively well during the recession compared to their for profit counterparts due to substantial partnerships with government agencies across a wide variety of fields. This strategic partnership allowed nonprofits to continue to serve vulnerable communities even at a time when the number of those in need expanded due to the negative financial, physical, and emotional impact of the recession. Of course, nonprofit organizations had other coping strategies such as increased fundraising efforts, increased collaborative work, staff consolidation and greater reliance on volunteers (Salamon 2009).

In New York and Los Angeles, in particular, the impact of the recession and the subsequent coping mechanisms by nonprofit organizations is similar to many organizations across the country. The difference, however, may be the well-established partnerships between local governments and the nonprofit sector in New York and the relatively nascent ones in Los Angeles. As such, New York nonprofits may be more "buffered" from the economic recession relative to Los Angeles nonprofits. Despite the data showing that the New York region experienced a decrease in organizational foundings compared to Los Angeles in 2008, the effect of the recession on established nonprofits may be less severe.

NOTES

1. While there may be notable exceptions in other areas, the authors are aware of the following regional nonprofit sector studies: in Los Angeles by the UCLA Center for

Civil Society, previously directed by Helmut K. Anheier (http://civilsociety.ucla.
edu/); in New York by The New York City Nonprofits Project, co-directed by John
Seley and Julian Wolpert (http://www.nycnonprofits.org); in Indiana by the Center
on Philanthropy at Indiana University directed by Kirsten Gronbjerg (http://www.
indiana.edu/~nonprof/index.php); in San Diego, CA, by the Caster Family Center for
Nonprofit and Philanthropic Research at the University of San Diego; and finally the
"Listening Posts" project by the Center for Civil Society Studies at the Johns Hopkins
Institute for Policy Studies directed by Lester M. Salamon (http://www.ccss.jhu.
edu/).

2. As mentioned previously, while research on the nonprofit sector in each region has
   been conducted independently, we know of little work that has attempted to offer a
   comparative perspective.
3. The socioeconomic, cultural, political, and racial diversity of each region is well documented in other chapters of this book and will not be discussed in great detail here.
   The geographical boundaries for comparison will be New York City (e.g., New York,
   Bronx, Richmond, Queens, and Kings Counties) and Los Angeles County. For the purposes of this chapter, these two geographical boundaries are more comparable than
   the larger Consolidated Metropolitan Statistical Areas (CMSA) used to compare the
   two regions in the first volume of this book. While the boundaries represent two
   types of administrative structures (e.g., city and county governments), Los Angeles
   County captures a comparable population in terms of size and diversity compared to
   the City of New York. In 2009, the population estimates for both regions were 8.4
   million for New York City and about 10.4 million for Los Angeles County.
4. Employment data obtained from the Bureau of Labor Statistics Quarterly Census of
   Employment and Wages for local government employers in all industries, by county,
   2009.
5. Government expenditure data is drawn from the Comprehensive Annual Financial
   Reports for the City of New York; the County of Los Angeles, and the ten largest cities
   with Los Angeles County (City of Los Angeles; Long Beach, Glendale, Santa Clarita,
   Lancaster, Palmdale, Pomona, Torrance, Pasadena, El Monte) for FY 2009.
6. Using financial data reported by nonprofits to the IRS on its annual Form 990, the
   focus of this section will be on the comparative size, scale, and scope of the nonprofit
   sectors as measured by the number of organizations and total expenditures.
7. Source: National Center for Charitable Statistics; US Department of Commerce,
   Bureau of Economic Analysis.
8. New York City employment figures are estimated for 2011 based on findings from
   the 2002 New York City Nonprofits Project, which found that nonprofit employment
   accounted for about 14 percent of total employment in the City. Applying 14 percent
   to the most recent (November 2011) New York State Department of Labor data suggests that NYC nonprofit employment stands at about 530,000, nearly identical to
   what was reported in 2002.
9. Examples include the Foundation Center, the Nonprofit Finance Fund, etc.
10. Government contributions are defined by the IRS as "a grant or other payment from
    a governmental unit [for the] primary purpose [of enabling] the organization to pro-
    vide a service to, or maintain a facility for, the direct benefit of the public rather than
    to serve the direct and immediate needs of the governmental unit." These include
    construction of public facilities (i.e., museums, libraries) or payments to social service
    providers to better service members of the community (i.e., nursing homes, child care
    organizations, etc.) (2008 IRS Instructions for Form 990). Excluded are payments
    by governments to individuals in the form of vouchers. Vouchers are a form of "fees

for service, earned income, or program service revenue" (IRS Form 990) and revenue from private payers, as well as government-subsidized payers, is not distinguishable in the data. Contributions from a "government unit" may include local, state, and federal entities.

11. A note of caution is in order, as the government contribution line in the Form 990 only includes grant funding. However, most government funding comes in the form of contracting, which is not accounted for here. Revenues nonprofits receive through services provided under government contracts fall under Program Service Revenue and cannot easily (if at all) be parsed out from other forms of fee-related income. Therefore, it is best to interpret the data on government grants as the minimum public sector support of nonprofits.

12. Current New York Mayor Michael Bloomberg—himself a billionaire philanthropist—developed close ties to the local nonprofit sector. In Los Angeles, it was not until the creation of a dedicated post in the mayor's office on philanthropy in 2007 that local nonprofit leaders and the city government could connect institutionally.

BIBLIOGRAPHY

Abramson, Paul R., John H. Aldrich, and David W. Rohde. 2011. *Change and Continuity in the 2008 and 2010 Elections*. Washington, DC: Congressional Quarterly Press.

Abrahams, Michael. 2009. "Conceptual Design of an East River Storm Surge Barrier." ASCE Met Section Infrastructure Group, New York Academy of Sciences & Polytechnic Institute of NYU, Department of Civil Engineering. Available online: http://www.ascemetsection.org/content/view/274/725/#2009

Abu-Lughod, Janet L. 1999. *New York, Chicago, Los Angeles: America's Global Cities*. Minneapolis: University of Minnesota Press.

Abu-Lughod, Janet L. 2007. *Race, Space, and Riots in Chicago, New York, and Los Angeles*. New York: Oxford University Press.

Adams, James Ring. 1979. "The New York City Crisis: Centralization by Default." *Publius* 9(1) (Winter 1979): 97–104.

Airbnb.com. 2012. Available at www.airbnb.com/sandy.

Algar, Selim, Kieran Crowley, and Lucas Alport. 2008. "Hate Roots Not Skin Deep: Immigration Overflow Fuels LI Tension." *New York Post*, November 22.

Allard, S. W. 2009. *Out of Reach: Place, Poverty, and the New American Welfare State*. New Haven, CT: Yale University Press.

Allen, Robert C. 1999. "Home Alone Together: Hollywood and the 'Family Film.'" In *Hollywood Spectatorship: Changing Perception of Cinema Audiences*, edited by Melvyn Stokes and Richard Maltby. London: BFI Pub.

Aloff, Mindy. 1997. "Where China and Brooklyn Overlap." *New York Times*, February 7, C1.

Alpert, Daniel, Robert Hockett, and Nouriel Roubini. 2011. "The Way Forward: Moving from the Post-Bubble, Post-Bust Economy to Renewed Growth and Competitiveness." *New America Foundation*, October 10.

Alpert, G., et al. 2006. Analysis Group, Inc., Pedestrian and Motor Vehicle Post-Stop Data Analysis Report.

Al Sayyad, Nezar. 2006. *Cinematic Urbanism: A History of the Modern from Reel to Real*. London: Routledge.

Alter, Jonathan. 2010. "A Case of Senioritis." *Newsweek*, November 28.

American Community Survey. 2005–09. New York City Chinatown: http://www.socialexplorer.com/pub/reportdata/htmlresults.aspx?ReportId=R10099416&Page=3; Los Angeles Chinatown: http://www.socialexplorer.com/pub/reportdata/htmlresults.aspx?ReportId=R10100128.

Anderson, Nels. 1923. *The Hobo: The Sociology of the Homeless Man*. Chicago: University of Chicago Press.

Anderson, Troy. 2009. "LA Criticized as 'Meanest City' in America." *Los Angeles Daily News*, July 14, A1.

Andranovich, G., and G. Riposa. 1998. "Is Governance the Lost Hard 'G' in Los Angeles?" *Cities* 15(3): 185–92.

Angotti, Tom. 2008. *New York for Sale: Community Planning Confronts Global Real Estate.* Cambridge, MA: MIT Press.

Anheier, H. K. 2005. *Nonprofit Organizations: Theory, Management, Policy.* London and New York: Routledge.

Anheier, H. K., and D. Hammack, eds. 2010. *American Foundations.* Washington, DC: Brookings.

Anheier, H. K., and D. Howard. 2012. "Foundations in Los Angeles." UCLA, Luskin School of Public Affairs, Center for Civil Society, Los Angeles, unpublished manuscript.

Anheier, H. K., and L. M. Salamon. 2006. "The Nonprofit Sector in Comparative Perspective." In *The Nonprofit Sector: A Research Handbook,* edited by W. W. Powell and R. Steinberg, 89–114. New Haven, CT: Yale University Press.

Appelbaum, Binyamin. 2012. "A Federal Open Market Committee Meeting on March 28, 2006." *New York Times,* January 12.

Applebome, Peter. 2012. "Despite 2009 Deal, Affordable Housing Roils Westchester." *New York Times,* April 3.

Arax, Mark. 1987. "Monterey Park: The Nation's First Suburban Chinatown." *Los Angeles Times,* April 6, 1.

Arian, Asher, Arthur Golberg, John Mollenkopf, and Edward Rogowsky. 1991. *Changing New York City Politics.* New York: Routledge.

Assembly Select Committee on the California Middle Class. 1998. The Distribution of Income in California and Los Angeles: A Look at Recent Current Population Survey and State Taxpayer Data. Sacramento: California State Legislature.

Ayres, Ian, and Jonathan Borowsky. 2008. *Racial Profiling & the LAPD: A Study of Racially Disparate Outcomes in the Los Angeles Police Department.* Los Angeles: American Civil Liberties Union of Southern California. Available at: http://islandia.law.yale.edu/ ayres/Ayres%20LAPD%20Report.pdf.

Baade, Robert A. 2003. "Los Angeles City Controllers Report on Economic Impact: Staples Center." Los Angeles City Controller's Office. Available at: http://controller.lacity. org/stellent/groups/ElectedOfficials/@CTR_Contributor/documents/Contributor_ Web_Content/LACITYP_008662.pdf.

Bagli, Charles V. 2010. "Court Upholds Columbia Campus Expansion Plan." *New York Times,* June 24.

Barber, Stephen. 2002. *Projected Cities: Cinema and Urban Space.* London: Reaktion.

Barofsky, Neil M. 2011. "Where the Bailout Went Wrong." *New York Times,* March 29.

Baum, Geraldine. 2009. "Expert Who Helped New York City Avoid Bankruptcy in 1975 Has Some Advice for California: Felix Rohatyn Says the Key Is Gutsy Political Leadership and a Realistic Plan That Includes Sacrifices by Everybody." *Los Angeles Times,* May 23.

Baumgarten, Max. 2010. "Reel Movement: Hollywood's Depiction of Transportation in Los Angeles throughout the Postwar Era." UCLA Department of History, unpublished paper.

BBC News. 1999. "NYPD Officer Jailed for Brutality." Available at: http://news.bbc.co.uk/2/ hi/americas/563441.stm.

Been, Vicki, Caitlyn Brazill, Samuel Dastrup, Ingrid Gould Ellen, John Infranca, Simon McDonnell, Mary Weselcouch, and Michael Williams. 2011. "State of the City's Housing and Neighborhoods, 2011." New York: New York University, Furman Center for Real Estate and Urban Policy. Available at: http://furmancenter.org/research/ sonychan/.

Been, Vicki, Sewin Chan, Ingrid Gould Ellen, and Josiah R. Madar. 2011. "Decoding the Foreclosure Crisis: Causes, Responses, and Consequences." *Journal of Policy Analysis and Management* 30(2) (Spring): 388–96.

Belkin, David. 2010. "Wall Street Wages: A Rough Ride on Easy Street." Independent Budget Office Web Blog, June 8. Available at: http://ibo.nyc.ny.us/cgi-park/?p=169.

Belkin, David, and Eldar Beiseitov. 2007. "Comparing State and Local Taxes in Large U.S. Cities." Independent Budget Office. Available at: http://www.ibo.nyc.ny.us/ibore-ports/CSALTFINAL.pdf.

Berg, Bruce F. 2008. *New York City Politics: Governing Gotham*. New Brunswick, NJ: Rutgers University Press.

Berk, Richard A., and John MacDonald. 2010. "Policing the Homeless: An Evaluation of Efforts to Reduce Homeless-Related Crime." *Criminology and Public Policy* 9(4): 813–40.

Beveridge, Andrew. 2011. "Commonalities and Contrasts in the Development of Major United States Urban Areas: A Spatial and Temporal Analysis from 1910 to 2000." In *Navigating Time and Space in Population Studies*, edited by Myron Guttman, Glenn D. Deane, Emily R. Merchant, and Kenneth M. Sylvester. Dordrecht: Springer for the International Union for the Scientific Study of Population.

Bhakta, Priyesh. 2011. "Los Angeles Rent Stabilization Ordinance: A Closer Look." University of Southern California, Lusk Center for Real Estate, working paper.

Bielefeld, W. 2000. "Metropolitan Nonprofit Sectors: Findings from NCCS Data." *Nonprofit and Voluntary Sector Quarterly* 29(2): 298–314.

Bill and Melinda Gates Foundation. 2008. "All Students Ready for College, Careers and Life: Reflections on the Foundation's Education Investments 2000–2008." September. Available at: http://www.gatesfoundation.org/learning/Documents/reflections-fou ndations-education-investments.pdf.

"Bill Gates' School Crusade." 2010. *Bloomberg Businessweek Magazine*, July 15. Available at: http://www.businessweek.com/magazine/content/10_30/b4188058281758.htm.

Binham, Caroline. 2012. "US Woman Takes Fight to Banks in First Homeowner Libor Class Action," *Financial Times*, October 15.

Bishop, Bill, with Robert G. Cushing. 2008. *The Big Sort: Why the Clustering of Like-Minded America Is Tearing Us Apart*. Boston: Houghton Mifflin.

Black, Donald. 1980. *Manners and Customs of the Police*. San Diego, CA: Academic Press, Inc.

Blake, Richard. 2005. *Street Smart: The New York of Lumet, Allen, Scorsese, and Lee*. Lexington: University Press of Kentucky.

Blasi, Gary, and Forrest Stuart. 2008. "Has the Safer Cities Initiative in Skid Row Reduced Serious Crime?" Los Angeles: UCLA School of Law. Available at: http://lampcommu-nity.org/docs/skid/Has_the_Safer_Cities_Initiative_Reduced_Serious_Crime.pdf.

Blasi, Gary, and the UCLA School of Law Fact Investigation Clinic. 2007. "Policing Our Way Out of Homelessness?: The First Year of the Safer Cities Initiative on Skid Row." Los Angeles: Inter-University Consortium on Homelessness. Available at: http://www.lafla.org/pdf/policinghomelessness.pdf.

Bloom, Howard S., Saskia Levy Thompson, and Rebecca Unterman. 2010. *Transforming the High School Experience: How New York City's New Small Schools Are Boosting Student Achievement and Graduation Rates*. New York: MDRC.

Bloomberg, Michael. 2007. "PlaNYC: A Greener, Greater New York, NY." New York: The City of New York.

Bloomberg, Michael. 2011. "Mayor Bloomberg Op-Ed: N.Y.C. Deserves Better Treatment in Andrew Cuomo's State Budget." *NY Daily News*, February 2. Available at:

http://articles.nydailynews.com/2011-02-02/news/27738555_1_local-aid-pensio
n-benefits-state-budget.

Bloomberg, Michael. 2012. Mayor Bloomberg State of the City Address—NYC: Capital of
Innovation. January 12, 2012. Available at: http://www.mikebloomberg.com/index.
cfm?objectid=CD40EE15-C29C-7CA2-F853754735274DC2.

Blume, Howard. 2008a. "Charter Schools Get Boost; L.A. Philanthropist Eli Broad is
Donating $23.3 Million to Create 17 New Campuses Run by Two Major Groups." *Los
Angeles Times*, January 17.

Blume, Howard. 2008b. "Power to Change Schools Sought." *Los Angeles Times*, June 28.

Blume, Howard, 2008c. "School Rejects Aid by Riordan." *Los Angeles Times*, October 15.

Blume, Howard. 2008d. "Space for Charter Schools Rescinded." *Los Angeles Times*, May 1.

Blume, Howard. 2008e. "Villaraigosa and His Partners Set for School to Start." *Los Angeles
Times*, July 1.

Blumstein, Alfred J. 1995–96. "Youth Violence, Guns, and the Illicit-Drug Industry."
Journal of Criminal Law & Criminology 86: 10–36.

Blumstein, Alfred J., and Joel Wallman, eds. 2000. *The Crime Drop in America*. New York:
Cambridge University Press.

Boburg, Shawn, and John Reitmeyer. 2012. "Dozens of Port Authority Jobs go to Christie
Loyalists." *The Record*, January 28.

Boghossian, Naush. 2008. "School Chief's Duties Shift: Cortines Takes Over Day-to-Day
Operations for Superintendent Brewer." *Daily News* (Los Angeles, CA), May 2.

Bowers, Josh. (2010). "Legal Guilt, Normative Innocence, and the Equitable Decision Not
to Prosecute," *Columbia Law Review* 110: 1655–1726.

Bowles, Samuel, Steve Durlauf, and Karla Hoff, eds. 2006. *Poverty Traps*. Princeton, NJ:
Princeton University Press.

Box, R. C. and Musso, J. 2004. "Experiments with Local Federalism: Secession and the
Neighborhood Council Movement in Los Angeles." *American Review of Public
Administration* 34: 259–76.

Bradley, Ann. 2008. "LA District, Charter Groups Settle Lawsuit over Facilities." *Education
Week*, February 20.

Braithwaite, Tom, and Aline van Duyn. 2011. "A Disappearing Act?" *Financial Times*, July 21.

Bratton, William, and Peter Knobler. 1998. *The Turnaround: How America's Top Cop Reversed
the Crime Epidemic*. New York: Random House.

Braude, Marvin, and Zev Yaroslavsky. 1987. "Pro U: Debate Goes on." *Los Angeles Times*.
March 29, 17.

Brewer, David L. 2008. Superintendent's Strategic Plan for High Priority Schools [July
2008 to June 2013]. Los Angeles, CA: Los Angeles Unified School District.

Briffault, Richard. 1999. "The Business Improvement District Comes of Age." *Drexel Law
Review* 3: 19–33.

Brint, Steven, et al. 2007. "A New Generation: Ethnicity, Socioeconomic Status, Immigration
and the Undergraduate Experience at the University of California." Berkeley: Center
for Studies in Higher Education, Student Experience Research Project. Available at:
http://cshe.berkeley.edu/publications/docs/SERU.NewGenerationReport2007.pdf.

Broad Foundation. 2012. "Become a Leader in Education." Available at: http://www.broad-
center.org/residency/.

Brooklyn Chinese-American Association. 2011. "The Bluer Sky: A History of the Brooklyn
Chinese-American Association". Available at: http://www.bca.net/eng/about.html.

Brown, Peter Hendee. 2009. *America's Waterfront Revival*. Philadelphia: University of
Pennsylvania Press.

Bruch, Elizabeth E., and Robert D. Mare. 2006. "Neighborhood Choice and Neighborhood
Change." *American Journal of Sociology* 112: 667–709.

Bryant, Nelson. 1968. "Wood, Field and Stream; Sierra Club Joins Protest of the Paving of Jamaica Bay to Expand Airport." *New York Times,* April 30, 56.

Buchheister, Carl. 1969. "Jamaica Bay's Wildlife." *New York Times,* July 28, 30.

Buckley, Cara. 2011. "Albany Deal Closes Rent Regulation Loophole for Landlords." *New York Times,* June 23. Available at: http://www.nytimes.com/2011/06/23/nyregion/albany-deal-closes-rent-regulation-loophole-for-landlords.html?ref=carabuckley.

Buder, Leonard. 1989. "New York School Board Faulted for the Disarray of Local Districts." *New York Times,* January 7.

Bureau of Economic Analysis, U.S. Department of Commerce. 2011. "GDP by Metropolitan Area, Advance 2010, and Revised 2007–2009." September 13, table 1. Available at: http://www.bea.gov/newsreleases/regional/gdp_metro/gdp_metro_newsrelease.htm.

Burgess, E. W. 1925. "The Growth of the City." In *The City,* edited by R. E. Park, E. W. Burgess, and R. D. McKenzie. Reprint. Chicago: University of Chicago Press.

California Air Resources Board (CARB). 2008. "Methodology for Estimating Premature Deaths Associated with Long Term Exposure to Fine Airborne Particulate Matter in California." October 2008. Available at: http://www.arb.ca.gov/research/health/pm-mort/PMmortalityreportFINALR10–24–08.pdf.

California Department of Finance. 2012. "2011–2012 Budget, Introduction." Available at: http://2011–12.archives.ebudget.ca.gov/pdf/Enacted/BudgetSummary/FullBudgetSummary.pdf.

California State Controller. Various years. *Community Redevelopment Agencies Annual Report.*

Calmes, Jackie. 2012. "In Speech, Obama to Draw Line on the Economy." *New York Times,* January 22.

Camarillo, Albert. 2004. "Black and Brown in Compton: Demographic Change, Suburban Decline, and Intergroup Relations in a South Central Los Angeles Community, 1950–2000." In *Not Just Black and White: Immigration, Race, and Ethnicity in Historical and Comparative Perspective in the United States,* edited by Nancy Foner and George Fredrickson. New York: Russell Sage Foundation.

Cannato, Vincent. 2002. *The Ungovernable City: John V. Lindsay and His Struggle to Save New York City.* New York: Basic Books.

Cardwell, Diane. 2003. "Mayor Says New York is Worth the Cost." *New York Times,* January 8.

Cassuto, David. 2010. "The CAFO Hothouse: Climate Change, Industrial Agriculture and the Law." Animals & Society Institute Policy Paper. Available at SSRN: http://ssrn.com/abstract=1646484.

Castells, Manuel. 1989. *The Informational City: Information Technology, Economic Restructuring, the Urban-Regional Process.* Oxford: Basil Blackwell.

Cavanagh, Sean. 2011. "Race to Top Winners Feel Heat on Teacher Evaluations." *Education Week,* September 14.

Cech, Sharon. 2010. "A California Network of Regional Food Hubs." Los Angeles: Urban & Environmental Policy Institute, September. Available at: http://departments.oxy.edu/uepi/publications/RFH-N.pdf.

Center for Research on Education Outcomes. 2009. "Multiple Choice: Charter School Performance in 16 States." Stanford, CA: Stanford University, CREDO. Available at: http://credo.stanford.edu/reports/MULTIPLE_CHOICE_CREDO.pdf.

Center for Research on Education Outcomes. 2010. Charter School Performance in New York City. Stanford, CA: Stanford University, CREDO. Available at: http://credo.stanford.edu/reports/NYC%202009%20_CREDO.pdf.

Central Intelligence Agency. 2011. *The World Factbook*. Available at: https://www.cia.gov/library/publications/the-world-factbook/rankorder/2172rank.html.

Chen, Sewell, and Louise Story. 2010. "Goldman Pays $550 Million to Settle Fraud Case." *New York Times*, July 15.

Chaves, M. 2002. "Religious Congregations." In *State of Nonprofit America*, edited by L. M. Salamon. Washington, DC: Brookings Institution Press.

Chernick, H. 2005. "Introduction." In *Resilient City*, edited by H. Chernick. New York: Russell Sage Foundation.

Chin, Margaret M. 2005a. *Sewing Women: Immigrants and the New York City Garment Industry*. New York: Columbia University Press.

Chin, Margaret M. 2005b. "Moving On: Chinese Garment Workers After 9/11." *In Wounded City*, edited by Nancy Foner. New York: Russell Sage Foundation.

Citizens Budget Commission. 2011. "A Poor Way to Pay for Medicaid: Why New York Should Eliminate Local Funding for Medicaid." December. Available at: http://www.cbcny.org/sites/default/files/REPORT_Medicaid_12122012.pdf.

Citizens Housing and Planning Council. 2002. "A Proposal to Enhance Tax and Zoning Incentives for New Housing Production." New York: CHPC Policy Paper. September.

City of Monterey Park. 2011. "Atlantic Times Square Project." Available at: http://www.ci.monterey-park.ca.us/Index.aspx?page=1403.

Clarke, David, ed. 1997. *The Cinematic City*. New York: Routledge.

Clemens, E. S., and Guthrie, D. 2010. *Politics & Partnerships: The Role of Voluntary Associations in America's Political Past and Present*. Chicago and London: University of Chicago Press.

Clinton, Bill. 2011. *Back to Work: Why We Need Smart Government for a Strong Economy*. New York: Knopf.

CNN/Money.com. 2011. "Fortune 500: Our Annual Ranking of America's Largest Corporations." Available at: http://money.cnn.com/magazines/fortune/fortune500/2010/snapshots/2255.html.

Cohan, William. 2011. "Don't Let Go of the Anger." *New York Times*, May 11.

Cohen, Jerry, and William S. Murphy. 1966. *Burn, Baby, Burn!: The Los Angeles Race Riot, August 1965*. New York: E. Dutton.

Commercial Club of Chicago. 2009. "Still Left Behind: Student Learning in Chicago's Public Schools." Civic Committee of the Commercial Club of Chicago. June. Available at: http://www.civiccommittee.org/Still%20Left%20Behind%20v2.pdf.

Common Dreams. 2003. "New York City Council Adopts Resolution Approving Iraq War." Available at: http://www.commondreams.org/headlines.shtml?/headlines 03/0312-12.htm.

Community Service Society of New York. 2003. "CSS Helps Families in Need Save their Homes through Jiggetts Relief." Social Services Department.

Comptroller of the City of Los Angeles. 2006–07. Annual Financial Report for Fiscal Year.

Comptroller of the City of New York. 2006–07. Comprehensive Financial Report for Fiscal Year.

Confessore, Nicholas. 2012. "Campaign Aid Is Now Surging into 8 Figures." *New York Times*, June 13.

Congressional Budget Office. 2011. "Trends in the Distribution of Household Income, between 1979 and 2007." October.

Connell, Rich. 1986. "Prop. U Backers See It as Start of Land-Use Revolt." *Los Angeles Times*, October 12, 1.

Conway, Nick. 2003. "San Gabriel Valley Regional Demographic Profile: Indicator Report." Pasadena: San Gabriel Council of Governments.

Cook, Philip J., and John H. Laub. 1998. "The Unprecedented Epidemic of Youth Violence." *Crime and Justice: A Review of Research* 24: 27–64.

Cook, Philip J., and John H. Laub. 2002. "After the Epidemic: Recent Trends in Youth Violence in the United States." *Crime and Justice: A Review of Research* 29: 1–37.

Corcoran, Sean. 2010. *Can Teachers be Evaluated by their Students' Test Scores? Should They Be?: The Use of Value-Added Measures of Teacher Effectiveness in Policy and Practice.* Annenberg Institute for School Reform at Brown University. Providence, RI: Brown University.

Cordero-Guzman, Hector R. 2011. "Main Stream Support for a Mainstream Movement: The 99% Movement Comes From and Looks Like the 99%." School of Public Affairs, Baruch College. Available at: http://www.occupywallst.org/media/pdf/OWS-profile 1-10-18-11-sent-v2-HRCG.pdf.

County of Los Angeles Public Health. 2010. "Trends in Diabetes: A Reversible Public Health Crisis." November. Available at: http://publichealth.lacounty.gov/ha/reports/habriefs/2007/diabetes/Diabetes_Secure/Diabetes_2010_6pg_Sfinal.pdf.

Cunningham, Lynn. 1976. "Venice, California: From City to Suburb." Ph.D. dissertation, UCLA.

Currid, E. 2007. *The Warhol Economy*. Princeton, NJ: Princeton University Press.

Cutler, David M., Edward L. Glaeser, and Jacob L. Vigdor. 1999. "The Rise and Decline of the American Ghetto." *Journal of Political Economy* 107: 455–506.

Dahmann, Nicholas. 2010. "For Maps! Working through Cartographic Anxiety in Downtown Los Angeles." *Urban Geography* 31(6): 717–23.

Danielson, Michael N., and Jameson W. Doig, 1982. *New York: The Politics of Urban Regional Development*. Berkeley: University of California Press.

Davey, Monica, and Steven Yaccino. 2012. "Teachers End Chicago Strike on Second Try." *New York Times*, September 18.

Davies, Garth, and Jeffrey Fagan. 2012. "Crime and Enforcement in Immigrant Neighborhoods: Evidence from New York City," *Annals of the American Society of Political and Social Science* 641: 99–124.

Davis, Mike. 1990. *City of Quartz: Excavating the Future in Los Angeles*. London: Haymarket Press.

Dawes, S. S., and J. R. Saidel. 1988. "The State and the Voluntary Sector: A Report of New York State Project 2000." Rockefeller Institute of Government, SUNY, The Foundation Center.

De Vany, Arthur. 2004. *Hollywood Economics: How Extreme Uncertainty Shapes the Film Industry*. London: Routledge.

De Vany, Arthur S., and W. David Walls. 1996. "Bose–Einstein Dynamics and Adaptive Contracting in the Motion Picture Industry." *Economic Journal* 439(106): 1493–1514.

Dear, Michael. 1992. "Understanding and Overcoming the NIMBY Syndrome." *Journal of the American Planning Association* 58(3) (Summer): 288–300.

Dear, M., and S. Flusty. 1998. "Postmodern Urbanism." *Annals of the Association of American Geographers* 88(1): 5–72.

Decker, Geoff. 2012. "New York has a 'Parent Trigger'-like Law that Mostly Sits Fallow." Gotham Schools (September 20). Available at: http://gothamschools.org.

Department of Neighborhood Empowerment. 2008. "Neighborhood Council Status Report." April 9. Available at: http://ens.lacity.org/done/certreport/donenewsflash_c94014785_10222003.pdf.

Deverell, William Francis. 1994. *Railroad Crossing: Californians and the Railroad, 1850–1910*. Berkeley: University of California Press.

DeVerteuil, Geoffrey. 2006. "The Local State and Homeless Shelters: Beyond Revanchism?" *Cities* 23(2): 109–20.

Devine, Theresa. 2010. "New York City's Long-Term Unemployment Continues to Outpace U.S. Rate." Independent Budget Office Web Blog, July 30.

Dickey, Christopher. 2009. *Securing the City: Inside America's Best Counterterror Force*. New York: Simon and Schuster.

Dillon, Sam. 2007. "Union-Friendly Maverick Leads New Charge for Charter Schools." *New York Times*, July 24.

DiMassa, Cara Mia. 2007. "Downtown Booms, Civic Center Fizzles." *Los Angeles Times*, July 28, B1.

Dimendberg, Edward. 2004. *Film Noir and the Spaces of Modernity*. Cambridge, MA: Harvard University Press.

DiPasquale, Denise, and Edward Glaeser. 1999. "Incentives and Social Capital: Are Homeowners Better Citizens?" *Journal of Urban Economics* 45: 354–84.

Doig, Jameson W. 1966. *Metropolitan Transportation Politics and the New York Region*. New York: Columbia University Press.

Doig, Jameson W. 2001. *Empire on the Hudson: Entrepreneurial Vision and Political Power at the Port of New York Authority*. New York: Columbia University Press.

Doig, Jameson W. 2012. "Restore Integrity at the Port Authority." *New York Times* (online), February 21.

Domanico, Ray. 2011. "Mayor's Plan for School Budget Savings Overstates Need for Teacher Layoffs." Independent Budget Office Web Blog, June 1. Available at: http://ibo.nyc.ny.us/cgi-park/?p=351.

Downtown Center Business Improvement District. 2006. "The Downtown Los Angeles Renaissance: Economic & Revenue Impacts." Report prepared by Los Angeles County Economic Development Corporation and Lauren Schlau Consulting. Available at: http://www.downtownla.com/pdfs/econ_developments/DCBID%20Economic%20 Impact%20Study%202006%20FINAL.pdf.

Dreier, Peter, et al. 2006. "Movement Mayor: Can Antonio Villaraigosa Change Los Angeles?" *Dissent*, Summer. Available at: http://www.dissentmagazine.org/ article/?article=656.

Dugger, Celia W. 1996. "Queens Old-Timers Uneasy as Asian Influence Grows." *New York Times*, March 31, A1.

Dunstan, Roger. 1995. "Overview of New York City's Fiscal Crisis." California Research Bureau, California State Library, CRB Note, Vol. 3 No. 1, March 1. Available at: http://www.library.ca.gov/crb/95/notes/v3n1.pdf.

Dwyer, Rachel E. 2007. "Expanding Homes and Increasing Inequalities: US Housing Development and the Residential Segregation of the Affluent." *Social Problems* 54(1): 23–46.

Dyble, Louise Nelson. 2009. "Reconstructing Transportation." *Technology and Culture* 50: 237–38.

"Editorial: Too Many Chiefs; LAUSD Has Two Superintendents—One Actual, One a Figurehead." 2008. *Daily News* (Los Angeles, CA), June 19.

Edwards, Richard C. 1979. *Contested Terrain: The Transformation of the Workplace in Twentieth Century*. New York: Harper Torchbooks.

Eisinger, Peter. 2000. "The Politics of Bread and Circuses." *Urban Affairs Review* 35(3): 316–33.

Eliashberg, Jehoshua, Anita Elberse, and Mark Leenders. 2006. "The Motion Picture Industry." *Marketing Science* 25: 638–61.

Eljera, Bert. 1996. "The Chinese Beverly Hills," *Asianweek*, May 24–30. Available at: http://www.asianweek.com/052496/LittleTaipei.html.

Ellen, Ingrid Gould. 2000. "Is Segregation Bad for Your Health? The Case of Low Birth Weight." *Brookings-Wharton Papers on Urban Affairs* 1: 203–38.

Ellen, Ingrid Gould. 2012. "The Housing Crisis and Foreclosures." Paper presented at the Eastern Sociological Society, February.

Ellen, Ingrid Gould, Michael H. Schill, Amy Ellen Schwartz, and Scott Susin. 2001. "Building Homes, Reviving Neighborhoods: Spillovers from Subsidized Construction of Owner-Occupied Housing in New York City." *Journal of Housing Research* 12(2): 185–216.

Employment Development Department, Labor Market Information Division, State of California. 2012. "Industry Employment and Labor Force Information, Table for Los Angeles County." Available at: http://www.calmis.ca.gov/htmlfile/county/califhtm.htm.

English, T. J. 2011. *The Savage City: Race, Murder and a Generation on the Edge*. New York: William Morrow.

Erie, Steven. 2004. *Globalizing L.A.: Trade, Infrastructure, and Regional Development*. Stanford, CA: Stanford University Press.

Erie, Steven. 2006. *Beyond Chinatown: The Metropolitan Water District, Growth, and the Environment in Southern California*. Stanford, CA: Stanford University Press.

Eterno, John A., and Eli B. Silverman. 2012. *The Crime Numbers Game: Management by Manipulation*. New York: CRC Press.

Fagan, J. A. 1990. "Intoxication and Aggression." *Drugs and Crime—Crime and Justice: An Annual Review of Research* 13: 241–320.

Fagan, Jeffrey A. 1992. "Drug Selling and Licit Income in Distressed Neighborhoods: The Economic Lives of Street-Level Drug Users and Dealers." In *Drugs, Crime and Social Isolation: Barriers to Urban Opportunity*, edited by George E. Peterson and Adelle V. Harrell. Washington, DC: Urban Institute Press.

Fagan, Jeffrey A. 1994. "Do Criminal Sanctions Deter Drug Offenders?" In *Drugs and Criminal Justice: Evaluating Public Policy Initiatives*, edited by Doris MacKenzie and Craig Uchida. Newbury Park, CA: Sage Publications.

Fagan, Jeffrey, and Garth Davies. 2000. "Street Stops and Broken Windows: *Terry*, Race and Disorder in New York City." *Fordham Urban Law Journal* 28: 457–504.

Fagan, Jeffrey, and Garth Davies. 2007. "Immigration, Neighborhood Selection and Crime in New York City: Race- and Ethnicity-Specific Effects." Paper presented at the Annual Meeting of the American Society of Criminology, Los Angeles, November.

Fagan, Jeffrey, and Tracey L. Meares. 2008. "Punishment, Deterrence and Social Control: The Paradox of Punishment in Minority Communities." *Ohio State Journal of Criminal Law* 6: 173–229.

Fagan, Jeffrey, Franklin E. Zimring, and June Kim. 1998. "Declining Homicide in New York: A Tale of Two Trends." *Journal of Criminal Law and Criminology* 88: 1277–1324.

Fagan, Jeffrey, Amanda Geller, Garth Davies, and Valerie West. 2010. "Street Stops and Broken Windows Revisited: Race and Order Maintenance Policing in a Safe and Changing City." In *Exploring Race, Ethnicity and Policing: Essential Readings*, edited by S. Rice and M. White. New York: New York University Press.

Fainstein, Susan S. 2001. "Inequality in Global City-Regions." In *Global City-Regions*, edited by Allen J. Scott. New York: Oxford University Press.

Fainstein, Susan S., Ian Gordon, and Michael Harloe. 2011 "Ups and Downs in the Global City: London and New York in the Twenty-First Century. In *The Blackwell Companion to the City*, edited by Gary Bridge and Sophie Watson. 2nd ed. Oxford: Blackwell.

Farley, Reynolds. 2011. "The Waning of American Apartheid?" *Contexts* 103: 36–43.

Farley, Reynolds, and William H. Frey. 1994. "Changes in the Segregation of Whites from Blacks during the 1980s: Small Steps towards a More Integrated Society." *American Sociological Review* 59(1): 23–45.

Farley, Reynolds, Howard Schuman, S. Bianchi, Diane Colasanto, and S. Hatchett. 1978. "Chocolate City, Vanilla Suburbs: Will the Trend toward Racially Separate Communities Continue?" *Social Science Research* 74: 319–44.

Farley, Reynolds, Charlotte Steeh, Tara Jackson, Maria Krysan, and Keith Reeves. 1993. "Continued Racial Residential Segregation in Detroit: 'Chocolate City, Vanilla Suburbs' Revisited." *Journal of Housing Research* 41: 1–38.

Farrell, Robert, 1996. Chair of the Voluntary Advisory Council on Hunger (Memo to Mayor Richard Riordan). April 15.

FBI Uniform Crime Reports. Various years.

Federal Emergency Management Agency. 2012. Sandy Flood Maps. Available at: http://184.72.33.183/GISData/MOTF/.

Felch, Jason, Jason Song, and Doug Smith. 2010. "Who's Teaching L.A.'s Kids? A Times Analysis, Using Data Largely Ignored by LAUSD, Looks at Which Educators Help Students Learn, and Which Held Them Back." *Los Angeles Times*, August 14.

Ferrell, David. 2009. "Harder Than It Looks: Villaraigosa's 'Model' Schools Bite Back." *LA Weekly*, July 7.

Financial Crisis Inquiry Commission. 2011. "The Financial Crisis Inquiry Report: Final Report of the National Commission on the Causes of the Financial Crisis in the United States." New York: Public Affairs.

Fiscal Policy Institute. 2010. "Grow Together or Pull Further Apart? Income Concentration Trends in New York." New York: Fiscal Policy Institute. Available at; http://www.fiscalpolicy.org/FPI_GrowTogetherOrPullFurtherApart_20101213.pdf.

Fischer, Claude S., Gretchen Stockmayer, Jon Stiles, and Michael Hout. 2004. "Distinguishing the Geographic Levels and Social Dimensions of U.S. Metropolitan Segregation, 1960–2000." *Demography* 41(1): 37–59.

Fix, Michael, Margie McHugh, Aaron Terrazas, and Lauren Laglagoran. 2008. *Los Angeles on the Leading Edge: Immigrant Integration Indicators and their Policy Implications.* Washington, DC: Migration Policy Institute. Available at: http://www.migrationpolicy.org/pubs/NCIIP_Los_Angeles_on_the_Leading_Edge.pdf.

Fliegel, Seymour. 1993. *Miracle in East Harlem: The Fight for Choice in Public Education.* New York: Crown.

Foley, Eileen. 2010. *Approaches of Bill & Melinda Gates Foundation-Funded Intermediary Organizations to Structuring and Supporting Small High Schools in New York City.* Washington, DC: Policy Studies Association. February.

Foner, Nancy. 2000. *From Ellis Island to JFK: New York's Two Great Waves of Immigration.* New Haven, CT: Yale University Press.

Foner, Nancy. 2005. *In a New Land: A Comparative View of Immigration.* New York: New York University Press.

Foner, Nancy. 2007. "How Exceptional is New York? Migration and Multiculturalism in the Empire City." *Ethnic and Racial Studies* 30: 999–1023.

Foner, Nancy. 2011. "Remaking the New York Mainstream: The Impact of the Immigrant Past on the Immigrant Present in America's Quintessential Immigrant City." Paper presented at Amsterdam-New York conference, University of Amsterdam, January.

Foner, Nancy. Forthcoming. "Immigration History and the Remaking of New York." In *New York and Amsterdam: Immigration and the New Urban Landscape,* edited by Nancy Foner, Jan Rath, Jan Willem Duyvendak, and Rogier van Reekum. New York: New York University Press.

Fong, Joe C. 2003. *Complementary Education and Culture in the Global/Local Chinese Community.* San Francisco: China Books and Periodicals.

Fong, Timothy. 1994. *The First Suburban Chinatown: The Remaking of Monterey Park, California*. Philadelphia: Temple University Press.

Fox, Julian. 1996. *Woody: Movies from Manhattan*. London: B. T. Bratsford.

Franks, Nino. 1946. "Un nouveau genre 'policier': L'aventure criminelle." *L'Ecranfrancais* 61 (August 28): 14–16.

Frieden, Bernard J., and Lynne B. Sagalyn. 1991. *Downtown, Inc.: How America Rebuilds Cities*. Cambridge, MA: MIT Press.

Friedman, Paul David. 1978. "Fear of Flying: The Development of Los Angeles International Airport and the Rise of Public Protest over Jet Aircraft Noise." M.A. thesis, University of California, Santa Barbara.

Friedmann, Jonathan. 1986. "The World City Hypothesis." *Development and Change* 17(1); 69–83.

Fruchter, Norm. 2008. "'Plus Ca Change....': Mayoral Control in New York City." In *The Transformation of Great American School Districts: How Big Cities are Reshaping Public Education*, edited by William Lowe Boyd, Charles Taylor Kerchner, and Mark Blyth. Cambridge, MA: Harvard Education Press.

Fuchs, Ester. 1992. *Mayors and Money: Fiscal Policy in New York and Chicago*. American Politics and Political Economy Series. Chicago: University of Chicago Press.

Fukuyama, Francis. 1992. *The End of History and the Last Man*. New York: Free Press.

Fuller, Bruce. 2010. "Palace Revolt in Los Angeles?" *Education Next* 10 (Summer): 20–28. Available at: http://educationnext.org/palace-revolt-in-los-angeles/.

Fulton, William. 2001. *The Reluctant Metropolis: The Politics of Urban Growth in Los Angeles*. Baltimore, MD: The Johns Hopkins University Press.

Fung, Amanda. 2012. "Wall St. Checks out of NY Housing." *Crain's New York Business Review*, February 6.

Furman Center for Real Estate and Urban Policy at New York University. 2011. "State of New York's Subsidized Housing: 2011." Available at: http://furmancenter.org/files/publications/SHIPReportFinal.pdf.

Futch, David. 2008. "Echo Park's Gentrification Woes: A Nasty Neighborhood Council Election Marks a Divide Emerging Citywide." *L.A. Weekly*, June 26.

Gabler, Neal. 1988. *An Empire of their Own: How the Jews Invented Hollywood*. New York: Doubleday Anchor.

Gandy, Matthew. 1999. *Concrete and Clay: Reworking Nature in New York City*. Cambridge, MA: MIT Press.

Gans, Herbert. 1974. *Popular Culture and High Culture*. New York: Basic Books.

Gapper, John. 2012. "The ascent of New York meets the rise of the Oceans." *Financial Times,* November 1.

Gardner, K., and S. Sittig. 2010. "Economic Impact of University of Rochester and its Affiliates." Center for Governmental Research. Available at: http://www.cgr.org/reports/10_R-1612_Economic%20Impact%20of%20UR%20and%20Affiliates.pdf.

Garland, David. 2001. *Culture of Control: Crime and Social Order in Contemporary Society* Chicago: University of Chicago Press.

Garrison, Jessica. 2004. "Class Struggle on Venice Boardwalk." *Los Angeles Times*, July 12, A1.

Garrison, Jessica, et al. 2004. "Wal-Mart to Push Southland Agenda." *Los Angeles Times*, April 8.

Garvin, Alexander. 2002. *The American City: What Works and What Doesn't*. 2nd ed. New York: McGraw Hill.

Gascón, George. 2005. "CompStat Plus: In-Depth Auditing, Mentorship, Close Collaboration." *The Police Chief* 72 (May): 34–43.

Gates, Bill. 2008. "A Forum on Education in America: Bill Gates." Bill & Melinda Gates Foundation. Available at: http://www.gatesfoundation.org/speeches-commentary/ Pages/bill-gates-2008-education-forum-speech.aspx.

Gauderman, W. J., E. Avol, F. Gilliland, et al. 2004. "The Effect of Air Pollution on Lung Development from 10 to 18 Years of Age." *New England Journal of Medicine* 351:1057–67.

Gauderman, W. J., H. Vora, R. McConnell, K. Berhane, F. Gilliland, D. Thomas, F. Lurmann, E. Avol, N. Kunzli, M. Jerrett, and J. Peters. 2007. "Effect of Exposure to Traffic on Lung Development from 10 to 18 Years of Age: A Cohort Study." *Lancet* 369(9561): 571–77.

Gebeloff, Robert, and Shaila Dewan. 2012. "Measuring the Top 1% by Wealth, Not Income." *New York Times, Economix Blog,* January 17.

Geller, A. & Fagan, J. 2010. "Pot as Pretext: Marijuana, Race, and the New Disorder in New York City Street Policing". *Journal of Empirical Legal Studies* 7(4): 591–633.

Gelman, Andrew, Jeffrey Fagan, and Alex Kiss. 2007. "An Analysis of the NYPD's Stop-and-Frisk Policy in the Context of Claims of Racial Bias." *Journal of the American Statistical Association* 102: 813–23.

Giles, David. 2011. "Behind the Curb." New York: Center for an Urban Future.

Giuliano, Genevieve, Christian Redfearn, Ajay Agarwal, Chen Li, and Duan Zhuang. 2007. "Employment Concentrations in Los Angeles, 1980–2000." *Environment and Planning A* 39(12): 2935–57.

Gladstone, David L., and Susan S. Fainstein. 2001. "Tourism in US Global Cities: A Comparison of New York and Los Angeles." *Journal of Urban Affairs* 23(1): 23–41.

Gladstone, David L., and Susan S. Fainstein. 2003. "The New York and Los Angeles Economies." In *New York and Los Angeles: Politics, Society, and Culture: A Comparative View,* edited by David Halle. Chicago: University of Chicago.

Glaeser, Edward, and Joseph Gyourko. 2003. "The Impact of Zoning on Housing Affordability." *Federal Reserve Bank of New York Economic Policy Review* 9(3): 21–40.

Glaeser, Edward, and Lloyd James. 2011. *Triumph of the City.* New York: Penguin Books.

Glaeser, Edward, and Erzo Luttmer. 1997. "The Misallocation of Housing under Rent Control." Working Paper 6220. Cambridge, MA: National Bureau of Economic Research.

Glaeser, Edward, and Jesse M. Shapiro. 2002. "The Benefits of the Home Mortgage Deduction." Discussion paper. Cambridge, MA: Harvard Institute for Economic Research.

Glaeser, Edward, and Jacob Vigdor. 2012. "The End of the Segregated Century." *Civic Report* 66, The Manhattan Institute.

Glazer, Nathan, and Daniel Moynihan. 1970. *Beyond the Melting Pot.* 2nd ed. Cambridge, MA: MIT Press.

Glenn, Russell W., Barbara Raymond, Dionne Barnes-Proby, Elizabeth Williams, John Christian, Matthew W. Lewis, Scott Gerwehr, and David Brannan. 2003. "Training the 21st Century Police Officer: Redefining Police Professionalism for the Los Angeles Police Department." Report No. MR1745. Santa Monica, CA: RAND Corporation.

Goering, John. 2004. "Segregation, Race, and Bias: The Role of the US Census, Comments." US Bureau of the Census. Available at: http://www.census.gov/hhes/www/housing/ housing_patterns/pdf/goering.pdf.

Goetz, Edward G. 1992. "Land Use and Homeless Policy in Los Angeles." *International Journal of Urban and Regional Research* 16(4): 540–54.

Goetz, Edward. 2011. "Gentrification in Black and White: The Racial Impact of Public Housing Demolition." *Urban Studies* 48(8): 1581–1604.

Gold, Adam and Matt Apuzzo. 2012. NYPD: Muslim Spying Led to No Leads, Terror Cases. New York: Associated Press. Available at http://www.ap.org/Content/AP-In-The-News/2012/NYPD-Muslim-spying-led-to-no-leads-terror-cases

Goldstein, Paul J. 1985. "The Drugs/Violence Nexus: A Tripartite Conceptual Framework." *Journal of Drug Issues* 15(4): 493–506.

Goldstein, Paul J., Henry H. Brownstein, Patrick J. Ryan, and Patricia A. Bellucci. 1989. "Crack and Homicide in New York City, 1988: A Conceptually Based Event Analysis." *Contemporary Drug Problems* 16(4): 651–87.

Goodman, Peter S. 2008. "Taking a Hard New Look at a Greenspan Legacy." *New York Times*, October 8.

Goodnough, Abby. 2002. "Edward Stancik, 47, New York Schools Investigator, Dies." *New York Times*, March 13.

Gothamist, 2012. "New SI Ferry from Great Kills to Wall Street Starting!" Available at http://gothamist.com/2012/11/20/staten_island_ferry_from_great_kill.php.

Gottlieb, Robert, and Anupama Joshi. 2010. *Food Justice*. Cambridge, MA: MIT Press.

Gottlieb, Robert, et al. 2006. *The Next Los Angeles: The Struggle for a Livable City*. Berkeley: University of California Press.

Greene, Jack R. 1998. "The Road to Community Policing in Los Angeles." A case study in *Community Policing: Contemporary Readings*, edited by G. Alpert and A. Piquero. Prospect Heights, IL: Waveland Press.

Greene, Jack R. 2007. *The Encyclopedia of Police Science*. 3rd ed. New York: Routledge.

Greene, Robert. 2004. "Not in My Neighborhood Council: What Can Save L.A.'s Broken Neighborhood Councils?" *L.A. Weekly*, August 26. Available at: http://www.laweekly.com/content/printVersion/38841/.

Greener Buildings Staff. 2009. "Los Angeles Building Retrofit Designed to Boost Green Jobs." *Greener Buildings*, April 9. Available at: http://www.greenbiz.com/news/2009/04/09/los-angeles-building-retrofit-designed-boost-green-jobs.

Greenhouse, Steven. 2001. "Los Angeles Warms to Labor Unions as Immigrants Look to Escape Poverty." *New York Times*, April 6.

Greider, Thomas, and L. Garkovich. 1994. "Landscapes: The Social Construction of Nature and the Environment." *Rural Sociology* 59: 1–24.

Grind, Kirsten. 2012. *The Lost Bank: The Story of Washington Mutual, the Biggest Bank Failure in American History*. New York: Simon and Schuster.

Grønbjerg, K. A., and L. Paarlberg. 2001. "Community Variations in the Size and Scope of the Nonprofit Sector." *Nonprofit and Voluntary Sector Quarterly* 30(4): 684–706.

Grossman, D. A., L. M. Salamon, and D. M. Altschuler. 1986. *The New York Non Profit Sector in a Time of Government Retrenchment*. Washington, DC: The Urban Institute.

Grossvogel, David. 2003. *Scenes in the City: Film Visions of Manhattan before 9/11*. New York: Lang.

Gyourko, Joseph, and Peter Linneman. 1989. "Equity and Efficiency Aspects of Rent Control: An Empirical Study of New York City." *Journal of Urban Economics* 26: 54–74.

Hacker, Jacob S., and Paul Pierson. 2010. *Winner-Take-All Politics: How Washington Made the Rich Richer—and Turned Its Back on the Middle Class*. New York: Simon and Schuster.

Haimson, Leonnie, and Ann Kjellberg, eds. 2009. *New York City Schools under Bloomberg and Klein: What Parents, Teachers, and Policymakers Need to Know*. New York: Lulu.

Halbfinger, David M., Michael Barbaro, and Fernanda Santos. 2010. "A Trailblazer with an Eye on the Bottom Line." *New York Times*, November 18.

Hall, Stephanie. 2008. "Spinning the Green Wheel." *Pacific Shipper*, October 13.

Halle, David, ed. 2003. *New York & Los Angeles: Politics, Society, and Culture: A Comparative View*. Chicago: University of Chicago Press.

Halle, David and Elisabeth Tiso. 2013. *New York's Far West Side Story: Contemporary Art, The High Line, Mega Projects &Urban Change on Manhattan's Last Frontier*. Chicago: University of Chicago Press, forthcoming.

Harbor Survey Program Report. 2006. Department of Environmental Protection, New York City.

Harcourt, Bernard E. 2005. "Policing L.A.'s Skid Row: Crime and Real Estate Development in Downtown Los Angeles (An Experiment in Real Time)." University of Chicago Legal Forum.

Harcourt, Bernard E., and Jens Ludwig. 2006. "Broken Windows: New Evidence from New York City and a Five-City Social Experiment." *University of Chicago Law Review* 73(1): 271–320.

Harding, Robin, and Tom Braithwaite. 2010. "European Banks Took Big Slice of Fed Aid." *Financial Times*, December 2.

Hasenfeld, Z., H. J. Kil, M. Chen, and W. Parent. 2011. *Stressed and Stretched: The Recession, Poverty, and Human Services Nonprofits in Los Angeles*. Los Angeles: UCLA Center for Civil Society.

Hathaway, Dennis. 2007. "Why Defend the Venice Specific Plan?" *The Free Venice Beachhead*. No. 312.

Haughwout, Andrew, James Orr, and David Bedoll, 2008, The price of land in the New York metropolitan area, Federal Reserve Bank of New York, Current Issues in Economics and Finance: Second District Highlights 14 (3): 1–7.

Hawthorne, Christopher. 2006. "Critic's Notebook: Grand Yes, but Public Expects More." *Los Angeles Times*, April 24, A1.

Hawthorne, Christopher. 2010. "Critic's Notebook: No Game Plan." *Los Angeles Times*. December 30, D1.

Hawthorne, Christopher. 2011. "Architecture Review: HL23 in Manhattan," *Los Angeles Times*, April 4.

Haynes, Bruce, and Ray Hutchison. 2008, "The Ghetto: Origins, History, Discourse." *City & Community* 7: 347–52.

Healy, Jack. 2009. "U.S. Regional Economies Slip and Trade Deficit Grows." *New York Times*, June 11, B3.

Healy, Jack, and Bettina Wassener. 2009. "U.S. Trade Deficit Widens as Value of Exports Falls More than Imports." *New York Times*, May 15, B4.

Heaton, Paul. 2010. "Hidden in Plain Sight: What Cost-of-Crime Research Can Tell Us About Investing in Police." Santa Monica, CA: RAND Corporation. Available at: http://www.rand.org/content/dam/rand/pubs/occasional_papers/2010/RAND_OP279.pdf.

Hemenway, David. 2004. *Private Guns, Public Health*. Ann Arbor: University of Michigan Press.

Hemphill, Clara, and Kim Nauer, with Helen Zelon, Thomaws Jacobs, Alessandra Raimondi, Sharon McCloskey, and Rajeev Yerneni. 2010. "Managing by the Numbers: Empowerment and Accountability in New York City's Schools." Center for New York City Affairs, The New School, June 16. Available at: http://www.newschool.edu/milano/nycaffairs/documents/ManagingByTheNumbers.pdf.

Hendrie, Caroline. 2002. "'Shadow' L.A. District Idea in the Works." *Education Week*, November 27.

Hendrie, Caroline. 2003. "Romer Raises Stakes in L.A. Charter Fight." *Education Week*, May 21.

Henig, Jeffrey R., and Wilbur C. Rich. 2004a. *Mayors in the Middle: Politics, Race, and Mayoral Control of Urban Schools*. Princeton, NJ: Princeton University Press.

Henig, Jeffrey R. and Wilbur C. Rich. 2004b. "Concluding Observations: Governance Structure as a Tool, Not a Solution." In *Mayors in the Middle: Politics, Race, and Mayoral Control of Urban Schools*, edited by Jeffrey R. Henig and Wilbur C. Rich. Princeton, NJ: Princeton University Press.

Hennelley, Robert. 2012. "Amid Budget Wrangling, Council Takes Aim at Soaring NYPD Payouts." WNYC News, May 20. Available at: http://www.wnyc.org/articles/wnyc-news/2012/may/20/nypd-tort/.

Herbert, Bob. 1998a. "A Cop's View." *New York Times*, March 15.

Herbert, Bob. 1998b. "Day of Humiliation." *New York Times*, March 8.

Herbert, Bob, 2008. "'Drop Dead' Is Not an Option." *New York Times*, November 17.

Herbert, Keith. 2012. "JFK Night Arrivals Rise, Complaints Follow." *Newsday*, February 26.

Hernandez, Javier. C. 2010. "Departing Schools Chief: 'We Weren't Bold Enough.'" *New York Times*, December 26.

Herszenhorn, David M. 2004. "Bloomberg Wins on School Tests after Firing Foes." *New York Times*, March 16.

Hill Paul T., Lydia Rainey, and Andrew Rotherham. 2006. *The Future of Charter Schools and Teachers Unions: Results of a Symposium*. National Charter School Research Project, Progressive Policy Institute, Center on Reinventing Public Education, Daniel J. Evans School of Public Affairs, University of Washington, Seattle.

Hinojosa-Ojeda, Raul, and Marshall Fitz. 2011. "Revitalizing the Golden State: What Legalization over Deportation Could Mean to California and Los Angeles County." Center for American Progress, Immigration Policy Center.

Hoch, Charles, and Robert A. Slayton. 1989. *New Homeless and Old: Community and the Skid Row Hotel*. Philadelphia: Temple University Press.

Hogen-Esch, Tom. 2001. "Urban Secession and the Politics of Growth: The Case of Los Angeles." *Urban Affairs Review* 36(6): 783–809.

Holli, Melvin. 1999. *The American Mayor: The Best and Worst Big-City Leaders*. University Park: Pennsylvania State University Press.

Hornblower, Luke. 2011. "Outsourcing Fraud Detection: The Analyst as Dodd-Frank Whistleblower." *Journal of Business and Technology Law*, June 3.

Horton, John. 1995. *The Politics of Diversity: Immigration, Resistance, and Change in Monterey Park, California*. Philadelphia: Temple University Press.

Hricko, Andrea. 2008. "Global Trade Comes Home: Community Impacts of Goods Movement." *Environmental Health Perspectives* 116(2): A78–A81.

HUD USER. 2008. "Picture of Subsidized Households—2008." Available at: http://www.huduser.org/portal/picture2008/index.html.

Hum, Tarry. 2003. "Mapping Global Production in New York City's Garment Industry: The Role of Sunset Park, Brooklyn's Immigrant Economy." *Economic Development Quarterly* 17(3): 294–309.

Human Rights Watch. 1998. "Shielded from Justice: Police Brutality and Accountability in the United States." New York: Human Rights Watch. Available at: http://www.hrw.org/legacy/reports98/police/index.htm.

Iceland, John. 2009. *Where We Live Now*. Berkeley, CA: University of California Press.

Immergluck, Dan. 2009. *Foreclosed: High-Risk Lending, Deregulation, and the Undermining of America's Mortgage Market*. Ithaca, NY: Cornell University Press.

Independent Budget Office. 2000. "Analysis of the Mayor's Executive Budget Capital Plan for 2001–2004." IBO Report. June Available at: http://www.ibo.nyc.ny.us/iboreports/CapitalBudget.pdf.

Independent Budget Office. 2007a. "Analysis of the Mayor's Executive Budget for 2008." May 15.

Independent Budget Office. 2007b. "City's Fiscal Picture Continues to Brighten." January.

Independent Budget Office. 2008. "Tax Revenues Slip, Labor Costs Rise: City's Fiscal Outlook Dims."

Independent Budget Office. 2010. "Fiscal Outlook: While Tax Revenues Improve, Cuts in State Aid Could Widen Gap. December. Available at: http://www.ibo.nyc.ny.us/iboreports/fiscaloutlookdec2010.pdf.

Independent Budget Office. 2011a. "Analysis of the Mayor's Preliminary Budget for 2012." New York: New York City Independent Budget Office. Available at: http://www.scribd.com/doc/51113671/finalmarch2011.

Independent Budget Office. 2011b. "New York City Public School Indicators: Demographics, Resources, Outcomes." Annual Report 2011. New York City: IBO.

Independent Budget Office. 2012a. Debt Service History, http://www.ibo.nyc.ny.us/RevenueSpending/debtservice.xls.

Independent Budget Office. 2012b. Re-estimating the Mayor's Plan: An Analysis of the 2013 Executive Budget and Financial Plan Through 2016.

Independent Budget Office. 2012c. Revenue and Spending Since 1980, http://www.ibo.nyc.ny.us/RevenueSpending/RevandExpSummary.xls.

Independent Commission on the Los Angeles Police Department (Christopher Commission). 1991. Report of the Independent Commission on the Los Angeles Police Department.

Independent Commission on the Los Angeles Police Department (Christopher Commission). 1998. Final Report. Available at: http://www.hrw.org.

Istrate, Emilia, Jonathan Townsend Rothwell, and Bruce Katz. 2010. *Export Nation: How U.S. Metros Lead National Export Growth and Boost Competitiveness*. Washington, DC: Metropolitan Policy Program at Brookings.

Ivry, Bob, Bradley Keoun, and Phil Kuntz. 2011. "Secret Fed Loans Gave Banks $13 Billion Undisclosed to Congress." *Bloomberg Markets Magazine*, November 27.

Jacobs, Michael. 2011. "Analyzing Income Distribution in NYC and Relative NYC Personal Income Tax Liability." Independent Budget Office. December.

Jamaica Bay Eco-Watchers. http://www.jamaicabayecowaters.org.

Jansen, Peter and P. Dircke. 2009. "Verrazano Narrows Storm Surge Barrier." ASCE Met Section Infrastructure Group, New York Academy of Sciences & Polytechnic Institute of NYU, Department of Civil Engineering. Available online: http://www.ascemetsection.org/content/view/274/725/#2009.

Jeffery, C. Ray. 1977. *Crime Prevention through Environmental Design*. Beverly Hills, CA: Sage.

Jeffries, Eric, Robert Kaminski, Steven Holmes, and Dana Hanley. 1997. "The Effect of a Videotaped Arrest on Public Perceptions of Police Use of Force." *Journal of Criminal Justice* 25: 381–95.

Jennings, Jennifer. 2008. "The NYC High School Progress Reports Meet Credit Recovery." Eduwonkette Blog, *Education Week*, November 13.

Jennings, Jennifer L., and Andrew A. Beveridge. 2009. "How Does Test Exemption Affect Schools' and Students' Academic Performance?" *Educational Evaluation and Policy Analysis* (June): 153–75.

Jennings, Jennifer, and Leonie Haimson. 2009. "Discharge and Graduation Rates." In *New York City Schools under Bloomberg and Klein: What Parents, Teachers, and Policymakers Need to Know*, edited by Leonie Haimson and Ann Kjellberg. New York: Lulu.

Jennings, Jennifer, and Aaron Pallas. 2009. "The Racial Achievement Gap." In *New York City Schools under Bloomberg and Klein: What Parents, Teachers, and Policymakers Need to Know*, edited by Leonie Haimson and Ann Kjellberg. New York: Lulu.

Johnson, Bruce D., Terry Williams, Kojo A. Dei, and Harry Sanabria. 1990. "Drug Abuse in the Inner City: Impact on Hard-Drug Users and the Community." *Crime and Justice* (Drugs and Crime) 13: 9–67.

Johnson, James H., Jr., Walter C. Farrell, Jr., and Chandra Guinn. 1999. "Immigration Reform and the Browning of America: Tensions, Conflicts, and Community Instability in Metropolitan Los Angeles." In *The Handbook of International Migration*, edited by Charles Hirschman, Philip Kasinitz, and Josh DeWind, New York: Russell Sage Foundation.

Johnson, Simon, and James Kwak. 2010. *13 Bankers: The Wall Street Takeover and the Next Financial Meltdown*. New York: Pantheon.

Johnston, David Cay. 2005. *Perfectly Legal: The Covert Campaign to Rig Our Tax System to Benefit the Super Rich—and Cheat Everybody Else*. New York: Portfolio.

Jun, Kyu-Nahm. 2007. "Event History Analysis of the Formation of Los Angeles Neighborhood Councils." *Urban Affairs Review* 43(1): 107–22.

Karmen, Andrew. 2000. *New York Murder Mystery: The True Story behind the Crime Crash of the 1990s*. New York: New York University Press.

Keating, Dennis, and Mitch Kahn. 2001. "Rent Control in the New Millenium." *Shelterforce Online*. May/June. Available at: http://www.nhi.org/online/issues/117/KeatingKahn.html.

Kelling, George, and Catherine Cole. 1996. *Fixing Broken Windows*. New York: Free Press.

Kennedy, Christopher, et al. 2009. "Greenhouse Gas Emissions from Global Cities." *Environmental Science & Technology* 43: 7297–7302.

Kerchner, Charles Taylor, David Menefee-Libey, and Laura Steen Mulfinger. 2008. "Comparing the Progressive Model and Contemporary Formative Ideas and Trends." In *The Transformation of Great American School Districts: How Big Cities are Reshaping Public Education*, edited by William Lowe Boyd, Charles Taylor Kerchner, and Mark Blyth. Cambridge, MA: Harvard Education Press.

Kerner Commission (National Advisory Commission on Civil Disorders). 1968. *Report of the National Advisory Commission on Civil Disorders*. Washington, DC: US Government Printing Office. Available at: http://www.eisenhowerfoundation.org/docs/kerner.pdf. Also known as *The Kerner Commission Report*.

King, Anthony, ed. 1996. *Re-Presenting the City: Ethnicity, Capital, and Culture in the Twenty-first Century Metropolis*. New York: New York University Press.

King, Geoff. 2002. *New Hollywood Cinema*. New York: Columbia University Press

Klein, Joel. 2011. Klein, Joel. 2011. "A Response from Joel Klein on Status Quo Apologists." In Valerie Strauss, "The Answer Sheet Column,*Washington Post*, June 23. Available at: http://www.washingtonpost.com/blogs/answer-sheet/post/a-response-from-joel-klein-on-status-quo-apologists/2011/06/22/AGQMAGgH_blog.html.

Klinenberg, Eric, 2011. Going Solo: *The Extraordinary Rise and Surprising Appeal of Living Alone*. New York: Penguin Press HC.

Koch, Edward I. 1985. "The State of the City: Housing Initiatives". Undated text of speech dated January 30.

Kocieniewski, David. 1998. "Man Framed by Police Officers Wins Payments." *New York Times*, February 12.

Kocieniewski, David. 2012. "Since 1980s, the Kindest of Tax Cuts for the Rich." *New York Times*, January 18.

Kogan, Vladimir. 2011. "Interview with Vladimir Kogan." Email, November 23.

Koren, James Rufus. 2012. "Ports Face Drive for More Drivers." *Los Angeles Business Journal*, February 13.

Koshalek, R., T. Mayne, and D. Hutt. 2002. *LA Now*. Vol. I. Berkeley: University of California Press.

KPCC News Services. 2010. "LA City Council Rejects Hiring Freeze." Available at: http://www.scpr.org/news/2010/04/14/14122/la-city-council-rejects-lapd-hiring-freeze/.

Kraus, Clifford. 1995. "Bratton Assailed on Ouster of Top Official." *New York Times*, January 29.

Krugman, Paul. 2011. "We Are the 99.9 %." *New York Times*, November 24.

Krysan, Maria, Mick P. Couper, Reynolds Farley, and Tyrone A. Forman. 2009. "Does Race Matter in Neighborhood Preferences? Results from a Video Experiment." *American Journal of Sociology* 1152: 527–59.

LA Curbed. 2010. "Madness in Monterey Park: Atlantic Times Square Behemoth Nearly Done." Available at: http://la.curbed.com/archives/2010/02/madness_in_monterey_park_latest_look_at_atlantic_times_square.php.

Labaton, Stephen. 2008. "Agency's '04 Rule Let Banks Pile up New Debt." *New York Times*, October 2.

Lambert, Bruce. 1997. "At 50, Levittown Contends with its Legacy of Bias." *New York Times*, December 28.

Landler, Mark. 2008. "World Bank Expects Pain Worldwide." *New York Times*, December 10, B1.

Landsberg, Mitchell. 2010. "Teachers Unions' Clout in Question: Some See Them as Obstacles and Even Sympathizers Agree their Voice is Muted." *Los Angeles Times*, November 7.

Lazo, Alejandro. 2012. "Housing Market may be on Rise at Last." *Los Angeles Times*, April 25.

Lea, Michael. 2010. "International Comparisons of Mortgage Product Offerings." San Diego, CA: Research Institute for Housing America. September. Available at: http://www.housingamerica.org/RIHA/RIHA/Publications/74023_10122_Research_RIHA_Lea_Report.pdf.

Lenzer, Anna, and J. Murphy. 2007. "City Limits Investigates New York's Sewage Stream." *City Limits Weekly*, No. 597, July 23. Available at: http://www.citylimits.org/.

Leonhardt, David. 2009. "The Looting of America's Coffers." *New York Times*, March 10.

Leopold, Aldo, and Charles Walsh Schwartz (illustrator). 1949. *A Sand County Almanac*. New York: Oxford University Press.

Letwin, Michael. 1990. "Report from the Front Line: The Bennett Plan, Street-Level Drug Enforcement in New York City, and the Legalization Debate." *Hofstra Law Review* 18: 795.

Levinson, Marc. 2006. *The Box: How the Shipping Container Made the World Smaller and the World Economy Bigger*. Princeton, NJ: Princeton University Press.

Levitin, Adam, and Susan Wachter. 2011. "Information Failure and the U.S. Mortgage Crisis." In *The American Mortgage System: Rethink and Reform*, edited by Susan Wachter and Marty Smith. Philadelphia: University of Pennsylvania Press.

Lewis, Michael. 2010. *The Big Short: Inside the Doomsday Machine*. New York: Norton.

Li, Wei. 1998a. "Building Ethnoburbia: The Emergence and Manifestation of the Chinese Ethnoburb in Los Angeles' San Gabriel Valley." *Journal of Asian American Studies* 2(1): 1–28.

Li, Wei. 1998b. "Ethnoburb versus Chinatown: Two Types of Urban Ethnic Communities in Los Angeles." *Cybergeo* 70, October. Available at: http://www.cybergeo.presse.fr/culture/weili/weili.htm.

Li, Wei, Gary Dymski, Yu Zhou, Maria Chee, and Carolyn Akdana. 2002. "Chinese-American Banking and Community Development in Los Angeles County." *Annals of the Association of American Geographers* 92(4): 777–96.

Lichtenstein, Nelson. 2009. *The Retail Revolution: How Wal-Mart Created a Brave New World of Business*. New York: Metropolitan Books.

Light, Ivan. 2006. *Deflecting Immigration: Networks, Markets, and Regulations in Los Angeles.* New York: Russell Sage Foundation.

Lii, Jane H. 1996. "Neighborhood Report: Northern Queens, Common Heritage, But No Common Ground." *New York Times*, April 21, 11.

Lim, Nelson, Carl Matthies, Greg Ridgeway, and Brian Gifford. 2009. "To Protect and to Serve: Enhancing the Efficiency of LAPD Recruiting." Report No. MG-881-RMPF. Santa Monica, CA: RAND Corporation.

Lin, Jan. 1998. *Reconstructing Chinatown: Ethnic Enclave, Global Change.* Minneapolis: University of Minnesota Press.

Linthicum, Kate. 2010. "Downtown Project Facing More Delays." *Los Angeles Times*, August 27, AA1.

Linthicum, Kate. 2011. "Occupy L.A. Receives Offer to Decamp." *Los Angeles Times*, November 22.

Linthicum, Kate. 2012. "L.A. Mayor Avoids Talk of Layoffs." *Los Angeles Times*, April 19.

Linthicum, Kate, and David Zahniser. 2012. "In New L.A. Budget, Villaraigosa Calls for Elimination of 669 City Jobs." *Los Angeles Times*, April 21.

LIS Cross-National Data Center in Luxembourg. 2011. "Inequality and Poverty." Available at: http://www.lisdatacenter.org/data-access/key-figures/download-key-figures/.

Liu, John C. 2012. "Comprehensive Annual Report of the Comptroller for the Fiscal Year Ended June 30, 2011." New York: Office of the Comptroller of the City of New York. Available at: http://www.comptroller.nyc.gov/bureaus/acc/cafr-pdf/CAFR2011.pdf.

Llanos, Connie. 2010. "Campus under LAUSD's School Choice Plan Opens." *The Daily News*, August 18.

Lobo, Arun Peter, and Joseph Salvo. 2013. "A Portrait of New York's Immigrant Melange." In *One Out of Three: Immigrant New York in the 21st Century*, edited by Nancy Foner. New York: Columbia University Press.

"Long Beach OKs Port Security Projects." 2004. *Journal of Commerce*, April 6.

Lopatto, Paul. 2010. "Recession's Divide: Food Stamp Caseload Soars, Welfare Caseload Does Not." Independent Budget Office Web Blog, September 13.

Los Angeles Alliance for a New Economy (LAANE). 2009. "Transforming the Gateway to L.A.: The Economic Benefits of a Sustainable Tourism Model." Los Angeles: Los Angeles Alliance for a New Economy. December 2. Available at: http://www.laane. org/downloads/LW_whitepaper.pdf.

Los Angeles, City of. 2011. *Your Chance to Balance LA's City Budget*, 2011. Available at: http://labudgetchallenge.lacity.org/budgetchallenge/sim/budget_master.html.

Los Angeles City Administrative Officer. 2012. "Four Year Budget Outlook and Update to the Three-Year Plan for Fiscal Sustainability." April.

Los Angeles City Administrative Officer. 2009. First Financial Status Report, September.

Los Angeles Community Design Center. 1976. "Skid Row: Recommendations to Citizens' Advisory Committee on the Central Business District Plan for the City of Los Angeles: Part 4, Physical Containment." Los Angeles.

Los Angeles Community Food Security and Hunger Partnership. 1999a. Meeting Minutes, February 18.

Los Angeles Community Food Security and Hunger Partnership. 1999b. "Community Garden Policy Meeting" (minutes), March 18.

Los Angeles Community Redevelopment Administration (CRA). 2011. Available at: http://www.crala.org/internet-site/About/index.cfm.

Los Angeles Convention and Visitors Bureau. 2010. "Los Angeles Tourism by Numbers, 2010 Quick Facts." Available at; http://discoverlosangeles.com/business-services/research-and-reports/2010tourismfactsnew.pdf.

Los Angeles County Economic Development Corporation. 2001. Press Release, July 30.

Los Angeles County Economic Development Corporation. 2008. *Southern California Consensus Group Projects TCIF Application Economic Analysis*. Los Angeles: LAEDC.

Los Angeles Department of Water and Power. 2011. Press Release: "Mayor Villaraigosa Announces Historic Renewable Energy Achievement." Los Angeles. January 13.

Los Angeles Economic Development Corporation. 2011. "2011–2012 Economic Forecast and Industrial Outlook." February.

Los Angeles Food Policy Task Force. 2010. "The Good Food for All Agenda: Creating a New Regional Food System for L.A." Los Angeles Food Policy Task Force, June. Available at: http://www.goodfoodla.org.

Los Angeles Housing Department. 2012. "Rent Stabilization Ordinance Information." Available at: http://lahd.lacity.org/lahdinternet/RentStabilization/tabid/247/language/en-US/Default.aspx.

Los Angeles Unified School District. 2012. Charter Schools Division: Mission. http://notebook.lausd.net/portal/page?_pageid=33,205129&_dad=ptl&_schema=PTL_EP.

Luce, Edward. 2011. "Mr President, It's Time to Panic." *Financial Times*, November 14.

Lueck, Thomas J. 2000. "Giuliani Suggests Privatizing Failing Schools." *New York Times*, January 12.

Lukes, Steven. 1974. *Power: A Radical View*. New York: Macmillan.

Luu, Amy. 2007. "The Chinese American Experience in the San Gabriel Valley."

MacDonald, John M., John Hipp, and Charlotte Gill. 2012. "The Effects of Immigrant Concentration on Changes in Neighborhood Crime Rates?" *Journal of Quantitative Criminology*. Online first (June 2). DOI 10.1007/s10940–012–9176–8.

Mackenzie, Michael. 2012. "Volcker Downplays Risks to Bond Markets." *Financial Times*, January 31.

MacVean, Mary. 2011. "Connecting WIC Participants with Farm Fresh Produce." *Los Angeles Times*, August 18. Available at: http://www.latimes.com/features/food/la-fo-farm-wic-20110818,0,4961107.story.

Malone, N., K. F. Baluja, J. M. Costanzo, and C. J. Davis. 2003. "The Foreign-Born Population: 2000." Census 2000 brief. US Census Bureau, Washington DC. Available at: http://www.census.gov/prod/2003pubs/c2kbr-34.pdf.

Malpezzi, Stephen, and Kerry Vandell. 2002. "Does the Low-Income Housing Tax Credit Increase the Supply of Housing?" *Journal of Housing Economics* 11(4): 330–59.

Malpezzi, Stephen, Gregory H. Chun, and Richard K. Green. 1998. "New Place-to-Place Housing Price Indices for U.S. Metropolitan Areas, and their Determinants." *Real Estate Economics* 26(2): 235–74.

Maple, Jack, and Christopher Mitchell. 1999. *The Crime Fighter: Putting the Bad Guys Out of Business*. New York: Broadway Books.

Marcuse, Peter. 1989. "Dual City: A Muddy Metaphor for a Quartered City." *International Journal of Urban and Regional Research* 13(4): 697–708.

Marcuse, Peter, and Ronald van Kempen. 2000. "Introduction." In *Globalizing Cities: A New Spatial Order?* edited by Peter Marcuse and Ronald van Kempen. Oxford: Blackwell.

Marks, Mara A. 2004. "Shifting Ground: The Rise and Fall of the Los Angeles Community Redevelopment Agency." *Southern California Quarterly* 86(3): 241–90.

Markusen, Ann, and Vicky Gwiasda. 1994. "Multipolarity and the Layering of Functions in World Cities: New York City's Struggle to Stay on Top." *International Journal of Urban and Regional Research* 18(2): 167–93.

Markusen, Ann, Peter Hall, Scott Campbell, and Sabina Deitrick. 1991. *The Rise of the Gunbelt*. New York: Oxford University Press.

Marroquin, Art. 2008. "I.D. Plan for Ports Dragging." *Daily News of Los Angeles*, April 6.

Marroquin, Art. 2009. "U.S. and Canadian Ports Gear up for Trade War." *Daily Breeze*, October 23.

Marsh, Julie A., John F. Pane, and Laura S. Hamilton. 2006. "Making Sense of Data-Driven Decision Making in Education." RAND Occasional Paper. Santa Monica, CA. Available at: http://www.rand.org/pubs/occasional_papers/OP170.html.

Martinez, Adrian. 2010. "And the Winner Is... The Communities of San Pedro and Wilmington." NRDC Switchboard. Posted October 27. Available at: http://switch-board.nrdc.org/blogs/amartinez/and_the_winner_isthe_communiti.html.

Martinez, Barbara. 2010. "Charter-School Advocates Raise Cap." *Wall Street Journal*, May 29.

Martinez, R., Jr, J. I. Stowell, and M. T. Lee. 2010. "Immigration and Crime in Era of Transformation: A Longitudinal Analysis of Homicides in San Diego Neighborhoods, 1980–2000." *Criminology* 48: 797–830.

Mason, J. W. 2009. "Federal Stimulus and Medicaid: How Big a Savings for the City?" Independent Budget Office Web Blog, January 16. Available at: http://ibo.nyc.ny.us/cgi-park/?p=7.

Massey, Douglas S., and Nancy A. Denton. 1988. "The Dimensions of Residential Segregation." *Social Forces* 67(2) (December): 281–315.

Massey, Douglas S., and Nancy Denton. 1993. *American Apartheid: Segregation and the Making of the Underclass*. Cambridge, MA: Harvard University Press.

Matsuoka, M., A. Hricko, R. Gottlieb, and J. DeLara. 2011. "Global Trade Impacts: Addressing the Health, Social and Environmental Consequences of Moving International Freight through Our Communities." March. Available at: http://scholar.oxy.edu/uep_faculty/411.

Maxwell, Lesli A. 2007. "Leaders in L.A. District at Odds Over School Reforms." *Education Week*, April 11.

Maxwell, Lesli A. 2008. "Broad Foundation to Spend $23 Million on L.A. Charter Schools." *Education Week*, January 17,

Maxwell, Lesli A. 2010. "Union Takes on High-Stakes Test in Running Troubled L.A. Schools." *Education Week*, March 10.

Maynard, John Arthur. 1991. *Venice West: The Beat Generation in Southern California*. New Brunswick and London: Rutgers University Press.

Maynard, Micheline. 2008. "Airports Grow Apace, but the Timing Seems Off." *New York Times*, October 30, A21.

Mayor's Office, City of Los Angeles. 2012. Press Release. "Mayor Villaraigosa Celebrates Milestone in Clean Truck Program at Port of Los Angeles." Mayor's Office, City of Los Angeles, January 4.

McAdam, Doug. 1982. *Political Process and the Development of Black Insurgency, 1930–1970*. Chicago: University of Chicago Press.

McClung, William Alexander. 2000. *Landscapes of Desire: Anglo Mythologies of Los Angeles*. Berkeley: University of California Press.

McCone Commission. 1965. *Violence in the City: An End or a Beginning?* Final Report of the Governor's Commission on the Los Angeles Riots. Available at: http://www.usc.edu/libraries/archives/cityinstress/mccone/contents.html.

McGreal, Chris. 2009. "Banned by Bush, UN Investigator Reveals America's Housing Shame." *The Guardian*, November 13, 26.

McGreevy, Patrick, and Steve Hymon. 2007. "Last-Minute Bill Boosts Anschutz's L.A. Project." *Los Angeles Times*, September 13, B1.

McGregor, Richard, and John Dunbar. 2012. "Attack of the Super-Pacs." *Financial Times*, February 2.

McMahon, Thomas L., Larian Angelo, Timothy A. Ross, Regina P. Ryan. 1998. "New York City's Middle Class: The Need for a New Urban Agenda." New York: New York City Council.

Medina, Jennifer. 2010a. "At California School, Parents Force an Overhaul." *New York Times*, December 7.

Medina, Jennifer. 2010b. "New York State Votes to Expand Charter Schools." *New York Times*, May 29.

Mediner, Jennifer. 2010c. "Standards Raised, More Students Fail Tests." *New York Times*, July 28.

Medina, Jennifer. 2012. "In Years since the Riots, a Changed Complexion in South Central." *New York Times*, April 24.

Medina, Jennifer, and Robert Gebeloff. 2010. "New York Charter Schools Lag in Enrolling Hispanics." *New York Times*, June 14.

Meier, Deborah. 2002. *The Power of Their Ideas: Lessons for America from a Small School in Harlem*. Boston: Beacon Press.

Meyer, Peter. 2008. "The Mayor, the Schools, and the 'Rinky-Dink' Candy Store." *Education Next* 8(2). Available at: http://educationnext.org/new-york-citys-education-battles/.

Milkman, Ruth. 2006. *LA Story: Immigrant Workers and the Future of the U.S. Labor Movement*. New York: Russell Sage Foundation.

Milkman, Ruth, and Laura Braslow. 2010. "The State of the Union: A Profile of 2009–2010 Union Membership in New York City, New York State, and the United States." New York: Joseph Murphy Institute for Worker Education and Labor Studies, the Center for Urban Research, and the NYC Labor Market Information Service, City University of New York.

Milkman, Ruth, and Bongoh Kye. 2006. "Union Membership in 2006: A Profile of Los Angeles, California, and the United States." Los Angeles: UCLA Institute on Labor and Employment. Available at: http://www.irle.ucla.edu/research/pdfs/unionmembership06-bw.pdf.

Miller, John W. 2009. "WTO Predicts Global Trade will Slide 9% This Year." *Wall Street Journal*, March 24, A8.

Miller, Toby, Nitin Govil, John McMurria, Richard Maxwell, and Ting Wang. 2005. *Global Hollywood 2*. London: British Film Institute.

Milo, Paul. 2012. "Baraka Wants City to Run Airport." *Patch* (Newark), February 24.

Mindiola, Jr., Tacho, Yolanda Flores Niemann, and Nestor Rodriguez. 2002. *Black–Brown Relations and Stereotypes*. Austin: University of Texas Press.

Minsky, Hyman. 2008. *Stabilizing an Unstable Economy*. New York: McGraw-Hill.

Mollen, Milton (Chair). 1994. "Anatomy of Failure: Path to Success. Report of the City of New York Commission to Investigate Allegations of Police Corruption and the Anti-Corruption Procedures of the Police Department." New York: Commission to Combat Police Corruption. Available at: http://www.parc.info/client_files/Special%20Reports/4%20-%20Mollen%20Commission%20-%20NYPD.pdf

Mollenkopf, John Hull. 1992. *A Phoenix in the Ashes*. Princeton, NJ: Princeton University Press.

Mollenkopf, John. 1993. *A Phoenix in the Ashes: The Rise and Fall of the Koch Coalition in New York City Politics*. Princeton, NJ: Princeton University Press.

Mollenkopf, John. 2003. "New York: Still the Great Anomaly." In *Racial Politics in American Cities*, edited by Rufus Browning, Dale R. Marshall, and David Tabb. New York: Longman.

Mollenkopf, John Hull, and Manuel Castells. 1991. *Dual City: Restructuring New York*. New York: Russell Sage.

Mollenkopf, John, and Raphael Sonenshein. 2009. "The New Urban Politics of Integration: A View from the Gateway Cities." In *Bringing Outsiders In: Transatlantic Perspectives on Immigrant Political Incorporation*, edited by Jennifer Hochschild and John Mollenkopf. Ithaca, NY: Cornell University Press.

Moore, Mark H. 2002. "Recognizing Value in Policing." Washington, DC: Police Executive Research Forum.

Morenoff, Jeffrey D., and A. Astor. 2006. "Immigrant Assimilation and Crime: Generational Differences in Youth Violence in Chicago." In *Immigration and Crime: Race, Ethnicity and Violence*, edited by R. Martinez, Jr. and A. Valenzuela, Jr. New York: New York University Press.

Morenoff, Jeffrey D., and Robert J. Sampson. 1997. "Violent Crime and the Spatial Dynamics of Neighborhood Transition: Chicago, 1970–1990." *Social Forces* 76(1): 31–64.

Morgenson, Gretchen, and Joshua Rosner. 2011. *Reckless Endangerment: How Outsized Ambition, Greed, and Corruption Led to Economic Armageddon*. New York: Henry Holt & Company.

Morris, Charles R. 1981. *The Cost of Good Intentions: New York City and the Liberal Experiment, 1960–1975*. New York: McGraw Hill.

Morrison, Patt. 2001. " Hahn Pulls Ahead of Villaraigosa in the Polls, but by What Method?" *Los Angeles Times*, 30 May.

Moscovitch, Ruth, Alan R. Sadovnik, Jason M. Barr, Tara Davidson, Teresa L. Moore, Roslyn Powell, Paul L. Trachtenberg, Eric Wagman, and Peijia Zha. 2010. *Governance and Urban School Improvement: Lessons for New Jersey from Nine Cities*. Newark, NJ: The Institute on Education Law and Policy, Rutgers-Newark, September.

Mouawad, Jad. 2012. "Airports Focus on the Ground." *New York Times*, June 15, B1.

Munch, J. R., and M. Svarer. 2002. "Rent Control and Tenancy Duration." *Journal of Urban Economics* 52: 542–60.

Murphy, Jarrett. 2008. "Waterways May Brighten through Stormwater Bill." *City Limits Weekly*, No. 625, February 4. Available at: http://www.citylimits.org/news/articles/3493/waterways-may-brighten.

Murphy, Lawrence and T. Schoettle. 2009. "Arthur Kill Storm Surge BarrierDesign Concept." ASCE Met Section Infrastructure Group, New York Academy of Sciences & Polytechnic Institute of NYU, Department of Civil Engineering. Available online: http://www.ascemetsection.org/content/view/274/725/#2009.

Murray, M. 1983. "Subsidized and Unsubsidized Housing Starts: 1961–1977." *Review of Economics and Statistics* 65(4): 590–97.

Murray, M. 1999. "Subsidized and Unsubsidized Housing Stocks 1935–1987: Crowding Out and Cointegration." *Journal of Real Estate Economics and Finance* 18(1): 107–24.

Musso, Juliet, Christopher Weare, and Kyu-Nahm Jun. 2009. "Democracy by Design: The Institutionalization of Community Participation Networks in Los Angeles." Paper presented at the Harvard Networks Conference.

Musso, Juliet A., Christopher Weare, Nail Oztas, and William E. Logges. 2006. "Neighborhood Governance Reform and Networks of Community Power in Los Angeles." *American Review of Public Administration* 36(1): 79–97.

Musso, Juliet, Christopher Weare, Mark Elliot, Alicia Kitsuse, and Ellen Shiau. 2007. "Toward Community Engagement in City Governance: Evaluating Neighborhood Council Reform in Los Angeles." University of Southern California Urban Policy Brief. Available at: http://www.usc-cei.org/pdfs/Full%20Brief%208[1].0.pdf.

Mustain, Gene. 1997. "Chinatown Grows in Brooklyn, Too." *Daily News*, October 27, 34.

Nagin, Daniel S. 2005. *Group-Based Modeling of Development*. Cambridge, MA: Harvard University Press.

Nagourney, Adam. 2011. "In Los Angeles, a Police Department Transformed." *New York Times*, August 12.

Nagy, J. 1995. "Increased Duration and Sample Attrition in New York City's Rent Controlled Sector." *Journal of Urban Economics* 38: 127–37.

Naremore, James. 1998. *More Than Night: Film Noir and Its Context.* Berkeley and Los Angeles: University of California Press.

Nasiripour, Shahien. 2012. "Home Foreclosure Prevention Scheme Fails to Reach Enough Borrowers." *Financial Times*, January 31.

National Alliance for Public Charter Schools. 2012. "Count of States Authorizing Charter Schools." Available at: http://dashboard.publiccharters.org/dashboard/policy/year/2012.

National Center for Education Statistics. 2011a. *The Nation's Report Card: Reading 2011.* (NCES 2012–457). Institute of Education Sciences, U.S. Department of Education: Washington, D.C. Available at: http://nces.ed.gov/pubsearch/pubsinfo.asp?pubid=2012457.

National Center for Education Statistics. 2011b. *The Nation's Report Card: Mathematics 2011.* (NCES 2012–450.) Institute of Education Sciences, U.S. Department of Education: Washington, D.C. Available at: http://nces.ed.gov/pubsearch/pubsinfo.asp?pubid=2012458.

National Commission on Law Observance and Enforcement (Eisenhower Commission). 1931. "Proposals to Improve Enforcement of Criminal Laws of the United States." Washington, DC: US Department of Justice. Also known as the Wickersham Commission.

National Commission on the Causes and Prevention of Violence. 1969. "To Establish Justice, to Insure Domestic Tranquility: The Final Report of the National Commission on the Causes and Prevention of Violence." Washington, DC: US Government Printing Office. Available at: http://www.eisenhowerfoundation.org/docs/National%20Violence%20Commission.pdf. Also known as the Eisenhower Commission Report.

National Park Service (NPS). 2003. "The Evolving Legacy of Jamaica Bay." Washington, DC: US Department of Interior. Available at: http://nbii-nin.ciesin.columbia.edu/jamaicabay/stakeholder/LegacyofJB_110503_NPS.pdf.

Navarro, Mireya. 2011. "New York Floats Rules for Cleaner Heating Oil." *New York Times*, January 28. Available at: http://green.blogs.nytimes.com/2011/01/28/new-york-floats-rules-for-cleaner-heating-oil/.

Navigant. 2012. "Phase II Report to the Board of Commissioners, Port Authority of New York and New Jersey. " September.

Newton, Jim. 2010. "One Coffee One Vote." *Los Angeles Times*, December 21, A25.

Newton, Jim. 2012. "How L.A.'s Shortfall Adds Up." *Los Angeles Times*, April 16.

Newtown Creek Alliance. Available at: http://www.newtowncreekalliance.org.

New York City. 2005. "The New Housing Marketplace Plan: Creating Housing for the Next Generation, 2004–2013." Available at: http://www.nyc.gov/html/hpd/downloads/pdf/10yearHMplan.pdf.

New York City, Department of City Planning. 2004. "The Newest New Yorkers, 2000." New York: New York City Department of City Planning.

New York City, Department of City Planning. 2011. *Vision 2020: New York City Comprehensive Waterfront Plan.* Available online: www.nyc.gov/waterfront,

New York City, Department of Education. 2012. "About Us." Available at: http://schools.nyc.gov/AboutUs/default.htm.

New York City, Department of Environmental Protection. 2006. "The 2006 New York Harbor Water Quality Report." New York: The City of New York. Available at: http://nyc.gov/html/dep/html/news/hwqs.shtml.

New York City, Department of Environmental Protection. 2008. "The NYC DEP Climate Change Program Assessment and Action Plan." New York: The City of New York. Available at: http://home2.nyc.gov/html/dep/html/news/climate_change_report_05-08.shtml.

New York City, Department of Finance. 2007. "Annual Report of Tax Expenditures." New York: New York City Department of Finance.

New York City, Department of Finance. 2011. "Glossary of Property Assessment Terms, 2011." Available at: http://www.nyc.gov/html/dof/html/property/property_val_glossary.shtml.

New York City, Department of Housing Preservation and Development. 1989. "The 10 Year Plan." New York: Department of Housing Preservation and Development.

New York City, Department of Housing Preservation and Development. 2002. "The New Housing Marketplace: Creating Housing for the Next Generation." Available at: http://www.nyc.gov/html/hpd/downloads/pdf/new-marketplace.pdf.

New York City, Housing Development Corporation. 2011. "Mission Statement". Available at: http://www.nychdc.com/about/about.html.

New York City, Mayor's Office 2012. "Update on City Recovery and Assistance Efforts." Press release 430-12, November 18, 2012. http://www.nyc.gov/portal/site/nycgov/menuitem.c0935b9a57bb4ef3daf2f1c701c789a0/index.jsp?pageID=mayor_press_release&catID=1194&doc_name=http%3A%2F%2Fwww.nyc.gov%2Fhtml%2Fom%2Fhtml%2F2012b%2Fpr401-12.html&cc=unused1978&rc=1194&ndi=1.

New York Power Authority. Available at: http://www.nypa.gov/organization.htm.

New York State, Department of Labor. 2009. "2009: Employment and Unemployment Data." Available at: http://www.labor.state.ny.us/workforceindustrydata/lslaus.shtm.

New York State, Department of Taxation and Finance, Office of Tax Policy and Analysis. 2012. "Annual statistical report; New York Adjusted Gross Income and Tax Liability." Retrieved August 2, 2012 from http://tax.ny.gov/research/stats/stat_pit/analysis_of_state_personal_income_tax_returns_by_place_of_residence.htm.

New York State, Division of Housing and Community Renewal. 2011a. "Fact Sheet #5: Vacancy Leases in Rent Stabilized Apartments." Available at: http://www.dhcr.state.ny.us/Rent/FactSheets/orafac5.pdf.

New York State, Division of Housing and Community Renewal. 2011b. "Fact Sheet #1: Rent Stabilization and Rent Control." Available at: http://www.dhcr.state.ny.us/Rent/FactSheets/orafac1.pdf.

New York State, Education Department. 2010. "Regents Approve Scoring Changes to Grade 3–8 Math and English Tests." July 19. Available at: http://www.oms.nysed.gov/press/Regents_Approve_Scoring_Changes.html.

New York Times. 1987. "Schools in Chicago are Called the Worst by Education Chief." November 8. AP Report.

New York State, Office of the Comptroller. 2011. "The Securities Industry in New York City." October.

New York Times. 1994a. "Policing the Police." Editorial. May 1.

New York Times. 1994b. "Tough Cops, Not Brutal Cops." Editorial. May 5.

New York Times. 2010. "Mistrust and the Mosque." Editorial. September 3.

New York Times. 2012. "What They Don't Want to Talk About." Editorial. January 15.

New Yorkers Debate Flood Protection, *Journal of Light Construction*, November 5, 2012. Available at http://www.jlconline.com/hurricanes/new-yorkers-debate-flood-protection.aspx.

Niblack, Preston. 2001. "Ten Year Plan Commitments and Expenditures." New York: New York City Independent Budget Office.

Nickelsburg, Jerry. 2007. "Richer and Poorer: Income Inequality in Los Angeles." *The UCLA Anderson Report*, March. Available at: http://www.uclaforecast.com/forecast/forecastDisplay.asp?iForecastID=127&iFileID=1623&iAccess=1&sForecastType=Article.

Nocera, Joe. 2010. "The Give and Take of Liar Loans." *New York Times*, November 26.

Nocera, Joe. 2011a. "The Banking Miracle." *New York Times*, June 18, A19.

Nocera, Joe. 2011b. "This is Considered Punishment?" *New York Times*, July 26, A23.

Nocera, Joe. 2011c. "9/11's White Elephant." *New York Times*. August 20, A17.

Nocera, Joe. 2011d "To Fix Housing, See the Data." *New York Times*, November 5.

Nussbaum, David. 2010. "LABJ Weekly Lists." *Los Angeles Business Journal*. Available at: http://www.labusinessjournal.com/la-single-lists/.

NYC & Company, Inc. NYC statistics. n.d. Unpublished data. Available at: http://www.nycgo.com/articles/nyc-statistics-page.

Oberschall, Anthony. 1968. "The Los Angeles Riot of August 1965." *Social Problems* 15(3): 322–41.

O'Brien, Bernard. 2009. "When It Comes to Making Labor Contracts Readily Accessible, Albany's Got Us Beat." Independent Budget Office Web Blog, August 13.

OECD Factbook 2011. "2011: Economic, Environmental and Social Statistics."

Office of Management and Budget. 2009. "Financial Plan for Fiscal Years 2009–2013, January 2009," Available at http://www.nyc.gov/html/omb/publications/finplan01_09.html

Office of Management and Budget. 2012a. Adopted Budget June 2012.

Office of Management and Budget November 2012b. "Financial Plan Update," Available at: http://www.nyc.gov/html/omb/downloads/pdf/fpu11_12.pdf.

Office of the State Controller. 2011. "The Securities Industry in New York City." Available at: http://www.osc.state.ny.us/osdc/rpt9–2013.pdf.

Olsen, Edgar. 2001. "Housing Programs for Low Income Households." Working paper 8208. Cambridge, MA: National Bureau of Economic Research.

Olson, Eric. 2008. "Restoring New York's Oysters: How Volunteers and Scientists are Fighting an Uphill Battle to Bring the Mollusk Back to the City's Waters." *Scienceonline*, September 10. Available at: http://scienceline.org/2008/09/env-olson-oysters/.

Orfield, Gary, John Kucsera, and Genevieve Siegel-Hawley. 2012. *E Pluribus... Separation: Deepening Double Segregation for More Students*. Los Angles: The Civil Rights Project. Available at: http://civilrightsproject.ucla.edu/research/k-12-education/integration-and-diversity/mlk-national/e-pluribus...separation-deepening-double-segregation-for-more-students.

Orleans Parish Assessor, 2012, "Search records."Available at November 25, 2012 at www.nolaassessor.com.

Orlov, Rick. 2008. "Mayor's Schools Test Starts." *Daily News* (Los Angeles, CA), July 1.

Orlov, Rick, and Beth Barrett. 2005. "Antonio Villaraigosa Challenges L.A.: 'Dream with Me' Inaugural Speech's Themes as Diverse as its Audience." *Los Angeles Daily News*, July 2.

Osborne, George. 2012. "The West Faces a Crisis of Confidence, not a Crisis of Capitalism." *Financial Times*, January 29.

Osofsky, Gilbert. 1966. *Harlem: The Making of a Ghetto Negro New York, 1890–1930*. New York: Harper and Row.

Otterman, Sharon. 2010a. "Harlem Children's Zone Gets $20 Million Gift." *New York Times*, September 16.

Otterman, Sharon. 2010b. "With Deal, Bloomberg's Pick Wins Helm of City Schools." *New York Times*, November 30.

Otterman, Sharon, and Robert Gebeloff. 2010. "Triumph Fades on Racial Gap in City Schools." *New York Times*, August 15.

Otterman, Sharon, and Allison Kopicki. 2011. "New Yorkers Say Mayor Has Not Improved Schools." *New York Times*, September 6.

Ouroussoff, Nicolai. 2004. "Grand Plans, Flawed Process." *Los Angeles Times*, April 4, E1.

Padron, Dennis and G. Forsyth. 2009. "NY-NJ Outer Harbor Gateway." ASCE Met Section Infrastructure Group, New York Academy of Sciences & Polytechnic Institute of NYU, Department of Civil Engineering. Available online: http://www.ascemetsection.org/content/view/274/725/#2009.

Pallas, Aaron. 2011. "Same Data, Different Story: Debating Progress in NYC Schools." *A Sociological Eye on Education*. June 27. Available at: http://eyeoned.org/content/same-data-different-story-debating-progress-in-nyc-schools_245/.

Parlow, Matthew J. 2002. "Publicly Financed Sports Facilities: Are They Economically Justifiable? A Case Study of the Los Angeles Staples Center." *University of Miami Business Law Review* 10(3): 483–545.

Partnership for Los Angeles Schools. 2008. "About the Partnership." Available at: http://www.partnershiplaw.org.

Partnoy, Frank. 2012. "Time to Rebuild the Twin Pillars of 1930s Wall Street." *Financial Times*, May 14.

Parvin, Jean. 1991. "Immigrants Migrate to International City." *Crain's New York Business* 7(27) (July 8): 22.

Pasanen, Glenn. 2010. "Bloomberg's Management Style Offers Some Surprises." *Gotham Gazette*, August 25. Available at: http://www.gothamgazette.com/index.php/city/archives/585-bloombergs-management-style-offers-some-surprises.

Passel, Jeffrey, and Roberto Suro. 2005. "Rise, Peak, and Decline: Trends in U.S. Immigration 1992–2004." PEW Hispanic Research Center. Available at: http://www.pewhispanic.org/files/reports/53.pdf.

Paulais, Thierry. 2009. "Local Governments and the Financial Crisis: An Analysis." Washington, DC: The Cities Alliance.

Payne, Charles M. 2008. *So Much Reform, So Little Change: The Persistence of Failure in Urban Schools*. Cambridge, MA: Harvard University Press.

Perlstein, Rick. 2008. *Nixonland: The Rise of a President and the Fracturing of America*. New York: Simon and Schuster.

Philbin, Brett. 2012. "Wall Street Cash Bonus Pool Reflects 'Difficult Year'—NY State Comptroller." *Wall Street Journal* March 1s. Available at: http://online.wsj.com/article/SB10001424052970203986604577253111846696908.html

Phillips, Anna M. 2011. "More Schools are Struggling, City Progress Repoorts Show." School Book. *New York Times*, September 23. http://www.schoolbook.org/2011/09/23/more-schools-are-struggling-city-progress-reports-show.

Pilkey, Orrin. 2012. "We Need to Retreat from the Beach." *New York Times*, November 15.

Pitt, L., and Pitt, D. 1997. *Los Angeles from A to Z*. Berkeley: University of California Press.

Pollakowski, Henry. 2003. "Who Really Benefits from New York City's Rent Regulation System?" Civic Report 34. New York: Manhattan Institute.

Pollard, Kelvin, and Mark Mather. 2008. "10% of U.S. Counties Now 'Majority-Minority.'" Population Reference Bureau, August. Available at: http://www.prb.org/Articles/2008/majority-minority.aspx.

Port Authority of New York and New Jersey. 2009. "2008 Annual Report."

Port Authority of New York and New Jersey. 2012. Special Committee of the Board of Commissioners. Letter to the Governors, with enclosure (Navigant, "Phase I Report). Janaury 31.

Port of Long Beach. 2005. "Long Beach Harbor Department Green Port Policy—White Paper."

Port of Long Beach. 2009. "Strategic Plan 2009 Update."

Port of Los Angeles and Port of Long Beach. 2006. "San Pedro Bay Ports Clean Air Action Plan."

Port of Los Angeles. 2007. "Port of Los Angeles Strategic Plan for Safety and Security."

Port of Los Angeles. 2009. Press release: "Los Angeles Harbor Board Approves First Terminal Lease under San Pedro Bay Ports Clean Air Action Plan." August. Available at: http://www.portoflosangeles.org/newsroom/2009_releases/news_081309_tra-pac.asp.

Portes, Alejandro, and Ruben Rumbaut. 1990. *Immigrant America: A Portrait*. Berkeley: University of California Press.

Powell, Michael. 2012. "No Room for Dissent in a Police Department Consumed by the Numbers." *New York Times*, May 7, A22.

Powell, W. W., and Steinberg, R., eds. 2006. *The Nonprofit Sector: A Research Handbook*. 2nd ed. New Haven, CT: Yale University Press.

Preble, Edward J., and John J. Casey. 1969. "Taking Care of Business: The Heroin User's Life on the Street." *International Journal of the Addictions* 4(1): 1–24.

Pritchett, Wendell. 2002. *Brownsville, Brooklyn: Blacks, Jews, and the Changing Face of the Ghetto*. Chicago: University of Chicago Press.

Protess, Ben, and Peter Eavis. 2012. "Progress is Seen in Advancing a Final Volcker Rule." *New York Times*, May 3.

Purcell, Mark. 1997. "Ruling Los Angeles: Neighborhood Movements, Urban Regimes, and the Production of Space in Southern California." *Urban Geography* 18(8): 684–704.

Purcell, Mark. 2000. "The Decline of Political Census for Urban Growth: Evidence from Los Angeles." *Journal of Urban Affairs* 22(1): 85–100.

Puzzanghera, Jim. 2012. "U.S. Watchdog Doubts TARP will Turn a Profit for Taxpayers." *Los Angeles Times*, April 26.

Puzzanghera, Jim, and Alejandro Lazo. 2012. "Rough Road for Obama Housing Plan." *Los Angeles Times,* January 26.

Queenan, Charles F. 1983. *The Port of Los Angeles: From Wilderness to World Port*. Los Angeles, Calif.: Los Angeles Harbor Dept.

Queenan, Charles F. 1986. *Long Beach and Los Angeles: A Tale of Two Ports*. Northridge, CA: Windsor Publications.

Quinn, Christine. 2010. "Food Works: A Vision to Improve NYC's Food System." NYC City Council, Christine Quinn, New York: NYC City Council, November. Available at: http://council.nyc.gov/html/food/files/foodworks_fullreport_11_22_10.pdf.

Quinn, Lois M. 2004. "Assumptions and Limitations of the Census Bureau Methodology Ranking Racial and Ethnic Residential Segregation in Cities and Metro Areas." University of Wisconsin-Milwaukee Employment and Training Institute, October.

Quint, Janet C., Jannell K. Smith, Rebecca Unterman, and Alma E. Moedano. 2010. "New York City's Changing High School Landscape: High Schools and their Characteristics, 2002–2008." New York: MDRC. February.

Rampart Independent Review Panel. 2000. "Final Report of the Rampart Independent Review Panel." Available at: http://www.ci.la.ca.us/oig/rirprpt.pdf.

Ravitch, Diane. n.d. "A History of Public School Governance in New York City." New York: Commission on School Governance, Office of the Public Advocate, Betsy Gotbaum.

Ravitch, Diane. 2007. "Power Struggle in New York City." Bridging Differences blog, *Education Week*, March 2. Available at: http://blogs.edweek.org/edweek/ Bridging-Differences/2007/03/power_struggle_in_new_york_cit.html.

Ravitch, Diane. 2008. "Why I Resigned." *The Sun*, February 15.

Ravitch, Diane. 2010. "Arne Ducan at ED: Year One." *Education Week*, January 26. Available at: http://blogs.edweek.org/edweek/Bridging-Differences/2010/01/arne_duncan_ at_ed_year_one.html.

Rawsthorn, Alice. 2011. "Elements of Style as Occupy Movement Evolves." *New York Times*, November 20.

Rayman, Graham. 2012. "The NYPD Tapes Confirmed." *Village Voice*, March 7. Available at: http://www.villagevoice.com/2012–03–07/news/the-nypd-tapes-confirmed/.

Reckless, Walter C., and Mapheus Smith. 1932. *Juvenile Delinquency*. New York: McGraw Hill.

Regional Plan Association (New York). 2011. "Upgrading to World Class: The Future of the New York Region's Airports." New York: Regional Plan Association. January. Available at: http://www.rpa.org/2011/01/major-new-rpa-study-finds-new-airpor t-capacity-needed.html.

Reinhart, Carmen, and Kenneth Rogoff. 2009. *This Time is Different: Eight Centuries of Financial Folly*. Princeton, NJ: Princeton University Press.

Reiss, Albert J., Jr. 1971. *The Police and the Public*. New Haven, CT: Yale University Press.

Reynolds, Christopher. 2010. "Urbane Renewal: Two Hotels are the Final Puzzle Pieces at the (Mostly) Family-Friendly L.A. Live." *Los Angeles Times*, May 2, L1.

Ridgeway, Greg. 2007. "Analysis of Racial Disparities in the New York Police Department's Stop, Question, and Frisk Practices." RAND Corporation, TR-534. Available at: http://www.rand.org/pubs/technical_reports/2007/RAND_TR534.pdf.

Rieder, John. 1987. *Canarsie: The Jews and Italians of Brooklyn against Liberalism*. Cambridge, MA: Harvard University Press.

Riordan, Richard. 1996. "Volunteer Advisory Council on Hunger (VACH)—Proposed Hunger Policy for the City of Los Angeles," Memo to Robert Farrell, January 25.

Roberts, Sam. 2009. "Westchester Adds Housing to Desegregation Pact." *New York Times*, August 10.

Roberts, Sam. 2011. "New York City's Population Barely Rose in the Last Decade, the Census Finds." *New York Times*, March 24, A23.

Roberts, Sam. 2012. "Income Data Shows Widening Gap Between New York City's Richest and Poorest." *New York Times*, September 20.

Robinson, Gail. 2005. "Charter Schools." *Gotham Gazette*, November 14.

Rogoff, Kenneth. 2011. "The Bullets Yet to be Fired to Stop the Crisis." *Financial Times*, August 9.

Ronald D. White, "Local Ports Upgrade to Build on Their Lead," *Los Angeles Times*, July 20, 2012.

Rosenfeld, Richard A., Robert Fornango, and Eric Baumer. 2005. "Did *Ceasefire, Compstat, And Exile* Reduce Homicide?" *Criminology & Public Policy* 4: 419–49.

Rossi, Peter H. 1989. *Down and Out in America: The Origins of Homelessness*. Chicago: University of Chicago Press.

Rozhon, Tracie, with N. R. Kleinfield. 1995. "Getting Into Co-ops: The Money Bias." *New York Times*, October 31.

Rubin, Joel. 2009. "U.S. Judge Ends Federal Oversight of the LAPD," *Los Angeles Times*, July 18. Available at: http://articles.latimes.com/2009/jul/18/local/me-consent-decree18.

Ruggles, Steven J., Trent Alexander, Katie Genadek, Ronald Goeken, Matthew B. Schroeder, and Matthew Sobek. 2010. Integrated Public Use Microdata Series: Version 5.0 [Machine-readable database]. Minneapolis: University of Minnesota.

Russo, Alexander. 2003. "Political Educator: Paul Vallas Became the Nation's Most Sought-After Superintendent by Bringing Order and Energy to Chicago's Moribund School System." *Education Next* 3(1): 38–43. Available at: http://educationnext.org/files/ednext20031_38.pdf.

Ruth, David. 1996. *Inventing the Public Enemy: The Gangster in American Culture, 1918–1934.* Chicago: University of Chicago Press.

Sabagh, Georges, and Mehdi Bozorgmehr. 2003. "From 'Give Me Your Poor' to 'Save Our State': New York and Los Angeles as Immigrant Cities and Regions." In *New York & Los Angeles: Politics, Society, and Culture: A Comparative View*, edited by David Halle. Chicago: University of Chicago Press.

Saito, Leland. 1998. *Race and Politics: Asian and Latino and White in Los Angeles Suburbs.* Urbana: University of Illinois Press.

Salamon, L. M. 1995. *Partners in Public Service.* Baltimore: Johns Hopkins University Press.

Salamon, L. M. 2009. *The Resilient Sector: The State of Nonprofit America.* Washington, DC: Brookings Institution Press.

Salamon, L. M. 2012. *The State of Nonprofit America.* 2nd ed. Washington, DC: Brookings Institution Press.

Salas, Nashla. 2011. "Despite Cut in Capital Spending, Mayor Plans to Build a New Jail, Renovate Others." Independent Budget Office Web Blog, June 15. Available at: http://ibo.nyc.ny.us/cgi-park/?p=357.

Saltzstein, Alan L., and Raphael J. Sonenshein. 1991. "Los Angeles: Transformation of a Governing Coalition." In *Big City Politics in Transition*, edited by H. V. Savitch and John Clayton Thomas. Newbury Park, CA: Sage Publications.

Sampson, Robert J. 2008. "Rethinking Crime and Immigration." *Contexts* 7(1): 28–33.

Sampson, Robert J., and Jeffrey Morenoff. 2006. "Durable Inequality: Spatial Dynamics, Social Processes, and the Persistence of Poverty in Chicago Neighborhoods." In *Poverty Traps*, edited by Samuel Bowles, Steve Durlauf, and Karla Hoff. Princeton, NJ: Princeton University Press.

Sampson, Robert J., Stephen W. Raudenbush, and Felton Earls. 1997. "Neighborhoods and Violent Crime: A Multilevel Study of Collective Efficacy." *Science* 277: 918–24.

Samuels, Christina. 2011. "Los Angeles Skips Search, Names New Leader." *Los Angeles Times*, January 11.

Sanders, James. 2003. *Celluloid Skyline: New York in the Movies.* New York: Knopf.

Sassen, Saskia. 1994. *Cities in a World Economy.* Thousand Oaks, CA: Pine Forge Press.

Sassen, Saskia. 2000. *Cities in a World Economy.* 2nd ed. Thousand Oaks, CA: Pine Forge.

Sassen, Saskia. 2001. *The Global City.* 2nd ed. Princeton, NJ: Princeton University Press.

Sassen, Saskia, and Frank Roost. 1999. "The City: Strategic Site for the Global Entertainment Industry." In *The Tourist City*, edited by Dennis R. Judd and Susan S. Fainstein. New Haven, CT: Yale University Press.

Scanlon, Rosemary, and Hope Cohen. 2009. "Assessing New York's Property Tax—Yet Again." Newsletter, The Manhattan Institute's Center for Rethinking Development, March/April 2009.

Schatz, Thomas. 1981. *Hollywood Genres: Formulas, Filmmaking, and the Studio System.* New York: McGraw-Hill.

Schatz, Thomas. 2008. "The Studio System and Conglomerate Hollywood." In *The Contemporary Hollywood Film Industry*, edited by Paul McDonald and Janet Wasko. Oxford: Blackwell.

Schill, Michael, Ioan Voicu, and Jonathan Miller. 2007. "The Condominium versus Cooperative Puzzle: An Empirical Analysis of Housing in New York City." *Journal of Legal Studies* 36: 275–324.

Schill, Michael, Ingrid Gould Ellen, Amy Schwartz, and Ioan Voicu. 2002. "Revitalizing Inner-City Neighborhoods: New York City's Ten Year Plan for Housing." *Housing Policy Debate* 13(3): 529–66.

"Schools in Chicago are Called the Worst by Education Chief." 1987. *New York Times*, November 8.

Schrag, Peter. 2004. *Paradise Lost: California's Experience, America's Future*. Updated with a new Preface. Berkeley: University of California Press.

Schultz, Harold, Jerilyn Perine, and Daniela Feibusch. 2011. *The Future of Real Estate Tax Incentives for Affordable Housing in New York City*. New York, New York: Citizen's Housing and Planning Council. Available at: http://www.chpcny.org/wp-content/uploads/2012/01/Tax-Incentives-Final-1-19-12.pdf.

Schwartz, Alex. 1999. "New York City and Subsidized Housing: Impacts and Lessons of the City's $5 Billion Capital Budget Housing Plan." *Housing Policy Debate* 10(4): 839–77.

Schwartz, Alex. 2009. *Housing Policy in the United States*. New York: Routledge.

Schwartz, Amy Ellen, Ingrid Gould Ellen, Michael Schill, and Ioan Voicu. 2006. "The External Effects of Subsidized Housing." *Regional Science and Urban Economics* 36: 679–707.

Schwartz, Amy E., Scott Susin, and Ivan Voicu. 2003. "Has Falling Crime Driven New York City's Real Estate Boom?" *Journal of Housing Research* 14(1): 101–35.

Schwartz, Joanna C. 2010. "Myths and Mechanics of Deterrence: The Role of Lawsuits in Police Department Decision Making." *UCLA Law Review* 57: 1023–94.

Schwartz, John. 2012. "U.S. Ports Expand, With an Eye on Panama." *New York Times*, August 21, A10.

Schweitzer, Lisa. 2012. "Keeping 30/10 on Track." *Los Angeles Times*, April 16.

Scott, Allen. 2005. *On Hollywood: The Place, the Industry*. Princeton, NJ: Princeton University Press.

Sears, David, and Jack Citrin. 1982. *Tax Revolt: Something for Nothing in California*. Cambridge, MA: Harvard University Press.

Sellin, Thorsten. 1938. "Culture Conflict and Crime." *American Journal of Sociology* 44(1): 97–103.

Semple, Kirk. 2010. "Staten Island Neighborhood Reels after Wave of Attacks on Mexicans." *New York Times*, July 31, A14.

Semuels, Alana. 2009. "More Pain Forecast for California." *Los Angeles Times*, July 22, B1.

Shahien Nasiripour. 2012. "US Mortgage Writedowns Could Cost Taxpayers $100bn." *Financial Times*, January 24.

Shalala, Donna E., and Carol Bellamy. 1977. "A State Saves a City: The New York Case." *Duke Law Journal* 1976(6): 1119–32.

Shaw, Clifford R., and Henry D. McKay. 1942. *Juvenile Delinquency and Urban Areas*. Chicago: University of Chicago Press.

Shefter, Martin. 1985. *Political Crisis/Fiscal Crisis: Collapse and Revival of New York City*. New York: Basic Books.

Sherman, Douglas, and Bernard Pipkin. 2005. "The Coastal Southern California: From Santa Monica to Dana Point." In *Living with the Changing California Coast*, edited by Gary Griggs, Kiki Patsch, and Lauret Savoy. Berkeley and Los Angeles: University of California Press.

Sherman, William, and Adam Lisberg. 2010. "Mayor Bloomberg Slams Arizona's Anti-Immigration Law." *New York Daily News*, April 28.

Shiel, Mark, and Tony Fitzmaurice, eds. 2001. *Cinema and the City: Film and Urban Societies in a Global Context*. Oxford: Blackwell.

Shiller, Robert. 2011. "I Just Got Here, but I Know Trouble When I See It: A Tax Credit to Fix a Housing Mess." *New York Times*, December 31.

Shipps, Dorothy. 2008. "Neo-Progressivism as School Reform in Chicago: Big Change, Little Difference?" In *The Transformation of Great American School Districts: How Big Cities are Reshaping Public Education*, edited by William Lowe Boyd, Charles Taylor Kerchner, and Mark Blyth. Cambridge, MA: Harvard Education Press.

Silver, Alain. 1979. *Film Noir: An Encyclopedic Reference to the American Style*. Woodstock, NY: Overlook Press.

Silver, Alain, and James Ursini. 2005. *L.A. Noir: The City as Character*. Santa Monica, CA: Santa Monica Press LLC.

Sinai, Todd, and Joel Waldfogel. 2005. "Do Low-Income Housing Subsidies Increase Housing Consumption?" *Journal of Public Economics* 89(11–12): 2137–64.

Skelton, George, 2010. "Brown Is Lucky—And Needs to be Luckier." *Los Angeles Times*, September 16.

Sklar, Robert. [1975] 1994. *Movie-Made America: A Cultural History of American Movies*. New York: Random House.

Skogan, Wesley G. 1990. *Disorder and Decline*. New York: Free Press.

Skogan, Wesley G. 2006. *Police and Community in Chicago: A Tale of Three Cities*. New York: Oxford University Press.

Skogan, Wesley G., and Kathleen Frydl. 2004. *Fairness and Effectiveness in Policing: The Evidence*. Washington, DC: National Academies Press.

Smerd, Jeremy. 2011. "Guv Preps for Second Act; Cuomo Won Big in his Rookie Year. A Repeat Performance won't be Easy." *Crain's*, November 21.

Smith, David J. 2008. "The Foundations of Legitimacy." In *Legitimacy and Criminal Justice in Comparative Perspective*, edited by T. Tyler et al. New York: Russell Sage Foundation Press.

Smith, Dennis C., and Robert Purtell. 2007. "An Empirical Assessment of NYPD's 'Operation Impact': A Targeted Zone Crime Reduction Strategy." Unpublished paper. Available at: http://wagner.nyu.edu/news/impactzoning.doc.

Social Explorer, Provides Downloadable Versions of Tabulated Data from United States Census and Housing from 1790 to 2010and the American Community Survey from 2005 to the present. Complete documentation of all data tables available on the site. Available at www.socialexplorer.com. (Note the professional version requires a subscription.

Soffer, Jonathan. 2010. "Creating Affordable Housing: How Koch Did It." *Gotham Gazette*, October. Available at: http://www.gothamgazette.com/article/housing/20101018/10/3385.

Sonenshein, Raphael J. 1994. *Politics in Black and White: Race and Power in Los Angeles*. Princeton, NJ: Princeton University Press.

Sonenshein, Raphael J. 2004. *The City at Stake: Secession, Reform, and the Battle for Los Angeles*. Princeton, NJ: Princeton University Press.

Sonenshein, Raphael. 2006. *Los Angeles: Structure of a City Government*. Los Angeles, CA: League of Women Voters of Los Angeles. http://www.lwvlosangeles.org/files/Structure_of_a_City.pdf

Sonenshein, Raphael J., and Tom Hogen-Esch. 2006. "Bringing the State (Government) Back In: Home Rule and the Politics of Secession in Los Angeles and New York City." *Urban Affairs Review* 41(4): 467–91.

Song, Jason, and Jason Felch. 2011. "Times Updates and Expands Value-Added Ratings for Los Angeles Elementary School Teachers." *Los Angeles Times*, May 7.

Sorkin, Andrew Ross. 2009. *Too Big to Fail: The Inside Story of How Wall Street and Washington Fought to Save the Financial System—and Themselves*. New York: Viking.

Sorkin, Andrew Ross. 2012. "Volcker Rule Stirs Up Opposition Overseas." *New York Times*, January 31.

South Coast Air Quality Management District (SCAQMD). 2008. "Multiple Air Toxics Exposure Study in the South Coast Air Basin (Mates III). Final Report." September.

Spitzer, Elliott. 1999. "The New York City Police Department's 'Stop and Frisk' Practices." Office of the New York State Attorney General. Available at: http://www.oag.state. ny.us/bureaus/civil_rights/pdfs/stp_frsk.pdf.

Spivack, Donald R. 1998. "CRA's Role in the History and Development of Skid Row Los Angeles." Los Angeles: Community Redevelopment Agency.

Stancik, Edward. 1993. *From Chaos to Corruption: An Investigation into the 1993 Community School Board Election*. City of New York: The Special Commissioner of Investigation for the New York City School District, December.

Stanton, Jeffrey. 2005. *Venice California: "Coney Island of the Pacific."* Centennial Edition. Los Angeles: Jeffrey Stanton.

Steinhauer, Jennifer. 2006. "Los Angeles Mayor Gains Control of the Schools, but Hardly Total Control." *New York Times*, August 31.

Stenger, Josh Alen. 2001. "What Price Hollywod? Producing and Consuming Culture Myth and Cinematic Landscape in Los Angeles." Ph.D. dissertation, Syracuse University.

Stern, Sol. 2009. "Wrong on Curriculum, Wrong on Pedagogy." In *New York City Schools under Bloomberg and Klein: What Parents, Teachers, and Policymakers Need to Know*, edited by Leonie Haimson and Ann Kjellberg. New York: Lulu.

Stiglitz, Joseph. 2010. "Watchdogs Need Not Bark Together." *Financial Times*, February 9.

Stiglitz, Joseph. 2012. *The Price of Inequality: How Today's Divided Society Endangers Our Future*. New York: W. W. Norton & Co.

Stokes, Melvyn, and Richard Maltby, eds. 1999. *Identifying Hollywood's Audiences: Cultural Identity and the Movies*. London: BFI Pub.

Stone, Christopher, Todd Fogelsong, and Christine M. Cole. 2009. *Policing Los Angeles under a Consent Decree: Dynamics of Change at the LAPD*. Cambridge, MA: Program in Criminal Justice, Harvard Kennedy School, Harvard University. Available at: http://www.lapdonline.org/assets/pdf/Harvard-LAPD%20Study.pdf.

Stowell, Jacob I., Steven F. Messner, Kelly Mcgeever, and L. E. Raffalovich. 2009. "Immigration and the Recent Violent Crime Drop in the United States: A Pooled, Cross-Sectional Time-Series Analysis of Metropolitan Areas." *Criminology* 47: 889–928.

Strunk, Katharine O., and Jason A. Grissom. 2010. "Do Strong Unions Shape District Policies? Collective Bargaining, Teacher Contract Restrictiveness, and the Political Power of Teachers' Unions." *Educational Evaluation and Policy Analysis* 32 (September): 389–406.

Strunsky, Steve. 2012. "Failed Christie court nominee gets Port Authority job." *Star-Ledger*, July 27.

Stuart, Forrest. 2011. "Race, Space, and the Regulation of Surplus Labor: Policing African-Americans in Skid Row." *Souls* 13(2) 197–212.

Stuntz, Wiliam J. 2011. *The Collapse of American Criminal Justice*. Cambridge, MA: Harvard University Press.

Summers, Larry. 2012. "Growth, not Austerity, is the Best Remedy for Europe." *Financial Times* (London), April 30.

Summers, Lawrence. 2011. "How to Save the Eurozone." *Financial Times*, July 18.

Sutherland, Edward. 1934. *Principles of Criminology*. 2nd ed. Philadelphia: J. B. Lippincott.

Sweeting, George. 1998. "Coop/Condo Abatement and Residential Property Tax Reform in New York City." New York City Independent Budget Office.

Swertlow, Frank. 1999. "Out of the Spotlight." In *The Book of Lists 1999*. Los Angeles: Los Angeles Business Journal.

SWIM—Storm Water Infrastructure Matters. Available at: http://swimmablenyc.info.

Sze, Julie. 2007. *Noxious New York: The Racial Politics of Urban Health and Environmental Justice*. Cambridge, MA: MIT Press.

Taleb, Nassim. 2007. *The Black Swan: The Impact of the Highly Improbable*. New York: Random House.

Taueber, Karl E., and Alma F. Taueber. 1965. *Negroes in Cities: Residential Segregation and Neighborhood Change*. Chicago: University of Chicago Press.

Tavernise, Sabrina. 2012. "Survey Finds Rising Perception of Class Tension." *New York Times*, January 12.

Taylor, J., G. Catalano, and D. R. F. Walker. 2002. "Measurement of the World City Network." *Urban Studies* 39(13): 2367–76.

Taylor, Martin. 2012. "The Banking Brontosaurus Nibbles at its Own Tail." *Financial Times*, May 9.

Terrazas, Aaron, and Jeanne Batalova. 2010. "Chinese Immigrants in the United States." *Migration Information Source*. Washington, DC: Migration Policy Institute.

Tett, Gillian. 2009. *Fool's Gold: How the Bold Dream of a Small Tribe at J. P. Morgan Was Corrupted by Wall Street Greed and Unleashed a Catastrophe*. New York: Free Press.

Tett, Gillian. 2011. "TARP Shows That US can Break Political Deadlock." Insight, *Financial Times*, May 13.

Tett, Gillian. 2012a. "Forget the Big Bonuses: A Pay Squeeze is Coming." *Financial Times*, January 31.

Tett, Gillian. 2012b. "How 'Good' Does a Shampoo Need to be?" *Financial Times*, February 3.

Thibodeau, Thomas. 1995. "House Price Indices from the 1984–1992 MSA American Housing Surveys." *Journal of Housing Research* 6(3): 439–81.

Thompson, J. Philli 1999. "Public Housing in New York City." In *Housing and Community Development in New York City: Facing the Future*, edited by Michael H. Schill. Albany: State University of New York Press.

Toby, Jackson. 1957. "Social Disorganization and Stake in Conformity: Complementary Factors in the Predatory Behavior of Hoodlums." *Journal of Criminal Law, Criminology, and Police Science* 48(1): 12–17.

Tolbert, Charles, Patrick M. Horan, and E. M. Beck. 1980. "The Structure of Economic Segmentation: A Dual Economy Approach." *American Journal of Sociology* 85(5): 1095–1116.

Tolchin, Martin. 1975. "Ford Again Denies Fiscal Aid to City." *New York Times*, October 17.

Tonry, Michael. 1997. "Ethnicity, Crime, and Immigration." *Crime and Justice* 21: 1–29.

Tornoe, Rob. 2012. "Christie's Port Authority – the house that pork built." *NewsWorks: New Jersey*, August 6.

Toyota, Tritia. 2009. *Envisioning America: New Chinese Americans and the Politics of Belonging*. Stanford: Stanford University Press.

Trounson, Rebecca, and Sandra Poindexter. 2012. "Low-Income Southland Households Had Biggest Recession Losses." *Los Angeles Times*, September 19.

Tseng, Yen-Fen. 1994. "Suburban Ethnic Economy: Chinese Business Communities in Los Angeles." Ph.D. dissertation, University of California Los Angeles.

Tuch, Stephen, and Ronald Weitzer. 1997. "The Polls-Trends: Racial Differences in Attitudes toward the Police." *Public Opinion Quarterly* 61: 642–63.

Turetsky, Doug. 2012. "Where the Jobs are Growing the Money isn't Always So Good." Independent Budget Office Web Blog, January 18. Available at: http://ibo.nyc.ny.us/cgi-park/?p=416.

Tyler, Tom R. 1990. *Why People Obey the Law*. New Haven, CT: Yale University Press.

Tyler, Tom R. 2010. *Why People Cooperate: The Role of Social Motivations*. Princeton, NJ: Princeton University Press.

Tyler, Tom R., and Jeffrey Fagan. 2008. "Legitimacy, Compliance and Cooperation: Procedural Justice and Citizen Ties to the Law." *Ohio State Journal of Criminal Law* 6: 231–75.

Ulam, Alex. 2011. "Why a Mortgage Cramdown Bill Is Still the Best Bet to Save the Economy." *The Nation*, October 20.

United Federation of Teachers. 2010a. *Research Notes: Special Education in Charters and District Schools*. April 29. UFT: New York City. Available at: http://www.uft.org/files/attachments/uft-report-2010–04-special-ed-in-charters.pdf.

United Federation of Teachers. 2010b. *The Failure of New York City Charter Schools to Serve the City's Neediest Students*. January. UFT: New York City. Available at: http://www.uft.org/files/attachments/uft-report-2010-01-separate-and-unequal.pdf.

"The Untidy Revolution." 2007. *The Economist*, November 10.

Urban and Environmental Policy Institute, Occidental College. 2001. "Re-Envisioning the Los Angeles River: A Program of Community and Ecological Revitalization." Report to the California Council of the Humanities, Los Angeles: Urban & Environmental Policy Institute. Available at: http://organizations.oxy.edu/lariver/publications/Re-envisioning%20the%20LA%20River%20Community%20and%20Eco%20Revitalization.pdf.

Urban and Environmental Policy Institute, Occidental College. 2002. "A Taste of Justice: Report on the November 3, 2001 Taste of Justice Conference." Los Angeles: Occidental College, Urban & Environmental Policy Institute

Urban Institute. 2011. *The Nonprofit Almanac*. Washington, DC: The Urban Institute.

US Bureau of the Census. Various years. "Population of the 100 Largest Urban Places."

US Bureau of Labor Statistics. 2000–12. Unemployment Statistics.

US Census Bureau. 1977–97. *County Business Patterns*. Washington, DC: Government Printing Press.

US Census Bureau. 1980. "Census of Population and Housing, Summary Tape File 1A" on CD-ROM.

US Census Bureau. 1990. "Census of Population and Housing, Summary Tape File 1A" on CD-ROM.

US Census Bureau. 1992. "1990 Census."

US Census Bureau. 2000. "State & County Quickfacts." Available at: http://quickfacts.census.gov/qfd/.

US Census Bureau. 2001. "Statistical Abstract of the United States."

US Census Bureau. 2002. "Census 2000."

US Census Bureau. 2011a. "American FactFinder." Available at: http://factfinder2.census.gov/faces/nav/jsf/pages/index.xhtml.

US Census Bureau. 2011b. County Business Patterns. Available at: http://www.census.gov/econ/cbp/historical.htm.

US Census Bureau. 2011c. "Statistical Abstract of the United States." Available at: http://www.census.gov/compendia/statab/2011/tables/11s0039.pdf.

US Census Bureau. 2011d. "Table MS-2. Estimated Median Age at First Marriage, by Sex: 1890 to the Present." Available at http://www.census.gov/population/socdemo/hh-fam/ms2.pdf.

US Census Bureau. 2012a. "Population Estimates for Counties 2010 to 2011." US Bureau of the Census.

US Census Bureau. 2012b. "Summary of Estimates of Coverage for Persons in the United States." US Census Bureau.

US Census Bureau. 2012c. "Population Estimates for Cities and Towns 2010 to 2011." US Bureau of the Census.

US Department of Commerce, Bureau of Economic Analysis. 2009. "Regional Economic Accounts, 2009." Available at: http://www.bea.gov/regional/reis/action.cfm.

US Department of Commerce. 2010. Bureau of the Census, FT 920 U.S. Merchandise Trade: Selected Highlights. Washington, DC. December.

US Department of Education. 2012. ESEA Flexibility. Available at: http://www.ed.gov/esea/flexibility.

US Department of Transportation. 2011. Research and Innovative Technology Administration, Bureau of Transportation Statistics, *Pocket Guide to Transportation*.

US Senate. 2011. "The Financial Crisis Inquiry Report: Final Report of the National Commission on the Causes of the Financial Crisis in the United States, Conclusions." New York: Public Affairs.

Vallianatos, Mark, and Elizabeth Medrano. 2009. "The Transformation of the School Food Environment in Los Angeles: The Link between Grass Roots Organizing and Policy Development and Implementation." Los Angeles: Urban & Environmental Policy Institute. July. Available at: http://departments.oxy.edu/uepi/publications/trans-formation_of_school_food_Environment.pdf.

Van Ryzin, Greg, and Andrew Genn. 1999. "Neighborhood Change and the City of New York's Ten-Year Housing Plan." *Housing Policy Debate* 10: 799.

Vesselinov, Elena. 2012. "Segregation by Design: Mechanisms of Selection of Latinos and Whites into Gated Communities." *Urban Affairs Review* 48 (May): 417–54.

Vesselinov, Elena, and Andrew A. Beveridge. 2011. "Avenue to Wealth or Road to Financial Ruin? Home Ownership and Racial Distribution of Mortgage Foreclosures." In *Forging a New Housing Policy: Opportunity in the Wake of Crisis*, edited by Christopher Niedt and Marc Silver. Hempstead, NY: National Center for Suburban Studies, Hofstra University.

Vielkind, Jimmy, and Tom DiNapoli. 2012. "Wall Street Bonuses down 14 Percent, Profits down Half." *Capitol Confidential*, February 29. Available at: http://blog.timesunion.com/capitol/archives/118031/wall-street-bonuses-down-14-percent-profits-down-half/.

Villancourt, Ryan. 2012. "LAPD Sends Surge of Officers to Downtown, Addition of Up to 50 Cops Designed to Help Police Skid Row." *Los Angeles Downtown News*, April 25. Available at: http://www.ladowntownnews.com/news/lapd-sends-surge-of-officers-to-downtown/article_7b421140–8f1f-11e1-a322–0019bb2963f4.html?mode=story.

Villaraigosa, Antonio. 2005a. "City of Dreams." Remarks of Los Angeles Mayor Antonio Villaraigosa, Los Angeles: Town Hall. November 9. Available at: http://www.ci.la.ca.us/mayor/stellent/groups/electedofficials/@myr_ch_contributor/documents/contributor_web_content/lacity_mayors_003973.pdf

Villaraigosa, Antonio. 2005b. "City of Dreams: Inaugural Address of Los Angeles Mayor Antonio Villaraigosa." July 1. Available at: http://www.ci.la.ca.us/

mayor/stellent/groups/electedofficials/@myr_ch_contributor/documents/contrib-
utor_web_content/lacity_mayors_003970.pdf.

Villaraigosa, Antonio. 2010a. "Boycott Arizona." *Huffington Post*, April 20.

Villaraigosa, Antonio. 2010b. "It is Time for Teachers Unions to Join the Educational Reform
Team," *The Blog*. Office of the Mayor of Los Angeles, December 7. Available at: http://
www.mayor.lacity.org/MeettheMayor/TheBlog/index.htm#education_reform.

"Villaraigosa's Frustration: California's Schools." 2007. *The Economist*, March 8.

Vitullo-Martin, Julia. 2008. "A Step toward Market-Rate Housing for NYCHA." Monthly
Newsletter, Center for Rethinking Development, Manhattan Institute, November
2008.

Vogel, Harold L. 2010. *Entertainment Industry Economics: A Guide for Financial Analysis*. 8th
ed. Cambridge: Cambridge University Press.

Voorsanger, Catherine, and John K. Howat. 2000. *Art and the Empire City*. New York:
Metropolitan Museum of Art; New Haven, CT: Yale University Press.

Waldinger, Roger. 1996a. "Ethnicity and Opportunity in the Plural City." In *Ethnic Los
Angeles*, edited by Roger Waldinger and Mehdi Bozorgmehr. New York: Russell Sage
Foundation.

Waldinger, Roger. 1996b. "From Ellis Island to LAX: Immigrant Prospects in the American
City." *International Migration Review* 30: 1078–86.

Waldinger, Roger, ed. 2001. *Strangers at the Gates: New Immigrants in Urban America*.
Berkeley: University of California Press.

Waldinger, Roger, and Mehdi Bozorgmehr, eds. 1997. *Ethnic Los Angeles*. New York: Russell
Sage Foundation.

Waldinger, Roger, and Yenfen Tseng. 1992. "Divergent Diasporas: The Chinese
Communities of New York and Los Angeles Compared." *Revue Europeenne des
Migrations Internationales* 8(3): 91–115.

Waldman, John. 1999. *Heartbeats in the Muck: The History, Sea Life, and Environment of New
York Harbor*. New York: Lyons Press.

Walker, Anders. 2012. "Theatres of Procedure." Available at SSRN: http://ssrn.com/
abstract=1999471.

Walker, Samuel. 1993. *Taming the System: The Control of Discretion in Criminal Justice,
1950 1990*. Oxford: Oxford University Press.

Wang, Xueying. 1996. *A View from Within: A Case Study of Chinese Heritage Community
Language Schools in the United States*. Baltimore: The National Foreign Language
Center, the Johns Hopkins University.

Ward, Christopher. 2011. "Ground Zero Rebuilding." *New York Times*, August 28, A22.

Wasko, Janet. 1994. *Hollywood in the Information Age*. Austin: University of Texas Press.

Wasko, Janet. 2003. *How Hollywood Works*. London, Thousand Oaks, CA, and New Delhi:
Sage.

Weikel, Dan. 2009. "LAX Suffers in Weak Economy." *Los Angeles Times*, January 21, B4.

Weikel, Dan. 2010. "Ontario Seeks to Take Control of Airport." *Los Angeles Times*, September
15, B1.

Weikel, Dan, and Peter Pae. 2008. "A Dizzying Descent at Airport." *Los Angeles Times*,
August 6, B1.

Weimer, Nicole. 1999. "Jordan, Capone Put a Double-team on Tourists' Cash." *Chicago
Tribune*, July 25.

Weinberg, Daniel H., and John Iceland. 2002 *Racial and Ethnic Residential Segregation in the
United States: 1980–2000*. US Bureau of the Census. Available at: http://www.census.
gov/hhes/www/housing/resseg/pdf/front_toc.pdf.

Weiner, N.A., and M. E. Wolfgang. 1985. "The Extent and Character of Violent Crime in America, 1969 to 1982." In *American Violence and Public Policy*, edited by L. A. Curtis. New Haven, CT: Yale University Press.

Weintraub, Daniel. 2007. "A Murky Picture." *Education Next* 7(Summer): 49–54. Available at: http://educationnext.org/a-murky-picture/.

Weisburd, David, Shawn Bushway, Cynthia Lum, and Sue-Ming Yang. 2004. "Trajectories of Crime at Places: A Longitudinal Study of Street Segments in the City of Seattle." *Criminology* 42: 283–321.

Weitzer, Ronald. 2002. "Perceptions of Racial Profiling: Race, Class, and Personal Experience." *Journal of Criminal Justice* 30(5): 397–408.

Weitzer, Ronald, and Tuch, Stephen A. 2006. *Race and Policing in America: Conflict and Reform*. New York: Cambridge University Press.

Weitzer, Ronald, Stephen A. Tuch, and Wesley G. Skogan. 2008. "Police–Community Relations in a Majority Black City." *Journal of Research in Crime & Delinquency* 45: 398–428.

Whitaker, Linda. 2003. "Los Angeles Council Adopts Resolution Against Iraq War." *The New York Times*. February 22. Available at: http://www.nytimes.com/2003/02/22/national/22COUN.html.

White, Ronald D. 2009a. "Port Cargo Levels are Sinking Fast." *Los Angeles Times*, March 2, C1.

White, Ronald D. 2009b. "Rail Route Takes a Hit." *Los Angeles Times*, May 15, B1.

White, Ronald D. 2009c. "Shipping Industry in Deep Water." *Los Angeles Times*, July 8, B1.

White, Ronald D. 2012. "Local Ports Upgrade to Build on Their Lead." *Los Angeles Times*, July 20.

Wilhelm, M., and B. Ritz. 2005. "Local Variations in CO and Particulate Air Pollution and Adverse Birth Outcomes in Los Angeles County, California, USA." *Environmental Health Perspectives* 113(9): 1212–21.

Williams, Joe. 2005. "Bloomberg and Klein Seek to Repair a Failure Factory." *Education Next* (5)4: 17–21.

Williams, Mark. 2011. "MF Global Gives the Fed a Lesson in How to Pick its Friends." *Financial Times*, November 6.

Willon, Phil. 2009. "Villaraigosa's Future, Once Bright, Now Tarnished." *Los Angeles Times*, June 21.

Wilson, James Q., and George L. Kelling. 1982. "Broken Windows: The Police and Neighborhood Safety." *Atlantic Monthly*, March: 29–38.

Winton, Richard, and Kristina Sauerwein. 2003. "LAPD Tests New Policing Strategy; Chief Picks Three Areas as Proving Grounds for His 'Broken Windows' System to Fight Crime." *Los Angeles Times*, February 1, A1.

Wolch, Jennifer, and Michael Dear. 1993. *Malign Neglect: Homelessness in an American City*. San Francisco: Jossey-Bass Publishers.

Wolch, Jennifer, John P. Wilson, and Jed Fehrenbach. 2002. "Parks and Park Funding in Los Angeles: An Equity Mapping Analysis." Los Angeles: USC Sustainable Cities Program.

Wolch, J., M. Dear, G. Blasi, D. Flaming, P. Tepper, and P. Koegel. 2007. *Ending Homelessness in 2007*. Los Angeles: Inter-University Consortium Against Homelessness.

Wolf, Martin. 2012. "Seven Ways to Fix the System's Flaws." *Financial Times*, January 22.

Wong, Charles Cloy. 1989. *Monterey Park: A Community Transition*. Pullman: Washington State University Press.

Wong, Kenneth K., Francis X. Shen, Dorothea Anagnostopoulos, and Stacey Rutledge. 2007. *The Education Mayor: Improving America's Schools*. Washington, DC: Georgetown University Press.

World Bank, 2012. "Fertility Rate, Total (Births per Woman)." World Bank, Washington, DC. Available at: http://data.worldbank.org/indicator/SP.DYN.TFRT.IN.

"World Trade: Unpredictable Tides." 2009. *The Economist*, July 23.

Wrigley, Julia. 1982. *Class Politics and Public Schools: Chicago, 1900–1950*. New Brunswick, NJ: Rutgers University Press.

Wyatt, Edward. 2012. "Consumer Inquiry Focuses on Bank Overdraft Fees." *New York Times*, February 22.

Yadron, Danny. 2010. "How 'Race to the Top' is rewriting U.S. education." *McClatchy Newspapers*, August 20, 2010. Available at: http://www.mcclatchydc.com/2010/08/08/v-print/98560/how-race-to-the-top-is-rewriting.html.

Yoon, In-Jin. 1991. "The Changing Signification of Ethnic and Class Resources in Immigrant Businesses: The Case of Korean Immigrant Businesses in Chicago." *International Migration Review* 35(2): 303–31.

Zahniser, David. 2012. "L.A. Employee Union Lashes out at Villaraigosa." *Los Angeles Times*, April 3.

Zahniser, David, Ari Bloomekatz, and Kate Linthicum. 2012. "Vallaraiogosa's Legacy Rides on Transit Plan." *Los Angeles Times*, April 18.

Zavis, Alexandra. 2010. "Not All Welcome Skid Row Charity." *Los Angeles Times*, September 12, A39.

Zepeda-Millan, Chris. 2011. "Dignity's Revolt: Threat, Identity, and Immigrant Mass Mobilization." Ph.D. dissertation, Cornell University.

Zhou, Min. 1992. *Chinatown: The Socioeconomic Potential of an Urban Enclave*. Philadelphia, PA: Temple University Press.

Zhou, Min. 1998. "'Parachute Kids' in Southern California: The Educational Experience of Chinese Children in Transnational Families." *Educational Policy* 12(6): 682–704.

Zhou, Min. 2009. *Contemporary Chinese America: Immigration, Ethnicity, and Community Transformation*. Philadelphia, PA: Temple University Press.

Zhou, Min, and James V. Gatewood. 2000. "Mapping the Terrain: Asian American Diversity and the Challenges of the Twenty-First Century." *Asian American Policy Review* 9: 5–29.

Zhou, Min, and Rebecca Y. Kim. 2001. "Formation, Consolidation, and Diversification of the Ethnic Elite: The Case of the Chinese Immigrant Community in the United States." *Journal of International Migration and Integration* 2(2): 227–47.

Zhou, Min, and Susan S. Kim. 2006. "Community Forces, Social Capital, and Educational Achievement: The Case of Supplementary Education in the Chinese and Korean Immigrant Communities." *Harvard Educational Review* 76(1): 1–29.

Zhou, Min, and Xiyuan Li. 2003. "Ethnic Language Schools and the Development of Supplementary Education in the Immigrant Chinese Community in the United States." *New Directions for Youth Developmen, Number 100t: Understanding the Social Worlds of Immigrant Youth*, 57–73.

Zhou, Min, Yen-fen Tseng, and Rebecca Y. Kim. 2008. "Rethinking Residential Assimilation through the Case of Chinese Ethnoburbs in the San Gabriel Valley, California." *Amerasia Journal* 34(3): 55–83.

Zhou, Yu. 1996. "Ethnic Networks as Transactional Networks: Chinese Networks in the Producer Service Sectors of Los Angeles." Ph.D. dissertation, University of Minnesota.

Zhou, Yu. 1998. "Beyond Ethnic Enclaves: Location Strategies of Chinese Producer Service Firms in Los Angeles County." *Economic Geography* 74(3): 228–52.

Zillow, 2012, "New Orleans Land for New Orleans Lots for Sale." Available at http://www.zillow.com/new-orleans-la/land/.

Zimmer, Lynn A. 1984. "Operation Pressure Point: The Disruption of Street-Level Drug Trade on New York's Lower East Side." New York: New York University School of Law, Center for Crime and Justice.

Zimring, Franklin E. 2006. The Great American Crime Decline. New York: Oxford University Press.

Zimring, Franklin E. 2011. *The City That Became Safe*. New York: Oxford University Press.

Zimring, Franklin E., and Gordon Hawkins. 1997. *Crime is Not the Problem: Lethal Violence in America*. New York: Oxford University Press.

INDEX